An Introduction to Programming Using

Visual Basic® 2008

with Visual Studio® Express Edition DVD

Seventh Edition

David I. Schneider

University of Maryland

PEARSON

Prentice
Hall

Pearson Education International

Editorial Director, Computer Science and Engineering: *Marcia J. Horton*
Executive Editor: *Tracy Dunkelberger*
Director of Marketing: *Margaret Waples*
Marketing Manager: *Christopher Kelly*
Associate Editor: *Melinda Haggerty*
Senior Managing Editor: *Scott Disanno*
Production Editor: *Irwin Zucker*
Art Director: *Kenny Beck*
Art Editor: *Gregory Dulles*
Manufacturing Manager: *Alan Fischer*
Manufacturing Buyer: *Lisa McDowell*

Pearson Education Ltd., *London*
Pearson Education Singapore, Pte. Ltd.
Pearson Education Canada, Inc.
Pearson Education—Japan
Pearson Education Australia PTY, Limited
Pearson Education North Asia Ltd., *Hong Kong*
Pearson Educación de Mexico, S.A. de C.V.
Pearson Education Malaysia, Pte. Ltd.
Pearson Education Inc., Upper Saddle River, New Jersey

10 9 8 7 6 5 4 3 2 1

ISBN 10: 0-13-814943-7
ISBN 13: 978-0-13-814943-7

CONTENTS

PREFACE

Since its introduction in 1991, Visual Basic has been the most widely used programming language in the world. The latest incarnation of Visual Basic, called Visual Basic 2008, brings the language into the Internet age by incorporating the .Net Framework. Visual Basic programmers are enthusiastically embracing the new features of the language. Likewise, students who are learning their first programming language will find VB 2008 the ideal tool to understand the development of computer programs.

My objectives when writing this text were as follows:

1. *To develop focused chapters.* Rather than covering many topics superficially, I concentrate on important subjects and cover them thoroughly.

2. *To use examples and exercises that students can relate to, appreciate, and feel comfortable with.* I frequently use real data. Examples do not have so many embellishments that students are distracted from the programming techniques illustrated.

3. *To produce compactly written text that students will find both readable and informative.* The main points of each topic are discussed first, and then the peripheral details are presented as comments.

4. *To teach good programming practices that are in step with modern programming methodology.* Problem solving techniques and structured programming are discussed early and used throughout the book. The style follows object-oriented programming principles.

5. *To provide insights into the major applications of computers.*

Unique and Distinguishing Features

Exercises for Most Sections. Each section that teaches programming has an exercise set. The exercises both reinforce the understanding of the key ideas of the section and challenge the student to explore applications. Most of the exercise sets require the student to trace programs, find errors, and write programs. The answers to all the odd-numbered exercises in Chapters 2 through 8 and selected odd numbered exercises from Chapters 9, 10, and 11 are given at the end of the text.

Practice Problems. Practice Problems are carefully selected exercises located at the end of a section, just before the exercise set. Complete solutions are given following the exercise set. The practice problems often focus on points that are potentially confusing or are best appreciated after the student has worked on them. The reader should seriously attempt the practice problems and study their solutions before moving on to the exercises.

Programming Projects. Beginning with Chapter 3, every chapter contains programming projects. The programming projects not only reflect the variety of ways that computers are used in the business community, but also present some games and general-interest topics. The large number and wide range of difficulty of the programming projects provide the flexibility to adapt the course to the interests and abilities of the students. Some programming projects in later chapters can be assigned as end-of-the-semester projects.

Comments. Extensions and fine points of new topics are deferred to the "Comments" portion at the end of each section so that they will not interfere with the flow of the presentation.

Case Studies. Each of the four case studies focuses on an important programming application. The problems are analyzed and the programs are developed with top-down charts and pseudo-code. The programs can be found on the companion website at http://int.prenhall.com/schneider.

Chapter Summaries. In Chapters 2 through 11, the key results are stated and the important terms are summarized at the end of the chapter.

Arrays. Arrays are introduced gently in two sections. The first section presents the basic definitions and avoids procedures. The second section presents the techniques for manipulating arrays and shows how to pass arrays to procedures.

"How To" Appendix. Appendix B provides a compact, step-by-step reference on how to carry out standard tasks in the Visual Basic environment.

Appendix on Debugging. Placing of the discussion of Visual Basic's sophisticated debugger in Appendix D allows the instructor flexibility in deciding when to cover this topic.

Appendix on Converting from Visual Basic 6.0 to Visual Basic 2008. This appendix is included primarily to assist the instructor who is familiar with VB 6.0 and is new to using VB 2008.

Companion Website. The companion website (http://int.prenhall.com/schneider) contains all the examples, case studies, and data files referenced in the book. (Details can be found on page 15).

Instructor Supplements. In addition to the materials on the companion website, solutions to every exercise and programming project, a test item file for each chapter, and PowerPoint lecture slides for each chapter are available to instructors. Contact your local Pearson sales representative for information on how to access these resources.

Pearson offers many different products around the world to facilitate learning. In countries outside the United States, some products and services related to this textbook may not be available due to copyright and/or permissions restrictions. If you have questions, you can contact your local office by visiting www.pearsonhighered.com/international, or you can contact your local Pearson representative.

What's New in the Seventh Edition

1. The version of Visual Basic has been upgraded from Visual Basic 2005 to Visual Basic 2008 and relevant new features of Visual Basic 2008 have been incorporated.

2. Suggestions from students and reviewers have been incorporated as much as possible.

3. Chapter 1 has been shortened considerably and combined with Chapter 2. (Some of the material from the previous Chapter 1 has been moved to the Appendices.)

4. Chapter 3 has been split into two chapters.

5. Chapter 4 (General Procedures) of the previous edition has been moved to follow the chapter on decision structures.

6. The concept of *scope* is discussed earlier in the book.

7. The real-life data in the examples and exercises have been updated and revised.

8. Text files are dealt with inside the Visual Basic environment instead of with Notepad.

9. All screen captures have been updated to show the Microsoft® Windows Vista operating system.

10. Message boxes are invoked with MessageBox.Show instead of MsgBox.

ACKNOWLEDGMENTS

Many talented instructors, students, and programmers provided helpful comments and constructive suggestions during the preparation of this text. For their contributions to the quality of the first six editions of the book I extend my gratitude to A. Abonomah, University of Akron; Timothy Babbitt, Rochester Institute of Technology; William Barnett, Northwestern State University; Sherry Barriclow, Grand Valley State University; Robert Berman, Wayne State University; William Burrows, University of Washington; David Chao, San Francisco State University; Christopher Chisolm, University of Nebraska, Omaha; Robert Coil, Cincinnati State Technical and Community College; Gary Cornell, University of Connecticut; Ronit Dancis; John DaPonte, Southern Connecticut State University; Ward Deutschman, Briarcliff; Ralph Duffy, North Seattle Community College; Charles Fairchild; Pat Fenton, West Valley College; David Fichbohm, Golden Gate University; Robert Fritz, American River College; Matthew Goddard, New Hampshire Technical College; Mickie Goodro, Casper College; Wade T. Graves, Grayson Community College; Christine Griffin; Gary Haw, MIPS Software Development Inc.; Shelly Hawkins, Microsoft; Tom Janicki, Kent State University; Dana Johnson, North Dakota State University; Dan Joseph, Rochester Institute of Technology; Del Kimber, Clemson University; Wanda Kunkle, Rowan College; Paul Lecoq, San Francisco Community College; David Leitch, DeVry Institute; David Letcher, The College of New Jersey; Kieran Mathieson, Oakland University; Charlie Miri, Delaware Tech; George Nezlek, DePaul University; Ron Notes, Hebrew Academy of Greater Washington; Mike Paul, Berry University; T. S. Pennington, Maple Woods Community College; Arland Richmond, Computer Learning Center; David Rosser, Essex County College; Arturo Salazar, San Francisco State; Susanne Peterson, Microsoft; Janie Schwark, Microsoft; Mike Talber, Portland Community College; Steve Turek, DeVry Institute of Technology, Kansas City; Jac Van Deventer, Washington State University; Randy Weinberg, St. Cloud State University; Laurie Werner, Miami University; Melinda, White, Santa Fe Community College; Ronald Williams, Central Piedmont Community College; Amit Kalani, CIStems Solutions LLC; Priti Kalani, MobiEcast Corporation; Chris Panell, Heald College; Kevin Parker, Idaho State University; TJ Racoosin, rSolutions; and Bill Tinker, Aries Software.

The current edition benefited greatly from the valuable comments of the following knowledgeable reviewers:

Paul Bladek, Edmonds Community College (WA)
Jason Blazzard, Lewis Clark State College & Washington State
Douglas Bock, Southern Illinois University
Joe Brady, University of Delaware
Peter Chan, Canyon College (CA)
Debra Chapman, University of South Alabama
Chakib Chraibi, Barry University
Ronald Greenberg, Loyola University of Chicago
Dennis Higgins, SUNY- Oneonta
Duke Hutchins, Bowling Green State University
Stephen Klein, Ramapo College (NJ)
Kathleen Lynch, University of Wisconsin (Oshkosh)
Joe Mast, Eastern Mennonite University
Tom McCollough, Hillsborough CC (FL)
Jim McKeown, Dakota State University

Josh Pauli, Dakota State University
Markita Price, University of Missouri
Paula Ruby, Arkansas State University
Sara Rushinek, University of Miami
Cheryl Schlitter, University of Colorado - Colorado Springs
Syd Shewchuk, Heald College
Debbie Tesch, Xavier University
Sangsuree Vasupongayya, Portland State University
Keith Weber, Idaho State University

Many people are involved in the successful publication of a book. I wish to thank the dedicated team at Pearson whose support and diligence made this textbook possible, especially Marcia Horton, Editor-in-Chief, and Scott Disanno, Senior Managing Editor.

I am grateful to Jeremy Schneider, Paul Mailhot, and Zane Lang for their careful proofreading. Production editor Irwin Zucker did a fantastic job producing the book and keeping it on schedule.

I extend special thanks to my editor Tracy Dunkelberger. Her ideas and enthusiasm helped immensely with the preparation of the book.

THE COMPANION WEBSITE FOR STUDENTS AND INSTRUCTORS

How to Access the Companion Website

All the programs from the examples, case studies, text files for the exercises, database files and BMP images can be downloaded by students and instructors at http://int.prenhall.com/schneider.

Students

The companion website, located at http://int.prenhall.com/schneider, contains all the programs from the examples and case studies set forth in this textbook, all the text files needed for the exercises, all databases needed for the exercises, and several picture files. All these files are contained in the folders "Ch02", "Ch03", "Ch04", and so on. Each chapter file contains a subfolder named "Text_Files_for_Exercises" which contains the text files needed for that chapter's exercises. The folder "Ch09" has a subfolder named "Pictures" that contains the picture files. The folder "Ch10" has a subfolder named "MajorDatabases" containing all the databases needed for the exercises.

Each program is contained in a folder with a name in the form *chapter–section–number*. For instance, the program in Chapter 3, Section 1, Example 2 is contained in the folder "3-1-2". Many of the programs make use of a text file in the subfolder *Debug* of the program's folder named *bin*.

Instructors

Instructor resources include solutions to the exercises, PowerPoint lecture slides, all the example programs and data files used by students throughout the book, and multiple-choice and true/false questions. Contact your local Pearson sales representative to gain access to this material.

Notice: This book contains many screen captures. When you run one of the programs downloaded from the website, what you see on your monitor might not look exactly like the screen capture shown in the book. To make them appear the same, you must check that your monitor is set to display 96 DPI (Dots Per Inch). To determine and/or change the DPI setting for your monitor, see the first item under "Utilize the Windows Environment" in Appendix B on pages 622-23.

Using This Book for a Short or Condensed Course

This book provides more than enough material for a complete semester course. The topics must be trimmed for courses lasting considerably less than a full semester. The following syllabus provides one possible way to present an abbreviated introduction to programming.

1

An Introduction to Computers and Problem Solving

1.1   An Introduction to Computers

An Introduction to Programming Using Visual Basic 2008 is a book about problem solving using computers. The programming language used is Visual Basic 2008 (hereafter shortened to Visual Basic), but the principles taught apply to many modern programming languages. The examples and exercises present a sampling of the ways that computers are used in the real world. Here are some questions that you might have about computers and programming.

Question: *What are the main components of a personal computer?*

Answer: Hidden from view inside the system unit are several components, including the microprocessor, memory, and hard drive of the computer. The *central processing unit* (CPU), sometimes referred to as the *microprocessor*, can be thought of as the computer's brain, which carries out all of the computations. The *memory*, often referred to as *random access memory* (RAM), stores instructions and data while they are being used by the computer. When the computer's power is turned off, the contents of memory are lost. A *hard disk drive* is used to store instructions and data when they are not being used in memory and when the computer is turned off. Inside the system unit there are also device cards, such as a graphics card, sound card, network card, and a modem. A *graphics card* is used to send an image to the monitor, and a *sound card* is used to send audio to a set of speakers attached to the computer. *Network cards* can be used to connect to a *local area network* (LAN) of computers, while a *modem* uses a telephone line or cable to connect to another computer.

The personal computer also has several *input* and *output devices*, which are used to communicate with the computer. Standard input devices include the keyboard and mouse. Standard output devices include the monitor and printer. Instructions are entered into the computer by typing them on the keyboard, clicking a mouse, or loading them from a file located on a disk drive or downloaded from a network. Information processed by the computer can be displayed on the monitor, printed on the printer, or recorded on a disk drive.

Question: *What are some topics covered in this text that students could use immediately?*

Answer: Computer files can be created to hold lists of names, addresses, and phone numbers, which can be alphabetized and displayed in their entirety or selectively. Mathematical computations can be carried out for science, business, and engineering courses. Personal financial transactions, such as bank deposits and loans, can be recorded, organized, and analyzed. Line charts, pie charts, and bar charts can be created to enhance the data in a term paper.

Question: *How do we communicate with the computer?*

Answer: Many languages are used to communicate with the computer. At the lowest level, there is *machine language*, which is understood directly by the microprocessor, but is awkward for humans. Visual Basic is an example of a *higher-level language*. It consists of instructions to which people can relate, such as Click, If, and Do.

Question: *How do we get computers to perform complicated tasks?*

Answer: Tasks are broken down into a sequence of instructions that can be expressed in a computer language. (This text uses the language Visual Basic.) This sequence of instructions is called a *program*. Programs can range in size from two or three instructions to millions of instructions. Instructions are typed on the keyboard, or read in from a file on a disk, and stored in the computer's memory. The process of executing the instructions is called *running* the program.

Question: *Are there certain features that all programs have in common?*

Answer: Most programs do three things: take in data, manipulate them, and give desired information. These operations are referred to as *input*, *processing*, and *output*. The input data might be held in a portion of the program, reside on a disk drive, or be provided by the computer operator in response to requests made by the computer while the program is running. The processing of the input data occurs inside the computer and can take from a fraction of a second to many hours. The output data are either displayed on the monitor, printed on the printer, or recorded on a disk. As a simple example, consider a program that computes sales tax. An item of input data is the cost of the thing purchased. The processing consists of multiplying the cost by a certain percentage. An item of output data is the resulting product, the amount of sales tax to be paid.

Question: *What are the meanings of the terms "hardware" and "software?"*

Answer: *Hardware* refers to the physical components of the computer, including all peripherals, the central processing unit, disk drives, and all mechanical and electrical devices. Programs are referred to as *software*.

Question: *What are the meanings of the terms "programmer" and "user?"*

Answer: A *programmer* is a person who solves problems by writing programs on a computer. After analyzing the problem and developing a plan for solving it, he or she writes and tests the program that instructs the computer how to carry out the plan. The program might be run many times, either by the programmer or by others. A *user* is any person who uses a program. While working through this text, you will function both as a programmer and as a user.

Question: *What is meant by problem solving?*

Answer: Problems are solved by carefully reading them to determine what data are given and what outputs are requested. Then a step-by-step procedure is devised to process the given data and produce the requested output. This procedure is called an *algorithm*. Finally, a computer program is written to carry out the algorithm. Algorithms are discussed in Section 1.4.

Question: *What types of problems are solved in this text?*

Answer: Carrying out business computations, creating and maintaining records, alphabetizing lists, and displaying tabular data are some of the types of problems we will solve.

Question: *When did the concept of computers and programming first appear?*

Answer: The first general-purpose computer, called the Analytical Engine, was described by Charles Babbage in 1837. Although it was never built, its logical design was essentially modern. (In 1939, the first general-purpose computer was actually built by John Atanasoff.) In 1843, Augusta Ada Byron showed how to carry out certain complex mathematical computations with the Analytical Engine, thereby establishing herself as the first computer programmer. For a historical perspective of the evolution of modern computers and programming languages, see Appendix E, *A Biographical History of Computing*.

Question: *How did Visual Basic 2008 evolve?*

Answer: In the early 1960s, two mathematics professors at Dartmouth College developed BASIC to provide their students with an easily learned language that could tackle complicated programming projects. As the popularity of BASIC grew, refinements were introduced that permitted structured programming, which increases the reliability of programs. Visual Basic 1.0 is a version of BASIC developed in 1991 by the Microsoft Corporation to allow easy, visual-oriented development of Windows applications. Visual Basic 2008 is a language similar to the original Visual Basic, but more powerful. It is targeted for what is known as the .NET run time, which is a program that executes Visual Basic 2008 as well as programs from other languages that are targeted for the .NET run time. This will ultimately allow programs written in Visual Basic to be run on devices other than computers, such as cell phones and handheld devices. Other features of Visual Basic 2008 include full object-oriented programming capabilities and the development of Web services. Object-oriented programming is discussed in Chapter 11.

Question: *Are there any prerequisites to learning Visual Basic 2008?*

Answer: Since Visual Basic is used to write Windows applications, you should be familiar with Windows and understand how folders and files are managed with Windows. The key concepts are presented succinctly in Section 1.2 and discussed in detail in Appendix F.

Question: *Will it matter whether I use Windows XP or Windows Vista as the operating system?*

Answer: Visual Basic runs fine with either Windows XP or Windows Vista. However, the screens will vary in appearance. Figure 1.1 shows how the appearance of a Visual Basic program differs with the operating system. In this book, all screens have the Windows Vista appearance.

(a) Windows XP   (b) Windows Vista

FIGURE 1.1   A Visual Basic window.

1.2   Windows, Folders, and Files

This preliminary section presents some terms used in this book.

■ Windows and its Little Windows

Windows gets its name from the way it organizes the screen into rectangular regions. When you run a program, the program runs inside a bordered rectangular box.

Unfortunately Windows jargon calls these *windows*, so there's only a lowercase "w" to distinguish them from the operating system called Windows. Figure 1.2 shows the window that results from running one of the programs in this book. In Visual Basic terminology, such a window is also called a **form**.

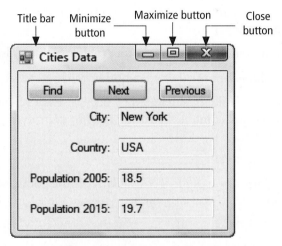

FIGURE 1.2 A Visual Basic window.

Mouse Actions

Hover: Linger the mouse at a particular place and wait for a message (such as a tool tip) to appear.

Drag an object: Move the mouse pointer until it is at the object, press the left mouse button and hold it down, move the mouse pointer until the object moves to where you want it to be, and finally, release the mouse button. (Sometimes this whole activity is called *drag-and-drop*.)

Right-click: Press and release the right mouse button once.

Click: Press and release the left mouse button once. (sometimes referred to as *single-click* or *left-click*)

Double-click: Click the left mouse button twice in quick succession.

Note: An important Windows convention is that clicking selects an object so you can give Windows further directions about it, but double-clicking tells it to perform a default operation. For example, double-clicking on a folder will open that folder.

Files and Folders

(A detailed discussion of files and folders can be found in Appendix F.)

Disk: Either the hard disk, a diskette, a CD, or DVD. Each disk drive is identified by a letter followed by a colon.

File:　Either a program file or a data file. Its name typically consists of letters, digits, and spaces. The name of the file is also called the *base name*.

Extension of a file name:　One or more letters, preceded by a period, that identify the type of file. For example, files created with Word have the extension *doc* or *docx*.

Filename:　The combination of the base name, the period, and the extension. The only characters that cannot be used in filenames are \, /, :, *, ?, <, >, ", and |. Filenames are not case sensitive.

Folder:　A container holding files and other folders. Folders also are known as *directories*.

Subfolder:　A folder contained inside another folder.

Path:　A sequence of folders, separated by backslashes (\ ), where each folder is a sub-folder of the folder preceding it. Paths are used to identify the locations of folders and files. An example is:

```
Programs\Ch07\Text_Files_for_Exercises
```

Filespec:　An abbreviation of *file specification*, it is the combination of a drive letter followed by a colon, a path, and a filename. An example is:

```
C:\Programs\Ch07\Text_Files_for_Exercises\USPRES.TXT
```

In practice, you rarely have to type a filespec, since both Windows and Visual Basic provide Browse facilities that locate files and folders for you.

Windows Explorer:　A program used to view, organize, and manage the folders and files on your disks. The details are presented in Appendix B in the section *Manage Files and Folders with Windows Explorer*. To invoke Windows Explorer, right-click the Windows Start button and click on Explore in the context menu that appears.

Displaying File Extensions:　By default, Windows shows only the base names of files. The following steps get Windows to also display the extensions. (In this book we assume that extensions are always shown).

Windows XP

1. From Windows Explorer, press Alt/T/O to display the Folder Options dialog box.
2. Click on the View tab in the dialog box. (The dialog box in Figure 1.3 will appear.)
3. If there is a check mark in the box next to "Hide extensions for known file types," click on the box to remove the check mark.
4. Click on the OK button to close the Folder Options dialog box.

Windows Vista

1. Click on the Start button.
2. Type Folder Options into the Start Search box (just above the Start button) and press the Enter key. (The Folder Options dialog box appears.)
3. Click on the View tab in the Folder Options dialog box. (The dialog box will appear as in Figure 1.4.)

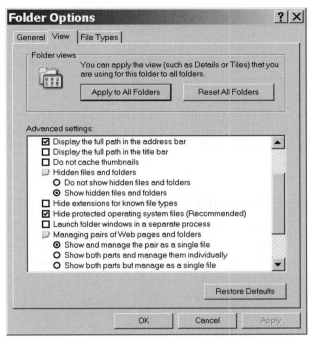

FIGURE 1.3 **XP Folder Options dialog box.**

4. If there is a check mark in the box next to "Hide extensions for known file types," click on the box to remove the check mark.

5. Click on the OK button to close the Folder Options dialog box.

FIGURE 1.4 **Vista Folder Options dialog box.**

1.3   Program Development Cycle

We learned in Section 1.1 that hardware refers to the machinery in a computer system (such as the monitor, keyboard, and CPU) and software refers to a collection of instructions, called a **program**, that directs the hardware. Programs are written to solve problems or perform tasks on a computer. Programmers translate the solutions or tasks into a language the computer can understand. As we write programs, we must keep in mind that the computer will only do what we instruct it to do. Because of this, we must be very careful and thorough with our instructions. **Note:** A program is also known as a **project, application,** or **solution**.

■ Performing a Task on the Computer

The first step in writing instructions to carry out a task is to determine what the **output** should be—that is, exactly what the task should produce. The second step is to identify the data, or **input**, necessary to obtain the output. The last step is to determine how to **process** the input to obtain the desired output, that is, to determine what formulas or ways of doing things can be used to obtain the output.

This problem-solving approach is the same as that used to solve word problems in an algebra class. For example, consider the following algebra problem:

How fast is a car traveling if it goes 50 miles in 2 hours?

The first step is to determine the type of answer requested. The answer should be a number giving the speed in miles per hour (the output). (*Speed* is also called *velocity*.) The information needed to obtain the answer is the distance and time the car has traveled (the input). The formula

$$speed = distance/time$$

is used to process the distance traveled and the time elapsed in order to determine the speed. That is,

$$speed = 50 \text{ miles}/2 \text{ hours}$$

$$= 25 \text{ miles/hour}$$

A pictorial representation of this problem-solving process is

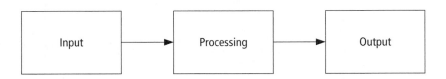

We determine what we want as output, get the needed input, and process the input to produce the desired output.

In the following chapters we discuss how to write programs to carry out the preceding operations. But first we look at the general process of writing programs.

■ Program Planning

A baking recipe provides a good example of a plan. The ingredients and the amounts are determined by what is to be baked. That is, the *output* determines the *input* and the *processing*. The recipe, or plan, reduces the number of mistakes you might make if you tried to bake with no plan at all. Although it's difficult to imagine an architect building a bridge or a factory without a detailed plan, many programmers (particularly students in their first programming course) try to write programs without first making a careful plan. The more complicated the problem, the more complex the plan may be. You will spend much less time working on a program if you devise a carefully thought out step-by-step plan and test it before actually writing the program.

Many programmers plan their programs using a sequence of steps, referred to as the **program development cycle**. The following step-by-step process will enable you to use your time efficiently and help you design error-free programs that produce the desired output.

1. *Analyze:* Define the problem.

   Be sure you understand what the program should do, that is, what the output should be. Have a clear idea of what data (or input) are given and the relationship between the input and the desired output.

2. *Design:* Plan the solution to the problem.

   Find a logical sequence of precise steps that solve the problem. Such a sequence of steps is called an **algorithm**. Every detail, including obvious steps, should appear in the algorithm. In the next section, we discuss three popular methods used to develop the logic plan: flowcharts, pseudocode, and top-down charts. These tools help the programmer break a problem into a sequence of small tasks the computer can perform to solve the problem. Planning also involves using representative data to test the logic of the algorithm by hand to ensure that it is correct.

3. *Choose the interface:* Select the objects (text boxes, buttons, etc.).

   Determine how the input will be obtained and how the output will be displayed. Then create objects to receive the input and display the output. Also, create appropriate buttons and menus to allow the user to control the program.

4. *Code:* Translate the algorithm into a programming language.

   Coding is the technical word for writing the program. During this stage, the program is written in Visual Basic and entered into the computer. The programmer uses the algorithm devised in Step 2 along with a knowledge of Visual Basic.

5. *Test and debug:* Locate and remove any errors in the program.

   Testing is the process of finding errors in a program, and **debugging** is the process of correcting errors that are found. (An error in a program is called a **bug.**) As the program is typed, Visual Basic points out certain types of program errors. Other types of errors will be detected by Visual Basic when the program is executed; however, many errors due to typing mistakes, flaws in the algorithm, or incorrect use of the Visual Basic language rules can be uncovered and corrected only by careful detective work. An example of such an error would be using addition when multiplication was the proper operation.

6. *Complete the documentation:* Organize all the material that describes the program. Documentation is intended to allow another person, or the programmer at a later date, to understand the program. Internal documentation (comments) consists of statements in the program that are not executed, but point out the purposes of various parts of the program. Documentation might also consist of a detailed description of what the program does and how to use the program (for instance, what type of input is expected). For commercial programs, documentation includes an instruction manual and on-line help. Other types of documentation are the flowchart, pseudocode, and hierarchy chart that were used to construct the program. Although documentation is listed as the last step in the program development cycle, it should take place as the program is being coded.

1.4　Programming Tools

This section discusses some specific algorithms and develops three tools used to convert algorithms into computer programs: flowcharts, pseudocode, and hierarchy charts.

You use algorithms every day to make decisions and perform tasks. For instance, whenever you mail a letter, you must decide how much postage to put on the envelope. One rule of thumb is to use one stamp for every five sheets of paper or fraction thereof. Suppose a friend asks you to determine the number of stamps to place on an envelope. The following algorithm will accomplish the task.

1. Request the number of sheets of paper; call it Sheets.　　　　　　*(input)*
2. Divide Sheets by 5.　　　　　　*(processing)*
3. Round the quotient up to the next highest whole number;
   call it Stamps.　　　　　　*(processing)*
4. Reply with the number Stamps.　　　　　　*(output)*

The preceding algorithm takes the number of sheets (Sheets) as input, processes the data, and produces the number of stamps needed (Stamps) as output. We can test the algorithm for a letter with 16 sheets of paper.

1. Request the number of sheets of paper; Sheets = 16.
2. Dividing 5 into 16 gives 3.2.
3. Rounding 3.2 up to 4 gives Stamps = 4.
4. Reply with the answer, 4 stamps.

This problem-solving example can be pictured by

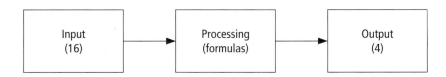

Of the program design tools available, three popular tools are the following:

Flowcharts: Graphically depict the logical steps to carry out a task and show how the steps relate to each other.

Pseudocode: Uses English-like phrases with some Visual Basic terms to outline the task.

Hierarchy charts: Show how the different parts of a program relate to each other.

■ Flowcharts

A flowchart consists of special geometric symbols connected by arrows. Within each symbol is a phrase presenting the activity at that step. The shape of the symbol indicates the type of operation that is to occur. For instance, the parallelogram denotes input or output. The arrows connecting the symbols, called **flowlines**, show the progression in which the steps take place. Flowcharts should "flow" from the top of the page to the bottom. Although the symbols used in flowcharts are standardized, no standards exist for the amount of detail required within each symbol.

Symbol	Name	Meaning
	Flowline	Used to connect symbols and indicate the flow of logic.
	Terminal	Used to represent the beginning (Start) or the end (End) of a task.
	Input/Output	Used for input and output operations, such as reading and displaying. The data to be read or displayed are described inside.
	Processing	Used for arithmetic and data-manipulation operations. The instructions are listed inside the symbol.
	Decision	Used for any logic or comparison operations. Unlike the input/ouput and processing symbols, which have one entry and one exit flowline, the decision symbol has one entry and two exit paths. The path chosen depends on whether the answer to a question is "yes" or "no."
	Connector	Used to joint different flowlines.
	Offpage Connector	Used to indicate that the flowchart continues to a second page.
	Predefined Process	Used to represent a group of statements that perform one processing task.
	Annotation	Used to provide additional information about another flowchart symbol.

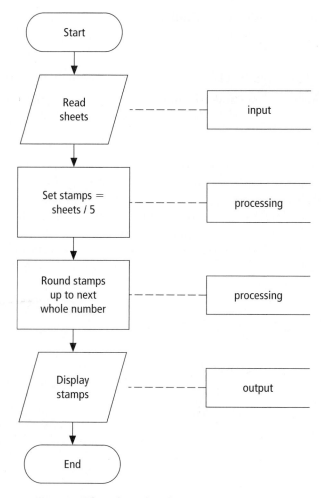

FIGURE 1.5   **Flowchart for the postage stamp problem.**

The table of the flowchart symbols shown on the previous page has been adopted by the American National Standards Institute (ANSI). Figure 1.5 shows the flowchart for the postage stamp problem.

The main advantage of using a flowchart to plan a task is that it provides a pictorial representation of the task, which makes the logic easier to follow. We can clearly see every step and how each is connected to the next. The major disadvantage with flowcharts is that when a program is very large, the flowcharts may continue for many pages, making them difficult to follow and modify.

▓ Pseudocode

Pseudocode is an abbreviated plain English version of actual computer code (hence, *pseudocode*). The geometric symbols used in flowcharts are replaced by English-like statements that outline the process. As a result, pseudocode looks more like computer code than does a flowchart. Pseudocode allows the programmer to focus on the steps required to solve a problem rather than on how to use the computer language. The programmer can describe the algorithm in Visual Basic-like form without being restricted by the rules of Visual Basic. When the pseudocode is completed, it can be easily translated into the Visual Basic language.

The following is pseudocode for the postage stamp problem:

Program: Determine the proper number of stamps for a letter
Read Sheets   (*input*)
Set the number of stamps to Sheets / 5   (*processing*)
Round the number of stamps up to the next whole number   (*processing*)
Display the number of stamps   (*output*)

Pseudocode has several advantages. It is compact and probably will not extend for many pages as flowcharts commonly do. Also, the plan looks like the code to be written and so is preferred by many programmers.

■ Hierarchy Chart

The last programming tool we'll discuss is the **hierarchy chart**, which shows the overall program structure. Hierarchy charts are also called structure charts, HIPO (Hierarchy plus Input-Process-Output) charts, top-down charts, or VTOC (Visual Table of Contents) charts. All these names refer to planning diagrams that are similar to a company's organization chart.

Hierarchy charts depict the organization of a program but omit the specific processing logic. They describe what each part, or **module**, of the program does and they show how the modules relate to each other. The details on how the modules work, however, are omitted. The chart is read from top to bottom and from left to right. Each module may be subdivided into a succession of submodules that branch out under it. Typically, after the activities in the succession of submodules are carried out, the module to the right of the original module is considered. A quick glance at the hierarchy chart reveals each task performed in the program and where it is performed. Figure 1.6 shows a hierarchy chart for the postage stamp problem.

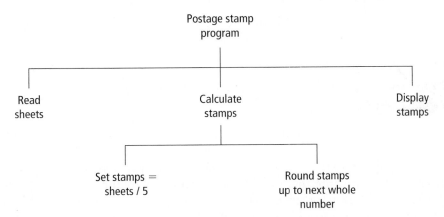

FIGURE 1.6   Hierarchy chart for the postage stamp problem.

The main benefit of hierarchy charts is in the initial planning of a program. We break down the major parts of a program so we can see what must be done in general. From this point, we can then refine each module into more detailed plans using flowcharts or pseudocode. This process is called the **divide-and-conquer** method.

The postage stamp problem was solved by a series of instructions to read data, perform calculations, and display results. Each step was in a sequence; that is, we moved from one line to the next without skipping over any lines. This kind of structure is called a **sequence structure**. Many problems, however, require a decision to determine whether a series of instructions should be executed. If the answer to a question is "Yes," then one group of instructions is executed. If the answer is "No," then another is executed. This structure is called a **decision structure**. Figure 1.7 contains the pseudocode and flowchart for a decision structure.

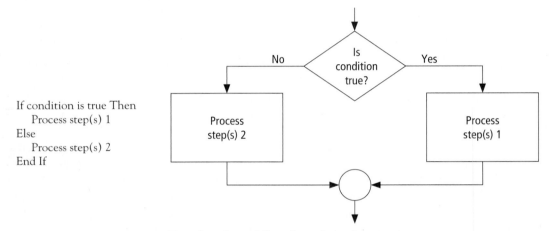

If condition is true Then
    Process step(s) 1
Else
    Process step(s) 2
End If

FIGURE 1.7 **Pseudocode and flowchart for a decision structure.**

The sequence and decision structures are both used to solve the following problem.

■ Direction of Numbered NYC Streets Algorithm

Problem: Given a street number of a one-way street in New York, decide the direction of the street, either eastbound or westbound.

Discussion: There is a simple rule to tell the direction of a one-way street in New York: Even-numbered streets run eastbound.

Input: Street number

Processing: Decide if the street number is divisible by 2.

Output: "Eastbound" or "Westbound"

Figures 1.8 through 1.10 show the flowchart, pseudocode, and hierarchy chart for the New York City numbered streets problem.

The solution to the next problem requires the repetition of a series of instructions. A programming structure that executes instructions many times is called a **loop structure**.

We need a test (or decision) to tell when the loop should end. Without an exit condition, the loop would repeat endlessly (an infinite loop). One way to control the number of times a loop repeats (often referred to as the number of passes or iterations)

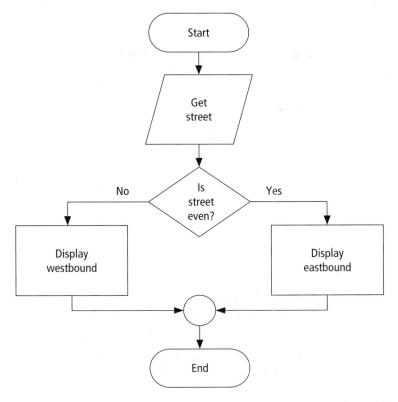

FIGURE 1.8 Flowchart for the New York City numbered streets problem.

Program: Determine the direction of a numbered NYC street.
Get street
If street is even Then
   Display Eastbound
Else
   Display Westbound
End If

FIGURE 1.9 Pseudocode for the New York City numbered streets problem.

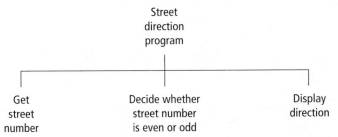

FIGURE 1.10 Hierarchy chart for the New York City numbered streets problem.

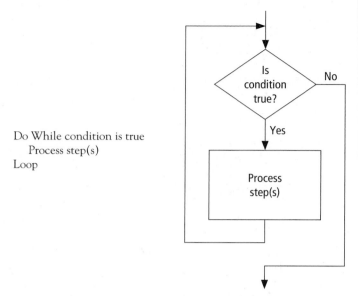

Do While condition is true
    Process step(s)
Loop

FIGURE 1.11 Pseudocode and flowchart for a loop.

is to check a condition before each pass through the loop and continue executing the loop as long as the condition is true. See Figure 1.11.

■ Class Average Algorithm

Problem: Calculate and report the grade-point average for a class.

Discussion: The average grade equals the sum of all grades divided by the number of students. We need a loop to read and then add (accumulate) the grades for each student in the class. Inside the loop, we also need to total (count) the number of students in the class. See Figures 1.12 to 1.14.

Input: Student grades

Processing: Find the sum of the grades; count the number of students; calculate average grade = sum of grades / number of students.

Output: Average grade

■ Comments

1. Tracing a flowchart is like playing a board game. We begin at the Start symbol and proceed from symbol to symbol until we reach the End symbol. At any time, we will be at just one symbol. In a board game, the path taken depends on the result of spinning a spinner or rolling a pair of dice. The path taken through a flowchart depends on the input.

2. The algorithm should be tested at the flowchart stage before being coded into a program. Different data should be used as input, and the output checked. This process is known as **desk checking**. The test data should include nonstandard data as well as typical data.

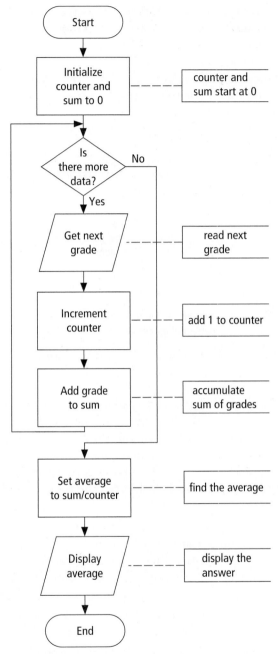

FIGURE 1.12   Flowchart for the class average problem.

3. Flowcharts, pseudocode, and hierarchy charts are universal problem-solving tools. They can be used to construct programs in any computer language, not just Visual Basic.

4. Flowcharts are used throughout this text to provide a visualization of the flow of certain programming tasks and Visual Basic control structures. Major examples of pseudocode and hierarchy charts appear in the case studies.

Program: Calculate and report the average grade of a class.
Initialize Counter and Sum to 0
Do While there is more data
    Get the next Grade
    Increment the Counter
    Add the Grade to the Sum
Loop
Compute Average = Sum/Counter
Display Average

FIGURE 1.13   Pseudocode for the class average problem.

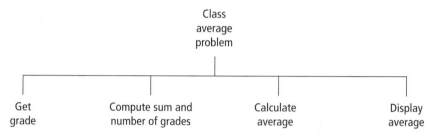

FIGURE 1.14   Hierarchy chart for the class average problem.

5. There are four primary logical programming constructs: sequence, decision, loop, and unconditional branch. Unconditional branch, which appears in some languages as GoTo statements, involves jumping from one place in a program to another. Structured programming uses the first three constructs but forbids the fourth. One advantage of pseudocode over flowcharts is that pseudocode has no provision for unconditional branching and thus forces the programmer to write structured programs.

6. Flowcharts are time consuming to write and difficult to update. For this reason, professional programmers are more likely to favor pseudocode and hierarchy charts. Because flowcharts so clearly illustrate the logical flow of programming techniques, however, they are a valuable tool in the education of programmers.

7. There are many styles of pseudocode. Some programmers use an outline form, whereas others use a form that looks almost like a programming language. The pseudocode appearing in the case studies of this text focuses on the primary tasks to be performed by the program and leaves many of the routine details to be completed during the coding process. Several Visual Basic keywords, such as, If, Else, Do, and While, are used extensively in the pseudocode appearing in this text.

8. Many people draw rectangles around each item in a hierarchy chart. In this text, rectangles are omitted in order to make hierarchy charts easier to draw and thereby to encourage their use.

2

Visual Basic, Controls, and Events

2.1   An Introduction to Visual Basic 2008

Visual Basic 2008 is the latest generation of Visual Basic, a language used by millions of software developers. Visual Basic was designed to make user-friendly programs easier to develop. Prior to the creation of Visual Basic, developing a friendly user interface usually required a programmer to use a language such as C or C++, often requiring hundreds of lines of code just to get a window to appear on the screen. Now the same program can be created with much less time and fewer instructions.

■ Why Windows and Why Visual Basic?

What people call **graphical user interfaces**, or GUIs (pronounced "gooies"), have revolutionized the computer industry. Instead of the confusing textual prompts that earlier users once saw, today's users are presented with such devices as icons, buttons, and drop-down lists that respond to mouse clicks. Accompanying the revolution in how programs look was a revolution in how they feel. Consider a program that requests information for a database. Figure 2.1 shows how a program written before the advent of GUIs got its information. The program requests the six pieces of data one at a time, with no opportunity to go back and alter previously entered information. Then the screen clears and the six inputs are again requested one at a time.

> **Enter name (Enter EOD to terminate): <u>Mr. President</u>**
> **Enter Address: <u>1600 Pennsylvania Avenue</u>**
> **Enter City: <u>Washington</u>**
> **Enter State: <u>DC</u>**
> **Enter Zipcode: <u>20500</u>**
> **Enter Phone Number: <u>202-456-1414</u>**

FIGURE 2.1   Input screen of a pre-Visual Basic program to fill a database.

Figure 2.2 shows how an equivalent Visual Basic program gets its information. The boxes may be filled in any order. When the user clicks on a box with the mouse, the cursor moves to that box. The user can either type in new information or edit the existing information. When the user is satisfied that all the information is correct, he or she just clicks on the "Write to Database" button. The boxes will clear, and the data

FIGURE 2.2   Input screen of a Visual Basic program to fill a database.

for another person can be entered. After all names have been entered, the user clicks on the Exit button. In Figure 2.1, the program is in control; in Figure 2.2, the user is in control!

◼ How You Develop a Visual Basic Program

One of the key elements of planning a Visual Basic program is deciding what the user sees—in other words, designing the screen. What data will he or she be entering? How large a window should the program use? Where will you place the buttons the user clicks on to activate actions by the program? Will the program have places to enter text (text boxes) and places to display output? What kind of warning boxes (message boxes) should the program use? In Visual Basic, the responsive objects a program designer places on windows are called *controls*. Two features make Visual Basic different from traditional programming tools:

1. You literally draw the user interface, much like using a paint program.
2. Perhaps more important, when you're done drawing the interface, the buttons, text boxes, and other objects that you have placed in a blank window will automatically recognize user actions such as mouse movements and button clicks. That is, the sequence of procedures executed in your program is controlled by "events" that the user initiates rather than by a predetermined sequence of procedures in your program.

In any case, only after you design the interface does anything like traditional programming occur. Objects in Visual Basic recognize events like mouse clicks; how the objects respond to them depends on the instructions you write. You always need to write instructions in order to make controls respond to events. This makes Visual Basic programming fundamentally different from conventional programming. Programs in traditional programming languages ran from the top down. For these programming languages, execution started from the first line and moved with the flow of the program to different parts as needed. A Visual Basic program works differently. Its core is a set of independent groups of instructions that are activated by the events they have been told to recognize. This event-driven methodology is a fundamental shift. The user decides the order in which things happen, not the programmer.

Most of the programming instructions in Visual Basic that tell your program how to respond to events like mouse clicks occur in what Visual Basic calls *event procedures*. Essentially, anything executable in a Visual Basic program either is in an event procedure or is used by an event procedure to help the procedure carry out its job. In fact, to stress that Visual Basic is fundamentally different from traditional programming languages, Microsoft uses the term *project*, rather than *program*, to refer to the combination of programming instructions and user interface that makes a Visual Basic program possible. Here is a summary of the steps you take to design a Visual Basic program:

1. Design the appearance of the window that the user sees.
2. Determine the events that the controls on the window should recognize.
3. Write the event procedures for those events.

Now here is what happens when the program is running:

1. Visual Basic monitors the controls in the window to detect any event that a control can recognize (mouse movements, clicks, keystrokes, and so on).

2. When Visual Basic detects an event, it examines the program to see if you've written an event procedure for that event.

3. If you have written an event procedure, Visual Basic executes the instructions that make up that event procedure and goes back to Step 1.

4. If you have not written an event procedure, Visual Basic ignores the event and goes back to Step 1.

These steps cycle continuously until the program ends. Usually, an event must happen before Visual Basic will do anything. Event-driven programs are reactive more than active—and that makes them more user friendly.

■ The Different Versions of Visual Basic

Visual Basic 1.0 first appeared in 1991. It was followed by version 2.0 in 1992, version 3.0 in 1993, version 4.0 in 1995, version 5.0 in 1997, and version 6.0 in 1998. VB.NET, initially released in February 2002, was not backward compatible with the earlier versions of Visual Basic. It incorporated many features requested by software developers, such as true inheritance and powerful Web capabilities. Visual Basic 2005, released in November 2005, and Visual Basic 2008, released in November 2007 are significantly improved versions of VB.NET.

2.2   Visual Basic Controls

Visual Basic programs display a Windows-style screen (called a **form**) with boxes into which users type (and in which users edit) information and buttons that they click to initiate actions. The boxes and buttons are referred to as **controls**. In this section, we examine forms and four of the most useful Visual Basic controls.

■ Starting a New Visual Basic Program

For our purposes, Visual Basic programs are also known as **applications**, **solutions**, or **projects**. Each program is saved (as several files and subfolders) in its own folder. Before starting a new program, you should use Windows Explorer to create a folder to hold the folders for your programs.

The process for invoking Visual Basic varies slightly with the edition of Visual Basic installed on the computer. To invoke Visual Basic from a computer that has Visual Basic Express installed, click the Windows Start button, hover over All Programs, and then click on Microsoft Visual Basic 2008 Express Edition. With the other editions of Visual Basic, hover over All Programs, hover over Microsoft Visual Studio 2008, and then click on Microsoft Visual Studio 2008 in the short list that is revealed.

The window that appears after Visual Basic is invoked is called the **Start Page** and is similar to the window shown in Figure 2.3. (The information in the large section in the middle of the screen comes from the Microsoft Web site and will differ each time Visual Basic is invoked.) The first item on the Start Page menu bar is "File." Click on File, and then click on New Project to produce a New Project dialog box. Figure 2.4 shows the

Menu bar

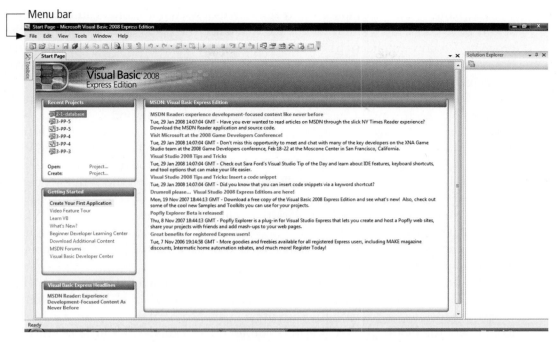

FIGURE 2.3 The Visual Basic 2008 Express Edition Start Page.

New Project dialog box produced by Visual Basic Express. The "Windows Forms Application" icon should be selected as the installed template. If this is not the case, click on "Windows Forms Application" to select it. (The other editions of Visual Basic contain a pane identifying a Project type. You should select "Visual Basic" as the Project type.)

Note: The number of project types and icons showing will vary depending on the version of Visual Basic you are using. Figure 2.4 was created from the Express Edition.

FIGURE 2.4 The Visual Basic Express New Project dialog box.

The name of the program, initially set to WindowsApplication1, can be specified at this time. Since we will have a chance to change the name later, let's just call the program WindowsApplication1 for now. Click on the OK button to invoke the Visual Basic programming environment See Figure 2.5. The Visual Basic programming environment is referred to as the **Integrated Development Environment** or **IDE**.

Very likely, your screen will look different than Figure 2.5. The IDE is extremely configurable. Each window in Figure 2.5 can have its location and size altered. New windows can be displayed in the IDE, and any window can be closed or hidden behind a tab. For instance, in Figure 2.5 the Toolbox window is hidden behind a tab. The View menu is used to add additional windows to the IDE. If you would like your screen to look exactly like Figure 2.5, click on "Reset Windows Layout" in the Windows menu, and then click on "Yes."

The **Menu bar** of the IDE displays the commands you use to work with Visual Basic. Some of the menus, like File, Edit, View, and Window, are common to most Windows applications. Others, such as Project, Build, and Debug, provide commands specific to programming in Visual Basic.

The **Toolbar** holds a collection of icons that carry out standard operations when clicked. For example, you use the fifth icon, which looks like a stack of three diskettes, to save the files associated with the current program. To reveal the purpose of a Toolbar icon, hover the mouse pointer over the icon for a few seconds. The little information rectangle that pops up is called a **tooltip**.

The **Main area** currently holds the rectangular **Form window**, or **form** for short. The form becomes a Windows window when a program is executed. Most information displayed by the program appears on the form. The information usually is displayed in

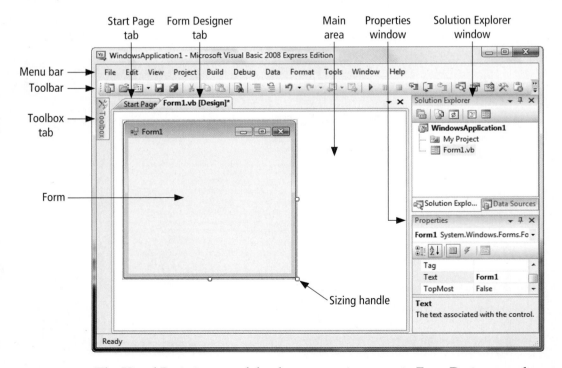

FIGURE 2.5 **The Visual Basic integrated development environment in Form Designer mode.**

controls that the programmer has placed on the form. You can change the size of the form by dragging one of its sizing handles.

The **Properties window** is used to change how objects look and react.

The **Solution Explorer** window displays the files associated with the program and provides access to the commands that pertain to them. (**Note:** If the Solution Explorer or the Properties window is not visible, click on it in the View menu.)

The **Toolbox** holds icons representing objects (called controls) that can be placed on the form. If your screen does not show the Toolbox, hover the mouse over the Toolbox tab at the left side of the screen. The Toolbox will slide into view. Then click on the pushpin icon in the title bar at the top of the Toolbox to keep the Toolbox permanently displayed in the IDE. (**Note:** If there is no tab marked Toolbox, click on Toolbox in the View menu.)

The controls in the Toolbox are grouped into categories such as All Windows Forms and Common Controls. Figure 2.6 shows the Toolbox after the plus sign to the left of "Common Controls" has been clicked. Nearly all the controls discussed in this text can be found in the list of common controls. (You can obtain a description of a control by hovering the mouse over the control.) The four controls discussed in this chapter are text boxes, labels, buttons, and list boxes. In order to see all the group names, click on each of the minus signs appearing to the left of a group name.

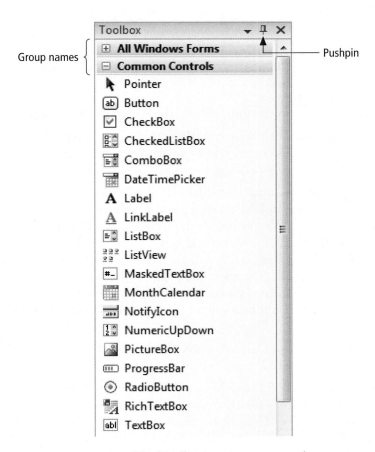

FIGURE 2.6 **The Toolbox's common controls.**

Text boxes: You use a text box to get information from the user, referred to as **input**, or to display information produced by the program, referred to as **output**.

Labels: You place a label near a text box to tell the user what type of information is displayed in the text box.

Buttons: The user clicks a button to initiate an action.

List boxes: In the first part of the book, we use list boxes to display tables or several lines of output. Later, we use list boxes to make selections.

■ A Text Box Walkthrough

1. Double-click on the text box icon in the Common Controls portion of the Toolbox. A rectangle with two small squares, called **sizing handles**, appears at the upper left corner of the form. (You can alter the width of the text box by dragging one of the sizing handles.) Move the mouse arrow to any point of the text box other than a sizing handle, hold down the left mouse button, and drag the text box to the center of the form. See Figure 2.7. **Note:** The Tasks button will be discussed in Chapter 3.

FIGURE 2.7   A text box with sizing handles.

2. Click anywhere on the form outside the rectangle to deselect the text box.

3. Click on the rectangle to restore the handles. An object showing its handles is said to be **selected**. A selected text box can have its width altered, location changed, and other properties modified.

4. Move the mouse arrow to the handle in the center of the right side of the text box. The cursor should change to a double arrow ($\leftrightarrow$). Hold down the left mouse button, and move the mouse to the right. The text box is stretched to the right. Similarly, grabbing the text box on the left side and moving the mouse to the left stretches the text box to the left. You also can use the handles to make the text box smaller. Steps 1 and 4 allow you to place a text box of any width anywhere on the form. **Note:** The text box should now be selected; that is, its sizing handles should be showing. If not, click anywhere inside the text box to select it.

5. Press the delete key, Del, to remove the text box from the form. Step 6 gives an alternative way to place a text box of any width at any location on the form.

6. Click on the text box icon in the Toolbox. Then move the mouse pointer to any place on the form. (When over the form, the mouse pointer becomes a pair of crossed thin lines.) Hold down the left mouse button, and drag the mouse on a diagonal to generate a rectangle. Release the mouse button to obtain a selected

text box. You can now alter the width and location as before. **Note:** The text box should now be selected. If not, click anywhere inside the text box to select it.

7. Press F4 to activate the Properties window. (You also can activate the Properties window by clicking on it, clicking on the Properties window icon in the right part of the Toolbar, selecting Properties Window from the View menu, or clicking on the text box with the right mouse button and selecting Properties.) See Figure 2.8. The first line of the Properties window (called the **Object box**) reads "TextBox1 etc." TextBox1 is the current name of the text box. The first two buttons below the Object box permit you to view the list of properties either grouped into categories or alphabetically. Use the up- and down-arrow keys (or the up- and down-scroll arrows) to move through the list. The left column gives the property names, and the right column gives the current settings of the properties. We discuss four properties in this walkthrough.

Categorized view   Alphabetic view   Properties window icon

FIGURE 2.8   Text box Properties window.

Note 1: The third and fourth buttons below the Object box, the Properties button and the Events button, determine whether properties or events are displayed in the Properties window. Normally the Properties button is highlighted. If not, click on the Properties button.

Note 2: If the Description pane is not visible, right-click on the Properties window, and then click on "Description." The Description pane describes the currently highlighted property.

8. Move to the Text property with the up- and down-arrow keys. (Alternatively, scroll until the property is visible, and click on the property.) The Text property, which determines the words displayed in the text box, is now highlighted. Currently, there is no text displayed in the **Settings box** on the right.

9. Type your first name. Then press the Enter key, or click on another property. Your name now appears in both the Settings box and the text box. See Figure 2.9.

FIGURE 2.9   Setting the Text property to David.

10. Click at the beginning of your name in the Text Settings box, and add your title, such as Mr., Ms., or The Honorable. (If you mistyped your name, you can easily correct it now.) Then, press Enter.

11. Use the up-arrow key or the mouse to move to the ForeColor property. This property determines the color of the information displayed in the text box.

12. Click on the down arrow in the right part of the Settings box, and then click on the Custom tab to display a selection of colors. See Figure 2.10. Click on one of the

FIGURE 2.10   Setting the ForeColor property.

colors, such as *blue* or *red*. Notice the change in the color of your name. (**Note:** The sixteen white boxes at the bottom of the grid are used to create custom colors. See item J under "Design a Form" in Appendix B for details.)

13. Highlight the Font property with a single click of the mouse. The current font is named Microsoft Sans Serif.

14. Click on the ellipsis (…) box in the right part of the Settings box to display a dialog box. See Figure 2.11. The three lists give the current name (Microsoft Sans Serif), current style (Regular), and current size (8) of the font. You can change any of these attributes by clicking on an item in its list or by typing into the box at the top of the list. Click on Bold in the style list, and click on 12 in the size list. Now click on the OK button to see your name displayed in a larger bold font. The text box will be longer so that it can accommodate the larger font.

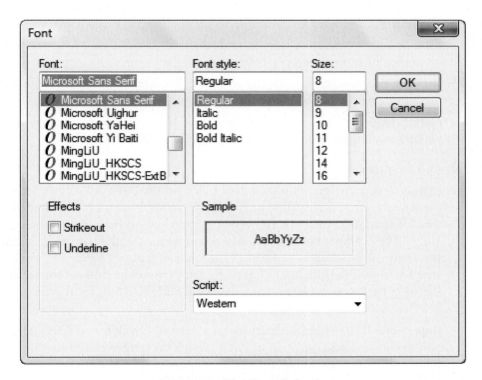

FIGURE 2.11   The Font dialog box.

15. Click on the text box and resize it to be about 3 inches wide.

Visual Basic programs consist of three parts: interface, values of properties, and code. Our interface consists of a form with a single object, a text box. We have set a few properties for the text box—the text (namely, your name), the foreground color, the font style, and the font size. In Section 2.3, we discuss how to place code into a program. Visual Basic endows certain capabilities to programs that are independent of any code we will write. We will now run the existing program without adding any code in order to experience these capabilities.

16. Press F5 to run the program. (Alternatively, a program can be run from the menu by pressing Alt/D/S or by clicking on the Start Debugging icon, the fourteenth or fifteenth icon on the Toolbar.) After a brief delay, a copy of the form appears that has neither the form nor the text box selected.

17. Your name is highlighted. Press the End key to move the cursor to the end of your name. Now type in your last name, and then keep typing. Eventually, the words will scroll to the left.

18. Press Home to return to the beginning of the text. You have a miniature word processor at your disposal. You can place the cursor anywhere you like to add or delete text. You can drag the cursor across text to select a block, place a copy of the block in the Clipboard with Ctrl+C, and then duplicate it elsewhere with Ctrl+V.

19. To end the program, press Alt + F4. Alternatively, you can end a program by clicking on the form's Close button at the right corner of the title bar.

20. Select the text box, activate the Properties window, select the ReadOnly property, click on the down-arrow button, and finally click on True. Notice that the background color is now gray.

21. Run the program, and try typing into the text box. You can't. Such a text box is used for output. Only code can display information in the text box.

    Note: In this textbook, whenever a text box will be used only for the purpose of displaying output, we will always set the ReadOnly property to True.

22. End the program.

23. Let's now save the program on a disk. Click on the Save All icon to save the work done so far. (The Save All icon is the fifth or sixth icon on the Toolbar. It shows three fanned diskettes. Alternately, you can click on Save All in the File menu.) You will be prompted for the name of the program and the path to the folder where you want the program to be saved. Type a name, such as "VBdemo". You can either type a path or use Browse to locate a folder. (This folder will automatically be used the next time you click on the Save All icon.) The files for the program will be held in a subfolder of the selected folder.

    Important: If the "Create directory for solution" check box is checked, then click on the check box to uncheck it. Finally, click on the Save button.

24. Create a new program as before by clicking on "New Project" on the File menu. (Or, you can click on the New Project icon, the first icon on the Toolbar.) A New Project dialog box will appear.

25. Give a name to the project, such as My Program, and then click on the OK button.

26. Place three text boxes on the form. (If you use the double-click technique, move the text boxes so that they do not overlap.) Notice that they have the names TextBox1, TextBox2, and TextBox3.

27. Run the program. Notice that the cursor is in TextBox1. We say that TextBox1 has the **focus**. (This means that TextBox1 is the currently selected object and any keyboard actions will be sent directly to this object.) Any text typed will display in that text box.

28. Press Tab once. Now, TextBox2 has the focus. When you type, the characters appear in TextBox2.

29. Press Tab several times, and then press Shift+Tab a few times. With Tab, the focus cycles through the objects on the form in the order the objects were created. With Shift+Tab, the focus cycles in the reverse order.

30. End the program you created.

31. We would now like to return to the first program. Click on "Open Project" from the File menu. An Open Project dialog box will appear stating that "You must choose to either save or discard changes in the current project before opening a project." There is no need to save this program, so click on the Discard button. Then a second Open Project dialog box will appear.

32. Find the folder corresponding to the program you saved earlier, double-click on the folder, and double-click on the file with extension *sln*. You have now recovered the first program.

    Note: As an alternative to using the Open Project dialog box in Steps 31 and 32 to return to the first program, click on the Start Page tab at the top of the Main area, and click on the program in the Recent Projects pane of the Start Page.

33. If you do not see the Form Designer for the program, double-click on Form1.vb in the Solution Explorer.

■ A Button Walkthrough

1. Click on the New Project icon to start a new program. (Give a name, such as ButtonProg, to the program, and click on OK.)

2. Double-click on the Button icon in the Toolbox to place a button on the form. (The Button icon is the second icon in the Common Controls portion of the Toolbox.)

3. Move the button to the center of the form.

4. Activate the Properties window, highlight the Text property, type "Please Push Me," and press Enter. See Figure 2.12. The button is too small.

FIGURE 2.12   Setting the Text property.

5. Click on the button to select it, and then enlarge it to accommodate the phrase "Please Push Me" on one line.

6. Run the program, and click on the button. The button appears to move in and then out. In Section 2.3, we will write code that is executed when a button is pushed.

7. End the program and select the button.

8. From the Properties window, edit the Text setting by inserting an ampersand (&) before the first letter, P. Press the Enter key, and notice that the first letter P on the button is now underlined. See Figure 2.13. Pressing Alt+P while the program is running triggers the same event as clicking the button. However, the button will not appear to move in and out. Here, P is referred to as the **access key** for the button. (The access key is always specified as the character following the ampersand.)

FIGURE 2.13 **Designating P as an access key.**

■ A Label Walkthrough

1. Click on the New Project icon to begin a new program. Feel free to select the default name, such as WindowsApplication1.

2. Double-click on the label icon to place a label on the form. (The label icon is a large letter A.) Move the label to the center of the form.

3. Activate the Properties window, highlight the Text property, type "Enter Your Phone Number:", and press Enter. (Such a label would be placed next to a text box into which the user will type a phone number.) Notice that the label widened to accommodate the text. This happened because the AutoSize property of the label is set to True by default.

4. Change the AutoSize property to False. Press Enter. Notice that the label now has eight sizing handles when selected.

5. Make the label narrower and longer until the words occupy two lines.

6. Activate the Properties window, and click on the down arrow to the right of the setting for the TextAlign property. Experiment by clicking on the various rectangles and observing their effects. The combination of sizing and alignment permits you to design a label easily.

7. Run the program. Nothing happens, even if you click on the label. Labels just sit there. The user cannot change what a label displays unless you write code to make the change.

8. End the program.

A List Box Walkthrough

1. Click on the New Project icon to begin a new program. Feel free to select the default name, such as WindowsApplication1.

2. Place a list box on the form. (The list box icon is the ninth icon in the Common Controls group of the Toolbox.)

3. Press F4 to activate the Properties window and notice that the list box does not have a Text property. The word ListBox1 is actually the setting for the Name property.

4. Also place a text box, a button and a label on the form.

5. Click on the Object box of the Properties window. The name of the form and the names of the four controls are displayed. If you click on one of the names, that object will become selected and its properties displayed in the Properties window.

6. Run the program. Notice that the word ListBox1 has disappeared, but the words Button1 and Label1 are still visible. The list box is completely blank. In subsequent sections, we will write code to place information into the list box.

The Name Property

Every control has a Name property. It is used in code to refer to the control. By default, controls are given names like TextBox1 and TextBox2. You can use the Properties window to change the Name property of a control to a more meaningful name. (The Name property is always the third property in the alphabetized list of properties. A control's name must begin with a letter and can be a maximum of 215 characters. It can include numbers and underline (_) characters, but cannot include punctuation or spaces.) Also, it is good coding practice to have each name begin with a three- or four-letter prefix that identifies the type of the control. See Table 2.1. The form itself also has a Name property. Beginning with Section 2.3, we will use suggestive names and these prefixes whenever possible.

TABLE 2.1	Some controls and their three-letter prefixes.		
Control	Prefix	Example	
form	frm	frmLottery	
button	btn	btnComputeTotal	
label	lbl	lblInstructions	
list box	lst	lstOutput	
text box	txt	txtAddress	

The Name property of the form itself also can be changed. Suppose you want to change the name of the form from Form1 to frmPayroll. The most efficient way to set the name of the form is to change the name of the file Form1.vb appearing in the Solution Explorer window to frmPayroll.vb. To make the change, right-click on Form1.vb in the

Solution Explorer window, click on Rename, type in the new name (frmPayroll.vb), and press Enter.

Important: Make sure that the new filename has the extension "vb".

The Name and Text properties of a button are both initially set to something like Button1. However, changing one of these properties does not affect the setting of the other property, and similarly for the Name and Text properties of forms, text boxes, and labels. The Text property of a form specifies the words appearing in the form's title bar.

■ Two Help Walkthroughs

The Help menu provides four ways for you to obtain information about Visual Basic. You can browse topic titles using the Contents window, search for topics by keyword using the Index window, search the full text of topics using the Search page, or browse for topics by category using How Do I. The following walkthroughs demonstrate the Index and How Do I features.

Index Walkthrough

1. Click on Index in the Help menu to invoke the Index window.
2. If the "Filtered by:" box does not say "Visual Basic" or "Visual Basic Express Edition," click on the down arrow and select one of them from the drop-down list.
3. Type "buttons" into the "Look for" box, look down the list of subheadings of "buttons," and then click on "introducing." (The page that appears has the title "Interacting with the User: Using Buttons.")
4. Read the first few paragraphs of the discussion.

"How Do I" Walkthrough

1. Click on "How Do I" in the Help menu. The page that appears contains a short list of underlined links.
2. Click on the underlined link "Learn the Visual Basic Language (How Do I in Visual Basic Express)." The page that appears contains another list of underlined links under the heading "In Visual Basic Express."
3. Click on the underlined link "Introduction to the Visual Basic Programming Language."
4. Read the introductory discussion of Visual Basic in the page that appears.

■ Fonts

The default font for controls is Microsoft Sans Serif. Two other useful fonts are Courier New and Wingdings.

Courier New is a fixed-width font; that is, each character has the same width. With such a font, the letter i occupies the same space as the letter m. Fixed-width fonts are used with tables when information is to be aligned in columns.

The Wingdings font consists of assorted small pictures and symbols, each corresponding to a character on the keyboard. For instance if one of the characters %, (, 1, or J is typed into the Text setting of a control whose Font is Wingdings, the control will display a bell, phone, open folder, or smiling face, respectively.

To view the character set for a Windows font, click on the Windows Start button in the Windows task bar and successively select All Programs, Accessories, System Tools, and Character Map. Then click on Character Map, or press the Enter key. After selecting the font, click on any item to enlarge it. You can insert the keyboard character for the item into the Clipboard by pressing the Select button and then the Copy button. To place the character into the Text property of a control having that font, just move the cursor to the Settings box for the Text property and press Ctrl+V.

■ Auto Hide

The Auto Hide feature allows you to make more room for the Main area of the screen by hiding windows (such as the Toolbox, Solution Explorer, or Properties window). Let's illustrate the feature with a walkthrough using the Toolbox window. We start by discussing the situation where the feature is *disabled*.

1. If the Toolbox window is currently visible and the pushpin icon in the window title is vertical, then the Auto Hide feature is disabled. (If the Toolbox window is not visible, press Alt/V/X to select Toolbox from the View menu. If the pushpin icon is horizontal, then click on the icon to make it vertical.) When the Auto Hide feature is disabled, the Toolbox window stays stationary and is always ready for use.

2. Click the mouse cursor somewhere outside of the Toolbox window and note that the Toolbox window stays fixed.

3. Click on the pushpin icon to make it horizontal. The Auto Hide feature is now *enabled*.

4. Move the mouse cursor somewhere outside of the Toolbox window and note that the window slides into a tab on the left side of the screen. The name and icon of the Toolbox window appear on the tab.

5. Hover the mouse cursor over the tab. The window slides into view and is ready for use.

6. Place a new control on the form, and then move the cursor away from the Toolbox window. The window automatically slides back to its tab on the edge of the screen.

   Note: We recommend that you keep the Toolbox, Solution Explorer, and Properties windows displayed unless you are creating a program with a very large form and need extra space.

■ Positioning and Aligning Controls

Visual Basic provides several tools for positioning and aligning controls on a form. **Proximity lines** are short line segments that help you place controls a comfortable distance from each other and from the sides of the form. **Snap lines** are horizontal and vertical line segments that help you align controls. The **Format menu** is used to align controls, center controls horizontally and vertically in a form, and make a group of selected controls the same size.

A *Positioning and Aligning Walkthrough*

1. Begin a new program.
2. Place a button near the center of the form.
3. Drag the button toward the upper-right corner of the form until two short line segments appear. See Figure 2.14(a). The button is now a comfortable distance from the two sides of the form.
4. Place a second button below the first button and drag it upwards until a proximity line appears between the two buttons. The buttons are now a comfortable distance apart.
5. Resize and position the two buttons as shown in Figure 2.14(b).
6. Drag Button2 upwards until a blue line appears along the bottoms of the two buttons. See Figure 2.14(c). This blue line is called a *snap line*. The bottoms of the two buttons are now aligned.
7. Continue dragging Button2 upwards until a purple snap line appears just underneath the words Button1 and Button2. See Figure 2.14(d). The middles of the two buttons are now aligned. If we were to continue dragging Button2 upwards, a blue snap line would tell us when the tops are aligned. Step 10 shows another way to align the controls.

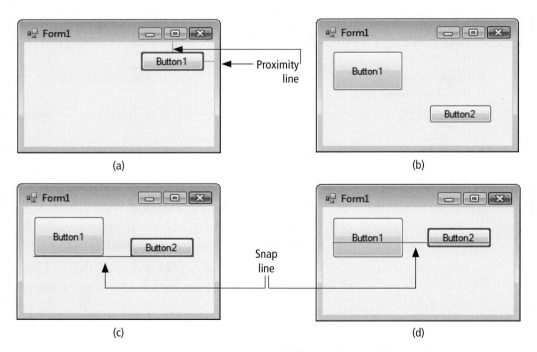

FIGURE 2.14 Positioning Controls.

8. Click on Button1 and then hold down the Ctrl key and click on Button2. After the mouse button is released, both buttons will be selected.

Note: This process (called **selection of multiple controls**) can be repeated to select a group of any number of controls.

9. With the two buttons still selected, press F4 to open the Properties window. Then set the ForeColor property to Blue. Notice that the ForeColor property has been altered for both buttons at the same time. Actually, any property that is common to every control in selected multiple controls can be set simultaneously for the entire group.

10. With the two buttons still selected, open the Format menu in the Menu bar, hover over Align, and click on Tops. The tops of the two buttons are now aligned. Precisely, Button1 (the first button selected) will stay fixed, and Button2 will move up so that its top is aligned with the top of Button1.

The most common uses of the submenus of the Format menu are as follows:

Align: Align middles or corresponding sides of a group of selected controls.

Make Same Size: Make the width and/or height of a group of selected controls the same.

Horizontal Spacing: Equalize the horizontal spacing between a group of three or more selected controls arranged in a row.

Vertical Spacing: Equalize the vertical spacing between a group of three or more selected controls arranged in a column.

Center in Form: Center a selected control either horizontally or vertically in a form.

When multiple controls are selected with the Ctrl key, the first control selected (called the **primary control** of the group) will have white sizing handles, while the other controls will have black sizing handles. All alignment and sizing statements initiated from the Format menu will keep the primary control fixed, and align (or size) the other controls with respect to the primary control.

After multiple controls have been selected, they can be dragged as a group and deleted as a group. Exercises 35 and 36 show how the arrow keys can be used to move and size a control. The arrow keys also can be used to move and size multiple controls as a group.

A group of controls also can be selected by clicking the mouse outside the controls, dragging it across the controls, and releasing it. The Select All command from the Edit menu (or the key combination Ctrl + A) causes all the controls on the form to be selected. Although these methods are easy to apply, they do not allow the programmer to choose the primary control.

■ Setting Tab Order

Each time the Tab key is pressed while a program is running, the focus moves from one control to another. The following walkthrough explains how to determine the order in which the focus moves and how that order can be changed.

1. Start a new program.

2. Place a button, a text box, and a list box on a form.

3. Run the program, and successively press the Tab key. Notice that the controls receive the focus in the order they were placed on the form.

4. End the program.

5. Click on Tab Order in the View menu. The screen appears as in Figure 2.15(a). The controls are numbered from 0 to 2 in the order they were created. Each of the numbers is referred to as a **tab index**.

6. Click on the list box, then the button, and finally the text box. Notice that the tab indexes change as shown in Figure 2.15(b).

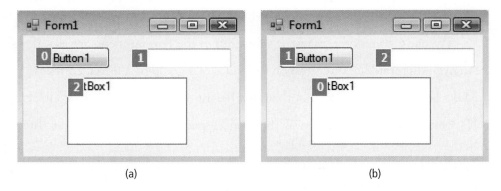

(a)   (b)

FIGURE 2.15

7. Click again on Tab Order in the View menu to set the new tab order.

8. Run the program again, and successively press Tab. Notice that the controls receive the focus according to the new tab order.

9. End the program.

10. Add a label to the form, rerun the program, and successively press Tab. Notice that the label does not receive the focus.

Whether or not a control can receive the focus is determined by the setting of its TabStop property. By default, the setting for TabStop property is True for buttons, text boxes, and list boxes, and False for labels. In this book we always use these default settings. **Note:** Even though labels do not receive the focus while tabbing, they are still assigned a tab index.

■ Comments

1. While you are working on a program, the program resides in memory. Removing a program from memory is referred to as **closing** the program. A program is automatically closed when you begin a new program. Also, it can be closed directly with the Close Project command from the File menu.

2. Three useful properties that have not been discussed are the following:

   (a) BackColor: This property specifies the background color for the form or a control.

(b) Visible: Setting the Visible property to False causes an object to disappear when the program is run. The object can be made to reappear with code.

(c) Enabled: Setting the Enabled property of a control to False restricts its use. It appears grayed and cannot receive the focus. Controls sometimes are disabled temporarily if they do not apply to the current state of the program.

3. Most properties can be set or altered with code as the program is running instead of being preset from the Properties window. For instance, a button can be made to disappear with a line such as `Button1.Visible = False`. The details are presented in Section 2.3.

4. If you inadvertently double-click on a form, a window containing text will appear. (The first line is Public Class Form1.) This is the Code Editor, which is discussed in the next section. Press Ctrl+Z to undo the addition of this new code. To return to the Form Designer, click on the tab above the Main area labeled "Form1.vb [Design]."

5. We have seen two ways to place a control onto a form. A third method is to drag the control from the Toolbox to the form.

6. The Recent Projects pane in the Start Page not only displays a list of recently updated programs, it also lets you open existing programs and create new programs. To open *any* existing program or to create a new program, click on the appropriate word "Project…" at the bottom of the pane.

7. The Getting Started pane in the Start Page displays a list of Help topics, Web sites, technical articles, and other sources that highlight features in the product.

Practice Problems 2.2

1. What is the difference between the Text and the Name properties of a button?

2. The first two group names in the Toolbox are "All Windows Forms" and "Common Controls." How many groups are there?

EXERCISES 2.2

1. Create a form with two buttons, run the program, and click on each button. Do you notice anything different about a button after it has been clicked?

2. While a program is running, a control is said to lose focus when the focus moves from that control to another control. In what three ways can the user cause a control to lose focus?

In Exercises 3 through 24, carry out the task. Use a new program for each exercise.

3. Place "CHECKING ACCOUNT" in the title bar of a form.

4. Create a text box containing the words "PLAY IT, SAM" in blue letters.

5. Create a text box with a yellow background.

6. Create a text box named txtGreeting and containing the word "HELLO" in large italic letters.

7. Create a label containing the sentence "After all is said and done, more is said than done." The sentence should occupy three lines, and each line should be centered horizontally in the label.

8. Create a read-only text box containing the words "Visual Basic" in bold white letters on a red background.

9. Create a text box named txtLanguage and containing the words "Visual Basic 2008" in Courier New font.

10. Create a yellow button named btnPush and containing the word "PUSH".

11. Create a white button containing the word "PUSH" in large italic letters.

12. Create a button containing the word "PUSH" in bold letters in which the letter P is underlined.

13. Create a button containing the word "PUSH" with the letter H as the access key.

14. Create a label containing the word "ALIAS" in white on a blue background.

15. Create a label named lblAKA and containing the centered italicized word "ALIAS".

16. Place BALANCE SHEET in the title bar of a form, where the form has a yellow background.

17. Create a label containing VISUAL on the first line and BASIC on the second line. Each word should be right justified.

18. Create a form named frmHello whose title bar reads "Hello World".

19. Create a label containing a picture of a diskette. (**Hint:** Use the Wingdings character <.) Make the diskette as large as possible.

20. Create a label containing the bold word "ALIAS" in the Courier New font.

21. Create a list box with a yellow background.

22. Create a list box that will be invisible when the program is run.

23. Create a form named frmYellow with a yellow background.

24. Create a button containing a picture of a red bell. (**Hint:** Use the Wingdings character %.) Make the bell as large as possible.

In Exercises 25 through 30, create the interface shown in that figure. (These exercises give you practice creating controls and assigning properties. The interfaces do not necessarily correspond to actual programs.)

25.

26.

27.

28.

29.

30.

31. Create a replica of your bank check on a form. Words common to all checks, such as "PAY TO THE ORDER OF," should be contained in labels. Items specific to your checks, such as your name at the top left, should be contained in text boxes. Make the check on the screen resemble your personal check as much as possible.

32. Create a replica of your campus ID on a form. Words that are on all student IDs, such as the name of the college, should be contained in labels. Information specific to your ID, such as your name and Social Security number, should be contained in text boxes. Simulate your picture with a text box containing a smiling face—a size 24 Wingdings J.

33. Consider the form shown in Exercise 25. Assume the Batman button was added to the form before the Robin button. What is the tab index of the Robin button?

34. Consider the form shown in Exercise 26. Assume the first control added to the form was the label. What is the tab index of the label?

The following hands-on exercises develop additional techniques for manipulating and accessing controls placed on a form.

35. Place a text box on a form and select the text box. What is the effect of pressing the various arrow keys?

36. Place a text box on a form and select the text box. What is the effect of pressing the various arrow keys while holding down the Shift key?

37. Repeat Exercise 36 for selected multiple controls.

38. Repeat Exercise 35 for selected multiple controls.

39. Place a label and a list box on a form and change their font sizes to 12 at the same time.

40. Place a button in the center of a form and select it. Hold down the Ctrl key and press an arrow key. Repeat this process for each of the other arrow keys. Describe what happens.

41. Place a label and a text box on a form with the label to the left of and above the text box. Select the label. Hold down the Ctrl key and press the down-arrow key twice. With the Ctrl key still pressed, press the right-arrow key. Describe what happens.

42. Place two buttons on a form with one button to the right of and below the other button. Select the lower button, hold down the Ctrl key, and press the left-arrow key. With the Ctrl key still pressed, press the up-arrow key. Describe the effect of pressing the two arrow keys.

43. Experiment with the Align command on the Format menu to determine the difference between the *center* and the *middle* of a control.

44. Place four large buttons vertically on a form. Use the Format menu to make them the same size and to make the spacing between them uniform.

45. Place a text box on a form, select the text box, and open its Properties window. Double-click on the name (not the Settings box) of the ReadOnly property. Double-click again. What is the effect of double-clicking on a property whose possible settings are True and False?

46. Place a button on a form, select the button, and open its Properties window. Double-click on the name (not the Settings box) of the ForeColor property. Double-click repeatedly. Describe what is happening.

Solutions to Practice Problems 2.2

1. The text is the words appearing on the button, whereas the name is the designation used to refer to the button. Initially, they have the same value, such as Button1. However, each can be changed independently of the other.

2. 11 groups. Figure 2.16 shows the Toolbox after each of the ⊟ signs preceding group names have been converted to ⊞ signs.

Until Chapter 9, all of the controls discussed in this book can be found in the Common Controls group. The group General, which holds text fragments rather than controls, will first be used in Section 3.3 to hold snippets of programming code.

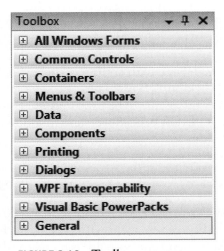

FIGURE 2.16   Toolbox group names

2.3   Visual Basic Events

When a Visual Basic program runs, the form and its controls appear on the screen. Normally, nothing happens until the user takes an action, such as clicking a control or pressing a key. We call such an action an **event.** The programmer writes code that reacts to an event by performing some functionality.

The three steps in creating a Visual Basic program are as follows:

1. Create the interface; that is, generate, position, and size the objects.
2. Set properties; that is, configure the appearance of the objects.
3. Write the code that executes when events occur.

Section 2.2 covered Steps 1 and 2; this section is devoted to Step 3. Code consists of statements that carry out tasks. In this section, we limit ourselves to statements that change properties of a control or the form while a program is running.

Properties of controls are changed in code with statements of the form

```
controlName.property = setting
```

where *controlName* is the name of the control, *property* is one of the properties of the control, and *setting* is a valid setting for that property. Such statements are called **assignment statements**. They assign values to properties. Three examples of assignment statements are as follows:

1. The statement

```
txtBox.Text = "Hello"
```

displays the word *Hello* in the text box.

2. The statement

```
btnButton.Visible = True
```

makes the button visible.

3. The statement

```
txtBox.ForeColor = Color.Red
```

sets the color of the characters in the text box named txtBox to red.

Most events are associated with controls. The event "click on btnButton" is different from the event "click on lstBox." These two events are specified btnButton.Click and lstBox.Click. The statements to be executed when an event occurs are written in a block of code called an **event procedure**. The first line of an event procedure (called the **header**) has the form

```
Private Sub objectName_event(ByVal sender As System.Object,
        ByVal e As System.EventArgs) Handles objectName.event
```

Since we do not make any use of the lengthy text inside the parentheses in this book, for the sake of readability we replace it with an ellipsis. However, it will automatically appear in our programs each time Visual Basic creates the header for an event procedure. The structure of an event procedure is

```
Private Sub objectName_event(...) Handles objectName.event
  statements
End Sub
```

where the three dots (that is, the ellipsis) represent

```
ByVal sender As System.Object, ByVal e As System.EventArgs
```

Words such as "Private," "ByVal," "As," "Sub," "Handles," and "End" have special meanings in Visual Basic and are referred to as **keywords** or **reserved words**. The Visual Basic editor automatically capitalizes the first letter of a keyword and displays the word in blue. The word "Sub" in the first line signals the beginning of the procedure, and the first line identifies the object and the event occurring to that object. The last line signals the termination of the event procedure. The statements to be executed appear between these two lines. (**Note:** The word "Private" indicates that the event procedure cannot be invoked by another form. This will not concern us until much later in the book. The expression following Handles identifies the object and the event happening to that object. The expression **"objectName_event"** is the default name of the procedure and can be changed if desired. In this book, we always use the default name. The word "Sub" is an abbreviation of *Subroutine*.) For instance, the event procedure

```
Private Sub btnButton_Click(...) Handles btnButton.Click
  txtBox.ForeColor = Color.Red
End Sub
```

changes the color of the words in the text box to red when the button is clicked.

■ An Event Procedure Walkthrough

The form in Figure 2.17, which contains two text boxes and a button, will be used to demonstrate what event procedures are and how they are created. Three event procedures will be used to alter the appearance of a phrase appearing in a text box. The event procedures are named txtFirst_TextChanged, btnRed_Click, and txtFirst_Leave.

OBJECT	PROPERTY	SETTING
frmDemo	Text	Demonstration
txtFirst		
txtSecond		
btnRed	Text	Change Color to Red

FIGURE 2.17   The interface for the event procedure walkthrough.

1. Create the interface in Figure 2.17 in the Form Designer. The Name properties of the form, text boxes, and button should be set as shown in the Object column. The Text property of the form should be set to Demonstration, and the Text property of the button should be set to Change Color to Red. No properties need be set for the text boxes.

2. Click the right mouse button anywhere on the Main area, and click on View Code. The Form Designer IDE is replaced by the **Code Editor IDE** (also known as the *Code view* or the *Code window*). See Figure 2.18.

FIGURE 2.18   The Visual Basic IDE in Code Editor mode.

The tab labeled frmDemo.vb corresponds to the Code Editor. You press the tab labeled frmDemo.vb [Design], when you want to return to the Form Designer. Just below the tabs are two drop-down list boxes. The left box is called the **Class Name box**, and the right box is called the **Method Name box**. (When you hover the mouse pointer over one of these list boxes, its type appears in a tooltip.) We will place our program code between the two lines shown. Let's refer to this region as the **program region**.

Figure 2.18 shows that the Code Editor IDE has a Toolbox, Solution Explorer, and Properties window that support Auto Hide. The Solution Explorer window for the Code Editor functions exactly like the one for the Form Designer. The Code Editor's Toolbox has just one group, General, that is used to store code fragments which can be copied into a program when needed. The Code Editor's Properties window will not be used in this textbook.

3. Click on the tab labeled "frmDemo.vb [Design]" to return to the Form Designer. (You also can invoke the Form Designer by clicking Designer in the View menu, or by right-clicking the Code Editor and clicking View Designer.)

4. Double-click on the first text box. The Code Editor reappears, but now the following two lines of code have been added to the program region and the cursor is located on the blank line between them.

```
Private Sub txtFirst_TextChanged(...) Handles txtFirst.TextChanged

End Sub
```

The first line is the header for the event procedure named txtFirst_TextChanged. This procedure is triggered by the event txtFirst.TextChanged. That is, whenever there is a change in the text displayed in the text box txtFirst, the code between the two lines just shown will be executed.

5. Type the line

```
txtFirst.ForeColor = Color.Blue
```

at the cursor location. When you type the first period, a list containing all the properties of text boxes appears. See Figure 2.19(a). (Each property is preceded by a little Properties window icon. The list also contains something called *methods*, which we will discuss later.) At this point, you can scroll up the list and double-click on ForeColor to automatically enter that property. See Figure 2.19(b). Or, you can keep typing. After you have typed "For," the list shortens to the single word ForeColor. At that point, you can press the Tab key to enter the word "ForeColor." This feature, known as **Member Listing**, is one of the features of Visual Basic that use a Microsoft context-sensitive help technology called **IntelliSense**.

FIGURE 2.19 IntelliSence at work.

6. Return to the Form Designer and double-click on the button. The Code window reappears, and the first and last lines of the event procedure btnRed_Click appear in the program region. Type the line that sets the ForeColor property of txtFirst to Red. The event procedure will now appear as follows:

```
Private Sub btnRed_Click(...) Handles btnRed.Click
  txtFirst.ForeColor = Color.Red
End Sub
```

7. Click on the down-arrow button to the right of the Class Name box and then click on txtFirst in the drop-down list.

8. Click on the down-arrow button to the right of the Method Name box and then click on Leave in the drop-down list box. (The event txtFirst.Leave is triggered when the focus is removed from the text box.) The first and last lines of the event procedure txtFirst_Leave will be displayed. In this procedure, type the line that sets the ForeColor property of txtFirst to Black. The Code Editor will now look as follows:

```
Public Class frmDemo
  Private Sub txtFirst_Leave(...) Handles txtFirst.Leave
    txtFirst.ForeColor = Color.Black
  End Sub

  Private Sub txtFirst_TextChanged(...) Handles txtFirst.TextChanged
    txtFirst.ForeColor = Color.Blue
  End Sub

  Private Sub btnRed_Click(...) Handles btnRed.Click
    txtFirst.ForeColor = Color.Red
  End Sub
End Class
```

9. Hover the cursor over the word "ForeColor." Visual Basic now displays information about the foreground color property. This illustrates another help feature of Visual Basic.

10. Now run the program by pressing F5.

11. Type something into the text box. In Figure 2.20, the blue word "Hello" has been typed. (Recall that a text box has the focus whenever it is ready to accept typing—that is, whenever it contains a blinking cursor.)

FIGURE 2.20 Text box containing input.

12. Click on the second text box. The contents of the first text box will become black. When the second text box was clicked, the first text box lost the focus; that is, the event Leave happened to txtFirst. Thus, the event procedure txtFirst_Leave was invoked, and the code inside the procedure was executed.

13. Click on the button. This invokes the event procedure btnRed_Click, which changes the color of the words in txtFirst to Red.

14. Click on the first text box, and type the word "Friend" after the word "Hello." As soon as typing begins, the text in the text box is changed and the TextChanged event is triggered. This event causes the color of the contents of the text box to become blue.

15. You can repeat Steps 11 through 14 as many times as you like. When you are finished, end the program by pressing Alt+F4, clicking the Stop Debugging icon on the Toolbar, or clicking the Close button (X) on the form.

■ Properties and Event Procedures of the Form

You can assign properties to the form itself in code. However, a statement such as

```
frmDemo.Text = "Demonstration"
```

will not work. The form is referred to by the keyword *Me*. Therefore, the proper statement is

```
Me.Text = "Demonstration"
```

To display a list of the events associated with frmDemo, select "(frmDemo Events)" from the Class Name box and then open the Method Name box.

■ The Header of an Event Procedure

As mentioned earlier, in a header for an event procedure such as

```
Private Sub btnOne_Click(...) Handles btnOne.Click
```

btnOne_Click is the name of the event procedure, and btnOne.Click identifies the event that triggers the procedure. The name can be changed at will. For instance, the header can be changed to

```
Private Sub ButtonPushed(...) Handles btnOne.Click
```

Also, an event procedure can be triggered by more than one event. For instance, if the previous line is changed to

```
Private Sub ButtonPushed(...) Handles btnOne.Click, btnTwo.Click
```

the event will be triggered if either btnOne or btnTwo is clicked.
We have been using ellipses (. . .) as place holders for the phrase

```
ByVal sender As System.Object, ByVal e As System.EventArgs
```

In Chapter 5, we will gain a better understanding of this type of phrase. Essentially, the word "sender" carries a reference to the object that triggered the event, and the letter "e" carries some additional information that the sending object wants to communicate. We will not make use of either "sender" or "e".

■ Context-Sensitive Help

Consider the program created in the event procedure walkthrough. If you click on the word *txtFirst* and then press the F1 key, a discussion of the Textbox control will appear. This feature of Visual Basic is called **context-sensitive help**. You can click on any element of a program and press F1 to obtain information relevant to that element. For instance, if you click on Sub and press F1, you will obtain information about procedures.

■ Text Files

Programs often make use of data stored in files. In Chapter 10 we work with sophisticated data files called databases. Until then we will rely on simple data files known as **text files**. Text files can be created, viewed, and modified with sophisticated word processors such as Word, or with elementary word processors such as the Windows accessories WordPad and Notepad. They differ from files normally created with Word in that they have no formatting. They are pure text and nothing else – hence the name *text file*.

The Visual Basic IDE provides simple ways to create and manage text files. The following walkthrough creates a text file:

1. Click on the New Project icon to start a new program.
2. Give a name, such as TextFileProg, to the program, and click on OK.
3. If the Solution Explorer window is not visible, click on Solution Explorer in the View menu.
4. Highlight the name of the program at the top of the Solution Explorer window.
5. Press Alt/P/W to invoke Add New Item from the Project menu. Alternately, click on the Add New Item icon in the Toolbar. (An Add New Item dialog box will appear.)
6. Select the Text File icon in the dialog box, and enter the filename PAYROLL.TXT in the Name text box. (Had we omitted the extension, Visual Basic would have automatically added the extension ".txt" to the name.)
7. Click the Add button. (The Text Editor, an elementary word processor, will appear in the Main area, and the filename will appear in the Solution Explorer window.)
8. Type the following information into the Text Editor. (It gives the names of employees, their hourly wages, and the number of hours worked in the past week. This text file will be used in Section 3.3.)

   ```
   Mike Jones
   9.35
   35
   John Smith
   10.75
   33
   ```

9. Right-click on the tab containing the filename PAYROLL.TXT and click on "Save PAYROLL.TXT."
10. Right-click on the tab containing the filename PAYROLL.TXT and click on Close.

■ Viewing All Possible Event Procedures for a Control

All the event procedures associated with the selected control can be displayed and described in the Form Designer Properties window by clicking on the Events button (pictured as a lightning bolt) on the toolbar at the top of the Properties window. Figure 2.21 shows some of the 58 events for the button from the preceding event procedure walk-through. A description of the selected event appears in the Description pane. Don't be alarmed by the large number of events. There is only one event that is used extensively throughout this book – the Click event for buttons. *Note:* After viewing events in the Properties window, click on the Properties button (to the left of the Events button) to return to displaying properties in the window.

FIGURE 2.21 Events displayed in the Properties window.

■ Opening a Program

Beginning with the next chapter, each example contains a program. These programs can be downloaded from my Prentice-Hall website for this book. See the discussion on page xv for details. The process of placing a program stored on a disk into the Visual Basic environment is referred to as **opening** the program. Let's open the downloaded program 7-1-3 from Chapter 7. That program allows you to enter the name of a football team, and then displays the numbers of Super Bowls the team won.

1. From Visual Basic, click on Open Project in the File menu. (An Open Project dialog box will appear.)
2. Display the contents of the Ch07 subfolder downloaded from the website.
3. Double-click on 7-1-3.
4. Double-click on 7-1-3.sln.
5. If the Solution Explorer window is not visible, click on Solution Explorer in the View menu.

6. In the Solution Explorer window, click on frmBowl.vb. (Five buttons will appear at the top of the Solution Explorer window. See Figure 2.22.) At any time you can click on the View Code button to invoke the Code Editor, or you can click on the View Designer button to invoke the Form Designer.

FIGURE 2.22   Solution Explorer window.

7. Press F5 to run the program.

8. Type in the name of a football team (such as 49ers or Giants), and press the "Display Games Team Won" button. (See Figure 2.23.) You can repeat this process as many times as desired.

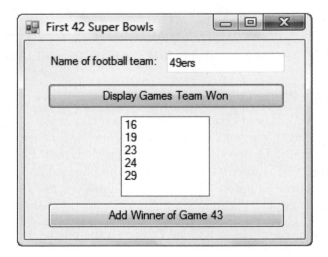

FIGURE 2.23   Output for program 7-1-3.

9. To end the program, click the Close button (X).

The program just executed uses a text file named SBWINNERS.TXT. To view the text file, open the folder *bin*, open the subfolder *Debug*, and click on SBWINNERS.TXT.

(If the *bin* folder is not visible, click on the Show All Files button. If SBWINNERS.TXT is not listed in the *Debug* subfolder, click the Refresh button and reopen the folders. After reading Chapter 3, you will understand why text files are placed in the *Debug* subfolder of the *bin* folder.) The first line of the file gives the winner of the first Super Bowl, the second line gives the winner of the second Super Bowl, and so on. To close the text file, right-click on the tab labeled SBWINNERS.TXT, and click on Close.

■ Comments

1. The Visual Basic editor automatically indents the statements inside procedures. In this book, we indent by two spaces. To instruct your editor to indent by two spaces, select Options from the Tools menu, and uncheck the "Show all settings" box in the Options window that appears. Expand "Text Editor Basic" or "Text Editor," click on "Editor," enter 2 into the "Indent size:" box, and click on OK.

2. The event *control*.Leave is triggered when the specified control loses the focus. Its counterpart is the event *control*. Enter which is triggered when the specified control gets the focus. A related statement is

```
control.Focus()
```

which moves the focus to the specified control.

3. We have ended our programs by clicking the Stop Debugging icon or pressing Alt + F4. A more elegant technique is to create a button, call it btnQuit, with caption Quit and the following event procedure:

```
Private Sub btnQuit_Click(...) Handles btnQuit.Click
  End
End Sub
```

4. For statements of the form

```
object.Text = setting
```

the expression for *setting* must be surrounded by quotes. (For instance, lblName. Text = "Name".) For properties where the proper setting is one of the words True or False, these words should *not* be surrounded by quotation marks.

5. Names of existing event procedures associated with an object are not automatically changed when you rename the object. You must change them yourself. However, the event that triggers the procedure (and all other references to the control) will change automatically. For example, suppose an event procedure is

```
Private Sub btnOne_Click(...) Handles btnOne.Click
  btnOne.Text = "Press Me"
End Sub
```

and, in the Form Designer, you change the name of btnOne to btnTwo. Then, when you return to the Code Editor the procedure will be

```
Private Sub btnOne_Click(...) Handles btnTwo.Click
  btnTwo.Text = "Press Me"
End Sub
```

6. The Code Editor has many features of a word processor. For instance, the operations cut, copy, paste, undo, and redo can be carried out with the sixth through ninth icons from the Toolbar. These operations, and several others, also can be initiated from the Edit menu.

7. The Code Editor can detect certain types of errors. For instance, if you type

```
txtFirst.Text = hello
```

and then move away from the line, the automatic syntax checker will underline the word "hello" with a blue squiggle to indicate that something is wrong. When the mouse cursor is hovered over the offending wording, the editor will display a message explaining what is wrong. If you try to run the program without correcting the error, the dialog box in Figure 2.24 will appear.

FIGURE 2.24 Error dialog box.

8. When you double-click on a control in the Form Designer, the header for the most used event procedure is placed in the Code Editor. The event that appears most frequently in this book is the Click event for button controls.

9. Font properties, such as the name, style, and size, are usually specified at design time. The setting of the properties can be displayed in code with statements such as

```
lstBox.Items.Add(txtBox.Font.Name)
lstBox.Items.Add(txtBox.Font.Bold)
lstBox.Items.Add(txtBox.Font.Size)
```

However, a font's name, style, and size properties cannot be altered in code with statements of the form

```
txtBox.Font.Name = "Courier New"
txtBox.Font.Bold = True
txtBox.Font.Size = 16
```

10. When you make changes to a program, asterisks appear as superscripts on the tabs labeled "frmName.vb [design]" and "frmName.vb." The asterisks disappear when the program is saved or run.

Note: If the program has been saved to disk, all files for the program will be automatically updated on the disk whenever the program is saved or run.

Practice Problem 2.3

1. What event procedure is displayed when you double-click on each of the following controls in the Form Designer?
   (a) text box
   (b) button
   (c) label
   (d) list box

2. Give a statement that will prevent the user from typing into txtBox.

EXERCISES 2.3

In Exercises 1 through 6, describe the contents of the text box after the button is clicked.

1.
```
Private Sub btnOutput_Click(...) Handles btnOutput.Click
    txtBox.Text = "Hello"
End Sub
```

2.
```
Private Sub btnOutput_Click(...) Handles btnOutput.Click
    txtBox.ForeColor = Color.Red
    txtBox.Text = "Hello"
End Sub
```

3.
```
Private Sub btnOutput_Click(...) Handles btnOutput.Click
    txtBox.BackColor = Color.Orange
    txtBox.Text = "Hello"
End Sub
```

4.
```
Private Sub btnOutput_Click(...) Handles btnOutput.Click
    txtBox.Text = "Goodbye"
    txtBox.Text = "Hello"
End Sub
```

5.
```
Private Sub btnOutput_Click(...) Handles btnOutput.Click
    txtBox.Text = "Hello"
    txtBox.Visible = False
End Sub
```

6.
```
Private Sub btnOutput_Click(...) Handles btnOutput.Click
    txtBox.BackColor = Color.Yellow
    txtBox.Text = "Hello"
End Sub
```

In Exercises 7 through 10, assume that the three objects on the form were created in the order txtFirst, txtSecond, and lblOne. Determine the output displayed in lblOne when the program is run and the Tab key is pressed. *Note:* Initially, txtFirst has the focus.

7.
```
Private Sub txtFirst_Leave(...) Handles txtFirst.Leave
    lblOne.ForeColor = Color.Green
    lblOne.Text = "Hello"
End Sub
```

8. ```
Private Sub txtFirst_Leave(...) Handles txtFirst.Leave
    lblOne.BackColor = Color.White
    lblOne.Text = "Hello"
End Sub
```

9. ```
Private Sub txtSecond_Enter(...) Handles txtSecond.Enter
    lblOne.BackColor = Color.Gold
    lblOne.Text = "Hello"
End Sub
```

10. ```
Private Sub txtSecond_Enter(...) Handles txtSecond.Enter
    lblOne.Visible = False
    lblOne.Text = "Hello"
End Sub
```

In Exercises 11 through 16, determine the errors.

11. ```
Private Sub btnOutput_Click(...) Handles btnOutput.Click
    Form1.Text = "Hello"
End Sub
```

12. ```
Private Sub btnOutput_Click(...) Handles btnOutput.Click
    txtBox.Text = Hello
End Sub
```

13. ```
Private Sub btnOutput_Click(...) Handles btnOutput.Click
    txtFirst.ForeColor = Red
End Sub
```

14. ```
Private Sub btnOutput_Click(...) Handles btnOutput.Click
    txtBox = "Hello"
End Sub
```

15. ```
Private Sub btnOutput_Click(...) Handles btnOutput.Click
    txtBox.Font.Size = 20
End Sub
```

16. ```
Private Sub btnOutput_Click(...) Handles btn1.Click, btn2.Click
    Me.Color = Color.Yellow
End Sub
```

In Exercises 17 through 28, write a line (or lines) of code to carry out the task.

17. Display "E.T. phone home." in lblTwo.

18. Display "Play it, Sam." in lblTwo.

19. Display "The stuff that dreams are made of." in red letters in txtBox.

20. Display "Life is like a box of chocolates." in txtBox with blue letters on a gold background.

21. Disable txtBox.

22. Change the words in the form's title bar to "Hello World."

23. Make lblTwo disappear.
```

24. Change the color of the letters in lblName to red.

25. Enable the disabled button btnOutcome.

26. Give the focus to btnCompute.

27. Give the focus to txtBoxTwo.

28. Change the background color of the form to White.

29. Describe the Enter event in your own words.

30. Describe the Leave event in your own words.

31. The label control has an event called DoubleClick that responds to a double-clicking of the left mouse button. Write a simple program to test this event. Determine whether you can trigger the DoubleClick event without also triggering the Click event.

32. Write a simple program to demonstrate that a button's Click event is triggered when you press the Enter key while the button has the focus.

In Exercises 33 through 38, the interface and initial properties are specified. Write the program to carry out the stated task.

33. When one of the three buttons is pressed, the words on the button are displayed in the text box with the stated alignment. *Note:* Rely on IntelliSense to provide you with the proper settings for the TextAlign property.

OBJECT	PROPERTY	SETTING
frmAlign	Text	Text Alignment
txtBox	ReadOnly	True
btnLeft	Text	Left Justify
btnCenter	Text	Center
btnRight	Text	Right Justify

34. When one of the buttons is pressed, the face changes to a smiling face (Wingdings character "J") or a frowning face (Wingdings character "L").

OBJECT	PROPERTY	SETTING
frmFace	Text	Face
lblFace	Font Name	Wingdings
	Font Size	24
	Text	K
btnSmile	Text	Smile
btnFrown	Text	Frown

35. Pressing the buttons alters the background and foreground colors in the text box.

OBJECT	PROPERTY	SETTING
frmColors	Text	Colorful Text
lblBack	Text	Background
btnRed	Text	Red
btnBlue	Text	Blue
txtBox	Text	Beautiful Day
	TextAlign	Center
lblFore	Text	Foreground
btnWhite	Text	White
btnYellow	Text	Yellow

36. When one of the three text boxes receives the focus, its text becomes red. When it loses the focus, the text returns to black. The buttons set the alignment in the text boxes to Left or Right. **Note:** Rely on IntelliSense to provide you with the proper settings for the TextAlign property.

OBJECT	PROPERTY	SETTING
frm123	Text	One, Two, Three
txtOne	Text	One
txtTwo	Text	Two
txtThree	Text	Three
btnLeft	Text	Left
btnRight	Text	Right

37. When the user moves the focus to one of the three small text boxes at the bottom of the form, an appropriate saying is displayed in the large text box. Use the sayings "I like life, it's something to do."; "The future isn't what it used to be."; and "Tell the truth and run."

OBJECT	PROPERTY	SETTING
frmQuote	Text	Sayings
txtQuote	ReadOnly	True
txtLife	Text	Life
txtFuture	Text	Future
txtTruth	Text	Truth

38. The user can disable or enable the text box by clicking on the appropriate button. After the user clicks the Enable button, the text box should receive the focus.

OBJECT	PROPERTY	SETTING
frmTextBox	Text	Text Box
txtBox		
btnDisable	Text	Disable Text Box
btnEnable	Text	Enable Text Box

In Exercises 39 through 44, write a program with a Windows-style interface to carry out the task.

39. The form contains four square buttons arranged in a rectangular array. Each button has the caption "Push Me." When the user clicks on a button, the button disappears and the other three become or remain visible.

40. A form contains two text boxes and one large label between them with no preset caption. When the first text box receives the focus, the label reads "Enter your full name." When the second text box receives the focus, the label reads "Enter your phone number, including area code."

41. Use the same form and properties as in Exercise 34, with the captions for the buttons replaced with Vanish and Reappear. Clicking a button should produce the stated result.

42. Simulate a traffic light with three small square text boxes placed vertically on a form. Initially, the bottom text box is solid green and the other text boxes are dark gray. When the Tab key is pressed, the middle text box turns yellow and the bottom text box turns dark gray. The next time Tab is pressed, the top text box turns red and the middle text box turns dark gray. Subsequent pressing of the Tab key cycles through the three colors. **Hint:** First place the bottom text box on the form, then the middle text box, and finally the top text box.

43. The form contains a single read-only text box and two buttons. When the user clicks on one of the buttons, the sentence "You just clicked on a button." is displayed in the text box. The program should consist of a single event procedure.

44. The form contains two text boxes into which the user types information. When the user clicks on one of the text boxes, it becomes blank and its contents are displayed in the other text box. **Note:** A text box can be cleared with the statement `txtBox.Clear()` or the statement `txtBox.Text = ""`.

> **Solutions to Practice Problem 2.3**

1. **(a)** TextChanged
   (b) Click
   (c) Click
   (d) SelectedIndexChanged

2. Three possibilities are

```
txtBox.Enabled = False
txtBox.ReadOnly = True
txtBox.Visible = False
```

CHAPTER 2 SUMMARY

1. The Visual Basic Form Designer displays a *form* that can hold a collection of *controls* for which various properties can be set. Some examples of controls are text boxes, labels, buttons, and list boxes. Some useful properties are Text (sets the text displayed in a control), Name (used to give a meaningful name to a control), Font.Name (selects the name of the font used), Font.Size (sets the size of the text displayed), Font.Bold (displays boldface text), Font.Italic (displays italics text), BackColor (sets the background color), ForeColor (sets the color of the text), ReadOnly (determines whether text can be typed into a text box when the program is running), TextAlign (sets the type of alignment for the text in a control), Enabled (determines whether a control can respond to user interaction), and Visible (determines whether an object can be seen or is hidden).

2. An *event procedure* is executed when something happens to a specified object. Some events are *object*.Click (*object* is clicked), *object*.TextChanged (a change occurred in the value of the object's Text property), *object*.Leave (*object* loses the focus), and *object*.Enter (*object* receives the focus). **Note:** The statement *object*.Focus() moves the focus to the specified object.

3. *Text files*, which can be created and managed in the Visual Basic IDE, provide a convenient device for holding data to be accessed by a program.

4. Programming assistance can be accessed through the *Help menu*, or via *IntelliSense* and *context-sensitive help*.

5. *Tab order*, the order in which the user moves the focus from one control to another by pressing the Tab key while the program is running, can be set from the View menu.

3

Variables, Input, and Output

3.1   Numbers

Much of the data processed by computers consists of numbers. In computerese, numbers are called **numeric literals**. This section discusses the operations that are performed with numbers and the ways numbers are displayed.

■ Arithmetic Operations

The five standard arithmetic operations in Visual Basic are addition, subtraction, multiplication, division, and exponentiation. Addition, subtraction, and division are denoted in Visual Basic by the standard symbols +, −, and /, respectively. However, the notations for multiplication and exponentiation differ from the customary mathematical notations as follows:

Mathematical Notation	Visual Basic Notation
$a \cdot b$ or $a \times b$	$a * b$
a^r	$a \wedge r$

(The asterisk [*] is the upper character of the 8 key. The caret [^] is the upper character of the 6 key.)

One way to show a number on the screen is to display it in a list box. If *n* is a number, then the instruction

```
lstBox.Items.Add(n)
```

displays the number *n* as the last item in the list box. *Add* is called a **method**. (Generally, a method is a process that performs a task for a particular object.) If the parentheses contain a combination of numbers and arithmetic operations, the *Add* method carries out the operations and displays the result. Another important method is *Clear*. The statement

```
lstBox.Items.Clear()
```

erases all the items displayed in the list box lstBox.

Example 1   The following program applies each of the five arithmetic operations. Preceding the program is the form design and a table showing the names of the objects on the form and the settings, if any, for properties of these objects. This form design is also used in the discussion and examples in the remainder of this section.

The word "Run" in the phrasing [Run . . .] indicates that F5 should be pressed to execute the program. Notice that in the output 3 / 2 is displayed in decimal form. Visual Basic never displays numbers as common fractions. In the evaluation of 2 * (3 + 4), the operation inside the parentheses is calculated first.

Note: All programs appearing in examples and case studies are provided on the companion website for this book. See the discussion on page 15 for details.

OBJECT	PROPERTY	SETTING
frmArithmetic	Text	3-1-1
lstResults		
btnCompute	Text	Compute

```
Private Sub btnCompute_Click(...) Handles btnCompute.Click
    lstResults.Items.Clear()
    lstResults.Items.Add(3 + 2)
    lstResults.Items.Add(3 - 2)
    lstResults.Items.Add(3 * 2)
    lstResults.Items.Add(3 / 2)
    lstResults.Items.Add(3 ^ 2)
    lstResults.Items.Add(2 * (3 + 4))
End Sub
```

[Run, and then click the button.]

■ Variables

In applied mathematics problems, quantities are referred to by names. For instance, consider the following high school algebra problem: "If a car travels at 50 miles per hour, how far will it travel in 14 hours? Also, how many hours are required to travel 410 miles?" The solution to this problem uses the well-known formula

$$\text{distance} = \text{speed} \times \text{time elapsed}$$

Here's how this problem would be solved with a computer program:

```
Private Sub btnCompute_Click(...) Handles btnCompute.Click
    Dim speed As Double
```

```
Dim timeElapsed As Double
Dim distance As Double
lstResults.Items.Clear()
speed = 50
timeElapsed = 14
distance = speed * timeElapsed
lstResults.Items.Add(distance)
distance = 410
timeElapsed = distance / speed
lstResults.Items.Add(timeElapsed)
End Sub
```

[Run, and then click the button. The following is displayed in the list box.]

```
700
8.2
```

Skip the second, third, and fourth lines of the event procedure for now. We will return to them soon. The sixth line sets the speed to 50, and the seventh line sets the time elapsed to 14. The eighth line multiplies the value for the speed by the value for the time elapsed and sets the distance to this product. The next line displays the answer to the distance-traveled question. The three lines before the End Sub statement answer the time-required question in a similar manner.

The names *speed*, *timeElapsed*, and *distance*, which hold values, are referred to as **variables**. Consider the variable *timeElapsed*. In the seventh line, its value was set to 14. In the eleventh line, its value was changed as the result of a computation. On the other hand, the variable *speed* had the same value, 50, throughout the program.

In general, a variable is a name that is used to refer to an item of data. The value assigned to the variable may change during the execution of the program. In Visual Basic, variable names can be up to 16,383 characters long, must begin with a letter or an underscore, and can consist only of letters, digits, and underscores. (The shortest variable names consist of a single letter.) Visual Basic does not distinguish between uppercase and lowercase letters used in variable names. Some examples of variable names are *total*, *numberOfCars*, *taxRate_2008*, and *n*. As a convention, we write variable names in lowercase letters except for the first letters of additional words (as in *gradeOnFirstExam*). This convention is called **camel casing**.

If *var* is a variable and *n* is a literal, then the statement

```
var = n
```

assigns the number *n* to the variable *var*. (Such a statement is another example of an **assignment statement**.)

A variable is declared to be of a certain type depending on the sort of data that can be assigned to it. The most versatile type for holding numbers is called **Double**. A variable of type Double can hold whole, fractional, or mixed numbers between about $-1.8 \cdot 10^{308}$ and $1.8 \cdot 10^{308}$. Dim statements (also called **declaration statements**) declare the names and types of the variables to be used in the program. The second, third, and fourth lines of this event procedure declare three variables of type Double and give them the names *speed*, *timeElapsed*, and *distance*.

In general, a statement of the form

```
Dim varName As Double
```

declares a variable named *varName* to be of type Double. Actually, the Dim statement causes the computer to set aside a location in memory with the name *varName*. Since *varName* is a numeric variable, the Dim statement initially places the number zero in that memory location. (We say that zero is the **initial value** or **default value** of the variable.) Each subsequent assignment statement having *varName* to the left of the equal sign will change the value of the number.

The initial value can be set to a value other than zero. To specify a nonzero initial value, follow the declaration statement with an equal sign followed by the initial value. The statement

```
Dim varName As Double = 50
```

declares the specified variable as a variable of type Double and gives it the initial value 50.

The statement

```
lstBox.Items.Add(varName)
```

looks into this memory location for the current value of the variable and displays that value in the list box.

A combination of literals, variables, and arithmetic operations that can be evaluated to yield a number is called a **numeric expression**. Expressions are evaluated by replacing each variable by its value and carrying out the arithmetic. Some examples of expressions are $2*\text{distance} + 7$, $n + 1$, and $(a + b)/3$.

 Example 2   The following program displays the default value of a variable and the value of an expression:

```
Private Sub btnCompute_Click(...) Handles btnCompute.Click
  Dim a As Double
  Dim b As Double = 3
  lstResults.Items.Clear()
  lstResults.Items.Add(a)
  lstResults.Items.Add(b)
  a = 5
  lstResults.Items.Add(a * (2 + b))
End Sub
```

[Run, and then click the button. The following is displayed in the list box.]

```
0
3
25
```

If *var* is a variable, then the assignment statement

```
var = expression
```

first evaluates the expression on the right and *then* assigns its value to the variable on the left. For instance, the event procedure in Example 2 can be written as

```
Private Sub btnCompute_Click(...) Handles btnCompute.Click
  Dim a As Double
  Dim b As Double
  Dim c As Double
  lstResults.Items.Clear()
  a = 5
  b = 3
  c = a * (2 + b)
  lstResults.Items.Add(c)
End Sub
```

The expression a*(2 + b) is evaluated to 25, and then this value is assigned to the variable *c*.

■ Incrementing the Value of a Variable

Because the expression on the right side of an assignment statement is evaluated *before* an assignment is made, a statement such as

```
var = var + 1
```

is meaningful. It first evaluates the expression on the right (that is, it adds 1 to the original value of the variable *var*) and then assigns this sum to the variable *var*. The effect is to increase the value of the variable *var* by 1. In terms of memory locations, the statement retrieves the value of *var* from *var*'s memory location, uses it to compute *var* + 1, and then places the sum back into *var*'s memory location. This type of calculation is so common that Visual Basic provides a special operator to carry it out. The statement **var = var + 1** can be replaced with the statement

```
var += 1
```

In general, if *n* has a numeric value, then the statement

```
var += n
```

adds *n* to the value of *var*.

■ Built-In Functions: Math.Sqrt, Int, Math.Round

There are several common operations that we often perform on numbers other than the standard arithmetic operations. For instance, we may take the square root of a number or round a number. These operations are performed by built-in functions. Functions associate with one or more values called the *input*, and a single value called the *output*. The function is said to **return** the output value. The three functions considered here have numeric input and output.

The function Math.Sqrt calculates the square root of a number. The function Int finds the greatest integer less than or equal to a number. Therefore, Int discards the decimal part of positive numbers. The value of Math.Round(*n*, *r*) is the number *n* rounded to *r* decimal places. The parameter *r* can be omitted. If so, *n* is rounded to a whole number. Some examples follow:

Math.Sqrt(9) is 3.   Int(2.7) is 2.   Math.Round(2.7) is 3.

Math.Sqrt(0) is 0.   Int(3) is 3.   Math.Round(2.317, 2) is 2.32.

Math.Sqrt(2) is 1.414214.   Int(−2.7) is −3.   Math.Round(2.317, 1) is 2.3.

The terms inside the parentheses can be numbers (as shown), numeric variables, or numeric expressions. Expressions are first evaluated to produce the input.

Example 3   The following program evaluates each of the functions for a specific input given by the value of the variable *n*:

```
Private Sub btnCompute_Click(...) Handles btnCompute.Click
  Dim n As Double
  Dim root As Double
  n = 6.76
  root = Math.Sqrt(n)
  lstResults.Items.Clear()
  lstResults.Items.Add(root)
  lstResults.Items.Add(Int(n))
  lstResults.Items.Add(Math.Round(n, 1))
End Sub
```

[Run, and then click the Compute button. The following is displayed in the list box.]

```
2.6
6
6.8
```

Example 4   The following program evaluates each of the preceding functions at an expression:

```
Private Sub btnCompute_Click(...) Handles btnCompute.Click
  Dim a As Double
  Dim b As Double
  a = 2
  b = 3
  lstResults.Items.Clear()
  lstResults.Items.Add(Math.Sqrt(5 * b + 1))
  lstResults.Items.Add(Int(a ^ b + 0.8))
  lstResults.Items.Add(Math.Round(a / b, 3))
End Sub
```

[Run, and then click the button. The following is displayed in the list box.]

```
4
8
0.667
```

■ The Integer Data Type

In this text, we sometimes need to use variables of type Integer. An Integer variable is declared with a statement of the form

```
Dim varName As Integer
```

and can be assigned only whole numbers from about −2 billion to 2 billion. Integer variables are used primarily for counting.

■ Multiple Declarations

Several variables of the same type can be declared with a single Dim statement. For instance, the two Dim statements in Example 2 can be replaced by the single statement

```
Dim a, b As Double
```

Two other types of multiple-declaration statement are

```
Dim a As Double, b As Integer
Dim c As Double = 2, b As Integer = 5
```

■ Parentheses

Parentheses cannot be used to indicate multiplication, as is commonly done in algebra. For instance, the expression $x(y + z)$ is not valid. It must be written as $x*(y + z)$.

Parentheses should be used when necessary to clarify the meaning of an expression. When there are no parentheses, the arithmetic operations are performed in the following order: (1) exponentiations; (2) multiplications and divisions; (3) additions and subtractions. In the event of ties, the leftmost operation is carried out first. Table 3.1 summarizes these rules. **Note:** If you use parentheses liberally, you will not have to rely on the precedence table for arithmetic operations. For instance, write (2 * 3) + 4 instead of 2 * 3 + 4. Write (2 ^ 3) + 4 instead of 2 ^ 3 + 4.

TABLE 3.1   Level of precedence for arithmetic operations.

( )	Inner to outer, left to right
^	Left to right in expression
* /	Left to right in expression
+ −	Left to right in expression

■ Three Types of Errors

Grammatical errors, such as misspellings, omissions, or incorrect punctuations, are called **syntax errors**. Most syntax errors are spotted by the Code Editor when they are entered. The editor underlines the syntax error with a blue squiggly line and displays a description of the error when the mouse cursor is hovered over the squiggly line. Some incorrect statements and their errors are as follows:

Statement	*Reason for Error*
lstBox.Itms.Add(3)	The word Items is misspelled.
lstBox.Items.Add(2+)	The number following the plus sign is missing.
Dim m; n As Integer	The semicolon should be a comma.

Errors that occur while a program is running are called **run-time errors** or **exceptions**. They usually result from the inability of the computer to carry out the intended task. For instance, if the file DATA.TXT is not in the root folder of the C drive, then a statement that refers to the file by the filespec "C:\DATA.TXT" will cause the program to stop executing and produce a message box with the title

```
FileNotFoundException was unhandled.
```

Also, a yellow arrow will appear at the left side of the line of code that caused the error. At that point, you should end the program.

A third type of error is the so-called **logical error**. Such an error occurs when a program does not perform the way it was intended. For instance, the line

```
average = firstNum + secondNum / 2
```

is syntactically correct. However, the missing parentheses in the line of code are responsible for an incorrect value being generated. Appendix D discusses debugging tools that can be used to detect and correct logical errors.

■ The Error List Window

Syntax errors are not only indicated in the Code Editor, but also are listed in the Error List window. (*Note:* If the Error List window is not visible in the IDE, click on Error List in the View menu.)

 Example 5 The following program contains three errors.

```
Private Sub btnCompute_Click(...) Handles btnCompute.Click
  Dim m; n As Double
  lstResults.Items.Add(5
  lstResults.Items.Add(a)
End Sub
```

[Press Alt/V/I to display the Error List window.]

Error List

	Description	File	Line	Column	Project
⊗ 1	Character is not valid.	frmShowErrors.vb	4	10	3-1-5
⊗ 2	')' expected.	frmShowErrors.vb	5	26	3-1-5
⊗ 3	Name 'a' is not declared.	frmShowErrors.vb	6	26	3-1-5

The Private Sub statement is in line 3. (Line 1 contains the Public Class statement and line 2 is a blank line.) Click on one of the three errors in the Error List window and then press F1 to see a discussion of that error.

■ Comments

1. Declaring variables at the beginning of each event procedure is regarded as good programming practice because it makes programs easier to read and helps prevent certain types of errors.

2. Keywords (reserved words) cannot be used as names of variables. For instance, the statements **Dim private as Double** and **Dim sub As Double** are not valid. To obtain a complete list of Visual Basic keywords, look up *reserved keywords* in Help's Index.

3. Names given to variables are sometimes referred to as *identifiers*.

4. In math courses, *literals* are referred to as *constants*. However, the word "constant" has a special meaning in programming languages.

5. Numeric literals used in expressions or assigned to variables must not contain commas, dollar signs, or percent signs. Also, mixed numbers, such as 8 1/2, are not allowed.

6. Although requesting the square root of a negative number does not terminate the execution of the program, it can produce unexpected results. For instance, the statement

```
lstBox.Items.Add(Math.Sqrt(-1))
```

displays **NaN**. **Note:** NaN is an abbreviation for "Not a Number."

7. If the value of *numVar* is 0 and *numVar* has type Double, then the statements

```
numVarInv = 1 / numVar
lstBox.Items.Add(numVarInv)
lstBox.Items.Add(1 / numVarInv)
```

cause the following items to be displayed in the list box:

```
Infinity
0
```

8. When *n* is halfway between two successive whole numbers (such as 1.5, 2.5, 3.5, and 4.5), then it rounds to the nearest even number. For instance, Math.Round (2.5) is 2 and Math.Round(3.5) is 4.

9. In addition to the five arithmetic operators discussed at the beginning of this section, the **Mod operator** and the **integer division operator (\)** are two other useful operators. Let *m* and *n* be positive whole numbers. When you use long division to divide *m* by *n*, you obtain an integer result and an integer remainder. The result is *m* \ *n* and the remainder is *m* Mod *n*. For instance,

14 \ 3 is 4 and 14 Mod 3 is 2
19 \ 5 is 3 and 19 Mod 5 is 4
10 \ 2 is 5 and 10 Mod 2 is 0.

10. In scientific notation, numbers are written in the form $b \cdot 10^r$, where *b* is a number of magnitude from 1 up to (but not including) 10, and *r* is an integer. Visual Basic displays very large numbers in **scientific notation** where $b \cdot 10^r$ is written as *bEr*. (The letter E is an abbreviation for *exponent*.) For instance, when the statement **lstBox.Items.Add(123 * 10 ^ 15)** is executed, 1.23E+17 is displayed in the list box.

11. When you first enter a statement such as `Dim n As Double`, a squiggle will appear under the variable name and the Error List window will record a warning. The squiggle merely indicates that the variable has not yet been assigned a value. If the squiggle is still present after the entire event procedure has been entered, this will tell you that the variable was never used and that the declaration statement should be removed.

Practice Problems 3.1

1. Evaluate $2 + 3 * 4$.

2. Explain the difference between the assignment statement

```
var1 = var2
```

and the assignment statement

```
var2 = var1
```

3. Complete the table by filling in the value of each variable after each line is executed.

	a	b	c
`Private Sub btnEvaluate_Click(...) Handles btnEvaluate.Click`			
`    Dim a, b, c As Double`	0	0	0
`    a = 3`	3	0	0
`    b = 4`	3	4	0
`    c = a + b`			
`    a = c * a`			
`    lstResults.Items.Add(a - b)`			
`    b = b * b`			
`End Sub`			

4. Write a statement that increases the value of the numeric variable *var* by 5%.

EXERCISES 3.1

In Exercises 1 through 6, evaluate the numeric expression without the computer, and then use Visual Basic to check your answer.

1. $3 * 4$ **2.** 7^2

3. $1/(2^3)$ **4.** $8 - 5 - 2$

5. $(7 - 3) - (2 + 1)$ **6.** $3 * ((-2)^5)$

In Exercises 7 through 10, evaluate the expression.

7. $7 \backslash 3$ **8.** 3 Mod 7

9. 7 Mod 3   **10.** $14 \backslash 4$

In Exercises 11 through 16, determine whether the name is a valid variable name.

11. sales.2008   **12.** room&Board

13. fOrM_1040   **14.** Integer

15. expenses?   **16.** Overall Total

In Exercises 17 through 22, evaluate the numeric expression where a = 2, b = 3, and c = 4.

17. $(a*b) - c$

18. $a*(b + c)$

19. $(1 + b)*c$

20. $a^{\wedge}(b - a)$

21. $b^{\wedge}(c - a)$

22. $(c - a)^{\wedge}b$

In Exercises 23 through 28, write an event procedure to calculate and display the value of the expression.

23. $7 \cdot 8 + 5$

24. $(1 + 2 \cdot 9)^3$

25. 2.5% of 25

26. $10 - 2(3 + 2^3)$

27. $17(3 + 162)$

28. $4\ 1/2 - 3\ 5/8$

In Exercises 29 and 30, complete the table by filling in the value of each variable after each line is executed.

29.

	x	y
`Private Sub btnEvaluate_Click(...) Handles btnEvaluate.Click`		
`Dim x, y As Double`		
`x = 1`		
`y = 3 + x`		
`x = y + 5`		
`lstResults.Items.Clear()`		
`lstResults.Items.Add(x + 4)`		
`y = y + 1`		
`End Sub`		

30.

	bal	inter	withDr
`Private Sub btnEvaluate_Click(...) Handles btnEvaluate.Click`			
`Dim bal, inter, withDr As Double`			
`bal = 100`			
`inter = 0.05`			
`withDr = 25`			
`bal += inter * bal`			
`bal = bal - withDr`			
`End Sub`			

In Exercises 31 through 38, determine the output displayed in the list box by the lines of code.

31.
```
Dim amount As Double
amount = 10
lstOutput.Items.Add(amount - 4)
```

32.
```
Dim a, b As Integer
a = 4
```

```
   b = 5 * a
   lstOutput.Items.Add(a + b)
```

33. ```
    Dim n As Integer = 7
    n += 1
    lstOutput.Items.Add(1)
    lstOutput.Items.Add(n)
    lstOutput.Items.Add(n + 1)
    ```

34. ```
    Dim num As Integer = 5
    num = 7 Mod num
    lstOutput.Items.Add(num)
    ```

35. ```
    Dim a, b As Integer
    lstOutput.Items.Add(a + 1)
    a = 4
    b = a * a
    lstOutput.Items.Add(a * b)
    ```

36. ```
    Dim tax As Double
    tax = 200
    tax = 25 + tax
    lstOutput.Items.Add(tax)
    ```

37. ```
    Dim x As Double = 3
    x += 4
    lstOutput.Items.Add(x * x)
    lstOutput.Items.Add(x + 3 * x)
    ```

38. ```
    Dim n As Double = 2, m As Double = 5
    lstOutput.Items.Add(3 * n)
    n += n
    lstOutput.Items.Add(n + m)
    lstOutput.Items.Add(n - m)
    ```

In Exercises 39 through 44, identify the errors.

39. ```
    Dim a, b, c As Double
    a = 2
    b = 3
    a + b = c
    lstOutput.Items.Add(c)
    ```

40. ```
    Dim a, b, c, d As Double
    a = 2
    b = 3
    c = d = 4
    lstOutput.Items.Add(5((a + b) / (c + d))
    ```

41. ```
    Dim balance, deposit As Double
    balance = 1,000,5
    deposit = $100
    lstOutput.Items.Add(balance + deposit)
    ```
    ```

42.
```
Dim interest, balance As Double
0.05 = interest
balance = 800
lstOutput.Itmes.Add(interest * balance)
```

43.
```
Dim 9W As Double
9W = 2 * 9W
lstOutput.Items.Add(9W)
```

44.
```
Dim n As Double = 1.2345
lstOutput.Items.Add(Round(n, 2))
```

In Exercises 45 and 46, rewrite the code using one line.

45.
```
Dim quantity As Integer
quantity = 12
```

46.
```
Dim m As Integer
Dim n As Double
m = 2
n = 3
```

In Exercises 47 through 52, find the value of the given function.

47. $\text{Int}(10.75)$ 48. $\text{Int}(9 - 3 - 2)$ 49. $\text{Math.Sqrt}(3 * 12)$

50. $\text{Math.Sqrt}(64)$ 51. $\text{Math.Round}(3.1279, 3)$ 52. $\text{Int}(-1.82)$

In Exercises 53 through 58, find the value of the given function where a and b are numeric variables of type Double, $a = 5$ and $b = 3$.

53. $\text{Int}(-a/2)$ 54. $\text{Math.Round}(a / b)$ 55. $\text{Math.Sqrt}(a - 8 \setminus 3 - 2)$

56. $\text{Math.Sqrt}(4 + a)$ 57. $\text{Math.Round}(a + .5)$ 58. $\text{Int}(b * 0.5)$

In Exercises 59 through 66, write an event procedure starting with a Private Sub btnCompute_Click(...) Handles btnCompute.Click statement, ending with an End Sub statement, and having one line for each step. Lines that display data should use the given variable names.

59. The following steps calculate a company's profit:

   (a) Declare all variables.
   (b) Assign the value 98456 to the variable *revenue*.
   (c) Assign the value 45000 to the variable *costs*.
   (d) Assign the difference between the variables *revenue* and *costs* to the variable *profit*.
   (e) Display the value of the variable *profit* in a list box.

60. The following steps calculate the amount of a stock purchase:

   (a) Declare all variables.
   (b) Assign the value 25.625 to the variable *costPerShare*.
   (c) Assign the value 400 to the variable *numberOfShares*.
   (d) Assign the product of *costPerShare* and *numberOfShares* to the variable *amount*.
   (e) Display the value of the variable *amount* in a list box.

61. The following steps calculate the price of an item after a 30% reduction:

    (a) Declare all variables.
    (b) Assign the value 19.95 to the variable *price*.
    (c) Assign the value 15 to the variable *discountPercent*.
    (d) Assign the value of (*discountPercent* divided by 100) times *price* to the variable *markDown*.
    (e) Decrease *price* by *markdown*.
    (f) Display the value of *price* in a list box.

62. The following steps calculate a company's break-even point, the number of units of goods the company must manufacture and sell in order to break even:

    (a) Declare all variables.
    (b) Assign the value 5000 to the variable *fixedCosts*.
    (c) Assign the value 8 to the variable *pricePerUnit*.
    (d) Assign the value 6 to the variable *costPerUnit*.
    (e) Assign the value *fixedCosts* divided by (the difference of *pricePerUnit* and *costPerUnit*) to the variable *breakEvenPoint*.
    (f) Display the value of the variable *breakEvenPoint* in a list box.

63. The following steps calculate the balance after two years when $100 is deposited in a savings account at 3% interest compounded annually:

    (a) Declare all variables.
    (b) Assign the value 500 to the variable *balance*.
    (c) Increase the variable *balance* by 3% of its value.
    (d) Increase the variable *balance* by 3% of its value.
    (e) Display the value of the variable *balance* in a list box.

64. The following steps calculate the balance at the end of three years when $100 is deposited at the beginning of each year in a savings account at 5% interest compounded annually:

    (a) Declare all variables.
    (b) Assign the value 100 to the variable *balance*.
    (c) Increase the variable *balance by* 5% of its value, and add 100.
    (d) Increase the variable *balance* by 5% of its value, and add 100.
    (e) Increase the variable *balance* by 5% of its value.
    (f) Display the value of the variable *balance* in a list box.

65. The following steps calculate the balance after 10 years when $100 is deposited in a savings account at 5% interest compounded annually:

    (a) Declare all variables.
    (b) Assign the value 100 to the variable *balance*.
    (c) Multiply the variable *balance* by 1.05 raised to the 10th power.
    (d) Display the value of the variable *balance* in a list box.

66. Using the following steps calculate the body mass index, BMI.

    (a) Declare all variables.
    (b) Assign the value 142 to the variable *weightInPounds*.

(c) Assign the value 65 to the variable *heightInInches*.

(d) Assign, to the variable *BMI*, 703 times the *weightInPounds* divided by *heightInInches* squared.

(e) Display the value of the variable *BMI* in the list box.

In Exercises 67 through 72, write an event procedure to solve the problem and display the answer in a list box. The program should use variables for each of the quantities.

67. Suppose each acre of farmland produces 18 tons of corn. How many tons of corn can be produced on a 30-acre farm?

68. The cost of a 1-ft by 1-ft tile is 3.90 dollars. How much will it cost to cover a 12-ft by 12-ft room with tiles?

69. If a car left Washington, D.C., at 2 o'clock and arrived in New York at 7 o'clock, what was its average speed? **Note:** New York is 233 miles from Washington.

70. A motorist wants to determine her gas mileage. At 23,352 miles (on the odometer), the tank is filled. At 23,695 miles the tank is filled again with 14 gallons. How many miles per gallon did the car average between the two fillings?

71. The cost of one yard of fabric is 17.57 dollars. It takes 8.5 yards to make a long curtain and 4.4 yards to make a short curtain. Determine the cost to make ten long curtains and five short ones.

72. Calculate the amount of energy obtained from a mass of 65 kilograms using Einstein's equation, $E = mc^2$. In the equation m represents mass in kilograms and c represents speed of light, 2.9979E8.

Solutions to Practice Problems 3.1

1. 24. Multiplications are performed before additions. If the intent is for the addition to be performed first, the expression should be written $(2 + 3)*4$.

2. The first assignment statement assigns the value of the variable *var2* to the variable *var1*, whereas the second assignment statement assigns *var1*'s value to *var2*.

3.

	a	b	c
Private Sub btnEvaluate_Click(...) Handles btnEvaluate.Click			
Dim a, b, c As Double	0	0	0
a = 3	3	0	0
b = 4	3	4	0
c = a + b	3	4	7
a = c * a	21	4	7
lstResults.Items.Add(a - b)	21	4	7
b = b * b	21	16	7
End Sub			

Each time an assignment statement is executed, only one variable (the variable to the left of the equal sign) has its value changed.

4. Each of the three following statements increases the value of *var* by 5%.

```
var = var + 0.05 * var
var = 1.05 * var
var += 0.05 * var
```

3.2 Strings

The most common types of data processed by Visual Basic are numbers and strings. Sentences, phrases, words, letters of the alphabet, names, telephone numbers, addresses, and Social Security numbers are all examples of strings. Formally, a **string literal** is a sequence of characters that is treated as a single item. String literals can be assigned to variables, displayed in text boxes and list boxes, and combined by an operation called concatenation (denoted by &).

■ Variables and Strings

A **string variable** is a name used to refer to a string. The allowable names of string variables are the same as those of numeric variables. The value of a string variable is assigned or altered with assignment statements and displayed in a list box like the value of a numeric variable. String variables are declared with statements of the form

```
Dim varName As String
```

 Example 1   The following code shows how assignment statements and the Add method are used with strings. The string variable *president* is assigned a value by the third line and this value is displayed by the sixth line. The quotation marks surrounding each string literal are not part of the literal and are not displayed by the Add method. (The form for this example contains a button and a list box.)

```
Private Sub btnDisplay_Click(...) Handles btnDisplay.Click
  Dim president As String
  president = "George Washington"
  1stOutput.Items.Clear()
  1stOutput.Items.Add("president")
  1stOutput.Items.Add(president)
End Sub
```

[Run, and then click the button. The following is displayed in the list box.]

```
president
George Washington
```

If *x*, *y*, . . . , *z* are characters and *strVar* is a string variable, then the statement

```
strVar = "xy...z"
```

assigns the string literal *xy . . . z* to the variable and the statement

```
lstBox.Items.Add("xy...z")
```

or

```
lstBox.Items.Add(strVar)
```

displays the string *xy...z* in a list box. If *strVar2* is another string variable, then the statement

```
strVar2 = strVar
```

assigns the value of the variable *strVar* to the variable *strVar2*. (The value of *strVar* will remain the same.) String literals used in assignment or lstBox.Items.Add statements must be surrounded by quotation marks, but string variables are never surrounded by quotation marks.

■ Option Explicit and Option Strict

Option Explicit and **Option Strict** are two options that affect programming. Throughout this book, we assume that both options are in effect. Having these two options working is considered good programming practice. Option Explicit requires that all variables be declared with Dim statements. The absence of this option can lead to errors resulting from the misspelling of names of variables. Option Strict requires explicit conversions in most cases where a value or variable of one type is assigned to a variable of another type. The absence of this option can lead to data loss.

Visual Basic provides a way to enforce Option Explicit and Option Strict for all programs you create. Press Alt/Tools/Options to open the Options dialog box. In the left pane, click on the symbol (+ or ▷) to the left of Projects and Solutions to expand that entry. Then click on the subentry VB Defaults. Four default project settings will appear on the right. (See Figure 3.1.) If the settings for Option Explicit and Object Strict are not already set to On, change them to On. **Note:** Option Infer is discussed in Chapter 6.

FIGURE 3.1 Option default project settings.

■ Using Text Boxes for Input and Output

The content of a text box is always a string. Therefore, statements such as

```
strVar = txtBox.Text
```

and

```
txtBox.Text = strVar
```

can be used to assign the contents of the text box to the string variable *strVar* and vice versa.

Numbers typed into text boxes are stored as strings. With Option Strict set to On, such strings must be converted to numeric values before they can be assigned to numeric variables or used in numeric expressions. The functions CDbl and CInt convert strings representing numbers into numbers of type Double and Integer, respectively. Going in the other direction, the function CStr converts a number into a string representation of the number. Therefore, statements such as

```
dblVar = CDbl(txtBox.Text)
```

and

```
txtBox.Text = CStr(dblVar)
```

can be used to assign the contents of a text box to the Double variable *dblVar* and vice versa. CDbl, CInt, and CStr, which stand for "convert to Double," "convert to Integer," and "convert to String," are referred to as **data-conversion** or **type-casting functions**.

  Example 2 The following program computes the sum of two numbers supplied by the user:

OBJECT	PROPERTY	SETTING
frmAdd	Text	Addition
lblFirstNum	AutoSize	False
	Text	First Number:
txtFirstNum		
lblSecondNum	AutoSize	False
	Text	Second Number:
txtSecondNum		
btnCompute	Text	Compute Sum
lblSum	Text	Sum:
txtSum	ReadOnly	True

```
Private Sub btnCompute_Click() Handles btnCompute.Click
  Dim num1, num2, sum As Double
  num1 = CDbl(txtFirstNum.Text)
  num2 = CDbl(txtSecondNum.Text)
  sum = num1 + num2
  txtSum.Text = CStr(sum)
End Sub
```

[Run, type 45 into the first text box, type 55 into the second text box, and click on the button.]

■ Auto Correction

The **Auto Correction** feature of IntelliSense suggests corrections when errors occur, and allows you to select a correction to be applied to the code. When a prohibited statement is entered, a blue squiggly error line appears under the offending part of the statement. If the squiggly line has a short red line segment at its right end, the Auto Correction feature is available for the error. When you hover the cursor over the squiggly line, a small box containing an exclamation mark inside a red circle appears. Clicking on the small box produces an Auto Correction helper box that describes the error and makes a suggestion for fixing it. Figure 3.2 shows a typical Auto Correction helper box for a data-type-conversion error. If you click on the line beginning "Replace," the change will be made for you.

FIGURE 3.2   An Auto Correction helper box.

■ Concatenation

Two strings can be combined to form a new string consisting of the strings joined together. The joining operation is called **concatenation** and is represented by an ampersand (&). For instance, "good" & "bye" is "goodbye". A combination of strings and ampersands that can be evaluated to form a string is called a **string expression**. The assignment statement and the Add method evaluate expressions before assigning them or displaying them.

Example 3   The following program illustrates concatenation. (The form for this example contains a button and a text box.) Notice the space at the end of the string assigned to *quote1*. If that space weren't present, then the statement that assigns a value to *quote* would have to be `quote = quote1 & " " & quote2`.

```
Private Sub btnDisplay_Click(...) Handles btnDisplay.Click
  Dim quote1, quote2, quote As String
  quote1 = "The ballgame isn't over, "
  quote2 = "until it's over."
  quote = quote1 & quote2
  txtOutput.Text = quote & "   Yogi Berra"
End Sub
```

[Run, and then click the button. The following is displayed in the text box.]

```
The ball game isn't over, until it's over.   Yogi Berra
```

Visual Basic also allows strings to be concatenated with numbers and allows numbers to be concatenated with numbers. In each case, the result is a string.

 Example 4   The following program concatenates a string with a number. Notice that a space was inserted after the word "has" and before the word "keys." (The form for this example contains a button and a text box.)

```
Private Sub btnDisplay_Click(...) Handles btnDisplay.Click
  Dim str As String, numOfKeys As Integer
  str = "The piano keyboard has "
  numOfKeys = 88
  txtOutput.Text = str & numOfKeys & " keys."
End Sub
```

[Run, and then click the button. The following is displayed in the text box.]

```
The piano keyboard has 88 keys.
```

The statement

```
strVar = strVar & strVar2
```

will append the value of *strVar2* to the end of the current value of *strVar*. The same result can be accomplished with the statement

```
strVar &= strVar2
```

■ String Properties and Methods: Length Property and ToUpper, ToLower, Trim, IndexOf, and Substring Methods

We have seen that controls, such as text and list boxes, have properties and methods. A control placed on a form is an example of an object. A string is also an object, and, like a control, has both properties and methods that are specified by following the string with a period and the name of the property or method. The Length property gives the number of characters in a string. The ToUpper and ToLower methods return an uppercase and lowercase version of the string. The Trim method returns the string with all leading and trailing spaces deleted. The Substring method returns a sequence of consecutive characters from the string. The IndexOf method searches for the first occurrence of one string in another and gives the position at which the string is found.

If *str* is a string, then

```
str.Length
```

is the number of characters in the string,

```
str.ToUpper
```

is the string with all its letters capitalized,

```
str.ToLower
```

is the string with all its letters in lowercase, and

```
str.Trim
```

is the string with all spaces removed from the front and back of the string. For instance,

```
"Visual".Length is 6.            "Visual".ToUpper is VISUAL.
"123 Hike".Length is 8.          "123 Hike".ToLower is 123 hike.
"a" & "  bcd  ".Trim & "efg" is abcdefg.
```

In Visual Basic, the **position** of a character in a string is identified with one of the numbers 0, 1, 2, 3, ... A **substring** of a string is a sequence of consecutive characters from the string. For instance, consider the string "Just a moment". The substrings "Jus", "mom", and "nt" begin at positions 0, 7, and 11, respectively.

If *str* is a string, then

```
str.Substring(m, n)
```

is the substring of *str* consisting of *n* characters beginning with the character in position *m* of *str*. If the comma and the number *n* are omitted, then the substring starts at position *m* and continues until the end of *str*. The value of

```
str.IndexOf(str2)
```

is −1 if *str2* is not a substring of *str*, and otherwise is the beginning position of the first occurrence of *str2* in *str*. Some examples using these two methods are as follows:

```
"fanatic".Substring(0, 3) is "fan". "fanatic".IndexOf("ati") is 3.
"fanatic".Substring(4, 2) is "ti".  "fanatic".IndexOf("a") is 1.
"fanatic".Substring(4) is "tic".            "fanatic".IndexOf("nt") is -1.
```

The IndexOf method has a useful extension. The value of `str.IndexOf(str2,n)`, where *n* is an integer, is the position of the first occurrence of *str2* in *str* in position *n* or greater. For instance, the value of `"Mississippi".IndexOf("ss",3)` is 5.

Like the numeric functions discussed before, string properties and methods also can be applied to variables and expressions.

Example 5   The following program uses variables and expressions with the property and methods just discussed:

```
Private Sub btnEvaluate_Click(...) Handles btnEvaluate.Click
  Dim str1, str2, str3 As String
  str1 = "Quick as "
  str2 = "a wink"
  lstResults.Items.Clear()
  lstResults.Items.Add(str1.Substring(0, 7))
  lstResults.Items.Add(str1.IndexOf("c"))
  lstResults.Items.Add(str1.Substring(0, 3))
  lstResults.Items.Add((str1 & str2).Substring(6, 6))
  lstResults.Items.Add((str1 & str2).ToUpper)
  lstResults.Items.Add(str1.Trim & str2)
  str3 = str2.Substring(str2.Length - 4)
  lstResults.Items.Add("The average " & str3 & " lasts .1 second.")
End Sub
```

[Run, and then click the button. The following is displayed in the list box.]

```
Quick a
3
Qui
as a w
QUICK AS A WINK
Quick asa wink
The average wink lasts .1 second.
```

Note: In Example 5, *c* is in the third position of *str1*, and there are three characters of *str1* to the left of *c*. In general, there are *n* characters to the left of the character in position *n*. This fact is used in Example 6.

Example 6   The following program parses a name. The fifth line locates the position, call it *n*, of the space separating the two names. The first name will contain *n* characters, and the last name will consist of all characters to the right of the *n*th character.

```
Private Sub btnAnalyze_Click(...) Handles btnAnalyze.Click
  Dim fullName, firstName, lastName As String
  Dim m As Integer
  Dim n As Integer
  fullName = txtName.Text
  n = fullName.IndexOf(" ")
  firstName = fullName.Substring(0, n)
  lastName = fullName.Substring(n + 1)
```

```
m = lastName.Length
lstResults.Items.Clear()
lstResults.Items.Add("First name: " & firstName)
lstResults.Items.Add("Your last name has " & m & " letters.")
End Sub
```

[Run, type "John Doe" into the text box, and then click the button.]

■ The Empty String

The string **""**, which contains no characters, is called the **empty string** or the **zero-length string**. It is different from **" "**, the string consisting of a single space.

The statement **lstBox.Items.Add("")** inserts a blank line into the list box. The contents of a text box can be cleared with either the statement

txtBox.Clear()

or the statement

txtBox.Text = ""

■ Initial Value of a String

When a string variable is declared with a Dim statement, it has the special value Nothing as its default value. To specify a different initial value, follow the declaration statement with an equal sign followed by the initial value. For instance, the statement

Dim pres As String = "Adams"

declares the variable *pres* to be of type String and assigns it the initial value "Adams."

An error occurs whenever an attempt is made to access a property or method for a string variable having the value Nothing or to display it in a list box. Therefore, unless a string variable is guaranteed to be assigned a value before being used, you should initialize it—even if you just assign the empty string to it.

■ Widening and Narrowing

The assignment of a value or variable of type Double to a variable of type Integer is called **narrowing** because the possible values of an Integer variable are a subset of the possible values of a Double variable. For the same reason, assigning in the reverse direction is called **widening**. Option Strict requires the use of a conversion function when narrowing, but allows widening without a conversion function. Specifically, a widening statement of the form

```
dblVar = intVar
```

is valid. However, a narrowing statement of the form

```
intVar = dblVar
```

is not valid. It must be replaced with

```
intVar = CInt(dblVar)
```

Great care must be taken when computing with Integer variables. For instance, the value of an expression involving division or exponentiation has type Double and therefore cannot be assigned to an Integer variable even if the value is a whole number. For instance, Option Strict makes each of the following two assignment statements invalid.

```
Dim m As Integer
m = 2 ^ 3
m = 6 / 2
```

In order to not have to worry about errors such as these, we restrict the use of Integer variables to counting rather than computation.

■ Internal Documentation

Program documentation is the inclusion of comments that specify the intent of the program, the purpose of the variables, and the tasks performed by individual portions of the program. To create a comment statement, just begin the line with an apostrophe. Such a statement appears green on the screen and is completely ignored when the program is executed. Comment lines appear whenever the program is displayed or printed. A line of code can be documented by adding an apostrophe, followed by the desired information, after the end of the line. The tenth and eleventh icons on the Toolbar can be used to comment out and uncomment selected blocks of code.

 Example 7 The following rewrite of Example 6 uses internal documentation. The first comment describes the entire program, the comment in line 5 gives the meaning of the variable, and the final comment describes the purpose of the three lines that follow it.

```
Private Sub btnAnalyze_Click(...) Handles btnAnalyze.Click
   'Determine a person's first name and the length of the second name
   Dim fullName, firstName, lastName As String
   Dim m As Integer
   Dim n As Integer    'location of the space separating the two names
   fullName = txtName.Text
   n = fullName.IndexOf(" ")
   firstName = fullName.Substring(0, n)
   lastName = fullName.Substring(n + 1)
```

```
m = lastName.Length
'Display the desired information in a list box
lstResults.Items.Clear()
lstResults.Items.Add("First name: " & firstName)
lstResults.Items.Add("Your last name has " & m & " letters.")
End Sub
```

Some of the benefits of documentation are as follows:

1. Other people can easily understand the program.

2. You can understand the program when you read it later.

3. Long programs are easier to read because the purposes of individual pieces can be determined at a glance.

Even though Visual Basic code is easy to read, it is difficult to understand the programmer's intentions without supporting documentation. Good programming practice dictates that programmers document their code at the same time that they are writing it. In fact, many software companies require a certain level of documentation before they release a version, and some judge their programmers' performances on how well their code is documented. A rule of thumb is that 10% of the effort developing a software program is the initial coding, while the remaining 90% is maintenance. Much of the anxiety surrounding the fixing of the "Year 2000" problem was due to the enormous amount of effort required by programmers to read and fix old, undocumented code. The challenge was compounded by the fact that most of the original programmers of the code were retired or could not recall how their code was written.

■ Line-Continuation Character

Thousands of characters can be typed in a line of code. If you use a statement with more characters than can fit in the window, Visual Basic scrolls the Code Editor toward the right as needed. However, most programmers prefer having lines that are no longer than the width of the Code Editor. A long statement can be split across two or more lines by ending each line (except the last) with the underscore character (_) preceded by a space. Make sure the underscore doesn't appear inside quotation marks, though. For instance, the line

```
msg = "640K ought to be enough for anybody. (Bill Gates, 1981)"
```

can be written as

```
msg = "640K ought to be enough for " & _
      "anybody. (Bill Gates, 1981)"
```

The line-continuation character does not work with comment statements. Therefore, each line of a comment statement must be preceded by an apostrophe.

■ Scope of a Variable

When a variable is declared in an event procedure with a Dim statement, a portion of memory is set aside to hold the value of the variable. As soon as the End Sub statement for the procedure executes, the memory location is freed up; that is, the variable ceases to exist. The variable is said to be **local** to the procedure or to have **local scope**. In general, the **scope** of a variable is the portion of the program that can refer to it.

When variables of the same name are declared with Dim statements in two different event procedures, Visual Basic gives the variables separate memory locations and treats them as two different variables. A value assigned to a variable in one procedure will not affect the value of the like-named variable in the other procedure.

Visual Basic provides a way to make a variable recognized by every procedure in a form's code. Such a variable is called a **class-level variable** and is said to have **class-level scope**. The Dim statement for a class-level variable can be placed anywhere between the statements **Public Class** *formName* and **End Class**, provided that the Dim statement is not inside an event procedure. Normally, we place the Dim statement just after the **Public Class** *formName* statement. (We refer to this region as the **Declarations section** of the Code Editor.) When a class-level variable has its value changed by a procedure, the value persists even after the procedure has finished executing. If an event procedure declares a local variable with the same name as a class-level variable, then the name refers to the local variable for code inside the procedure.

 Example 8   The following program uses a class-level variable to keep track of the number of times a button has been clicked.

```
Public Class frmCount
  Dim numTimes As Integer = 0    'Class-level variable
  Private Sub btnPushMe_Click(...) Handles btnPushMe.Click
    numTimes += 1
    txtOutput.Text = "The button has been clicked " & _
                     numTimes & " times."
  End Sub
End Class
```

[Run, and click the button three times.]

■ **Comments**

  1. From the Code Editor, you can determine the type of a variable by letting the mouse cursor hover over the variable name until a tooltip appears. This feature of IntelliSense is called **Quick Info**.

2. Variable names should describe the role of the variable. Also, some programmers use a prefix, such as *dbl* or *str*, to identify the type of a variable. For example, they would use names like *dblInterestRate* and *strFirstName*. This naming convention is not needed in Visual Basic for the reason mentioned in Comment 1, and is no longer recommended by Microsoft.

3. The functions CInt and CDbl are user friendly. If the user types a number into a text box, but types in a comma as the thousands separator, the values of CInt(txtBox.Text) and CDbl(txtBox.Text) will be the number with the comma removed.

4. The Trim method is useful when reading data from a text box. Sometimes users type spaces at the end of the input. Unless the spaces are removed, they can cause havoc elsewhere in the program.

5. There are several alternatives to CStr for casting a value to a string value. For instance, the statement

```
strVar = CStr(dblVar)
```

can be replaced with any of the following statements:

```
strVar = CType(dblVar, String)
strVar = Convert.ToString(dblVar)
strVar = dblVar.ToString
```

Some alternatives to the use of CInt and CDbl are

```
dblVar = CType(strVar, Double)
intVar = CType(strVar, Integer)
intVar = CType(dblVar, Integer)
intVar = Integer.Parse(strVar)
dblVar = Double.Parse(strVar)
dblVar = Convert.ToDouble(strVar)
intVar = Convert.ToInt32(strVar)
intVar = Convert.ToInt32(dblVar)
```

These alternatives are common to all the Visual Studio languages and therefore are preferred by advanced programmers. We have decided to use CStr, CDbl, and CInt for the following two reasons:

(a) These functions make statements less cluttered, and therefore easier for beginning programmers to read.

(b) When an incorrect conversion is detected by IntelliSense, the Auto Correction helper box recommends and implements the use of the CStr, CDbl, and CInt functions.

Practice Problems 3.2

1. What is the value of "Computer".IndexOf("E")?

2. What is the difference in the output produced by the following two statements? Why is CStr used in the first statement, but not in the second?

```
txtBox.Text = CStr(8 + 8)
txtBox.Text = 8 & 8
```

3. Give an example of a prohibited statement that invokes an Auto Correction helper box with the heading "Option Strict On disallows implicit conversion from 'String' to 'Double'." Also, give the suggestion for fixing the error.

EXERCISES 3.2

In Exercises 1 through 28, determine the output displayed in the text box or list box by the lines of code.

1. ```
txtBox.Text = "Computer Science"
```

2. ```
lstBox.Items.Add("Hello")
```

3. ```
Dim var As String
var = "Mathematics"
lstBox.Items.Add(var)
```

4. ```
Dim var As String
var = "Physics"
txtBox.Text = var
```

5. ```
txtBox.Text = "act" & "ion"
```

6. ```
lstBox.Items.Add("sun" & "flower")
```

7. ```
Dim var As Double
var = 222
txtBox.Text = CStr(var)
```

8. ```
Dim var As Double
var = 3
txtBox.Text = CStr(var + 5)
```

9. ```
txtBox.Text = "The cost is " & 25 & " dollars and " & 70 & _
    " cents."
```

10. ```
txtBox.Text = "Fred has " & 2 & " children."
```

11. ```
Dim r As String
r = "TO BE"
txtBox.Text = r & "OR NOT " & r
```

12. ```
Dim s As String, n As Integer
s = "trombones"
n = 76
txtBox.Text = n & " " & s
```

13. ```
Dim num As Double
txtBox.Text = "5"
num = 0.5 + CDbl(txtBox.Text)
txtBox.Text = CStr(num)
```

14. ```
Dim num As Integer = 2
txtBox.Text = CStr(num)
txtBox.Text = CStr(1 + CInt(txtBox.Text))
```

15. ```
txtBox.Text = "good"
txtBox.Text &= "bye"
```

16. ```
Dim var As String = "eight"
var &= "h"
txtBox.Text = var
```

17. ```
Dim var As String = "LIBER"
var &= var.trim & "TAS"
txtBox.Text = var
```

18. ```
txtBox.Text = "mur"
txtBox.Text &= txtBox.Text
```

19. ```
lstBox.Items.Add("aBc".ToUpper)
lstBox.Items.Add("Wallless".IndexOf("lll"))
lstBox.Items.Add("five".Length)
lstBox.Items.Add(" 55 ".Trim & " mph")
lstBox.Items.Add("UNDERSTUDY".Substring(5, 3))
```

20. ```
lstBox.Items.Add("8 Ball".ToLower)
lstBox.Items.Add("colonel".IndexOf("k"))
lstBox.Items.Add("23.45".Length)
lstBox.Items.Add("revolutionary".Substring(1))
lstBox.Items.Add("whippersnapper".IndexOf("pp", 5))
```

21. ```
Dim a As Integer = 4
Dim b As Integer = 2
Dim c As String = "Municipality"
Dim d As String = "pal"
lstBox.Items.Add(c.Length)
lstBox.Items.Add(c.ToUpper)
lstBox.Items.Add(c.Substring(a, b) & c.Substring(5 * b))
lstBox.Items.Add(c.IndexOf(d))
```

22. ```
Dim m As Integer = 4
Dim n As Integer = 3
Dim s As String = "Microsoft"
Dim t As String = "soft"
lstOutput.Items.Add(s.Length)
lstOutput.Items.Add(s.ToLower)
lstOutput.Items.Add(s.Substring(m, n - 1))
lstOutput.Items.Add(s.IndexOf(t))
```

23. How many positions does a string of sixteen characters have?

24. What is the highest numbered position for a string of eight characters?

25. (True or False) If *n* is the length of *str*, then `str.Substring(n - 1)` is the string consisting of the last character of *str*.

26. (True or False) If *n* is the length of *str*, then `str.Substring(n - 1)` is the string consisting of the last two characters of *str*.

In Exercises 27 through 32, identify any errors.

27. ```
Dim phoneNumber As Double
phoneNumber = "234-5678"
txtBox.Text = "My phone number is " & phoneNumber
```
```

28. ```
Dim quote As String
    quote = I came to Casablanca for the waters.
    txtBox.Text = quote & ": " & "Bogart"
```

29. ```
Dim sub As String
    sub = "ham"
    txtBox.Text = sub & " and cheese"
```

30. ```
Dim hiyo As String
    hiyo = "Silver"
    txtBox = "Hi-Yo " & hiYo
```

31. ```
Dim num As Double = 1234
    txtBox.Text = CStr(num.IndexOf("2"))
```

32. ```
Dim num As Integer = 45
    txtBox.Text = CStr(num.Length)
```

**In Exercises 33 through 36, write an event procedure starting with a** Private Sub btnCompute_Click( ... ) Handles btnCompute.Click **statement, ending with an** End Sub **statement, and having one line for each step. Display each result by assigning it to the** txtOutput.Text **property. Lines that display data should use the given variable names.**

33. The following steps give the name and birth year of a famous inventor:

    (a) Declare all variables used in steps (b)–(e).
    (b) Assign "Thomas" to the variable *firstName*.
    (c) Assign "Alva" to the variable *middleName*.
    (d) Assign "Edison" to the variable *lastName*.
    (e) Assign 1847 to the variable *yearOfBirth*.
    (f) Display the inventor's full name followed by a comma and his year of birth.

34. The following steps compute a final grade after adding extra credit to it.

    (a) Declare all variables used in steps (b)–(d).
    (b) Assign 85 to the variable *grade*.
    (c) Assign 10 to the variable *extraCredit*.
    (d) Assign the sum of variables *grade* and *extraCredit* to the variable *finalGrade*.
    (e) Display the phrase "Final grade is 95."

35. The following steps display a copyright statement:

    (a) Declare the variable used in step (b).
    (b) Assign "Prentice Hall, Inc." to the variable *publisher*.
    (c) Display the phrase "(c) Prentice Hall, Inc."

36. The following steps give advice:

    (a) Declare the variable used in step (b).
    (b) Assign "Fore" to the variable *prefix*.
    (c) Display the phrase "Forewarned is Forearmed."

**In Exercises 37 and 38, write a line of code to carry out the task. Specify where in the program the line of code should be placed.**

37. Declare the variable *str* as a string variable visible to all parts of the program.
```

38. Declare the variable *str* as a string variable visible only to the btnTest_Click event procedure.

In Exercises 39 through 42, the interface is specified. Write the code to carry out the stated task.

39. If *n* is the number of seconds between lightning and thunder, the storm is *n*/5 miles away. Write a program that reads the number of seconds between lightning and thunder and reports the distance of the storm. A sample run is shown in Figure 3.3.

FIGURE 3.3 **Sample output of Exercise 39.**

40. The American College of Sports Medicine recommends that you maintain your *training heart rate* during an aerobic workout. Your training heart rate is computed as $.7*(220 - a) + .3*r$, where *a is* your age and *r is* your resting heart rate (your pulse when you first awaken). Write code to read a person's age and resting heart rate and display the training heart rate. (Determine *your* training heart rate.) A sample run is shown in Figure 3.4.

FIGURE 3.4 **Sample output of Exercise 40.**

41. The number of calories burned per hour by bicycling, jogging, and swimming are 200, 475, and 275, respectively. A person loses 1 pound of weight for each 3500 calories burned. Write code to read the number of hours spent at each activity and then display the number of pounds worked off. A sample run is shown in Figure 3.5.

FIGURE 3.5   Sample output of Exercise 41.

42. Total Cholesterol (TC), HDL cholesterol, and triglyceride (TG) levels are counted directly from a blood sample. LDL cholesterol is calculated by using the formula LDL = TC - HDL - TG / 5. Write a program that asks the user to input TC, HDL, and TG. When the user presses the *Compute LDL Cholesterol* button, the text box below the button should output the LDL cholesterol value calculated from the input data. A sample run is shown in Figure 3.6. A sample run is shown in Figure 3.6.

FIGURE 3.6   Sample output of Exercise 42.

In Exercises 43 through 48, write a program with a Windows-style interface to carry out the task. The program should use variables for each of the quantities and display the outcome in a text box with a label as in Example 2.

43. Request a company's annual revenue and expenses as input, and display the company's net income (revenue minus expenses). (Test the program with the amounts $550,000 and $410,000.)

44. Request the amount of money that a student has saved and the percentage of the amount he wants to spend for housing. Display the amount allocated for housing and remaining amount to be used for all other expenses.

45. Calculate the amount of a waiter's tip, given the amount of the bill and the percentage tip as input. (Test the program with $20 and 15 percent.)

46. Convert a percentage to a decimal. For instance, if the user enter 125% into a text box, then the output should be 1.25.

47. Write a program with a form that contains two buttons labeled Increase and Decrease, respectively, and a read-only text box initially containing 0. Each time the button Increase is pressed, the number in the text box should increase by 1. Each time the button Decrease is pressed, the number in the text box should decrease by 1.

48. Write a program that requests a (complete) phone number in a text box and then displays the area code in another text box when a button is pressed.

49. Write a program that requests a sentence and a word in the sentence. Display the resulting sentence obtained by omitting the first occurrence of the input word in the sentence.

50. Write a program that requests a letter, converts it to uppercase, and gives its first position in the sentence "THE QUICK BROWN FOX JUMPS OVER A LAZY DOG." For example, if the user responds by typing *b* into the text box, then the message "B first occurs in position 10." is displayed.

51. The formula $s = \sqrt{24d}$ gives an estimate of the speed of a car in miles per hour that skidded *d* feet on dry concrete when the brakes were applied. Write a program that requests the distance skidded and then displays the estimated speed of the car. (Try the program for a car that skids 54 feet.)

52. Write a program that requests a positive number containing a decimal point as input and then displays the number of digits to the left of the decimal point and the number of digits to the right of the decimal point.

53. Write a program that allows scores to be input one at a time, and then displays the average of the scores upon request. (See Figure 3.7.) The user should type a score into the top text box and then press the Record button. This process can be repeated as many times as desired. At any time the user should be able to press the Calculate button to display the average of all the scores that were entered so far. **Note:** This program requires two class-level variables.

FIGURE 3.7 **Form for Exercise 53.**

54. Write a program that allows furniture sales (item and price) to be displayed in a list box one at a time, and then shows the total commission of the sales (6%) upon request. (See Figure 3.8.) The user should type each item and price into the text boxes and then press the Display button. This process can be repeated as many

FIGURE 3.8 Form for Exercise 54.

times as desired. At any time the user should be able to press the Show button to display the total commission of all the sales that were entered. **Note:** This program requires a class-level variable.

55. Add an event procedure to Example 2 so that txtSum will be cleared whenever either the first number or the second number is changed.

Solutions to Practice Problems 3.2

1. −1. There is no uppercase letter E in the string "Computer". IndexOf distinguishes between uppercase and lowercase.

2. The first statement displays 16 in the text box, whereas the second statement displays 88. With Option Strict in effect, the first statement would not be valid if CStr were missing, since 8 + 8 is a number and txtBox.Text is a string. Visual Basic treats the second statement as if it were

```
txtBox.Text = CStr(8) & CStr(8)
```

3. Some possibilities are

PROHIBITED STATEMENT	SUGGESTION FOR FIXING
`Dim x As Double = "23"`	Replace '"23"' with 'CDbl("23")'.
`dblVar = txtBox.Text`	Replace 'txtBox.Text' with 'CDbl(txtBox.Text)'.
`dblVar = 2 & 3`	Replace '2 & 3' with 'CDbl(2 & 3)'.

3.3   Input and Output

■ Formatting Output with Format Functions

The Format functions are used to display numbers in familiar forms. Here are some examples of how numbers are converted to strings with Format functions:

FUNCTION	STRING VALUE
`FormatNumber(12345.628, 1)`	12,345.6
`FormatCurrency(12345.628, 2)`	$12,345.63
`FormatPercent(0.185, 2)`	18.50%

The value of FormatNumber(n, r) is the string containing the number n rounded to r decimal places and displayed with commas as thousands separators. The value of FormatCurrency(n, r) is the string consisting of a dollar sign followed by the value of FormatNumber(n, r). FormatCurrency uses the accountant's convention of denoting negative amounts with surrounding parentheses. The value of FormatPercent(n, r) is the string consisting of the number n displayed as a percent and rounded to r decimal places. With all three functions, r can be omitted. If so, the number is rounded to two decimal places. Strings corresponding to numbers less than one in magnitude have a zero to the left of the decimal point. Also, n can be a number, a numeric expression, or even a string corresponding to a number.

FUNCTION	STRING VALUE
`FormatNumber(1 + Math.Sqrt(2), 3)`	2.414
`FormatCurrency(-1000)`	($1,000.00)
`FormatPercent(".05")`	5.00%

■ Formatting Output with Zones

Data can be displayed in tabular form in a list box. In order to have the items line up nicely in columns, you must

1. use a fixed-width font such as Courier New so that each character will have the same width;
2. divide the line into zones with a format string.

Figure 3.9 shows a line of a list box divided into zones of widths 15 characters, 10 characters, and 8 characters. The leftmost zone is referred to as zone 0, the next zone is zone 1, and so on. These zones are declared in a string with the statement

```
Dim fmtStr As String = "{0, 15}{1, 10}{2, 8}"
```

Note: The pairs of numbers are surrounded by curly brackets, not parentheses.

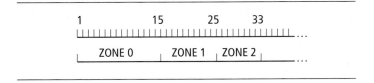

FIGURE 3.9   Zones.

If *data0*, *data1*, and *data2* are strings or numbers, the statement

```
lstOutput.Items.Add(String.Format(fmtStr, data0, data1, data2))
```

displays the pieces of data right justified into the zones. If any of the width numbers (such as 15, 10, or 8) is preceded with a minus sign, the data placed into the corresponding zone will be left justified.

Example 1 The following program displays information about two colleges in the United States. *Note:* The endowments are in billions of dollars. The final column tells what fraction of the student body attended public secondary schools.

OBJECT	PROPERTY	SETTING
frmColleges	Text	College Data
lstColleges	Font	Courier New
btnDisplay Table	Text	Display

```
Private Sub btnDisplay_Click(...) Handles btnDisplay.Click
  Dim fmtStr As String = "{0,-10}{1,12}{2,14}{3,12}"
  lstColleges.Items.Clear()
  lstColleges.Items.Add(String.Format(fmtStr, "College", _
                    "Enrollment", "Endowment", "Public SS"))
  lstColleges.Items.Add(String.Format(fmtStr, "Harvard", 6715, 45.9, 0.659))
  lstColleges.Items.Add(String.Format(fmtStr, "Yale", 5316, 22.5, 0.532))
End Sub
```

[Run, and click on the button.]

There is no limit to the number of zones, and the zones can be of any widths. In addition, by placing a colon and formatting symbols after the width, you can instruct Visual Basic to specially format numeric data. (String data are not affected.) The most used formatting symbols consist of a letter (*N* for number, *C* for currency, or *P* for percent) followed by a digit specifying the number of decimal places. If there is no digit after the letter, two decimal places are displayed. Here are some examples of such formatting:

ZONE FORMAT TERM	NUMBER TO BE FORMATTED	NUMBER DISPLAYED
{1, 12:N3}	1234.5679	1,234.568
{1, 12:N0}	34.6	34
{1, 12:C1}	1234.567	$1,234.6
{1, 12:P}	0.569	56.90%

If the second line of the program in Example 1 is replaced with

```
Dim fmtStr As String = "{0,-10}{1,12:N0}{2,14:C}{3,12:P0}"
```

the output will be as follows.

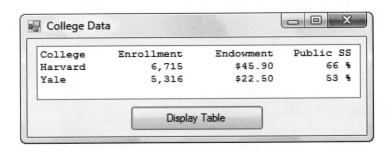

The format strings considered so far consist of a sequence of pairs of curly brackets. We also can insert spaces between successive pairs of brackets. If so, the corresponding zones in the output will be separated by those spaces. The lines of code

```
Dim fmtStr As String = "{0, 5}  {1, -5}"   'Two spaces after the
'                                           first right curly bracket
lstOutput.Items.Add("12345678901234567890")
lstOutput.Items.Add(String.Format(fmtStr, 1, 2))
```

produce the output

```
12345678901234567890
   1  2
```

▇ Reading Data from Files

So far, we have relied on assignment statements and text box controls to assign data to variables. Data also can be stored in text files and accessed with a StreamReader object or supplied by the user with an input dialog box.

In Chapter 2, we saw how to create text files with the Visual Basic Text Editor. We will assume that the text files have one item of information per line. Figure 3.10 shows a sample file giving payroll information. Each set of three lines gives the name of a person, their hourly wage, and the number of hours that person worked during the week.

Mike Jones
9.35
35
John Smith
10.75
33

FIGURE 3.10   Contents of PAYROLL.TXT.

Data stored in a text file can be read in order (that is, sequentially) and assigned to variables with the following steps:

1. Execute a statement of the form

```
Dim readerVar As IO.StreamReader
```

A StreamReader is an object from the Input/Output class that can read a stream of characters coming from a disk or coming over the Internet. The Dim statement declares the variable *readerVar* to be of type StreamReader.

2. Execute a statement of the form

```
readerVar = IO.File.OpenText(filespec)
```

where *filespec* identifies the file to be read. This statement establishes a communications link between the computer and the disk drive for reading data *from* the disk. Data then can be input from the specified file and assigned to variables in the program. This assignment statement is said to "open the file for input."

Just as with other variables, the declaration and assignment statements in Steps 1 and 2 can be combined into the single statement

```
Dim readerVar As IO.StreamReader = IO.File.OpenText(filespec)
```

3. Read items of data in order, one at a time, from the file with the ReadLine method. Each datum is retrieved as a string. A statement of the form

```
strVar = readerVar.ReadLine
```

causes the program to look in the file for the next unread line of data and assign it to the variable *strVar*. The data can be assigned to a numeric variable if it is first converted to a numeric type with a statement such as

```
numVar = CDbl(readerVar.ReadLine)
```

Note: The OpenText method sets a pointer to the first line of data in the specified file. Each time a ReadLine method is executed, the line pointed to is read, and the pointer is then moved to the next line. If all the data in a file have been read by ReadLine methods and another item is requested by a ReadLine method, the item retrieved will have the value Nothing.

4. After the desired items have been read from the file, terminate the communications link set in Step 2 with the statement

```
readerVar.Close()
```

Each Visual Basic program is contained in a folder with the name that was specified when the program was saved. The Solution Explorer window has the name of that folder as its first line. (If only a few entries appear in the Solution Explorer, click the Show All Files button at the top of the Solution Explorer window to display all the files and subfolders.) One subfolder is named *bin*. The folder *bin* has a subfolder named *Debug*. If the *filespec* in Step 2 above consists only of a filename (that is; if no path is given) Visual Basic will look for the file in the *Debug* subfolder of the program's *bin* folder. **Throughout this book, we assume that every text file** accessed by a program is located in the program's *Debug* subfolder of *bin.* Every program downloaded from my Prentice-Hall website has this feature.

 Example 2 Consider the following program that displays the address of the White House. (The form design for this and subsequent examples in this section consists of a button and a text or list box.)

```
Private Sub btnDisplay_Click(...) Handles btnDisplay.Click
  Dim houseNumber As Double
  Dim street, address As String
  houseNumber = 1600
  street = "Pennsylvania Ave."
  address = houseNumber & " " & street
  txtAddr.Text = "The White House is located at " & address
End Sub
```

[Run, and then click the button. The following is displayed in the text box.]

```
The White House is located at 1600 Pennsylvania Ave.
```

Let's now rewrite this program so that it uses a file for input and produces the same output. First, use the Visual Basic Text Editor to create the file DATA.TXT containing the following two lines:

```
1600
Pennsylvania Ave.
```

In the following code, the fifth line of the event procedure reads the first row of data as the string "1600", converts its type to Double, and assigns it to the variable *houseNumber.* (Visual Basic records that this row of data has been used.) The sixth line looks for the next available row of data, "Pennsylvania Ave.", and assigns it to the string variable *street.*

```
Private Sub btnDisplay_Click(...) Handles btnDisplay.Click
  Dim sr As IO.StreamReader = IO.File.OpenText("DATA.TXT")
  Dim houseNumber As Double
  Dim street, address As String
  houseNumber = CDbl(sr.ReadLine)
  street = sr.ReadLine
  sr.Close()
  address = houseNumber & " " & street
  txtAddr.Text = "The White House is located at " & address
End Sub
```

 Example 3 The following program uses the file PAYROLL.TXT shown in Figure 3.10 on page 98.

```
Private Sub btnCompute_Click(...) Handles btnCompute.Click
  Dim sr As IO.StreamReader = IO.File.OpenText("PAYROLL.TXT")
```

```
'The file PAYROLL.TXT is in the Debug subfolder
'of the bin subfolder of the folder 3-3-3.
Dim name As String
Dim hourlyWage, hoursWorked, salary As Double
name = sr.ReadLine
hourlyWage = CDbl(sr.ReadLine)
hoursWorked = CDbl(sr.ReadLine)
salary = hourlyWage * hoursWorked
lstPayroll.Items.Add(name & "    " & FormatCurrency(salary))
name = sr.ReadLine
hourlyWage = CDbl(sr.ReadLine)
hoursWorked = CDbl(sr.ReadLine)
salary = hourlyWage * hoursWorked
lstPayroll.Items.Add(name & "    " & FormatCurrency(salary))
sr.Close()
End Sub
```

[Run, and then click the button. The following is displayed in the list box.]

```
Mike Jones    $327.25
John Smith    $354.75
```

In certain situations, we must read the data in a file more than once. This is accomplished by closing the file and then reopening it with a second assignment statement of the form **sr = IO.File.OpenText(*filespec*)**. ***Note:*** The Close method only disconnects the StreamReader from the file. The variable *sr* continues to be recognized by the event procedure as a StreamReader variable.

 Example 4 The following program takes the average annual amounts of money spent by single-person households for several categories and converts these amounts to percentages. The data are read once to compute the total amount of money spent and then read again to calculate the percentage for each category. ***Note:*** These figures were compiled for 2006 by the Bureau of Labor Statistics.

The file COSTS.TXT consists of the following eight lines:

Transportation
4234
Housing
10463
Food
3162
Other
10229

```
Private Sub btnCompute_Click(...) Handles btnCompute.Click
   Dim sr As IO.StreamReader = IO.File.OpenText("COSTS.TXT")
   Dim total As Double              'Total annual amount spent
   Dim category As String
```

```
Dim amount As Double              'Amount spent on category
Dim fmtStr As String = "{0,-15}{1,8:P}"
category = sr.ReadLine            'Read the first category from the file
total += CDbl(sr.ReadLine)        'Increment total by the amount
'                                  associated with the category
category = sr.ReadLine            'Read the next category from the file
total += CDbl(sr.ReadLine)
category = sr.ReadLine
total += CDbl(sr.ReadLine)
category = sr.ReadLine
total += CDbl(sr.ReadLine)
sr.Close()
sr = IO.File.OpenText("COSTS.TXT")  'Open the file anew
category = sr.ReadLine
amount = CDbl(sr.ReadLine)
lstPercent.Items.Add(String.Format(fmtStr, category, amount / total))
category = sr.ReadLine
amount = CDbl(sr.ReadLine)
lstPercent.Items.Add(String.Format(fmtStr, category, amount / total))
category = sr.ReadLine
amount = CDbl(sr.ReadLine)
lstPercent.Items.Add(String.Format(fmtStr, category, amount / total))
category = sr.ReadLine
amount = CDbl(sr.ReadLine)
lstPercent.Items.Add(String.Format(fmtStr, category, amount / total))
sr.Close()
End Sub
```

[Run, and then click the button. The following is displayed in the list box.]

Transportation	15.07 %
Housing	37.25 %
Food	11.26 %
Other	36.42 %

■ Getting Input from an Input Dialog Box

Normally, a text box is used to obtain input, where the type of information requested is specified in a label adjacent to the text box. Sometimes, we want just one piece of input and would rather not have a text box and label stay on the screen forever. The problem can be solved with an **input dialog box**. When a statement of the form

stringVar = InputBox(*prompt*, *title*)

is executed, an input dialog box similar to the one shown in Figure 3.11 pops up on the screen. After the user types a response into the text box at the bottom of the dialog box and presses Enter (or clicks OK), the response is assigned to the string variable. The *title* argument is optional and provides the text that appears in the Title bar. The *prompt* argument is a string that tells the user what information to type into the text box.

FIGURE 3.11   Sample input dialog box.

When you type the opening parenthesis following the word InputBox, the Code Editor displays a line containing the general form of the InputBox statement. See Figure 3.12. This feature of IntelliSense is called **Parameter Info**. Optional parameters are surrounded by square brackets. All the parameters in the general form of the InputBox statement are optional except for *prompt*.

```
Dim prompt, title, name As String
prompt = "Enter the name of the file containing the information."
title = "Name of File"
name=InputBox (
```

InputBox (**Prompt As String**, [Title As String = ""], [DefaultResponse As String = ""], [XPos As Integer = -1], [YPos As Integer = -1]) As String
Prompt:
Required String expression displayed as the message in the dialog box. The maximum length of Prompt is approximately 1024 characters, depending on the width of the characters used. If Prompt consists of more than one line, you can separate the lines using a carriage return character (Chr(13)), a line feed character (Chr(10)), or a carriage return/line feed combination (Chr(13) & Chr(10)) between each line.

FIGURE 3.12   Parameter Info feature of IntelliSense.

 Example 5   In the following enhancement to Example 2, the file name is provided by the user in an input dialog box.

```
Private Sub btnDisplay_Click(...) Handles btnDisplay.Click
  Dim sr As IO.StreamReader
  Dim fileName, prompt, title, street As String
  Dim houseNumber As Double
  prompt = "Enter the name of the file containing the information."
  title = "Name of File"
  fileName = InputBox(prompt, title)
  'We assume the file is located in the subfolder Debug
  'of the bin subfolder of the folder 3-3-5.
  sr = IO.File.OpenText(fileName)
  houseNumber = CDbl(sr.ReadLine)
  street = sr.ReadLine
  sr.Close()
  txtAddr.Text = "The White House is located at " & _
                 houseNumber & " " & street
End Sub
```

[Run, and then click the button. The input dialog box of Figure 3.11 appears on the screen. Type "DATA.TXT" into the input dialog box, and click on OK. The input dialog box disappears, and the following appears in the text box.]

`The White House is located at 1600 Pennsylvania Ave.`

The response typed into an input dialog box is treated as a single string value, no matter what is typed. (Quotation marks are not needed and, if included, are considered as part of the string.) Numeric data typed into an input dialog box should be converted to a number with CDbl or CInt before being assigned to a numeric variable or used in a calculation. Just as with a text box or file, the typed data must be a literal. It cannot be a variable or an expression. For instance, *num*, 1/2, and 2 + 3 are not acceptable.

■ Using a Message Dialog Box for Output

Sometimes you want to grab the user's attention with a brief message such as "Correct" or "Nice try, but no cigar." You want this message only to appear on the screen until the user has read it. This task is easily accomplished with a **message dialog box** such as the one shown in Figure 3.13.

FIGURE 3.13   Sample message dialog box.

When a statement of the form

`MessageBox.Show(prompt, title)`

is executed, where *prompt* and *title* are strings or numbers, a message dialog box appears with *prompt* displayed and the Title bar caption *title*, and stays on the screen until the user presses Enter, clicks on the box in the upper-right corner, or clicks OK. For instance, the statement

`MessageBox.Show("Nice try, but no cigar.", "Consolation")`

produces Figure 3.13. You can omit the value for *title* and just execute `MessageBox.Show(prompt)`. If you do, the Title bar will be blank and the rest of the message dialog box will appear as before.

■ Using a Masked Text Box for Input

Problems can arise when the wrong type of data is entered as input into a text box. For instance, if the user replies to the request for an age by entering "twenty-one" into a text box, the program can easily crash. Sometimes this type of predicament can be avoided by using a masked text box for input. (In later chapters, we will consider other ways of insuring the integrity of input.)

In the Toolbox, the icon for the MaskedTextBox control consists of a rectangle containing the two characters # and _. The most important property of a masked text box is the Mask property that can be used to restrict the characters entered into the box. Also, the Mask property can be used to show certain characters in the control—to give users a visual cue that they should be entering a phone number or a social security number, for example. Some possible settings for the Mask property are shown in Table 3.2. The first four settings can be selected from a list of specified options. The last three settings generalize to any number of digits, letters, or ampersands. If the Mask property is left blank, then the MaskedTextBox control is nearly identical to the TextBox control.

TABLE 3.2 **Some settings for the Mask property.**

Setting	Effect
000-00-0000	The user can enter a social security number.
000-0000	The user can enter a phone number (without an area code).
(000)000-0000	The user can enter a phone number (with an area code).
00/00/0000	The user can enter a date.
0000000	The user can enter a positive integer consisting of up to 7 digits.
LLLLL	The user can enter a string consisting of up to 5 letters.
&&&&&&&&	The user can enter a string consisting of up to 8 characters.

Suppose a form contains a masked text box whose Mask property has the setting 000-00-0000. When the program is run, the string "___-__-____" will appear in the masked text box. The user will be allowed to type a digit in place of each of the eight underscore characters. The hyphens cannot be altered, and no characters can be typed anywhere else in the masked text box.

During run time, the characters 0, L, and & in the setting for a Mask property are replaced by underscore characters that are place holders for digits, letters, and characters, respectively. (Spaces are also allowed. However, trailing spaces are dropped.) When the characters "-", "(", ")", or "/" appear in a setting for a Mask property, they appear as themselves in the masked text box and cannot be altered. There are some other mask settings, but these seven will suffice for our purposes.

Figure 3.14 (a) shows a masked text box during design time. It looks like an ordinary text box. However, the Tasks button for the masked text box is used to set the Mask property rather than the Multiline property. Figure 3.14 (b) shows the result of clicking on the Tasks button. Then, clicking on "Set Mask . . . " brings up the Input Mask dialog box shown in Figure 3.15 on the next page. (This input dialog box is the same input dialog box that is invoked when you click on the ellipses in the Mask property's Settings box.) You can use this input dialog box to select a commonly used value for the Mask property,

(a)   (b)

FIGURE 3.14 **The Masked TextBox control.**

FIGURE 3.15 **Input dialog box used to set the Mask property of a masked text box.**

such as the social security number or phone number mask, or set and test a custom-designed mask you create with characters such as 0, &, and L. We will use the prefix *mtxt* for the names of masked text boxes.

■ Comments

1. *Importing an Existing Text File into a Program.* All text files required for the exercises in this chapter are located in the subfolder *Text Files_for_Exercises* of the folder *Ch03* downloaded from the companion website. The following steps import an existing text file into a program.

   (a) Highlight the name of the program at the top of the Solution Explorer window. (**Note:** If the Solution Explorer window is not visible, click on Solution Explorer in the View menu.)

   (b) Click on "Add Existing Item" in the Project menu. (An "Add Existing Item" dialog box will appear.)

   (c) There is a drop-down box for displaying file types near the bottom of the dialog box. Click on its down-arrow and click on "All Files (*.*)."

   (d) Locate the text file and double-click on it. (The text file will be copied, and the filename will appear in the Solution Explorer window.)

   (e) Locate the text file in the Solution Explorer window and move it to the *Debug* subfolder of *bin*. The move can be accomplished either by drag-and-drop or by Cut-and-Paste. (**Note:** If the *bin* folder does not show in the Solution Explorer window, click on the "Show All Files" icon in the Solution Explorer toolbar.)

2. The statement `Dim sr As IO.StreamReader = IO.File.OpenText("DATA.TXT")` will be used frequently in this book, albeit with a different file name each time. You can

store this line of code (or any frequently used fragment of code) for later use by highlighting it and dragging it from the Code Editor into the Toolbox. To reuse the code, just drag it back from the Toolbox to the Code Editor. A copy of the code will remain in the Toolbox for further use. Alternately, you can click on the location in the Code Editor where you want the code to be inserted, and then double-click on the code in the Toolbox.

3. In Example 4 the pair of lines

```
category = sr.ReadLine
total += CDbl(sr.ReadLine)
```

are repeated four times, as are the triplet of lines

```
category = sr.ReadLine
amount = CDbl(sr.ReadLine)
lstPercent.Items.Add(String.Format(fmtStr, category, amount / total))
```

Chapter 6 presents repetition structures that allow the lines to execute four times, yet appear just once in the code.

Practice Problems 3.3

1. Is the statement

```
txtOutput.Text = FormatNumber(12345.628, 1)
```

correct, or should it be written

```
txtOutput.Text = CStr(FormatNumber(12345.628, 1))
```

2. What is the difference in the outcomes of the following two sets of code?

```
strVar = InputBox("How old are you?", "Age")
numVar = CDbl(strVar)
txtOutput.Text = numVar

numVar = CDbl(InputBox("How old are you?", "Age")
txtOutput.Text = numVar
```

EXERCISES 3.3

In Exercises 1 through 30, determine the output produced by the lines of code.

1. `txtOutput.Text = FormatNumber(123.4567, 1)`

2. `txtOutput.Text = FormatNumber(-12.3456, 3)`

3. `txtOutput.Text = FormatNumber(1234, 2)`

4. `txtOutput.Text = FormatNumber(12345)`

5. `txtOutput.Text = FormatNumber(0.1234, 2)`

6. `txtOutput.Text = FormatNumber(22 * (10 ^ -2), 1)`

7. `txtOutput.Text = FormatNumber(-2 / 3)`

8.
```
Dim numVar As Double = Math.Round(1.9876, 1)
txtOutput.Text = FormatNumber(numVar, 2)
```

9.
```
Dim numVar As Double = Math.Round(19876.54)
txtOutput.Text = FormatNumber(numVar, 3)
```

10.
```
Dim numVar As Double = Math.Round(12.5)
txtOutput.Text = FormatNumber(numVar, 0)
```

11.
```
Dim numVar As Double = Math.Round(55.5)
txtOutput.Text = FormatNumber(numVar, 0)
```

12.
```
txtOutput.Text = FormatCurrency(1234.5)
```

13.
```
txtOutput.Text = FormatCurrency(123.4567, 0)
```

14.
```
txtOutput.Text = FormatCurrency(-1234567)
```

15.
```
txtOutput.Text = FormatCurrency(-0.225)
```

16.
```
txtOutput.Text = FormatCurrency(32 * (10 ^ 3))
```

17.
```
txtOutput.Text = FormatCurrency(4 / 5)
```

18.
```
txtOutput.Text = FormatPercent(0.088, 2)
```

19.
```
txtOutput.Text = FormatPercent(0.055)
```

20.
```
txtOutput.Text = FormatPercent(-.05, 3)
```

21.
```
txtOutput.Text = FormatPercent(1)
```

22.
```
txtOutput.Text = FormatPercent(0.01)
```

23.
```
txtOutput.Text = FormatPercent(2 / 3)
```

24.
```
txtOutput.Text = FormatPercent(3 / 4, 1)
```

25.
```
txtOutput.Text = "Pay amount " & FormatCurrency(222222)
```

26.
```
txtOutput.Text = "Manhattan was purchased for " & FormatCurrency(24)
```

27.
```
Dim popUSover24 As Double = 177.6        'Million
Dim collegeGrads As Double = 45.5        'Million
'                                        45.5/177.6 = 0.2561937
txtOutput.Text = FormatPercent(collegeGrads / popUSover24, 1) & _
    " of the U.S. population 25+ years old are college graduates."
```

28.
```
Dim degrees As String = FormatNumber(1711500, 0)
txtOutput.Text = degrees & " degrees were conferred."
```

29.
```
txtOutput.Text = "The likelihood of Heads is " & _
                 FormatPercent(1 / 2, 0)
```

30.
```
txtOutput.Text = "Pi = " & FormatNumber(3.1415926536, 4)
```

In Exercises 31 through 40, determine the output produced by the lines of code. Assume that Courier New is the font for the list box.

31.
```
Dim fmtStr As String = "{0,-10}{1,10}" 'two spaces
lstOutput.Items.Add("12345678901234567890012345")
lstOutput.Items.Add(String.Format(fmtStr, 5, 3))
```

32.
```
Dim fmtStr As String = "{0,10}{1,10}" 'two spaces
lstOutput.Items.Add("12345678901234567890012345")
lstOutput.Items.Add(String.Format(fmtStr, 5, 3))
```

33.
```
Dim fmtStr As String = "{0,10}{1,-10}" 'two spaces
lstOutput.Items.Clear()
lstOutput.Items.Add("123456789012345678901 2345")
lstOutput.Items.Add(String.Format(fmtStr, 5, 3))
```

34.
```
Dim fmtStr As String = "{0,-10}{1,-10}" 'two spaces
lstOutput.Items.Add("123456789012345678901 2345")
lstOutput.Items.Add(String.Format(fmtStr, 5, 3))
```

35.
```
Dim fmtStr As String = "{0,3}{1,10}"
lstOutput.Items.Add("12345678901234567890")
lstOutput.Items.Add(String.Format(fmtStr, "A", "Alice"))
```

36.
```
Dim fmtStr As String = "{0,-13}{1,-10}{2,-7:N0}"
lstOutput.Items.Add("123456789012345678901234567890")
lstOutput.Items.Add(String.Format(fmtStr, "Mountain", "Place", "Ht (ft)"))
lstOutput.Items.Add(String.Format(fmtStr, "K2", "Kashmir", 28250))
```

37.
```
Dim fmtStr As String = "{0,11}   {1,-11}"    'Three spaces
lstOutput.Items.Add("12345678901234567890")
lstOutput.Items.Add(String.Format(fmtStr, "College", "Mascot"))
lstOutput.Items.Add(String.Format(fmtStr, "Univ. of MD", "Terrapins"))
lstOutput.Items.Add(String.Format(fmtStr, "Duke", "Blue Devils"))
```

38.
```
'Toss coin twice
Dim fmtStr As String = "{0,8}   {1,-7:P0}"    'Two spaces
lstOutput.Items.Clear()
lstOutput.Items.Add("12345678901234567890")
lstOutput.Items.Add(String.Format(fmtStr, "Number", "Percent"))
lstOutput.Items.Add(String.Format(fmtStr, "of Heads", "of time"))
lstOutput.Items.Add(String.Format(fmtStr, 0, 1 / 4))
lstOutput.Items.Add(String.Format(fmtStr, 1, 1 / 2))
lstOutput.Items.Add(String.Format(fmtStr, 2, 1 / 4))
```

39.
```
'Elements in a 150 Pound Person
Dim fmtStr As String = "{0,-10}   {1,-10:N1}   {2,-10:P1}" '2 spaces
lstOutput.Items.Clear()
lstOutput.Items.Add("123456789012345678901234567890")
lstOutput.Items.Add(String.Format(fmtStr, "Element", "Weight", "Percent"))
lstOutput.Items.Add(String.Format(fmtStr, "Oxygen", 97.5, 97.5 / 150))
lstOutput.Items.Add(String.Format(fmtStr, "Carbon", 27, 27 / 150))
```

40.
```
Dim fmtStr As String = "{0,10}   {1,-10:C0}"    'Three spaces
lstOutput.Items.Clear()
lstOutput.Items.Add("12345678901234567890")
lstOutput.Items.Add(String.Format(fmtStr, "", "Tuition"))
lstOutput.Items.Add(String.Format(fmtStr, "College", "& Fees"))
lstOutput.Items.Add(String.Format(fmtStr, "Stanford", 24441))
lstOutput.Items.Add(String.Format(fmtStr, "Harvard", 25128))
```

In Exercises 41 through 52, assume that the file DATA.TXT (shown to the right of the code) has been accessed with the statement `Dim sr As IO.StreamReader =`

`IO.File.OpenText("DATA.TXT")` and closed afterwards with the statement `sr.Close()`. Determine the output displayed by the lines of code.

41.
```
Dim num As Double
num = CDbl(sr.ReadLine)
txtOutput.Text = CStr(num * 5)
```
DATA.TXT

4

42.
```
Dim word As String
word = sr.ReadLine
txtOutput.Text = "dis" & word
```
DATA.TXT

like

43.
```
Dim str1, str2 As String
str1 = sr.ReadLine
str2 = sr.ReadLine
txtOutput.Text = str1 & str2
```
DATA.TXT

soft

ball

44.
```
Dim num1, num2, num3 As Double
num1 = CDbl(sr.ReadLine)
num2 = CDbl(sr.ReadLine)
num3 = CDbl(sr.ReadLine)
txtOutput.Text = CStr((num1 + num2) / num3)
```
DATA.TXT

6

4

5

45.
```
Dim yrOfBirth, curYr As Double
yrOfBirth = CDbl(sr.ReadLine)
curYr = CDbl(sr.ReadLine) 'Current year
txtOutput.Text = "Age: " & (curYr - yrOfBirth)
```
DATA.TXT

1988

2008

46.
```
Dim str1, str2 As String
str1 = sr.ReadLine
str2 = sr.ReadLine
txtOutput.Text = str1 & " " & str2
```
DATA.TXT

A, my name is

Alice

47.
```
Dim building As String
Dim numRooms As Double
building = sr.ReadLine
numRooms = CDbl(sr.ReadLine)
txtOutput.Text = "The " & building & " has " & numRooms & " rooms."
```
DATA.TXT

White House

132

48.
```
Dim major As String
Dim percent As Double
major = sr.ReadLine
percent = CDbl(sr.ReadLine)
txtOutput.Text = "In 2007, " & percent & _
    "% of entering college freshmen majored in " & major & "."
```
DATA.TXT

Computer Science

1.1

49.
```
Dim num, sum, average As Double
sum = 0
num = CDbl(sr.ReadLine)
sum += num
num = CDbl(sr.ReadLine)
sum += num
txtOutput.Text = "Sum: " & sum & _ & " and average= " & sum/2 & "."
```
DATA.TXT

111

222

50.
```
Dim grade, total, average As Double
Dim numGrades As Integer
total = 0
numGrades = 0
grade = CDbl(sr.ReadLine)
total += grade        'Increase value of total by value of grade
numGrades += 1        'Increase value of numGrades by 1
grade = CDbl(sr.ReadLine)
total += grade    'Increase value of total by value of grade
numGrades += 1    'Increase value of numGrades by 1
average = total / numGrades
txtOutput.Text = "Average grade: " & average
```

DATA.TXT
```
85
95
```

51.
```
Dim museum As String
museum = sr.ReadLine
lstOutput.Items.Add(museum)
sr.Close()
sr = IO.File.OpenText("DATA.TXT")
museum = sr.ReadLine
lstOutput.Items.Add(museum)
```

DATA.TXT
```
Metropoliten
Smithsonian
```

52.
```
Dim num As Integer, str As String
num = CInt(sr.ReadLine)
str = sr.ReadLine
lstOutput.Items.Add(num & " " & str)
sr.Close()
sr = IO.File.OpenText("DATA.TXT")
num = CInt(sr.ReadLine)
str = sr.ReadLine
lstOutput.Items.Add(num & " " & str)
```

DATA.TXT
```
4
calling birds
3
French hens
```

In Exercises 53 through 58, determine the output displayed.

53.
```
Dim bet As Double               'Amount bet at roulette
bet = CDbl(InputBox("How much do you want to bet?", "Wager"))
txtOutput.Text = "You might win " & 36 * bet & " dollars."
```

(Assume that the response is 10.)

54.
```
Dim word As String
word = InputBox("Word to negate:", "Negatives")
txtOutput.Text = "un" & word
```

(Assume that the response is "tied".)

55.
```
Dim lastName, message, firstName As String
lastName = "Jones"
message = "What is your first name Mr. " & lastName & "?"
firstName = InputBox(message, "Name")
txtOutput.Text = "Hello " & firstName & " " & lastName
```

(Assume that the response is "John".)

56.
```
Dim intRate, doublingTime As Double 'Current interest rate, time to double
   intRate = CDbl(InputBox("Current interest rate?", "Interest"))
   doublingTime = 72 / intRate
   lstOutput.Items.Add("At the current interest rate, money will")
   lstOutput.Items.Add("double in " & doublingTime & " years.")
```

(Assume that the response is 4.)

In Exercises 57 and 58, write a line of code to carry out the task.

57. Pop up a message dialog box with "Latin Quote" in the title bar and the message "Dies diem docet."

58. Pop up a message dialog box with "Latin Saying" in the title bar and the message "Divinum dare, humanum accipere."

In Exercises 59 through 66, identify any errors. If the code refers to a file, assume that DATA.TXT (on the right of the code) already has been opened for input.

59.
```
Dim num As Double
num = CDbl(sr.ReadLine)
txtOutput.Text = CStr(3 * num)
```
DATA.TXT

1 + 2

60.
```
'Each line triplet of DATA.TXT contains
'building, height, # of stories
Dim building As String
Dim ht As Double
Dim numStories As Integer
lstOutput.Items.Clear()
building = sr.ReadLine
ht = CDbl(sr.ReadLine)
lstOutput.Items.Add(building & " is " & ht & " feet tall.")
building = sr.ReadLine
ht = CDbl(sr.ReadLine)
lstOutput.Items.Add(building & " is " & ht & " feet tall.")
```
DATA.TXT

Sears Tower

1454

110

Empire State Building

1250

102

61.
```
Dim num As Double
num = InputBox("Pick a number from 1 to 5.")
txtOutput.Text = "Your number is " & num
```

62.
```
info = InputBox()
```

63.
```
Dim num As Double = FormatNumber(123456)
lstOutput.Items.Add(num)
```

64.
```
txtOutput.Text = FormatCurrency("5%")
```

65.
```
Dim fmtStr As String = "{0,20}{1,10}"
lstOutput.Items.Add(fmtStr, "Washington", "George")
```

66.
```
MessageBox("The Road", "Pulitzer Prize for Fiction")
```

In Exercises 67 through 70, write an event procedure starting with a `Private Sub btnCompute_Click(...) Handles btnCompute.Click` statement, ending with an `End`

Sub statement, and having one, two, or three lines for each step. Lines that display data should use the given variable names.

67. The following steps display information about Americans' eating habits. Assume that the three lines of the file SODA.TXT contain the following data: soft drinks, million gallons, 23.

    (a) Declare all variables used in step (c).
    (b) Open the file SODA.TXT for input.
    (c) Use ReadLine statements to assign values to the variables *food*, *units*, and *quantityPerDay*.
    (d) Display a sentence giving the quantity of a food item consumed by Americans in one day.

68. Use the following steps to calculate the number of moles for an element..

    (a) Declare all variables used in the steps that follow.
    (b) Request atomic weight for the element and assign it to variable *atomicWeight*.
    (c) Request weight in grams and assign it to variable *weight*.
    (d) Calculate the number of moles, *numberMoles*, as the ratio of *weight* and *atomicWeight*.
    (e) Report the number of moles in the output text box with a full sentence.

69. The following steps calculate the percent increase in a typical grocery basket of goods:

    (a) Declare all variables used in the steps that follow.
    (b) Assign 200 to the variable *begOfYearPrice*.
    (c) Request the price at the end of the year with an input dialog box, and assign it to the variable *endOfYearPrice*.
    (d) Assign 100*(*endOfYearPrice* − *begOfYearPrice*) / *begOfYearPrice* to the variable *percentIncrease*.
    (e) Display a sentence giving the percent increase for the year.

    (Test the program with a $215 end-of-year price.)

70. Use the following steps to calculate number of moles of a calcium carbonate ($CaCO_3$) compound.

    (a) Declare all variables used in the steps that follow.
    (b) Request atomic weight for calcium and assign it to variable *atomicWeightCa*.
    (c) Request atomic weight for carbon and assign it to variable *atomicWeightC*.
    (d) Request atomic weight for oxygen and assign it to variable *atomicWeightO*.
    (e) Request weight in grams for the given compound and assign it to variable *weight*.
    (f) Determine molecular weight *molecularWeight* as sum of *atomicWeightCa* plus *atomicWeightC* plus three times *atomicWeightO*.
    (g) Calculate the number of moles, *numberMoles*, as the ratio of *weight* and *molecularWeight*.
    (h) Report the number of moles for the CaCO3 compound in the output text box with a full sentence.

    (Test the program with a pledge of $2.00 and a 15-mile walk.)

In Exercises 71 through 76, give a setting for the Mask property of a masked text box used to input the stated information.

71. A number from 100 to 999.
72. A word of ten letters.

73. A Maryland license plate consisting of three letters followed by three digits. (*Example*: BHC365)

74. A California license plate consisting of a digit followed by three letters and then three digits. (*Example*: 7BHC365)

75. An ISBN number. [Every book is identified by a ten-character International Standard Book Number (ISBN). The first nine characters are digits and the last character is either a digit or the letter X.] (*Example*: 0-32-108599-X).

76. A Social Security number. (*Example*: 666-66-6666)

77. Table 3.3 summarizes the month's activity of three checking accounts. Write a program that displays the account number and the end-of-month balance for each account and then displays the total amount of money in the three accounts. Assume that the data are stored in a text file.

TABLE 3.3 Checking account activity.

Account Number	Beginning of Month Balance	Deposits	Withdrawals
AB4057	1234.56	345.67	100.00
XY4321	789.00	120.00	350.00
GH2222	321.45	143.65	0.00

78. Table 3.4 contains a list of colleges with their student enrollments and faculty sizes. Write a program to display the names of the colleges and their student/faculty ratios, and the ratio for the total collection of students and faculty. Assume that the data for the colleges are stored in a text file.

TABLE 3.4 Colleges.

	Enrollment	Faculty
Ohio State	52568	3025
Univ. of MD, College Park	36041	2896
Princeton	7055	850

79. Write a program to compute semester averages. Each set of five lines in a text file should contain a student's Social Security number and the grades for three hourly exams and the final exam. (The final exam counts as two hourly exams.) The program should display each student's Social Security number and semester average, and then the class average. Use the data in Table 3.5.

TABLE 3.5 Student grades.

Soc. Sec. No.	Exam 1	Exam 2	Exam 3	Final Exam
123-45-6789	67	85	90	88
111-11-1111	93	76	82	80
123-32-1234	85	82	89	84

80. Table 3.6 gives the year 2006 populations of three New England states. Write a program that calculates the average population and then displays the name of each state and the difference between its population and the average population. The states and their populations should be stored in a text file.

TABLE 3.6	2006 population (in thousands) of three New England states.

State	Population
Maine	1371
Massachusetts	6437
Connecticut	3504

81. Design a form with two text boxes labeled "Name" and "Address". Write an event procedure that shows a message dialog box stating "Enter first name, middle initial, and last name separated by spaces." when the first text box receives the focus. In addition, write another event procedure that shows a message dialog box stating "Enter street address, city, state, and zip code separated by commas." when the second text box receives the focus.

82. Write a program to calculate the volume of a sphere. Design a form with a button displaying "Compute Volume of a Sphere" and a text box to display the resulting volume. Radius should be obtained via input dialog box. The output should be complete sentence that reiterates the input and gives resulting volume. Determine volume using the formula: volume $= (4 / 3) * 3.14159 * \text{radius}^{\wedge} 3$.

FIGURE 3.16   Sample output for Exercise 82.

83. When P dollars are deposited in a savings account at interest rate r compounded annually, the balance after n years is $P(1 + r)^n$. Write a program to request the principal P and the interest rate r as input, and compute the balance after 10 years, as shown in Figure 3.17.

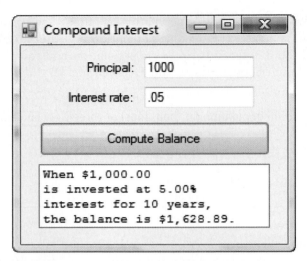

FIGURE 3.17 Sample output for Exercise 83.

In Exercises 84 and 85, write lines of code corresponding to the given flowchart. Assume that the data needed are contained in a file.

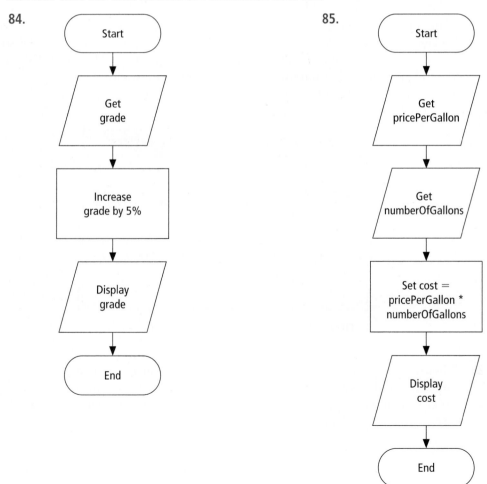

Solutions to Practice Problems 3.3

1. The first statement is correct, since FormatNumber evaluates to a string. Although the second statement is not incorrect, the use of CStr is redundant.

2. The outcomes are identical. In this text, we primarily use the second style.

CHAPTER 3 SUMMARY

1. Two types of *literals* that can be stored and processed by Visual Basic are numbers and strings.

2. Many Visual Basic tasks are carried out by methods such as Clear (erases the contents of a text box or list box), Add (places an item into a list box), ToUpper (converts a string to uppercase), ToLower (converts a string to lowercase), Trim (removes leading and trailing spaces from a string), IndexOf (searches for a specified character in a string and gives its position if found), and Substring (returns a sequence of consecutive characters from a string).

3. The standard *arithmetic operations* are $+$, $-$, $*$, $/$, and $\wedge$. The only string operation is &, concatenation. An *expression* is a combination of literals, variables, functions, and operations that can be evaluated.

4. A *variable* is a name used to refer to data. Variable names must begin with a letter or an underscore and may contain letters, digits, and underscores. Dim statements declare variables, specify the data types of the variables, and assign initial values to the variables. In this book, most variables have data types Double, Integer, or String.

5. Values are assigned to variables by *assignment statements*. The values appearing in assignment statements can be literals, variables, or expressions. String literals used in assignment statements must be surrounded by quotation marks.

6. *Comment statements* are used to explain formulas, state the purposes of variables, and articulate the purposes of various parts of a program.

7. *Option Explicit* requires that all variables be declared with Dim statements. *Option Strict* requires the use of conversion functions in certain situations.

8. The *Error List window* displays, and helps you find, errors in the code. The *Auto Correction* feature of IntelliSense suggests corrections when errors occur.

9. The *line continuation character* (an underscore preceded with a space) is used to extend a Visual Basic statement over two or more lines.

10. The *scope* of a variable is the portion of the program in which the variable is visible and can be used. A variable declared inside an event procedure is said to have *local* scope and is visible only inside the procedure. A variable declared in the Declarations section of a program is said to have *class-level* scope and is visible throughout the entire program.

11. *Format strings* can be used to line up data in tables uniformly and display them with dollar signs, commas, percent signs, and a specified number of decimal places.

12. A *StreamReader* object allows us to read data from a file that is specified with an OpenText method. The ReadLine method reads the next unread line from a file.

13. *Functions* can be thought of as accepting numbers or strings as input and returning numbers or strings as output.

FUNCTION	INPUT	OUTPUT
CDbl	string or number	number
CInt	string or number	number
CStr	number	string
FormatCurrency	number	string
FormatNumber	number	string
FormatPercent	number	string
InputBox	string, string	string
Int	number	number
Math.Round	number, number	number
Math.Sqrt	number	number

14. *Masked text boxes* are useful for input since they have a Mask property that specifies the type of data that can be typed into them.

CHAPTER 3   PROGRAMMING PROJECTS

1. Write a program that allows the user to specify two numbers and then adds, subtracts, or multiplies them when the user clicks on the appropriate button. The output should give the type of arithmetic performed and the result. See Figure 3.18. (**Note:** If one of the numbers in an input text box is changed, the output text box should be cleared.)

FIGURE 3.18   Sample run for Programming Project 1.

2. Suppose automobile repair customers are billed at the rate of $35 per hour for labor. Also, costs for parts and supplies are subject to a 5% sales tax. Write a program to display a simplified bill. The customer's name, the number of hours of labor, and the cost of parts and supplies should be entered into the program via text boxes. When a button is clicked, the customer's name (indented) and the three costs should be displayed in a list box, as shown in the sample run in Figure 3.19.

FIGURE 3.19   Sample run for Programming Project 2.

3. At the end of each month, a credit card company constructs the table in Figure 3.20 to summarize the status of the accounts. Write a program to produce this table. The first four pieces of information for each account should be read from a text file. The program should compute the finance charges (1.5% of the unpaid past due amount) and the current amount due.

```
  Credit Card Accounts                                        □ ▣ X

                        Display Account Summary

  Account   Past Due                         Finance    Current
  Number     Amount   Payments  Purchases    Changes    Amt Due
  123-AB    $123.45    $10.00    $934.00      $1.70    $1,049.15
  456-CD    $134.56   $134.56    $300.00      $0.00      $300.00
```

FIGURE 3.20   Status of credit card accounts.

4. Table 3.7 gives the 2007 distribution of the U.S. population (in thousands) by age group and sex. Write a program to produce the table shown in Figure 3.21. For each age group, the column labeled "%Males" gives the percentage of the people in that age group who are male, and the column labeled "%Females" gives this information about the female population. The last column gives the percentage of the total population in each age group. **Note:** Store the information in Table 3.7 in a text file. For instance, the first three lines in the file should contain the following data: Under 15, 31152, 29777. Read and add up the data once to obtain the total population, and then read the data again to produce the table.

TABLE 3.7	2007 U.S. population (in thousands).	
Age Group	Males	Females
Under 15	31,152	29,777
15–64	100,996	101,365
65+	15,858	21,991

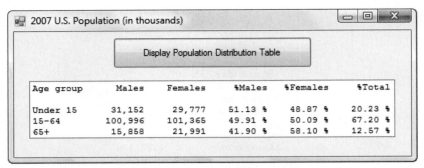

FIGURE 3.21 **Output of Programming Project 4.**

5. Write a program that requests change amount via a textbox and calculates the minimal number of coins for that amount. Let q, d, n, and p denote the number of quarters, dimes, nickels, and pennies, respectively. The following is the outline of the algorithm to produce the change.

amount = changeAmount * 100	'convert change amount into cents
q = amount \ 25	'get number of quarters by doing integer division
amount = amount − q * 25	'remaining amount after subtracting max number of quarters
d = amount \ 10	'get number of dimes
amount = amount − d * 10	'calculate remaining amount
. . .	'get nickels n and remaining amount
. . .	'pennies equal to the remaining amount

FIGURE 3.22 **Sample run for Programming Project 5.**

4

Decisions

4.1   Relational and Logical Operators

In Chapter 1, we discussed the two logical programming constructs *decision* and *loop*. In order to make a decision or control a loop, you need to specify a condition that determines the course of action.

A **condition** is an expression involving relational operators (such as < and =) that is either true or false. Conditions also may incorporate logical operators (such as And, Or, and Not). ANSI values determine the order used to compare strings with the relational operators. Boolean variables and literals can assume the values True or False.

■ ANSI Values

Each of the 47 different keys in the center typewriter portion of the keyboard can produce two characters, for a total of 94 characters. Adding 1 for the space character produced by the space bar makes 95 characters. These characters have numbers ranging from 32 to 126 associated with them. These values, called the ANSI (or ASCII) values of the characters, are given in Appendix A. Table 4.1 shows a few of the values.

TABLE 4.1	A few ANSI values.		
32 (space)	48 0	66 B	122 z
33 !	49 1	90 Z	123 {
34 "	57 9	97 a	125 }
35 #	65 A	98 b	126 ~

Most of the best known fonts, such as Courier New, Microsoft San Serif, and Times New Roman, are essentially governed by the ANSI standard, which assigns characters to the numbers from 0 to 255. Table 4.2 shows a few of the higher ANSI values.

TABLE 4.2	A few higher ANSI values.		
162 ¢	177 ±	181 μ	190 $^3/_4$
169 ©	178 ^{2}	188 $^1/_4$	247 ÷
176 °	179 ^{3}	189 $^1/_2$	248 ϕ

If *n* is a number between 0 and 255, then

```
Chr(n)
```

is the string consisting of the character with ANSI value *n*. If *str* is any string, then

```
Asc(str)
```

is the ANSI value of the first character of *str*. For instance, the statement

```
txtBox.Text = Chr(65)
```

displays the letter A in the text box, and the statement

```
lstBox.Items.Add(Asc("Apple"))
```

displays the number 65 in the list box.

Concatenation can be used with Chr to obtain strings using the higher ANSI characters. For instance, with one of the fonts that conforms to the ANSI standard, the statement

```
txtBox.Text = "32" & Chr(176) & " Fahrenheit"
```

displays 32° Fahrenheit in the text box.

The quotation-mark character (**"**) can be placed into a string by using Chr(34). For example, after the statement

```
txtBox.Text = "George " & Chr(34) & "Babe" & Chr(34) & " Ruth"
```

is executed, the text box contains

```
George "Babe" Ruth
```

■ Relational Operators

The relational operator *less than* (<) can be applied to both numbers and strings. The number *a* is said to be less than the number *b* if *a* lies to the left of *b* on the number line. For instance, $2 < 5$, $-5 < -2$, and $0 < 3.5$.

The string *a* is said to be less than the string *b* if *a* precedes *b* alphabetically when using the ANSI table to alphabetize their values. For instance, "cat" < "dog", "cart" < "cat", and "cat" < "catalog". Digits precede uppercase letters, which precede lowercase letters. Two strings are compared working from left to right, character by character, to determine which one should precede the other. Therefore, "9W" < "bat", "Dog" < "cat", and "Sales-99" < "Sales-retail".

Table 4.3 shows the different mathematical relational operators, their representations in Visual Basic, and their meanings.

TABLE 4.3   **Relational operators.**

Mathematical Notation	Visual Basic Notation	Numeric Meaning	String Meaning
=	=	equal to	identical to
≠	<>	not equal to	different from
<	<	less than	precedes alphabetically
>	>	greater than	follows alphabetically
≤	<=	less than or equal to	precedes alphabetically or is identical to
≥	>=	greater than or equal to	follows alphabetically or is identical to

Example 1   Determine whether each of the following conditions is true or false.

(a) $1 <= 1$

(b) $1 < 1$

(c) "car" < "cat"

(d) "Dog" < "dog"

SOLUTION

(a) True. The notation <= means "less than *or* equal to." That is, the condition is true provided either of the two circumstances holds. The second one (equal to) holds.

(b) False. The notation < means "strictly less than" and no number can be strictly less than itself.

(c) True. The characters of the strings are compared one at a time working from left to right. Because the first two match, the third character decides the order.

(d) True. Because uppercase letters precede lowercase letters in the ANSI table, the first character of "Dog" precedes the first character of "dog".

Conditions also can involve variables, numeric operators, and functions. To determine whether a condition is true or false, first compute the numeric or string values and then decide if the resulting assertion is true or false.

Example 2   Suppose the numeric variables *a* and *b* have values 4 and 3, and the string variables *c* and *d* have values "hello" and "bye". Are the following conditions true or false?

(a) $(a + b) < 2*a$

(b) $(c.Length - b) = (a/2)$

(c) $c < (\text{"good"} \& d)$

SOLUTION

(a) The value of a + b is 7 and the value of $2*a$ is 8. Because $7 < 8$, the condition is true.

(b) True, because the value of c.Length − b is 2, the same as (a / 2).

(c) The condition "hello" < "goodbye" is false, because "h" follows "g" in the ANSI table.

■ Logical Operators

Programming situations often require more complex conditions than those considered so far. For instance, suppose we would like to state that the value of a numeric variable, *n*, is strictly between 2 and 5. The proper Visual Basic condition is

$$(2 < n) \text{ And } (n < 5)$$

The condition $(2 < n)$ And $(n < 5)$ is a combination of the two conditions $2 < n$ and $n < 5$ with the logical operator And.

The three main logical operators are And, Or, and Not. If *cond1* and *cond2* are conditions, then the condition

`cond1 And cond2`

is true if both *cond1* and *cond2* are true. Otherwise, it is false. The condition

`cond1 Or cond2`

is true if either *cond1* or *cond2* (or both) is true. Otherwise, it is false. The condition

`Not cond1`

is true if *cond1* is false, and is false if *cond1* is true.

Example 3   Suppose the numeric variable *n* has value 4 and the string variable *answ* has value "Y". Determine whether each of the following conditions is true or false.

(a) (2 < n) And (n < 6)

(b) (2 < n) Or (n = 6)

(c) Not (n < 6)

(d) (answ = "Y") Or (answ = "y")

(e) (answ = "Y") And (answ = "y")

(f) Not (answ = "y")

(g) ((2 < n) And (n = 5 + 1)) Or (answ = "No")

(h) ((n = 2) And (n = 7)) Or (answ = "Y")

(i) (n = 2) And ((n = 7) Or (answ = "Y"))

SOLUTION

(a) True, because the conditions (2 < 4) and (4 < 6) are both true.

(b) True, because the condition (2 < 4) is true. The fact that the condition (4 = 6) is false does not affect the conclusion. The only requirement is that at least one of the two conditions be true.

(c) False, because (4 < 6) is true.

(d) True, because the first condition becomes ("Y" = "Y") when the value of *answ* is substituted for *answ*.

(e) False, because the second condition is false. Actually, this compound condition is false for every value of *answ*.

(f) True, because ("Y" = "y") is false.

(g) False. In this logical expression, the compound condition ((2 < n) And (n = 5 + 1)) and the simple condition (answ = "No") are joined by the logical operator Or. Because both of these conditions are false, the total condition is false.

(h) True, because the second Or clause is true.

(i) False. Comparing (h) and (i) shows the necessity of using parentheses to specify the intended grouping.

■ Boolean Data Type

A statement of the form

```
txtBox.Text = CStr(condition)
```

will display either True or False in the text box, depending on the truth value of the condition. Any variable or expression that evaluates to either True or False is said to have a **Boolean data type**. The following lines of code display False in the text box.

```
Dim x As Integer = 5
txtBox.Text = CStr((3 + x) < 7)
```

A variable is declared to be of type Boolean with a statement of the form

```
Dim varName As Boolean
```

The following lines of code will display True in the text box.

```
Dim boolVar as Boolean
Dim x As Integer = 2
Dim y As Integer = 3
boolVar = x < y
txtBox.Text = CStr(boolVar)
```

The answer to part (i) of Example 3 can be confirmed to be False by executing the following lines of code.

```
Dim n as Integer = 4
Dim answ as String = "Y"
txtBox.Text = CStr((n = 2) And ((n = 7) Or (answ = "Y")))
```

■ Comments

1. A condition involving numeric variables is different from an algebraic truth. The assertion $(a + b) < 2*a$, considered in Example 2, is not a valid algebraic truth because it isn't true for all values of a and b. When encountered in a Visual Basic program, however, it will be considered true if it is correct for the current values of the variables.

2. Conditions evaluate to either True or False. These two values often are called the possible **truth values** of the condition.

3. A condition such as $2 < n < 5$ should never be used, because Visual Basic will not evaluate it as intended. The correct condition is $(2 < n)$ And $(n < 5)$.

4. A common error is to replace the condition Not $(n < m)$ by the condition $(n > m)$. The correct replacement is $(n >= m)$.

Practice Problems 4.1

1. Is the condition "Hello " = "Hello" true or false?

2. Complete Table 4.4.

TABLE 4.4 Truth values of logical operators.

cond1	cond2	cond1 And cond2	cond1 Or cond2	Not cond2
True	True	True		
True	False		True	
False	True			False
False	False			

EXERCISES 4.1

In Exercises 1 through 6, determine the output displayed in the text box.

1. `txtBox.Text = Chr(72) & Chr(73)`

2. `txtBox.Text = "C" & Chr(35)`

3. `txtBox.Text = "The letter after M is: " & Chr(Asc("M") + 1)`

4. `txtBox.Text = Chr(Asc("B"))  'The ANSI value of B is 66`

5. ```
Dim quote, person, qMark As String
quote = "We're all in this alone."
person = "Lily Tomlin"
qMark = Chr(34)
txtBox.Text = qMark & quote & qMark & " - " & person
```

6. ```
Dim letter As String
letter = "D"
txtBox.Text = letter & " is the " & (Asc(letter) - Asc("A") + 1) & _
              "th letter of the alphabet."
```

In Exercises 7 through 18, determine whether the condition is true or false. Assume a = 2 and b = 3.

7. $3*a = 2*b$

8. $(8 + a)*b > 30$

9. $b <= 3$

10. $a^\wedge b = b^\wedge a$

11. $a^\wedge(4 - b) > 5$

12. $3E-02 < .01*a$

13. $(a < b)$ Or $(b < a)$

14. $(a*a > a*b)$ Or Not $(b*b < b)$

15. Not $((a < b)$ And $(a < (b + a)))$

16. Not $(a < b)$ Or Not $(a < (b + a))$

17. $((a = b)$ And $(a*a < b*b))$ Or $((b < a)$ And $(2*a < b))$

18. $((a = b)$ Or Not $(b < a))$ And $((a < b)$ Or $(b = a + 1))$

In Exercises 19 through 30, determine whether the condition is true or false.

19. "9W" <> "9w"

20. "Happy" < "Birthday"

21. "Car" < "Train"

22. "J" >= "J"

23. "50" > "Fifty"

24. "B" > "?"

25. ("Duck" < "pig") And ("pig" < "big")

26. "Duck" < "Duck" & "Duck"

27. Not (("H" = "h") And ("Happy" < "happy"))

28. Not ("B" = "b") And Not ("Big" < "big")

29. (("Ant" < "hill") And ("mole" > "hill")) Or Not (Not ("Ant" < "hill") Or Not ("Mole" > "hill"))

30. (25 > 15) And ("25" > "15")

In Exercises 31 through 40, determine whether or not the two conditions are equivalent—that is, whether they will be true or false for exactly the same values of the variables appearing in them.

31. a <= b; (a < b) Or (a = b)

32. Not (a < b); a > b

33. (a = b) And (a < c); (a = c)

34. Not ((a = b) Or (a = c)); (a <> b) And (a <> c)

35. (b > c) And ((b < d) Or (b < e));
    ((b > c) And (b < d)) Or ((b > c) And (b < e))

36. Not ((a = b + c) Or (a = b)); (a <> b) Or (a <> b + c)

37. Not (c <= d);
    (c >= d) And Not (c = d)

38. Not (a >= b); (a <= b) Or Not (a = b)

39. Not (a >= b); (a <= b) And Not (a = b)

40. (a = b) And ((b = c) Or (a = c)); (a = b) Or ((b = c) And (a = c))

In Exercises 41 through 45, write a condition equivalent to the negation of the given condition. (For example, a **<>** b is equivalent to the negation of a **=** b.)

41. a < c

42. (a = b) Or (a = d)

43. (a > b) Or (c = d)

44. Not ((a = b) Or (a > b))

45. (b <> 5) And (c < d) And (c.length < 7)

46. Rework Exercise 20 by evaluating a Boolean expression.

47. Rework Exercise 21 by evaluating a Boolean expression.

48. Rework Exercise 22 by evaluating a Boolean expression.

49. Rework Exercise 23 by evaluating a Boolean expression.

Solutions to Practice Problems 4.1

1. False. The first string has six characters, whereas the second has five. Two strings must be 100% identical to be called equal.

2.

cond1	cond2	cond1 And cond2	cond1 Or cond2	Not cond2
True	True	True	True	False
True	False	False	True	True
False	True	False	True	False
False	False	False	False	True

4.2   If Blocks

An **If block** allows a program to decide on a course of action based on whether certain conditions are true or false.

■ If Block

A block of the form:

```
If condition Then
   action1
Else
   action2
End If
```

causes the program to take *action1* if *condition* is true and *action2* if *condition* is false. Each action consists of one or more Visual Basic statements. After an action is taken, execution continues with the line after the If block. Figure 4.1 contains the pseudocode and flowchart for an If block.

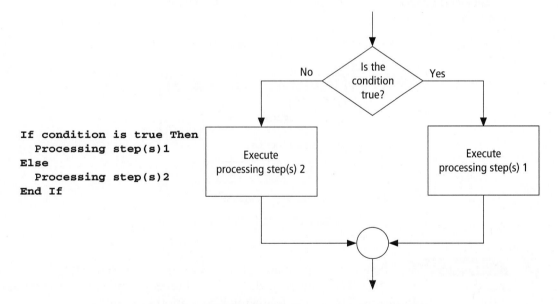

FIGURE 4.1   Pseudocode and flowchart for an If block.

✔   **Example 1**   The following program finds the larger of two numbers input by the user. The condition is

```
num1 > num2
```

and each action consists of a single assignment statement. With the inputs 3 and 7, the condition is false, and so the second action is taken.

OBJECT	PROPERTY	SETTING
frmMaximum	Text	Maximum
lblFirstNum	Text	First Number:
txtFirstNum		
lblSecondNum	Text	Second Number:
txtSecondNum		
btnFindLarger	Text	Find Larger Number
txtResult	ReadOnly	True

```
Private Sub btnFindLarger_Click(...) Handles btnFindLarger.Click
  Dim num1, num2, largerNum As Double
  num1 = CDbl(txtFirstNum.Text)
  num2 = CDbl(txtSecondNum.Text)
  If num1 > num2 Then
    largerNum = num1
  Else
    largerNum = num2
  End If
  txtResult.Text = "The larger number is " & largerNum & "."
End Sub
```

[Run, type 3 and 7 into the text boxes, and press the button.]

Example 2   The following program requests the costs and revenue for a company and displays the message "Break even" if the costs and revenue are equal; otherwise, it displays the profit or loss. The action following Else is another If block.

OBJECT	PROPERTY	SETTING
frmStatus	Text	Profit/Loss
lblCosts	Text	Costs:
txtCosts		
lblRev	Text	Revenue:
txtRev		
btnShow	Text	Show Financial Status
txtResult	ReadOnly	True

```
Private Sub btnShow_Click(...) Handles btnShow.Click
  Dim costs, revenue, profit, loss As Double
  costs = CDbl(txtCosts.Text)
  revenue = CDbl(txtRev.Text)
  If costs = revenue Then
    txtResult.Text = "Break even"
  Else
    If costs < revenue Then
      profit = revenue - costs
      txtResult.Text = "Profit is " & FormatCurrency(profit) & "."
    Else
      loss = costs - revenue
      txtResult.Text = "Loss is " & FormatCurrency(loss) & "."
    End If
  End If
End Sub
```

[Run, type 9500 and 8000 into the text boxes, and press the button.]

 Example 3   The If block in the following program has a logical operator in its condition.

OBJECT	PROPERTY	SETTING
frmQuiz	Text	A Quiz
lblQuestion	AutoSize	False
	Text	How many gallons does a ten-gallon hat hold?
txtAnswer		
btnEvaluate	Text	Evaluate Answer
txtSolution	ReadOnly	True

```
Private Sub btnEvaluate_Click(...) Handles btnEvaluate.Click
  'Evaluate answer
  Dim answer As Double
  answer = CDbl(txtAnswer.Text)
  If (answer >= 0.5) And (answer <= 1) Then
    txtSolution.Text = "Good, "
  Else
```

```
      txtSolution.Text = "No, "
    End If
    txtSolution.Text &= "it holds about 3/4 of a gallon."
End Sub
```

[Run, type 10 into the text box, and press the button.]

The Else part of an If block can be omitted. This important type of If block appears in the next example.

 Example 4 The following program offers assistance to the user before presenting a quotation.

OBJECT	PROPERTY	SETTING
frmQuotation	Text	Quotation
lblQuestion	Text	Do you know what the game of skittles is (Y/N)?
mtxtAnswer	Mask	L
btnDisplay	Text	Display Quotation
txtQuote	ReadOnly	True

```
Private Sub btnDisplay_Click(...) Handles btnDisplay.Click
  Dim message As String
  message = "Skittles is an old form of bowling in which a wooden " & _
            "disk is used to knock down nine pins arranged in a square."
  If mtxtAnswer.Text.ToUpper = "N" Then
    MessageBox.Show(message, "Definition")
  End If
  txtQuote.Text = "Life ain't all beer and skittles." & _
                " - Du Maurier (1894)"
End Sub
```

[Run, type "N" into the masked text box, and press the button.]

[Press OK.]

Note: Rerun the program, type "Y" into the masked text box, press the button, and observe that the description of the game is skipped.

■ ElseIf Clauses

An extension of the If block allows for more than two possible alternatives with the inclusion of ElseIf clauses. A typical block of this type is

```
If condition1 Then
    action1
ElseIf condition2 Then
    action2
ElseIf condition3 Then
    action3
Else
    action4
End If
```

This block searches for the first true condition, carries out its action, and then skips to the statement following End If. If none of the conditions are true, then Else's action is carried out. Execution then continues with the statement following the block. In general, an If block can contain any number of ElseIf clauses. As before, the Else clause is optional.

Example 5 The following program redoes Example 1 so that if the two numbers are equal, the program so reports:

```
Private Sub btnFindLarger_Click(...) Handles btnFindLarger.Click
  Dim num1, num2 As Double
  num1 = CDbl(txtFirstNum.Text)
  num2 = CDbl(txtSecondNum.Text)
  If (num1 > num2) Then
    txtResult.Text = "The larger number is " & num1
  ElseIf (num2 > num1) Then
    txtResult.Text = "The larger number is " & num2
  Else
    txtResult.Text = "The two numbers are equal."
  End If
End Sub
```

[Run, type 7 into both text boxes, and press the button.]

The If block in Example 6 allows us to calculate values that are not determined by a simple formula.

 Example 6 The Social Security or FICA tax has two components—the Social Security benefits tax, which in 2008 is 6.2 percent on the first $102,000 of earnings for the year, and the Medicare tax, which is 1.45 percent of earnings. The following program calculates an employee's FICA tax for the current pay period.

OBJECT	PROPERTY	SETTING
frmFICA	Text	FICA Taxes
lblToDate	AutoSize	False
	Text	Total earnings for this year prior to the current pay period:
txtToDate		
lblCurrent	Text	Earnings for the current pay period:
txtCurrent		
btnCalculate	Text	Calculate FICA Taxes
lblTax	Text	FICA taxes for the current pay period:
txtTax	ReadOnly	True

```
Private Sub btnCalculate_Click(...) Handles btnCalculate.Click
  'Calculate Social Security benefits tax and Medicare tax
  'for a single pay period in 2008
  Dim ytdEarnings, curEarnings As Double
  Dim socialSecurityBenTax, medicareTax, ficaTaxes As Double
  ytdEarnings = CDbl(txtToDate.Text)
  curEarnings = CDbl(txtCurrent.Text)
  If (ytdEarnings + curEarnings) <= 102000 Then
    socialSecurityBenTax = 0.062 * curEarnings
  ElseIf ytdEarnings < 102000 Then
    socialSecurityBenTax = 0.062 * (102000 - ytdEarnings)
  End If
  medicareTax = 0.0145 * curEarnings
  ficaTaxes = socialSecurityBenTax + medicareTax
  txtTax.Text = FormatCurrency(ficaTaxes)
End Sub
```

[Run, type 12345.67 and 543.21 into the top two text boxes and press the button.]

Comments

1. Constructs in which an If block is contained inside another If block are referred to as **nested** If blocks.

2. Care should be taken to make If blocks easy to understand. For instance, in Figure 4.2, the block on the left is difficult to follow and should be replaced by the clearer block on the right.

```
If cond1 Then              If cond1 And cond2 Then
  If cond2 Then              action
    action                 End If
  End If
End If
```

FIGURE 4.2   A confusing If block and an improvement.

3. In Appendix C, the section "Stepping through Programs Containing Decision Structures: Chapter 4" uses the Visual Basic debugging tools to trace the flow through an If block.

4. Some programs call for selecting among many possibilities. Although such tasks can be accomplished with complicated If blocks, the Select Case block (discussed in the next section) is often a better alternative.

Practice Problems 4.2

1. Suppose the user is asked to input a number into txtNumber for which the square root is to be taken. Fill in the If block so that the lines of code that follow will display either the message "Number can't be negative." or the square root of the number.

```
Private Sub btnSqrt_Click(...) Handles btnSqrt.Click
  'Check reasonableness of data
  Dim num As Double
  num = CDbl(txtNumber.Text)
  If


  End If
End Sub
```

2. Improve the block

```
If a < b Then
  If c < 5 Then
     txtBox.Text = "hello"
  End If
End If
```

EXERCISES 4.2

In Exercises 1 through 12, determine the output displayed in the text box when the button is clicked.

1.
```
Private Sub btnDisplay_Click(ByVal sender As System.Object, ByVal e As
System.EventArgs) Handles btnDisplay.Click
  Dim a As Double = 6
  If a > 5 Then
    txtOutput.Text = "a is greater than 5"
  Else
    If a = 6 Then
       txtOutput.Text = "a is equal to 6"
    End If
  End If
End Sub
```

2.
```
Private Sub btnDisplay_Click(...) Handles btnDisplay.Click
  Dim gpa As Double = 3.49
  txtOutput.Clear()
```

```vb
    If gpa >= 3.5 Then
        txtOutput.Text = "Honors "
    End If
 txtOutput.Text &= "Student"
    End Sub
```

3.
```vb
Private Sub btnDisplay_Click(ByVal sender As System.Object, ByVal e As
System.EventArgs) Handles btnDisplay.Click
    Dim a As Double = 15
    txtOutput.Clear()
    If (a - 5 * 2) < 20 Then
        txtOutput.Text = "Visual Basic"
    End If
    txtOutput.Text &= "Programming is Fun"
End Sub
```

4.
```vb
Private Sub btnDisplay_Click(...) Handles btnDisplay.Click
    Dim change As Double = 356     'Amount of change in cents
    If change >= 100 Then
        txtOutput.Text = "Your change contains "  & _
                        Int(change / 100) & " dollars."
    Else
        txtOutput.Text = "Your change contains no dollars."
    End If
End Sub
```

5.
```vb
Private Sub btnDisplay_Click(...) Handles btnDisplay.Click
    Dim a as Double = 2
    Dim b As Double = 3
    Dim c As Double = 5
    If a * b < c Then
        b = 7
    Else
        b = c * a
    End If
    txtOutput.Text = CStr(b)
End Sub
```

6.
```vb
Private Sub btnDisplay_Click(ByVal sender As System.Object, ByVal e As
System.EventArgs) Handles btnDisplay.Click
    Dim num1, num2 As Double
    num1 = CDbl(InputBox("Enter a number"))
    num2 = CDbl(InputBox("Enter a number"))
    If (num1 < num2) Then
        num1 += 5
    Else
        num2 += 5
    End If
    txtOutput.Text = num1 & "   " & num2
End Sub
```

(Assume input of 5 and 10)

7.
```
Private Sub btnDisplay_Click(...) Handles btnDisplay.Click
    'Cost of phone call from New York to London
    Dim length, cost As Double
    'Request the length of a phone call
    length = CDbl(InputBox("Duration of the call in minutes?"))
    'Calculate cost of phone call
    If length < 1 Then
      cost = 0.46
    Else
      cost = 0.46 + (length - 1) * 0.36
    End If
    'Display the cost of the call
    txtBox.Text = "Cost of call: " & FormatCurrency(cost)
End Sub
```
(Assume the response is *31.*)

8.
```
Private Sub btnDisplay_Click(ByVal sender As System.Object, ByVal e As
System.EventArgs) Handles btnDisplay.Click
    Dim num1 As Integer
    num1 = CInt(InputBox("Enter a number"))
    If (num1 Mod 2 = 0) Then
      txtOutput.Text = num1 & "  is an even number"
    Else
      txtOutput.Text = num1 & "  is an odd number"
    End If
End Sub
```
(Assume input of *24.*)

9.
```
Private Sub btnDisplay_Click(...) Handles btnDisplay.Click
    Dim vowel As Boolean = False
    Dim ltr As String
    ltr = InputBox("Enter a letter.")
    ltr = ltr.ToUpper
    If (ltr = "A") Or (ltr = "E") Or (ltr = "I") Or _
       (ltr = "O") Or (ltr = "U") Then
      vowel = True
    End If
    If vowel Then
      txtOutput.Text = ltr & " is a vowel."
    Else
      txtOutput.Text = ltr & " is not a vowel."
    End If
End Sub
```
(Assume the response is *a.*)

10.
```
Private Sub btnDisplay_Click(...) Handles btnDisplay.Click
    Dim a As Double = 5
    If (a > 2) And ((a = 3) Or (a < 7)) Then
```

```vbnet
      txtOutput.Text = "Hi"
    End If
  End Sub
```

11.
```vbnet
Private Sub btnDisplay_Click(...) Handles btnDisplay.Click
  Dim num As Double = 5
  If num < 0 Then
    txtOutput.Text = "neg"
  Else
    If num = 0 Then
       txtOutput.Text = "zero"
    Else
       txtOutput.Text = "positive"
    End If
  End If
End Sub
```

12.
```vbnet
Private Sub btnDisplay_Click(ByVal sender As System.Object, ByVal e As
System.EventArgs) Handles btnDisplay.Click
  Dim output As String, age As Integer
  output = "You can drive a car"
  age = CInt(InputBox("Enter your age: "))
  If (age >= 16) Then
    txtOutput.Text = output
  ElseIf (age >= 15) Then
    txtOutput.Text = output & " with an adult"
  Else
    txtOutput.Text = output & " in " & (16 - age) & " years"
  End If
End Sub
```

(Assume input of *14*)

13.
```vbnet
Private Sub btnDisplay_Click(...) Handles btnDisplay.Click
  Dim num As Double = 0.5
  If (1 < num < 3) Then
    txtOutput.Text = "Number is between 1 and 3."
  End If
End Sub
```

14.
```vbnet
Private Sub btnDisplay_Click(...) Handles btnDisplay.Click
  Dim num As Double = 6
  If num > 5 And < 9 Then
    txtOutput.Text = "Yes"
  Else
    txtOutput.Text = "No"
  End If
End Sub
```

15.
```
Private Sub btnDisplay_Click(ByVal sender As System.Object, ByVal e As
System.EventArgs) Handles btnDisplay.Click
   If ("a" <> "A")
      txtOutput.Text = "The Values are not equal"
   End If
End Sub
```

16.
```
Private Sub btnDisplay_Click(...) Handles btnDisplay.Click
   Dim major As String
   major = "Computer Science"
   If major = "Business" Or "Computer Science" Then
      txtOutput.Text = "Yes"
   End If
End Sub
```

17.
```
Private Sub btnDisplay_Click(...) Handles btnDisplay.Click
   Dim numName As String, num As Double
   numName = "Seven"
   num = CDbl(InputBox("Enter a number."))
   If num < numName Then
      txtOutput.Text = "Less than"
   Else
      txtOutput.Text = "Greater than"
   End If
End Sub
```

18.
```
Private Sub btnDisplay_Click(ByVal sender As System.Object, ByVal e As
System.EventArgs) Handles btnDisplay.Click
   'Switch answers from "yes" to "on", or from "no" to "yes"
   Dim answer As String
   answer = InputBox("Enter your answer: Yes or No.")
   If answer = "Yes" Then
      answer = "No"
   End If
   If answer = "No" Then
      answer = "Yes"
   End If
   txtOutput.Text = answer
End Sub
```

19.
```
Private Sub btnDisplay_Click(...) Handles btnDisplay.Click
   'Display "OK" if either j or k equals 4
   Dim j As Double = 2
   Dim k As Double = 3
   If j Or k = 4 Then
      txtOutput.Text = "OK"
   End If
End Sub
```

20.
```
Private Sub btnDisplay_Click(...) Handles btnDisplay.Click
    'Is your program correct?
    Dim query, answer1, answer2 As String
    query = "Are you sure everything in your program is correct?"
    answer1 = InputBox(query)
    answer1 = answer1.ToUpper.Substring(0, 1)
    If answer1 = "N" Then
      txtOutput.Text = "Don't patch bad code, rewrite it."
    Else
      query = "Does your program run correctly?"
      answer2 = InputBox(query)
      answer2 = answer2.ToUpper.Substring(0, 1)
      If answer2 = "Y" Then
         txtOutput.Text = "Congratulations."
      Else
         txtOutput.Text = "Something you are sure about is wrong."
      End If
    End If
End Sub
```

In Exercises 21 through 26, simplify the code.

21.
```
If (a = 2) Then
    a = 3 + a
Else
  a = 5
End If
```

22.
```
If Not (answer <> "y") Then
    txtOutput.Text = "YES"
Else
  If (answer = "y") Or (answer = "Y") Then
    txtOutput.Text = "YES"
  End If
End If
```

23.
```
If (j = 7) Then
  b = 1
Else
  If (j <> 7) Then
    b = 2
  End If
End If
```

24.
```
If (number1 < number2) Then
   If (number2 > number3) Then
     txtOutput.Text = "Number 1 is smaller than Number 2 and Number 3"
   End If
End If
```

25.
```
message = "Is Alaska bigger than Texas and California combined?"
answer = InputBox(message)
If (answer.Substring(0, 1) = "Y") Then
   answer = "YES"
End If
If (answer.Substring(0, 1) = "y") Then
   answer = "YES"
End If
If (answer = "YES") Then
  txtOutput.Text = "Correct"
Else
  txtOutput.Text = "Wrong"
End If
```

26.
```
message = "How tall (in feet) is the Statue of Liberty?"
feet = CDbl(InputBox(message))
If (feet <= 141) Then
  lstOutput.Items.Add("Nope")
End If
If (feet > 141) Then
  If (feet < 161) Then
    lstOutput.Items.Add("Close")
  Else
    lstOutput.Items.Add("Nope")
  End If
End If
lstOutput.Items.Add("The statue is 151 feet from base to torch.")
```

27. Write a program to determine how much to tip the server in a restaurant. The tip should be 15 percent of the check, with a minimum of $1.

28. A school supply store charges 15 cents each for pens sold in quantities of 10 or less and 10 cents each for quantities of more than 10. Write a program that requests the number of pens purchased and display the total cost.

    Test the program for ordering 10 and 15 pens

29. A store sells widgets at 25 cents each for small orders or at 20 cents each for orders of 100 widgets or more. Write a program that requests the number of widgets ordered and displays the total cost. (Test the program for purchases of 5 and 200 widgets.)

30. A copy center charges 5 cents per copy for the first 100 copies and 3 cents per copy for each additional copy. Write a program that requests the number of copies as input and displays the total cost. (Test the program with the quantities 25 and 125.)

31. Write a program to ask "Who created Mickey Mouse?" The program should answer "Correct" if the answer is "Walt Disney" or "Ub Iwerks" and "Sorry, Incorrect" for any other answer.

32. Suppose a program has a button with the caption "Quit." Suppose also that the Name property of this button is btnQuit. Write a btnQuit_Click event procedure that gives the user a second chance before ending the program. The procedure

should use an input box to request that the user confirm that the program should be terminated, and then end the program only if the user responds in the affirmative.

33. Write a program to handle an purchase made using a gift card. The program should request the gift card balance and the amount of the purchase. If the purchase amount is more than the balance, the program should display "Transaction denied, insufficient funds", otherwise the program should display "Transaction Approved" and the new balance on the gift card. A notice should be issued if the gift card balance is below $10.00.

34. A store is having a sale, buy 2 items and get the third item of equal or lower value for free. Write a program to request the price of three items and display the total sales price for this purchase.

35. A supermarket sells apples for $1.70 per pound. Write a cashier's program that requests the number of pounds and the amount of cash tendered as input and displays the change from the transaction. If the cash is not enough, the message "I need $x.xx more." should be displayed, where $x.xx is the difference between the cash and the total cost. (Test the program with six pounds and $20, and four pounds and $10.)

36. Federal law requires hourly employees be paid "time-and-a-half" for work in excess of 40 hours in a week. For example, if a person's hourly wage is $8 and he works 60 hours in a week, his gross pay should be

$$(40 \times 8) + (1.5 \times 8 \times (60 - 40)) = \$560$$

Write a program that requests as input the number of hours a person works in a given week and his hourly wage, and then displays his gross pay.

37. Write a program that requests a word (with lowercase letters) as input and translates the word into pig latin. The rules for translating a word into pig latin are as follows:

    (a) If the word begins with a consonant, move the first letter to the end of the word and add *ay*. For instance, *chip* becomes *hipcay*.
    (b) If the word begins with a vowel, add *way* to the end of the word. For instance, *else* becomes *elseway*.

38. The current calendar, called the Gregorian calendar, was introduced in 1582. Every year divisible by four was declared to be a leap year, with the exception of the years ending in 00 (that is, those divisible by 100) and not divisible by 400. For instance, the years 1600 and 2000 are leap years, but 1700, 1800, and 1900 are not. Write a program that requests a year as input and states whether it is a leap year. (Test the program on the years 2008, 2009, 1900, and 2000.)

39. Create a form with a text box and two buttons captioned Bogart and Raines. When Bogart is first pressed, the sentence "I came to Casablanca for the waters." is displayed in the text box. The next time Bogart is pressed, the sentence "I was misinformed." is displayed. When Raines is pressed, the sentence "But we're in the middle of the desert." is displayed. Run the program and then press Bogart, Raines, and Bogart to obtain a dialogue.

40. Write a program that allows the user to use a button to toggle the background color of the window (form) between Red and Blue.

41. Write a program that allows the user ten tries to answer the question, "Which U.S. President was born on July 4?" After three incorrect guesses, the program should display the hint, "He once said, 'If you don't say anything, you won't be called upon to

repeat it."' in a message box. After seven incorrect guesses, the program should give the hint, "His nickname was 'Silent Cal.'" The number of guesses should be displayed in a text box. (See Figure 4.3) **Note:** Calvin Coolidge was born on July 4, 1872.

FIGURE 4.3   Form for Exercise 41.

42. Write a program that reads a test score from a text box each time a button is clicked and then displays the two highest scores whenever a second button is clicked. Use two class-level variables to track the two highest scores.

43. The flowchart in Figure 4.4 (on the next page) calculates a state's income tax. Write a program corresponding to the flowchart. (Test the program with taxable incomes of $15,000, $30,000, and $60,000.)

44. Write a program to play "Hide and Seek" with the name of our programming language. When the button is pressed, the name should disappear and the caption on the button should change to "Show Name of Language." The next time the button is pressed, the name should reappear and the caption should revert to "Hide Name of Language," and so on.

OBJECT	PROPERTY	SETTING
frmHideSeek	Text	Hide and Seek
lblLanguage	Text	VB 2008
	Font.Size	26
btnDisplay	Text	Hide Name of Language

45. The campus bookstore is having a sale on T-Shirts that normally cost $8.00. You will receive 10% off the purchase of 1 t-shirt, 20% off the purchase of 2 t-shirts, and 30% off the purchase of 3 or more t-shirts. Write a program that asks the user to specify the number of t-shirts to be purchased, and then displays the total price of the purchase.

Solutions to Practice Problems 4.2

```
1. If (num < 0) Then
     MessageBox.Show("Number can't be negative.", "Input Error")
     txtNumber.Clear()
     txtNumber.Focus()
   Else
     txtSquareRoot.Text = CStr(Math.Sqrt(num))
   End If
```

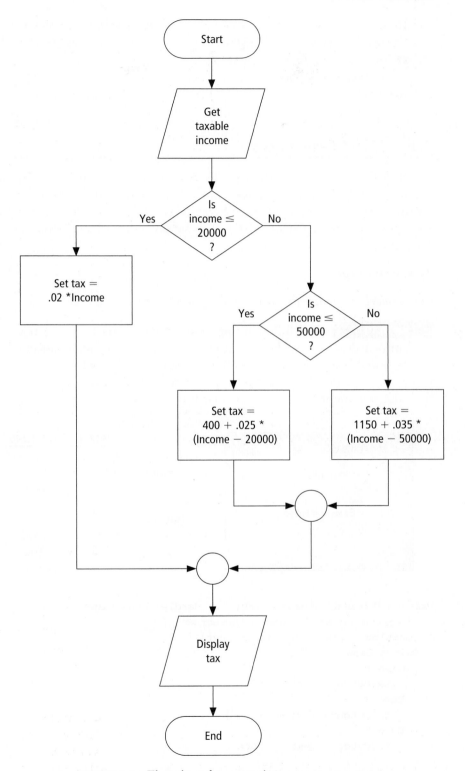

FIGURE 4.4   Flowchart for a state's income tax program.

2. The word "hello" will be displayed when $(a < b)$ is true and $(c < 5)$ is also true. That is, it will be displayed when both of these two conditions are true. The clearest way to write the block is

```
If (a < b) And (c < 5) Then
   txtBox.Text = "hello"
End If
```

4.3   Select Case Blocks

A Select Case block is an efficient decision-making structure that simplifies choosing among several actions. It avoids complex If constructs. If blocks make decisions based on the truth value of a condition; Select Case choices are determined by the value of an expression called a **selector**. Each of the possible actions is preceded by a clause of the form

Case *valueList*

where *valueList* itemizes the values of the selector for which the action should be taken.

 Example 1   The following program converts the finishing position in a horse race into a descriptive phrase. After the variable *position* is assigned a value from txtPosition, Visual Basic searches for the first Case clause whose value list contains that value and executes the succeeding statement. If the value of *position* is greater than 5, then the statement following Case Else is executed.

OBJECT	PROPERTY	SETTING
frmRace	Text	Horse Race
lblPosition	AutoSize	False
	Text	Finishing position (1, 2, 3, . . .):
txtPosition		
btnEvaluate	Text	Evaluate Position
txtOutcome	ReadOnly	True

```
Private Sub btnEvaluate_Click(...) Handles btnEvaluate.Click
   Dim position As Integer    'selector
   position = CInt(txtPosition.Text)
   Select Case position
     Case 1
        txtOutcome.Text = "Win"
     Case 2
        txtOutcome.Text = "Place"
     Case 3
        txtOutcome.Text = "Show"
```

```
      Case 4, 5
         txtOutcome.Text = "You almost placed in the money."
      Case Else
         txtOutcome.Text = "Out of the money."
   End Select
End Sub
```

[Run, type 2 into the text box, and press the button.]

Example 2   In the following variation of Example 1, the value lists specify ranges of values. The first value list provides another way to stipulate the numbers 1, 2, and 3. The second value list covers all numbers from 4 on.

```
Private Sub btnEvaluate_Click(...) Handles btnEvaluate.Click
   'Describe finishing positions in a horse race
   Dim position As Integer
   position = CInt(txtPosition.Text)
   Select Case position
      Case 1 To 3
         txtOutcome.Text = "In the money. Congratulations."
      Case Is >= 4
         txtOutcome.Text = "Not in the money."
   End Select
End Sub
```

[Run, type 2 into the text box, and press the button.]

A typical form of the Select Case block is

```
Select Case selector
  Case valueList1
    action1
  Case valueList2
    action2
  Case Else
    action of last resort
End Select
```

where Case Else (and its action) is optional, and each value list contains one or more of the following types of items:

1. a literal;
2. a variable;
3. an expression;
4. an inequality sign preceded by Is and followed by a literal, variable, or expression;
5. a range expressed in the form **a To b**, where *a* and *b* are literals, variables, or expressions.

Different items appearing in the same list must be separated by commas. Each action consists of one or more statements. After the selector is evaluated, Visual Basic looks for the first value-list item including the value of the selector and carries out its associated action. (If the value of the selector appears in two different value lists, only the action associated with the first value list will be carried out.) If the value of the selector does not appear in any of the value lists and there is no Case Else clause, execution of the program will continue with the statement following the Select Case block.

Figure 4.5 (on the next page) contains the flowchart for a Select Case block. The pseudocode for a Select Case block is the same as for the equivalent If block.

 Example 3 The following program uses several different types of value lists. With the response shown, the second action was selected.

OBJECT	PROPERTY	SETTING
frmRhyme	Text	One, Two, Buckle My Shoe
lblEnterNum	Text	Enter a number from 1 to 10:
txtNumber		
btnInterpret	Text	Interpret Number
txtPhrase	ReadOnly	True

```
Private Sub btnInterpret_Click(...) Handles btnInterpret.Click
  'One, Two, Buckle My Shoe
  Dim x As Integer = 2, y As Integer = 3
  Dim num As Integer
  num = CInt(txtNumber.Text)
```

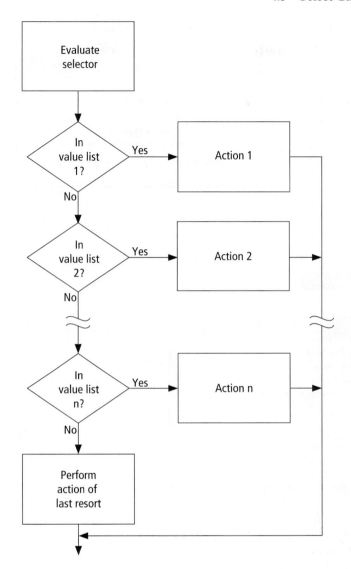

FIGURE 4.5   Flowchart for a Select Case block.

```
Select Case num
   Case y - x, x
     txtPhrase.Text = "Buckle my shoe."
   Case Is <= 4
     txtPhrase.Text = "Shut the door."
   Case x + y To x * y
     txtPhrase.Text = "Pick up sticks."
   Case 7, 8
     txtPhrase.Text = "Lay them straight."
   Case Else
     txtPhrase.Text = "Start all over again."
  End Select
End Sub
```

[Run, type 4 into the text box, and press the button.]

In each of the three preceding examples, the selector was a numeric variable; however, the selector also can be a string variable or an expression.

 Example 4   The following program has the string variable *firstName* as a selector.

OBJECT	PROPERTY	SETTING
frmQuiz	Text	Quiz
lblQuestion	AutoSize	False
	Text	What was President Wilson's first name?
txtName		
btnInterpret	Text	Interpret Answer
txtReply	ReadOnly	True

```
Private Sub btnInterpret_Click(...) Handles btnInterpret.Click
    'Quiz
    Dim firstName As String
    firstName = txtName.Text.ToUpper
    Select Case firstName
        Case "THOMAS"
            txtReply.Text = "Correct."
        Case "WOODROW"
            txtReply.Text = "Sorry, his full name was " & _
                            "Thomas Woodrow Wilson."
        Case "PRESIDENT"
            txtReply.Text = "Are you for real?"
        Case Else
            txtReply.Text = "Nice try, but no cigar."
    End Select
End Sub
```

[Run, type "Woodrow" into the text box, and press the button.]

 Example 5 The following program has the string selector *anyString.Substring (0, 1)*. In the sample run, only the first action was carried out, even though the value of the selector was in both of the first two value lists. Visual Basic stops looking as soon as it finds the value of the selector.

OBJECT	PROPERTY	SETTING
frmAnalyze	Text	Analyze First Character of a String
lblEnter	Text	Enter a string:
txtString		
btnAnalyze	Text	Analyze
txtResult	ReadOnly	True

```
Private Sub btnAnalyze_Click(...) Handles btnAnalyze.Click
    'Analyze the first character of a string
    Dim anyString As String
    anyString = txtString.Text.ToUpper
    Select Case anyString.Substring(0, 1)
        Case "S", "Z"
            txtResult.Text = "The string begins with a sibilant."
        Case "A" To "Z"
            txtResult.Text = "The string begins with a nonsibilant."
        Case "0" To "9"
            txtResult.Text = "The string begins with a digit."
        Case Is < "0"
            txtResult.Text = "The string begins with a character of " & _
                             "ANSI value less than 48."
        Case Else
            txtResult.Text = "The string begins with :  ;  <  =  > " & _
                             " ?  @  [  \  ]  ^  _  or '  . "
    End Select
End Sub
```

[Run, type "Sunday" into the text box, and press the button.]

 Example 6 The color of the beacon light atop Boston's John Hancock Building forecasts the weather according to the following rhyme:

Steady blue, clear view.
Flashing blue, clouds due.
Steady red, rain ahead.
Flashing red, snow instead.

The following program requests a color (Blue or Red) and a mode (Steady or Flashing) as input and displays the weather forecast. The program contains a Select Case block with a string expression as selector.

OBJECT	PROPERTY	SETTING
frmWeather	Text	Weather Beacon
lblColor	Text	Color of the light (B or R):
mtxtColor	Mask	L
lblMode	Text	Mode (S or F):
mtxtMode	Mask	L
btnInterpret	Text	Interpret Beacon
txtForecast	ReadOnly	True

```
Private Sub btnInterpret_Click(...) Handles btnInterpret.Click
  'Interpret a weather beacon
  Dim color, mode As String
  color = mtxtColor.Text
  mode = mtxtMode.Text
  Select Case mode.ToUpper & color.ToUpper
    Case "SB"
      txtForecast.Text = "CLEAR VIEW"
    Case "FB"
      txtForecast.Text = "CLOUDS DUE"
    Case "SR"
      txtForecast.Text = "RAIN AHEAD"
```

```
      Case "FR"
         txtForecast.Text = "SNOW AHEAD"
   End Select
End Sub
```

[Run, type "R" and "S" into the masked text boxes, and press the button.]

Example 7 Select Case is useful in calculating values that are not determined by a formula. The following program assumes that the current year is not a leap year:

OBJECT	PROPERTY	SETTING
frmSeasons	Text	Seasons
lblSeason	Text	Season:
txtSeason		
btnNumber	Text	Number of Days
txtNumDays	ReadOnly	True

```
Private Sub btnNumber_Click(...) Handles btnNumber.Click
   'Determine the number of days in a season
   Dim season As String, numDays As Integer
   season = txtSeason.Text
   Select Case season.ToUpper
     Case "WINTER"
       numDays = 87
     Case "SPRING"
       numDays = 92
     Case "SUMMER", "AUTUMN", "FALL"
       numDays = 93
   End Select
   txtNumDays.Text = season & " has " & numDays & " days."
End Sub
```

[Run, type "Summer" into the text box, and press the button.]

■ Comments

1. In a Case clause of the form **Case b To c**, the value of *b* should be less than or equal to the value of *c*. Otherwise, the clause is meaningless.

2. If the word **Is**, which should precede an inequality sign in a value list, is accidentally omitted, the editor will automatically insert it when checking the line.

3. The items in the value list must evaluate to a literal of the same type as the selector. For instance, if the selector evaluated to a string value, as in

```
Dim firstName As String
firstName = txtBox.Text
Select Case firstName
```

then the clause

```
Case firstName.Length
```

would be meaningless.

4. Any variable declared inside an If or Select Case block has **block-level scope**; that is, the variable cannot be referred to by code outside of the block.

5. In Appendix D, the section "Stepping through Programs Containing Selection Structures: Chapter 4" uses the Visual Basic debugging tools to trace the flow through a Select Case block.

Practice Problems 4.3

1. Suppose the selector of a Select Case block is the numeric variable *num*. Determine whether each of the following Case clauses is valid.

   (a) `Case 1, 4, Is < 10`
   (b) `Case Is < 5, Is >= 5`
   (c) `Case num = 2` (where the selector *num* is of type Double)

2. Do the following two programs always produce the same output for a whole-number grade from 0 to 100?

```
grade = CDbl(txtBox.Text)              grade = CDbl(txtBox.Text)
Select Case grade                      Select Case grade
  Case Is >= 90                          Case Is >= 90
     txtOutput.Text = "A"                   txtOutput.Text = "A"
```

```
    Case Is >= 60                        Case 60 To 89
      txtOutput.Text = "Pass"              txtOutput.Text = "Pass"
    Case Else                            Case 0 To 59
      txtOutput.Text = "Fail"              txtOutput.Text = "Fail"
  End Select                           End Select
```

EXERCISES 4.3

In Exercises 1 through 8, for each of the responses shown in the parentheses, determine the output displayed in the text box when the button is clicked.

1.
```
Private Sub btnDisplay_Click(...) Handles btnDisplay.Click
   Dim age, price As Double
   age = CDbl(InputBox("What is your age?"))
   Select Case age
     Case Is < 6
       price = 0
     Case 6 To 17
       price = 3.75
     Case Is >= 17
       price = 5
   End Select
   txtOutput.Text = "The price is " & FormatCurrency(price)
End Sub
```
   (8.5, 17)

2.
```
Private Sub btnDisplay_Click(...) Handles btnDisplay.Click
   Dim n As Double
   n = CDbl(InputBox("Enter a number from 5 to 12"))
   Select Case n
     Case 5
       txtOutput.Text = "case 1"
     Case 5 To 7
       txtOutput.Text = "case 2"
     Case 7 To 12
       txtOutput.Text = "case 3"
   End Select
End Sub
```
   (7, 5, 11.2)

3.
```
Private Sub btnDisplay_Click(ByVal sender As System.Object, ByVal e As
System.EventArgs) Handles btnDisplay.Click
   Dim birthYear As Integer
   birthYear = CInt(InputBox("Enter the year of your Birth"))
   Select Case birthYear
     Case Is < 1946
       txtOutput.Text = "Greatest Generation"
     Case 1946 To 1960
       txtOutput.Text = "Baby Boomer"
```

```
      Case 1960 To 1981
        txtOutput.Text = "Generation X"
      Case 1981 To 2001
        txtOutput.Text = "Generation Y"
      Case Else
        txtOutput.Text = "Generation I"
    End Select
  End Sub
```

(1933, 1960, 2000)

4.
```
Private Sub btnDisplay_Click(ByVal sender As System.Object, ByVal e As
  System.EventArgs) Handles btnDisplay.Click
    Dim yearENIAC As Integer
    'Ask question and obtain answer
    Dim message As String
    message = "In what year did man first land on the moon?"
    yearMoon = CInt(InputBox(message))
    'Respond to answer
    Select Case yearMoon
      Case 1969
        txtOutput.Text = "Correct"
      Case 1967 To 1971
        txtOutput.Text = "Close, 1969"
      Case Is < 1967
        txtOutput.Text = "Sorry, the correct answer is 1969"
      Case Is > 1971
        txtOutput.Text = "Sorry, by this time man had already been to the
                          moon"
    End Select
  End Sub
```

(1961, 1969, 1973)

5.
```
Private Sub btnDisplay_Click(...) Handles btnDisplay.Click
    Dim name As String
    name = InputBox("Who developed the stored-program concept?")
    Select Case name.ToUpper
      Case "JOHN VON NEUMANN", "VON NEUMANN"
        txtOutput.Text = "Correct."
      Case "JOHN MAUCHLY", "MAUCHLY", "J. PRESPER ECKERT", "ECKERT"
        txtOutput.Text = "He worked with the developer, " & _
                          "von Neumann, on the ENIAC."
      Case Else
        txtOutput.Text = "Nope."
    End Select
  End Sub
```

(Grace Hopper, Eckert, John von Neumann)

6.
```
Private Sub btnDisplay_Click(...) Handles btnDisplay.Click
    Dim message As String, a, b, c As Double
    message = "Analyzing solutions to the quadratic equation "
    message &= "AX^2 + BX + C = 0.  Enter the value for "
    a = CDbl(InputBox(message & "A"))
    b = CDbl(InputBox(message & "B"))
    c = CDbl(InputBox(message & "C"))
    Select Case (b ^ 2) - (4 * a * c)
      Case Is < 0
        txtOutput.Text = "The equation has no real solutions."
      Case 0
        txtOutput.Text = "The equation has exactly one solution."
      Case Is > 0
        txtOutput.Text = "The equation has two solutions."
    End Select
End Sub
```
(1,2,3; 1,5,1; 1,2,1)

7.
```
Private Sub btnDisplay_Click(...) Handles btnDisplay.Click
    'State a quotation
    Dim num1, num2 As Double
    Dim word As String = "hello"
    num1 = 3
    num2 = CDbl(InputBox("Enter a number"))
    Select Case (2 * num2 - 1)
      Case num1 * num1
        txtBox.Text = "Less is more."
      Case Is > word.Length
        txtBox.Text = "Time keeps everything from happening at once."
      Case Else
        txtBox.Text = "The more things change, the less " & _
                      "they remain the same."
    End Select
End Sub
```
(2, 5, 6)

8.
```
Private Sub btnDisplay_Click(...) Handles btnDisplay.Click
    Dim whatever As Double
    whatever = CDbl(InputBox("Enter a number:"))
    Select Case whatever
      Case Else
        txtOutput.Text = "Hi"
    End Select
End Sub
```
(7, −1)

In Exercises 9 through 16, identify the errors.

9.
```
Private Sub btnDisplay_Click(ByVal sender As System.Object, ByVal e As
System.EventArgs) Handles btnDisplay.Click
    Dim a As String = "Hi"
    Select Case a
      txtOutput.Text = "Hello"
    End Select
End Sub
```

10.
```
Private Sub btnDisplay_Click(...) Handles btnDisplay.Click
    Dim num1 As Double = 5
    Dim num2 As Double = 2
    Select Case num1
      Case 3 <= num1 <= 10
        txtOutput.Text = "between 3 and 10."
      Case num2 To 5; 4
        txtOutput.Text = "near 5."
    End Select
End Sub
```

11.
```
Private Sub btnDisplay_Click(...) Handles btnDisplay.Click
    Dim color As String
    color = InputBox("Enter a color")
    Select Case color
      Case color = "red"
        txtOutput.Text = "I like red"
      Case Else
    End Select
End Sub
```

12.
```
Private Sub btnDisplay_Click(...) Handles btnDisplay.Click
    Dim word As String = "hello"
    Select Case word.Substring(0,1)
      Case h
        txtOutput.Text = "begins with h."
    End Select
End Sub
```

13.
```
Private Sub btnDisplay_Click(...) Handles btnDisplay.Click
    Dim word As String
    word = InputBox("Enter a word from the United States motto.")
    Select Case word.ToUpper
      Case "E"
        txtOutput.Text = "This is the first word of the motto."
      Case word.Substring(0,1) = "P"
        txtOutput.Text = "The second word is PLURIBUS."
      Case Else
        txtOutput.Text = "The third word is UNUM."
    End Select
End Sub
```

14.
```
Private Sub btnDisplay_Click(ByVal sender As System.Object, ByVal e As
    System.EventArgs) Handles btnDisplay.Click
    Dim num As Integar = 15
    Select Case num
      Case 15, Is <> 15
        txtOutput.Text = "fifteen"
      Case Is > 15
        txtOutput.Text = "Bigger than fifteen"
      Case Is < 15
        txtOutput.Text = "Smaller than fifteen"
    End Select
End Sub
```

15.
```
Private Sub btnDisplay_Click(...) Handles btnDisplay.Click
    Dim fruit As String = "Peach"
    Select Case fruit.ToUpper
      Case Is >= "Peach"
        txtOutput.Text = "Georgia"
      Case "ORANGE To PEACH"
        txtOutput.Text = "Ok"
     End Select
End Sub
```

16.
```
Private Sub btnDisplay_Click(ByVal sender As System.Object, ByVal e As
    System.EventArgs) Handles btnDisplay.Click
    Dim hoursPassed As Integer
    hoursPassed = CInt(InputBox("Class hours passed"))
    Select Case hoursPassed
      Case Is < 31
        txtOutput.Text = "Student is a Freshman"
      Case Is 32 To 63
        txtOutput.Text = "Student is a Sophomore"
      Case Is 64 To 95
        txtOutput.Text = "Student is a Junior"
      Case Is > 95
        txtOutput.Text = "Student is a Senior"
    End Select
End Sub
```

In Exercises 17 through 22, suppose the selector of a Select Case block, *word*,
evaluates to a String value. Determine whether the Case clause is valid.

17. `Case "un" & "til"`

18. `Case "happy", Is < "sad"`

19. `Case 0 To 9`

20. `Case word <> "Great"`

21. `Case "abc".Substring(0, 1)`

22. `Case Is <> "Hello"`

In Exercises 23 through 26, rewrite the code using a Select Case block.

23.
```
If input = "R" Then
    txtOutput.Text = "Color is Red"
ElseIf input = "B" Then
    txtOutput.Text = "Color is Blue"
Else
    txtOutput.Text = "Color is Black"
End If
```

24.
```
If a = 1 Then
    lstOutput.Items.Add("lambs")
End If
If ((a <= 3) And (a < 4)) Then
    lstOutput.Items.Add("eat")
End If
If ((a = 5) Or (a > 7)) Then
    lstOutput.Items.Add("ivy")
End If
```

25.
```
If input >= 90 Then
    txtOutput.Text = "Letter Grade is A"
ElseIf input >= 80 Then
    txtOutput.Text = "Letter Grade is B"
ElseIf input >= 70 Then
    txtOutput.Text = "Letter Grade is C"
ElseIf input >= 60 Then
    txtOutput.Text = "Letter Grade is D"
Else
    txtOutput.Text = "Letter Grade is F"
End If
```

26.
```
If a = 3 Then
    a = 1
End If
If a = 2 Then
    a = 3
End If
If a = 1 Then
    a = 2
End If
```

27. Table 4.5 gives the terms used by the National Weather Service to describe the degree of cloudiness. Write a program that requests the percentage of cloud cover as input and then displays the appropriate descriptor.

28. Table 4.6 shows the location of books in the library stacks according to their call numbers. Write a program that requests the call number of a book as input and displays the location of the book.

TABLE 4.5	Cloudiness descriptors.
Percentage of Cloud Cover	Descriptor
0–30	clear
31–70	partly cloudy
71–99	cloudy
100	overcast

TABLE 4.6	Location of library books.
Call Numbers	Location
100 to 199	basement
200 to 500 and over 900	main floor
501 to 900 except 700 to 750	upper floor
700 to 750	archives

29. Write a program that requests a month of the year and then gives the number of days in the month. If the month is February, the user should be asked whether the current year is a leap year.

30. Figure 4.6 shows some geometric shapes and formulas for their areas. Write a program that requests the user to select one of the shapes, requests the appropriate lengths, and then gives the area of the figure. The areas should be computed by Function procedures.

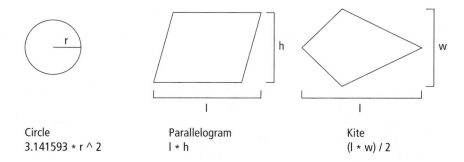

Circle	Parallelogram	Kite
3.141593 * r ^ 2	l * h	(l * w) / 2

FIGURE 4.6 Areas of geometric shapes.

31. Write a program that requests an exam score and assigns a letter grade with the scale 90–100 (A), 80–89 (B), 70–79 (C), 60–69 (D), 0–59 (F). (Test the program with the grades 84, 100, and 57.)

32. Table 4.7 contains information on NBA Basketball teams. Write a program that requests a team name and category (city or arena) as input and displays the requested information. If the item requested is not in the table, the program should inform the user.

TABLE 4.7	Team name, City and Arena.	
Team Name	**City**	**Arena**
Hawks	Atlanta	Phillips Arena
Bulls	Chicago	United Center
Nuggets	Denver	Pepsi Center
Heat	Miami	American Airlines Arena

33. IRS informants are paid cash awards based on the value of the money recovered. If the information was specific enough to lead to a recovery, the informant receives 10 percent of the first $75,000, 5 percent of the next $25,000, and 1 percent of the remainder, up to a maximum award of $50,000. Write a program that requests the amount of the recovery as input and displays the award. (Test the program on the amounts $10,000, $125,000, and $10,000,000.)(**Note:** The source of this formula is *The Book of Inside Information*, Boardroom Books, 1993.)

34. Table 4.8 contains the meanings of some abbreviations doctors often use for prescriptions. Write a program that requests an abbreviation and gives its meaning. The user should be informed if the meaning is not in the table.

TABLE 4.8	Physicians' abbreviations.	
	Abbreviation	**Meaning**
	ac	before meals
	ad lib	freely as needed
	bid	twice daily
	gtt	a drop
	hs	at bedtime
	qid	four times a day

35. Write a program that, given the last name of one of the five recent presidents beginning with Carter, displays his state and a colorful fact about him. (**Hint:** The program might need to request further information.) **Note:** Carter: Georgia; The only soft drink served in the Carter White House was Coca-Cola. Reagan: California; His Secret Service code name was Rawhide. George H. W. Bush: Texas; He was the third left-handed president. Clinton: Arkansas; In college he did a good imitation of Elvis Presley. George W. Bush: Texas; He once owned the Texas Rangers baseball team.

36. The user enters a number into a masked text box and then clicks on the appropriate button to have either one of three pieces of humor or one of three insults displayed in a text box below the buttons. If the number entered is not between 1 and 3, the masked text box should be cleared. **Note:** Some possible bits of humor are "I can resist everything except temptation," "I just heard from Bill Bailey. He's not coming home," and "I have enough money to last the rest of my life, unless I buy something." Some possible insults are "How much would you charge to haunt a house?" "I bet you have no more friends than an alarm clock," and "When your IQ rises to 30, sell."

OBJECT	PROPERTY	SETTING
frmExercise 36	Text	4.3 Exercise 36
lblNumber	Text	Number (1–3):
mtxtNumber	Mask	0
btnHumor	Text	&Humor
btnInsult	Text	&Insult
txtSentence	ReadOnly	True

Solutions to Practice Problems 4.3

1. (a) Valid. These items are redundant because 1 and 4 are just special cases of **Is < 10**. However, this makes no difference in Visual Basic.

(b) Valid. These items are contradictory. However, Visual Basic looks at them one at a time until it finds an item containing the value of the selector. The action following this Case clause will always be carried out.

(c) Not valid. It should be **Case 2**.

2. Yes. However, the program on the right is clearer and therefore preferable.

CHAPTER 4   SUMMARY

1. The function Chr associates a character with each number from 0 through 255 as determined by the ANSI table. The function Asc is the inverse of the Chr function.

2. The *relational operators* are <, >, =, <>, <=, and >=.

3. The principal *logical operators* are And, Or, and Not.

4. A *condition* is an expression involving literals, variables, functions, and operators (arithmetic, relational, or logical) that can be evaluated as either True or False.

5. The value of a variable or expression of Boolean data type is either True or False.

6. An *If block* decides what action to take depending on the truth values of one or more conditions. To allow several courses of action, the If, ElseIf, and Else parts of an If statement can contain other If statements.

7. A *Select Case block* selects from one of several actions depending on the value of an expression, called the *selector*. The entries in the *value lists* should have the same type as the selector.

CHAPTER 4   PROGRAMMING PROJECTS

1. Table 4.9 gives the price schedule for Eddie's Equipment Rental. Full-day rentals cost one-and-a-half times half-day rentals. Write a program that displays Table 4.9 in a list box when an appropriate button is clicked and displays a bill in another list box based on the item number and time period chosen by a customer. The bill should include a $30.00 deposit. A possible form layout and sample output are shown in Figure 4.7.

TABLE 4.9	Price schedule for Eddie's Equipment Rental.		
Piece of Equipment		Half-Day	Full-Day
1. Rug cleaner		$16.00	$24.00
2. Lawn mower		$12.00	$18.00
3. Paint sprayer		$20.00	$30.00

FIGURE 4.7 Form layout and sample output for Programming Project 1.

2. The American Heart Association suggests that at most 30 percent of the calories in our diet come from fat. Although food labels give the number of calories and amount of fat per serving, they often do not give the percentage of calories from fat. This percentage can be calculated by multiplying the number of grams of fat in one serving by 9, dividing that number by the total number of calories per serving, and multiplying the result by 100. Write a program that requests the name, number of calories per serving, and the grams of fat per serving as input, and tells us whether the food meets the American Heart Association recommendation. A sample run is as in Figure 4.8.

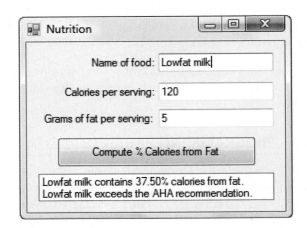

FIGURE 4.8 Sample run of Programming Project 2.

3. Table 4.10 gives the 2007 federal income tax rate schedule for single taxpayers. Write a program that requests taxable income and calculates federal income tax.

TABLE 4.10	2007 federal income tax rates for single tax payers.		
Taxable Income Over	But Not Over	The Tax Is	Of Amount Over
$0	$7,825	10%	$0
$7,825	$31,850	$782.50 + 15%	$7.825
$31,850	$77,100	$4,386.25 + 25%	$31,850
$77,100	$160,850	$15,698.75 + 28%	$77,100
$160,850	$349,700	$39,148.75 + 33%	$160,850
$349,700		$101,469.25 + 35%	$349,700

4. Write a program to determine the real roots of the quadratic equation $ax^2 + bx + c = 0$ (where $a \neq 0$) after requesting the values of a, b, and c. Use a Sub procedure to ensure that a is nonzero. **Note:** The equation has 2, 1, or 0 solutions depending on whether the value of $b^2 - 4*a*c$ is positive, zero, or negative. In the first two cases, the solutions are given by the quadratic formula $(-b \pm \text{Math.Sqrt}(b^2 - 4*a*c))/(2*a)$. Test the program with the following sets of coefficients:

$a = 1$ $b = -11$ $c = 28$ Solutions are 4 and 7
$a = 1$ $b = -6$ $c = 9$ Solution is 3
$a = 1$ $b = 4$ $c = 5$ No solution

5. Write a program to analyze a mortgage. The user should enter the amount of the loan, the annual rate of interest, and the duration of the loan in months. When the user clicks on the button, the information that was entered should be checked to make sure it is reasonable. If bad data have been supplied, the user should be so advised. Otherwise, the monthly payment and the total amount of interest paid should be displayed. The formula for the monthly payment is

$$\text{payment} = p*r/(1 - (1 + r)^{\wedge}(-n)),$$

where p is the amount of the loan, r is the monthly interest rate (annual rate divided by 12) given as a number between 0 (for 0 percent) and 1 (for 100 percent), and n is the duration of the loan in months. The formula for the total interest paid is

$$\text{total interest} = n*\text{payment} - p.$$

(Test the program for a mortgage of $240,000 at 6% annual rate of interest, and duration 360 months. Such a mortgage will have a monthly payment of $1,438.92 and total interest of $278,011.65.)

5

General Procedures

5.1 Sub Procedures, Part I

Visual Basic has two devices, **Sub procedures** and **Function procedures**, that are used to break complex problems into small problems to be solved one at a time. To distinguish them from event procedures, Sub and Function procedures are referred to as **general procedures**. General procedures also eliminate repetitive code and can be reused in other programs.

In this section, we show how Sub procedures are defined and used. The programs in this section are designed to demonstrate the use of Sub procedures rather than to accomplish sophisticated programming tasks. Later chapters of the book use them for more substantial programming efforts.

A **Sub procedure** is a part of a program that performs one or more related tasks, has its own name, and is written as a separate part of the program. The simplest sort of Sub procedure has the form

```
Sub ProcedureName()
  statement(s)
End Sub
```

A Sub procedure is invoked with a statement consisting only of the name of the procedure, that is, a statement of the form

```
ProcedureName()
```

Such a statement is said to *call* the Sub procedure and is referred to as a **Call statement**.

The rules for naming general procedures are identical to the rules for naming variables. The name chosen for a Sub procedure should describe the task it performs. Sub procedures are typed directly into the Code Editor.

Consider the following program that calculates the sum of two numbers. This program will be revised to incorporate Sub procedures.

OBJECT	PROPERTY	SETTING
frmAdd	Text	Arithmetic
btnAdd	Text	Add Numbers
lstResult		

```
Private Sub btnAdd_Click(...) Handles btnAdd.Click
  'Display the sum of two numbers
  Dim num1, num2, sum As Double
  lstResult.Items.Clear()
  lstResult.Items.Add("This program displays a sentence")
  lstResult.Items.Add("identifying two numbers and their sum.")
  lstResult.Items.Add("")
  num1 = 2
  num2 = 3
```

```
   sum = num1 + num2
   lstResult.Items.Add("The sum of " & num1 & " and " & _
                       num2 & " is " & sum & ".")
End Sub
```

[Run, and then click the button. The following is displayed in the list box:]

```
This program displays a sentence
identifying two numbers and their sum.

The sum of 2 and 3 is 5.
```

The tasks performed by this program can be summarized as follows:

Task #1: Explain purpose of program.

Task #2: Display numbers and their sum.

Sub procedures allow us to write and read a program in such a way that we first focus on the tasks and later on how to accomplish each task.

Example 1 The following program uses a Sub procedure to accomplish the first task of the preceding program. When the statement **ExplainPurpose()** is reached, execution jumps to the **Sub ExplainPurpose()** statement. The lines between **Sub ExplainPurpose()** and **End Sub** are executed, and then execution continues with the line following the Call statement.

```
Private Sub btnAdd_Click(...) Handles btnAdd.Click
  'Display the sum of two numbers
  Dim num1, num2, sum As Double
  lstResult.Items.Clear()
  ExplainPurpose()
  lstResult.Items.Add("")
  num1 = 2
  num2 = 3
  sum = num1 + num2
  lstResult.Items.Add("The sum of " & num1 & " and " & _
                      num2 & " is " & sum & ".")
End Sub

Sub ExplainPurpose()
  'Explain the task performed by the program
  lstResult.Items.Add("This program displays a sentence")
  lstResult.Items.Add("identifying two numbers and their sum.")
End Sub
```

Note 1: When you type **Sub ExplainPurpose** and then press the Enter key, the editor automatically inserts the parentheses, the line **End Sub**, and a blank line separating the two lines of code. Also, the smart indenting feature of the Code Editor automatically indents all lines in the block of code between the Sub and End Sub statements.

Note 2: We recommend that you type in the Sub procedure before typing the calling statement. If so, after you type in the first few letters of the procedure name IntelliSense's **Word Completion** feature will help you complete the name of the Sub procedure.

In Example 1, the btnAdd_Click event procedure is referred to as the **calling procedure** and the ExplainPurpose Sub procedure is referred to as the **called procedure**. The second task performed by the addition program also can be handled by a Sub procedure. The values of the two numbers, however, must be transmitted to the Sub procedure. This transmission is called **passing**.

 Example 2   The following revision of the program in Example 1 uses a Sub procedure to accomplish the second task. The statement `DisplaySum(2, 3)` causes execution to jump to the `Sub DisplaySum(ByVal num1 As Double, ByVal num2 As Double)` statement, which assigns the number 2 to *num1* and the number 3 to *num2*.

DisplaySum(2, 3)

Sub DisplaySum (ByVal num1 As Double, ByVal num2 As Double)

After the lines between `Sub DisplaySum(ByVal num1 As Double, ByVal num2 As Double)` and `End Sub` are executed, execution continues with the line following `DisplaySum(2, 3)`, namely, the `End Sub` statement in the event procedure. **Note:** If you don't type in the word *ByVal* from the Sub DisplaySum line, the editor will automatically insert it when you either press the Enter key or move the cursor away from the line. In the next section, we consider an alternative to the keyword *ByVal*. For now we needn't be concerned with *ByVal*.

```
Private Sub btnAdd_Click(...) Handles btnAdd.Click
  'Display the sum of two numbers
  lstResult.Items.Clear()
  ExplainPurpose()
  lstResult.Items.Add("")
  DisplaySum(2, 3)
End Sub

Sub DisplaySum(ByVal num1 As Double, ByVal num2 As Double)
  'Display two numbers and their sum
  Dim sum As Double
  sum = num1 + num2
  lstResult.Items.Add("The sum of " & num1 & " and " & _
                    num2 & " is " & sum & ".")
End Sub

Sub ExplainPurpose()
  'Explain the task performed by the program
  lstResult.Items.Add("This program displays sentences")
  lstResult.Items.Add("identifying two numbers and their sum.")
End Sub
```

Sub procedures make a program easy to read, modify, and debug. The event procedure gives a description of what the program does, and the Sub procedures fill in the details. Another benefit of Sub procedures is that they can be called several times during the execution of the program. This feature is especially useful when there are many statements in the Sub procedure.

Example 3   The following extension of the program in Example 2 displays several sums:

```
Private Sub btnAdd_Click(...) Handles btnAdd.Click
  'Display the sum of two numbers
  lstResult.Items.Clear()
  ExplainPurpose()
  lstResult.Items.Add("")
  DisplaySum(2, 3)
  DisplaySum(4, 6)
  DisplaySum(7, 8)
End Sub

Sub DisplaySum(ByVal num1 As Double, ByVal num2 As Double)
  'Display two numbers and their sum
  Dim sum As Double
  sum = num1 + num2
  lstResult.Items.Add("The sum of " & num1 & " and " & _
                      num2 & " is " & sum & ".")
End Sub

Sub ExplainPurpose()
  'Explain the task performed by the program
  lstResult.Items.Add("This program displays sentences")
  lstResult.Items.Add("identifying two numbers and their sum.")
End Sub
```

[Run, and then click the button. The following is displayed in the list box.]

```
This program displays sentences
identifying pairs of numbers and their sum.

The sum of 2 and 3 is 5.
The sum of 4 and 6 is 10.
The sum of 7 and 8 is 15.
```

The variables *num1* and *num2* appearing in the Sub procedure DisplaySum are called **parameters**. They are merely temporary place holders for the numbers passed to the Sub procedure; their names are not important. The only essentials are their type, quantity, and order. In this DisplaySum Sub procedure, the parameters must be numeric variables of type Double and there must be two of them. For instance, the Sub procedure could have been written

```
Sub DisplaySum(ByVal this As Double, ByVal that As Double)
  'Display two numbers and their sum
  Dim sum As Double
  sum = this + that
  lstResult.Items.Add("The sum of " & this & " and " & _
                      that & " is " & sum & ".")
End Sub
```

When a parameter is defined in a Sub procedure, it is automatically available to the code between the Sub and End Sub lines. That is, the code "this As Double" that defines a parameter behaves similarly to the "Dim this As Double" code that defines a variable. A string also can be passed to a Sub procedure. In this case, the receiving parameter in the Sub procedure must be followed by the type declaration "As String".

 Example 4   The following program passes a string and two numbers to a Sub procedure. When the Sub procedure is first called, the string parameter *state* is assigned the value "Hawaii", and the numeric parameters *pop* and *area* are assigned the values 1275194 and 6471, respectively. The Sub procedure then uses these parameters to carry out the task of calculating the population density of Hawaii. The second Call statement assigns different values to the parameters.

OBJECT	PROPERTY	SETTING
frmDensities	Text	5-1-4
btnDisplay	Text	Display Demographics
lstDensity		

```
Private Sub btnDisplay_Click(...) Handles btnDisplay.Click
  'Calculate the population densities of states
  lstDensity.Items.Clear()
  CalculateDensity("Hawaii", 1275194, 6471)
  lstDensity.Items.Add("")
  CalculateDensity("Alaska", 663661, 591000)
End Sub

Sub CalculateDensity(ByVal state As String, _
                 ByVal pop As Double, ByVal area As Double)
  Dim rawDensity, density As Double
  'The density (number of people per square mile)
  'will be displayed rounded one decimal place
  rawDensity = pop / area
  density = Math.Round(rawDensity, 1)      'Round to one decimal place
  lstDensity.Items.Add("The density of " & state & " is " & density)
  lstDensity.Items.Add("people per square mile.")
End Sub
```

[Run, and then click the button. The following is displayed in the list box.]

```
The density of Hawaii is 197.1
people per square mile.

The density of Alaska is 1.1
people per square mile.
```

The parameters in the density program can have any valid variable names, as with the parameters in the addition program of Example 3. The only restriction is that the first parameter be a string variable and that the last two parameters have type Double. When nondescriptive names are used for parameters, the Sub procedure should contain comments giving the meanings of the variables.

■ Variables and Expressions as Arguments

The items appearing in the parentheses of a Call statement are called **arguments**. These should not be confused with parameters, which appear in the header of a Sub procedure. Each parameter defined for a Sub procedure corresponds to an argument passed in a Call statement for that procedure. In Example 3, the arguments of the DisplaySum statements were literals. These arguments also could have been variables or expressions. For instance, the event procedure could have been written as follows. See Figure 5.1.

```
Private Sub btnAdd_Click(...) Handles btnAdd.Click
    'Display the sum of two numbers
    Dim x, y, z As Double
    lstResult.Items.Clear()
    ExplainPurpose()
    lstResult.Items.Add("")
    x = 2
    y = 3
    DisplaySum(x, y)
    DisplaySum(x + 2, 2 * y)
    z = 7
    DisplaySum(z, z + 1)
End Sub
```

This feature allows values obtained as input from the user to be passed to a Sub procedure.

FIGURE 5.1 **Passing arguments to parameters.**

 Example 5 The following variation of the addition program requests the two numbers as input from the user. Notice that the names of the arguments, *x* and *y*, are different from the names of the parameters. The names of the arguments and parameters may be the same or different; what matters is that the *order, number,* and *types* of the arguments and parameters match.

OBJECT	PROPERTY	SETTING
frmAdd	Text	Add Two Numbers
lblFirstNum	Text	First Number:
txtFirstNum		
lblSecondNum	Text	Second Number:
txtSecondNum		
btnCompute	Text	Compute Sum
txtResult	ReadOnly	True

```
Private Sub btnCompute_Click(...) Handles btnCompute.Click
  'This program requests two numbers and
  'displays the two numbers and their sum.
  Dim x, y As Double
  x = CDbl(txtFirstNum.Text)
  y = CDbl(txtSecondNum.Text)
  DisplaySum(x, y)
End Sub

Sub DisplaySum(ByVal num1 As Double, ByVal num2 As Double)
  'Display two numbers and their sum
  Dim sum As Double
  sum = num1 + num2
  txtResult.Text = "The sum of " & num1 & " and " & _
                   num2 & " is " & sum & "."
End Sub
```

[Run, type 23 and 67 into the text boxes, and then click the button.]

 Example 6 The following variation of Example 4 obtains its input from the file DEMOGRAPHICS.TXT. The second Call statement uses different variable names for the arguments to show that using the same argument names is not necessary. See Figure 5.2. DEMOGRAPHICS.TXT contains the following lines:

Hawaii
1275194
6471
Alaska
663661
591000

FIGURE 5.2   Passing arguments to parameters in Example 6.

```vb
Private Sub btnDisplay_Click(...) Handles btnDisplay.Click
  'Calculate the population densities of states
  Dim state As String, pop, area As Double
  Dim s As String, p, a As Double
  Dim sr As IO.StreamReader = IO.File.OpenText("DEMOGRAPHICS.TXT")
  lstDensity.Items.Clear()
  state = sr.ReadLine
  pop = CDbl(sr.ReadLine)
  area = CDbl(sr.ReadLine)
  CalculateDensity(state, pop, area)
  lstDensity.Items.Add("")
  s = sr.ReadLine
  p = CDbl(sr.ReadLine)
  a = CDbl(sr.ReadLine)
  sr.Close()
  CalculateDensity(s, p, a)
End Sub

Sub CalculateDensity(ByVal state As String, _
                     ByVal pop As Double, ByVal area As Double)
  'The density (number of people per square mile)
  'will be displayed rounded to one decimal place
  Dim rawDensity, density As Double
  rawDensity = pop / area
  density = Math.Round(rawDensity, 1)      'Round to one decimal place
  lstDensity.Items.Add("The density of " & state & " is " & density)
  lstDensity.Items.Add("people per square mile.")
End Sub
```

[Run, and then click the button. The following is displayed in the list box.]

```
The density of Hawaii is 197.1
people per square mile.

The density of Alaska is 1.1
people per square mile.
```

■ Sub Procedures Calling Other Sub Procedures

A Sub procedure can call another Sub procedure. If so, after the End Sub of the called Sub procedure is reached, execution continues with the line in the calling Sub procedure that follows the Call statement.

Example 7   In the following program, the Sub procedure FirstPart calls the Sub procedure SecondPart. After the statements in SecondPart are executed, execution continues with the remaining statements in the Sub procedure FirstPart before returning to the event procedure. The form contains a button and a list box.

```
Private Sub btnDisplay_Click(...) Handles btnDisplay.Click
  'Demonstrate a Sub procedure calling another Sub procedures
  FirstPart()
  lstOutput.Items.Add(4)
End Sub

Sub FirstPart()
  lstOutput.Items.Add(1)
  SecondPart()
  lstOutput.Items.Add(3)
End Sub

Sub SecondPart()
  lstOutput.Items.Add(2)
End Sub
```

[Run, and click the button. The following is displayed in the list box.]

```
1
2
3
4
```

Arguments and parameters also can be used to pass values from Sub procedures back to event procedures or other Sub procedures. This important property is explored in detail in the next section.

■ Comments

1. Sub procedures allow programmers to focus on the main flow of a complex task and defer the details of implementation. Modern programs use them liberally. This method of program construction is known as **modular** or **top-down** design. As a rule, a Sub procedure should perform only one task, or several closely related tasks, and should be kept relatively small.

2. In this text, Sub procedure names begin with uppercase letters in order to distinguish them from variable names. Like variable names, however, they can be written with any combination of upper- and lowercase letters. ***Note:*** Parameters appearing in a Sub statement are not part of the Sub procedure name.

3. The first line inside a Sub procedure is often a comment statement describing the task performed by the Sub procedure. If necessary, several comment statements are devoted to this purpose. Conventional programming practice also recommends that all variables used by the Sub procedure be listed in comment statements with their meanings. In this text, we give several examples of this practice, but adhere to it only when the variables are especially numerous or lack descriptive names.

4. In this section we have passed variables of type String and Double to Sub procedures. Actually, any type of variable can be passed to a Sub procedure. When a variable of type StreamReader is passed to a Sub procedure, the header contains the phrase **ByVal sr As IO.StreamReader**.

5. After a Sub procedure has been defined, Visual Basic automatically reminds you of the Sub procedure's parameters when you type in a Call statement. As soon as you type in the left parenthesis of a Call statement, a Parameter Info banner appears giving the names and types of the parameters. See Figure 5.3. A syntax error occurs if there are a different number of arguments in a Call statement than there are parameters in the called Sub procedure. Also, having an argument of a different data type than the corresponding parameter is a syntax error. If you type in the Sub procedure before typing any Call statements, Parameter Info will help you prevent both of these types of syntax errors.

```
frmAdd.vb*  Start Page                                    ▼ ✕

  btnAdd                          ▼     Click                        ▼

    Private Sub btnAdd_Click(ByVal sender As System.Object,
         'Display the sum of two numbers
         lstResult.Items.Clear()
         ExplainPurpose()
         lstResult.Items.Add("")
         DisplaySum(
    En  DisplaySum (num1 As Double, num2 As Double)
```

FIGURE 5.3   The Parameter Info help feature.

Practice Problems 5.1

1. What is the difference between an event procedure and a Sub procedure?

2. What is wrong with the following code?

```
Private Sub btnDisplay_Click(...) Handles btnDisplay.Click
  Dim phone As String
  phone = mtxtPhoneNum.Text
  AreaCode(phone)
End Sub

Sub AreaCode()
  txtOutput.Text = "Your area code is " & phone.Substring(1, 3)
End Sub
```

In Exercises 1 through 34, determine the output displayed when the button is clicked.

1. ```
Private Sub btnDisplay_Click(...) Handles btnDisplay.Click
   lstBox.Items.Clear()
   lstBox.Items.Add("There's no great loss")
   Consolation()
End Sub

Private Sub Consolation()
   lstBox.Items.Add ("without some small gain.")
End Sub
```

2. ```
Private Sub btnDisplay_Click(...) Handles btnDisplay.Click
   Dim name as String
   name = InputBox("Name")
   PigLatin(name)
End Sub

Private Sub PigLatin(ByVal name as String)
   txtOutput.Text= name.substring(1) & name.substring(0,1) & "ay"
End Sub
```

3. ```
Private Sub btnDisplay_Click(...) Handles btnDisplay.Click
   lstBox.Items.Clear()
   lstBox.Items.Add("Nothing is certain but")
   Certainties()
End Sub

Private Sub Certainties()
   lstBox.Items.Add("Death and Taxes")
End Sub
```

4. ```
Private Sub btnDisplay_Click(...) Handles btnDisplay.Click
   lstBox.Items.Clear()
   lstBox.Items.Add("A short horse")
   GroomingTime()
End Sub

Private Sub GroomingTime()
   lstBox.Items.Add("is soon curried.")
End Sub
```

5.
```
Private Sub btnDisplay_Click(...) Handles btnDisplay.Click
    lstBox.Items.Clear()
    lstBox.Items.Add("All's well")
    OldAdage()
End Sub

Private Sub OldAdage()
    lstBox.Items.Add("that ends well.")
End Sub
```

6.
```
Private Sub btnDisplay_Click(...) Handles btnDisplay.Click
    lstBox.Items.Clear()
    lstBox.Items.Add("A dog that will fetch a bone")
    WhatDogsDo()
End Sub

Private sub WhatDogsDo()
    lstBox.Items.Add("will carry a bone.")
End Sub
```

7.
```
Private Sub btnDisplay_Click(...) Handles btnDisplay.Click
    Dim s as String="Ooh la la"
    lstBox.Items.Clear()
    SpinAround(s)
    lstBox.Items.Add(s)
End Sub

Private Sub SpinAround(ByRef s as String)
    s = s.ToUpper()
    Dim A, B As String
    A = s.Substring(0, 2)
    B = s.Substring(4, 2)
    s = "H" & A & B & "H" & A & "P"
End Sub
```

8.
```
Private Sub btnDisplay_Click(...) Handles btnDisplay.Click
    Answer()
    Question()
End Sub

Sub Answer()
    lstOutput.Items.Add("The answer is 9W.")
    lstOutput.Items.Add("What is the question?")
End Sub

Sub Question()
    'Note: "Wagner" is pronounced "Vagner"
    lstOutput.Items.Add("Do you spell your name with a V,")
    lstOutput.Items.Add("Mr. Wagner?")
End Sub
```

9.
```
Private Sub btnDisplay_Click(...) Handles btnDisplay.Click
    Piano(88)
End Sub

Sub Piano(ByVal num As Integer)
  txtOutput.Text = num & " keys on a piano"
End Sub
```

10.
```
Private Sub btnDisplay_Click(...) Handles btnDisplay.Click
    'Opening line of Moby Dick
    FirstLine("Ishmael")
End Sub

Sub FirstLine(ByVal name As String)
  'Display first line
  txtOutput.Text = "Call me " & name & "."
End Sub
```

11.
```
Private Sub btnDisplay_Click(...) Handles btnDisplay.Click
    'Beginning of Tale of Two Cities
    Times("best")
    Times("worst")
End Sub

Sub Times(ByVal word As String)
  'Display sentence
  lstOutput.Items.Add("It was the " & word & " of times.")
End Sub
```

12.
```
Private Sub btnDisplay_Click(...) Handles btnDisplay.Click
    Potato(1)
    Potato(2)
    Potato(3)
    lstOutput.Items.Add(4)
End Sub

Sub Potato(ByVal quantity As Integer)
  lstOutput.Items.Add(quantity & " potato")
End Sub
```

13.
```
Private Sub btnDisplay_Click(...) Handles btnDisplay.Click
    'Analyze a name
    Dim name As String = "Gabriel"
    AnalyzeName(name)
End Sub

Sub AnalyzeName(ByVal name As String)
  'Display length and first letter
  lstBox.Items.Add("Your name has " & name.Length & " letters.")
  lstBox.Items.Add("The first letter is " & name.Substring(0, 1))
End Sub
```

14.
```
Private Sub btnDisplay_Click(...) Handles btnDisplay.Click
    Dim color As String
    color = InputBox("What is your favorite color?")
    Flattery(color)
End Sub

Sub Flattery(ByVal color As String)
    txtOutput.Text = "You look dashing in " & color & "."
End Sub
```
(Assume that the response is *blue*.)

15.
```
Private Sub btnDisplay_Click(...) Handles btnDisplay.Click
    Dim num As Integer
    num = CInt(InputBox("Give a number from 1 to 26."))
    Alphabet(num)
End Sub

Sub Alphabet(ByVal num As Integer)
    txtOutput.Text = "abcdefghijklmnopqrstuvwxyz".Substring(0, num)
End Sub
```
(Assume that the response is 5.)

16.
```
Private Sub btnDisplay_Click(...) Handles btnDisplay.Click
    Dim size As Double
    size = 435
    House(size)
    lstOutput.Items.Add("of Representatives")
End Sub

Sub House(ByVal size As Double)
    lstOutput.Items.Add(size & " members in the House")
End Sub
```

17.
```
Private Sub btnDisplay_Click(...) Handles btnDisplay.Click
    Dim num As Double
    num = 144
    Gross(num)
End Sub

Sub Gross(ByVal amount As Double)
    txtOutput.Text = amount & " items in a gross"
End Sub
```

18.
```
Private Sub btnDisplay_Click(...) Handles btnDisplay.Click
    Dim a As String = "mile"
    Acres(a)
End Sub

Sub Acres(ByVal length As String)
    txtOutput.Text = "640 acres in a square " & length
End Sub
```

19.
```
Private Sub btnDisplay_Click(...) Handles btnDisplay.Click
    Dim candy As String
    candy = "M&M's Plain Chocolate Candies"
    Brown(candy)
End Sub

Sub Brown(ByVal item As String)
    txtOutput.Text = "30% of " & item & " are brown."
End Sub
```

20.
```
Private Sub btnDisplay_Click(...) Handles btnDisplay.Click
    Dim annualRate As Double = 0.08
    Balance(annualRate)
End Sub

Sub Balance(ByVal r As Double)
    Dim p As Double
    p = CDbl(InputBox("What is the principal?"))
    txtOutput.Text = "The balance after 1 year is " & (1 + r) * p
End Sub
```
(Assume that the response is *100*.)

21.
```
Private Sub btnDisplay_Click(...) Handles btnDisplay.Click
    Dim hours As Double
    hours = 24
    Minutes(60 * hours)
End Sub

Sub Minutes(ByVal num As Double)
    txtOutput.Text = num & " minutes in a day"
End Sub
```

22.
```
Private Sub btnDisplay_Click(...) Handles btnDisplay.Click
    Dim a, b As String
    a = "United States"
    b = "acorn"
    Display(a.Substring(0, 3) & b.Substring(1, 4))
End Sub

Sub Display(ByVal word As String)
    txtOutput.Text = word
End Sub
```

23.
```
Private Sub btnDisplay_Click(...) Handles btnDisplay.Click
    Dim word As String
    word = InputBox("Enter a word.")
    T(word.IndexOf("t"))
End Sub

Sub T(ByVal num As Integer)
    txtBox.Text = "t is the " & (num + 1) & "th letter of the word."
End Sub
```
(Assume that the response is *computer*.)

24.
```
Private Sub btnDisplay_Click(...) Handles btnDisplay.Click
    Dim states, senators As Double
    states = 50
    senators = 2
    Senate(states * senators)
End Sub

Sub Senate(ByVal num As Double)
    txtBox.Text = "The number of U.S. Senators is " & num
End Sub
```

25.
```
Private Sub btnDisplay_Click(...) Handles btnDisplay.Click
    DisplaySource()
    Occupation("Computer support specialist", 44350)
    Occupation("Database administrator", 67460)
    Occupation("Computer programmer", 69500)
    Occupation("Computer systems analyst", 72230)
End Sub

Sub DisplaySource()
    lstOutput.Items.Add("According to the " & _
                        "Bureau of Labor Statistics,")
    lstOutput.Items.Add("the average salaries for " & _
                        "computer occupations")
    lstOutput.Items.Add("in 2006 were as follows:")
    lstOutput.Items.Add("")
End Sub

Sub Occupation(ByVal job As String, ByVal salary As Double)
    lstOutput.Items.Add(job & "s earned " & _
                        FormatCurrency(salary, 0) & ".")
End Sub
```

26.
```
Private Sub btnDisplay_Click(...) Handles btnDisplay.Click
    'Sentence using number, thing, and place
    Sentence(168, "hour", "a week")
    Sentence(76, "trombone", "the big parade")
End Sub

Sub Sentence(ByVal num As Double, ByVal thing As String, _
             ByVal where As String)
    lstOutput.Items.Add(num & " " & thing & "s in " & where)
End Sub
```

27.
```
Private Sub btnDisplay_Click(...) Handles btnDisplay.Click
    Dim pres, college As String
    Dim sr As IO.StreamReader = IO.File.OpenText("CHIEF.TXT")
    pres = sr.ReadLine
    college = sr.ReadLine
    PresAlmaMater(pres, college)
    pres = sr.ReadLine
```

```
      college = sr.ReadLine
      PresAlmaMater(pres, college)
      sr.Close()
   End Sub

   Sub PresAlmaMater(ByVal pres As String, ByVal college As String)
      lstBox.Items.Add("President " & pres & " is a graduate of " & _
                       college & ".")
   End Sub
```

(Assume that the four lines of the file CHIEF.TXT contain the following data: B. Clinton, Georgetown University, G. Bush, Yale University.)

28.
```
   Private Sub btnDisplay_Click(...) Handles btnDisplay.Click
      Dim name As String, yob As Integer
      name = InputBox("Name?")
      yob = CInt(InputBox("Year of birth?"))
      AgeIn2010(name, yob)
   End Sub

   Sub AgeIn2010(ByVal name As String, ByVal yob As Integer)
      txtBox.Text = name & ", in the year 2010 your age will be " & _
                    (2010 - yob) & "."
   End Sub
```

(Assume that the responses are *Gabriel* and *1980*.)

29.
```
   Private Sub btnDisplay_Click(...) Handles btnDisplay.Click
      Dim word As String, num As Integer
      word = "Visual Basic"
      num = 6
      FirstPart(word, num)
   End Sub

   Sub FirstPart(ByVal term As String, ByVal digit As Integer)
      txtOutput.Text = "The first " & digit & " letters are " & _
                       term.Substring(0, digit) & "."
   End Sub
```

30.
```
   Private Sub btnDisplay_Click(...) Handles btnDisplay.Click
      Dim statue As String, tons As Double
      statue = "The Statue of Liberty"
      tons = 250
      HowHeavy(statue, tons)
   End Sub

   Sub HowHeavy(ByVal what As String, ByVal weight As Double)
      txtOutput.Text = what & " weighs " & weight & " tons."
   End Sub
```

31.
```
   Private Sub btnDisplay_Click(...) Handles btnDisplay.Click
      Dim word As String
      word = "worldly"
```

```
      Negative("un" & word, word)
   End Sub

   Sub Negative(ByVal neg As String, ByVal word As String)
      txtOutput.Text = "The negative of " & word & " is " & neg
   End Sub
```

32.
```
   Private Sub btnDisplay_Click(...) Handles btnDisplay.Click
      Dim age, yrs As Integer, major As String
      age = CInt(InputBox("How old are you?"))
      yrs = CInt(InputBox("In how many years will you graduate?"))
      major = InputBox("What sort of major do you have " & _
                    "(Arts or Sciences)?")
      Graduation(age + yrs, major.Substring(0, 1))
   End Sub

   Sub Graduation(ByVal num As Integer, ByVal letter As String)
      txtOutput.Text = "You will receive a B" & letter.ToUpper & _
                    " degree at age " & num
   End Sub
```

(Assume that the responses are *19*, *3*, and *arts*.)

33.
```
   Private Sub btnDisplay_Click(...) Handles btnDisplay.Click
      HowMany(24)
      lstOutput.Items.Add("a pie.")
   End Sub

   Sub HowMany(ByVal num As Integer)
      What(num)
      lstOutput.Items.Add("baked in")
   End Sub

   Sub What(ByVal num As Integer)
      lstOutput.Items.Add(num & " blackbirds")
   End Sub
```

34.
```
   Private Sub btnDisplay_Click(...) Handles btnDisplay.Click
      txtOutput.Text = "All's"
      PrintWell()
      PrintWords(" that ends")
      PrintWell()
      txtOutput.Text &= "."
   End Sub

   Sub PrintWell()
      txtOutput.Text &= " well"
   End Sub

   Sub PrintWords(ByVal words As String)
      txtOutput.Text &= words
   End Sub
```

In Exercises 35 through 38, find the errors.

35.
```
Private Sub btnDisplay_Click(...) Handles btnDisplay.Click
   Dim n As Integer = 5
   Alphabet()
End Sub

Sub Alphabet(ByVal n As Integer)
   txtOutput.Text = "abcdefghijklmnopqrstuvwxyz".Substring(0, n)
End Sub
```

36.
```
Private Sub btnDisplay_Click(...) Handles btnDisplay.Click
   Dim word As String, number As Double
   word = "seven"
   number = 7
   Display(word, number)
End Sub

Sub Display(ByVal num As Double, ByVal term As String)
   txtOutput.Text = num & " " & term
End Sub
```

37.
```
Private Sub btnDisplay_Click(...) Handles btnDisplay.Click
   Dim name As String
   name = InputBox("Name")
   Handles(name)
End Sub

Sub Handles(ByVal moniker As String)
   txtOutput.Text = "Your name is " & moniker
End Sub
```

38.
```
Private Sub btnDisplay_Click(...) Handles btnDisplay.Click
   Dim num As Integer = 2
   Tea(num)
End Sub

Sub Tea()
   txtOutput.Text = "Tea for " & num
End Sub
```

In Exercises 39 through 42, rewrite the program with the output performed by a call to a Sub procedure.

39.
```
Private Sub btnDisplay_Click(...) Handles btnDisplay.Click
   'Display a lucky number
   Dim num As Integer = 7
   txtOutput.Text = num & " is a lucky number."
End Sub
```

40.
```
Private Sub btnDisplay_Click(...) Handles btnDisplay.Click
   'Greet a friend
   Dim name As String = "Jack"
   txtOutput.Text = "Hi, " & name
End Sub
```

41.
```
Private Sub btnDisplay_Click(...) Handles btnDisplay.Click
    'Information about trees
    Dim tree As String, ht As Double
    Dim sr As IO.StreamReader = IO.File.OpenText("TREES.TXT")
    lstBox.Items.Clear()
    tree = sr.ReadLine
    ht = CDbl(sr.ReadLine)
    lstBox.Items.Add("The tallest " & tree & " in the U.S. is " & _
                    ht & " feet.")
    tree = sr.ReadLine
    ht = CDbl(sr.ReadLine)
    lstBox.Items.Add("The tallest " & tree & " in the U.S. is " & _
                    ht & " feet.")
    sr.Close()
End Sub
```

(Assume that the four lines of the file TREES.TXT contain the following data: redwood, 362, pine, 223.)

42.
```
Private Sub btnDisplay_Click(...) Handles btnDisplay.Click
    Dim city As String, salary As Double
    Dim sr As IO.StreamReader = IO.File.OpenText("DATA.TXT")
    lstBox.Items.Clear()
    city = sr.ReadLine
    salary = CDbl(sr.ReadLine)
    lstBox.Items.Add("In 2008, the average salary for " & city & _
                " residents was " & FormatCurrency(salary, 0) & ".")
    city = sr.ReadLine
    salary = CDbl(sr.ReadLine)
    lstBox.Items.Add("In 2008, the average salary for " & city & _
                " residents was " & FormatCurrency(salary, 0) & ".")
    sr.Close()
End Sub
```

(Assume that the four lines of the file DATA.TXT contain the following data: San Jose, 83089, Hartford, 46000.) **Note:** San Jose is located in Silicon Valley, and Hartford is the center of the insurance industry.

43. Write a program that requests a number as input and displays three times the number. The output should be produced by a call to a Sub procedure named Triple.

44. Write a program that requests a word as input and displays the word followed by the number of letters in the word. The output should be produced by a call to a Sub procedure named HowLong.

45. Write a program that requests a word of at most ten letters and a width from 10 through 20 as input and displays the word right-justified in a zone having the specified width. The output should be produced by a call to a Sub procedure named PlaceNShow.

46. Write a program that requests three numbers as input and displays the average of the three numbers. The output should be produced by a call to a Sub procedure named Average.

In Exercises 47 through 50, write a program that, when btnDisplay is clicked, will display in lstOutput the output shown. The last two lines of the output should be displayed by one or more Sub procedures using data passed by variables from an event procedure.

47. (Assume that the following is displayed.)

```
According to a 2007 survey of college freshmen
taken by the Higher Educational Research Institute:

17.7 percent said they intend to major in business.
1.1 percent said they intend to major in computer science.
```

48. (Assume that the current date is 12/31/2008, the label for txtBox reads "What is your year of birth?", and the user types 1982 into txtBox before btnDisplay is clicked.)

```
You are now 26 years old.
You have lived for more than 9490 days.
```

49. (Assume that the label for txtBox reads "What is your favorite number?", and the user types 7 into txtBox before btnDisplay is clicked.)

```
The sum of your favorite number with itself is 14.
The product of your favorite number with itself is 49.
```

50. (Assume that the following is displayed.)

```
In a recent year,
823 thousand college students took a course in Spanish
206 thousand college students took a course in French
```

51. Write a program to display three verses of "Old McDonald Had a Farm." The primary verse, with variables substituted for the animals and sounds, should be contained in a Sub procedure. The program should use the file FARM.TXT. The eight lines of the file FARM.TXT contain the following data: lamb, baa, firefly, blink, computer, beep.

The first verse of the output should be

```
Old McDonald had a farm. Eyi eyi oh.
And on his farm he had a lamb. Eyi eyi oh.
With a baa baa here, and a baa baa there.
Here a baa, there a baa, everywhere a baa baa.
Old McDonald had a farm. Eyi eyi oh.
```

52. Write a program that displays the word WOW vertically in large letters. Each letter should be drawn in a Sub procedure. For instance, the Sub procedure for the letter W follows. **Hint:** Use the font *Courier New* in the list box.

```
Sub DrawW()
    'Draw the letter W
    lstWOW.Items.Add("**          **")
    lstWOW.Items.Add(" **         **")
    lstWOW.Items.Add("  **   **   **")
    lstWOW.Items.Add("   **     **")
    lstWow.Items.Add("")
End Sub
```

53. Write a program to display the data from Table 5.1. The occupations and numbers of jobs for 2006 and 2016 should be contained in the file GROWTH.TXT. A Sub procedure, to be called four times, should read the first three pieces of data for an occupation, calculate the percent increase from 2006 to 2016, and display the four items. **Note:** The percent increase is calculated as (2016 value − 2006 value)/(2006 value).

TABLE 5.1	Occupations projected to experience large job growth, 2006–2016 (numbers in thousands of jobs).		
Occupation	2006	2016	Increase
Network system analyst	262	402	53.4%
Home health aide	787	1171	48.7%
Software engineer	507	733	44.6%
Medical assistant	417	565	35.4%

Source: U.S. Department of Labor.

54. Write a program to compute tips for services rendered. The program should request the person's occupation, the amount of the bill, and the percentage tip as input and pass this information to a Sub procedure to display the person and the tip. A sample run is shown in Figure 5.4.

FIGURE 5.4   Sample run of Exercise 54.

55. *Computerized quiz show.* Write a program that asks the contestant to select one of the numbers 1, 2, or 3 and then calls a Sub procedure that asks the question and requests the answer. The program should then tell the contestant if the answer is correct. Use the following three questions:

   1. Who was the only living artist to have his work displayed in the Grand Gallery of the Louvre?

   2. Who said, "Computers are useless. They can only give you answers."?

   3. By what name is Pablo Blasio better known?

   Note: These questions have the same answer, Pablo Picasso.

Solutions to Practice Problems 5.1

1. An event procedure always has the two parameters *sender* and *e* and ends with a phrase of the form "Handles *object.event*." It is triggered when the specified object experiences the specified event. On the other hand, a Sub procedure is triggered by a line of code containing the name of the Sub procedure.

2. The statement `Sub AreaCode()` must be replaced by `Sub AreaCode(ByVal phone As String)`. Whenever a value is passed to a Sub procedure, the Sub statement must provide a parameter to receive the value.

5.2 Sub Procedures, Part II

The previous section introduced the concept of a Sub procedure, but left some questions unanswered. Why can't the value of a variable be passed from an event procedure to a Sub procedure by just using the variable in the Sub procedure? How do Sub procedures pass values back to an event procedure? The answers to these questions provide a deeper understanding of the workings of Sub procedures and reveal their full capabilities.

■ Passing by Value

In Section 5.1, all parameters appearing in Sub procedures were preceded by the word ByVal, which stands for "By Value." When a variable is passed to such a parameter, we say that the variable is "passed by value." A variable that is passed by value will retain its original value after the Sub procedure terminates—regardless of what was done to the corresponding parameter inside the Sub procedure. Example 1 illustrates this feature.

 Example 1   The following program illustrates the fact that changes to the value of a parameter passed by value have no effect on the value of the calling argument:

```
Private Sub btnDisplay_Click(...) Handles btnDisplay.Click
  'Illustrate that a change in value of parameter does not alter the
  'value of the argument
  Dim amt As Double = 2
  lstResults.Items.Add(amt)
  Triple(amt)
  lstResults.Items.Add(amt)
End Sub

Sub Triple(ByVal num As Double)
  'Triple a number
  lstResults.Items.Add(num)
  num = 3 * num
  lstResults.Items.Add(num)
End Sub
```

[Run, and then click the button. The following is displayed in the list box.]

```
2
2
6
2
```

When a variable is passed by value, two memory locations are involved. At the time the Sub procedure is called, a temporary second memory location for the parameter is set aside for the Sub procedure's use and the value of the argument is copied into that location. After the completion of the Sub procedure, the temporary memory location is released, and the value in it is lost. So, for instance, the outcome in Example 1 would be the same even if the name of the parameter were *amt*.

■ Passing by Reference

Another way to pass a variable to a Sub procedure is "By Reference." In this case the parameter is preceded by the reserved word ByRef. Suppose a variable, call it *arg*, appears as an argument in a Call statement, and its corresponding parameter in the Sub procedure's header, call it *par*, is preceded by ByRef. After the Sub procedure is executed, *arg* will have whatever value *par* had in the Sub procedure. Hence, not only is the value of *arg* passed to *par*, but the value of *par* is passed back to *arg*.

In Example 1, if the first line of the Sub procedure is changed to

```
Sub Triple(ByRef num As Double)
```

then the last number of the output will be 6.

Although this feature may be surprising at first glance, it provides a vehicle for passing values from a Sub procedure back to the place from which the Sub procedure was called. Different names may be used for an argument and its corresponding parameter, but only one memory location is involved. Initially, the btnDisplay_Click() event procedure allocates a memory location to hold the value of *amt* (Figure 5.5(a)). When the Sub procedure is called, the parameter *num* becomes the Sub procedure's name for this memory location (Figure 5.5(b)). When the value of *num* is tripled, the value in the memory location becomes 6 (Figure 5.5(c)). After the completion of the Sub procedure, the parameter name *num* is forgotten; however, its value lives on in *amt* (Figure 5.5(d)). The variable *amt* is said to be **passed by reference**.

amt	amt	amt	amt
2	2	6	6
	num	num	
(a)	(b)	(c)	(d)

FIGURE 5.5 **Passing a variable by reference to a Sub procedure.**

Passing by reference has a variety of uses. In the next example, it is used as a vehicle to transport a value from a Sub procedure back to an event procedure.

Example 2 The following variation of Example 5 from the previous section uses a Sub procedure to acquire the input. The variables *x* and *y* are not assigned values prior to the execution of the first Call statement. Therefore, before the Call statement is executed, they have the value 0. After the Call statement is executed, however, they have the values entered into the text boxes. These values then are passed by the second Call statement to the Sub procedure DisplaySum.

OBJECT	PROPERTY	SETTING
frmAdd	Text	Add Two Numbers
lblFirstNum	Text	First Number:
txtFirstNum		
lblSecondNum	Text	Second Number:
txtSecondNum		
btnCompute	Text	Compute Sum
txtResult	ReadOnly	True

```
Private Sub btnCompute_Click(...) Handles btnCompute.Click
  'This program requests two numbers and
  'displays the two numbers and their sum.
  Dim x, y As Double
  GetNumbers(x, y)
  DisplaySum(x, y)
End Sub

Sub GetNumbers(ByRef x As Double, ByRef y As Double)
  'Record the two numbers in the text boxes
  x = CDbl(txtFirstNum.Text)
  y = CDbl(txtSecondNum.Text)
End Sub

Sub DisplaySum(ByVal num1 As Double, ByVal num2 As Double)
  'Display two numbers and their sum
  Dim sum As Double
  sum = num1 + num2
  txtResult.Text = "The sum of " & num1 & " and " & _
                   num2 & " is " & sum & "."
End Sub
```

[Run, type 2 and 3 into the text boxes, and then click the button.]

In some situations, a variable with no preassigned value is used as an argument of a Call statement for the sole purpose of carrying back a value from the Sub procedure.

Example 3   The following variation of Example 2 allows the btnCompute_Click event procedure to be written in the input-process-output style. Just before the Call statement `CalculateSum(x, y, s)` is executed, the value of *s* is 0. After the call, the value of *s* will be the sum of the two numbers in the text boxes.

```
Private Sub btnCompute_Click(...) Handles btnCompute.Click
  'This program requests two numbers and
  'displays the two numbers and their sum.
  Dim x As Double        'First number
  Dim y As Double        'Second number
  Dim s As Double        'Sum
  GetNumbers(x, y)
  CalculateSum(x, y, s)
  DisplayResult(x, y, s)
End Sub

Sub GetNumbers(ByRef num1 As Double, ByRef num2 As Double)
  'Retrieve the two numbers in the text boxes
  num1 = CDbl(txtFirstNum.Text)
  num2 = CDbl(txtSecondNum.Text)
End Sub

Sub CalculateSum(ByVal num1 As Double, ByVal num2 As Double, _
                 ByRef sum As Double)
  'Add the values of num1 and num2
  sum = num1 + num2
End Sub

Sub DisplayResult(ByVal num1 As Double, ByVal num2 As Double, _
                  ByVal sum As Double)
  txtResult.Text = "The sum of " & num1 & " and " & num2 & _
                   " is " & sum & "."
End Sub
```

Visual Basic provides a way to override passing by reference, even if the ByRef keyword precedes the parameter. If you enclose the variable in the call statement in an extra pair of parentheses, then the variable will be passed by value.

For instance, in Example 1, if you change the Call statement to

```
Triple((amt))
```

then the fourth number of the output will be 2 even if the parameter *num* is preceded with ByRef.

■ Lifetime and Scope of a Variable

When a variable is declared inside a Sub or event procedure with a Dim statement, a portion of memory is set aside to hold the value of the variable. That portion of memory is released when the procedure's End Sub statement is reached. The **lifetime** of a variable is the period during which it remains in memory. (Its value can change over its lifetime, but it always holds some value.) The **scope** of a variable is the portion of the program that can refer to it. A variable declared in a procedure with a Dim statement is a **local variable** and is said to have **local scope**. (It cannot be accessed outside of the procedure.) When variables declared in two different procedures have the same name, Visual Basic treats them as two different variables.

A variable declared outside of a procedure has **class-level scope** and can be referred to by any Sub or event procedure. A variable declared inside an If or a Select Case block has **block-level scope** and cannot be accessed outside the block. Good programming practice dictates that the scope of a variable be as small as possible. This minimizes the chance of code referring to the wrong variable.

 Example 4　The following program illustrates the fact that each time a Sub procedure is called, its variables are set to their initial values.

```
Private Sub btnDisplay_Click(...) Handles btnDisplay.Click
  'Demonstrate that variables declared in a Sub procedure
  'do not retain their values in subsequent calls
  Three()
  Three()
End Sub

Sub Three()
  'Display the value of num and assign it the value 3
  Dim num As Double
  lstResults.Items.Add(num)
  num = 3
End Sub
```

[Run, and then click the button. The following is displayed in the list box.]

```
0
0
```

 Example 5　The following program illustrates the fact that variables are local to the part of the program in which they reside. The variable x in the event procedure and the variable x in the Sub procedure are treated as different variables. Visual Basic handles them as if their names were separate, such as xbtnDisplay_Click and xTrivial. Also, each time the Sub procedure is called, the value of variable x inside the Sub procedure is reset to 0.

```
Private Sub btnDisplay_Click(...) Handles btnDisplay.Click
  'Demonstrate the local nature of variables
  Dim x As Double = 2
  lstResults.Items.Clear()
  lstResults.Items.Add(x & " : event procedure")
  Trivial()
  lstResults.Items.Add(x & " : event procedure")
  Trivial()
```

```
    lstResults.Items.Add(x & " : event procedure")
End Sub

Sub Trivial()
  'Do something trivial
  Dim x As Double
  lstResults.Items.Add(x & " : Sub procedure")
  x = 3
  lstResults.Items.Add(x & " : Sub procedure")
End Sub
```

[Run, and then click the button.]

Debugging

Programs with Sub procedures are easier to debug. Each Sub procedure can be checked individually before being placed into the program.

In Appendix D, the section "Stepping through a Program Containing a General Procedure: Chapter 5" uses the Visual Basic debugger to trace the flow through a program and observe the interplay between arguments and parameters.

Practice Problems 5.2

1. What does the following code display in the list box when the button is clicked?

```
Private Sub btnDisplay_Click(...) Handles btnDisplay.Click
  Dim b As Integer = 1, c As Integer = 2
  Rhyme()
  lstOutput.Items.Add(b & " " & c)
End Sub

Sub Rhyme()
  Dim b, c As Integer
  lstOutput.Items.Add(b & " " & c & " buckle my shoe.")
  b = 3
End Sub
```

2. Determine the output displayed in the list box when the button is clicked.

```
Private Sub btnDisplay_Click(...) Handles btnDisplay.Click
  Dim amt1 As Integer = 1, amt2 As Integer = 2
  lstOutput.Items.Add(amt1 & " " & amt2)
  Swap(amt1, amt2)
  lstOutput.Items.Add(amt1 & " " & amt2)
End Sub

Sub Swap(ByRef num1 As Integer, ByRef num2 As Integer)
  'Interchange the values of num1 and num2
  Dim temp As Integer
  temp = num1
  num1 = num2
  num2 = temp
  lstOutput.Items.Add(num1 & " " & num2)
End Sub
```

3. In Problem 2, change the Sub statement to

```
Sub Swap(ByRef num1 As Integer, ByVal num2 As Integer)
```

and determine the output.

4. In Problem 2, change the calling statement to

```
Swap((amt1), (amt2))
```

and determine the output.

EXERCISES 5.2

In Exercises 1 through 18, determine the output displayed when the button is clicked.

1.
```
Private Sub btnDisplay_Click(...) Handles btnDisplay.Click
  Dim num As Double = 7
  AddTwo(num)
  txtOutput.Text = CStr(num)
End Sub

Sub AddTwo(ByRef num As Double)
  num += 2
End Sub
```

2.
```
Private Sub btnDisplay_Click(...) Handles btnDisplay.Click
  Dim term As String = "Fall"
  Plural(term)
  txtOutput.Text = term
End Sub

Sub Plural(ByRef term As String)
  'Concatenate the letter "s" to the value of term
  term &= "s"
End Sub
```

3.
```
Private Sub btnDisplay_Click(...) Handles btnDisplay.Click
    Dim dance As String
    dance = "Can "
    Twice(dance)
    txtOutput.Text = dance
End Sub

Sub Twice(ByRef dance As String)
    'Concatenate the value of dance to itself
    dance &= dance
End Sub
```

4.
```
Private Sub btnCompute_Click(...) Handles btnCompute.Click
    Dim a As Integer = 1, b As Integer = 3
    lstOutput.Items.Add(a & " " & b)
    Combine(a, b)
    lstOutput.Items.Add(a & " " & b)
    Combine((a), b)
    lstOutput.Items.Add(a & " " & b)
End Sub

Sub Combine(ByRef x As Integer, ByVal y As Integer)
    x = y - x
    y = x + y
    lstOutput.Items.Add(x & " " & y)
End Sub
```

5.
```
Private Sub btnDisplay_Click(...) Handles btnDisplay.Click
    Dim a As Double = 5
    Square(a)
    txtOutput.Text = CStr(a)
End Sub

Sub Square(ByRef num As Double)
    num = num * num
End Sub
```

6.
```
Private Sub btnDisplay_Click(...) Handles btnDisplay.Click
    Dim name As String = "Terry Jones"
    Abbreviate(name)
    txtOutput.Text = name
End Sub

Sub Abbreviate(ByRef a As String)
    Dim b As Integer = a.IndexOf("")
    a = a.SubString(0, 1) & " . " & a.SubString(b + 1, 1) & "."
End Sub
```

7.
```
Private Sub btnDisplay_Click(...) Handles btnDisplay.Click
    Dim word As String = ""
    GetWord(word)
    txtOutput.Text = "Less is " & word & "."
End Sub
```

```
Sub GetWord(ByRef w As String)
  w = "more"
End Sub
```

8. ```
Private Sub btnDisplay_Click(...) Handles btnDisplay.Click
  Dim hourlyWage, annualWage As Double
  hourlyWage = 10
  CalcAnnualWage(hourlyWage, annualWage)
  txtOutput.Text = "Approximate Annual Wage: " & _
                  FormatCurrency(annualWage)
End Sub

Sub CalcAnnualWage(ByVal hWage As Double, ByRef aWage As Double)
  'A year contains about 2000 work hours
  aWage = 2000 * hWage
End Sub
```

9. ```
Private Sub btnDisplay_Click(...) Handles btnDisplay.Click
  Dim name As String = ""
  Dim yob As Integer
  GetVita(name, yob)
  txtOutput.Text = name & " was born in the year " & yob
End Sub

Sub GetVita(ByRef name As String, ByRef yob As Integer)
  name = "Gabriel"
  yob = 1980    'Year of birth
End Sub
```

10. ```
Private Sub btnDisplay_Click(...) Handles btnDisplay.Click
  'Display a quotation
  Dim word1, word2 As String
  word1 = "fail"
  word2 = "plan"
  txtOutput.Text = "If you "
  Sentence(word1, word2)
  txtOutput.Text &= ","z
  Exchange(word1, word2)
  txtOutput.Text &= " then you "
  Sentence(word1, word2)
  txtOutput.Text &= "."
End Sub

Sub Exchange(ByRef word1 As String, ByRef word2 As String)
  Dim temp As String
  temp = word1
  word1 = word2
  word2 = temp
End Sub

Sub Sentence(ByVal word1 As String, ByVal word2 As String)
  txtOutput.Text &= word1 & " to " & word2
End Sub
```
```

11.
```
Private Sub btnDisplay_Click(...) Handles btnDisplay.Click
    Dim state As String = "Ohio "
    Team()
End Sub

Sub Team()
    Dim state As String
    txtOutput.Text = state
    txtOutput.Text &= "Buckeyes"
End Sub
```

12.
```
Private Sub btnDisplay_Click(...) Handles btnDisplay.Click
    Dim a As Double = 5
    Multiply(7)
    lstOutput.Items.Add(a * 7)
End Sub

Sub Multiply(ByRef num As Double)
    Dim a As Double
    a = 11
    lstOutput.Items.Add(a * num)
End Sub
```

13.
```
Private Sub btnDisplay_Click(...) Handles btnDisplay.Click
    Dim a As Double = 5
    Multiply(7)
End Sub

Sub Multiply(ByVal num As Double)
    Dim a As Double
    txtOutput.Text = CStr(a * num)
End Sub
```

14.
```
Private Sub btnDisplay_Click(...) Handles btnDisplay.Click
    Dim name, n As String
    name = "Ray"
    Hello(name)
    lstOutput.Items.Add(n & " and " & name)
End Sub

Sub Hello(ByRef name As String)
    Dim n As String
    n = name
    name = "Bob"
    lstOutput.Items.Add("Hello " & n & " and " & name)
End Sub
```

15.
```
Private Sub btnDisplay_Click(...) Handles btnDisplay.Click
    Dim num As Double = 1
    Amount(num)
    Amount(num)
End Sub
```

```
    Sub Amount(ByVal num As Double)
      Dim total As Double
      total += num 'Add the value of num to the value of total
      lstOutput.Items.Add(total)
    End Sub
```

16.
```
    Private Sub btnDisplay_Click(...) Handles btnDisplay.Click
      Dim river As String
      river = "Wabash"
      Another()
      lstOutput.Items.Add(river & " River")
      Another()
    End Sub

    Sub Another()
      Dim river As String
      lstOutput.Items.Add(river & " River")
      river = "Yukon"
    End Sub
```

17.
```
    Private Sub btnCompute_Click(...) Handles btnCompute.Click
      Dim n As Integer = 4, word As String = "overwhelming"
      lstOutput.Items.Add(n & " " & word)
      Crop(n, word)
      lstOutput.Items.Add(n & " " & word)
      Crop(n, (word))
      lstOutput.Items.Add(n & " " & word)
    End Sub

    Sub Crop(ByVal n As Integer, ByRef word As String)
      n = word.Length - n
      word = word.Substring(word.Length - n)
      lstOutput.Items.Add(n & " " & word)
    End Sub
```

18.
```
    Private Sub btnCompute_Click(...) Handles btnCompute.Click
      Dim tax, price, total As Double
      tax = 0.05
      GetPrice("bicycle", price)
      ProcessItem(price, tax, total)
      DisplayResult(total)
    End Sub

    Sub DisplayResult(ByVal total As Double)
      txtOutput.Text = "With tax, price is " & FormatCurrency(total)
    End Sub

    Sub GetPrice(ByVal item As String, ByRef price As Double)
      Dim strVar As String
      strVar = InputBox("What is the price of a " & item & "?")
      price = CDbl(strVar)
    End Sub
```

```
Sub ProcessItem(ByVal price As Double, ByVal tax As Double, _
                ByRef total As Double)
  total = (1 + tax) * price
End Sub
```

(Assume that the cost of the bicycle is $200.)

In Exercises 19 and 20, find the errors.

19.
```
Private Sub btnCompute_Click(...) Handles btnCompute.Click
    Dim a, b, c As Double
    a = 1
    b = 2
    Sum(a, b, c)
    txtOutput.Text = "The sum is " & c
End Sub

Sub Sum(ByVal x As Double, ByVal y As Double)
    Dim c As Double
    c = x + y
End Sub
```

20.
```
Private Sub btnDisplay_Click(...) Handles btnDisplay.Click
    Dim vowels As Integer    'Number of vowels
    ExamineLetter(vowels)
    ExamineLetter(vowels)
    ExamineLetter(vowels)
    txtOutput.Text = "The number of vowels is " & vowels
End Sub

Sub ExamineLetter(ByRef vowels As Integer)
    Dim ltr As String
    ltr = InputBox("Enter a letter.")
    ltr = ltr.ToUpper
    If (ltr = "A") Or (ltr = "E") Or (ltr = "I") Or _
       (ltr = "O") Or (ltr = "U") Then
      vowels += 1
    End If
End Sub
```

(Assume the three responses are U, b, and a.)

In Exercises 21 through 24, rewrite the program so input, processing, and output are each performed by calls to Sub procedures.

21.
```
Private Sub btnCompute_Click(...) Handles btnCompute.Click
    'Calculate sales tax
    Dim price, tax, cost As Double
    lstOutput.Items.Clear()
    price = CDbl(InputBox("Enter the price of the item:"))
    tax = .05 * price
    cost = price + tax
    lstOutput.Items.Add("Price:   " & price)
```

```
        lstOutput.Items.Add("Tax:     " & tax)
        lstOutput.Items.Add("-------")
        lstOutput.Items.Add("Cost:    " & cost)
    End Sub
```

22. ```
    Private Sub btnDisplay_Click(...) Handles bnDisplay.Click
        'Letter of acceptance
        Dim name, firstName As String, n As Integer
        lstOutput.Items.Clear()
        name = InputBox("What is your full name?")
        n = name.IndexOf(" ")
        firstName = name.Substring(0, n)
        lstOutput.Items.Add("Dear " & firstName & ",")
        lstOutput.Items.Add("")
        lstOutput.Items.Add("We are proud to accept you to Yale.")
    End Sub
    ```

23. ```
    Private Sub btnDisplay_Click(...) Handles bnDisplay.Click
        'Determine the area of a rectangle
        Dim length, width, area As Double
        length = CDbl(txtLength.Text)
        width = CDbl(txtWidth.Text)
        area = length * width
        txtOutput.Text = "The area of the rectangle is " & area
    End Sub
    ```

24. ```
    Private Sub btnCompute_Click(...) Handles btnCompute.Click
        'Convert feet and inches to centimeters
        Dim str As String
        Dim feet, inches, totalInches, centimeters As Double
        str = "Give the length in feet and inches. "
        feet = CDbl(InputBox(str & "Enter the number of feet."))
        inches = CDbl(InputBox(str & "Enter the number of inches. "))
        totalInches = 12 * feet + inches
        centimeters = 2.54 * totalInches
        txtOutput.Text = "The length in centimeters is " & centimeters
    End Sub
    ```

In Exercises 25 through 30, write a program to perform the stated task. The input, processing, and output should be performed by calls to Sub procedures.

25. Given three double parameters (length of the sides of a triangle) determine if the triangle formed by these dimensions is "Equilateral" (if all the values are positive and the same), "Isosceles" (if just two values match) or "Scalene".

26. Radiometric dating techniques date materials usually using radioactive isotopes. It is the principal source of information about the age of rocks, and can be used to date natural and man-made materials. **Radiocarbon dating** uses the naturally occurring isotope carbon-14 to determine the age of carbonaceous materials up to about 60,000 years old. **Uranium-lead** is one of the oldest and most refined radio-
    ```

metric dating schemes, with a routine age range of about 1 million years to over 4.5 billion years. **Potassium-Argon** dating is most applicable for dating minerals and rocks more than 100,000 years old. Devise a function that accepts a double parameter (the approximate date of the material to be tested) and returns as a String the best dating technique to use. Return "No Dating" in the event the material can not be dated using an available scheme.

27. Write a program to implement a game where the computer will guess the number you are thinking of. Provide 3 buttons named btnTooHigh, btnTooLow and btnCorrect. The program should prompt you with a MessageBox to think of a number between 1 and 100 (inclusive). The program will make a series of guesses which should be displayed in a listbox, along with the guess number. For each guess, you must press the appropriate button indicating that the guess is too high, too low or correct. The program will make its guesses by averaging two number, low and high. Set integer field values low to 1 and high to 101 (why?) in form load. Write a Sub procedure called GetGuess which accepts the low and high values as parameters. It adjusts field values guess and guesscount and displays these in a listbox. Note, the integer guess is computed as (low+high)\2. If the player presses the "too high" button, then replace high with guess and call GetGuess. If the player presses the "too low" button replace low with guess and call GetGuess. When "correct" button is selected display "Game Over" and disable the buttons.

28. Sound travels a little over 1000 feet per second at sea level, and the speed of light across short distances is near instantaneous. Consequently, the distance away of lighting in feet is about 1000*s where s is the count of seconds from seeing the lightening until hearing the thunder. Write a function which takes an integer parameter **seconds** and returns the distance away **in miles** of the lightening as a double. Recall, there are 5280 feet in a mile.

29. A *4-digit Base Converter*. Suppose the user may enter a 4-digit value representing a number in a base from 2 to 10, as well as the base of the number. Write a Sub procedure to convert the input value into its equivalent form in base 10 by breaking it into its separate digits. If the base of the number is called b and the digits of the number are called *d1* (one's place), *d2, d3* and *d4*, then the equivalent base 10 representation of this value can be computed as $(((d4*b+d3)*b)+d2)*b+d1$. Display this in a text box with an identifying label.

30. Write a function to determine the absolute value of a double variable. The absolute value is the positive distance from zero of the number, so the absolute value of -5 is 5, and so is the absolute value of 5.

31. *Taxi-cab distance.* Imagine the grid of roads that make up a city's streets, laid out horizontally and vertically. A taxi cab travels $(x1-x2) + (y1-y2)$. To get to locations which are not on the same street, the taxi must drive a distance up (or down) town, or across town. For example, to get from address (3, 5) to address (1, 1) we go 2+4 or 6 miles. (Notice, to go from $(-1, -1)$ to $(6, -8)$ we go $abs(-1 -6)+abs(-1 +8)$, or 14 miles.) Write a function TaxiCab which accepts four doubles, the starting and ending coordinates of the trip and returns the taxi

ride cost as a double if a flat rate of $10 per mile is charged. A function which returns the absolute value of its argument is handy for this problem.

32. Instead of a taxi, we'll use a helicopter to travel from one building (top) to another. Use the Cartesian distance formula $((x2-x1)^2 +(y2-y1)^2))^{0.5}$. Write a function Helicopter which accepts four double values of the starting and ending coordinates of the trip and, assuming all distances are in miles, returns the copter ride cost if a flat rate of $100 per mile is charged.

33. *Summing the integers from 1 to n.* A useful formula exists for computing the sum of the first n integers: $1+2+3+ \ldots +n = n*(n+1)/2$. Write a program which uses an InputBox to prompt for a non-negative integer. Write a function to calculate the sum and use a text box to display the sum of the integers $1+2+3+ \ldots +n$ using the formula.

FIGURE 5.6 Sample output for Exercise 33.

Solutions to Practice Problems 5.2

1. **0 0 buckle my shoe.**
    1 2

    This program illustrates the local nature of the variables in a Sub procedure. Notice that the variables *b* and *c* appearing in the Sub procedure have no relationship whatsoever to the variables of the same name in the event procedure. In a certain sense, the variables inside the Sub procedure can be thought of as having alternate names, such as *bRhyme* and *cRhyme*.

2. **1 2**
    2 1
    2 1

    Both variables are passed by reference and so have their values changed by the Sub procedure.

3. **1 2**
    2 1
    2 2

    Here *amt1* is passed by reference and *amt2* is passed by value. Therefore, only *amt1* has its value changed by the Sub procedure.

4. **1 2**
    2 1
    1 2

Both variables are passed by value, so their values are not changed by the Sub procedure.

5.3   Function Procedures

Visual Basic has many built-in functions. In one respect, functions are like miniature programs. They use input, they process the input, and they have output. Some functions we encountered earlier are listed in Table 5.2.

Although the input can involve several values, the output always consists of a single value. The items inside the parentheses can be literals (as in Table 5.2), variables, or expressions.

TABLE 5.2   Some Visual Basic built-in functions.

Function	Example	Input	Output
Int	Int(2.6) is 2	number	number
Chr	Chr(65) is "A"	number	string
Asc	Asc("Apple") is 65	string	number
FormatNumber	FormatNumber(12345.628, 1) is 12,345.6	number, number	string

In addition to using built-in functions, we can define functions of our own. These new functions, called **Function procedures** or **user-defined functions**, are defined in much the same way as Sub procedures and are used in the same way as built-in functions. Like built-in functions, Function procedures have a single output that can be of any data type. Function procedures can be used in expressions in exactly the same way as built-in functions. Programs refer to them as if they were literals, variables, or expressions. Function procedures are defined by function blocks of the form

```
Function FunctionName(ByVal var1 As Type1, _
                ByVal var2 As Type2, ...) As DataType
   statement(s)
   Return expression
End Function
```

The variables appearing in the top line are called **parameters**. The discussion of lifetime and scope for variables declared in Sub and event procedures also applies to variables declared in Function procedures. Function names should be suggestive of the role performed and must conform to the rules for naming variables. The type *DataType*, which specifies the type of the output, will be one of String, Integer, Double, and so on. In the preceding general code, the next-to-last line specifies the output, which must be of type *DataType*. Like Sub procedures, Function procedures are typed directly into the

Code Editor. (The last line, End Function, will appear automatically after the first line is entered into the Code Editor.) A variable passed to a Function procedure is normally passed by value. It can also be passed by reference and thereby possibly have its value changed by the Function procedure. However, passing a variable by reference violates good design principles, since a function is intended to only create a single result and not cause any other changes.

Two examples of Function procedures are as follows:

```
Function FtoC(ByVal t As Double) As Double
  'Convert Fahrenheit temperature to Celsius
  Return (5 / 9) * (t - 32)
End Function

Function FirstName(ByVal name As String) As String
  'Extract the first name from a full name
  Dim firstSpace As Integer
  firstSpace = name.IndexOf(" ")
  name = name.Substring(0, firstSpace)
  Return name
End Function
```

The value of each of the preceding functions is assigned by a statement of the form **Return** *expression*. The variables *t* and *name* appearing in the preceding functions are parameters. They can be replaced with any variable of the same type without affecting the function definition.

Example 1   The following program uses the Function procedure FtoC.

OBJECT	PROPERTY	SETTING
frmConvert	Text	Convert Fahrenheit to Celsius
lblTempF	Text	Temperature (Fahrenheit)
txtTempF		
btnConvert	Text	Convert to Celsius
lblTempC	Text	Temperature (Celsius)
txtTempC	ReadOnly	True

```
Private Sub btnConvert_Click(...) Handles btnConvert.Click
  Dim fahrenheitTemp, celsiusTemp As Double
  fahrenheitTemp = CDbl(txtTempF.Text)
  celsiusTemp = FtoC(fahrenheitTemp)
  txtTempC.Text = CStr(celsiusTemp)
  'Note: The above four lines can be replaced with the single line
  'txtTempC.Text = CStr(FtoC(CDbl(txtTempF.Text)))
End Sub

Function FtoC(ByVal t As Double) As Double
  'Convert Fahrenheit temperature to Celsius
  Return (5 / 9) * (t - 32)
End Function
```

[Run, type 212 into the text box, and then click the button.]

 Example 2   The following program uses the Function procedure FirstName.

OBJECT	PROPERTY	SETTING
frmFirstName	Text	Extract First Name
lblName	Text	Name:
txtFullName		
btnDetermine	Text	Determine First Name
lblFirstName	Text	First Name:
txtFirstName	ReadOnly	True

```
Private Sub btnDetermine_Click(...) Handles btnDetermine.Click
  'Determine a person's first name
  Dim name As String
  name = txtFullName.Text
  txtFirstName.Text = FirstName(name)
End Sub

Function FirstName(ByVal name As String) As String
  'Extract the first name from a full name
  Dim firstSpace As Integer
  firstSpace = name.IndexOf(" ")
  name = name.Substring(0, firstSpace)
  Return name
End Function
```

[Run, type Franklin Delano Roosevelt into the text box, and then click the button.]

User-Defined Functions Having Several Parameters

The input to a user-defined function can consist of one or more values. Two examples of Function procedures with several parameters follow. One-letter variable names have been used so the mathematical formulas will look familiar and be readable. Because the names are not descriptive, the meanings of these variables are carefully spelled out in comment statements.

```
Function Hypotenuse(ByVal a As Double, ByVal b As Double) As Double
  'Calculate the hypotenuse of a right triangle
  'having sides of lengths a and b
  Return Math.Sqrt(a ^ 2 + b ^ 2)
End Function

Function FutureValue(ByVal p As Double, ByVal r As Double, _
          ByVal c As Double, ByVal n As Double) As Double
  'Find the future value of a bank savings account
  'p principal, the amount deposited
  'r annual rate of interest (expressed as a decimal)
  'c number of times interest is compounded per year
  'n number of years
  Dim i As Double  'interest rate per period
  Dim m As Double  'total number of times interest is compounded
  i = r / c
  m = c * n
  Return p * ((1 + i) ^ m)
End Function
```

 Example 3 The following program uses the Hypotenuse Function procedure.

OBJECT	PROPERTY	SETTING
frmPythagoras	Text	Right Triangle
lblSideOne	AutoSize	False
	Text	Length of one side
txtSideOne		
lblSideTwo	AutoSize	False
	Text	Length of other side
txtSideTwo		
btnCalculate	Text	Calculate Hypotenuse
lblHyp	AutoSize	False
	Text	Length of Hypotenuse
txtHyp	ReadOnly	True

```
Private Sub btnCalculate_Click(...) Handles btnCalculate.Click
  'Calculate the length of the hypotenuse of a right triangle
  Dim a, b As Double
  a = CDbl(txtSideOne.Text)
  b = CDbl(txtSideTwo.Text)
  txtHyp.Text = CStr(Hypotenuse(a, b))
End Sub

Function Hypotenuse(ByVal a As Double, ByVal b As Double) As Double
  'Calculate the hypotenuse of a right triangle
  'having sides of lengths a and b
  Return Math.Sqrt(a ^ 2 + b ^ 2)
End Function
```

[Run, type 3 and 4 into the text boxes, and then click the button.]

 Example 4　　The following program uses the Function procedure FutureValue. With the responses shown, the program computes the balance in a savings account when $100 is deposited for five years at 4% interest compounded quarterly. Interest is earned four times per year at the rate of 1% per interest period. There will be 4 * 5, or 20, interest periods.

OBJECT	PROPERTY	SETTING
frmBank	Text	Bank Deposit
lblAmount	Text	Amount of bank deposit:
txtAmount		
lblRate	Text	Annual rate of interest:
txtRate		
lblNumComp	AutoSize	False
	Text	Number of times interest is compounded per year:
txtNumComp		
lblNumYrs	Text	Number of years:
txtNumYrs		
btnCompute	Text	Compute Balance
lblBalance	Text	Balance:
txtBalance	ReadOnly	True

```
Private Sub btnCompute_Click(...) Handles btnCompute.Click
  'Find the future value of a bank deposit
  Dim p As Double    'principal, the amount deposited
  Dim r As Double    'annual rate of interest (expressed as a decimal)
  Dim c As Double    'number of times interest is compounded per year
  Dim n As Double    'number of years
  InputData(p, r, c, n)
  DisplayBalance(p, r, c, n)
End Sub

Sub InputData(ByRef p As Double, ByRef r As Double, _
              ByRef c As Double, ByRef n As Double)
  'Get the four values from the text boxes
  p = CDbl(txtAmount.Text)
  r = CDbl(txtRate.Text)
  c = CDbl(txtNumComp.Text)
  n = CDbl(txtNumYrs.Text)
End Sub

Sub DisplayBalance(ByVal p As Double, ByVal r As Double, _
                   ByVal c As Double, ByVal n As Double)
  'Display the balance in a text box
  Dim balance As Double
  balance = FutureValue(p, r, c, n)
  txtBalance.Text = FormatCurrency(balance)
End Sub

Function FutureValue(ByVal p As Double, ByVal r As Double, _
                     ByVal c As Double, ByVal n As Double) As Double
  'Find the future value of a bank savings account
  'p  principal, the amount deposited
  'r  annual rate of interest
  'c  number of times interest is compounded per year
  'n  number of years
  Dim i As Double    'interest rate per period
  Dim m As Double    'total number of times interest is compounded
  i = r / c
  m = c * n
  Return p * ((1 + i) ^ m)
End Function
```

[Run, type 100, .04, 4, and 5 into the text boxes, then click the button.]

User-Defined Functions Having No Parameters

Function procedures, like Sub procedures, need not have any parameters.

 Example 5 The following program uses a parameterless Function procedure.

```
Private Sub btnDisplay_Click(...) Handles btnDisplay.Click
  'Request and display a saying
  txtBox.Text = Saying()
End Sub

Function Saying() As String
  'Retrieve a saying from the user
  Dim strVar As String
  strVar = InputBox("What is your favorite saying?")
  Return strVar
End Function
```

[Run, click the button, and then type "Less is more." into the message box.]

The saying "Less is more." is displayed in the text box.

User-Defined Boolean-Valued Functions

So far, the values returned by Function procedures have been numbers or strings. However, a Function procedure can also return a Boolean value; that is, True or False.

 Example 6 The following program uses a Boolean-valued function to determine whether a word input by the user is a vowel word; that is, contains every vowel. Some examples of vowel words are "sequoia," "facetious," and "dialogue." The Function procedure IsVowelWord examines the word for vowels one at a time and terminates when a vowel is found to be missing.

```
Private Sub btnDetermine_Click(...) Handles btnDetermine.Click
  Dim word As String
  word = txtWord.Text.ToUpper
  If IsVowelWord(word) Then
    txtOutput.Text = word & " contains every vowel."
  Else
    txtOutput.Text = word & " does not contain every vowel."
  End If
End Sub

Function IsVowelWord(ByVal word As String) As Boolean
  If word.IndexOf("A") = -1 Then
    Return False
  End If
  If word.IndexOf("E") = -1 Then
    Return False
  End If
  If word.IndexOf("I") = -1 Then
    Return False
  End If
  If word.IndexOf("O") = -1 Then
    Return False
  End If
  If word.IndexOf("U") = -1 Then
    Return False
  End If
  Return True      'All vowels are present.
End Function
```

[Run, type a word into the top text box, and click the button.]

■ Comparing Function Procedures with Sub Procedures

Function procedures differ from Sub procedures in the way they are accessed. Sub procedures are invoked with Call statements, whereas functions are invoked by placing them where you would otherwise expect to find a literal, variable, or expression. Unlike a Function procedure, a Sub procedure can't be used in an expression.

Function procedures can perform the same tasks as Sub procedures. For instance, they can request input and display text. However, Function procedures are primarily used to calculate a single value. Normally, Sub procedures are used to carry out other tasks.

The Sub procedures considered in this book terminate only when End Sub is reached. On the other hand, Function procedures terminate as soon as the first Return statement is executed. For instance, if a Return statement is followed by a sequence of statements and the Return statement is executed, then the sequence of statements will not be executed.

■ Named Constants

Often a program uses a special constant whose value does not change during program execution. Some examples might be the minimum wage, the sales tax rate, and the name of a master file. Programs are often made easier to understand and maintain if such a constant is given a name. Visual Basic has an object, called a **named constant**, that serves this purpose. A named constant is declared and used in a manner similar to a variable. The two main differences are that in the declaration of a named constant, Dim is replaced with Const, and the value of the named constant cannot be changed by the program. Named constants can be thought of as read-only variables.

A named constant is declared and assigned a value with a statement of the form

```
Const CONSTANT_NAME As DataType = value
```

The standard convention is that the names be written in uppercase letters with words separated by underscore characters. Like a Dim statement, a Const statement can be placed in the Declaration sections of a program (for class-level scope) or in a procedure (for local scope). Named constant declarations in procedures usually are placed near the beginning of the procedure. Some examples of named constant declarations are

```
Const INTEREST_RATE As Double = 0.04
Const MINIMUM_VOTING_AGE As Integer = 18
Const MASTER_FILE As String = "CUSTOMERS.TXT"
```

Examples of statements using these named constants are

```
interestEarned = INTEREST_RATE * CDbl(txtAmount.Text)

If (age >= MINIMUM_VOTING_AGE) Then
  MessageBox.Show("You are eligible to vote")
End If

Dim sr As IO.StreamReader = IO.File.OpenText(MASTER_FILE)
```

Although the value of a named constant such as **INTEREST_RATE** will not change during the execution of a program, the value may change over time. The programmer can adjust to this change by altering just one line of code instead of searching through the entire program for each occurrence of the old interest rate.

Practice Problems 5.3

1. Suppose a program contains the lines
```
Dim n As Double, x As String
lstOutput.Items.Add(Arc(n, x))
```
What types of inputs (numeric or string) and output does the function Arc have?

2. What is displayed in the text box when btnCompute is clicked?

```
Private Sub btnCompute_Click(...) Handles btnCompute.Click
  'How many gallons of apple cider can we make?
  Dim gallonsPerBushel, apples As Double
  GetData(gallonsPerBushel, apples)
  DisplayNumOfGallons(gallonsPerBushel, apples)
End Sub

Function Cider(ByVal g As Double, ByVal x As Double) As Double
  Return g * x
End Function
Sub DisplayNumOfGallons(ByVal galPerBu As Double, _
                        ByVal apples As Double)
  txtOutput.Text = "You can make " & Cider(galPerBu, apples) & _
                  " gallons of cider."
End Sub

Sub GetData(ByRef gallonsPerBushel As Double, _
            ByRef apples As Double)
  'gallonsPerBushel: Number of gallons of cider one bushel makes
  'apples: Number of bushels of apples available
  gallonsPerBushel = 3
  apples = 9
End Sub
```

EXERCISES 5.3

In Exercises 1 through 10, determine the output displayed when the button is clicked.

1.
```
Private Sub btnConvert_Click(...) Handles btnConvert.Click
  'Convert Celsius to Fahrenheit
  Dim temp As Double = 95
  txtOutput.Text = CStr(CtoF(temp))
End Sub

Function CtoF(ByVal t As Double) As Double
  Return (9 / 5) * t + 32
End Function
```

2.
```
Private Sub btnDisplay_Click(...) Handles btnDisplay.Click
  Dim acres As Double 'Number of acres in a parking lot
  acres = 5
  txtOutput.Text = "You can park about " & Cars(acres) & " cars."
End Sub

Function Cars(ByVal x As Double) As Double
  'Number of cars that can be parked
  Return 100 * x
End Function
```

3.
```
Private Sub btnDisplay_Click(...) Handles btnDisplay.Click
  'Rule of 72
  Dim p As Double
```

```
   p = CDbl(txtPopGr.Text) 'Population growth as a percent
   txtOutput.Text = "The population will double in " & _
                    DoublingTime(p) & " years."
End Sub

Function DoublingTime(ByVal x As Double) As Double
   'Estimate time required for a population to double
   'at a growth rate of x percent
   Return 72 / x
End Function
```

(Assume the text box txtPopGr contains the number 3.)

4.
```
Private Sub btnDetermine_Click(...) Handles btnDetermine.Click
   Dim numOne, numTwo, numThree, numLowest As Double
   numOne = CDbl(txtOne.Text)
   numTwo = CDbl(txtTwo.Text)
   numThree = CDbl(txtThree.Text)
   numLowest = FindLowest(numOne, numTwo, numThree)
   txtLowest.Text = CStr(numLowest)
End Sub

Function FindLowest(ByVal x As Double, ByVal y As Double, _
                    ByVal z As Double) As Double
   'Find the lowest of three numbers denoted by x, y, and z
   Dim lowest As Double
   lowest = x
   If y < lowest Then
     lowest = y
   End If
   If z < lowest Then
     lowest = z
   End If
   Return lowest
End Function
```

(Assume the first three text boxes contain the numbers 7, 4, and 3.)

5.
```
Private Sub btnDisplay_Click(...) Handles btnDisplay.Click
   'Compute volume of a cylinder
   Dim r As Double = 1    'Radius
   Dim h As Double = 2    'Height
   DisplayVolume(r, h)
   r = 3
   h = 4
   DisplayVolume(r, h)
End Sub

Function Area(ByVal r As Double) As Double
   'Compute area of a circle of radius r
   Return 3.14159 * r ^ 2
End Function
```

```
Sub DisplayVolume(ByVal r As Double, ByVal h As Double)
  lstBox.Items.Add("Volume of cylinder having base area " & _
        Area(r) & " and height " & h & " is " & (h * Area(r)))
End Sub
```

6. ```
Private Sub btnDisplay_Click(...) Handles btnDisplay.Click
    'Determine the day of the week from its number
    Dim days As String, num As Integer
    days = "SunMonTueWedThuFriSat"
    num = CInt(InputBox("Enter the number of the day."))
    txtOutput.Text = "The day is " & DayOfWk(days, num) & "."
End Sub

Function DayOfWk(ByVal x As String, ByVal n As Integer) As String
  'x String containing 3-letter abbreviations of days
  'n The number of the day
  Dim position As Integer
  position = 3 * n - 3
  Return x.Substring(position, 3)
End Function
```

(Assume the response is 4.)

7. ```
Private Sub btnDisplay_Click(...) Handles btnDisplay.Click
    'Demonstrate local variables
    Dim word As String = "Choo "
    txtOutput.Text = TypeOfTrain()
End Sub

Function TypeOfTrain() As String
  'Concatenate the value of word with itself
  Dim word As String
  word &= word
  Return word & "train"
End Function
```

8. ```
Private Sub btnDisplay_Click(...) Handles btnDisplay.Click
    'Triple a number
    Dim num As Double = 5
    lstOutput.Items.Add(Triple(num))
    lstOutput.Items.Add(num)
End Sub

Function Triple(ByVal x As Double) As Double
  Dim num As Double = 3
  Return num * x
End Function
```

9. ```
Private Sub btnDisplay_Click(...) Handles btnDisplay.Click
    Dim word As String
    word = "moral"
    Negative(word)
```

```
    word = "political"
    Negative(word)
  End Sub

  Function AddA(ByVal word As String) As String
    Return "a" & word
  End Function

  Sub Negative(ByVal word As String)
    lstOutput.Items.Add(word & " has the negative " & AddA(word))
  End Sub
```

10.
```
Const POPULATION_UNIT As Double = 100000

Private Sub btnDisplay_Click(...) Handles btnDisplay.Click
  Dim city As String, pop, shrinks As Double
  Dim sr As IO.StreamReader = IO.File.OpenText("DOCS.TXT")
  city = sr.ReadLine
  pop = CDbl(sr.ReadLine)
  shrinks = CDbl(sr.ReadLine)
  DisplayData(city, pop, shrinks)
  city = sr.ReadLine
  pop = CDbl(sr.ReadLine)
  shrinks = CDbl(sr.ReadLine)
  DisplayData(city, pop, shrinks)
  sr.Close()
End Sub

Sub DisplayData(ByVal city As String, ByVal pop As Double, _
                ByVal shrinks As Double)
  lstBox.Items.Add(city & " has " & ShrinkDensity(pop, shrinks) & _
  " psychiatrists per " & FormatNumber(POPULATION_UNIT,0) & " people.")
End Sub

Function ShrinkDensity(ByVal pop As Double, _
                       ByVal shrinks As Double) As Double
  Return Int(POPULATION_UNIT * (shrinks / pop))
End Function
```

(Assume the six lines of the file DOCS.TXT contain the following data: Boston, 2824000, 8602, Denver, 1633000, 3217.)

In Exercises 11 and 12, identify the errors.

11.
```
Private Sub btnDisplay_Click(...) Handles btnDisplay.Click
  'Select a greeting
  Dim answer As Integer
  answer = CInt(InputBox("Enter 1 or 2."))
  txtOutput.Text = CStr(Greeting(answer))
End Sub

Function Greeting(ByVal x As Integer) As Integer
  Return "hellohi ya".Substring(5 * (x - 1), 5)
End Function
```

12.
```
Private Sub btnDisplay_Click(...) Handles btnDisplay.Click
    Dim word As String
    word = InputBox("What is your favorite word?")
    txtOutput.Text = "When the word is written twice, " & _
                    Twice(word) & " letters are used."
End Sub

Function Twice(ByVal w As String) As Integer
    'Compute twice the length of a string
    Dim len As Integer
    Return len = 2 * w.Length
End Function
```

In Exercises 13 through 21, construct user-defined functions to carry out the primary task(s) of the program.

13. To determine the number of square centimeters of tin needed to make a tin can, add the square of the radius of the can to the product of the radius and height of the can, and then multiply this sum by 6.283. Write a program that requests the radius and height of a tin can in centimeters as input and displays the number of square centimeters required to make the can.

14. According to Plato, a man should marry a woman whose age is half his age plus seven years. Write a program that requests a man's age as input and gives the ideal age of his wife.

15. The federal government developed the body mass index (BMI) to determine ideal weights. Body mass index is calculated as 703 times the weight in pounds, divided by the square of the height in inches, and then rounded to the nearest whole number. Write a program that accepts a person's weight and height as input and gives the person's body mass index. **Note:** A BMI of 19 to 25 corresponds to a healthy weight.

16. In order for exercise to be beneficial to the cardiovascular system, the heart rate (number of heart beats per minute) must exceed a value called the *training heart rate*, THR. A person's THR can be calculated from his age and resting heart rate (pulse when first awakening) as follows:

(a) Calculate the maximum heart rate as $220 -$ age.
(b) Subtract the resting heart rate from the maximum heart rate.
(c) Multiply the result in step (b) by 60%, and then add the resting heart rate.

Write a program to request a person's age and resting heart rate as input and display their THR. (Test the program with an age of 20 and a resting heart rate of 70, and then determine *your* training heart rate.)

17. The three components for a serving of popcorn at a movie theater are popcorn, butter substitute, and a bucket. Write a program that requests the cost of these three items and the price of the serving as input and then displays the profit. (Test the program where popcorn costs 5 cents, butter substitute costs 2 cents, the bucket costs 25 cents, and the selling price is $5.)

18. Rewrite the population-density program from Example 4 of Section 5.1 using a function to calculate the population density.

19. The original cost of airmail letters was 5 cents for the first ounce and 10 cents for each additional ounce. Write a program to compute the cost of a letter whose weight is given by the user in a text box. Use a function called Ceil that rounds noninteger numbers up to the next integer. The function Ceil can be defined by $\text{Ceil}(x) = -\text{Int}(-x)$. (Test the program with the weights 4, 1, 2.5, and .5 ounces.)

20. Suppose a fixed amount of money is deposited at the beginning of each month into a savings account paying 6% interest compounded monthly. After each deposit is made, [new balance] = 1.005 * [previous balance one month ago] + [fixed amount]. Write a program that requests the fixed amount of the deposits as input and displays the balance after each of the first four deposits. A sample outcome when 800 is typed into the text box for the amount deposited each month follows.

```
Month 1      800.00
Month 2    1,604.00
Month 3    2,412.02
Month 4    3,224.08
```

21. Write a program to request the name of a United States senator as input and display the address and greeting for a letter to the senator. Assume the name has two parts, and use a function to determine the senator's last name. A sample outcome when Robert Smith is typed into the input dialog box requesting the senator's name follows.

```
The Honorable Robert Smith
United States Senate
Washington, DC 20001

Dear Senator Smith,
```

Solutions to Practice Problems 5.3

---

1. The first argument, n, takes a value of type Double and the second argument, x, takes a String value; therefore, the input consists of a number and a string. From the two lines shown here, there is no way to determine the type of the output. This can be determined only by looking at the definition of the function.

2. **You can make 27 gallons of cider.** In this program, the function was called by a Sub procedure rather than by an event procedure.

5.4   Modular Design

▇ Top-Down Design

Full-featured software usually requires large programs. Writing the code for an event procedure in such a Visual Basic program might pose a complicated problem. One method programmers use to make a complicated problem more understandable is to divide it into smaller, less complex subproblems. Repeatedly using a "divide-and-conquer" approach to break up a large problem into smaller subproblems is called **stepwise refinement**. Stepwise refinement is part of a larger methodology of writing programs known as **top-down design.** The term top-down refers to the fact that the more general tasks occur near the top of the design and tasks representing their refinement occur below. Top-down design and structured programming emerged as techniques to enhance programming productivity. Their use leads to programs that are easier to read and maintain. They also produce programs containing fewer initial errors, with these errors being easier to find and correct. When such programs are later modified, there is a much smaller likelihood of introducing new errors.

The goal of top-down design is to break a problem into individual tasks, or **modules,** that can easily be transcribed into pseudocode, flowcharts, or a program. First, a problem is restated as several simpler problems depicted as modules. Any modules that remain too complex are broken down further. The process of refining modules continues until the smallest modules can be coded directly. Each stage of refinement adds a more complete specification of what tasks must be performed. The main idea in top-down design is to go from the general to the specific. This process of dividing and organizing a problem into tasks can be pictured using a hierarchy chart. When using top-down design, certain criteria should be met:

1. The design should be easily readable and emphasize small module size.

2. Modules proceed from general to specific as you read down the chart.

3. The modules, as much as possible, should be single minded. That is, they should only perform a single well-defined task.

4. Modules should be independent of each other as much as possible, and any relationships among modules should be specified.

This process is illustrated with the following example.

 Example 1 The chart in Figure 5.7 is a hierarchy chart for a program that gives certain information about a car loan. The inputs are the amount of the loan, the duration (in years), and the interest rate. The output consists of the monthly payment and the amount of interest paid during the first month. In the broadest sense, the program calls for obtaining the input, making calculations, and displaying the output. Figure 5.7 shows these tasks as the first row of a hierarchy chart.

FIGURE 5.7 **Beginning of a hierarchy chart for the car loan program.**

Each of these tasks can be refined into more specific subtasks. (See Figure 5.8 on the next page for the final hierarchy chart.) Most of the subtasks in the third row are straightforward and do not require further refinement. For instance, the first month's interest is computed by multiplying the amount of the loan by one-twelfth of the annual

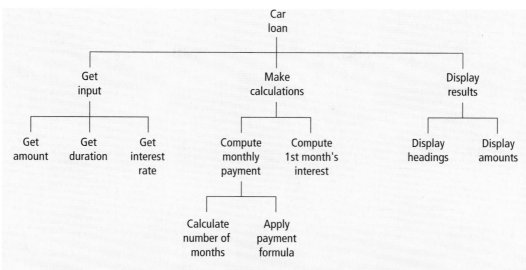

FIGURE 5.8   Hierarchy chart for the car loan program.

rate of interest. The most complicated subtask, the computation of the monthly payment, has been broken down further. This task is carried out by applying a standard formula found in finance books; however, the formula requires the number of payments.

It is clear from the hierarchy chart that the top modules manipulate the modules beneath them. While the higher-level modules control the flow of the program, the lower-level modules do the actual work. By designing the top modules first, specific processing decisions can be delayed.

■ Structured Programming

A program is said to be **structured** if it meets modern standards of program design. Although there is no formal definition of the term **structured program**, computer scientists are in uniform agreement that such programs should have modular design and use only the three types of logical structures discussed in Chapter 1: sequences, decisions, and loops.

Sequences: Statements are executed one after another.

Decisions: One of several blocks of program code is executed based on a test for some condition.

Loops (iteration): One or more statements are executed repeatedly as long as a specified condition is true.

Chapters 4 and 6 are devoted to decisions and loops, respectively.

One major shortcoming of the earliest programming languages was their reliance on the GoTo statement. This statement was used to branch (that is, jump) from one line of a program to another. It was common for a program to be composed of a convoluted tangle of branchings that produced confusing code referred to as **spaghetti code**. At the heart of structured programming is the assertion of E. W. Dijkstra that GoTo statements should be eliminated entirely because they lead to complex and confusing programs. Two Italians, C. Bohm and G. Jacopini, were able to prove that GoTo

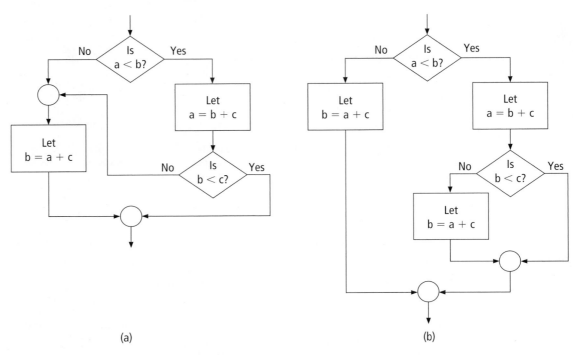

(a)

(b)

FIGURE 5.9 Flowcharts illustrating the removal of a GoTo statement.

statements are not needed and that any program can be written using only the three types of logic structures discussed before.

Structured programming requires that all programs be written using sequences, decisions, and loops. Nesting of such statements is allowed. All other logical constructs, such as GoTos, are not allowed. The logic of a structured program can be pictured using a flowchart that flows smoothly from top to bottom without unstructured branching (GoTos). The portion of a flowchart shown in Figure 5.9(a) contains the equivalent of a GoTo statement and, therefore, is not structured. A correctly structured version of the flowchart in which the logic flows from the top to the bottom appears in Figure 5.9(b).

■ Advantages of Structured Programming

The goal of structured programming is to create correct programs that are easy to write, understand, and change. Let us now take a closer look at the way modular design, along with a limited number of logical structures, contributes to attaining these goals.

1. *Easy to write*.

Modular design increases the programmer's productivity by allowing him or her to look at the big picture first and focus on the details later. During the actual coding, the programmer works with a manageable chunk of the program and does not have to think about an entire complex program.

Several programmers can work on a single large program, each taking responsibility for a specific module.

Studies have shown structured programs require significantly less time to write than standard programs.

Often, procedures written for one program can be reused in other programs requiring the same task. Not only is time saved in writing a program, but reliability is enhanced, because reused procedures will already be tested and debugged. A procedure that can be used in many programs is said to be **reusable**.

2. *Easy to debug.*

Because each procedure is specialized to perform just one task or several related tasks, a procedure can be checked individually to determine its reliability. A dummy program, called a **driver**, is set up to test the procedure. The driver contains the minimum definitions needed to call the procedure to be tested. For instance, if the procedure to be tested is a function, the driver program assigns diverse values to the arguments and then examines the corresponding function return values. The arguments should contain both typical and special-case values.

The program can be tested and debugged as it is being designed with a technique known as **stub programming**. In this technique, the key event procedures and perhaps some of the smaller procedures are coded first. Dummy procedures, or stubs, are written for the remaining procedures. Initially, a stub procedure might consist of a message box to indicate that the procedure has been called, and thereby confirm that the procedure was called at the right time. Later, a stub might simply display values passed to it in order to confirm not only that the procedure was called, but also that it received the correct values from the calling procedure. A stub also can assign new values to one or more of its parameters to simulate either input or computation. This provides greater control of the conditions being tested. The stub procedure is always simpler than the actual procedure it represents. Although the stub program is only a skeleton of the final program, the program's structure can still be debugged and tested. (The stub program consists of some coded procedures and the stub procedures.)

Old-fashioned unstructured programs consist of a sequence of instructions that are not grouped for specific tasks. The logic of such a program is cluttered with details and therefore difficult to follow. Needed tasks are easily left out and crucial details easily neglected. Tricky parts of the program cannot be isolated and examined. Bugs are difficult to locate because they might be present in any part of the program.

3. *Easy to understand.*

The interconnections of the procedures reveal the modular design of the program.

The meaningful procedure names, along with relevant comments, identify the tasks performed by the modules.

The meaningful variable names help the programmer to recall the purpose of each variable.

4. *Easy to change.*

Because a structured program is self-documenting, it can easily be deciphered by another programmer.

Modifying a structured program often amounts to inserting or altering a few procedures rather than revising an entire complex program. The programmer does not even have to look at most of the program. This is in sharp contrast to the situation with unstructured programs where one must understand the entire logic of the program before any changes can be made with confidence.

■ Object-Oriented Programming

An object is an encapsulation of data and code that operates on the data. Like controls, objects have properties, respond to methods, and raise events. The most effective type of programming for complex problems is called **object-oriented** design. An object-oriented program can be viewed as a collection of cooperating objects. Most modern programmers use a blend of traditional structured programming along with object-oriented design.

Visual Basic.NET was the first version of Visual Basic that was truly object-oriented; in fact, every element such as a control or a string is actually an object. This book illustrates the building blocks of Visual Basic in the initial chapters and then puts them together using object-oriented techniques in Chapter 11. Throughout the book, an object-oriented approach is taken whenever feasible.

■ A Relevant Quote

We end this section with a few paragraphs from *Dirk Gently's Holistic Detective Agency*, by Douglas Adams, Pocketbooks, 1987:

> "What really is the point of trying to teach anything to anybody?"
> This question seemed to provoke a murmur of sympathetic approval from up and down the table.
> Richard continued, "What I mean is that if you really want to understand something, the best way is to try and explain it to someone else. That forces you to sort it out in your own mind. And the more slow and dim-witted your pupil, the more you have to break things down into more and more simple ideas. And that's really the essence of programming. By the time you've sorted out a complicated idea into little steps that even a stupid machine can deal with, you've certainly learned something about it yourself. The teacher usually learns more than the pupil. Isn't that true?"

5.5   A Case Study: Weekly Payroll

This case study processes a weekly payroll using the 2008 Employer's Tax Guide. Table 5.3 shows typical data used by a company's payroll office. (**Note:** A withholding allowance is sometimes referred to as an exemption.) These data are processed to produce the information

TABLE 5.3	Employee data.				
Name	Hourly Wage	Hours Worked	Withholding Allowances	Marital Status	Previous Year-to-Date Earnings
Al Clark	$45.50	38	4	Married	$88,600.00
Ann Miller	$44.00	35	3	Married	$68,200.00
John Smith	$17.95	50	1	Single	$30,604.75
Sue Taylor	$25.50	43	2	Single	$36,295.50

in Table 5.4 that is supplied to each employee along with his or her paycheck. The program should request the data from Table 5.3 for an individual as input and produce output similar to that in Table 5.4.

TABLE 5.4	Payroll information.				
Name	Current Earnings	Yr. to Date Earnings	FICA Taxes	Income Tax Wh.	Check Amount
Al Clark	$1,729.00	$90,329.00	$132.27	$188.09	$1,408.64

The items in Table 5.4 should be calculated as follows:

Current Earnings: hourly wage times hours worked (with time-and-a-half after 40 hours)

Year-to-Date Earnings: previous year-to-date earnings plus current earnings

FICA Taxes: sum of 6.2 percent of first $102,000 of earnings (Social Security benefits tax) and 1.45 percent of total wages (Medicare tax)

Federal Income Tax Withheld: subtract $67.31 from the current earnings for each withholding allowance and use Table 5.5 or Table 5.6, depending on marital status

Check Amount: [current earnings] − [FICA taxes] − [income tax withheld]

TABLE 5.5	2008 Federal income tax withheld for a single person paid weekly.
Adjusted Weekly Income	Income Tax Withheld
$0 to $51	$0
Over $51 to $198	10% of amount over $51
Over $198 to $653	$14.70 + 15% of amount over $198
Over $653 to $1,533	$82.95 + 25% of amount over $653
Over $1,533 to $3,202	$302.95 + 28% of amount over $1,533
Over $3,202 to $6,916	$770.27 + 33% of amount over $3,202
Over $6,916	$1,995.89 + 35% of amount over $6,916

TABLE 5.6	2008 Federal income tax withheld for a married person paid weekly.
Adjusted Weekly Income	Income Tax Withheld
$0 to $154	$0
Over $154 to $453	10% of amount over $154
Over $453 to $1,388	$29.90 + 15% of amount over $453
Over $1,388 to $2,651	$170.15 + 25% of amount over $1,388
Over $2,651 to $3,994	$485.90 + 28% of amount over $2,651
Over $3,994 to $7,021	$861.94 + 33% of amount over $3,994
Over $7,021	$1,860.85 + 35% of amount over $7,021

Designing the Weekly Payroll Program

After the data for an employee have been gathered from the text boxes, the program must compute the five items appearing in Table 5.4 and then display the payroll information. The five computations form the basic tasks of the program:

1. Compute current earnings.

2. Compute year-to-date earnings.

3. Compute FICA tax.

4. Compute federal income tax withheld.

5. Compute paycheck amount (that is, take-home pay).

Tasks 1, 2, 3, and 5 are fairly simple. Each involves applying a formula to given data. (For instance, if hours worked are at most 40, then [Current Earnings] = [Hourly Wage] times [Hours Worked].) Thus, we won't break down these tasks any further. Task 4 is more complicated, so we continue to divide it into smaller subtasks.

4. *Compute Federal Income Tax Withheld.* First, the employee's pay is adjusted for withholding allowances, and then the amount of income tax to be withheld is computed. The computation of the income tax withheld differs for married and single individuals. Task 4 is, therefore, divided into the following subtasks:

4.1. Compute pay adjusted by withholding allowances.

4.3. Compute income tax withheld for single employee.

4.3. Compute income tax withheld for married employee.

The hierarchy chart in Figure 5.10 shows the stepwise refinement of the problem.

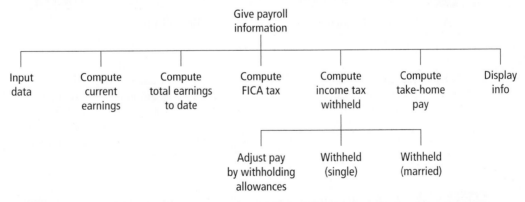

FIGURE 5.10 **Hierarchy chart for the weekly payroll program.**

Pseudocode for the Display Payroll Event

INPUT employee data (Sub procedure InputData)
COMPUTE CURRENT GROSS PAY (Function Gross_Pay)
COMPUTE TOTAL EARNINGS TO DATE (Function Total_Pay)
COMPUTE FICA TAX (Function FICA_Tax)
COMPUTE INCOME TAX WITHHELD (Function Fed_Tax)

Adjust pay for withholding allowances
If employee is single Then
    COMPUTE INCOME TAX WITHHELD (Function TaxSingle)
Else
    COMPUTE INCOME TAX WITHHELD (Function TaxMarried)
End If
COMPUTE PAYCHECK AMOUNT (Function Net_Check)
DISPLAY PAYROLL INFORMATION (Sub procedure ShowPayroll)

▇ Writing the Weekly Payroll Program

The btnDisplay_Click event procedure calls a sequence of seven procedures. Table 5.7 shows the tasks and the procedures that perform the tasks.

TABLE 5.7   Tasks and their procedures.

Task	Procedure
0. Input employee data.	InputData
1. Compute current earnings.	Gross_Pay
2. Compute year-to-date earnings.	Total_Pay
3. Compute FICA tax.	FICA_Tax
4. Compute federal income tax withheld.	Fed_Tax
4.1 Compute adjusted pay.	Fed_Tax
4.2 Compute amount withheld for single employee.	TaxSingle
4.3 Compute amount withheld for married employee.	TaxMarried
5. Compute paycheck amount.	Net_Check
6. Display payroll information.	ShowPayroll

▇ The Program and the User Interface

Figure 5.11 and Table 5.8 define the user interface for the Weekly Payroll Program. Figure 5.12 shows a sample output.

FIGURE 5.11   Template for entering payroll data.

TABLE 5.8	Objects and initial properties for the weekly payroll program.	
Object	Property	Setting
frmPayroll	Text	Weekly Payroll
lblName	Text	Employee name:
txtName		
lblWage	Text	Hourly wage:
txtWage		
lblHours	Text	Number of hours worked:
txtHours		
lblAllowances	AutoSize	False
	Text	Number of withholding allowances:
txtAllowances		
lblMarital	Text	Marital status (M or S):
mtxtMarital	Mask	L
lblPriorPay	Text	Total pay prior to this week:
txtPriorPay		
btnDisplay	Text	Display Payroll
btnNext	Text	Next Employee
btnQuit	Text	Quit
lstResults	Font	Courier New

FIGURE 5.12 Sample output of weekly payroll program.

```
Private Sub btnDisplay_Click(...) Handles btnDisplay.Click
    Dim empName As String = ""    'Name of employee
    Dim hrWage As Double          'Hourly wage
    Dim hrsWorked As Double       'Hours worked this week
    Dim allowances As Integer     'Number of withholding allowances
    '                                for employee
    Dim mStatus As String = ""    'Marital status: S - Single; M - Married
    Dim prevPay As Double         'Total pay for year excluding this week
    Dim pay As Double             'This week's pay before taxes
    Dim totalPay As Double        'Total pay for year including this week
```

```
    Dim ficaTax As Double        'FICA taxes for this week
    Dim fedTax As Double         'Federal income tax withheld this week
    Dim check As Double          'Paycheck this week (take-home pay)
    'Obtain data, compute payroll, display results
    InputData(empName, hrWage, hrsWorked, allowances, _
                                      mStatus, prevPay)     'Task 0
    pay = Gross_Pay(hrWage, hrsWorked)                      'Task 1
    totalPay = Total_Pay(prevPay, pay)                     'Task 2
    ficaTax = FICA_Tax(pay, prevPay, totalPay)            'Task 3
    fedTax = Fed_Tax(pay, allowances, mStatus)            'Task 4
    check = Net_Check(pay, ficaTax, fedTax)               'Task 5
    ShowPayroll(empName, pay, totalPay, ficaTax, fedTax, check)  'Task 6
End Sub

Private Sub btnNext_Click(...) Handles btnNext.Click
    'Clear all text boxes for next employee's data
    txtName.Clear()
    txtWage.Clear()
    txtHours.Clear()
    txtAllowances.Clear()
    mtxtMarital.Clear()
    txtPriorPay.Clear()
    lstResults.Items.Clear()
End Sub

Private Sub btnQuit_Click(...) Handles btnQuit.Click
    End
End Sub

Sub InputData(ByRef empName As String, ByRef hrWage As Double, _
            ByRef hrsWorked As Double, ByRef allowances As Integer, _
            ByRef mStatus As String, ByRef prevPay As Double)
    'Task 0: Get payroll data for employee
    empName = txtName.Text
    hrWage = CDbl(txtWage.Text)
    hrsWorked = CDbl(txtHours.Text)
    allowances = CInt(txtAllowances.Text)
    mStatus = mtxtMarital.Text.ToUpper.Substring(0, 1)   'M or S
    prevPay = CDbl(txtPriorPay.Text)
End Sub

Function Gross_Pay(ByVal hrWage As Double, ByVal hrsWorked As Double) _
        As Double
    'Task 1: Compute weekly pay before taxes
    If hrsWorked <= 40 Then
      Return hrsWorked * hrWage
    Else
      Return 40 * hrWage + (hrsWorked - 40) * 1.5 * hrWage
    End If
End Function

Function Total_Pay(ByVal prevPay As Double, _
                   ByVal pay As Double) As Double
    'Task 2: Compute total pay before taxes
    Return prevPay + pay
End Function
```

```vb
Function FICA_Tax(ByVal pay As Double, ByVal prevPay As Double, _
                 ByVal totalPay As Double) As Double
  'Task 3: Compute social security and medicare tax
  Dim socialSecurity As Double        'Social Security tax for this week
  Dim medicare As Double              'Medicare tax for this week
  Dim sum As Double                   'Sum of above two taxes
  If totalPay <= 102000 Then
    socialSecurity = 0.062 * pay
  ElseIf prevPay < 102000 Then
    socialSecurity = 0.062 * (102000 - prevPay)
  End If
  medicare = 0.0145 * pay
  sum = socialSecurity + medicare
  Return Math.Round(sum, 2)           'Round to nearest cent
End Function

Function Fed_Tax(ByVal pay As Double, ByVal allowances As Integer, _
                 ByVal mStatus As String) As Double
  'Task 4.1: Compute federal income tax rounded to two decimal places
  Dim adjPay As Double
  Dim tax As Double                   'Unrounded federal tax
  adjPay = pay - (67.31 * allowances)
  If adjPay < 0 Then
    adjPay = 0
  End If
  If mStatus = "S" Then
    tax = TaxSingle(adjPay)           'Task 4.2
  Else
    tax = TaxMarried(adjPay)          'Task 4.3
  End If
  Return Math.Round(tax, 2)           'Round to nearest cent
End Function

Function TaxSingle(ByVal adjPay As Double) As Double
  'Task 4.2: Compute federal tax withheld for single person
  Select Case adjPay
    Case 0 To 51
      Return 0
    Case 51 To 198
      Return 0.1 * (adjPay - 51)
    Case 198 To 653
      Return 14.7 + 0.15 * (adjPay - 198)
    Case 653 To 1533
      Return 82.95 + 0.25 * (adjPay - 653)
    Case 1533 To 3202
      Return 302.95 + 0.28 * (adjPay - 1533)
    Case 3202 To 6916
      Return 720.27 + 0.33 * (adjPay - 3202)
    Case Is > 6916
      Return 1995.89 + 0.35 * (adjPay - 6916)
  End Select
End Function

Function TaxMarried(ByVal adjPay As Double) As Double
  'Task 4.3: Compute federal tax withheld for married person
```

```
    Select Case adjPay
      Case 0 To 154
        Return 0
      Case 154 To 453
        Return 0.1 * (adjPay - 154)
      Case 453 To 1388
        Return 29.9 + 0.15 * (adjPay - 453)
      Case 1388 To 2651
        Return 170.15 + 0.25 * (adjPay - 1388)
      Case 2651 To 3994
        Return 485.9 + 0.28 * (adjPay - 2651)
      Case 3994 To 7021
        Return 861.94 + 0.33 * (adjPay - 3994)
      Case Is > 7021
        Return 1860.85 + 0.35 * (adjPay - 7021)
    End Select
End Function

Function Net_Check(ByVal pay As Double, ByVal ficaTax As Double, _
                   ByVal fedTax As Double) As Double
  'Task 5: Compute amount of money given to employee
  Return pay - ficaTax - fedTax
End Function

Sub ShowPayroll(ByVal empName As String, ByVal pay As Double, _
                ByVal totalPay As Double, ByVal ficaTax As Double, _
                ByVal fedTax As Double, ByVal check As Double)
  'Task 6: Display results of payroll computations
  Dim fmtStr As String = "{0,24} {1,-10:C}"
    lstResults.Items.Clear()
    lstResults.Items.Add("Payroll results for " & empName)
    lstResults.Items.Add("")
    lstResults.Items.Add(String.Format(fmtStr, "Gross pay this period:", pay))
    lstResults.Items.Add("")
    lstResults.Items.Add(String.Format(fmtStr, "Year-to-date earnings:", _
                        totalPay))
    lstResults.Items.Add("")
    lstResults.Items.Add(String.Format(fmtStr, "Fica Taxes this period:", _
                        ficaTax))
    lstResults.Items.Add("")
    lstResults.Items.Add(String.Format(fmtStr, "Income tax withheld:", fedTax))
    lstResults.Items.Add("")
    lstResults.Items.Add(String.Format(fmtStr, "Net pay (check amount):", _
                        check))
End Sub
```

■ Comments

1. In the function FICA_Tax, care has been taken to avoid computing Social Security benefits tax on income in excess of $102,000 per year. The logic of the program makes sure an employee whose income for the year crosses the $102,000 threshold during a given week is taxed only on the difference between $102,000 and his previous year-to-date income.

2. The two functions TaxMarried and TaxSingle use Select Case blocks to incorporate the tax brackets given in Tables 5.5 and 5.6 for the amount of federal income tax withheld. The upper limit of each Case clause is the same as the lower limit of the next Case clause. This ensures that fractional values for *adjPay*, such as 51.50 in the TaxSingle function, will be properly treated as part of the higher salary range.

CHAPTER 5   SUMMARY

1. A *general procedure* is a portion of a program that is accessed by event procedures or other general procedures. The two types of general procedures are *Sub procedures* and *Function procedures*.

2. *Sub procedures* are defined in blocks beginning with Sub statements and ending with End Sub statements. A Sub procedure is accessed (called) by a statement consisting of the name of the procedure.

3. *Function procedures* are defined in blocks beginning with Function statements and ending with End Function statements. A function is invoked by a reference in an expression and returns a value.

4. In any procedure, the *arguments* appearing in the calling statement must match the *parameters* of the Sub or Function statement in number, type, and order. They need not match in name.

5. The *lifetime* of a variable is the period during which it remains in memory. (Its value can change over its lifetime, but it always holds some value.) The *scope* of a variable is the portion of the program that can refer to it. A variable declared inside a Sub or Function procedure has *local* scope and is visible only inside the procedure.

6. Variables declared with a Dim statement inside a procedure are *local* to the procedure. The values of these variables are reinitialized each time the procedure is called. A variable with the same name appearing in another part of the program is treated as a different variable.

7. *Named constants* store values that do not change during the execution of a program. They are declared with Const statements and given meaningful names.

8. *Structured programming* uses modular design to refine large problems into smaller subproblems. Programs are coded using the three logical structures of sequences, decisions, and loops.

CHAPTER 5   PROGRAMMING PROJECTS

1. There are formulas in Mathematics for all sorts of sums. One due to Archimedes is a formula for the sum of the first n-1 squares:
$$1 + 4 + 9 + \ldots + (n-1)^2 = n^3/3 - n^2/2 + n/6.$$
Write a Sub procedure to calculate the sum of the squares of the integers up to $(n-1)^2$, ie., $1 + 4 + 9 + \ldots + (n-1)^2$ and use a text box to display the sum.

2. Write the Boolean-valued function Equilateral which accepts three doubles representing the sides of a triangle and which returns True if the three values sent are positive numbers and equal, and False otherwise.

3. Write the Boolean-valued function isDigit which takes a String of length 1 as a parameter and returns True if the String contains a digit (ie., "0" or "1" or "2" and so on) and False otherwise.

4. Write the Boolean-valued Sub function isAlpha which takes a String of length 1 as a parameter and returns True if the String contains a single alphabet character, upper or lower case (ie., "a" or "A" , "b" or "B" and so on) and False otherwise.

5. Use the isDigit function to create a Sub procedure CheckPhoneFormat which takes a ByVal String parameter and displays in a text box txtOutput whether or not the String has the correct format for a phone number with an area code, that is (DDD)DDD-DDDD where the Ds represent digit characters, position 0 must contain "(" , position 4 must contain ")" and position 8 contains "−".

6. There is a relationship between the ANSI ASCII code assigned to the characters '0', '1', and so on, and the numerical values of the digits they represent. The ANSI ASCII code for '0' is 48, the code for '1' is 49, and so on up to '9' whose code is 57. In Visual Basic, the function ASC takes a String argument and returns the ANSI ASCII code for its first character. So, for example, ASC ("9") is 57. Write a function procedure which accepts a String containing a digit character as a parameter and returns its appropriate digit value. Return a −1 value to signal an error if the String contains more than one character or if the String's character value is not in the range "0" . "9".

7. Two ways to convert strings to a particular case are the Visual Basic functions ToUpper and ToLower which convert the String argument to the given case. Using ToUpper and the substring function of String, write a Sub procedure which accepts a String as a parameter in the form "first last" and returns the name with proper capitalization. So, if the String parameter were "john smith" the function would return "John Smith".

8. Reformat a name which appears in the form "First Last" into the form, "Last, F." so "John Smith" would become "Smith, J."

6

Repetition

6.1   Do Loops

A **loop**, one of the most important structures in Visual Basic, is used to repeat a sequence of statements a number of times. At each repetition, or **pass**, the statements act upon variables whose values are changing.

The **Do loop** repeats a sequence of statements either as long as or until a certain condition is true. A Do statement precedes the sequence of statements, and a Loop statement follows the sequence of statements. The condition, preceded by either the word "While" or the word "Until", follows the word "Do" or the word "Loop". When Visual Basic executes a Do loop of the form

```
Do While condition
  statement(s)
Loop
```

it first checks the truth value of *condition*. If *condition* is false, then the statements inside the loop are not executed, and the program continues with the line after the Loop statement. If *condition* is true, then the statements inside the loop are executed. When the statement Loop is encountered, the entire process is repeated, beginning with the testing of *condition* in the Do While statement. In other words, the statements inside the loop are repeatedly executed only as long as (that is, while) the condition is true. Figure 6.1 contains the pseudocode and flowchart for this loop.

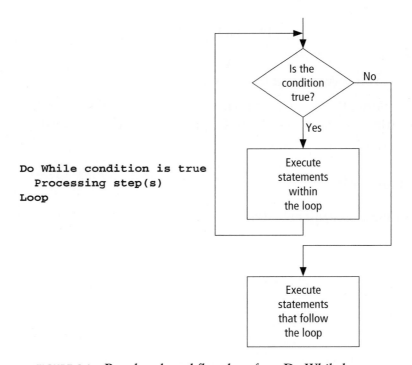

```
Do While condition is true
  Processing step(s)
Loop
```

FIGURE 6.1   Pseudocode and flowchart for a Do While loop.

Example 1   The following program, in which the condition in the Do loop is "num <= 7", displays the numbers from 1 through 7. (After the Do loop executes, the value of *num* will be 8.)

```
Private Sub btnDisplay_Click(...) Handles btnDisplay.Click
  'Display the numbers from 1 to 7
  Dim num As Integer = 1
  Do While num <= 7
    lstNumbers.Items.Add(num)
    num += 1     'Add 1 to the value of num
  Loop
End Sub
```

[Run, and click the button. The following is displayed in the list box.]

```
1
2
3
4
5
6
7
```

Do loops are commonly used to ensure that a proper response is received from the InputBox function.

 Example 2   The following program requires the user to enter a number from 1 through 3. The Do loop repeats the request until the user gives a proper response.

OBJECT	PROPERTY	SETTING
frmMovie	Text	6-1-2
btnDisplay	Text	Display a Movie Quotation
txtQuotation	ReadOnly	True

```
Private Sub btnDisplay_Click(...) Handles btnDisplay.Click
  Dim response As Integer, quotation As String = ""
  response = CInt(InputBox("Enter a number from 1 to 3."))
  Do While (response < 1) Or (response > 3)
    response = CInt(InputBox("Enter a number from 1 to 3."))
  Loop
  Select Case response
    Case 1
      quotation = "Plastics."
```

```
    Case 2
      quotation = "Rosebud."
    Case 3
      quotation = "That's all folks."
  End Select
  txtQuotation.Text = quotation
End Sub
```

[Run, and click the button.]

[Type 3 into the box and press the OK button.]

In Examples 1 and 2, the condition was checked at the top of the loop—that is, before the statements were executed. Alternatively, the condition can be checked at the bottom of the loop when the statement Loop is reached. When Visual Basic encounters a Do loop of the form

```
Do
  statement(s)
Loop Until condition
```

it executes the statements inside the loop and then checks the truth value of *condition*. If *condition* is true, then the program continues with the line after the Loop statement. If *condition* is false, then the entire process is repeated beginning with the Do statement. In other words, the statements inside the loop are executed once and then are repeatedly executed *until* the condition is true. Figure 6.2 shows the pseudocode and flowchart for this type of Do loop.

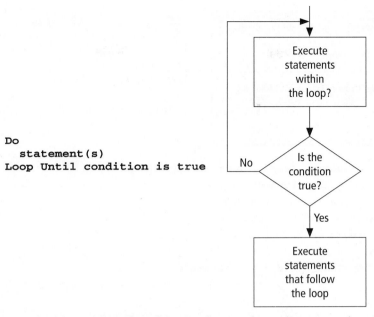

```
Do
   statement(s)
Loop Until condition is true
```

FIGURE 6.2   Pseudocode and flowchart for a Do loop with condition tested at the bottom.

  Example 3   The following program is equivalent to Example 2, except that the condition is tested at the bottom of the loop:

```
Private Sub btnDisplay_Click(...) Handles btnDisplay.Click
  Dim response As Integer, quotation As String = ""
  Do
    response = CInt(InputBox("Enter a number from 1 to 3."))
  Loop Until (response >= 1) And (response <= 3)
  Select Case response
    Case 1
      quotation = "Plastics."
    Case 2
      quotation = "Rosebud."
    Case 3
      quotation = "That's all folks."
  End Select
  txtQuotation.Text = quotation
End Sub
```

Do loops allow us to calculate useful quantities for which we might not know a simple formula.

Example 4   Suppose you deposit money into a savings account and let it accumulate at 6 percent interest compounded annually. The following program determines when you will be a millionaire:

```
Private Sub btnYears_Click(...) Handles btnYears.Click
  'Compute years required to become a millionaire
```

OBJECT	PROPERTY	SETTING
frmMillionaire	Text	6% Interest
lblAmount	Text	Amount Deposited:
txtAmount		
btnCalculate	Text	Calculate Years to Become a Millionaire
txtWhen	ReadOnly	True

```
Dim balance As Double, numYears As Integer
balance = CDbl(txtAmount.Text)
Do While balance < 1000000
  balance += 0.06 * balance
  numYears += 1
Loop
txtWhen.Text = "In " & numYears & _
               " years you will have a million dollars."
End Sub
```

[Run, type 100000 into the text box, and press the button.]

■ Comments

1. Be careful to avoid infinite loops—that is, loops that are never exited. The following loop is infinite, because the condition "balance < 1000" will always be true.

Note: Click on the form's Close button at the upper right corner of the title bar to end the program.

```
Private Sub btnButton_Click(...) Handles btnButton.Click
  'An infinite loop
  Dim balance As Double = 100, intRate As Double
  Do While balance < 1000
    balance = (1 + intRate) * balance
  Loop
  txtBalance.Text = FormatCurrency(balance)
End Sub
```

Notice that this slip-up can be avoided by adding something like **= 0.04** to the end of the Dim statement.

2. Visual Basic provides a way to break out of a Do loop. When the statement **Exit Do** is encountered in the body of a loop, execution jumps immediately to the statement following the Loop statement.

3. A variable declared inside a Do loop has block-level scope; that is, the variable cannot be referred to by code outside of the Do loop.

4. Visual Basic allows the use of the words "While" and "Until" at either the top or bottom of a Do loop. In this text, the usage of these words is restricted for the following reasons:

(a) Because any While statement can be easily converted to an Until statement and vice versa, the restriction produces no loss of capabilities and the programmer has one less matter to think about.

(b) Restricting the use simplifies reading the program. The word "While" proclaims testing at the top, and the word "Until" proclaims testing at the bottom.

(c) Certain other major structured languages only allow "While" at the top and "Until" at the bottom of a loop. Therefore, following this convention will make life easier for people already familiar with or planning to learn one of these languages.

(d) Standard pseudocode uses the word "While" to denote testing a loop at the top and the word "Until" to denote testing at the bottom.

Practice Problems 6.1

1. How do you decide whether a condition should be checked at the top of a loop or at the bottom?

2. Change the following code segment so it will be executed at least once:

```
Do While continue = "Yes"
  answer = InputBox("Do you want to continue? (Y or N)")
  If answer.ToUpper = "Y" Then
    continue = "Yes"
  Else
    continue = "No"
  End If
Loop
```

EXERCISES 6.1

In Exercises 1 through 6, determine the output displayed when the button is clicked.

```
1. Private Sub btnDisplay_Click(...) Handles btnDisplay.Click
    Dim q As Double
    q = 3
    Do While q < 15
      q = 2 * q - 1
    Loop
    txtOutput.Text = CStr(q)
  End Sub
```

2.
```
Private Sub btnDisplay_Click(...) Handles btnDisplay.Click
    Dim balance As Double = 1000
    Dim interest As Double = 0.1
    Dim n As Integer = 0            'Number of years
    Do
      lstOutput.Items.Add(n & " " & balance)
      balance = (1 + interest) * balance
      n += 1
    Loop Until (balance > 1200)
    lstOutput.Items.Add(n)
End Sub
```

3.
```
Private Sub btnDisplay_Click(...) Handles btnDisplay.Click
    'Display a message
    Dim num As Double = 4
    Dim message As String = ""
    Do
      Select Case num
        Case 1
          message = "grammer!"
          num = -1
        Case 2
          message = "re a su"
          num = (5 - num) * (3 - num)
        Case 3
          message = "per pro"
          num = 4 - num
        Case 4
          message = "You a"
          num = 2 * num - 6
      End Select
      txtOutput.Text &= message
    Loop Until (num = -1)
End Sub
```

4.
```
Private Sub btnQuiz_Click(...) Handles btnQuiz.Click
    Dim prompt As String, firstYear As Integer
    'Computer-assisted instruction
    prompt = "In what year was the IBM PC first produced?"
    lstQuiz.Items.Clear()
    Do
      firstYear = CInt(InputBox(prompt))
      Select Case firstYear
        Case 1981
          lstQuiz.Items.Add("Correct. The computer was an instant")
          lstQuiz.Items.Add("success. By the end of 1981, there")
          lstQuiz.Items.Add("was such a backlog of orders that buyers")
          lstQuiz.Items.Add("had a three-month waiting period.")
```

```
        Case Is < 1981
          lstQuiz.Items.Add("Later. The Apple II, which preceded")
          lstQuiz.Items.Add("the IBM PC, appeared in 1977.")
        Case Is > 1981
          lstQuiz.Items.Add("Earlier. The first successful IBM PC")
          lstQuiz.Items.Add("clone, the Compaq Portable, ")
          lstQuiz.Items.Add("appeared in 1983.")
      End Select
      lstQuiz.Items.Add("")
    Loop Until firstYear = 1981
  End Sub
```

(Assume that the first response is 1980 and the second response is 1981.)

5.
```
Private Sub btnDisplay_Click(...) Handles btnDisplay.Click
    'Calculate the remainder in long division
    txtOutput.Text = CStr(Remainder(3, 17))
End Sub

Function Remainder(ByVal divisor As Double, _
                   ByVal dividend As Double) As Double
  Dim sum As Double = 0
  Do While (dividend - sum) >= divisor
    sum += divisor
  Loop
  Return (dividend - sum)
End Function
```

6.
```
Private Sub btnDisplay_Click(...) Handles btnDisplay.Click
    'Simulate IndexOf; search for the letter t
    Dim info As String = "Potato"
    Dim letter As String = "t"
    Dim answer As Integer
    answer = IndexOf(info, letter)
    txtOutput.Text = CStr(answer)
End Sub

Function IndexOf(ByVal word As String, ByVal letter As String) _
              As Integer
  Dim counter As Integer = 0
  Dim current As String = ""
  Do While counter < word.Length
    current = word.Substring(counter, 1)
    If letter = current Then
      Return counter
    End If
    counter += 1 'Add 1 to the value of counter
  Loop
  'If not found then the answer is -1
  Return -1
End Function
```

In Exercises 7 through 10, identify the errors.

7.
```
Private Sub btnDisplay_Click(...) Handles btnDisplay.Click
   Dim q As Double
   q = 1
   Do While q > 0
     q = 3 * q - 1
     lstOutput.Items.Add(q)
   Loop
End Sub
```

8.
```
Private Sub btnDisplay_Click(...) Handles btnDisplay.Click
   'Display the numbers from 1 to 5
   Dim num As Integer
   Do While num <> 6
     num = 1
     lstOutput.Items.Add(num)
     num += 1
   Loop
End Sub
```

9.
```
Private Sub btnDisplay_Click(...) Handles btnDisplay.Click
   'Repeat until a yes response is given
   Dim answer As String = "N"
   Loop
     answer = InputBox("Did you chop down the cherry tree (Y/N)?")
   Do Until (answer.ToUpper = "Y")
End Sub
```

10.
```
Private Sub btnDisplay_Click(...) Handles btnDisplay.Click
   'Repeat as long as desired
   Dim n As Integer, answer As String = ""
   Do
     n += 1
     lstOutput.Items.Add(n)
     answer = InputBox("Do you want to continue (Y/N)?")
   Until answer.ToUpper = "N"
End Sub
```

In Exercises 11 through 20, replace each phrase containing "Until" with an equivalent phrase containing "While", and vice versa. For instance, the phrase (Until sum = 100) would be replaced by (While sum <> 100).

11. `Until num < 7`

12. `Until name = "Bob"`

13. `While response = "Y"`

14. `While total = 10`

15. `While name <> ""`

16. `Until balance >= 100`

```
17. While (a > 1) And (a < 3)
18. Until (ans = "") Or (n = 0)
19. Until Not (n = 0)
20. While (ans = "Y") And (n < 7)
```

In Exercises 21 and 22, write simpler and clearer code that performs the same task as the given code.

```
21. Private Sub btnDisplay_Click(...) Handles btnDisplay.Click
        Dim name As String
        name = InputBox("Enter a name:")
        lstOutput.Items.Add(name)
        name = InputBox("Enter a name:")
        lstOutput.Items.Add(name)
        name = InputBox("Enter a name:")
        lstOutput.Items.Add(name)
    End Sub
```

```
22. Private Sub btnDisplay_Click(...) Handles btnDisplay.Click
        Dim loopNum As Integer, answer As String = ""
        Do
          If loopNum >= 1 Then
            answer = InputBox("Do you want to continue (Y/N)?")
            answer = answer.ToUpper
          Else
            answer = "Y"
          End If
          If (answer = "Y") Or (loopNum = 0) Then
            loopNum += 1
            txtOutput.Text = CStr(loopNum)
          End If
        Loop Until (answer <> "Y")
    End Sub
```

23. Write a program that displays a Celsius-to-Fahrenheit conversion table. Entries in the table should range from −40 to 40 degrees Celsius in increments of 5 degrees. **Note:** The formula $f = (9/5)*c + 32$ converts Celsius to Fahrenheit.

24. The world population doubled from 3 billion in 1959 to 6 billion in 1999. Assuming that the world population has been doubling every 40 years, write a program to determine when in the past the world population was less than 6 million.

25. The world population reached 6.64 billion people in January 2008 and was growing at the rate of 1.17 percent each year. Assuming that the population will continue to grow at the same rate, write a program to determine when the population will reach 10 billion.

26. Write a program to display all the numbers between 1 and 100 that are perfect squares. (A perfect square is an integer that is the square of another integer; 1, 4, 9, and 16 are examples of perfect squares.)

27. Write a program to display all the numbers between 1 and 100 that are part of the Fibonacci sequence. The Fibonacci sequence begins 1, 1, 2, 3, 5, 8, . . . , where each new number in the sequence is found by adding the previous two numbers in the sequence.

28. Write a program to request positive numbers one at a time from the user in an input dialog box. The user should be instructed to enter -1 after all the positive numbers have been supplied. At that time, the program should display the sum of the numbers.

29. An old grandfather clock reads 6:00 p.m. Sometime not too long after 6:30 p.m., the minute hand will pass directly over the hour hand. Write a program using a loop to make better and better guesses as to what time it is when the hands exactly overlap. Keep track of the positions of both hands using the minutes at which they are pointing. (At 6:00 p.m., the minute hand points at 0 while the hour hand points at 30.) You will need to use the fact that when the minute hand advances m minutes, the hour hand advances $m/12$ minutes. (For example, when the minute hand advances 60 minutes, the hour hand advances 5 minutes from one hour mark to the next.) To make an approximation, record how far the minute hand is behind the hour hand, then advance the minute hand by this much and the hour hand by 1/12 this much. The loop should terminate when the resulting positions of the minute and hour hands differ by less than .0001 minute. (The exact answer is 32 and 8/11 minutes after 6.)

30. Write a program that requests a word containing the two letters r and n as input and determines which of the two letters appears first. If the word does not contain both of the letters, the program should so advise the user. (Test the program with the words "colonel" and "merriment.")

31. The coefficient of restitution of a ball, a number between 0 and 1, specifies how much energy is conserved when a ball hits a rigid surface. A coefficient of .9, for instance, means a bouncing ball will rise to 90 percent of its previous height after each bounce. Write a program to input a coefficient of restitution and an initial height in meters, and report how many times a ball bounces when dropped from its initial height before it rises to a height of less than 10 centimeters. Also report the total distance traveled by the ball before this point. The coefficients of restitution of a tennis ball, basketball, super ball, and softball are .7, .75, .9, and .3, respectively.

In Exercises 32 through 35, write a program to solve the stated problem.

32. *Savings Account.* $15,000 is deposited into a savings account paying 5 percent interest and $1000 is withdrawn from the account at the end of each year. Approximately how many years are required for the savings account to be depleted?

    Note: If at the end of a certain year the balance is $1000 or less, then the final withdrawal will consist of that balance and the account will be depleted.

33. Rework Exercise 32 so that the amount of money deposited initially is input by the user and the program computes the number of years required to deplete the account. **Note:** Be careful to avoid an infinite loop.

34. Consider an account in which $1000 is deposited upon opening the account and an additional $1000 is deposited at the end of each year. If the money earns interest at the rate of 5 percent, how long will it take before the account contains at least $1 million?

35. A person born in 1980 can claim, "I will be *x* years old in the year *x* squared." Write a program to determine the value of *x*.

36. Illustrate the growth of money in a savings account. When the user presses the button, values for Amount and Interest Rate are obtained from text boxes and used to calculate the number of years until the money doubles and the number of years until the money reaches a million dollars. Use the form design shown below.

    Note: The balance at the end of each year is $(1 + r)$ times the previous balance, where *r* is the annual rate of interest in decimal form.

OBJECT	PROPERTY	SETTING
frmInterest	Text	Compound Interest
lblAmount	Text	Amount:
txtAmount		
lblRate	AutoSize	False
	Text	Interest Rate: [Annual]
txtRate		
btnDetermine	Text	Determine Years
lblDouble	AutoSize	False
	Text	Doubling time: [Years]
txtDouble	ReadOnly	True
lblMillion	AutoSize	False
	Text	Reach a Million: [Years]
txtMillion	ReadOnly	True

37. Allow the user to enter a sentence. Then, depending on which button the user clicks, display the sentence entirely in capital letters or with just the first letter of each word capitalized.

In Exercises 38 and 39, write a program corresponding to the flowchart.

38. The flowchart in Figure 6.3 (on the next page) requests a whole number greater than 1 as input and factors it into a product of prime numbers. **Note:** A number is prime if its only factors are 1 and itself. Test the program with the numbers 660 and 139.

39. The flowchart in Figure 6.4 (on page 251) finds the greatest common divisor (the largest integer that divides both) of two positive integers input by the user. Write a program that corresponds to the flowchart. Use the Visual Basic operator Mod. The value of *m* Mod *n* is the remainder when *m* is divided by *n*.

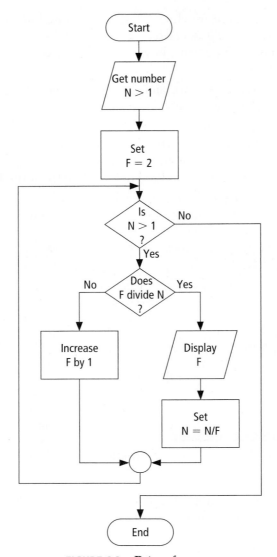

FIGURE 6.3 Prime factors.

Solutions to Practice Problems 6.1

1. As a rule of thumb, the condition is checked at the bottom if the loop should be executed at least once.

2. Either precede the loop with the statement **continue = "Yes"**, or change the first line to **Do** and replace the Loop statement with **Loop Until continue <> "Yes"**.

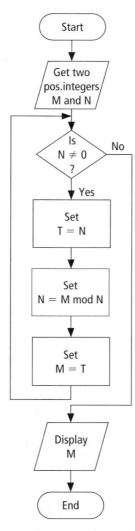

FIGURE 6.4   **Greatest common divisor.**

6.2   **Processing Lists of Data with Do Loops**

One of the main applications of programming is the processing of lists of data. Do loops are used to display all or selected items from lists, search lists for specific items, and per-form calculations on the numerical entries of a list. This section introduces several devices that facilitate working with lists. The **Peek method** is used to determine when the end of a file has been reached, **counters** calculate the number of elements in lists, **accumulators** sum numerical values in lists, and **flags** record whether certain circum-stances have occurred. **Nested loops** add yet another dimension to repetition.

■ **Peek Method**

Data to be processed are often retrieved from a file by a Do loop. Visual Basic has a use-ful method that will tell us if we have reached the end of the file from which we are reading. Suppose a text file has been opened with a StreamReader object named *sr*. At any time, the value of

```
sr.Peek
```

is the ANSI value of the first character of the line about to be read with ReadLine. If the end of the file has been reached, the value of `sr.Peek` is −1.

One of the programs I wrote when I got my first personal computer in 1982 stored a list of names and phone numbers and printed a phone directory. I stored the names in a file so I could easily add, change, or delete entries.

 Example 1   The following program displays the contents of a telephone directory. The names and phone numbers are contained in the file PHONE.TXT. The loop will repeat as long as there is still data in the file.

PHONE.TXT contains the following eight lines:

Bert
123-4567
Ernie
987-6543
Grover
246-8321
Oscar
135-7900

OBJECT	PROPERTY	SETTING
frmPhone	Text	Directory
btnDisplay	Text	Display Phone Numbers
lstNumbers		

```
Private Sub btnDisplay_Click(...) Handles btnDisplay.Click
  Dim name, phoneNum As String
  Dim sr As IO.StreamReader = IO.File.OpenText("PHONE.TXT")
  lstNumbers.Items.Clear()
  Do While sr.Peek <> -1
    name = sr.ReadLine
    phoneNum = sr.ReadLine
    lstNumbers.Items.Add(name & "    " & phoneNum)
  Loop
  sr.Close()
End Sub
```

[Run, and press the button.]

The program in Example 1 illustrates the proper way to process a list of data contained in a file. The Do loop should be tested at the top with an end-of-file condition. (If the file is empty, no attempt is made to input data from the file.) The first set of data should be input after the Do statement, and then the data should be processed. Figure 6.5 contains the pseudocode and flowchart for this technique.

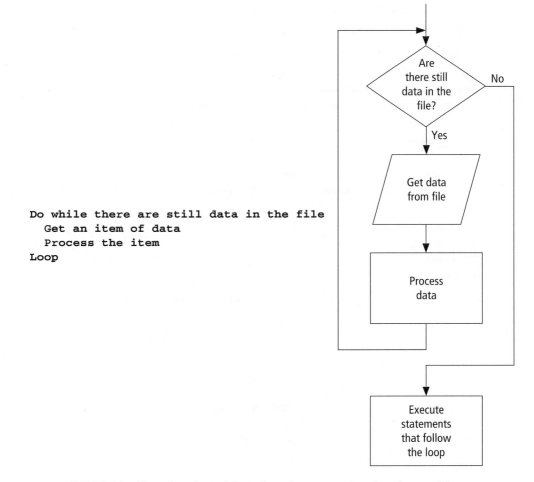

```
Do while there are still data in the file
  Get an item of data
  Process the item
Loop
```

FIGURE 6.5   Pseudocode and flowchart for processing data from a file.

Text files can be quite large. Rather than list the entire contents, we typically search the file for a specific piece of information.

 Example 2 The following program modifies the program in Example 1 to search the telephone directory for a name specified by the user. If the name does not appear in the directory, the user is so notified. We want to keep searching as long as there is no match and we have not reached the end of the list. Therefore, the condition for the Do While statement is a compound logical expression with the operator And. After the last pass through the loop, we will know whether the name was found and will be able to display the requested information.

OBJECT	PROPERTY	SETTING
frmPhone	Text	Phone Number
lblName	Text	Name to look up:
txtName		
btnDisplay	Text	Display Phone Number
txtNumber	ReadOnly	True

```
Private Sub btnDisplay_Click(...) Handles btnDisplay.Click
  Dim name As String = "",  phoneNum As String = ""
  Dim sr As IO.StreamReader = IO.File.OpenText("PHONE.TXT")
  Do While (name <> txtName.Text) And (sr.Peek <> -1)
    name = sr.ReadLine
    phoneNum = sr.ReadLine
  Loop
  If (name = txtName.Text) Then
    txtNumber.Text = name & "     " & phoneNum
  Else
    txtNumber.Text = "Name not found."
  End If
  sr.Close()
End Sub
```

[Run, type "Grover" into the text box, and press the button.]

■ Counters and Accumulators

A **counter** is a numeric variable that keeps track of the number of items that have been processed. An **accumulator** is a numeric variable that totals numbers.

 Example 3   The following program counts and finds the value of coins listed in a file. The file COINS.TXT contains the following entries, one per line: 1, 1, 5, 10, 10, 25. The fifth and sixth lines of the event procedure are not needed, since the counter *numCoins* and the accumulator *sum* have the initial value 0 by default. However, since these default values show the starting points for the two variables, the two assignment statements add clarity to the program.

OBJECT	PROPERTY	SETTING
frmCoins	Text	Coins
btnAnalyze	Text	Analyze Change
txtValue	ReadOnly	True

```
Private Sub btnAnalyze_Click(...) Handles btnAnalyze.Click
  Dim numCoins As Integer, coin As String
  Dim sum As Double
  Dim sr As IO.StreamReader = IO.File.OpenText("COINS.TXT")
  numCoins = 0
  sum = 0
  Do While (sr.Peek <> -1)
    coin = sr.ReadLine
    numCoins += 1      'Add 1 to the value of numCoins
    sum += CDbl(coin)  'Add the value of the current coin to the sum
  Loop
  sr.Close()
  txtValue.Text = "The value of the " & numCoins & _
                  " coins is " & sum & " cents."
End Sub
```

[Run, and press the button.]

The value of the counter, *numCoins*, was initially 0 and changed on each execution of the loop to 1, 2, 3, 4, 5, and finally 6. The accumulator, *sum*, initially had the value 0 and increased with each execution of the loop to 1, 2, 7, 17, 27, and finally 52.

■ Flags

A **flag** is a variable that keeps track of whether a certain situation has occurred. The data type most suited to flags is the **Boolean data type**. Variables of type Boolean can assume just two values: True and False. (As a default, Boolean variables are initialized to False.) Flags are used within loops to provide information that will be utilized after the loop terminates. Flags also provide an alternative method of terminating a loop.

 Example 4 The following program counts the number of words in the file WORDS.TXT and then reports whether the words are in alphabetical order. In each execution of the loop, a word is compared to the next word in the list. The flag variable, called *orderFlag*, is initially assigned the value True and is set to False if a pair of adjacent words is out of order. The technique used in this program will be used in Chapter 7 when we study sorting. **Note:** The first time through the loop, the value of *word1* is the empty string. Each word must first be read into the variable *word2*.

WORDS.TXT contains the following winning words from the U.S. National Spelling Bee, one word per line: cambist, croissant, deification, hydrophyte, incisor, maculature, macerate, narcolepsy, shallon.

OBJECT	PROPERTY	SETTING
frmWords	Text	Word Analysis
btnAnalyze	Text	Analyze Words
lblNumber	Text	Number of words:
txtNumber	ReadOnly	True
lblAlpha	Text	Alphabetical order?
txtAlpha	ReadOnly	True

```vb
Private Sub btnAnalyze_Click(...) Handles btnAnalyze.Click
  'Count words.  Are they in alphabetical order?
  Dim orderFlag As Boolean, wordCounter As Integer
  Dim word1 As String = "", word2 As String
  Dim sr As IO.StreamReader = IO.File.OpenText("WORDS.TXT")
  orderFlag = True
  Do While (sr.Peek <> -1)
    word2 = sr.ReadLine
    wordCounter += 1              'Increment the word count by 1
    If word1 > word2 Then         'Two words are out of order
      orderFlag = False
    End If
    word1 = word2
  Loop
  sr.Close()
  txtNumber.Text = CStr(wordCounter)
```

```
    If orderFlag = True Then
      txtAlpha.Text = "YES"
    Else
      txtAlpha.Text = "NO"
    End If
End Sub
```

[Run, and press the button.]

Nested Loops

The statements within a Do loop can contain another Do loop. Such a configuration is referred to as **nested loops** and is useful in repeating a single data-processing routine several times.

  Example 5   The following program allows the user to look through several lists of names. Suppose we have several different phone directories, the names of which are listed in the file LISTS.TXT. (For instance, the file LISTS.TXT might contain the entries CLIENTS.TXT, FRIENDS.TXT, and KINFOLK.TXT.) A sought-after name might be in any one of the files. The statements in the inner Do loop will be used to look up names as before. At least one pass through the outer Do loop is guaranteed, and passes will continue as long as the name is not found and phone lists remain to be examined.

OBJECT	PROPERTY	SETTING
frmPhone	Text	Phone Number
lblName	Text	Name to look up:
txtName		
btnDisplay	Text	Display Phone Number
txtNumber	ReadOnly	True

```
Private Sub btnDisplay_Click(...) Handles btnDisplay.Click
  Dim foundFlag As Boolean
  Dim fileName As String
  Dim name As String = ""
  Dim phoneNum As String = ""
  Dim sr1 As IO.StreamReader = IO.File.OpenText("LISTS.TXT")
```

```
'The next line is not needed. It is added for clarity.
foundFlag = False
Do While (foundFlag = False) And (sr1.Peek <> -1)
  fileName = sr1.ReadLine
  Dim sr2 As IO.StreamReader = IO.File.OpenText(fileName)
  Do While (name <> txtName.Text) And (sr2.Peek <> -1)
    name = sr2.ReadLine
    phoneNum = sr2.ReadLine
  Loop
  sr2.Close()
  If name = txtName.Text Then
    txtNumber.Text = name & "      " & phoneNum
    foundFlag = True
  End If
Loop
sr1.Close()
If foundFlag = False Then
  txtNumber.Text = "Name not found."
End If
End Sub
```

■ Comments

1. In Appendix D, the section "Stepping through a Program Containing a Do Loop: Chapter 6" uses the Visual Basic debugging tools to trace the flow through a Do loop.

2. When *flagVar* is a variable of Boolean type, the statements

   ```
   If flagVar = True Then  and  If flagVar = False Then
   ```

   can be replaced by

   ```
   If flagVar Then  and  If Not flagVar Then
   ```

   Similarly, the statements

   ```
   Do While flagVar = True  and  Do While flagVar = False
   ```

   can be replaced by

   ```
   Do While flagVar  and  Do While Not flagVar
   ```

Practice Problems 6.2

1. Determine the output of the following program, where the three lines of the file SCORES.TXT contain the scores 150, 200, and 300:

```
Private Sub btnCompute_Click(...) Handles btnCompute.Click
  'Find the sum of a collection of bowling scores
  Dim sum, score As Double
```

```
Dim sr As IO.StreamReader = IO.File.OpenText("SCORES.TXT")
sum = 0
score = CDbl(sr.ReadLine)
Do While (sr.Peek <> -1)
  sum += score    'Add value of score to value of sum
  score = CDbl(sr.ReadLine)
Loop
sr.Close()
txtTotal.Text = CStr(sum)
End Sub
```

2. Why didn't the preceding program produce the intended output?

3. Correct the preceding program so it has the intended output.

In Exercises 1 through 10, determine the output displayed when the button is clicked.

1.
```
Private Sub btnDisplay_Click(...) Handles btnDisplay.Click
  Dim flag As Boolean, word As String
  Dim sr As IO.StreamReader = IO.File.OpenText("FRUITS.TXT")
  Do While (sr.Peek <> -1)
    word = sr.ReadLine
    If word.IndexOf("A") <> -1 Then
      flag = True
    End If
  Loop
  sr.Close()
  If flag Then
    txtOutput.Text = "At least one word contains the letter A."
  Else
    txtOutput.Text = "No word contains the letter A."
  End If
End Sub
```
(Assume that the four lines of the file DATA.TXT have the following entries: AL, GORE, VIDAL, SASSOON.)

2.
```
Private Sub btnDisplay_Click(...) Handles btnDisplay.Click
  Dim name As String
  Dim sr As IO.StreamReader = IO.File.OpenText("DATA.TXT")
  Do While (sr.Peek <> -1)
    name = sr.ReadLine
    txtOutput.Text &= name
  Loop
  sr.Close()
End Sub
```
(Assume that the two lines of the file DATA.TXT contain the following entries: Ben, son.)

3.
```
Private Sub btnDisplay_Click(...) Handles btnDisplay.Click
  'Display list of desserts
  Dim dessert As String
  Dim sr As IO.StreamReader = IO.File.OpenText("DESSERTS.TXT")
  Do While (sr.Peek <> -1)
    dessert = sr.ReadLine
    lstOutput.Items.Add(dessert)
  Loop
  sr.Close()
End Sub
```

(Assume that the three lines of the file DESSERTS.TXT contain the following entries: pie, cake, melon.)

4.
```
Private Sub btnDisplay_Click(...) Handles btnDisplay.Click
  Dim city As String, pop As Double
  Dim sr As IO.StreamReader = IO.File.OpenText("CITYPOPS.TXT")
  Do While (sr.Peek <> -1)
    city = sr.ReadLine
    pop = CDbl(sr.ReadLine)
    If pop >= 3 Then
      lstOutput.Items.Add(city & "  " & pop)
    End If
  Loop
  sr.Close()
End Sub
```

(Assume that the eight lines of the file CITYPOPS.TXT contain the following data, where each pair of lines gives a city and its population in millions: New York, 8.2, Los Angeles, 3.8, Chicago, 2.8, Houston, 2.1.)

5.
```
Private Sub btnDisplay_Click(...) Handles btnDisplay.Click
  Dim firstLetter As String = "", fruit As String = ""
  Dim sr As IO.StreamReader = IO.File.OpenText("FRUITS.TXT")
  Do While (sr.Peek <> -1)
    fruit = sr.ReadLine
    If fruit.Substring(0, 1) <> firstLetter Then
      If firstLetter <> "" Then
        lstOutput.Items.Add("")
      End If
      firstLetter = fruit.Substring(0, 1)
      lstOutput.Items.Add("   " & firstLetter)
    End If
    lstOutput.Items.Add(fruit)
  Loop
  sr.Close()
End Sub
```

(Assume that the eight lines of the file FRUITS.TXT contain the following entries: Apple, Apricot, Avocado, Banana, Blueberry, Grape, Lemon, Lime.)

6.
```
Private Sub btnDisplay_Click(...) Handles btnDisplay.Click
    'Display list of numbers
    Dim num As Double
    Dim sr As IO.StreamReader = IO.File.OpenText("DATA.TXT")
    num = CDbl(sr.ReadLine)
    Do While (sr.Peek <> -1)
      lstOutput.Items.Add(num)
      num = CDbl(sr.ReadLine)
    Loop
    sr.Close()
End Sub
```

(Assume the four lines of the file DATA.TXT contain the entries 2, 3, 8, 5.)

7.
```
Private Sub btnDisplay_Click(...) Handles btnDisplay.Click
    Dim animal As String = "", groupName As String = ""
    InputAnimal(animal)
    If animal <> "" Then
      SearchList(animal, groupName)
      DisplayResult(animal, groupName)
    End If
End Sub

Sub DisplayResult(ByVal anml As String, ByVal gName As String)
  If gName = "" Then
    txtOutput.Text = "Animal not found."
  Else
    txtOutput.Text = "A " & gName & " of " & anml & "s."
  End If
End Sub

Sub InputAnimal(ByRef anml As String)
  'Request the name of an animal as input
  anml = InputBox("Please enter the name of an animal.")
End Sub

Sub SearchList(ByVal anml As String, ByRef gName As String)
  Dim creature, groupName As String
  creature = ""
  Dim sr As IO.StreamReader = IO.File.OpenText("ANIMALS.TXT")
  Do While (creature <> anml) And (sr.Peek <> -1)
    creature = sr.ReadLine
    groupName = sr.ReadLine
  Loop
  If (sr.Peek = -1) Then
    gName = ""
  Else
    gName = groupName
  End If
  sr.Close()
End Sub
```

(The six lines of the file ANIMALS.TXT contain the following entries: lion, pride, duck, brace, bee, swarm. Each pair of lines give an animal and the name of a group of those animals. Assume that the response is "duck".)

8.
```
Private Sub btnDisplay_Click(...) Handles btnDisplay.Click
    Dim excerpt As String
    excerpt = "I think I can. "
    Duplicate30(excerpt)
    excerpt = "We're off to see the wizard, " & _
              "the wonderful wizard of Oz."
    Duplicate30(excerpt)
End Sub

Sub Duplicate30(ByVal sentence As String)
    Dim flag As Boolean
    flag = False    'Flag tells whether loop has been executed
    Do While sentence.Length < 30
        flag = True
        sentence &= sentence
    Loop
    If flag = True Then
        lstOutput.Items.Add(sentence)
    Else
        lstOutput.Items.Add("Loop not executed.")
    End If
End Sub
```

9.
```
Private Sub btnDisplay_Click(...) Handles btnDisplay.Click
    Dim word As String = "", cWord As String = ""
    Dim sr As IO.StreamReader = IO.File.OpenText("WORDS.TXT")
    Do While (sr.Peek <> -1)
        word = sr.ReadLine
        If word.Substring(0, 1) = "c" Then
            cWord = word
        End If
    Loop
    sr.Close()
    txtOutput.Text = cWord
End Sub
```

(Assume that the 11 lines of the file WORDS.TXT contain the following items: time, is, a, child, idly, moving, counters, in, a, game, Heraclitus.)

10.
```
Private Sub btnDisplay_Click(...) Handles btnDisplay.Click
    Dim max, value, rowMax As Double
    Dim sr As IO.StreamReader = IO.File.OpenText("DATA.TXT")
    Do While (sr.Peek <> -1)
        value = CDbl(sr.ReadLine)
        rowMax = 0
```

```
      Do While value <> -2
        If value > rowMax Then
          rowMax = value
        End If
        value = CDbl(sr.ReadLine)
      Loop
      lstOutput.Items.Add(rowMax)
      If rowMax > max Then
        max = rowMax
      End If
    Loop
    sr.Close()
    lstOutput.Items.Add(max)
  End Sub
```

(Assume that the 12 lines of the file DATA.TXT contain the following entries: 5, 7, 3, −2, 10, 12, 6, 4, −2, 1, 9, −2.)

In Exercises 11 through 14, identify the errors.

11.
```
Private Sub btnDisplay_Click(...) Handles btnDisplay.Click
  Dim num As Double
  Dim sr As IO.StreamReader = IO.File.OpenText("DATA.TXT")
  Do While (sr.Peek <> -1) And (num > 0)
    num = CDbl(sr.ReadLine)
    lstOutput.Items.Add(num)
    sr.Close()
End Sub
```

(Assume that the five lines of the file DATA.TXT contain the following entries: 7, 6, 0, −1, 2.)

12.
```
Private Sub btnDisplay_Click(...) Handles btnDisplay.Click
  Dim flag As Boolean, num, sum As Double
  Do While flag = False
    num = CDbl(InputBox("Enter a number"))
    sum += num
    If num * num < 0 Then
      flag = True
    End If
  Loop
  txtOutput.Text = CStr(sum)
End Sub
```

13.
```
Private Sub btnDisplay_Click(...) Handles btnDisplay.Click
  'Display names of four U.S. Presidents
  Dim president As String
  Dim sr As IO.StreamReader = IO.File.OpenText("PRES.TXT")
  president = sr.ReadLine
```

```
    Do
       lstOutput.Items.Add(president)
       president = sr.ReadLine
    Loop Until (sr.Peek = -1)
     sr.Close()
  End Sub
```

(Assume that the lines of the file PRES.TXT contain the following entries: Lincoln, Washington, Kennedy, Jefferson.)

14.
```
  Private Sub btnDisplay_Click(...) Handles btnDisplay.Click
    Dim num As Double
    Dim sr As IO.StreamReader = IO.File.OpenText("DATA.TXT")
    If (sr.Peek = -1) Then
       num = 0
    Else
       num = CDbl(sr.ReadLine)
    End If
    Do While 1 < num < 5
       lstOutput.Items.Add(num)
       If (sr.Peek = -1) Then
          num = 0
       Else
          num = CDbl(sr.ReadLine)
       End If
    Loop
     sr.Close()
  End Sub
```

(Assume that the five lines of the file DATA.TXT contain the following entries: 3, 2, 4, 7, 2.)

15. Write a program to find and display the largest of a collection of positive numbers contained in a text file. (Test the program with the collection of numbers 89, 77, 95, and 86.)

16. Write a program to find and display those names that are repeated in a text file. Assume that the file has already been sorted into alphabetical order. When a name is found to be repeated, display it only once.

17. Suppose that the file FINAL.TXT contains student grades on a final exam. Write a program that displays the average grade on the exam and the percentage of grades that are above average.

18. Suppose that the file BIDS.TXT contains a list of bids on a construction project. Write a program to analyze the list and report the two highest bids.

19. Suppose that the file USPRES.TXT contains the names of the United States presidents in order from George Washington to George W. Bush. Write a program that asks the user to type a number from 1 to 43 into a text box and then, when the user clicks a button, displays the name of the president corresponding to that number.

20. Table 6.1 shows the different grades of eggs and the minimum weight required for each classification. Write a program that processes the text file EGGS.TXT containing a list of the weights of a sample of eggs. The program should report the number of eggs in each grade and the weight of the lightest and heaviest egg in the sample. Figure 6.6 shows a possible output of the program. **Note:** Eggs weighing less than 1.5 ounces cannot be sold in supermarkets.

TABLE 6.1	Grades of eggs.	
	Grade	Weight (in ounces)
	Jumbo	2.5
	Extra Large	2.25
	Large	2
	Medium	1.75
	Small	1.5

```
57 Jumbo eggs
95 Extra Large eggs
76 Large eggs
96 Medium eggs
77 Small eggs
Lightest egg: 1 ounces
Heaviest egg: 2.69 ounces
```

FIGURE 6.6   Possible output for Exercise 20.

21. Write a program to request a positive integer as input and carry out the following algorithm. If the number is even, divide it by 2. Otherwise, multiply the number by 3 and add 1. Repeat this process with the resulting number and continue repeating the process until the number 1 is reached. After the number 1 is reached, the program should display how many iterations were required. **Note:** A number is even if **num Mod 2 = 0**. (Test the program with the numbers 9, 21, and 27.)

22. Suppose that the file USPRES.TXT contains the names of the first 43 United States presidents, and the file USSENATE.TXT contains the names of all former and present U.S. senators. Write a program with nested loops that uses these files to display the names of the presidents who served in the Senate.

23. Suppose that the file SONNET.TXT contains Shakespeare's Sonnet #18. Each entry in the file consists of a line of the sonnet. Write a program using nested loops to analyze this file line by line and report the average number of words in a line and the total number of words in the sonnet.

24. Suppose that the file SALES.TXT contains information on the sales during the past week at a new car dealership. The file contains the following information for each salesperson at the dealership: the name of the salesperson, pairs of numbers giving the final sales price and the dealer cost for each sale made by that salesperson, and a pair of zeros to indicate the end of data for that salesperson. The first fourteen lines of the file contain the following data: Tom Jones, 18100, 17655, 22395, 21885, 15520, 14895, 0, 0, Bill Smith, 16725, 16080, 0, 0. Write a program

to display the name of each salesperson and the commission earned for the week. Assume that the commission is 15% of the profit on each sale.

25. Write a program that uses a flag and does the following:

    (a) Ask the user to input a sentence containing parentheses. **Note:** The closing parenthesis should not directly precede the period.

    (b) Display the sentence with the parentheses and their contents removed. Test the program with the following sentence as input: BASIC (Beginners All-purpose Symbolic Instruction Code) was the world's most widely known computer language.

26. The salespeople at a health club keep track of the members who have joined in the last month. Their names and types of membership (Bronze, Silver, or Gold) are stored in the text file NEWMEMBERS.TXT. Write a program that displays all the Bronze members, then the Silver members, and finally the Gold members.

27. Table 6.2 gives the prices of various liquids. Write a program that requests an amount of money as input and displays the names of all liquids for which a gallon could be purchased with that amount of money. The information from the table should be read from a file. As an example, if the user has $2.35, then the following should be displayed in the list box:

```
You can purchase one gallon of any of the following liquids:
Bleach
Milk
```

TABLE 6.2 **Some comparative prices per gallon of various liquids.**

Liquid	Price	Liquid	Price
Apple Cider	2.60	Milk	2.30
Beer	6.00	Gatorade	4.20
Bleach	1.40	Perrier	6.85
Coca-Cola	2.55	Pancake Syrup	15.50
Gasoline	3.25	Spring Water	4.10

28. The text file CRAYONS.TXT contains the 120 Crayola crayon colors. Write a program that requests a color as input in a text box and then determines whether or not the color is in the text file. The program should use the Boolean-valued Function procedure IsCrayola that returns the value True if the color in the text box is a Crayola color.

Solutions to Practice Problems 6.2

1. 350

2. When the third score was read from the file, sr.Peek assumed the value −1. With sr.Peek = −1, the loop terminated and the third score was never added to *sum*.

```
3. Private Sub btnCompute_Click(...) Handles btnCompute.Click
     'Find the sum of a collection of bowling scores
     Dim sum, score As Double
     Dim sr As IO.StreamReader = IO.File.OpenText("SCORE.TXT")
     Do While (sr.Peek <> -1)
       score = CDbl(sr.ReadLine)
       sum += score
     Loop
     sr.Close()
     txtTotal.Text = CStr(sum)
   End Sub
```

6.3   For . . . Next Loops

When we know exactly how many times a loop should be executed, a special type of loop, called a For . . . Next loop, can be used. For . . . Next loops are easy to read and write, and have features that make them ideal for certain common tasks. The following code uses a For . . . Next loop to display a table:

```
Private Sub btnDisplayTable_Click(...) Handles btnDisplayTable.Click
  'Display a table of the first 5 numbers and their squares
  'Assume the font for lstTable is Courier New
  For i As Integer = 1 To 5
    lstTable.Items.Add(i & "   " & i ^ 2)
  Next
End Sub
```

[Run, and click on btnDisplayTable. The following is displayed in the list box.]

```
1   1
2   4
3   9
4   16
5   25
```

A similar program written with a Do loop is as follows.

```
Private Sub btnDisplayTable_Click(...) Handles btnDisplayTable.Click
  'Display a table of the first 5 numbers and their squares
  Dim i As Integer
  i = 1
  Do While i <= 5
    lstTable.Items.Add(i & "   " & i ^ 2)
    i += 1     'Add 1 to i
  Loop
End Sub
```

In general, a portion of a program of the form

constitutes a For . . . Next loop. The pair of statements For and Next cause the statements between them to be repeated a specified number of times. The For statement declares a numeric variable, called the **control variable**, that is initialized and then automatically changes after each execution of the loop. Also, the For statement gives the range of values this variable will assume. The Next statement increments the control variable. If $m \leq n$, then i is assigned the values $m, m + 1, \ldots, n$ in order, and the body is executed once for each of these values. If $m > n$, then the body is skipped and execution continues with the statement after the For . . . Next loop.

When program execution reaches a For . . . Next loop, such as the one shown previously, the For statement assigns to the control variable i the **initial value** m and checks to see whether i is greater than the **terminating value** n. If so, then execution jumps to the line following the Next statement. If $i <= n$, the statements inside the loop are executed. Then, the Next statement increases the value of i by 1 and checks this new value to see if it exceeds n. If not, the entire process is repeated until the value of i exceeds n. When this happens, the program moves to the line following the loop. Figure 6.7 contains the pseudocode and flowchart of a For . . . Next loop.

The control variable can be any numeric variable. The most common single-letter names are i, j, and k; however, if appropriate, the name should suggest the purpose of the control variable.

The control variable, and any variable declared inside a For... Next loop, has **block-level scope**; that is, the variable cannot be referred to by code outside of the loop.

A control variable also can be declared with a Dim statement outside of the For ... Next loop. For instance, the following program produces the same output as the program shown at the beginning of this section.

```
Private Sub btnDisplay_Click(...) Handles btnDisplay.Click
  'Display a table of the first 5 numbers and their squares
  'Assume the font for lstTable is Courier New
  Dim i As Integer
  For i = 1 To 5
    lstTable.Items.Add(i & "   " & i ^ 2)
  Next
End Sub
```

In this case, the variable i does not have block-level scope, and therefore violates the principle that the scope of a variable should be as small as possible. In this book, we never declare a control variable outside of a For ... Next loop.

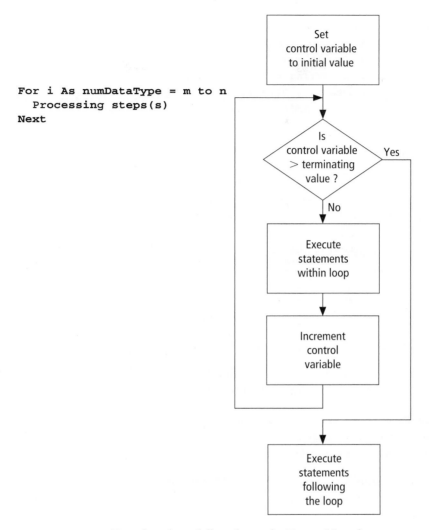

```
For i As numDataType = m to n
   Processing steps(s)
Next
```

FIGURE 6.7 **Pseudocode and flowchart of a For . . . Next loop.**

 Example 1 Suppose the population of a city is 300,000 in the year 2008 and is growing at the rate of 3 percent per year. The following program displays a table showing the population each year until 2012.

OBJECT	PROPERTY	SETTING
frmPopulation	Text	POPULATION GROWTH
btnDisplay	Text	Display Population
lstTable	Font	Courier New

```
Private Sub btnDisplay_Click(...) Handles btnDisplay.Click
  'Display population from 2008 to 2012
  Dim pop As Double = 300000
  Dim fmtStr As String = "{0,4}{1,12:N0}"
  For yr As Integer = 2008 To 2012
    lstTable.Items.Add(String.Format(fmtStr, yr, pop))
    pop += 0.03 * pop
  Next
End Sub
```

[Run, and click the button.]

The initial and terminating values can be literals, variables, or expressions. For instance, the For statement in the preceding program can be replaced by

```
Dim firstYr As Integer = 2008
Dim lastYr As Integer = 2012
For yr As Integer = firstYr To lastYr
```

In Example 1, the control variable was increased by 1 after each pass through the loop. A variation of the For statement allows any number to be used as the increment. The statement

```
For i As numDataType = m To n Step s
```

instructs the Next statement to add *s* to the control variable instead of 1. The numbers *m*, *n*, and *s* do not have to be whole numbers. The number *s* is called the **step value** of the loop. *Note:* If the control variable will assume values that are not whole numbers, then the variable must be of type Double.

 Example 2 The following program displays the values of the index of a For . . . Next loop for terminating and step values input by the user:

OBJECT	PROPERTY	SETTING
frmIndex	Text	For index = 0 To n Step s
lblN	Text	n:
txtEnd		
lblS	Text	s:
txtStep		
btnDisplay	Text	Display Values of Index
lstValues		

```
Private Sub btnDisplay_Click(...) Handles btnDisplay.Click
  'Display values of index ranging from 0 to n Step s
  Dim n, s As Double
  n = CDbl(txtEnd.Text)
  s = CDbl(txtStep.Text)
  lstValues.Items.Clear()
  For index As Double = 0 To n Step s
    lstValues.Items.Add(index)
  Next
End Sub
```

[Run, type 3.2 and .5 into the text boxes, and click the button.]

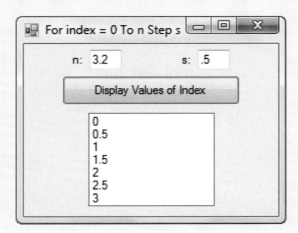

In the examples considered so far, the control variable was successively increased until it reached the terminating value. However, if a negative step value is used and the initial value is greater than the terminating value, then the control value is decreased until reaching the terminating value. In other words, the loop counts backward or downward.

Example 3 The following program accepts a word as input and displays it backwards:

OBJECT	PROPERTY	SETTING
frmBackwards	Text	Write Backwards
lblWord	Text	Enter word:
txtWord		
btnReverse	Text	Reverse Letters
txtBackwards	ReadOnly	True

```
Private Sub btnReverse_Click(...) Handles btnReverse.Click
  txtBackwards.Text = Reverse(txtWord.Text)
End Sub

Function Reverse(ByVal info As String) As String
  Dim m As Integer, temp As String = ""
  m = info.Length
  For j As Integer = m - 1 To 0 Step -1
    temp &= info.Substring(j, 1)
  Next
  Return temp
End Function
```

[Run, type "SUEZ" into the text box, and click the button.]

Note: The initial and terminating values of a For . . . Next loop can be expressions. For instance, the third and fourth lines of the function in Example 3 can be consolidated to

```
For j As Integer = info.Length - 1 To 0 Step -1
```

■ Nested For . . . Next Loops

The body of a For . . . Next loop can contain any sequence of Visual Basic statements. In particular, it can contain another For . . . Next loop. However, the second loop must be completely contained inside the first loop and must have a different control variable. Such a configuration is called **nested For . . . Next loops**.

Example 4   The following program displays a multiplication table for the integers from 1 to 3. Here *j* denotes the left factors of the products, and *k* denotes the right factors. Each factor takes on a value from 1 to 3. The values are assigned to *j* in the outer loop (lines 4–11) and to *k* in the inner loop (lines 6–8). Initially, *j* is assigned the value 1, and then the inner loop is traversed three times to produce the first row of products. At the end of these three passes, the value of *j* will still be 1, and the value of *k* will have been incremented to 4. The first execution of the outer loop is then complete. Following this, the statement Next increments the value of *j* to 2. The statement beginning "For k" is then executed. It resets the value of *k* to 1. The second row of products is displayed during the next three executions of the inner loop and so on.

OBJECT	PROPERTY	SETTING
frmTable	Text	Multiplication Table
btnDisplay	Text	Display Table
lstTable	Font	Courier New

```
Private Sub btnDisplay_Click(...) Handles btnDisplay.Click
  Dim row, entry As String
  lstTable.Items.Clear()
  For j As Integer = 1 To 3
    row = ""
    For k As Integer = 1 To 3
      entry = j & " x " & k & " = " & (j * k)
      row &= entry & "     "
    Next
    lstTable.Items.Add(row)
  Next
End Sub
```

[Run, and press the button.]

■ Local Type Inference (This material is optional.)

Local type inference (also referred to as *implicit typing*), a new-to-VB 2008 feature, allows you to declare and initialize a local variable without explicitly stating its type in an As clause. Local type inference is enabled if Option Infer is set to On in the VB Defaults dialog box shown in Figure 3.1 of Section 3.2. (It is enabled by default.) Although we will not make use of local type inference in this book, you might see it used in other Visual Basic books. If you decide to make use of local type inference in your programming assignments, first get permission from your instructor.

Some examples of the use of local type inference are as follows:

Standard Declaration	Local Type Inference Equivalent
For i As Integer = 1 To 3	For i = 1 To 3
For i As Double = 1 To 3 Step 0.5	For i = 1 To 3 Step 0.5
Dim count As Integer = 5	Dim count = 5
Dim rate as Double = 0.05	Dim rate = 0.05
Dim name As String = "Fred"	Dim name = "Fred"

With local type inference, the type of a local variable is determined by the values following the equal sign. If the values are all whole number (written without a decimal point) and in the range of values for Integers, then the variable is declared to be of type Integer. If any of the values are numbers containing a decimal point or are outside the range of values for Integers, then the variable is declared to be of type Double. If the value is surrounded in quotes, then the variable is declared to be of type String. **Note:** This feature *does not* apply to class-level variables.

The following walkthrough (which assumes that Option Infer is On) demonstrates how local type inference works in a For…Next loop.

1. Create a new program consisting of a form having a button (btnConfirm) and a list box (lstBox).

2. Enter the following code.

```
Private Sub btnConfirm_Click(...) Handles btnConfirm.Click
  For i = 1 To 5 Step 2
    lstBox.Items.Add(i)
  Next
  lstBox.Items.Add(i)
End Sub
```

3. In the Code Editor, hover the mouse cursor over the variable *i*. (The tooltip `Dim i As Integer` appears to confirm that the variable *i* has indeed been declared as type Integer.)

4. In the header of the For … Next loop, change the 5 to 5.0 and again hover the cursor over the letter *i*. (This time the tooltip reads `Dim i As Double .`)

5. Hover the cursor over the variable *i* in the line following the For … Loop. (The tooltip `Name 'i' is not declared.` appears to confirm that the variable *i* is now out of scope.)

■ Comments

1. For and Next statements must be paired. If one is missing, the automatic syntax checker will complain with a wavy underline and a message such as "A 'For' must be paired with a 'Next'."

2. Consider a loop beginning with For $i = m$ To n Step s. The loop will be executed exactly once if m equals n no matter what value s has. The loop will not be executed at all if m is greater than n and s is positive, or if m is less than n and s is negative.

3. The value of the control variable should not be altered within the body of the loop; doing so might cause the loop to repeat indefinitely or have an unpredictable number of repetitions.

4. Non-integer Step values in For . . . Next loops can result in unexpected outcomes. For instance, if you run Example 2 with $n = 2$ and $s = .1$, the last number displayed will not be 2 as intended. In general, the use of control variables of type Double is poor programming practice and should be avoided. From now on, all control variables appearing in this book will have type Integer.

5. Visual Basic provides a way to skip an iteration in a For . . . Next loop. When the statement **Continue For** is encountered in the body of the loop, execution immediately jumps to the Next statement. An analogous statement **Continue Do** is available for Do loops.

6. Visual Basic provides a way to back out of a For . . . Next loop. When the statement **Exit For** is encountered in the body of the loop, execution jumps immediately to the statement following the Next statement.

Practice Problems 6.3

1. Why won't the following lines of code work as intended?

```
For i As Integer = 15 To 1
   lstBox.Items.AddItem(i)
Next
```

2. When is a For . . . Next loop more appropriate than a Do loop?

EXERCISES 6.3

In Exercises 1 through 12, determine the output displayed in the list box when the button is clicked.

```
1. Private Sub btnDisplay_Click(...) Handles btnDisplay.Click
      For i As Integer = 1 To 4
        lstBox.Items.Add("Pass #" & i)
      Next
   End Sub
```

2.
```
Private Sub btnDisplay_Click(...) Handles btnDisplay.Click
  For i As Integer = 3 To 6
    lstBox.Items.Add(2 * i)
  Next
End Sub
```

3.
```
Private Sub btnDisplay_Click(...) Handles btnDisplay.Click
  For j As Integer = 2 To 8 Step 2
    lstBox.Items.Add(j)
  Next
  lstBox.Items.Add("Who do we appreciate?")
End Sub
```

4.
```
Private Sub btnDisplay_Click(...) Handles btnDisplay.Click
  For countdown As Integer = 10 To 1 Step -1
    lstBox.Items.Add(countdown)
  Next
  lstBox.Items.Add("blastoff")
End Sub
```

5.
```
Private Sub btnDisplay_Click(...) Handles btnDisplay.Click
  Dim num As Integer
  num = 5
  For i As Integer = num To (2 * num - 3)
    lstBox.Items.Add(i)
  Next
End Sub
```

6.
```
Private Sub btnDisplay_Click(...) Handles btnDisplay.Click
  For i As Integer = -9 To -1 Step 3
    lstBox.Items.Add(i)
  Next
End Sub
```

7.
```
Private Sub btnDisplay_Click(...) Handles btnDisplay.Click
  'First entry in text file is number of records in file
  Dim recCount As Integer
  Dim name, mileTime As String
  Dim sr As IO.StreamReader = IO.File.OpenText("MILER.TXT")
  recCount = CInt(sr.Readline)
  For miler As Integer = 1 To recCount
    name = sr.Readline
    mileTime = sr.Readline
    lstBox.Items.Add(name & "   " & mileTime)
  Next
  sr.Close()
End Sub
```

(Assume that the seven lines of the file MILER.TXT contain the following entries: 3, Hicham El Guerrouj, 3:43.13, Alan Webb, 3:46.91, Svetlana Masterkova, 4:12.56)

8.
```
Private Sub btnDisplay_Click(...) Handles btnDisplay.Click
    'First entry in text file is number of records in file
    Dim recCount, total, score As Integer
    Dim sr As IO.StreamReader = IO.File.OpenText("SCORES.TXT")
    recCount = CInt(sr.Readline)
    For i As Integer = 1 To recCount
      score = CInt(sr.Readline)
      total += score 'Add the value of score to the value of total
    Next
    sr.Close()
    lstBox.Items.Add("Average = " & total / recCount)
End Sub
```
(Assume the file SCORES.TXT contains the entries 4, 89, 85, 88, 98.)

9.
```
Private Sub btnDisplay_Click(...) Handles btnDisplay.Click
    Dim row, entry As String
    For i As Integer = 0 To 2
      row = ""
      For j As Integer = 0 To 3
        entry = CStr(i + (3 * j) + 1)
        row &= entry & "     "
      Next
      lstBox.Items.Add(row)
    Next
End Sub
```

10.
```
Private Sub btnDisplay_Click(...) Handles btnDisplay.Click
    Dim row As String
    For i As Integer = 1 To 5
      row = ""
      For j As Integer = 1 To i
        row &= "*"
      Next
      lstBox.Items.Add(row)
    Next
End Sub
```

11.
```
Private Sub btnDisplay_Click(...) Handles btnDisplay.Click
    Dim word As String
    Dim num1, num2 As Integer
    word = InputBox("Please enter a word.")
    num1 = CInt(Int((20 - word.Length) / 2))
    num2 = 20 - num1 - word.Length
    lstBox.Items.Add(Asterisks(num1) & word & Asterisks(num2))
End Sub

Function Asterisks(ByVal num As Integer) As String
    Dim chain As String = ""
    For i As Integer = 1 To num
```

```
        chain &= "*"
    Next
    Return chain
End Function
```

(Assume that the response is *Hooray.*)

12.
```
Private Sub btnDisplay_Click(...) Handles btnDisplay.Click
    'Display an array of letters
    Dim info As String, letter As String
    info = "DATA"
    For i As Integer = 1 To info.Length
      letter = info.Substring(i - 1, 1)
      lstBox.Items.Add(RepeatFive(letter))
    Next
End Sub

Function RepeatFive(ByVal letter As String) As String
    Dim chain As String = ""
    For i As Integer = 1 To 5
      chain &= letter
    Next
    Return chain
End Function
```

In Exercises 13 through 16, identify the errors.

13.
```
Private Sub btnDisplay_Click(...) Handles btnDisplay.Click
    For j As Integer = 1 To 25 Step -1
      lstBox.Items.Add(j)
    Next
End Sub
```

14.
```
Private Sub btnDisplay_Click(...) Handles btnDisplay.Click
    For i As Integer = 1 To 3
      lstBox.Items.Add(i & " " & 2 ^ i)
End Sub
```

15.
```
Private Sub btnDisplay_Click(...) Handles btnDisplay.Click
    'Display all numbers from 0 through 20 except for 13
    For i As Integer = 20 To 0
      If i = 13 Then
        i = 12
      End If
      lstBox.Items.Add(i)
    Next
End Sub
```

16.
```
Private Sub btnDisplay_Click(...) Handles btnDisplay.Click
    For j As Integer = 1 To 4 Step 0.5
```

```
    lstBox.Items.Add(j)
  Next
End Sub
```

In Exercises 17 and 18, rewrite the program using a For ... Next loop.

17.
```
Private Sub btnDisplay_Click(...) Handles btnDisplay.Click
  Dim num As Integer = 1
  Do While num <= 9
    lstBox.Items.Add(num)
    num += 2     'Add 2 to value of num
  Loop
End Sub
```

18.
```
Private Sub btnDisplay_Click(...) Handles btnDisplay.Click
  lstBox.Items.Add("hello")
  lstBox.Items.Add("hello")
  lstBox.Items.Add("hello")
  lstBox.Items.Add("hello")
End Sub
```

In Exercises 19 through 38, write a program to complete the stated task.

19. Display a row of 10 stars (asterisks).

20. Request a number from 1 to 20 and display a row of that many stars (asterisks).

21. Display a 10-by-10 array of stars.

22. Request a number and then call a Sub procedure to display a rectangle having that number of stars on each side.

23. Find the sum $1 + 1/2 + 1/3 + 1/4 + \cdots + 1/100$.

24. Find the sum of the odd numbers from 1 through 99.

25. You are offered two salary options for ten days of work. Option 1: $100 per day. Option 2: $1 the first day, $2 the second day, $4 the third day, and so on, with the amount doubling each day. Write a program to determine which option pays better.

26. When $1000 is deposited at 5 percent simple interest, the amount grows by $50 each year. When money is invested at 5 percent compound interest, then the amount at the end of each year is 1.05 times the amount at the beginning of that year. Write a program to display the amounts for 10 years for a $1000 deposit at 5 percent simple and compound interest. The first few lines displayed in the list box should appear as in Figure 6.8.

Year	Amount Simple Interest	Amount Compound Interest
1	$1,050.00	$1,050.00
2	$1,100.00	$1,102.50
3	$1,150.00	$1,157.63

FIGURE 6.8   Growth of $1000 at simple and compound interest.

27. According to researchers at Stanford Medical School (as cited in *Medical Self Care*), the ideal weight for a woman is found by multiplying her height in inches by 3.5 and subtracting 108. The ideal weight for a man is found by multiplying his height in inches by 4 and subtracting 128. Request a lower and upper bound for heights and then produce a table giving the ideal weights for women and men in that height range. For example, when a lower bound of 62 and an upper bound of 65 are specified, Figure 6.9 shows the output displayed in the list box.

```
Height    Wt-Women    Wt-Men

  62        109        120
  63        112.5      124
  64        116        128
  65        119.5      132
```

FIGURE 6.9 Output for Exercise 27.

28. Table 6.3 gives historic and projected data (in millions) on personal computer sales and revenues. Read the data from the file PC.TXT, and generate an extended table with two additional columns, Pct Foreign (percent of personal computers sold outside the United States) and Avg Rev (average revenue per computer sold in the United States).

TABLE 6.3	Personal computer sales and revenues (in millions).		
Year	U.S. Sales	Worldwide Sales	U.S. Revenues
2000	46.0	130	86,900
2003	48.3	149	78,100
2005	56.6	181	84,500
2010	66.7	249	86,100

29. Request a sentence, and display the number of sibilants (that is, letters S or Z) in the sentence. The counting should be carried out by a Function procedure.

30. Request a whole number, n, from 1 to 30 and one of the letters S or P. Then, depending upon whether S or P was selected, calculate the sum or product of the numbers from 1 to n. The calculations should be carried out in Function procedures.

31. Suppose $800 is deposited into a savings account earning 4 percent interest compounded annually, and $100 is added to the account at the end of each year. Calculate the amount of money in the account at the end of 10 years. (Determine a formula for computing the balance at the end of one year based on the balance at the beginning of the year. Then write a program that starts with a balance of $800 and makes 10 passes through a loop containing the formula to produce the final answer.)

32. A TV set is purchased with a loan of $563 to be paid off with five monthly payments of $116. The interest rate is 1 percent per month. Display a table giving the balance on the loan at the end of each month.

33. *Radioactive Decay.* Cobalt 60, a radioactive form of cobalt used in cancer therapy, decays or dissipates over a period of time. Each year, 12 percent of the amount present at the beginning of the year will have decayed. If a container of cobalt 60 initially contains 10 grams, determine the amount remaining after five years.

34. *Supply and Demand.* This year's level of production and price (per bushel) for most agricultural products greatly affects the level of production and price next year. Suppose the current crop of soybeans in a country is 80 million bushels and experience has shown that for each year,

$$[\text{price this year}] = 20 - .1 * [\text{quantity this year}]$$

$$[\text{quantity next year}] = 5 * [\text{price this year}] - 10,$$

where quantity is measured in units of millions of bushels. Generate a table to show the quantity and price for each of the next 12 years.

35. Request a number greater than 3, and display a hollow rectangle similar to the one in Figure 6.10(a) with each outer row and column having that many stars. Use a fixed-width font such as Courier New so that the spaces and asterisks will have the same width.

FIGURE 6.10 Outputs for Exercises 35 and 36.

36. Request an odd number, and display a triangle similar to the one in Figure 6.10(b) with the input number of stars in the top row.

37. A man pays $1 to get into a gambling casino. He loses half of his money there and then has to pay $1 to leave. He goes to a second casino, pays another $1 to get in, loses half of his money again, and pays another $1 to leave. Then, he goes to a third casino, pays another $1 to get in, loses half of his money again, and pays another $1 to get out. After this, he's broke. Write a program to determine the amount of money he began with by testing $5, then $6, and so on.

38. Create the histogram in Figure 6.11. A file should hold the years and values. The first line in the file could be used to hold the title for the histogram.

```
2003    *   1
2004    * * * * * * * *   8
2005    * * * * * * * * * * * * * * * * * * * * * * * * * * * * * * * *   32
2006    * * * * * * * * * * * * * * * * * * * * * * * * * * * * * * * * * * * * * * * * * * * * * *   46
```

Worldwide iPod Sales in Millions

FIGURE 6.11 Histogram for Exercise 38.

39. Write a program to estimate how much a young worker will make before retiring at age 65. Request the worker's name, age, and starting salary as input. Assume the worker receives a 5 percent raise each year. For example, if the user enters Helen, 25, and 20000, then the text box should display the following:

```
Helen will earn about $2,415,995
```

40. Write a program that accepts a word as input and determines if its letters are in alphabetical order. (Test the program with the words "almost," "imply," and "biopsy.")

Solutions to Practice Problems 6.3

1. The loop will never be entered because 15 is greater than 1. The intended first line might have been

```
For i = 15 To 1 Step -1
```
or
```
For i = 1 To 15
```

2. If the exact number of times the loop will be executed is known before entering the loop, then a For . . . Next loop should be used. Otherwise, a Do loop is more appropriate.

6.4   A Case Study: Analyze a Loan

This case study develops a program to analyze a loan. Assume the loan is repaid in equal monthly payments and interest is compounded monthly. The program should request the amount (principal) of the loan, the annual rate of interest, and the number of years over which the loan is to be repaid. The four options to be provided by buttons are as follows:

1. Calculate the monthly payment. The formula for the monthly payment is

$$\text{payment} = p*r/(1 - (1 + r)^{\wedge}(-n)),$$

where p is the principal of the loan, r is the monthly interest rate (annual rate divided by 12) given as a number between 0 (for 0 percent) and 1 (for 100 percent), and n is the number of months over which the loan is to be repaid. When a payment computed in this manner includes fractions of a cent, the value should be rounded up to the next nearest cent. This corrected payment can be achieved using the formula

$$\text{correct payment} = \text{Math.Round}(\text{payment} + 0.005, 2).$$

2. Display an amortization schedule, that is, a table showing the balance on the loan at the end of each month for any year over the duration of the loan. Also show how much of each monthly payment goes toward interest and how much is used to repay the principal. Finally, display the total interest paid over the duration of the loan. The balances for successive months are calculated with the formula

$$\text{balance} = (1 + r)*b - m,$$

where r is the monthly interest rate (annual rate / 12, a fraction between 0 and 1), b is the balance for the preceding month (amount of loan left to be paid), and m is the monthly payment.

3. Show the effect of changes in the interest rate. Display a table giving the monthly payment for each interest rate from 1 percent below to 1 percent above the specified annual rate in steps of one-eighth of a percent.

4. Quit.

■ Designing the Analyze-a-Loan Program

For each of the tasks described in the preceding options 1 to 4, the program must first look at the text boxes to obtain the particulars of the loan to be analyzed. Thus, the first division of the problem is into the following tasks:

1. Input the principal, interest, and duration.
2. Calculate the monthly payment.
3. Calculate the amortization schedule.
4. Display the effects of interest-rate changes.
5. Quit.

Task 1 is a basic input operation and Task 2 involves applying the formula in Option 1; therefore, these tasks need not be broken down further. The demanding work of the program is done in Tasks 3 and 4, which can be divided into smaller subtasks.

3. *Calculate the amortization schedule.* This task involves simulating the loan month by month. First, the monthly payment must be computed. Then, for each month, the new balance must be computed together with a decomposition of the monthly payment into the amount paid for interest and the amount going toward repaying the principal. In addition, the total amount of interest paid is calculated. That is, Task 3 is divided into the following subtasks:

3.1 Calculate monthly payment.

3.2 Calculate new balance.

3.3 Calculate amount of monthly payment for principal.

3.4 Calculate amount of monthly payment for interest.

3.5 Calculate total interest paid.

4. *Display the effects of interest-rate changes.* A table is needed to show the effects of changes in the interest rate on the size of the monthly payment. First, the interest rate is reduced by one percentage point and the new monthly payment is computed. Then the interest rate is increased by regular increments until it reaches one percentage point above the original rate, with new monthly payment amounts computed for each intermediate interest rate. The subtasks for this task are then as follows:

4.1 Reduce the interest rate by 1 percent.

4.2 Calculate the new monthly payment.

4.3 Increase the interest rate by 1/8 percent.

4.4 Repeat until a certain condition is met.

The hierarchy chart in Figure 6.12 (on the next page) shows the stepwise refinement of the problem.

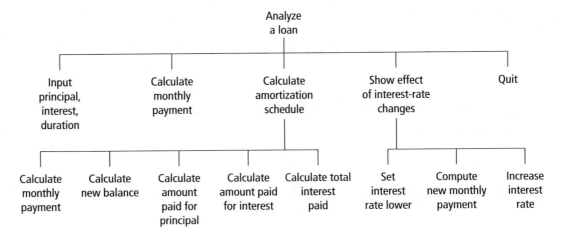

FIGURE 6.12   **Hierarchy chart for the Analyze-a-Loan Program.**

■ The User Interface

Figure 6.13 shows a possible form design and Table 6.4 gives the initial settings for the form and its controls. Figures 6.14, 6.15, and 6.16 show possible runs of the program for each task available through the buttons. The width and height of the list box were adjusted by trial and error to handle the extensive output generated.

FIGURE 6.13   **Template for the Analyze-a-Loan program.**

TABLE 6.4	Objects and initial properties for the Analyze-a-Loan program.		
	Object	Property	Setting
	frmLoan	Text	Analysis of a Loan
	lblPrincipal	Text	Amount of loan:
	txtPrincipal		
	lblYearlyRate	Text	Interest rate:
	txtYearlyRate		
	lblNumYears	Text	Number of loan years:
	txtNumYears		
	btnPayment	Text	Calculate Monthly Payment
	btnAmort	Text	Display Amortization Schedule
	btnRateTable	Text	Display Interest Rate Change Table
	btnQuit	Text	Quit
	lstResults		

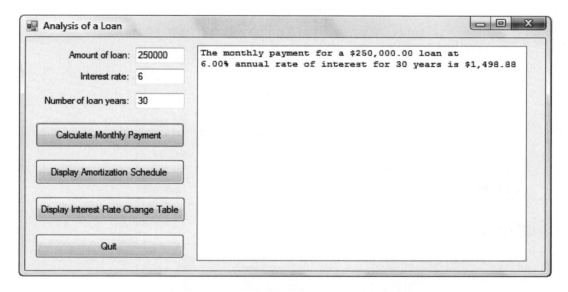

FIGURE 6.14   **Monthly payment on a 30-year loan.**

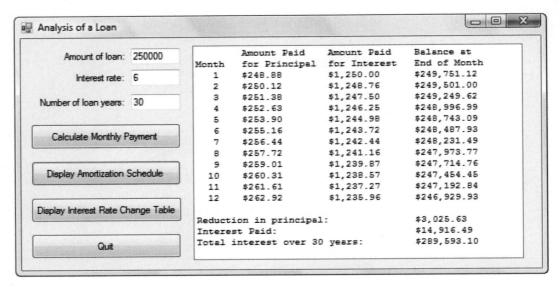

FIGURE 6.15   Amortization for year 30 of a loan.

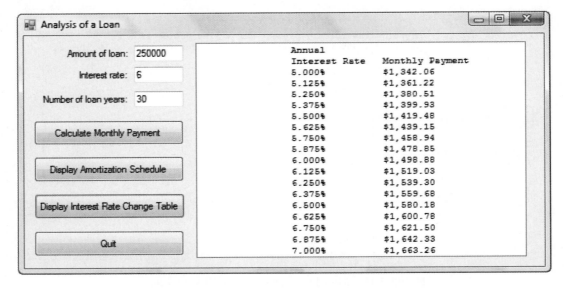

FIGURE 6.16   Interest-rate-change table for a 30-year loan.

■ Pseudocode for the Analyze-a-Loan Program

Calculate Monthly Payment button:
    INPUT LOAN DATA (Sub procedure InputData)
    COMPUTE MONTHLY PAYMENT (Function Payment)
    DISPLAY MONTHLY PAYMENT (Sub procedure ShowPayment)

Display Amortization Schedule button:
    INPUT LOAN DATA (Sub procedure InputData)

DISPLAY AMORTIZATION SCHEDULE
    (Sub procedure ShowAmortizationSchedule)
Compute monthly interest rate
COMPUTE MONTHLY PAYMENT (Function Payment)
Calculate and display amortization table
Display total interest paid

Display Interest Rate Change Table button:
    INPUT LOAN DATA (Sub procedure InputData)
    DISPLAY INTEREST RATE CHANGE TABLE
        (Sub procedure ShowInterestChanges)
    Decrease annual rate by .01
    Do
        Display monthly interest rate
        COMPUTE AND DISPLAY MONTHLY PAYMENT (Function Payment)
        Increase annual rate by .00125
    Loop Until annual rate > original annual rate + .01

■ Writing the Analyze-a-Loan Program

Table 6.5 shows each task discussed before and the procedure that carries out the task.

TABLE 6.5　Tasks and their procedures.

Task	Procedure
1. Input principal, interest, and duration.	InputData
2. Calculate monthly payment.	ShowPayment
3. Calculate amortization schedule.	ShowAmortizationSchedule
3.1 Calculate monthly payment.	Payment
3.2 Calculate new balance.	Balance
3.3 Calculate amount paid for principal.	ShowAmortizationSchedule
3.4 Calculate amount paid for interest.	ShowAmortizationSchedule
3.5 Calculate total interest paid.	ShowAmortizationSchedule
4. Display effect of interest-rate changes.	ShowInterestChanges
4.1 Reduce interest rate.	ShowInterestChanges
4.2 Compute new monthly payment.	Payment
4.3 Increase interest rate.	ShowInterestChanges
4.4 Repeat until a certain condition is met.	ShowInterestChanges

```
Private Sub btnPayment_Click(...) Handles btnPayment.Click
  Dim principal As Double        'Amount of loan
  Dim yearlyRate As Double       'Annual rate of interest
  Dim numMonths As Integer       'Number of months to repay loan
  InputData(principal, yearlyRate, numMonths)
  ShowPayment(principal, yearlyRate, numMonths)
End Sub
```

```
Private Sub btnAmort_Click(...) Handles btnAmort.Click
    Dim principal As Double              'Amount of loan
    Dim yearlyRate As Double             'Annual rate of interest
    Dim numMonths As Integer             'Number of months to repay loan
    InputData(principal, yearlyRate, numMonths)
    ShowAmortizationSchedule(principal, yearlyRate, numMonths)
End Sub

Private Sub btnRateTable_Click(...) Handles btnRateTable.Click
    Dim principal As Double              'Amount of loan
    Dim yearlyRate As Double             'Annual rate of interest
    Dim numMonths As Integer             'Number of months to repay loan
    InputData(principal, yearlyRate, numMonths)
    ShowInterestChanges(principal, yearlyRate, numMonths)
End Sub

Private Sub btnQuit_Click(...) Handles btnQuit.Click
    End
End Sub

Sub InputData(ByRef principal As Double, _
              ByRef yearlyRate As Double, ByRef numMonths As Integer)
    'Input the loan amount, yearly rate of interest, and duration
    Dim percentageRate As Double, numYears As Integer
    principal = CDbl(txtPrincipal.Text)
    percentageRate = CDbl(txtYearlyRate.Text)
    yearlyRate = percentageRate / 100
    numYears = CInt(txtNumYears.Text)
    numMonths = numYears * 12
End Sub

Sub ShowPayment(ByVal principal As Double, _
                ByVal yearlyRate As Double, ByVal numMonths As Integer)
    Dim monthlyRate As Double = yearlyRate / 12
    Dim monthlyPayment As Double
    'Calculate monthly payment
    monthlyPayment = Payment(principal, monthlyRate, numMonths)
    'Display results
    lstResults.Items.Clear()
    lstResults.Items.Add("The monthly payment for a " & _
                FormatCurrency(principal) & " loan at")
    lstResults.Items.Add(FormatNumber(yearlyRate * 100) & _
                        "% annual rate of interest for " & _
                        FormatNumber(numMonths / 12, 0) & _
                        " years is " & FormatCurrency(monthlyPayment))
End Sub

Sub ShowAmortizationSchedule(ByVal principal As Double, _
            ByVal yearlyRate As Double, ByVal numMonths As Integer)
    Dim questionYear As String
```

```vb
Dim startMonth As Integer
Dim monthlyRate As Double = yearlyRate / 12
Dim monthlyPayment As Double
Dim totalInterest As Double = 0
Dim yearInterest As Double = 0
Dim oldBalance, newBalance As Double
Dim numYears As Double = numMonths / 12
Dim principalPaid, interestPaid As Double
Dim principalReduced As Double
Dim fmtStr As String
'Ask for the year to display
questionYear = "Please enter year (1-" & numYears & _
                 ") for which amortization is to be shown:"
startMonth = 12 * CInt(InputBox(questionYear, "Which Year?")) - 11
'Display column headings
lstResults.Items.Clear()
fmtStr = "{0,-8}{1,-15}{2,-15}{3,-15}"
lstResults.Items.Add(String.Format(fmtStr, "", "Amount Paid", _
                                   "Amount Paid", "Balance at"))
lstResults.Items.Add(String.Format(fmtStr, "Month", _
                     "for Principal", "for Interest", "End of Month"))
monthlyPayment = Payment(principal, monthlyRate, numMonths)
oldBalance = principal
fmtStr = "{0,4}     {1,-15:C}{2,-15:C}{3,-15:C}"
'Loop for each month of the loan period
For monthNum As Integer = 1 To numMonths
  'Calculate the relevant figures
  newBalance = Balance(monthlyPayment, oldBalance, monthlyRate)
  principalPaid = oldBalance - newBalance
  interestPaid = monthlyPayment - principalPaid
  totalInterest = totalInterest + interestPaid
  'Display results if current year is the desired year to display
  If (monthNum >= startMonth) And (monthNum < startMonth + 12) Then
    lstResults.Items.Add(String.Format(fmtStr, monthNum, _
                       principalPaid, interestPaid, newBalance))
    yearInterest = yearInterest + interestPaid
  End If
  'Update the old balance for the next pass through the For loop
  oldBalance = newBalance
Next
'Display totals
principalReduced = 12 * monthlyPayment - yearInterest
fmtStr = "{0,-38}{1,-15:C}"
lstResults.Items.Add("")
lstResults.Items.Add(String.Format(fmtStr, _
                   "Reduction in principal:", principalReduced))
```

```
    lstResults.Items.Add(String.Format(fmtStr,"Interest Paid:", yearInterest))
    lstResults.Items.Add(String.Format(fmtStr, "Total interest over " & _
                        numYears & " years:", totalInterest))
End Sub

Function Balance(ByRef payment As Double, _
    ByVal oldBalance As Double, ByVal monthlyRate As Double) As Double
    'Compute balance at end of month
    Dim newBalance As Double
    newBalance = (1 + monthlyRate) * oldBalance
    'If balance is less than payment, then this
    'payment is the last one for this loan
    If newBalance <= payment Then
      payment = newBalance
      Return 0
    Else
      Return newBalance - payment
    End If
End Function

Function Payment(ByVal principal As Double, _
      ByVal monthlyRate As Double, ByVal numMonths As Integer) As Double
    Dim estimate As Double              'Estimate of monthly payment
    If numMonths = 0 Then
      'If no months then the loan must be repaid immediately
      estimate = principal
    ElseIf monthlyRate = 0 Then
      'If loan has no interest then just repay the principal over time
      estimate = principal / numMonths
    Else
      'Otherwise, use the formula for determining the monthly payment
      estimate = principal * monthlyRate / (1 - _
              (1 + monthlyRate) ^ (-numMonths))
    End If
    'Round the payment up if it there are fractions of a cent
    If estimate = Math.Round(estimate, 2) Then
      Return estimate
    Else
      Return Math.Round(estimate + 0.005, 2)
    End If
End Function

Sub ShowInterestChanges(ByVal principal As Double, _
              ByVal yearlyRate As Double, ByVal numMonths As Integer)
    Dim newRate As Double, monthlyRate As Double, monthlyPayment As Double
    Dim fmtStr As String = "{0,15} {1,-15} {2,-15}"
```

```
'Display effect of interest changes
lstResults.Items.Clear()
lstResults.Items.Add(String.Format(fmtStr, "", "Annual", ""))
lstResults.Items.Add(String.Format(fmtStr, "", _
        "Interest Rate", "Monthly Payment"))
'Set the annual rate's lower limit for the table
newRate = yearlyRate - 0.01
fmtStr = "{0,15} {1,-15} {2,-15:C}"
'Loop the annual rate from its lower limit to its upper limit
Do
    'Calculate the monthly payment for the corresponding monthly rate
    monthlyRate = newRate / 12
    monthlyPayment = Payment(principal, monthlyRate, numMonths)
    lstResults.Items.Add(String.Format(fmtStr, "", _
        FormatPercent(newRate, 3), monthlyPayment))
    newRate = newRate + 0.00125   'Increment by 1/8 of one percent for
    'the next pass through the loop
    'To avoid rounding errors, add 0.001 to the upper-limit condition
Loop Until newRate > yearlyRate + 0.01 + 0.001
End Sub
```

▨ Comments

1. Tasks 3.1 and 3.2 are performed by functions. Using functions to compute these quantities simplifies the computations in ShowAmortizationSchedule.

2. Because the payment was rounded up to the nearest cent, it is highly likely that the payment needed in the final month to pay off the loan will be less than the normal payment. For this reason, ShowAmortizationSchedule checks if the balance of the loan (including interest due) is less than the regular payment and, if so, makes appropriate adjustments.

3. The standard formula for computing the monthly payment cannot be used if either the interest rate is zero percent or the loan duration is zero months. Although both of these situations do not represent reasonable loan parameters, provisions are made in the function Payment so that the program can handle these esoteric situations.

CHAPTER 6   SUMMARY

1. A *Do loop* repeatedly executes a block of statements either as long as or until a certain condition is true. The condition can be checked either at the top of the loop or at the bottom.

2. The *Peek method* can be used to tell us if we have read to the end of a file.

3. As various items of data are processed by a loop, a *counter* can be used to keep track of the number of items, and an *accumulator* can be used to sum numerical values.

4. A *flag* is a Boolean variable, used to indicate whether a certain event has occurred.

5. A *For...Next loop* repeats a block of statements a fixed number of times. The *control variable* assumes an initial value and increments by one after each pass through the loop until it reaches the terminating value. Alternative increment values can be specified with the Step keyword.

6. A variable declared inside a Do loop or For...Next block has *block-level scope;* that is, the variable cannot be referred to by code outside of the loop or block.

CHAPTER 6   PROGRAMMING PROJECTS

1. Write a program to display a company's payroll report in a list box. The program should read each employee's name, hourly rate, and hours worked from a file and produce a report in the form of the sample run shown in Figure 6.17. Employees should be paid time-and-a-half for hours in excess of 40.

```
Payroll Report for week ending 11/17/08

Employee          Hourly Rate      Hours Worked      Gross Pay

Al Adams             $8.50             38            $323.00
Bob Brown            $7.70             50            $423.50
Carol Coe            $9.00             40            $360.00

Final Total                                        $1,106.50
```

FIGURE 6.17   Sample output from Programming Project 1.

2. Table 6.6 shows the standard prices for items in a department store. Suppose prices will be reduced for the annual President's Day Sale. The new price will be computed by reducing the old price by 10 percent, rounding up to the nearest dollar, and subtracting 1 cent. If the new price is greater than the old price, the old price is used as the sale price. Write a program to display in a list box the output shown in Figure 6.18.

TABLE 6.6   President's Day sale.

Item	Original Price
GumShoes	39.00
SnugFoot Sandals	21.00
T-Shirt	7.75
Maine Handbag	33.00
Maple Syrup	6.75
Flaked Vest	24.00
Nightshirt	26.00

```
Item                    Sale Price
  GumShoes                 35.99
  SnugFoot Sandals         18.99
  T-Shirt                   6.99
  Maine Handbag            29.99
  Maple Syrup               6.75
  Flaked Vest              21.99
  Nightshirt               23.99
```

FIGURE 6.18   Output of Programming Project 2.

3. The Rule of 72 is used to make a quick estimate of the time required for prices to double due to inflation. If the inflation rate is r percent, then the Rule of 72 estimates that prices will double in $72/r$ years. For instance, at an inflation rate of 6 percent, prices double in about $72/6$ or 12 years. Write a program to test the accuracy of this rule. The program should display a table showing, for each value of r from 1 to 20, the rounded value of $72/r$ and the actual number of years required for prices to double at an r percent inflation rate. (Assume prices increase at the end of each year.) Figure 6.19 shows the first few rows of the output.

```
Interest      Rule
Rate (%)     of 72    Actual
    1          72        70
    2          36        36
    3          24        24
```

FIGURE 6.19   Rule of 72 used in Programming Project 3.

4. Table 6.7 shows the number of bachelor degrees conferred in 1981 and 2005 in certain fields of study. Tables 6.8 and 6.9 (on the next page) show the percentage change and a histogram of 2005 levels, respectively. Write a program that allows the user to display any one of these tables as an option and quit as a fourth option.

TABLE 6.7   Bachelor degrees conferred in certain fields.

Field of Study	1981	2005
Business	200,521	311,574
Computer and info. science	15,121	54,111
Education	108,074	105,451
Engineering	63,642	64,906
Social sciences and history	100,513	156,892

Source: U.S. National Center of Education Statistics

TABLE 6.8	**Percentage change in bachelor degrees conferred.**

Field of Study	% Change (1981–2005)
Business	55.4
Computer and info. science	257.9
Education	−2.4
Engineering	2.0
Social sciences and history	56.1

TABLE 6.9	**Bachelor degrees conferred in 2005 in certain fields.**

Business	********************************	311,574
Computer and info. science	***** 54,111	
Education	*********** 105,451	
Engineering	****** 64,906	
Social sciences and history	*************** 156,892	

5. *Least-Squares Approximation.* Table 6.10 shows the 1988 prices of a gallon of gasoline and the amounts of fuel consumed for several countries. Figure 6.20 displays the data as points in the xy plane. For instance, the point with coordinates $(1, 1400)$ corresponds to the USA. Figure 6.20 also shows the straight line that best fits these data in the least-squares sense. (The sum of the squares of the distances of the 11 points from this line is as small as possible.) In general, if (x_1, y_1), (x_2, y_2), ..., (x_n, y_n) are n points in the xy coordinate system, then the least-squares approximation to these points is the line $y = mx + b$, where

$$m = \frac{n * (\text{sum of } x_i * y_i) - (\text{sum of } x_i) * (\text{sum of } y_i)}{n * (\text{sum of } x_i * x_i) - (\text{sum of } x_i)^2}$$

TABLE 6.10	**A comparison of 1988 gasoline prices and per capita fuel use.**

Country	Price per gallon in U.S. Dollars	Tons of Fuel per 1000 Persons	Country	Price per gallon in U.S. Dollars	Tons of Fuel per 1000 Persons
USA	$1.00	1400	France	$3.10	580
W. Ger.	$2.20	620	Norway	$3.15	600
England	$2.60	550	Japan	$3.60	410
Austria	$2.75	580	Denmark	$3.70	570
Sweden	$2.80	700	Italy	$3.85	430
Holland	$3.00	490			

Source: World Resources Institute

and

$$b = ((\text{sum of } y_i) - m * (\text{sum of } x_i))/n.$$

Write a program that calculates and displays the equation of the least-squares line. The program should then allow the user to enter a gasoline price and use the equation of the line to predict the corresponding consumption of fuel. (Place the numeric data from the table in a text file.) A sample run is shown in Figure 6.21.

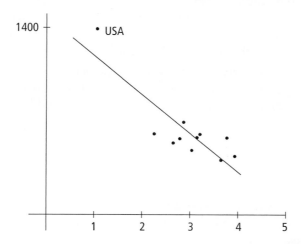

FIGURE 6.20   Least-squares fit to data from Table 6.10.

FIGURE 6.21   Sample run of Programming Project 5.

6. Write a program to provide information on the height of a ball thrown straight up into the air. The program should request the initial height, h feet, and the initial velocity, v feet per second, as input. The four options to be provided by buttons are as follows:

   (a) Determine the maximum height of the ball. **Note:** The ball will reach its maximum height after $v/32$ seconds.
   (b) Determine approximately when the ball will hit the ground. **Hint:** Calculate the height after every .1 second and observe when the height is no longer a positive number.
   (c) Display a table showing the height of the ball every quarter second for five seconds or until it hits the ground.
   (d) Quit.

The formula for the height of the ball after t seconds, $h + v*t - 16*t*t$, should be specified in a user-defined function. (Test the program with $v = 148$ and $h = 0$. This velocity is approximately the top speed clocked for a ball thrown by a professional baseball pitcher.)

7. *Depreciation to a Salvage Value of 0.* For tax purposes an item may be depreciated over a period of several years, n. With the *straight-line* method of depreciation, each year the item depreciates by 1/nth of its original value. With the *double-declining-balance* method of depreciation, each year the item depreciates by 2/nths of its value at the beginning of that year. (In the last year, it is depreciated by its value at the beginning of the year.) Write a program that performs the following tasks:

    (a) Requests a description of the item, the year of purchase, the cost of the item, the number of years to be depreciated (estimated life), and the method of depreciation. The method of depreciation should be chosen by clicking one of two buttons.

    (b) Displays a depreciation schedule for the item similar to the schedule shown in Figure 6.22.

```
Description: Computer
Year of purchase: 2005
Cost: $2,000.00
Estimated life: 5
Method of depreciation: double-declining-balance

            Value at      Amount Deprec     Total Depreciation
  Year      Beg of Yr      During Year        to End of Year
  2005      2,000.00          800.00               800.00
  2006      1,200.00          480.00             1,280.00
  2007        720.00          288.00             1,568.00
  2008        432.00          172.80             1,740.80
  2009        259.20          259.20             2,000.00
```

FIGURE 6.22 **Depreciation schedule for Programming Project 7.**

8. *The Twelve Days of Christmas.* Each year, PNC Advisors of Pittsburgh publishes a Christmas price list. See Table 6.11. Write a program that requests an integer from 1 through 12 and then lists the gifts for that day along with that day's cost. On the nth day, the n gifts are 1 partridge in a pear tree, 2 turtle doves, ..., n of the nth item. The program also should give the total cost of all twelve days. As an example, Figure 6.23 shows the output in the list box when the user enters 3.

TABLE 6.11	Christmas price list for 2007.		
Item	Cost	Item	Cost
partridge in a pear tree	164.99	swan-a-swimming	600.00
turtle dove	20.00	maid-a-milking	5.85
French hen	15.00	lady dancing	528.80
calling bird	149.99	lord-a-leaping	428.51
gold ring	79.00	piper piping	201.22
goose-a-laying	60.00	drummer drumming	199.82

```
The gifts for day 3 are
1 partridge in a pear tree
2 turtle doves
3 french hens
Cost: $249.99
Total cost for the twelve days: $78,100.30
```

FIGURE 6.23   Sample output for Programming Project 8.

9. A *palindrome* is a word or phrase that reads the same forwards and backwards, character for character, disregarding punctuation, case, and spaces. Some examples are "race-car", "Madam, I'm Adam.", and "Was it a cat I saw?". Write a program that allows the user to input a word or phrase and then determines if it is a palindrome. The program should use a Boolean-valued Function procedure named IsPalindrome that returns the value True if the word or phrase is a palindrome and the value False otherwise.

7

Arrays

7.1 Creating and Accessing Arrays

A **variable** (or simple variable) is a name to which Visual Basic can assign a single value. An **array variable** is a collection of simple variables of the same type to which Visual Basic can efficiently assign a list of values.

Consider the following situation: Suppose that you want to evaluate the exam grades for 30 students. Not only do you want to compute the average score, but you also want to display the names of the students whose scores are above average. You might place the 30 pairs of student names and scores in a text file and run the program outlined below. *Note:* Visual Basic prefers to begin numberings with 0 instead of 1. (We saw this preference in Chapter 3 where the numbering of the positions in a string began with 0.) Therefore we will number the 30 student names from 0 through 29 instead of from 1 through 30.

```
Private Sub btnDisplay_Click(...) Handles btnDisplay.Click
  Dim student0 As String, score0 As Double
  Dim student1 As String, score1 As Double
  Dim student2 As String, score2 As Double
        .
        .
  Dim student29 As String, score29 As Double
  'Analyze exam grades
  Dim sr As IO.StreamReader = IO.File.OpenText("SCORES.TXT")
  student0 = sr.ReadLine
  score0 = CDbl(sr.ReadLine)
  student1 = sr.ReadLine
  score1 = CDbl(sr.ReadLine)
        .
        .
  student29 = sr.ReadLine
  score29 = CDbl(sr.ReadLine)
  sr.Close()
  'Compute the average grade
        .
        .
  'Display names of above average students
        .
        .
End Sub
```

This program is going to be uncomfortably long. What's most frustrating is that the 30 Dim statements and 30 pairs of statements reading from the file are very similar and look as if they should be condensed into a short loop. A shorthand notation for the many related variables would be welcome. It would be nice if we could just write

```
For i As Integer = 0 To 29
  studenti = sr.ReadLine
  scorei = CDbl(sr.ReadLine)
Next
```

Of course, this will not work. Visual Basic will treat *studenti* and *scorei* as two variables and keep reassigning new values to them. At the end of the loop, they will have the values of the thirtieth student.

■ Declaring an Array Variable

Visual Basic provides a data structure called an **array** that lets us do what we tried to accomplish in the loop on the previous page. The variable names, similar to those in the preceding program, will be

```
student(0), student(1), student(2), student(3), ..., student(29)
```

and

```
score(0), score(1), score(2), score(3), ..., score(29)
```

We refer to these collections of variables as the array variables *student()* and *score()*. The numbers inside the parentheses of the individual variables are called **subscripts** or **indexes**, and each individual variable is called a **subscripted variable** or **element**. For instance, *student*(3) is the fourth subscripted variable of the array *student()*, and *score*(20) is the 21st subscripted variable of the array *score()*. The elements of an array are assigned successive memory locations. Figure 7.1 shows the memory locations for the array *score()*.

FIGURE 7.1   The array *score().*

Array variables have the same kinds of names as simple variables. If *arrayName* is the name of an array variable and *n* is an Integer literal, variable, or expression, then the declaration statement

```
Dim arrayName(n) As varType
```

reserves space in memory to hold the values of the subscripted variables *arrayName*(0), *arrayName*(1), *arrayName*(2), ..., *arrayName*(*n*). The value of *n* is called the **upper bound** of the array. The number of elements in the array, *n* + 1, is called the **size** of the array. The subscripted variables will all have the same data type; namely, the type specified by *varType*. For instance, they could be all String variables or all Integer variables. In particular, the statements

```
Dim student(29) As String
Dim score(29) As Double
```

declare the arrays needed for the preceding program. They each have 30 elements.

Values can be assigned to individual subscripted variables with assignment statements and displayed in text boxes and list boxes just as values of ordinary variables. The default initial value of each subscripted variable is the same as with an ordinary variable; that is, the keyword Nothing for String types and 0 for numeric types. The statement

```
Dim score(29) As Double
```

sets aside a portion of memory for the Double array *score*( ) and assigns the default value 0 to each element.

	score(0)	score(1)	score(2)	· · ·	score(29)
score( )	0	0	0	· · ·	0

The statements

```
score(0) = 87
score(1) = 92
```

assign values to the zeroth and first elements.

	score(0)	score(1)	score(2)	· · ·	score(29)
score( )	87	92	0	· · ·	0

The statements

```
For i As Integer = 0 To 2
  lstBox.Items.Add(score(i))
Next
```

then produce the following output in the list box:

```
87
92
0
```

As with an ordinary variable, an array declared in the Declarations section of the Code Editor is class-level. That is, it will be visible to all procedures in the form, and any values assigned to it in a procedure will persist when the procedure terminates. Array variables declared inside a procedure are local to that procedure and cease to exist when the procedure is exited.

 Example 1 The following program creates a String array consisting of the names of the first four Super Bowl winners. Figure 7.2 shows the array created by the program.

	teamName(0)	teamName(1)	teamName(2)	teamName(3)
teamName( )	Packers	Packers	Jets	Chiefs

FIGURE 7.2 **The array *teamName*( ) of Example 1.**

OBJECT	PROPERTY	SETTING
frmBowl	Text	Early Super Bowls
lblNumber	Text	Number from 1 to 4:
mtxtNumber	Mask	0
btnWhoWon	Text	Who Won?
lblWinner	Text	Winning Team:
txtWinner	ReadOnly	True

```
Private Sub btnWhoWon_Click(...) Handles btnWhoWon.Click
  Dim teamName(3) As String
  Dim n As Integer
  'Place Super Bowl Winners into the array
  teamName(0) = "Packers"
  teamName(1) = "Packers"
  teamName(2) = "Jets"
  teamName(3) = "Chiefs"
  'Access array
  n = CInt(mtxtNumber.Text)
  txtWinner.Text = teamName(n - 1)
End Sub
```

[Run, type 2 into the masked text box, and click the button.]

The Load Event Procedure

In Example 1, the array *teamName* was assigned values within the btnWhoWon_Click event procedure. Every time the button is clicked, the values are reassigned to the array. This manner of assigning values to an array can be very inefficient, especially in programs with large arrays where the task of the program (in Example 1, looking up a fact) may be repeated numerous times for different user input. When, as in Example 1, the data to be placed in an array are known at the time the program begins to run, a more efficient location for the statements that fill the array is in the form's Load event procedure. The Load event occurs automatically when the form is loaded into memory, before it becomes visible on the screen. The header and End Sub statements for the Load event procedure are placed in the Code Editor when you double-click on the form. A typical header looks like

```
Private Sub frmName_Load(...) Handles MyBase.Load
```

The keyword MyBase is similar to the Me keyword and refers to the form being loaded. Example 2 uses the frmBowl_Load procedure to improve on Example 1.

Example 2   The following improvement on Example 1 makes *teamName*() a class-level array and assigns values to the elements of the array in the frmBowl_Load procedure:

```
Dim teamName(3) As String

Private Sub btnWhoWon_Click(...) Handles btnWhoWon.Click
  Dim n As Integer
  n = CInt(mtxtNumber.Text)
  txtWinner.Text = teamName(n - 1)
End Sub

Private Sub frmBowl_Load(...) Handles MyBase.Load
  'Place Super Bowl Winners into the array
  teamName(0) = "Packers"
  teamName(1) = "Packers"
  teamName(2) = "Jets"
  teamName(3) = "Chiefs"
End Sub
```

Like ordinary variables, array variables can be declared and assigned initial values at the same time. A statement of the form

```
Dim arrayName() As DataType = {value0, value1, value2, ..., valueN}
```

declares an array having upper bound N and assigns *value0* to *arrayName*(0), *value1* to *arrayName*(1), *value2* to *arrayName*(2), ..., and *valueN* to *arrayName*(N). For instance, in Example 2, the Dim statement and frmBowl_Load event procedure can be replaced by the single line

```
Dim teamName() As String = {"Packers", "Packers", "Jets", "Chiefs"}
```

■ The GetUpperBound Method

The value of *arrayName*.GetUpperBound(0) is the upper bound of the array. For instance, in Example 1, the value of `teamName.GetUpperBound(0)` is 3.

■ ReDim Statement

After an array has been declared, its size (but not its type) can be changed with a statement of the form

```
ReDim arrayName(m)
```

where *arrayName* is the name of the already declared array and m is an Integer literal, variable, or expression. **Note:** Since the type cannot be changed, there is no need for an "As *dataType*" clause at the end of the ReDim statement.

Visual Basic allows you to declare an array without specifying an upper bound with a statement of the form

```
Dim arrayName() As DataType
```

Later, the size of the array can be stipulated with a ReDim statement.

The ReDim statement has one shortcoming: It causes the array to lose its current contents. That is, it resets all String values to Nothing and resets all numeric values to 0. This situation can be remedied by following ReDim with the word Preserve. The general form of a ReDim Preserve statement is

ReDim Preserve *arrayName*(*m*)

Of course, if you make an array smaller than it was, data in the eliminated elements will be lost.

Example 3   The following program reads the names of the winners of Super Bowl games from a file and places them into an array. The user can type a team's name into a text box and then display the numbers of the Super Bowl games won by that team. The user has the option of adding winners of subsequent games to the array of winners. The program uses the text file SBWINNERS.TXT whose lines contain the names of the winners in order. That is, the first four lines of the file contain the names Packers, Packers, Jets, and Chiefs.

```
Dim teamName() As String

Dim upperBound As Integer

Private Sub frmBowl_Load(...) Handles MyBase.Load
  Dim sr As IO.StreamReader = IO.File.OpenText("SBWINNERS.TXT")
  Dim name As String, numLines As Integer
  'Count number of lines in the file and assign it minus one to upperBound
  numLines = 0
  Do While (sr.Peek <> -1)
    name = sr.ReadLine
    numLines += 1
  Loop
  upperBound = numLines - 1
  sr.Close()
  'Specify the title bar of the form
  Me.Text = "First " & upperBound + 1 & " Super Bowls"
  'Specify the caption of the Next Winner button
  btnNextWinner.Text = "Add Winner of Game " & upperBound + 2
  'Specify the size of the array and fill it with the entries of the file
  ReDim teamName(upperBound)
  sr = IO.File.OpenText("SBWINNERS.TXT")
  For i As Integer = 0 To upperBound
    teamName(i) = sr.ReadLine
  Next
  sr.Close()
End Sub
```

```
Private Sub btnDisplay_Click(...) Handles btnDisplay.Click
  'Display the numbers of the games won by the team in the text box
  Dim noWins As Boolean = True 'Flag to detect if any wins
  lstGamesWon.Items.Clear()
  For i As Integer = 0 To upperBound
    If teamName(i).ToUpper = txtName.Text.ToUpper Then
      lstGamesWon.Items.Add(i + 1)
      noWins = False
    End If
  Next
  If noWins Then
    lstGamesWon.Items.Add("No Games Won")
  End If
End Sub

Private Sub btnNextWinner_Click(...) Handles btnNextWinner.Click
  'Add winner of next Super Bowl to the array
  Dim prompt As String
  upperBound += 1
  'Add one more element to the array
  ReDim Preserve teamName(upperBound)
  'Request the name of the next winner
  prompt = "Enter winner of game #" & upperBound + 1
  teamName(upperBound) = InputBox(prompt, , "")
  'Update the title bar of the form and the caption of the button
  'Note: "Me" refers to the form.
  Me.Text = "First " & upperBound + 1 & " Super Bowls"
  btnNextWinner.Text = "Add Winner of Game " & upperBound + 2
End Sub
```

[Run, type "Giants" into the text box, and press the Display button. Then, feel free to add subsequent winners. Your additions will be taken into account when you next press the Display button.]

Using an Array as a Frequency Table

An array can be used as either a checklist or a frequency table, as in the next example.

Example 4 The following program requests a sentence as input and records the frequencies of the letters occurring in the sentence. The first element of the array *charCount*( ) holds the frequency with which the letter A occurs in the sentence, and so on. Recall that the function Asc associates each character with its position in the ANSI table.

```
Private Sub btnAnalyze_Click(...) Handles btnAnalyze.Click
  'Count occurrences of the various letters in a sentence
  Dim index As Integer
  Dim sentence, letter As String
  Dim charCount(25) As Integer
  'Examine and tally each letter of the sentence
  sentence = (txtSentence.Text).ToUpper
  For letterNum As Integer = 1 To sentence.Length
    letter = sentence.Substring(letterNum - 1, 1)
    If (letter >= "A") And (letter <= "Z") Then
      index = Asc(letter) - 65   'The ANSI value of "A" is 65
      charCount(index) += 1
    End If
  Next
  'List the tally for each letter of alphabet
  lstCount.Items.Clear()
  For i As Integer = 0 To 25
    letter = Chr(i + 65)
    If charCount(i) > 0 Then
      lstCount.Items.Add(letter & "  " & charCount(i))
    End If
  Next
End Sub
```

[Run, type a sentence into the text box, and press the button.]

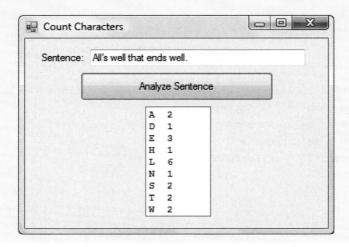

■ Assignment Statement for Arrays

If *arrayOne*( ) and *arrayTwo*( ) have been declared with the same data type, then the statement

```
arrayOne = arrayTwo
```

makes *arrayOne*( ) an exact duplicate of *arrayTwo*( ). It will have the same size and contain the same information. Such a statement is put to good use in Example 5. However, in general it must be used with care since after it is executed, arrayOne and arrayTwo will share the same portion of memory. Therefore, any value assigned to an element of one of the arrays will affect the other array.

■ User-Defined Array-Valued Functions

A Function procedure with a header of the form

```
Function FunctionName(ByVal var1 As Type1, _
                      ByVal var2 As Type2, ...) As DataType()
```

returns an array of type *DataType* as its value.

✔ | **Example 5**   The text file STATES.TXT lists the fifty U.S. states in the order they entered the union. (The first state is Delaware and the last state is Hawaii.) The following program asks the user to enter a number from 1 through 50 and then displays the corresponding state. The program uses the Function procedure FillArrayWithStates that returns an array.

```
Dim states() As String

Private Sub frmStates_Load(...) Handles MyBase.Load
  'Assume STATES.TXT is in the Debug subfolder of bin
  states = FillArrayWithStates("STATES.TXT")
End Sub

Private Sub btnDetermine_Click(...) Handles btnDetermine.Click
  txtOutput.Text = "State #" & txtNumber.Text & ": " & _
                  states(CInt(txtNumber.Text) - 1)
End Sub

Function FillArrayWithStates(ByVal file As String) As String()
  Dim temp(49) As String
  Dim sr As IO.StreamReader = IO.File.OpenText(file)
  For i As Integer = 0 To 49
    temp(i) = sr.ReadLine
```

```
    Next
    sr.Close()
    Return temp
End Function
```

[Run, type 49 into the top text box, and then click the button.]

■ Comments

1. Using a subscript greater than the upper bound of an array is not allowed. For instance, at run time the following two lines of code produce the error dialog box shown in Figure 7.3.

```
Dim trees() As String = {"Sequoia", "Redwood", "Spruce"}
txtBox.Text = trees(5)
```

FIGURE 7.3   Error dialog box.

2. An array can consume a large block of memory. After the array is no longer needed, the statement

Erase *arrayName*

can be executed to release all memory allocated to the array.

Practice Problems 7.1

1. Write code to declare an array with upper bound 10 and place the names of the five Great Lakes into the first five elements. Use one or two lines of code.
2. In Example 3, rewrite the btnDisplay_Click event procedure so that only the first Super Bowl won by the requested team is displayed. The loop should terminate when the team is found.
3. When should arrays be used to hold data?

EXERCISES 7.1

1. What is the size of an array whose upper bound is 500?
2. What is the upper bound of an array whose size is 500?

In Exercises 3 through 12, determine the output displayed when the button is clicked.

3.
```
Private Sub btnDisplay_Click(...) Handles btnDisplay.Click
    Dim num As Integer = 2
    Dim spoon(num) As String
    spoon(0) = "soup"
    spoon(1) = "dessert"
    spoon(2) = "tea"
    txtOutput.Text = "Have a " & spoon(num - 2) & " spoon."
End Sub
```

4.
```
Private Sub btnDisplay_Click(...) Handles btnDisplay.Click
    Dim a(20) As Integer
    a(5) = 3
    a(10) = 2
    a(15) = 7
    lstOutput.Items.Add(a(5) + a(10))
    lstOutput.Items.Add(a(5 + 5))
    lstOutput.Items.Add(a(20))
End Sub
```

5.
```
Dim sq(5) As Integer
Private Sub btnDisplay_Click(...) Handles btnDisplay.Click
    Dim t As Integer
    For i As Integer = 0 To 5
        sq(i) = i * i
    Next
    lstOutput.Items.Add(sq(3))
    t = 3
    lstOutput.Items.Add(sq(5 - t))
End Sub
```

6.
```
Dim fh(3) As String
Private Sub btnDisplay_Click(...) Handles btnDisplay.Click
    Dim n As Integer
    Dim sr As IO.StreamReader = IO.File.OpenText("HORSEMEN.TXT")
    For i As Integer = 0 To 3
        fh(i) = sr.ReadLine
```

```
    Next
    sr.Close()
    lstOutput.Items.Add(fh(fh.GetUpperBound(0)))
    n = 1
    lstOutput.Items.Add(fh(2 * n))
  End Sub
```

(Assume that the four lines of the file HORSEMEN.TXT contain the following entries: Miller, Layden, Crowley, Stuhldreher.)

7.
```
Dim s(4) As Integer
Private Sub btnDisplay_Click(...) Handles btnDisplay.Click
  Dim t As Integer
  Dim sr As IO.StreamReader = IO.File.OpenText("DATA.TXT")
  t = 0
  For k As Integer = 0 To 4
    s(k) = CInt(sr.ReadLine)
    t += s(k)
  Next
  txtOutput.Text = CStr(t)
  sr.Close()
End Sub
```

(Assume that the four lines of the file DATA.TXT contain the following entries: 7, 3, 5, 2, 1.)

8.
```
Dim a(4), b(4) As Integer
Dim c(4) As Double
Private Sub btnDisplay_Click(...) Handles btnDisplay.Click
  Dim sr As IO.StreamReader = IO.File.OpenText("DATA.TXT")
  For i As Integer = 0 To 4
    a(i) = CInt(sr.ReadLine)
    b(i) = CInt(sr.ReadLine)
  Next
  sr.Close()
  For i As Integer = 0 To c.GetUpperBound(0)
    c(i) = a(i) + b(i)
    lstOutput.Items.Add(c(i))
  Next
End Sub
```

(Assume that the eight lines of the file DATA.TXT contain the following entries: 8, 9, 2, 5, 3, 4, 1, 3, 7, 2.)

9.
```
Private Sub btnDisplay_Click(...) Handles btnDisplay.Click
  'Compare the values of two chess pieces
  Dim chess() As string = {"king", "queen", ""}
  chess(2) = "rook"
  ReDim Preserve chess(6)
  chess(3) = "bishop"
  txtOutput.Text = "A " & chess(2) & " is worth more than a " & chess(3)
End Sub
```

10.
```
Dim grade(1) As Double
Private Sub btnDisplay_Click(...) Handles btnDisplay.Click
  Dim average As Double
  ReDim grade(4)
  grade(2) = 70
  grade(3) = 80
  grade(4) = 60
  average = (grade(0) + grade(1) + grade(2) + grade(3) + grade(4)) / 5
    txtOutput.Text = "Your average is " & average
End Sub

Private Sub frmGrades_Load(...) Handles MyBase.Load
  grade(0) = 80
  grade(1) = 70
End Sub
```

11.
```
Dim score() As Double = {71, 68, 69}
Private Sub btnDisplay_Click(...) Handles btnDisplay.Click
  'Find the sum of four scores
  Dim total As Double
  ReDim Preserve score(3)
  score(3) = 72
  total = score(0) + score(1) + score(2) + score(3)
  txtOutput.Text = "Your total is " & total & "."
End Sub
```

12.
```
Dim band() As String = {"solo", "duet", "trio", "quartet"}
Private Sub btnDisplay_Click(...) Handles btnDisplay.Click
  Dim num As Integer
  ReDim Preserve band(7)
  band(4) = "quintet"
  band(5) = "sextet"
  band(6) = InputBox("What do you call a group of 7 musicians?")
  num = CInt(InputBox("How many musicians are in your group?"))
  txtOutput.Text = "You have a " & band(num - 1) & "."
End Sub
```

(Assume that the first response is *septet* and the second response is *7*.)

In Exercises 13 through 18, identify the errors.

13.
```
Dim companies(100) As String
Private Sub frmFirms_Load(...) Handles MyBase.Load
  Dim recCount As Integer
  Dim sr As IO.StreamReader = IO.File.OpenText("FIRMS.TXT")
  recCount = CInt(sr.ReadLine)
  ReDim companies(recCount - 1) As String
  For i As Integer = 0 To recCount - 1
    companies(i) = sr.ReadLine
  Next
  sr.Close()
End Sub
```

(Assume that the file FIRMS.TXT contains a list of companies and the first line of the file gives the number of companies.)

14.
```
Dim p(100) As Double
Private Sub btnDisplay_Click(...) Handles btnDisplay.Click
  For i As Integer = 0 To 200
    p(i) = i / 2
  Next
End Sub
```

15.
```
Dim a(10) As Integer
Private Sub btnDisplay_Click(...) Handles btnDisplay.Click
  Dim sr As IO.StreamReader = IO.File.OpenText("DATA.TXT")
  For i As Integer = 0 To 8
    a(i) = CInt(sr.ReadLine)
  Next
  sr.Close()
  For k As Integer = 0 To 8
    a(k) = a(5 - k)
  Next
End Sub
```

(Assume that the nine lines of the file DATA.TXT contain the following entries: 1, 2, 3, 4, 5, 6, 7, 8, 9.)

16.
```
Private Sub btnDisplay_Click(...) Handles btnDisplay.Click
  Dim films() As String = {"Gladiator", "Titanic"}
  lstOutput.Items.Add(films)
End Sub
```

17.
```
Private Sub btnDisplay_Click(...) Handles btnDisplay.Click
  Dim amount(2) As Integer = {7, 11, 14}
  Dim total As Integer = 0
  For i As Integer = 0 To 2
    total += amount(i)
  Next
  txtOutput.Text = CStr(total)
End Sub
```

18.
```
Private Sub frmNames_Load(...) Handles MyBase.Load
  Dim recCount As Integer
  Dim sr As IO.StreamReader = IO.File.OpenText("DATA.TXT")
  recCount = CInt(sr.ReadLine)
  ReDim names(recCount - 1) As String
  For i As Integer = 0 to recCount - 1
    names(i) = sr.ReadLine
  Next
  sr.Close()
End Sub
```

(Assume that the four lines of the file DATA.TXT contain the following entries: 3, Tom, Dick, Harry.)

19. Assuming that the array *river*() is as follows, fill in the empty rectangles to illustrate the progressing status of *river*() after the execution of each program segment:

	river(0)	river(1)	river(2)	river(3)	river(4)
river( )	Nile	Ohio	Amazon	Volga	Thames

```
temp = river(0)
river(0) = river(4)
river(4) = temp
```

	river(0)	river(1)	river(2)	river(3)	river(4)
river( )					

```
temp = river(0)
For i As Integer = 0 To 3
  river(i) = river(i + 1)
Next
river(4) = temp
```

	river(0)	river(1)	river(2)	river(3)	river(4)
river( )					

20. Assuming the array *cat*() is as follows, fill in the empty rectangles to show the final status of *cat*() after executing the nested loops:

	cat(0)	cat(1)	cat(2)	cat(3)
cat( )	Morris	Garfield	Socks	Felix

```
For i As Integer = 0 To 2
  For j As Integer = 0 To 3 - i
    If cat(j) > cat(j + 1) Then
      temp = cat(j)
      cat(j) = cat(j + 1)
      cat(j + 1) = temp
    End If
  Next
Next
```

	cat(0)	cat(1)	cat(2)	cat(3)
cat( )				

```
Dim gap As Integer = 2
Do While gap >= 1
  Do
    doneFlag = True
    For i As Integer = 0 To 3 - gap
      If cat(i) > cat(i + gap) Then
        temp = cat(i)
        cat(i) = cat(i + gap)
        cat(i + gap) = temp
        doneFlag = False
      End If
    Next
  Loop Until doneFlag = True
  gap = CInt(gap / 2)
Loop
```

	cat(0)	cat(1)	cat(2)	cat(3)
cat( )				

21. The subscripted variables of the array a() have the following values: $a(0) = 2$, $a(1) = 4$, $a(2) = 6$, $a(3) = 1$, $a(4) = 3$, $a(5) = 5$, $a(6) = 7$, $a(7) = 8$. Suppose $i = 2, j = 4$, and $k = 5$. What values are assigned to n when the following assignment statements are executed?

    (a) $n = a(k) + a(i)$ (c) $n = a(k) * a(i + 2)$
    (b) $n = a(k - i) - a(k - j)$ (d) $n = a(j - i) * a(j)$

22. The array *monthName*() holds the following three-character strings:

    ```
    monthName(0)="Jan", monthName(1)="Feb", ..., monthName(11)="Dec"
    ```

    (a) What is displayed by the following statement?

    ```
    txtMonth.Text = monthName(4) & " " & monthName(5)
    ```

    (b) What value is assigned to *summer* by the following statement?

    ```
    summer = monthName(5) & ", " & monthName(6) & ", " & monthName(7)
    ```

23. Assume that the text file NUMBERS.TXT contains a list of at most 100 integers. Write the Function procedure GetData for the following event procedure. GetData should return an array consisting of all the integers in the text file. The Function procedure should make just one pass through the text file, and should have the same size as the number of integers in the text file.

    ```
    Private Sub btnDisplay_Click(...) Handles btnDisplay.Click
      Dim numbers() As Integer
      numbers = GetData("NUMBERS.TXT")
    ```

```
    'Display the integers in the file
    For i As Integer = 0 To numbers.GetUpperBound(0)
       lstOutput.Items.Add(numbers(i))
    Next
  End Sub
```

24. Modify the program in Example 3 so that the text file SBWINNERS.TXT is only read once.

In Exercises 25 through 36, write a line of code or program segment to complete the stated task.

25. Suppose the Integer array *inventory*() has been declared with an upper bound of 1000 and data have been placed into several elements of the array. Write one line of code that will restore the values of all the elements to their default value of 0.

26. Write code to declare an array of size 20 and place the names Jerry, George, Elaine, and Kramer into the first four elements. Use one or two lines of code.

27. Declare the string array *marx*() with upper bound 3 so that the array is visible to all parts of the program. Assign the four values Chico, Harpo, Groucho, and Zeppo to the array before any buttons are pressed.

28. Declare the string array *stooges*() to have size 3 so that the array is local to the event procedure btnStooges_Click. Assign the three values Moe, Larry, and Curly to the array as soon as the button is clicked.

29. The arrays *a*() and *b*() have been declared to have upper bound 4, and values have been assigned to *a*(0) through *a*(4). Store these values in array *b*() in reverse order.

30. Given two arrays of type Integer, *p*() and *q*(), each with upper bound 99, compute the sum of the products of the corresponding array elements, that is,

```
p(0)*q(0) + p(1)*q(1) + p(2)*q(2) + ... + p(99)*q(99)
```

31. Display the values of the array *a*() having upper bound 29 in five columns, like the following:

$$
\begin{array}{ccccc}
a(0) & a(1) & a(2) & a(3) & a(4) \\
a(5) & a(6) & a(7) & a(8) & a(9) \\
\cdot & \cdot & \cdot & \cdot & \cdot \\
\cdot & \cdot & \cdot & \cdot & \cdot \\
\cdot & \cdot & \cdot & \cdot & \cdot \\
a(25) & a(26) & a(27) & a(28) & a(29)
\end{array}
$$

32. A list of 20 digits, all between 0 and 9, is contained in a text file. Display the frequency of each digit.

33. Compare two arrays *a*() and *b*() of size 10 to see if they hold identical values, that is, if *a*(*i*) = *b*(*i*) for all *i* from 0 through 9.

34. Calculate the sum of the entries with odd subscripts in an integer array *a*() of size 10.

35. Ten exam grades are stored in the array *exams*(). Curve the grades by adding 5 points to each grade.

36. Read 10 digits contained in a text file into an array and then display three columns in a list box as follows: column 1 should contain the original 10 digits, column 2 should contain these digits in reverse order, and column 3 should contain the averages of the corresponding digits' numbers in columns 1 and 2.

37. Thirty scores, each lying between 0 and 49, are given in a text file. Write a program that uses these scores to create an array *frequency*( ) as follows:

frequency(0) = # of scores < 10
frequency(1) = # of scores such that 10 <= score < 20
frequency(2) = # of scores such that 20 <= score < 30
frequency(3) = # of scores such that 30 <= score < 40
frequency(4) = # of scores such that 40 <= score < 50

The program should then display the results in tabular form as follows:

INTERVAL	FREQUENCY
0 to 9	frequency(0)
10 to 19	frequency(1)
20 to 29	frequency(2)
30 to 39	frequency(3)
40 to 49	frequency(4)

38. Write a program that asks the user for a month by number and then displays the name of that month. For instance, if the user inputs 2, the program should display February. **Hint:** Create an array of 12 strings, one for each month of the year.

39. The file USPRES.TXT contains the names of the first 43 U.S. Presidents in the order they served. Write a program that places the names in an array, supplies all presidents having a requested first name, and supplies all presidents for a requested range of numbers. Figure 7.4 shows one possible outcome.

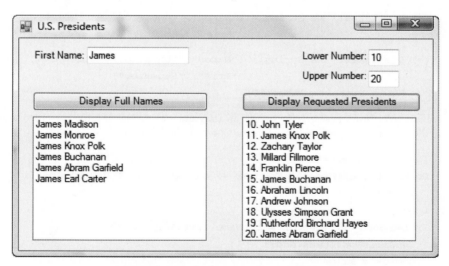

FIGURE 7.4 Sample run of Exercise 39.

40. The file COLORS.TXT contains the names of the colors of Crayola®* crayons in alphabetical order. Write a program to read the colors into an array and then display the colors beginning with a specified letter. The program should declare an array with upper bound 50 and then increase the size of the array by 10 elements whenever it runs out of space to store the colors. One possible outcome is shown in Figure 7.5.

---

*Crayola® is a registered trademark of Binney & Smith.

FIGURE 7.5 Sample run of Exercise 40.

41. An *anagram* of a word or phrase is another word or phrase that uses the same letters with the same frequency. Punctuation marks and spaces are ignored. Write a program that requests two words or phases as input and determines if they are anagrams of each other. (Test the program with the pair of phrases DWIGHT DAVID EISENHOWER and HE DID VIEW THE WAR DOINGS.)

Solutions to Practice Problems 7.1

1. Two possible answers are as follows:

   (a) ```
   Dim lakes() As String = {"Huron", "Ontario", "Michigan", _
                            "Erie", "Superior", "", "", "", "", "", ""}
   ```

   (b) ```
   Dim lakes() As String = {"Huron", "Ontario", "Michigan", _
                            "Erie", "Superior"}
       ReDim Preserve lakes(10)
   ```

2. This task consists of searching through an array and is carried out just like the task of searching a text file for a specified item. Replace the For loop with the following code:

   ```
   Dim i As Integer
   Do While (teamName(i).ToUpper <> txtName.Text.ToUpper) And (i < upperBound)
     i += 1
   Loop
   If teamName(i).ToUpper = txtName.Text.ToUpper Then
     lstGamesWon.Items.Add(i + 1)
     noWins = False
   End If
   ```

3. Arrays should be used when several pieces of data of the same type will be entered by the user; or computations must be made on the items in a text file after all of the items have been read.

7.2 Using Arrays

This section considers three aspects of the use of arrays: processing ordered arrays, reading part of an array, and passing arrays to procedures.

■ Ordered Arrays

An array is said to be **ordered** if its values are in either ascending or descending order. The following arrays illustrate the different types of ordered and unordered arrays. In an ascending ordered array, the value of each element is less than or equal to the value of the next element. That is,

$$[\text{each element}] \leq [\text{next element}].$$

For string arrays, the ANSI table is used to evaluate the "less than or equal to" condition.

Ordered Ascending Numeric Array

dates()	1492	1776	1812	1929	1969

Ordered Descending Numeric Array

discov()	1610	1541	1513	1513	1492

Ordered Ascending String Array

king()	Edward	Henry	James	John	Kong

Ordered Descending String Array

lake()	Superior	Ontario	Michigan	Huron	Erie

Unordered Numeric Array

rates()	8.25	5.00	7.85	8.00	6.50

Unordered String Array

char()	G	R	E	A	T

Ordered arrays can be searched more efficiently than unordered arrays. In this section, we use their order to shorten the search. The technique used here is applied to searching text files in Chapter 8.

Example 1   The following program places an ordered list of names into an array, requests a name as input, and informs the user if the name is in the list. Because the list is ordered, the search of the array ends when an element is reached whose value is greater than or equal to the input name. On average, only half the ordered array will be searched. Figure 7.6 shows the flowchart for this search.

```
'Create array to hold 10 strings
Dim nom() As String = {"AL", "BOB", "CARL", "DON", "ERIC", _
                "FRED", "GREG", "HERB", "IRA", "JACK"}
```

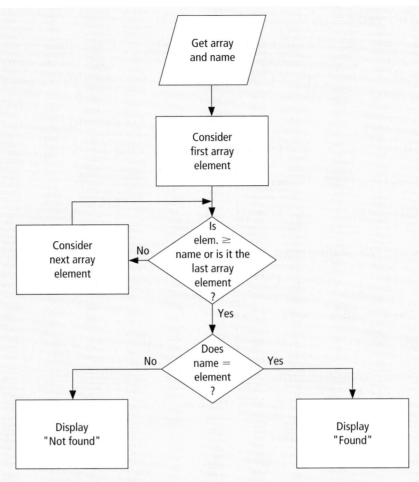

FIGURE 7.6 Flowchart for a search of an ordered array.

```
Private Sub btnSearch_Click(...) Handles btnSearch.Click
  'Search for a name in an ordered list
  Dim name2Find As String
  Dim n As Integer = -1
  name2Find = txtName.Text.ToUpper
  Do
    n += 1    'Add 1 to n
  Loop Until (nom(n) >= name2Find) Or (n = 9)
  'Interpret result of search
  If nom(n) = name2Find Then
    txtResult.Text = "Found."
  Else
    txtResult.Text = "Not found."
  End If
End Sub
```

[Run, type "Don" into the text box, and click the button.]

Using Part of an Array

In some programs, we must dimension an array before knowing how many pieces of data are to be placed into it. In these cases, we dimension the array large enough to handle all reasonable contingencies. For instance, if the array is to hold exam grades, and class sizes are at most 100 students, we use a statement such as **Dim grades(99) As Integer**. In such situations, we must employ a **counter variable** to keep track of the number of values actually stored in the array. We create this counter variable using a Dim statement in the Declarations section of the program so that all procedures will have access to it.

Example 2   The following program requests a list of companies and then displays them along with a count:

```
'Demonstrate using part of an array
Dim stock(99) As String
Dim counter As Integer

Private Sub btnRecord_Click(...) Handles btnRecord.Click
  If (counter < 99) Then
    counter += 1   'Increment counter by 1
    stock(counter - 1) = txtCompany.Text
    txtCompany.Clear()
    txtCompany.Focus()
    txtNumber.Text = CStr(counter)
  Else
    MessageBox.Show("No space to record additional companies.")
    txtCompany.Clear()
    btnSummarize.Focus()
  End If
End Sub

Private Sub btnSummarize_Click(...) Handles btnSummarize.Click
  'List stock companies that have been recorded
  lstStocks.Items.Clear()
  For i As Integer = 0 To counter - 1
    lstStocks.Items.Add(stock(i))
  Next
End Sub
```

[Run, type in the seven companies shown (press Record Name after each company name is typed), and press Summarize.]

■ Merging Two Ordered Arrays

Suppose that you have two ascending ordered lists of customers (possibly with some customers on both lists) and you want to consolidate them into a single ordered list. The technique for creating the third list, called the **merge algorithm**, is as follows:

1. Compare the two names at the top of the first and second lists.
   - (a) If one name alphabetically precedes the other, copy it onto the third list and cross it off its original list.
   - (b) If the names are the same, copy the name onto the third list and cross out the name from the first and second lists.
2. Repeat Step 1 with the current top names until you reach the end of either list.
3. Copy the names from the remaining list onto the third list.

 Example 3 The following program stores two lists of names in ascending ordered arrays and merges them into a third list. At most 10 names will be placed into the third array; duplicates will reduce this number. Because the variable r identifies the next position to insert a name in the third array, $r - 1$ is the number of names in the array.

```
Private Sub btnMerge_Click(...) Handles btnMerge.Click
  'Create arrays to hold list of names
  Dim list1() As String = {"Al", "Carl", "Don", "Greg", "Jack"}
  Dim list2() As String = {"Bob", "Carl", "Eric", "Greg", "Herb"}
  Dim newList(9) As String
  Dim m, n, r, numNames As Integer
  'Merge two lists of names
  m = 0    'Subscript for first array
  n = 0    'Subscript for second array
  r = 0    'Subscript and counter for third array
  Do While (m <= 4) And (n <= 4)
    Select Case list1(m)
```

```
      Case Is < list2(n)
        newList(r) = list1(m)
        m += 1      'Increase m by 1
      Case Is > list2(n)
        newList(r) = list2(n)
        n += 1      'Increase n by 1
      Case list2(n)
        newList(r) = list1(m)
        m += 1
        n += 1
    End Select
    r += 1          'Increase r by 1
  Loop
  'If one of the lists has items left over, copy them into the third list.
  'At most one of the following two loops will be executed.
  Do While m <= 4        'Copy rest of first array into third
    newList(r) = list1(m)
    r += 1
    m += 1
  Loop
  Do While n <= 4        'Copy rest of second array into third
    newList(r) = list2(n)
    r += 1
    n += 1
  Loop
  numNames = r - 1
  'Show result of merging lists
  lstMergedList.Items.Clear()
  For i As Integer = 0 To numNames
    lstMergedList.Items.Add(newList(i))
  Next
End Sub
```

[Run, and click the button.]

Passing Arrays to Procedures

An array that is not declared in the Declarations section, but rather is declared in a procedure, is local to that procedure and unknown in all other procedures. However, an entire local array can be passed to another procedure. The argument in the calling statement consists of the name of the array, written *without* a trailing empty set of parentheses. The corresponding parameter in the header for the procedure must consist of an array name *with* a trailing empty set of parentheses. Like all other parameters, the array parameter must be preceded with ByVal or ByRef and followed with an "As DataType" clause. The method GetUpperBound simplifies working with arrays that have been passed to a procedure.

 Example 4   The following program illustrates passing an array to a Function procedure. Notice that the function call is written Sum(score), not Sum(score()), and that the parameter declaration is written `ByVal s() As Integer`, not `ByVal s As Integer`.

```
Private Sub btnCompute_Click(...) Handles btnCompute.Click
  'Pass array to Function procedure
  Dim score() As Integer = {85, 92, 75, 68, 84, 86, 94, 74, 79, 88}
  txtAverage.Text = CStr(Sum(score) / 10)
End Sub

Function Sum(ByVal s() As Integer) As Integer
  'Add up scores
  Dim total As Integer
  total = 0
  For index As Integer = 0 To s.GetUpperBound(0)    'The upper bound is 9
    total += s(index)    'Add the value of s(index) to the value of total
  Next
  Return total
End Function
```

[Run, and click the button.]

Sometimes it is also necessary to pass a class-level array from one procedure to another. For example, you might have a sorting procedure (discussed in Section 7.3) and three class-level arrays to be sorted. The sorting procedure would be called three times, each time passing a different class-level array. The method for passing a class-level array to another procedure is the same as the method for passing a local array.

 Example 5   The following program incorporates all three topics discussed in this section. It places ordered lists of computer languages and spoken languages into class-level arrays, requests a new language as input, and inserts the language into its proper array position (avoiding duplication). The language arrays are declared to hold up to 21 names; the variables *numCompLangs* and *numSpokLangs* record the actual number of languages in each of the ordered arrays.

OBJECT	PROPERTY	SETTING
frmAdding	Text	Adding to an Ordered Array
lblLang	Text	New language:
txtLang		
btnAddComp	Text	Add to Computer List
btnAddSpok	Text	Add to Spoken List
lstAllLang		

```
Dim compLang() As String = {"ADA", "C++", "Cobol", _
                            "Fortran", "Java", "Visual Basic"}
Dim spokLang() As String = {"Cantonese", "English", "French", _
                            "Mandarin", "Russian", "Spanish"}
Dim numCompLangs As Integer = 6, numSpokLangs As Integer = 6

Private Sub frmAdding_Load(...) Handles MyBase.Load
  ReDim Preserve compLang(20)
  ReDim Preserve spokLang(20)
End Sub

Private Sub btnAddComp_Click(...) Handles btnAddComp.Click
  'Insert language into ordered array of computer languages
  AddALang(compLang, numCompLangs)
  DisplayArray(compLang, numCompLangs)
  txtLang.Clear()
  txtLang.Focus()
End Sub

Private Sub btnAddSpok_Click(...) Handles btnAddSpok.Click
  'Insert language into ordered array of spoken languages
  AddALang(spokLang, numSpokLangs)
  DisplayArray(spokLang, numSpokLangs)
  txtLang.Clear()
  txtLang.Focus()
End Sub

Sub AddALang(ByRef lang() As String, ByRef langCount As Integer)
  'Insert a language into an ordered array of languages
  Dim language As String
  Dim n As Integer = -1
  language = txtLang.Text.Trim
  Do
    n += 1    'Increase n by 1
  Loop Until ((lang(n).ToUpper >= language.ToUpper) Or (n = langCount - 1))
  If lang(n).ToUpper < language.ToUpper Then        'Insert language at end
```

```
      lang(langCount) = language
      langCount += 1
    ElseIf lang(n).ToUpper > language.ToUpper Then    'Insert before item n
      For i As Integer = (langCount - 1) To n Step -1
        lang(i + 1) = lang(i)
      Next
      lang(n) = language
      langCount += 1
    End If
End Sub

Sub DisplayArray(ByVal lang() As String, ByVal howMany As Integer)
    'Display the languages in the array
    lstAllLang.Items.Clear()
    For i As Integer = 0 To howMany - 1
        lstAllLang.Items.Add(lang(i))
    Next
End Sub
```

[Run, type "German," and click "Add to Spoken List."]

[Type "Fortran," and click "Add to Computer List."]

■ Comments

1. In Examples 1 and 5, we searched successive elements of an ordered list beginning with the first element. This is called a **sequential search**. An efficient alternative to the sequential search is the **binary search**, which is considered in Section 7.4.

2. A single element of an array can be passed to a procedure just like any ordinary numeric or string variable.

```
Private Sub btnDisplay_Click(...) Handles btnDisplay.Click
  Dim num(20) As Integer
  num(5) = 10
  lstOutput.Items.Add(Triple(num(5)))
End Sub

Function Triple(ByVal x As Integer) As Integer
  Return 3 * x
End Function
```

When the program is run and the button clicked, 30 will be displayed.

3. In Section 7.1, we noted that when an assignment statement is used to assign one array to another, the two arrays actually share the same memory location. Of course, this also happens when an array argument is passed to an array parameter with ByRef. Surprisingly, this also happens when an array is passed ByVal.

Practice Problems 7.2

1. Can an array be in both ascending and descending order at the same time?
2. How can the Select Case block in Example 3 be changed so all entries of both arrays (including duplicates) are merged into the third array?

EXERCISES 7.2

In Exercises 1 and 2, decide whether the array is ordered.

1. month()

January	February	March	April	May

2. pres()

Adams	Adams	Bush	Johnson	Johnson

In Exercises 3 through 8, determine the output displayed when the button is clicked.

```
3. Private Sub btnDisplay_Click(...) Handles btnDisplay.Click
     Dim lake(2) As String
     lake(0) = "Superior"
     lake(1) = "Michigan"
     lake(2) = "Ontario"
     DisplayFirst(lake)
   End Sub
```

```
Sub DisplayFirst(ByVal lake() As String)
  'Display the first element of an array
  txtOutput.Text = lake(0)
End Sub
```

4.
```
Private Sub btnDisplay_Click(...) Handles btnDisplay.Click
    Dim num As Integer
    Dim cube(10) As Double
    For i As Integer = 0 To 10
      cube (i) = i ^ 3
    Next
    num = CInt(InputBox("Enter a number from 1 to 10."))
    txtOutput.Text = "The sum of the " & num & _
                    " cubes is " & Total(cube, num)
End Sub

Function Total(ByVal list() As Double, ByVal n As Integer) As Double
    Dim sum As Double = 0
    For i As Integer = 1 To n
      sum += list(i)
    Next
    Return sum
End Function
```

(Assume that the response is 3.)

5.
```
Private Sub btnDisplay_Click(...) Handles btnDisplay.Click
    Dim value(5) As Integer
    FillArray(value)
    For i As Integer = 0 To 4
      Select Case value(i)
        Case Is < value(i + 1)
          lstOutput.Items.Add("less than")
        Case Is > value(i + 1)
          lstOutput.Items.Add("greater than")
        Case Else
          lstOutput.Items.Add("equals")
      End Select
    Next
End Sub

Private Sub FillArray(ByRef list() As Integer)
  'Place values into an array of six elements
  Dim sr As IO.StreamReader = IO.File.OpenText("DATA.TXT")
  For i As Integer = 0 To 5
    list(i) = CInt(sr.ReadLine)
  Next
  sr.Close()
End Sub
```

(Assume that the five lines of the file DATA.TXT contain the following entries: 3, 2, 6, 1, 4, 4.)

6.
```
Private Sub btnDisplay_Click(...) Handles btnDisplay.Click
    Dim ocean(5) As String
    ocean(0) = "Pacific"
    ocean(1) = "Atlantic"
    Magazine(ocean(1))
End Sub

Sub Magazine(ByVal mag As String)
    txtOutput.Text = mag & " Monthly"
End Sub
```

7.
```
Private Sub btnDisplay_Click(...) Handles btnDisplay.Click
    Dim rain(11) As Double
    rain(0) = 2.4
    rain(1) = 3.6
    rain(2) = 4.0
    rain(3) = 1.4
    rain(4) = 2.6
    rain(5) = 3.0
    txtOutput.Text = "total rainfall for second quarter: " & _
        Total(rain, 3, 5) & " inches"
End Sub

Function Total(ByVal rain() As Double, first As Integer, last as Integer)
As Double
    Dim sum As Double = 0
    For i As Integer = first To last
        sum += rain(i)
    Next
    Return sum
End Function
```

8.
```
Private Sub btnDisplay_Click(...) Handles btnDisplay.Click
    Dim num(9) As Integer
    Dim sr As IO.StreamReader = IO.File.OpenText("DATA.TXT")
    For i As Integer = 0 To 9
        num(i) = CInt(sr.ReadLine)
    Next
    sr.Close()
    txtOutput.Text = "The array has " & zero(num) & " zero entries."
End Sub

Function Zero(ByVal digit() As Integer) As Integer
    Dim count As Integer
    count = 0
    For i As Integer = 0 To 9
        If digit(i) = 0 Then
            count += 1
        End If
    Next
    Return count
End Function
```

(Assume that the ten lines of the file DATA.TXT contain the following data: 5, 0, 2, 1, 0, 3, 0, 7, 0, 7.)

In Exercises 9 through 14, identify the error.

9.
```
Private Sub btnDisplay_Click(...) Handles btnDisplay.Click
    Dim city(3) As String
    Assign(city)
    txtOutput.Text = city
End Sub

Sub Assign(ByRef town() As String)
    town(1) = "Chicago"
End Sub
```

10.
```
Private Sub btnDisplay_Click(...) Handles btnDisplay.Click
    Dim planet(8) As String
    Assign(planet)
    txtOutput.Text = planet(1)
End Sub

Sub Assign(ByRef planet As String)
    planet(1) = "Venus"
End Sub
```

11.
```
Private Sub btnDisplay_Click(...) Handles btnDisplay.Click
    'Multiply several positive numbers together
    Dim prompt As String
    Dim number, product, num(4) As Double
    Dim n As Integer = -1
    prompt = "Enter a positive number to multiply by, or, "
    prompt &= "to see the product, Enter a negative number. "
    prompt &= "(Five numbers maximum can be specified.)"
    Do
        n += 1
        number = CDbl(InputBox(prompt))
        If number > 0 Then
            num(n) = number
        End If
    Loop Until (number < 0) Or (n = 4)
    product = 1
    For i As Integer = 0 To n
        product = product * num(i)
    Next
    txtOutput.Text = "The product of the numbers entered is " & _
                    product & "."
End Sub
```

12.
```
Private Sub btnDisplay_Click(...) Handles btnDisplay.Click
    Dim hue(15) As String
    hue(1) = "Blue"
```

```
      Favorite(hue())
   End Sub

   Sub Favorite(ByVal tone() As String)
     tone(1) = hue(1)
     txtOutput.Text = tone
   End Sub
```

13.
```
Private Sub btnDisplay_Click(...) Handles btnDisplay.Click
   Dim a(10), b(10) As Double
   For i As Integer = 0 To 10
     a(i) = i ^ 2
   Next
   CopyArray(a, b)
   txtOutput.Text = CStr(b(10))
End Sub

Sub CopyArray(ByRef a() As Double, ByRef b() As Double)
   'Place a's values in b
   b() = a()
End Sub
```

14.
```
Private Sub btnDisplay_Click(...) Handles btnDisplay.Click
   Dim a(2) As Integer
   a(0) = 42
   a(1) = 7
   a(2) = 11
   FlipFirstTwo(a)
   txtOutput.Text = a(0) & " " & a(1) & " " & a(2)
End Sub

Sub FlipFirstTwo(ByRef a() As Integer)
   'Swap first two elements
   a(1) = a(0)
   a(0) = a(1)
End Sub
```

Suppose an array has been declared in the Declarations section of the Code Editor with the statement Dim scores(50) As Double and numbers assigned to the elements having subscripts 0 to 50 by the frmOrder_Load event procedure. In Exercises 15 through 18, write a procedure to perform the stated task.

15. Determine whether the array is in ascending order.

16. Determine whether the array is in descending order.

17. With a single loop, determine whether the array is in ascending order, descending order, both, or neither.

18. Assuming that the array is in ascending order, determine how many numbers appear more than once in the array.

In Exercises 19 and 20, suppose arrays $a()$, $b()$, and $c()$ are class-level and that arrays $a()$ and $b()$ have each been assigned 20 numbers in ascending order (duplications

may occur) by a frmNumbers_Load event procedure. For instance, array *a*() might hold the numbers 1, 3, 3, 3, 9, 9, ...

19. Write a procedure to place all the 40 numbers from arrays *a*() and *b*() into *c*() so that *c*() is also in ascending order. The array *c*() could contain duplications.

20. Write a procedure to place the numbers from *a*() and *b*() into *c*() so that *c*() also has ascending order, but contains no duplications.

21. Write a program to declare an array with the statement **Dim state(49) As String** and maintain a list of certain states. The list of states should always be in alphabetical order and occupy consecutive elements of the array. The buttons in the program should give the user the following options:

    (a) Take the state specified by the user in a text box and insert it into its proper position in the array. (If the state is already in the array, so report.)
    (b) Take the state specified by the user in a text box and delete it from the array. If the state is not in the array, so report.
    (c) Display the states in the array.

22. Write a program that requests a sentence one word at a time from the user and then checks whether the sentence is a *word palindrome*. A word palindrome sentence reads the same, word by word, backward and forward (ignoring punctuation and capitalization). An example is "You can cage a swallow, can't you, but you can't swallow a cage, can you?" The program should hold the words of the sentence in an array and use procedures to obtain the input, analyze the sentence, and declare whether the sentence is a word palindrome. (Test the program with the sentences, "Monkey see, monkey do." and "I am; therefore, am I?")

23. Write a program to display the average score and the number of above-average scores on an exam. Each time the user clicks a "Record Score" button, a grade should be read from a text box. The average score and the number of above-average scores should be displayed in a list box whenever the user clicks on a "Display Average" button. (Assume that the class has at most 100 students.) Use a function to calculate the average and another function to determine the number of above-average scores. **Note:** Pass the functions an array argument for the grades and a numeric argument for the number of elements of the array that have been assigned values.

24. Suppose that an array of 100 names is in ascending order. Write a procedure to search for a name input by the user. If the first letter of the name is found in *N* through *Z*, then the search should begin with the 100th element of the array and proceed backward.

25. At the beginning of 1990, a complete box of Crayola crayons had 72 colors (in the file PRE1990COLORS.TXT). During the 1990's, 8 colors were retired (in the file RETIREDCOLORS.TXT) and 56 new colors were added (in the file ADDED-COLORS.TXT). Each of the three files is in alphabetical order. Write a program that reads the text files into the arrays *colors*(), *retired*(), and *added*(), and then uses the arrays *retired*() and *added*() to update the array *colors*() so that it contains the current 120 colors.

Solutions to Practice Problems 7.2

1. Yes, provided each element of the array has the same value.

2. The third Case clause tests for duplicates and assigns only one array element to the third array if duplicates are found in the two arrays. Thus, we remove the third Case clause and change the first Case clause so it will process any duplicates. A situation where you would want to merge two lists while retaining duplications is the task of merging two ordered arrays of test scores.

```
Select Case list1(m)
  Case Is <= list2(n)
    newList(r) = list1(m)
    m += 1
  Case Is > list2(n)
    newList(r) = list2(n)
    n += 1
End Select
```

7.3   Some Additional Types of Arrays

So far, the array elements have been standard data types. This section considers arrays of controls and arrays of a new compound data type designed by the programmer.

■ Control Arrays

We have seen many examples of the usefulness of subscripted variables. They are essential for writing concise solutions to many programming problems. Because of the utility that subscripts provide, Visual Basic also provides for arrays of labels, text boxes, and buttons. Since labels, text boxes, and buttons are referred to generically in Visual Basic as controls, arrays of these objects (or of any other control) are called **control arrays**. *Note:* Since Visual Basic does not provide for arrays of masked text boxes, we will only use ordinary text boxes for input.

Control arrays are created in much the same way as any other array; that is, with a statement of the form

```
Dim arrayName(n) As ControlType
```

or

```
Dim arrayName() As ControlType
```

For instance, the following statements declare control arrays.

```
Dim lblTitle(10) As Label
Dim txtNumber(8) As TextBox
Dim btnAmount() As Button
```

Example 1   A department store has five departments. The following program requests the amount of sales for each department and displays the total sales for the store. The five labels identifying the departments are grouped into an array of labels and the five text boxes for the individual amounts are grouped into an array of text boxes. The initial settings for these labels are specified at run time in the frmSales_Load event procedure instead of being specified at design time. The Text properties of the labels are set to be "Department 1", "Department 2", and so on.

OBJECT	PROPERTY	SETTING
frmSales	Text	Daily Sales
Label1–Label5		
TextBox1–TextBox5		
btnCompute	Text	Compute Total Sales
lblTotal	Text	Total Sales:
txtTotal	ReadOnly	True

```
Dim lblDept(4) As Label
Dim txtDept(4) As TextBox


Private Sub frmSales_Load(...) Handles MyBase.Load
  lblDept(0) = Label1
  lblDept(1) = Label2
  lblDept(2) = Label3
  lblDept(3) = Label4
  lblDept(4) = Label5
  txtDept(0) = TextBox1
  txtDept(1) = TextBox2
  txtDept(2) = TextBox3
  txtDept(3) = TextBox4
  txtDept(4) = TextBox5
  'Set the labels' Text property to the corresponding department
  For depNum As Integer = 1 To 5
    lblDept(depNum - 1).Text = "Department " & depNum & ":"
  Next
End Sub


Private Sub btnCompute_Click(...) Handles btnCompute.Click
  Dim totalSales As Double = 0
  For depNum As Integer = 1 To 5
```

```
      totalSales += CDbl(txtDept(depNum - 1).Text)
   Next
   txtTotal.Text = FormatCurrency(totalSales)
End Sub
```

[Run, enter amounts into the text boxes, and then click the button.]

Structures

Often we work with two or more pieces of related data. For instance, we might be interested in a person's name, age, and phone number. Traditionally, the way to work with such related lists of data was to create three parallel arrays – one for names, a second for ages, and a third for phone numbers. The modern way of dealing with this situation is to work with a single array of a composite data type that holds several pieces of related data.

The data types we have worked with so far are Double, Integer, String, and Boolean. A **structure** provides a convenient way of packaging as a single unit several related variables of different types. In previous versions of Visual Basic a structure was called a user-defined type (UDT).

Three pieces of related information about colleges are "name," "state," and "year founded." A structure type capable of holding this data is defined by the following block of statements located in the Declarations section of the Code Editor.

```
Structure College
   Dim name As String
   Dim state As String
   Dim yearFounded As Integer
End Structure
```

Each of the three subvariables of the structure type is called a **member**. A structure variable of the type College is declared by a statement such as

```
Dim college1 As College
```

Each member is accessed by giving the name of the structure variable and the member, separated by a period. For instance, the three members of the structure variable *college1* are accessed as *college1.name*, *college1.state*, and *college1.yearFounded*.

In general, a structure type is defined by a Structure block of the form

```
Structure StructureType
   Dim memberName1 As MemberType1
   Dim memberName2 As MemberType2
      .
      .
      .
End Structure
```

where *StructureType* is the name of the user-defined data type; *memberName1*, *memberName2*, ..., are the names of the members of the structure; and *MemberType1*, *MemberType2*, ..., are the corresponding member types, such as String, Integer, Double, or Boolean.

A structure variable, *structureVar*, is declared to be of the user-defined type by a statement of the form

```
Dim structureVar As StructureType
```

 Example 2   The following program stores information about two colleges into structure variables of type College and uses the variables to determine which college is older. **Note:** In the third line of the btnOlder_Click event procedure, all the member values of *college1* are assigned simultaneously to *collegeOlder*.

OBJECT	PROPERTY	SETTING
frmFind	Text	Find Earlier College
btnFirst	Text	Get Data on First College
btnSecond	Text	Get Data on Second College
btnOlder	Text	Display Data on Older College
txtResult	ReadOnly	True

```
Structure College
   Dim name As String
   Dim state As String
   Dim yearFounded As Integer
End Structure

Dim college1, college2, collegeOlder As College

Private Sub btnFirst_Click(...) Handles btnFirst.Click
   Dim prompt As String
   college1.name = InputBox("Enter name of first college.", "Name")
   college1.state = InputBox("Enter state of first college.", "State")
   prompt = "Enter the year the first college was founded."
   college1.yearFounded = CInt(InputBox(prompt, "Year"))
End Sub
```

```
Private Sub btnSecond_Click(...) Handles btnSecond.Click
  Dim prompt As String
  college2.name = InputBox("Enter name of second college.", "Name")
  college2.state = InputBox("Enter state of second college.", "State")
  prompt = "Enter the year the second college was founded."
  college2.yearFounded = CInt(InputBox(prompt, "Year"))
End Sub


Private Sub btnOlder_Click(...) Handles btnOlder.Click
  If (college1.yearFounded < college2.yearFounded) Then
    collegeOlder = college1
  Else
    collegeOlder = college2
  End If
  txtResult.Text = collegeOlder.name & " was founded in " & _
          collegeOlder.state & " in " & collegeOlder.yearFounded & "."
End Sub
```

[Run, click the first button, and respond to the input boxes with Princeton University, New Jersey, 1746. Click the second button; respond to the input boxes with Yale University, Connecticut, 1701. Finally, click the third button.]

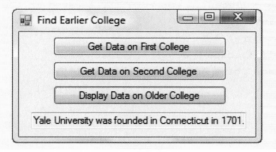

Example 3 The file COLLEGES.TXT holds the name, state, and year founded for each of the 27 colleges in the United States founded before 1800. The first three lines of the file contain the data Harvard University, MA, 1636. The following program places the information about the colleges into an array of structures. The array is then used to display the names of the colleges in a specified state. **Note:** The masked text box has Mask "LL".

```
Structure College
  Dim name As String
  Dim state As String
  Dim yearFounded As Integer
End Structure

Dim school(26) As College

Private Sub frmColleges_Load(...) Handles MyBase.Load
  'Place the data for each college into the array school()
  Dim i As Integer = -1
  Dim sr As IO.StreamReader = IO.File.OpenText("COLLEGES.TXT")
  Do While (sr.Peek <> -1)
    i += 1
    school(i).name = sr.ReadLine
    school(i).state = sr.ReadLine
    school(i).yearFounded = CInt(sr.ReadLine)
  Loop
  sr.Close()
End Sub

Private Sub btnDisplay_Click(...) Handles btnDisplay.Click
  'Display the colleges in COLLEGES.TXT located in the given state
  lstCollege.Items.Clear()
  For i As Integer = 0 To 26
    If (school(i).state = mtxtState.Text) Then
      lstCollege.Items.Add(school(i).name & " " & _
                          school(i).yearFounded)
    End If
  Next
End Sub
```

[Run, type the name of a state into the masked text box, and click the button.]

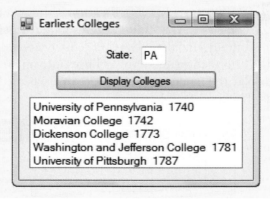

So far, the members of structures have had elementary types; such as String or Integer. However, the type for a member can be another structure or an array type. When a member is given an array type, the defining Dim statement must not specify the upper bound; this task must be left to a ReDim statement. Example 4 demonstrates the use of both of these nonelementary types of members. In addition, the example shows how to pass a structure variable to a Sub procedure.

   Example 4   The following program totals a person's college credits and determines whether they have enough credits for graduation. *Notes:* The structure variable *person* is local to the btnGet_Click event procedure. In the fourth line of the procedure, **person.name.firstName** should be thought of as **(person.name).firstName**.

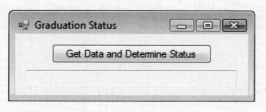

OBJECT	PROPERTY	SETTING
frmStatus	Text	Graduation Status
btnGet	Text	Get Data and Determine Status
txtResult	ReadOnly	True

```
Structure FullName
  Dim firstName As String
  Dim lastName As String
End Structure

Structure Student
  Dim name As FullName
  Dim credits() As Integer
End Structure

Private Sub btnGet_Click(...) Handles btnGet.Click
  Dim numYears As Integer
  Dim person As Student
  txtResult.Clear()
  person.name.firstName = InputBox("First Name:")
  person.name.lastName = InputBox("Second Name:")
  numYears = CInt(InputBox("Number of years completed:"))
  ReDim person.credits(numYears - 1)
  For i As Integer = 0 To numYears - 1
    person.credits(i) = CInt(InputBox("Credits in year " & i + 1))
  Next
  DetermineStatus(person)
End Sub

Sub DetermineStatus(ByVal person As Student)
  Dim total As Integer = 0
  For i As Integer = 0 To person.credits.GetUpperBound(0)
    total += person.credits(i)
  Next
```

```
If (total >= 120) Then
  txtResult.Text = person.name.firstName & " " & _
          person.name.lastName & " has enough credits to graduate."
Else
  txtResult.Text = person.name.firstName & " " & _
              person.name.lastName & " needs " & _
              (120 - total) & " more credits to graduate."
End If
End Sub
```

[Run, click the button, and respond to requests for input with Miranda, Smith, 3, 34, 33, 34.]

■ Displaying and Comparing Structure Values

Statements of the form

```
lstBox.Items.Add(structureVar)
```

where *structureVar* is a structure variable, do not perform as intended. Each member of a structure should appear separately in a lstBox.Items.Add statement. Also, comparisons involving structures using the relational operators <, >, =, <>, <=, and >= are valid only with individual members of the structures, not with the structures themselves.

Practice Problems 7.3

1. Find the errors in the following event procedure.

```
Sub btnDisplay_Click(...) Handles btnDisplay.Click
  Structure Team
    Dim school As String
    Dim mascot As String
  End Structure
  Team.school = "Rice"
  Team.mascot = "Owls"
  txtOutput.Text = Team.school & " " & Team.mascot
End Sub
```

2. Correct the code in Practice Problem 1.

In Exercises 1 through 4, use the form in Figure 7.7 (already filled in by the user) to determine the output displayed in the read-only text box at the bottom of the form when the button is clicked. The rectangular group of text boxes on the form consist of four arrays of text boxes—*txtWinter*(), *txtSpring*(), *txtSummer*(), and *txtFall*()—with each array having subscripts ranging from 0 to 3.

FIGURE 7.7   Form for Exercises 1–4.

1.
```
Private Sub btnProcess_Click(...) Handles btnProcess.Click
   Dim total As Double = 0
   For itemNum As Integer = 0 To 2
     total += CDbl(txtWinter(itemNum).Text)
   Next
   txtBox.Text = "Utility expenses for spring: " & FormatCurrency(total)
End Sub
```

2.
```
Private Sub btnProcess_Click(...) Handles btnProcess.Click
   Dim total As Double = 0
   total += CDbl(txtWinter(1).Text)
   total += CDbl(txtSpring(1).Text)
   total += CDbl(txtSummer(1).Text)
   total += CDbl(txtFall(1).Text)
   txtBox.Text = "Annual gas bill: " & FormatCurrency(total)
End Sub
```

3.
```
Private Sub btnProcess_Click(...) Handles btnProcess.Click
   Dim diff As Double
   Dim total As Double = 0
   For i As Integer = 0 To 3
     diff = CDbl(txtSummer(i).Text) - CDbl(txSpring(i).Text)
     total += diff
   Next
   txtBox.Text = "Summer bills top springer bills by " & _
     FormatCurrency(total)
End Sub
```

```
4. Private Sub btnProcess_Click(...) Handles btnProcess.Click
      Dim total As Double = 0
      Dim itemNum As Integer = 3
        total += TotalCateg(itemNum)
      txtBox.Text = "Total mortgage expenses: " & FormatCurrency(total)
   End Sub

   Function TotalCateg(ByVal itemNum As Integer) As Double
      Dim total As Double = 0
      total += CDbl(txtWinter(itemNum).Text)
      total += CDbl(txtSpring(itemNum).Text)
      total += CDbl(txtSummer(itemNum).Text)
      total += CDbl(txtFall(itemNum).Text)
      Return total
   End Function
```

In Exercises 5 through 8, determine the output displayed when the button is clicked.

```
5. Structure Appearance
      Dim height As Double
      Dim weight As Double
   End Structure

   Private Sub btnDisplay_Click(...) Handles btnDisplay.Click
      Dim person1, person2 As Appearance
      person1.height = 72
      person1.weight = 150
      person2.height = 12 * 5
      If person1.height <> person2.height Then
         lstOutput.Items.Add("heights are not the same")
      End If
      person2 = person1
      lstOutput.Items.Add(person2.weight)
   End Sub
```

```
6. Structure TestData
      Dim name As String
      Dim score As Double
   End Structure

   Dim sr As IO.StreamReader = IO.File.OpenText("SCORES.TXT")

   Private Sub btnDisplay_Click(...) Handles btnDisplay.Click
      Dim student As TestData
      For i As Integer = 1 to 4
         GetScore(student)
         DisplayScore(student)
      Next
      sr.Close()
   End Sub
```

```
Sub GetScore(ByRef student As TestData)
  student.name = sr.ReadLine
  student.score = CDbl(sr.ReadLine)
End Sub

Sub DisplayScore(ByVal student As testData)
  lstOutput.Items.Add(student.name & " " & student.score)
End Sub
```

(Assume that the eight lines of the file SCORES.TXT contain the following data: Tom, 78, Dick, 80, Harry, 95, Bill, 100.)

7.
```
Structure Address
  Dim street As String
  Dim city As String
  Dim state As String
End Structure

Structure Citizen
  Dim name As String
  Dim residence As Address
End Structure

Private Sub btnDisplay_Click(...) Handles btnDisplay.Click
  Dim person As Citizen
  person.name = "Bill Gates"
  person.residence.street = "1835 73rd Ave NE"
  person.residence.city = "Medina"
  person.residence.state = "Washington"
  txtOutput.Text = person.name & " lives in " & _
    person.residence.city & ", " & person.residence.state
End Sub
```

8.
```
Structure TaxData
  Dim socSecNum As String
  Dim hourlyWage As Double
End Structure

Structure Employee
  Dim name As String
  Dim hrsWorked As Double
  Dim taxInfo as TaxData
End Structure

Private Sub btnDisplay_Click(...) Handles btnDisplay.Click
  Dim worker as Employee
  worker.name = "Bill Gates"
  worker.hrsWorked = 4
  worker.taxInfo.hourlyWage = 2000
  txtOutput.Text = worker.name " & earned " & _
    FormatCurrency(worker.hrsWorked * worker.taxInfo.hourlyWage)
End Sub
```

In Exercises 9 through 11, determine the errors.

9.
```
Structure Nobel
    Dim peace as String
    Dim year as Integer
End Structure

Private Sub btnDisplay_Click(...) Handles btnDisplay.Click
  Dim prize As Nobel
  peace = "Al Gore"
  year = 2007
  txtBox.Text = peace & " won the " & year & " Nobel Peace Prize."
End Sub
```

10.
```
Structure Vitamins
    Dim a As Double
    Dim b As Double
End Structure

Private Sub btnDisplay_Click(...) Handles btnDisplay.Click
  Dim minimum As Vitamins
  minimum.b = 200
  minimum.a = 500
  1stOutput.Items.Add(minimum)
End Sub
```

11.
```
Structure BallGame
    Dim hits As Double
    Dim runs As Double
End Structure

Private Sub btnDisplay_Click(...) Handles btnDisplay.Click
  Dim game1, game2 As BallGame
  game1.hits = 15
  game1.runs = 8
  game2.hits = 17
  game2.runs = 10
  If game1 > game2 Then
    txtOutput.Text = "The first game was better."
  Else
    txtOutput.Text = "The second game was at least as good."
  End If
End Sub
```

12. Write a line or lines of code as instructed in Steps (a) through (e) to fill in the missing lines in the following program.

```
Structure Appearance
    Dim height As Double    'Inches
    Dim weight As Double    'Pounds
End Structure
```

```
Structure Person
  Dim name As String
  Dim stats As Appearance
End Structure

Private Sub btnDisplay_Click(...) Handles btnDisplay.Click
  Dim person1, person2 As Person
  (missing lines)
End Sub
```

(a) Give *person1* the name Michael.
(b) Set Michael's height and weight to 71 and 190, respectively.
(c) Give *person2* the name Jacob.
(d) Set Jacob's height and weight to 70 and 175, respectively.
(e) If one person is both taller and heavier than the other, display a sentence of the form "[name of bigger person] is bigger than [name of smaller person]."

A campus club has 10 members. The following program stores information about the students into an array of structures. Each structure contains the student's name and a list of the courses he or she is currently taking. Exercises 13 through 16 request that an additional event procedure be written for this program.

```
Structure Student
  Dim name As String
  Dim courses() As String
End Structure

Dim club(9) As Student

Private Sub frmStudents_Load(...) Handles MyBase.Load
  Dim pupil As student
  'Enter data for first student
  pupil.name = "Juan Santana"
  ReDim pupil.courses(2)
  pupil.courses(0) = "CMSC 100"
  pupil.courses(1) = "PHIL 200"
  pupil.courses(2) = "ENGL 120"
  club(0) = pupil
  'Enter data for second student
  pupil.name = "Mary Carlson"
  ReDim pupil.courses(3)
  pupil.courses(0) = "BIOL 110"
  pupil.courses(1) = "PHIL 200"
  pupil.courses(2) = "CMSC 100"
  pupil.courses(3) = "MATH 220"
  club(1) = pupil
  'Enter names and courses for remaining 8 people in the club
End Sub
```

13. Write the code for a btnDisplay_Click event procedure that will display the names of all the students in the club in a list box.

14. Write the code for a btnDisplay_Click event procedure that will display the names of all the students in the club who are registered for three courses.

15. Write the code for a btnDisplay_Click event procedure that will display the names of all the students in the club who are enrolled in CMSC 100.

16. Write the code for a btnDisplay_Click event procedure that will display the names of all the students in the club who are *not* enrolled in CMSC 100.

17. Write a program to compute a student's grade-point average for a semester. Allow for as many as six courses. For each course, the grades (A, B, ...) should be entered in an element of an array of six text boxes, and the semester hours credits entered into another array of six text boxes. After the student fills in the grades and clicks on a button, a Function procedure should compute the GPA. Then a Sub procedure should display the GPA along with one of two messages. A student with a GPA of 3 or more should be informed that he or she has made the honor roll. Otherwise, the student should be congratulated on having completed the semester.

18. Table 7.1 gives the U.S. Census Bureau projections for the populations (in millions) of the states predicted to be the most populous in the year 2030. Write a program that allows the user to enter the current populations of the states into an array of text boxes, computes the projected population growths for the states in an array of text boxes, and gives the percentage growth for the collection of five states. The growth is calculated with the formula

$$\text{growth} = (\text{projected pop.} - \text{current pop.})/\text{current pop}$$

Percentage growth can be displayed as FormatPercent(growth). Test the program with the current populations shown in Figure 7.8.

FIGURE 7.8 **Sample run for Exercise 18.**

TABLE 7.1	State populations in the year 2030.
State	Population in 2030
California	46.4
Texas	33.3
New York	19.5
Illinois	13.4
Florida	28.7

19. Write a program to look up data on notable tall buildings. The program should declare a user-defined data type named "Building" with the members "name", "city", "height", and "stories". This interactive program should allow the user to type the name of a building into a text box and then search through an array of structures to determine the city, height, and number of stories of the building when a button is pressed. If the building is not in the array, then the program should so report. Place the information in Table 7.2 into a text file, and read it into the array.

TABLE 7.2	Tallest buildings.		
Building	City	Height (ft)	Stories
Empire State	New York	1250	102
Sears Tower	Chicago	1454	110
Texas Commerce Tower	Houston	1002	75
Transamerica Pyramid	San Francisco	853	48

20. Given the following flight schedule, write a program to load this information into an array of structures, and ask the user to specify a flight number. Have the computer find the flight number and display the information corresponding to that flight. Account for the case where the user requests a nonexistent flight.

FLIGHT #	ORIGIN	DESTINATION	DEPARTURE TIME
117	Tucson	Dallas	8:45 a.m.
239	LA	Boston	10:15 a.m.
298	Albany	Reno	1:35 p.m.
326	Houston	New York	2:40 p.m.
445	New York	Tampa	4:20 p.m.

21. Table 7.3 contains the names and number of stores of the top 10 pizza chains in 2006. Write a program to place these data into an array of structures, compute the total number of stores for these 10 chains, and display a table giving the name and percentage of total stores for each of the companies.

TABLE 7.3	Top 10 pizza chains (and numbers of stores).		
Name	Stores	Name	Stores
1. Pizza Hut	11,179	6. Sbarro	974
2. Domino's	8,124	7. Papa Murphy's	880
3. Papa John's	2,924	8. Noble Romen's	800
4. Little Caesar's	2,000	9. NPC International	791
5. Casey's Carry-out	1,412	10. CiCi's Pizza	593

Source: *Pizza Marketing Quarterly*, September 2006

22. A retail store has five bins, numbered 1 to 5, each containing a different commodity. At the beginning of a particular day, each bin contains 45 items. Table 7.4 shows the cost per item for each of the bins and the quantity sold during that day.

Write a program to

(a) place the cost per item and the quantity sold from each bin into an array of structures;

(b) display a table giving the inventory at the end of the day and the amount of revenue obtained from each bin;

(c) compute the total revenue for the day;

(d) list the number of each bin that contains fewer than 20 items at the end of the day.

TABLE 7.4	Costs of items and quantities sold for Exercise 22.	
Bin	Cost per Item	Quantity Sold
1	3.00	10
2	12.25	30
3	37.45	9
4	7.49	42
5	24.95	17

Solutions to Practice Problems 7.3

1. The event procedure contains two errors. First, the definition of a structure cannot be inside a procedure; it must be typed into the Declarations section of the Code Editor. Second, the statements **Team.school = "Rice"** and **Team.mascot = "Owls"** are not valid. Team.school and Team.mascot are not valid. "Team" should be replaced by a variable of type Team that has previously been declared.

2.
```
Structure Team
    Dim school As String
    Dim mascot As String
End Structure
```

```
Private Sub btnDisplay_Click(...) Handles btnDisplay.Click
  Dim squad As Team
  squad.school = "Rice"
  squad.mascot = "Owls"
  txtOutput.Text = squad.school & " " & squad.mascot
End Sub
```

7.4   Sorting and Searching

A **sort** is an algorithm for ordering an array. Of the many different techniques for sorting an array we discuss two, the **bubble sort** and the **Shell sort**. Both require the interchange of values stored in a pair of variables. If *var1*, *var2*, and *temp* are all variables of the same data type (such as all String), then the statements

```
temp = var1
var1 = var2
var2 = temp
```

assign *var1*'s value to *var2* and *var2*'s value to *var1*.

 Example 1   The following program alphabetizes two words supplied in text boxes:

```
Private Sub btnAlphabetize_Click(...) Handles btnAlphabetize.Click
  'Alphabetize two words
  Dim firstWord, secondWord, temp As String
  firstWord = txtFirstWord.Text
  secondWord = txtSecondWord.Text
  If (firstWord > secondWord) Then     'Swap the two words
    temp = firstWord
    firstWord = secondWord
    secondWord = temp
  End If
  txtResult.Text = firstWord & " before " & secondWord
End Sub
```

[Run, type "beauty" and "age" into the text boxes, and click the button.]

■ Bubble Sort

The bubble sort is an algorithm that compares adjacent items and swaps those that are out of order. If this process is repeated enough times, the list will be ordered. Let's carry out this process on the list Pebbles, Barney, Wilma, Fred, and Dino. The steps for each pass through the list are as follows:

1. Compare the first and second items. If they are out of order, swap them.

2. Compare the second and third items. If they are out of order, swap them.

3. Repeat this pattern for all remaining pairs. The final comparison and possible swap are between the next-to-last and last items.

The first time through the list, this process is repeated to the end of the list. This is called the first pass. After the first pass, the last item (Wilma) will be in its proper position. Therefore, the second pass does not have to consider it and so requires one less comparison. At the end of the second pass, the last two items will be in their proper position. (The items that must have reached their proper position have been underlined.) Each successive pass requires one less comparison. After four passes, the last four items will be in their proper positions, and hence, the first will be also.

Example 2 The following program alphabetizes the names Pebbles, Barney, Wilma, Fred, and Dino. Sorting the list requires a pair of nested loops. The inner loop performs a single pass, and the outer loop controls the number of passes.

```
Dim person() As String = {"Pebbles", "Barney", "Wilma", "Fred", "Dino"}

Private Sub frmFlintstones_Load(...) Handles MyBase.Load
  'Display unsorted list
  For i As Integer = 0 To 4
    lstPeople.Items.Add(person(i))
  Next
End Sub

Private Sub btnSort_Click(...) Handles btnSort.Click
  'Bubble sort names
  Dim temp As String
  For passNum As Integer = 1 To 4      'Number of passes is 1 less than
    '                                   number of items
    For i As Integer = 1 To 5 - passNum    'Each pass needs 1 less comparison
      If (person(i - 1) > person(i)) Then
        temp = person(i - 1)
        person(i - 1) = person(i)
        person(i) = temp
      End If
    Next
  Next
  'Display alphabetized list
  lstPeople.Items.Clear()
  For i As Integer = 0 To 4
    lstPeople.Items.Add(person(i))
  Next
End Sub
```

[Run, and click the button.]

 Example 3 Table 7.5 contains facts about the 10 most populous states with listings in ascending order by state abbreviation. The following program sorts the table in descending order by population. Data are read from a file into an array of structures by the form's Load event procedure. When btnDisplayStats is clicked, the array is sorted based on the population field.

TABLE 7.5	The 10 most populous states (2006).		
State	Per Capita Income	% College Graduates	Population in Millions
CA	$37,036	29.8	36.5
FL	$33,219	27.2	18.1
GA	$31,121	28.1	9.4
IL	$36,120	31.2	12.8
MI	$33,116	26.1	10.1
NC	$30,553	25.6	8.9
NY	$40,507	32.2	19.3
OH	$32,478	23.3	11.5
PA	$34,897	26.6	12.4
TX	$32,462	25.5	23.5

Note: Column 3 gives the percentage of residents age 25 or older with a college degree.

```
Structure District
  Dim name As String
  Dim income As Double
  Dim collegeGrad As Double
  Dim population As Double
End Structure

Dim state(9) As District

Private Sub frmStates_Load(...) Handles MyBase.Load
  'Assume the data for state name, income, % college grads,
  'and population in millions are in the file "STATES.TXT"
  'First four lines of file contain the data CA, 37036, 29.8, 36.5
  Dim sr As IO.StreamReader = IO.File.OpenText("STATES.TXT")
  For i As Integer = 0 To 9
    state(i).name = sr.ReadLine
    state(i).income = CDbl(sr.ReadLine)
    state(i).collegeGrad = CDbl(sr.ReadLine)
    state(i).population = CDbl(sr.ReadLine)
  Next
  sr.Close()
End Sub

Private Sub btnDisplayStats_Click(...) Handles btnDisplayStats.Click
  SortData()
  ShowData()
End Sub

Sub ShowData()
  'Display ordered table
  Dim fmtStr As String = "{0,-4}{1,11:C0}{2,9:N1}{3,9:N1}"
  lstStats.Items.Clear()
```

```
  For i As Integer = 0 To 9
    lstStats.Items.Add(String.Format(fmtStr, state(i).name, _
      state(i).income, state(i).collegeGrad, state(i).population))
  Next
End Sub


Sub SortData()
  'Bubble sort table in descending order by population
  For passNum As Integer = 1 To 9
    For index As Integer = 1 To 10 - passNum
      If (state(index - 1).population < state(index).population) Then
        SwapData(index)
      End If
    Next
  Next
End Sub


Sub SwapData(ByVal index As Integer)
  'Swap entries
  Dim temp As District
  temp = state(index - 1)
  state(index - 1) = state(index)
  state(index) = temp
End Sub
```

[Run, and click the button.]

■ Shell Sort

The bubble sort is easy to understand and program. However, it is too slow for really long lists. The Shell sort, named for its inventor, Donald L. Shell, is much more efficient in such cases. It compares distant items first and works its way down to nearby items. The interval separating the compared items is called the **gap**. The gap begins as one-half the length of the list and is successively halved until eventually each item is compared with its neighbor as in the bubble sort. The algorithm for a list of $n + 1$ items referred to as item 0 through item n is as follows.

1. Begin with a gap of $g = \text{Int}([n + 1]/2)$.

2. Compare items 0 and g, items 1 and $1 + g$, 2 and $2 + g, \ldots, n - g$ and n. Swap any pairs that are out of order.

3. Repeat Step 2 until no swaps are made for gap g.

4. Halve the value of g.

5. Repeat Steps 2, 3, and 4 until the value of g is 0.

The Shell sort is illustrated in what follows, in which crossing arrows indicate that a swap occurred:

$$\text{Initial Gap} = \text{Int}([\text{Number of Items}]/2) = \text{Int}(5/2) = 2$$

Because there was a swap, use the same gap for the second pass.

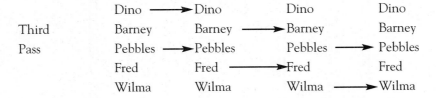

Again, there was a swap, so keep the current gap.

Third Pass

Dino ⟶ Dino   Dino   Dino
Barney   Barney ⟶ Barney   Barney
Pebbles ⟶ Pebbles   Pebbles ⟶ Pebbles
Fred   Fred ⟶ Fred   Fred
Wilma   Wilma   Wilma ⟶ Wilma

There were no swaps for the current gap of 2, so

$$\text{Next Gap} = \text{Int}([\text{Previous Gap}]/2) = \text{Int}(2/2) = 1.$$

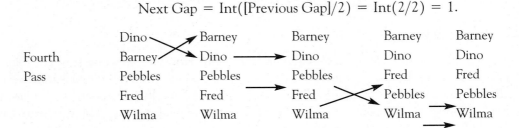

Because there was a swap (actually two swaps), keep the same gap.

	Barney ⟶	Barney	Barney	Barney	Barney
Fifth	Dino ⟶	Dino ⟶	Dino	Dino	Dino
Pass	Fred	Fred ⟶	Fred ⟶	Fred	Fred
	Pebbles	Pebbles	Pebbles ⟶	Pebbles ⟶	Pebbles
	Wilma	Wilma	Wilma	Wilma ⟶	Wilma

Because there were no swaps for the current gap, then

$$\text{Next Gap} = \text{Int}([\text{Previous Gap}]/2) = \text{Int}(1/2) = 0,$$

and the Shell sort is complete.

Notice that the Shell sort required 17 comparisons to sort the list, whereas the bubble sort required only 10 comparisons for the same list. This illustrates the fact that for very short lists, the bubble sort is preferable; however, for lists of 30 items or more, the Shell sort will consistently outperform the bubble sort. Table 7.6 shows the average number of comparisons required to sort arrays of varying sizes.

TABLE 7.6   **Efficiency of bubble and Shell sorts.**

Array Elements	Bubble Sort Comparisons	Shell Sort Comparisons
5	10	17
10	45	57
15	105	115
20	190	192
25	300	302
30	435	364
50	1225	926
100	4950	2638
500	124,750	22,517
1000	499,500	58,460

Example 4   The following program uses the Shell sort to alphabetize the parts of a running shoe. (See Figure 7.9 on the next page.) The data are read into an array whose size is large enough to guarantee sufficient space. In the form's Load event procedure, the variable *numParts* provides the subscripts for the array and serves as a counter. The final value of *numParts* is available to all procedures because the variable was created in the Declarations section of the Code Editor. The Sub procedure SortData uses a flag to indicate if a swap has been made during a pass.

FIGURE 7.9 Running shoe.

```
Dim part(50) As String
Dim numParts As Integer

Private Sub frmShoe_Load(...) Handles MyBase.Load
  'Read names of parts
  numParts = 0          'Number of parts
  Dim sr As IO.StreamReader = IO.File.OpenText("SHOEPART.TXT")
  Do While (sr.Peek <> -1) And (numParts < part.GetUpperBound(0))
    part(numParts) = sr.ReadLine
    numParts += 1
  Loop
  sr.Close()
End Sub

Private Sub btnDisplay_Click(...) Handles btnDisplay.Click
  'Sort and display parts of running shoe
  SortData()
  ShowData()
End Sub

Sub SortData()
  'Shell sort shoe parts
  Dim gap As Integer, doneFlag As Boolean
  Dim temp As String
  gap = CInt(Int(numParts / 2))
  Do While gap >= 1
    Do
      doneFlag = True
```

```
        For index As Integer = 0 To numParts - 1 - gap
          If part(index) > part(index + gap) Then
            temp = part(index)
            part(index) = part(index + gap)
            part(index + gap) = temp
            doneFlag = False
          End If
        Next
      Loop Until doneFlag = True     'Also can be Loop Until doneFlag
      gap = CInt(Int(gap / 2))       'Halve the length of the gap
    Loop
End Sub

Sub ShowData()
  'Display sorted list of parts
  lstParts.Items.Clear()
  For i As Integer = 0 To numParts - 1
    lstParts.Items.Add(part(i))
  Next
End Sub
```

[Run, and click the button.]

■ Searching

Suppose we had an array of 1000 names in alphabetical order and wanted to locate a specific person in the list. One approach would be to start with the first name and consider each name until a match was found. This process is called a **sequential search**. We would find a person whose name begins with "A" rather quickly, but 1000 comparisons might be necessary to find a person whose name begins with "Z." For much longer lists, searching could be a time-consuming matter. However, there is a method, called a **binary search**, that shortens the task considerably.

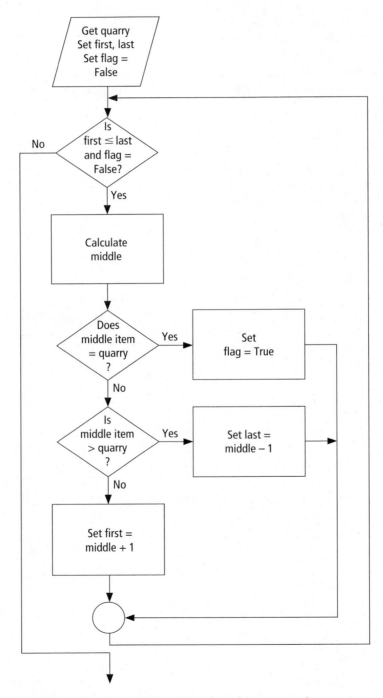

FIGURE 7.10 Flowchart for a binary search.

Let us refer to the sought item as *quarry*. The binary search looks for *quarry* by determining in which half of the list it lies. The other half is then discarded, and the retained half is temporarily regarded as the entire list. The process is repeated until the item is found. A flag can indicate if *quarry* has been found.

The algorithm for a binary search of an ascending list is as follows (Figure 7.10 shows the flowchart for a binary search):

1. At each stage, denote the subscript of the first item in the retained list by *first* and the subscript of the last item by *last*. Initially, the value of *first* is 0, the value of *last* is one less than the number of items in the list, and the value of *flag* is False.

2. Look at the middle item of the current list, the item having the subscript *middle* = Int((*first* + *last*)/2).

3. If the middle item is *quarry*, then *flag* is set to True and the search is over.

4. If the middle item is greater than *quarry*, then *quarry* should be in the first half of the list. So the subscript of *quarry* must lie between *first* and *middle* −1. That is, the new value of *last* is *middle* −1.

5. If the middle item is less than *quarry*, then *quarry* should be in the second half of the list of possible items. So the subscript of *quarry* must lie between *middle* +1 and *last*. That is, the new value of *first* is *middle* +1.

6. Repeat Steps 2 through 5 until *quarry* is found or until the halving process uses up the entire list. (When the entire list has been used up, *first* > *last*.) In the second case, *quarry* was not in the original list.

✔ **Example 5**   In the following program the array *firm*() contains the alphabetized names of up to 100 corporations. The program requests the name of a corporation as input and uses a binary search to determine whether the corporation is in the array.

```
Dim firm(99) As String
Dim numFirms As Integer

Private Sub frmCompanies_Load(...) Handles MyBase.Load
  'Fill array with data from FIRMS.TXT, which contains
  'the names of up to 100 companies
  Dim sr As IO.StreamReader = IO.File.OpenText("FIRMS.TXT")
  numFirms = 0
  Do While (sr.Peek <> -1) And (numFirms < firm.GetUpperBound(0))
    firm(numFirms) = sr.ReadLine
    numFirms += 1
  Loop
  sr.Close()
End Sub
```

```
Private Sub btnSearch_Click(...) Handles btnSearch.Click
  Dim corp, result As String
  corp = txtCorporation.Text.ToUpper
  result = ""
  BinarySearch(corp, result)
  'Display results of search
  txtResult.Text = corp & " " & result
End Sub

Sub BinarySearch(ByVal corp As String, ByRef result As String)
  'Array firm() assumed already ordered alphabetically
  'Binary search of firm() for corp
  Dim first, middle, last As Integer
  Dim foundFlag As Boolean = False
  first = 0
  last = numFirms - 1
  Do While (first <= last) And (Not foundFlag)
    middle = CInt(Int((first + last) / 2))
    Select Case firm(middle).ToUpper
      Case corp
        foundFlag = True
      Case Is > corp
        last = middle - 1
      Case Is < corp
        first = middle + 1
    End Select
  Loop
  If foundFlag Then
    result = "found"
  Else
    result = "not found"
  End If
End Sub
```

[Run, type "IBM" into the text box, and click the button.]

Suppose the array contains 100 corporations and the corporation input in Example 5 is in the second half of the array. On the first pass, *middle* would be assigned Int((0 + 99)/2) = Int(49.5) = 49 and then *first* would be altered to 49 + 1 = 50. On the second pass, *middle* would be assigned Int((50 + 99)/2) = Int(74.5) = 74. If the corporation is not the array element with subscript 74, then either *last* would be assigned 73 or *first* would be assigned 75, depending on whether the corporation appears before or after the 74th element. Each pass through the loop halves the range of subscripts containing the corporation until the corporation is located.

In Example 5, the binary search merely reported whether an array contained a certain item. After finding the item, its array subscript was not needed. However, if the search had been carried out on an array of structures (as in Table 7.5), the subscript of the found item could be used to retrieve the related information for the other members. This process, called a **table lookup**, is used in the following example.

Example 6   The following program uses a binary search procedure to locate the data for a state from Example 3 requested by the user. The program does not include a sort of the text file STATES.TXT, because the file is already ordered alphabetically by city name.

```
Structure District
    Dim name As String
    Dim income As Double
    Dim collegeGrad As Double
    Dim population As Double
End Structure

Dim state(9) As District

Private Sub frmStates_Load(...) Handles MyBase.Load
    'Assume that the data for state name, per capita income,
    '% college grads, and population in millions
    'have been placed in the file "STATES.TXT"
    'First four lines of file contain the data CA, 37036,29.8,36.5
    Dim sr As IO.StreamReader = IO.File.OpenText("STATES.TXT")
    For i As Integer = 0 To 9
        state(i).name = sr.ReadLine
        state(i).income = CDbl(sr.ReadLine)
        state(i).collegeGrad = CDbl(sr.ReadLine)
        state(i).population = CDbl(sr.ReadLine)
    Next
    sr.Close()
End Sub

Private Sub btnDisplayStats_Click(...) Handles btnDisplayStats.Click
    'Search for state in the populous states table
    Dim searchState As String, result As Integer
    searchState = mtxtState.Text.ToUpper
    result = FindState(searchState)
    If result >= 0 Then
        ShowData(result)
    Else
        MessageBox.Show(searchState & " not in file", "Not Found")
    End If
End Sub
```

```
Function FindState(ByVal searchState As String) As Integer
    'Binary search table for state name
    Dim first, middle, last As Integer
    first = 0
    last = 9
    Do While (first <= last)
        middle = CInt(Int((first + last) / 2))
        Select Case city(middle).name.ToUpper
            Case searchState
                Return middle      'Terminates function
            Case Is > searchState
                last = middle - 1
            Case Is < searchState
                first = middle + 1
        End Select
    Loop
    Return -1
End Function

Sub ShowData(ByVal result As Integer)
    'Display the data for the specified state
    Dim fmtStr As String = "{0,-4}{1,11:C0}{2,9:N1}{3,9:N1}"
    txtStats.text = String.Format(fmtStr, state(result).name, _
                    state(result).income, state(result).collegeGrad, _
                    state(result).population)
End Sub
```

[Run, type "OH" into the masked text box, and click the button.]

State Statistics			
Name of State: OH	Display Statistics		
State	Per Capita Income	% College Grads	Pop. in millions
OH	$32,478	23.3	11.5

■ Comments

1. Suppose that our bubble sort algorithm is applied to an ordered list. The algorithm will still make $n - 1$ passes through the list. The process could be shortened for some lists by flagging the presence of out-of-order items as in the Shell sort.

2. In Example 3, an array of structures already ordered by one member was sorted by another member. Usually, an array of structures is sorted by the member to be searched when accessing the array. This member is called the **key member**.

3. Suppose that an array of 2000 items is searched sequentially—that is, one item after another—in order to locate a specific item. The number of comparisons

would vary from 1 to 2000, with an average of 1000. With a binary search, the number of comparisons would be at most 11, because $2^{11} > 2000$.

4. The method ToUpper converts all the characters in a string to uppercase. ToUpper is useful in sorting and searching arrays of strings when the alphabetic case (upper or lower) is unimportant. For instance, Example 5 includes ToUpper in the Select Case comparisons, and so the binary search will locate "Mobil" in the array even if the user entered "MOBIL".

5. Visual Basic has a built-in sort routine that can be used to sort arrays. The statement

```
Array.Sort(arrayName)
```

sorts *arrayName* into ascending order. For instance, in Example 2 the event procedure can be replaced with the following code.

```
Private Sub btnSort_Click(...) Handles btnSort.Click
  Dim name() As String = {"Pebbles", "Barney", "Wilma", _
                          "Fred", "Dino"}
  Array.Sort(name)
  'Display alphabetized list
  lstNames.Items.Clear()
  For i As Integer = 0 To 4
    lstNames.Items.Add(name(i))
  Next
End Sub
```

Array.Sort cannot be used with arrays of structures and therefore is not sufficient for our purposes.

Practice Problems 7.4

1. The pseudocode for a bubble sort of an array of n items follows. Why is the terminating value of the outer loop $n - 1$ and the terminating value of the inner loop $n - j$?

```
For j As Integer = 1 To n - 1
  For k As Integer = 1 To n - j
    If [(k-1)st and kth items are out of order] Then [swap them]
  Next
Next
```

2. Complete the table that follows by filling in the values of each variable after successive passes of a binary search of an array of 20 items, where the sought item is in the position 13.

FIRST	LAST	MIDDLE
0	19	9
10	19	

EXERCISES 7.4

In Exercises 1 through 4, determine the output displayed in the list box when the button is clicked.

1.
```
Private Sub btnDisplay_Click(...) Handles btnDisplay.Click
    Dim p As Integer = 300
    Dim q As Integer = 500
    Dim r As Integer = p
    p = q
    q = r
    lstOutput.Items.Add(p)
    lstOutput.Items.Add(q)
End Sub
```

2.
```
Dim first() As String = {"Egg", "Chicken"}

Private Sub btnDisplay_Click(...) Handles btnDisplay.Click
    Dim temp As String
    If first(1) < first(0) Then
      temp = first(1)
      first(1) = first(0)
      first(0) = temp
    End If
    lstOutput.Items.Add(first(0))
    lstOutput.Items.Add(first(1))
End Sub
```

3.
```
Private Sub btnDisplay_Click(...) Handles btnDisplay.Click
    Dim x, y, t As Double
    Dim swappedFlag As Boolean = False
    x = 8
    y = 8
    If y > x Then
      t = x
      x = y
      y = t
      swappedFlag = True
    End If
    lstOutput.Items.Add(x)
    lstOutput.Items.Add(y)
    If swappedFlag Then
      lstOutput.Items.Add("Numbers swapped.")
    End If
End Sub
```

4.
```
Dim a(2) As Integer

Private Sub btnDisplay_Click(...) Handles btnDisplay.Click
    Dim temp As Integer
    For j As Integer = 0 To 1
```

```
      For k As Integer = 0 To 2 - j
        If a(k) > a(k + 1) Then
          temp = a(k)
          a(k) = a(k + 1)
          a(k + 1) = temp
        End If
      Next
    Next
    For j As Integer = 0 To 2
      lstOutput.Items.Add(a(j))
    Next
  End Sub

  Private Sub frmNumbers_Load(...) Handles MyBase.Load
    Dim sr As IO.StreamReader = IO.File.OpenText("DATA.TXT")
    For j As Integer = 0 To 2
      a(j) = CInt(sr.ReadLine)
    Next
    sr.Close()
  End Sub
```

(Assume that the three lines of the file DATA.TXT contain the following entries: 7, 4, 3.)

In Exercises 5 and 6, identify the errors.

5.
```
Dim c(3), d(3) As Integer

Private Sub btnDisplay_Click(...) Handles btnDisplay.Click
  'Swap two items
  c(3) = d(3)
  d(3) = c(3)
  lstOutput.Items.Add(c(3))
  lstOutput.Items.Add(d(3))
End Sub

Private Sub frmNumbers_Load(...) Handles MyBase.Load
  Dim sr As IO.StreamReader = IO.File.OpenText("DATA.TXT")
  For i As Integer = 0 To 3
    c(i) = CInt(sr.ReadLine)
    d(i) = CInt(sr.ReadLine)
  Next
  sr.Close()
End Sub
```

(Assume that the eight lines of the file DATA.TXT contain the following entries:1, 2, 3, 4, 5, 6, 7, 8.)

6.
```
Dim a(2), b(2) As Integer

Private Sub btnDisplay_Click(...) Handles btnDisplay.Click
  'Swap the two arrays
  Dim temp(2) As Integer
  a = b
  b = a
End Sub

Private Sub frmNumbers_Load(...) Handles MyBase.Load
  Dim sr As IO.StreamReader = IO.File.OpenText("DATA.TXT")
  For i As Integer = 0 To 2
    a(i) = CInt(sr.ReadLine)
    b(i) = CInt(sr.ReadLine)
  Next
  sr.Close()
End Sub
```

(Assume that the six lines of the file DATA.TXT contain the following entries:1, 3, 5, 7, 9, 11.)

7. Which type of search would be best for the following array?

0	1	2	3	4
Paul	Ringo	John	George	Pete

8. Which type of search would be best for the following array?

0	1	2	3	4
Beloit	Green Bay	Madison	Milwaukee	Oshkosh

9. Consider the items Bobby, Jimmy, Fred, and Billy in that order. After how many swaps in a bubble sort will the list be in alphabetical order?

10. How many comparisons will be made in a bubble sort of seven items?

11. How many comparisons will be made in a bubble sort of n items?

12. Modify the program in Example 2 so that it will keep track of the number of swaps and comparisons and display these numbers before ending.

13. Rework Exercise 9 using the Shell sort.

14. How many comparisons would be made in a Shell sort of six items if the items were originally in descending order and were sorted in ascending order?

15. If a list of six items is already in the proper order, how many comparisons will be made by a Shell sort?

16. Suppose a list of 5000 numbers is to be sorted, but the numbers consist of only 1, 2, 3, and 4. Describe a method of sorting the list that would be much faster than either the bubble or Shell sort.

17. What is the maximum number of comparisons required to find an item in a sequential search of 32 items? What is the average number of comparisons? What is the maximum number of comparisons required to find an item in a binary search of 32 items?

18. Redo Exercise 17 with 2^n items, where n is any positive integer.

In Exercises 19 through 26, write a program (or procedure) to complete the stated task.

19. Exchange the values of the variables x, y, and z so that x has y's value, y has z's value, and z has x's value.

20. Display the names of the seven dwarfs in alphabetical order. For the contents of a text file use Doc, Grumpy, Sleepy, Happy, Bashful, Sneezy, and Dopey.

21. The nation's capital has long been a popular staging area for political, religious, and other large public rallies, protest marches, and demonstrations. The events in Table 7.7 have drawn the largest crowds, according to estimates from D.C., U.S. Park, or Capitol police. Read the data into an array of structures and display a similar table with the event names in alphabetical order. *Note:* The data is contained in the file EVENTS.TXT.

TABLE 7.7 **Large Public Displays of Emotion in Washington, D.C.**

Event	Crowd Estimate (in thousands)
Lyndon Johnson inauguration (1/23/65)	1,200
Bicentennial fireworks (7/4/76)	1,000
Desert Storm rally (6/8/91)	800
Bill Clinton inauguration (1/20/93)	800
Beach Boys concert (7/4/85)	625
Washington Redskins victory parade (2/3/88)	600
Vietnam moratorium rally (11/15/69)	600
Ronald Reagan inauguration (1/20/81)	500
U.S. Iran hostage motorcade (1/28/81)	500

22. Table 7.8 presents statistics from a recent year on the five leading sneaker brands. Read the data into an array of structures, and display a similar table with wholesale revenue in descending order.

TABLE 7.8 **U.S. market share in sneakers.**

Brand	Wholesale Revenue (in millions)	Percentage Share of U.S. Market
Adidas USA	792	8.9
Fila	392	4.4
New Balance	1024	11.5
Nike	3231	36.3
Reebok	1086	12.1

Source: Morgan Stanley Dean Witter Research.

23. Accept 10 words to be input in alphabetical order, and store them in an array. Then accept an 11th word as input, and store it in the array in its correct alphabetical position.

24. An airline has a list of 200 flight numbers (between 1 and 1000) in ascending order in the file FLIGHTS.TXT. Accept a number as input and do a binary search of the list to determine if the flight number is valid.

25. Allow a number *n* to be input by the user. Then accept as input a list of *n* numbers. Place the numbers into an array and apply a bubble sort.

26. Rework Exercise 25, but use a flag to detect the presence of out-of-order items as in the Shell sort.

27. Write a program that accepts a word as input and converts it into Morse code. The dots and dashes corresponding to each letter of the alphabet are as follows:

A .–	H	O –––	V ...–
B –...	I ..	P .––.	W .––
C –.–.	J .–––	Q ––.–	X –..–
D –..	K –.–	R .–.	Y –.––
E .	L .–..	S ...	Z ––..
F ..–.	M ––	T –	
G ––.	N –.	U ..–	

28. Write a program that accepts an American word as input and performs a binary search to translate it into its British equivalent. Use the following list of words for data, and account for the case when the word requested is not in the list:

AMERICAN	BRITISH	AMERICAN	BRITISH
attic	loft	ice cream	ice
business suit	lounge suit	megaphone	loud hailer
elevator	lift	radio	wireless
flashlight	torch	sneakers	plimsolls
french fries	chips	truck	lorry
gasoline	petrol	zero	nought

29. Write a program that accepts a student's name and seven test scores as input and calculates the average score after dropping the two lowest scores.

30. Suppose letter grades are assigned as follows:

97 and above	A+	74–76	C
94–96	A	70–73	C–
90–93	A–	67–69	D+
87–89	B+	64–66	D
84–86	B	60–63	D–
80–83	B–	0–59	F
77–79	C+		

Write a program that accepts a grade as input and displays the corresponding letter.

Hint: This problem shows that when you search an array, you don't always look for equality. Set up an array of structures with the member *range* containing the values 97, 94, 90, 87, 84, ..., 0 and the member *letter* containing A+, A, A−, B+, ..., F. Next, perform a sequential search to find the first structure such that the value of the *range* member is less than or equal to the input grade.

31. The *median* of an ordered set of measurements is a number separating the lower half from the higher half. If the number of measurements *n is* odd, the median is the middle number when the measurements are arranged in ascending or descending order. If the number of measurements *n* is even, the median is the average of the two middle measurements when the measurements are arranged in ascending or descending order. Write a program that requests a number *n* and a set of *n* measurements as input and then displays the median.

32. Write a program with two buttons labeled Ascending Order and Descending Order that displays the eight vegetables in V8® in either ascending or descending alphabetic order. The vegetables (tomato, carrot, celery, beet, parsley, lettuce, watercress, and spinach) should be stored in a class-level array.

Solutions to Practice Problems 7.4

1. The outer loop controls the number of passes, one less than the number of items in the list. The inner loop performs a single pass, and the *j*th pass consists of $n - j$ comparisons.

2.

FIRST	LAST	MIDDLE
0	19	9
10	19	14
10	13	11
12	13	12
13	13	13

7.5   Two-Dimensional Arrays

Each array discussed so far held a single list of items. Such array variables are called **one-dimensional** or **single-subscripted variables**. An array can also hold the contents of a table with several rows and columns. Such array variables are called **two-dimensional** or **double-subscripted variables**. Two tables follow. Table 7.9 gives the road mileage between certain cities. It has four rows and four columns. Table 7.10 shows the leading universities in three graduate school programs. It has three rows and five columns.

TABLE 7.9   Road mileage between selected U.S. cities.

	Chicago	Los Angeles	New York	Philadelphia
Chicago	0	2054	802	738
Los Angeles	2054	0	2786	2706
New York	802	2786	0	100
Philadelphia	738	2706	100	0

TABLE 7.10 Rankings of U.S. university graduate school programs.

	1	2	3	4	5
Business	Harvard	Stanford	U of PA	MIT	U of Chicago
Engineering	MIT	Stanford	UC Berk	GA Tech	Cal Tech
Law	Yale	Harvard	Stanford	NYU	Columbia

Source: U.S. News and World Report, 2007.

Two-dimensional array variables store the contents of tables. They have the same types of names as other array variables. The only difference is that they have two subscripts, each with its own upper bound. The first subscript is determined by the number of rows in the table, and the second subscript is determined by the number of columns. The statement

```
Dim arrayName(m, n) As DataType
```

declares an array of type *DataType* corresponding to a table with rows labeled from 0 to m and columns labeled from 0 to n. The entry in the jth row, kth column is *arrayName(j, k)*. For instance, the data in Table 7.9 can be stored in an array named *rm()*. The statement

```
Dim rm(3, 3) As Double
```

will declare the array. Each element of the array has the form rm(row, column). The values of the elements of the array we use will be

$rm(0, 0) = 0$	$rm(0, 1) = 2054$	$rm(0, 2) = 802$	$rm(0, 3) = 738$
$rm(1, 0) = 2054$	$rm(1, 1) = 0$	$rm(1, 2) = 2786$	$rm(1, 3) = 2706$
$rm(2, 0) = 802$	$rm(2, 1) = 2786$	$rm(2, 2) = 0$	$rm(2, 3) = 100$
$rm(3, 0) = 738$	$rm(3, 1) = 2706$	$rm(3, 2) = 100$	$rm(3, 3) = 0$

The data in Table 7.10 can be stored in a two-dimensional string array named *univ()*. The appropriate array is declared with the statement

```
Dim univ(2, 4) As String
```

Some of the entries of the array are

univ(0, 0) = "Harvard"

univ(1, 2) = "UC Berk"

univ(2, 4) = "Columbia"

Since a one-dimensional array has a single subscript, it can be processed with a single For . . . Next loop. Processing a two-dimensional array usually requires a pair of nested For . . . Next loops — one for each of the two subscripts. The outer loop considers the rows one at a time. For each row, the inner loop cycles through the elements in that row.

Example 1   The following program stores and accesses the data from Table 7.9. Data are read from the text file DISTANCE.TXT into a two-dimensional class-level array using a pair of nested For . . . Next loops.

OBJECT	PROPERTY	SETTING
frmDistances	Text	Intercity Distances
lblCh	Text	1. Chicago
lblLA	Text	2. Los Angeles
lblNY	Text	3. New York
lblPh	Text	4. Philadelphia
lblOrig	Text	Origin:
mtxtOrig	Mask	0
lblDest	Text	Destination:
mtxtDest	Mask	0
btnShow	Text	Show Mileage Between Origin and Destination
lblMiles	Text	Mileage:
txtMiles	ReadOnly	True

```vb
Dim rm(3, 3) As Double

Private Sub frmDistances_Load(...) Handles MyBase.Load
  'Fill two-dimensional array with intercity mileages
  'Assume the data has been placed in the file "DISTANCE.TXT"
  '(First four lines of the file contain the numbers 0, 2054, 802, 738)
  Dim sr As IO.StreamReader = IO.File.OpenText("DISTANCE.TXT")
  For row As Integer = 0 To 3
    For col As Integer = 0 To 3
      rm(row, col) = CDbl(sr.ReadLine)
    Next
  Next
  sr.Close()
End Sub

Private Sub btnShow_Click(...) Handles btnShow.Click
  'Determine road mileage between cities
  Dim row, col As Integer
  row = CInt(mtxtOrig.Text)
  col = CInt(mtxtDest.Text)
  If (row >= 1 And row <= 4) And (col >= 1 And col <= 4) Then
    txtMiles.Text = CStr(rm(row - 1, col - 1))
  Else
    MessageBox.Show("Origin and Dest. must be numbers from 1 to 4", "Error")
  End If
End Sub
```

[Run, type 3 into the Origin box, type 1 into the Destination box, and click the button.]

An unsized two-dimensional array can be declared with a statement of the form

```
Dim arrayName(,) As varType
```

and a two-dimensional array can be declared and initialized at the same time with a statement of the form

```
Dim arrayName(,) As varType = {{ROW0}, {ROW1},... {ROWm}}
```

where ROW0 consists of the entries in the top row of the corresponding table separated by commas; ROW1 consists of the entries in the next row of the corresponding table separated by commas, and so on. For instance, in Example 1, the declaration statement and frmDistances_Load event procedure can be replaced by the single statement

```
Dim rm(,) As Double = {{0, 2054, 802, 738}, _
            {2054, 0, 2786, 2706}, {802, 2786, 0, 100}, _
            {738, 2706, 100, 0}}
```

An already-created array can be resized with

```
ReDim arrayName(r, s)
```

which loses the current contents, or with

```
ReDim Preserve arrayName(r, s)
```

which keeps the current values. However, when the keyword Preserve is used, only the last coordinate can be resized. The upper bound of the first coordinate of the array is given by **arrayName.GetUpperBound(0),** and the upper bound of the second coordinate is given by **arrayName.GetUpperBound(1).**

So far, two-dimensional arrays have been used only to store data for convenient lookup. In the next example, an array is used to make a valuable computation.

 Example 2   The Center for Science in the Public Interest publishes *The Nutrition Scorebook*, a highly respected rating of foods. The top two foods in each of five categories are shown in Table 7.11 along with some information on their composition. The following program computes the nutritional content of a meal. The table is read

TABLE 7.11	Composition of 10 top-rated foods.				
	Calories	Protein (grams)	Fat (grams)	Vit A (IU)	Calcium (mg)
Spinach (1 cup)	23	3	0.3	8100	93
Sweet potato (1 med.)	160	2	1	9230	46
Yogurt (8 oz.)	230	10	3	120	343
Skim milk (1 cup)	85	8	0	500	302
Whole wheat bread (1 slice)	65	3	1	0	24
Brown rice (1 cup)	178	3.8	0.9	0	18
Watermelon (1 wedge)	110	2	1	2510	30
Papaya (1 lg.)	156	2.4	0.4	7000	80
Tuna in water (1 lb)	575	126.8	3.6	0	73
Lobster (1 med.)	405	28.8	26.6	984	190

into an array, and then the program requests the quantities of each food item that is part of the meal. The program then computes the amounts of each nutritional component consumed by summing each column with each entry weighted by the quantity of the food item. Coding is simplified by using an array of labels to hold the food names and an array of text boxes to hold the amounts input by the user. The five nutrients of interest and the actual names and nutrient values of the foods to be used in building a meal are read from the text file NUTTABLE.TXT.

OBJECT	PROPERTY	SETTING
frmNutrition	Text	Nutrition in a Meal
Label1–Label10		
lblQnty	Text	Quantity in Meal
TextBox1–TextBox10		
btnAnalyze	Text	Analyze Meal Nutrition
lblStatement	AutoSize	False
	Text	This meal contains the following quantities of these nutritional components:
	Visible	False
lstAnalysis	Visible	False
	Font	Courier New

```
Dim lblarrayFood(9) As Label
Dim txtarrayQnty(9) As TextBox
Dim nutName(4) As String          'Nutrient names
Dim nutTable(9, 4) As Double      'Nutrient values for each food

Private Sub frmNutrition_Load(...) Handles MyBase.Load
  'Fill arrays, set text for labels
  lblarrayFood(0) = Label1
  lblarrayFood(1) = Label2
  lblarrayFood(2) = Label3
  lblarrayFood(3) = Label4
  lblarrayFood(4) = Label5
  lblarrayFood(5) = Label6
  lblarrayFood(6) = Label7
  lblarrayFood(7) = Label8
  lblarrayFood(8) = Label9
  lblarrayFood(9) = Label10
  txtarrayQnty(0) = TextBox1
  txtarrayQnty(1) = TextBox2
  txtarrayQnty(2) = TextBox3
  txtarrayQnty(3) = TextBox4
  txtarrayQnty(4) = TextBox5
  txtarrayQnty(5) = TextBox6
  txtarrayQnty(6) = TextBox7
  txtarrayQnty(7) = TextBox8
  txtarrayQnty(8) = TextBox9
  txtarrayQnty(9) = TextBox10
  Dim foodName As String
  'Fill arrays; assign label captions
  Dim sr As IO.StreamReader = IO.File.OpenText("NUTTABLE.TXT")
  For i As Integer = 0 To 4
    nutName(i) = sr.ReadLine
  Next
  For i As Integer = 0 To 9
    foodName = sr.ReadLine
    lblarrayFood(i).Text = foodName
    For j As Integer = 0 To 4
      nutTable(i, j) = CDbl(sr.ReadLine)
    Next
  Next
  sr.Close()
End Sub

Private Sub btnAnalyze_Click(...) Handles btnAnalyze.Click
  'Determine the nutritional content of a meal
  Dim quantity(9) As Double     'amount of food in meal
  GetAmounts(quantity)
  lblStatement.Visible = True
  lstAnalysis.Visible = True
```

```
    ShowData(quantity)
  End Sub

  Sub GetAmounts(ByRef quantity() As Double)
    'Obtain quantities of foods consumed
    For i As Integer = 0 To 9
      If txtarrayQnty(i).Text <> "" Then
        quantity(i) = CDbl(txtarrayQnty(i).Text)
      Else
        quantity(i) = 0
      End If
    Next
  End Sub

  Sub ShowData(ByVal quantity() As Double)
    'Display amount of each component
    Dim amount As Double
    Dim fmtStr As String = "{0,-15}{1,8}"
    lstAnalysis.Items.Clear()
    For col As Integer = 0 To 4
      amount = 0
      For row As Integer = 0 To 9
        amount = amount + quantity(row) * nutTable(row, col)
      Next
      lstAnalysis.Items.Add(String.Format(fmtStr, nutName(col), amount))
    Next
  End Sub
```

[Run, type quantities into the text boxes, and press the button.]

■ Comments

1. We can define three- (or higher-) dimensional arrays much as we do two-dimensional arrays. A three-dimensional array uses three subscripts, and the assignment of values requires a triple-nested loop. As an example, a meteorologist might use a three-dimensional array to record temperatures for various dates, times, and elevations. The array might be created by the statement

   ```
   Dim temps(30, 23, 14) As Double
   ```

2. A ReDim statement cannot change the number of dimensions of an array. For instance, it cannot change a one-dimensional array into a two-dimensional array.

Practice Problems 7.5

1. Consider the road-mileage program in Example 1. How can the program be modified so the actual names of the cities can be supplied by the user?
2. In what types of problems are two-dimensional arrays superior to arrays of structures?

EXERCISES 7.5

In Exercises 1 through 8, determine the output displayed when the button is clicked. All Dim statements for arrays are in the Declarations section of the Code Editor.

1.
```
Dim a(20, 30) As Double

Private Sub btnDisplay_Click(...) Handles btnDisplay.Click
   a(3, 5) = 6
   a(5, 3) = 2 * a(3, 5)
   txtOutput.Text = CStr(a(5, 3))
End Sub
```

2.
```
Dim years(100, 50) As Double

Private Sub btnDisplay_Click(...) Handles btnDisplay.Click
  Dim x As Integer = 7, y As Integer = 8
  years(x, y) = 1937
  txtOutput.Text = CStr(years(7, 8) + 60)
End Sub
```

3.
```
Dim w(10, 15) As String

Private Sub btnDisplay_Click(...) Handles btnDisplay.Click
  Dim d As String = "Dorothy", n As Integer = 1
  w(1, 1) = d
  txtOutput.Text = w(n, n)
End Sub
```

4.
```
Dim actor(5, 5) As String

Private Sub btnDisplay_Click(...) Handles btnDisplay.Click
  Dim a As Integer = 2, b As Integer = 3, temp As Integer
  actor(a, b) = "Bogart"
```

```
    temp = a
    a = b
    b = temp
    lstOutput.Items.Add("1. " & actor(a, b))
    lstOutput.Items.Add("2. " & actor(b, a))
  End Sub
```

5. `Dim a(,) As Integer`

```
  Private Sub btnDisplay_Click(...) Handles btnDisplay.Click
    Dim p, q, sum As Integer
    Dim sr As IO.StreamReader = IO.File.OpenText("DATA.TXT")
    p = CInt(sr.ReadLine)
    q = CInt(sr.ReadLine)
    ReDim a(p, q)
    For j As Integer = 0 To p
      sum = 0
      For k As Integer = 0 To q
        a(j, k) = CInt(sr.ReadLine)
        sum += a(j, k)
      Next
      lstOutput.Items.Add(sum)
    Next
    sr.Close()
  End Sub
```

(Assume that the eight lines of the file DATA.TXT contain the following data: 2, 1, 4, 1, 6, 5, 8, 2.)

6. `Dim a(4, 3) As Integer`

```
  Private Sub btnDisplay_Click(...) Handles btnDisplay.Click
    Dim row As String
    For j As Integer = 0 To 4
      row = ""
      For k As Integer = 0 To 3
        a(j, k) = k * j
        row &= a(j, k) & "  "
      Next
      lstOutput.Items.Add(row)
    Next
  End Sub
```

7. `Dim s(3, 3) As Double`

```
  Private Sub btnDisplay_Click(...) Handles btnDisplay.Click
    Dim sr As IO.StreamReader = IO.File.OpenText("DATA.TXT")
    For j As Integer = 0 To 3
      For k As Integer = 0 To 3
        s(j, k) = CDbl(sr.ReadLine)
      Next
    Next
```

```
    sr.Close()
    For j As Integer = 0 To 3
      lstOutput.Items.Add(s(j, j))
    Next
  End Sub
```

(Assume that the sixteen lines of the file DATA.TXT contain the following entries: 1, 1, 1, 1, 2, 2, 2, 2, 3, 3, 3, 3, 4, 4, 4, 4.)

8.
```
Dim m(,) As Integer
Private Sub btnDisplay_Click(...) Handles btnDisplay.Click
  Dim x, y As Integer
  Dim sr As IO.StreamReader = IO.File.OpenText("DATA.TXT")
  x = CInt(sr.ReadLine)
  y = CInt(sr.ReadLine)
  ReDim m(x, y)
  For j As Integer = 0 To x
    For k As Integer = 0 To y - j
      m(j, k) = CInt(sr.ReadLine)
      lstOutput.Items.Add(m(j, k) - k)
    Next
  Next
  sr.Close()
End Sub
```

(Assume that the 10 lines of the file DATA.TXT contain the following entries: 1, 3, 5, 3, 2, 4, 3, 4, 7, 8.)

In Exercises 9 and 10, identify the errors.

9.
```
Dim a(2, 3) As Integer
Private Sub btnDisplay_Click(...) Handles btnDisplay.Click
  'Fill an array
  Dim sr As IO.StreamReader = IO.File.OpenText("DATA.TXT")
  For j As Integer = 0 To 3
    For k As Integer = 0 To 2
      a(j, k) = CInt(sr.ReadLine)
    Next
  Next
  sr.Close()
End Sub
```

(Assume that the 12 lines of the file DATA.TXT contain the following entries: 1, 2, 3, 4, 5, 6, 7, 8, 9, 0, 1, 2.)

10.
```
Dim score(2, 2) As Integer
Private Sub frmScores_Load(...) Handles MyBase.Load
  'Fill array from text file
  Dim student As Integer
  Dim sr As IO.StreamReader = IO.File.OpenText("SCORES.TXT")
  For j As Integer = 0 To 2
```

```
    student = CInt(sr.ReadLine)
    For k As Integer = 0 To 2
      score(k, j) = CInt(sr.ReadLine)
    Next
  Next
End Sub

Private Sub btnDisplay_Click(...) Handles btnDisplay.Click
  'Report individual scores
  Dim student, exam As Integer
  student = CInt(txtStudent.Text)
  exam = CInt(txtExam.Text)
  If (student>=0 And student<=2) And (exam>=0 And exam<=2) Then
    txtOutput.Text = CStr(score(student, exam))
  End If
End Sub
```

(Assume that the 12 lines of the file SCORES.TXT contain the following data: 0, 80, 85, 90, 1, 72, 80, 88, 2, 87, 93, 90.)

In Exercises 11 through 14, write a procedure to perform the stated task.

11. Given an array declared with the statement `Dim a(5, 5) As Integer`, set the entries in the jth row to j (for $j = 0, \ldots, 5$).

12. Given an array declared with the statement `Dim a(5, 5) As integer`, and values assigned to each entry, compute the product of the values in row 5.

13. Given an array declared with the statement `Dim a(5, 5) As Double`, and values assigned to each entry, interchange the values in rows 3 and 4.

14. Given an array declared with the statement `Dim a(5, 10) As Double`, and values assigned to each entry, find the smallest value and the places (possibly more than one) at which it occurs.

In Exercises 15 through 25, write a program to perform the stated task.

15. A company has two stores (1 and 2), and each store sells three items (1, 2, and 3). The following tables give the inventory at the beginning of the day and the amount of each item sold during that day.

		Beginning Inventory ITEM						**Sales for Day** ITEM		
		1	2	3				1	2	3
Store	1	25	64	23		Store	1	7	45	11
	2	12	82	19			2	4	24	8

(a) Record the values of each table in an array.

(b) Adjust the values in the first array to hold the inventories at the end of the day and display these new inventories.

(c) Calculate and display the number of items in each store at the end of the day.

16. Table 7.12 gives the results of a survey on the uses of computers in the workplace. Each entry shows the percentage of respondents from the age category that use the computer for the indicated purpose.

   (a) Place the data from the table in an array. (Use 7-5-E16.TXT.)
   (b) Determine the average of the percentages in the Spreadsheets column.

TABLE 7.12 Workers using computers on the job.

Age	Word Processing	Spreadsheets	Internet/ e-mail	Calendar/ Schedule	Programming
18–24	57.9	56.0	62.1	48.9	12.4
25–29	67.8	66.2	75.6	58.3	18.8
30–39	69.8	68.0	78.3	61.8	18.0
40–49	69.7	66.9	77.1	59.0	17.7
50–59	68.1	62.5	76.5	54.6	15.1
60 and older	63.7	53.8	71.2	46.1	10.6

Source: U.S. Center of Educational Statistics, Digest of Educational Statistics, 2003

17. A university offers 10 courses at each of three campuses. The number of students enrolled in each is presented in Table 7.13.

   (a) Find the total number of course enrollments on each campus.
   (b) Find the total number of students taking each course.

TABLE 7.13 Number of students enrolled in courses.

		Course 1	2	3	4	5	6	7	8	9	10
	1	5	15	22	21	12	25	16	11	17	23
Campus	2	11	23	51	25	32	35	32	52	25	21
	3	2	12	32	32	25	26	29	12	15	11

18. Table 7.14 gives the 2005 and 2006 U.S. sales for the five top restaurant chains.

   (a) Place the data into an array.
   (b) Calculate the total change in sales for these five restaurant chains.

TABLE 7.14 Top restaurant chains.

	2005 Sales $MM	2006 Sales $MM
1. McDonald's	25.6	27.1
2. Burger King	8.4	8.5
3. Wendy's	7.7	7.8
4. Subway	7.1	7.7
5. Taco Bell	6.1	6.3

Source: QSR Magazine, Dec. 2007

19. The scores for the top four golfers at the 2008 Buick Invitational are shown in Table 7.15.

(a) Place the data into an array. (See GOLF.TXT.)
(b) Compute the total score for each player.
(c) Compute the average score for each round.

TABLE 7.15   2008 Buick Invitational.

| | \multicolumn{4}{c}{Round} | | | |
	1	2	3	4
Tiger Woods	67	65	66	71
Ryuji Imada	69	72	69	67
Rory Sabbatini	67	75	70	67
Stewart Cink	68	69	69	73

20. Table 7.16 contains part of the pay schedule for federal employees in Washington, D.C. Table 7.17 gives the number of employees in each classification in a certain division. Place the data from each table into an array and compute the amount of money this division pays for salaries during the year.

TABLE 7.16   2008 pay schedule for federal white-collar workers.

| | \multicolumn{4}{c}{Step} | | | |
	1	2	3	4
GS-1	17,046	17,615	18,182	18,746
GS-2	19,165	19,621	20,255	20,793
GS-3	20,911	21,608	22,305	23,002
GS-4	23,475	24,258	25,041	25,824
GS-5	26,264	27,139	28,014	28,889
GS-6	29,276	30,252	31,228	32,204
GS-7	32,534	33,618	34,702	35,786

TABLE 7.17   Number of employees in each category.

	1	2	3	4
GS-1	0	0	2	1
GS-2	2	3	0	1
GS-3	4	2	5	7
GS-4	12	13	8	3
GS-5	4	5	0	1
GS-6	6	2	4	3
GS-7	8	1	9	2

21. Consider Table 7.10, the rankings of three graduate school programs. Write a program that places the data into an array, allows the name of a university to be input, and gives the categories in which it appears. Of course, a university might appear more than once or not at all. (See RANKING.TXT.)

22. Table 7.18 gives the monthly precipitation for a typical Nebraska city during a five-year period. Write a program that reads the table from a text file into an array and then displays in a list box the output in Figure 7.11.

TABLE 7.18 **Monthly precipitation (in inches) for a typical Nebraska city.**

	Jan.	Feb.	Mar.	Apr.	May	June	July	Aug.	Sept.	Oct.	Nov.	Dec.
1986	0.88	1.11	2.01	3.64	6.44	5.58	4.23	4.34	4.00	2.05	1.48	0.77
1987	0.76	0.94	2.09	3.29	4.68	3.52	3.52	4.82	3.72	2.21	1.24	0.80
1988	0.67	0.80	1.75	2.70	4.01	3.88	3.72	3.78	3.55	1.88	1.21	0.61
1989	0.82	0.80	1.99	3.05	4.19	4.44	3.98	4.57	3.43	2.32	1.61	0.75
1990	0.72	0.90	1.71	2.02	2.33	2.98	2.65	2.99	2.55	1.99	1.05	0.92

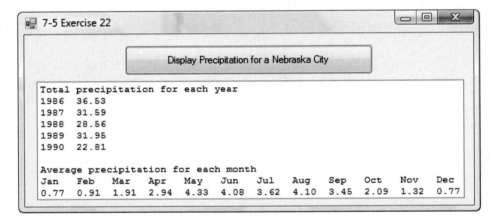

FIGURE 7.11 Outcome of Exercise 22.

23. Suppose that a course has 15 students enrolled and that five exams are given during the semester. Write a program that accepts each student's name and grades as input and places the names in a one-dimensional array and the grades in a two-dimensional array. The program should then display each student's name and semester average. Also, the program should display the median for each exam. (For an odd number of grades, the median is the middle grade. For an even number of grades, it is the average of the two middle grades.)

24. An *n*-by-*n* array is called a magic square if the sums of each row, each column, and each diagonal are equal. Write a program to determine if an array is a magic square and use it to determine if either of the following arrays is a magic square. **Hint:** If, at any time, one of the sums is not equal to the others, the search is complete.

(a)	1	15	15	4		(b)	11	10	4	23	17
	12	6	7	9			18	12	6	5	24
	8	10	11	5			25	19	13	7	1
	13	3	2	16			2	21	20	14	8
							9	3	22	16	15

25. A company has three stores (1, 2, and 3), and each store sells five items (1, 2, 3, 4, and 5). The following tables give the number of items sold by each store and category on a particular day, and the cost of each item.

(a) Place the data from the left-hand table in a two-dimensional array and the data from the right-hand table in a one-dimensional array.

(b) Compute and display the total dollar amount of sales for each store and for the entire company.

Number of Items Sold During Day

		ITEM						ITEM	COST PER ITEM
		1	2	3	4	5		1	$12.00
	1	25	64	23	45	14		2	$17.95
Store	2	12	82	19	34	63		3	$95.00
	3	54	22	17	43	35		4	$86.50
								5	$78.00

Solutions to Practice Problems 7.5

1. Replace the masked text boxes with ordinary text boxes to hold city names. The function FindCityNum can be used to determine the subscript associated with each city. This function and the modified event procedure btnShow_Click are as follows:

```
Function FindCityNum(ByVal city As String) As Integer
  Select Case city.ToUpper
    Case "CHICAGO"
      Return 1
    Case "LOS ANGELES"
      Return 2
    Case "NEW YORK"
      Return 3
    Case "PHILADELPHIA"
      Return 4
    Case Else
      Return 0
  End Select
End Function

Private Sub btnShow_Click(...) Handles btnShow.Click
  Dim orig, dest As String
  Dim row, col As Integer 'Determine road mileage between cities
  orig = txtOrig.Text
  dest = txtDest.Text
  row = FindCityNum(orig)
  col = FindCityNum(dest)
  If (row < 1) Or (row > 4) Then
    MessageBox.Show("City of origin not available", "Error")
  ElseIf (col < 1) Or (col > 4) Then
    MessageBox.Show("Destination city not available", "Error")
  Else
    txtMiles.Text = CStr(rm(row, col))
  End If
End Sub
```

2. Both arrays of structures and two-dimensional arrays are used to hold related data. If some of the data are numeric and some are string, then structures must be used, because all entries of a two-dimensional array must be of the same type. Arrays of structures should also be used if the data will be sorted. Two-dimensional arrays are best suited to tabular data.

7.6 A Case Study: A Sophisticated Cash Register

One of the most prevalent types of computer equipment today is the cash register. This machine has evolved considerably from the time when it functioned like an old-fashioned mechanical typewriter, recording the amount of each sale on a strip of paper and keeping a running sum. Today, cash registers are located not only in stores, but also within gasoline pumps and airport kiosks, performing many functions above and beyond printing receipts. The data from customers' purchases can be stored on a central computer and analyzed to determine trends in buying behavior. For example, a grocery store may glean from cash register transactions that customers who purchase potato chips are likely to also purchase soft drinks. This might lead the store to stock soft drinks in the same aisle as snacks. In the retail industry, the location of a cash register is called the "point of sale" (abbreviated as "POS").

■ The Design of the Program

This case study develops a sophisticated cash register that supports three main features: First, it accepts user input for the quantity, price, and department of a particular article. Second, it calculates the totals including sales tax and stores those data along with the payment method into an array. Finally, the program generates a report on the stored data. Each of these features is a task that is executed by clicking on a button:

1. Enter the price, quantity, and department of a new article to purchase. Display the article's data.
2. Display the subtotal, sales tax, and total, and record the purchase and payment method in an array.
3. Generate a report showing (a) the quantity and sales for each department and (b) the number of receipts and amounts for each payment method.

■ The User Interface

Two text boxes are used to collect input for quantity and price. Buttons that represent each department are used to record and display this data in an output list box. Each payment type is represented by a button that finalizes the purchase and displays the totals. A report button is enabled after a purchase is finalized and, when pressed, generates the report in the same list box. See Figure 7.12 and Table 7.19.

FIGURE 7.12   Sample output after pressing the bottom button.

TABLE 7.19   Controls that comprise the user interface.

Object	Property	Setting
frmCashRegister	Text	Sophisticated Cash Register
lblQuantity	Text	Quantity:
txtQuantity		
lblPrice	Text	Price:
txtPrice		
lblDepartment	Text	Department
btnWomens	Text	Womens
btnMens	Text	Mens
btnKids	Text	Kids
btnSportswear	Text	Sportswear
btnHousehold	Text	Household
btnHardware	Text	Hardware
lblMethod	Text	Payment Method
btnVisa	Text	Visa
btnMasterCard	Text	MasterCard
btnCash	Text	Cash
lblCash	Text	Tendered:
txtCash		
btnReport	Enabled	False
	Text	Display Department Sales and Receipts Report
lstOutput	Font	Courier New

▦ The Data Structures

The cash register inputs, stores, and processes data. These data are organized into related fields that lend themselves to structure data types. The program employs an Article structure that stores the data for each article that is purchased and a Purchase structure that stores all of the articles and the totals on one receipt. An array of Purchase structures is declared as a class-level variable and holds all of the data for the store. Figure 7.13 shows a representation of the way the structures are organized.

Article	
1	Article.department
2	Article.quantity
$25.00	Article.price

Purchase	
Articles()	Purchase.articles
2	Purchase.articleCount
$50.00	Purchase.subtotal
$52.50	Purchase.total
1	Purchase.method

FIGURE 7.13   Structures used in the Sophisticated Cash Register program.

▦ Coding the Program

The top row of Figure 7.14 shows the different events to which the program must respond. Table 7.20 identifies the corresponding event procedures and the general procedures they call. Let's examine each event procedure:

1. **frmCashRegister_Load** initializes the first Purchase structure by dimensioning its *articles* array to an initial upper bound of 4. It is necessary to do this in the Load procedure because arrays cannot be sized within the structure definition block, yet they must be dimensioned before they are accessed.

2. **RingupArticle** is called by the event procedures connected to the buttons that represent the department names (Womens, Mens, Kids, etc.). It takes as its parameter the number of the department that was clicked. The procedure stores the

FIGURE 7.14   Hierarchy chart for Sophisticated Cash Register program.

TABLE 7.20	Tasks and their procedures.
1. Initialize First Purchase	frmCashRegister_Load
2. Store and Display Article	RingupArticle
2.1 Store Article	RingupArticle
2.2 Display Article	DisplayArticle
3. Store and Display Purchase	TotalPurchase
3.1 Calculate Totals	TotalPurchase
3.2 Store Purchase	TotalPurchase
3.3 Display Purchase	DisplayTotals
3.4 Initialize Next Purchase	TotalPurchase
4. Analyze Data	btnReport_Click
4.1 Aggregate Data	btnReport_Click
4.2 Total and Display Department Statistics	btnReport_Click
4.2 Total and Display Payment Method Statistics	btnReport_Click

department, quantity, and price of the article into a new Article structure. If the quantity and price are valid (that is, they are greater than zero), then the new article is stored into the array that is a member of the current Purchase structure. If that array does not have room to accommodate the new article, the array is enlarged using a ReDim Preserve statement. Finally, the procedure calls the Display-Article procedure and resets the quantity to 1 for the next article.

The DisplayArticle procedure displays the quantity, department, price, and total (that is, quantity times price) for an article in the output list box. A heading is displayed along with the first purchase on the receipt. The department names are stored in a string array called *department()* that is declared as a class-level variable. The procedure displays the article's department name by using its department number as the subscript in the *department()* array.

3. TotalPurchase is called by the event procedures that are connected to the buttons representing the methods of payment (Visa, MasterCard, Cash). It takes as its parameter the number of the payment method that was clicked. The procedure first checks to see if any articles have been stored. If not, a message box is displayed. Otherwise, the articles are totaled, and sales tax is applied to calculate the purchase's subtotal and total. If the payment method is Cash, the procedure verifies that the amount tendered by the customer is at least the total amount. If it isn't, a message box is displayed. Otherwise, the purchase is stored, the DisplayTotals procedure is called, and the *articles* array in the next purchase structure is ReDimmed to the default upper bound of 4.

The technique used to store a purchase requires elaboration. The class-level array *purchases()* is declared with an initial upper bound of 30. The integer counter *count* keeps track of the number of stored purchases and is initialized to the default value of zero. New articles are stored in the *purchases()* element with subscript *count*. When a payment method is clicked, the purchase is finalized. The action that does this is the line `count += 1`, which increments the counter by one. Therefore, the new purchase is stored in the *purchases()* array all along, but it is only recognized as "stored" when its subscript is less than the counter.

The DisplayTotals procedure displays the subtotal, applicable sales tax, and total for the purchase. It also displays the payment method in the following manner: If the payment method is Cash (method #3), it displays the cash tendered and the change due. Otherwise it displays the type of credit card used.

4. **btnReport_Click** aggregates the data in the *purchases*() array and displays the resulting analysis. It first declares the arrays and variables that are used for the results. It then loops through all of the articles for each purchase (using a nested loop) to aggregate each article into a department result and a payment method result. It uses the department and payment method numbers as subscripts for the result arrays, the four arrays declared at the top of the procedure. The department statistics are totaled and displayed, then the payment method statistics are totaled and displayed.

```vb
'Define the Purchase and Article structures
Structure Article
    Dim department As Integer    'Department number, see department() below
    Dim quantity As Integer      'Quantity of articles purchased
    Dim price As Double          'Price of each article
End Structure

Structure Purchase
    Dim articles() As Article        'articles purchases
    Dim articleCount As Integer      'Number of articles purchased
    Dim subtotal As Double           'Subtotal of prices times quantities
    Dim total As Double              'Total of purchase including tax
    Dim method As Integer            'Method of payment, see method() below
End Structure

'Declare the class-level variables and named constants
Dim purchases(30) As Purchase    'Array that holds all purchases
Dim count As Integer             'Number of completed purchases
Dim department() As String = {"Womens", "Mens", "Kids", _
    "Sportswear", "Household", "Hardware"}
Dim method() As String = {"Visa", "MasterCard", "Cash"}
Const TAX_RATE As Double = 0.05      '5% sales tax

Private Sub frmCashRegister_Load(...) Handles MyBase.Load
    'Initialize the first purchase
    ReDim purchases(0).articles(4)
End Sub

Sub RingupArticle(ByVal dept As Integer)
    'Store the user's input into a new article
    Dim newarticle As Article    'New article to hold user input
    Dim size As Integer          'Size of the articles array
    newarticle.department = dept
    newarticle.quantity = CInt(txtQuantity.Text)
    'If blank price then use default of 0
    If txtPrice.Text = "" Then
```

```vb
      newarticle.price = 0
    Else
      newarticle.price = CDbl(txtPrice.Text)
    End If
    'If price and quantity are valid then store and display article
    If (newarticle.quantity > 0) And (newarticle.price > 0) Then
      'Increment the number of articles in the current purchase
      purchases(count).articleCount += 1
      'Ensure that Purchase's articles array has room for the new article
      size = purchases(count).articles.GetUpperBound(0)
      If purchases(count).articleCount >= size Then
        'If not enough room, increase the array size by 5
        ReDim Preserve purchases(count).articles(size + 5)
      End If
      'Store the new article into the purchase
      purchases(count).articles(purchases(count).articleCount-1) = newarticle
      'Display the article in the receipt
      DisplayArticle()
      'Reset the quantity and price for the next article
      'Disable the report button until the article is paid for
      btnReport.Enabled = False
      txtQuantity.Clear()
      txtPrice.Clear()
    End If
    btnReport.Enabled = False
    txtQuantity.Focus() 'Focus on the quantity for the next article
  End Sub

  Private Sub btnWomens_Click(...) Handles btnWomens.Click
    RingupArticle(0)
  End Sub

  Private Sub btnMens_Click(...) Handles btnMens.Click
    RingupArticle(1)
  End Sub

  Private Sub btnKids_Click(...) Handles btnKids.Click
    RingupArticle(2)
  End Sub

  Private Sub btnSportswear_Click(...) Handles btnSportswear.Click
    RingupArticle(3)
  End Sub

  Private Sub btnHousehold_Click(...) Handles btnHousehold.Click
    RingupArticle(4)
  End Sub

  Private Sub btnHardware_Click(...) Handles btnHardware.Click
    RingupArticle(5)
  End Sub
```

```
Sub DisplayArticle()
  Dim cost As Double
  Dim fmtStr As String = "{0,3} {1,-12} {2,7:C} {3,7:C}"
  'If article is the first then clear the display and display the header
  If purchases(count).articleCount = 1 Then
    lstOutput.Items.Clear()
    lstOutput.Items.Add("          Customer Receipt")
    lstOutput.Items.Add("")
    lstOutput.Items.Add(String.Format(fmtStr, "Qty", "Dept", _
                                      " Price", " Total"))
    lstOutput.Items.Add(String.Format(fmtStr, "---", "------------", _
                                      "-------", "-------"))

  End If
  'Display the article's information
  cost = _
    purchases(count).articles(purchases(count).articleCount - 1).quantity _
    * purchases(count).articles(purchases(count).articleCount - 1).price
  lstOutput.Items.Add(String.Format(fmtStr, _
    purchases(count).articles(purchases(count).articleCount - 1).quantity, _
    department(purchases(count).articles(purchases(count).articleCount - _
    1).department), _
    purchases(count).articles(purchases(count).articleCount-1).price, cost))
End Sub

Sub TotalPurchase(ByVal meth As Integer)
  Dim cash As Double          'Amount of cash tendered
  Dim flag As Boolean = True  'If purchase is valid
  'If no articles purchased then display message and exit
  If purchases(count).articleCount < 1 Then
    MessageBox.Show("No articles purchased.", "No sale")
    txtQuantity.Focus()
    flag = False
  End If
  'Calculate and store totals
  purchases(count).subtotal = 0
  For i As Integer = 0 To purchases(count).articleCount - 1
    purchases(count).subtotal += purchases(count).articles(i).price * _
      purchases(count).articles(i).quantity
  Next
  'Add sales tax to get total
  purchases(count).total = (1 + TAX_RATE) * purchases(count).subtotal
  'Store the method of payment
  purchases(count).method = meth
  'If cash method then get the amount tendered by customer
  If purchases(count).method = 2 Then
    If txtCash.Text = "" Then
      cash = 0
    Else
```

```vbnet
      cash = CDbl(txtCash.Text)
    End If
    'If tendered amount is not enough, then display message
    If (cash < purchases(count).total) Then
      MessageBox.Show("Not enough cash tendered (need " & _
        FormatCurrency(purchases(count).total) & ")", "Insufficient Cash")
      txtCash.Focus()              'Focus on cash for reinput
      flag = False
    End If
  End If
  'If purchase is valid then store and display it
  If flag Then
    'Increment the counter so the latest purchase is considered stored.
    count += 1
    'Display purchase totals
    DisplayTotals()
    'Make sure there is room for the next purchase and initialize it
    If purchases.GetUpperBound(0) <= count Then
      ReDim purchases(count + 5)
    End If
    ReDim purchases(count).articles(4)
  End If
  'Enable the report button
  btnReport.Enabled = True
End Sub

Sub DisplayTotals()
  'Display subtotal, tax and total
  Dim prompt As String = "Tax: (" & FormatPercent(TAX_RATE) & ")"
  Dim cash As Double
  Dim fmtStr As String = "{0,3} {1,-12} {2,7} {3,7:C}"
  lstOutput.Items.Add(String.Format(fmtStr, "", "", "", "-------"))
  lstOutput.Items.Add(String.Format(fmtStr, "", "Sub Total:", "", _
                                     purchases(count - 1).subtotal))
  lstOutput.Items.Add(String.Format(fmtStr, "", prompt, "", _
      purchases(count - 1).total - purchases(count - 1).subtotal))
  lstOutput.Items.Add(String.Format(fmtStr, "", "", "", "-------"))
  lstOutput.Items.Add(String.Format(fmtStr, "", "Total:", "", _
                                     purchases(count - 1).total))
  'If cash purchase, then display amount tendered and change
  If purchases(count - 1).method = 2 Then
    cash = CDbl(txtCash.Text)
    lstOutput.Items.Add("")
    lstOutput.Items.Add(String.Format(fmtStr, "", "Cash:", "", cash))
    lstOutput.Items.Add(String.Format(fmtStr, "", "Change:", "", _
                                      cash - purchases(count - 1).total))
  Else
```

```vb
        'If not cash, mention how tendered
        lstOutput.Items.Add(" Charged to " & _
                            method(purchases(count - 1).method))
    End If
    'Clear the cash and set focus to quantity for the next purchase
    txtCash.Clear()
    txtQuantity.Focus()
End Sub

Private Sub btnVisa_Click(...) Handles btnVisa.Click
    TotalPurchase(0)
End Sub

Private Sub btnMasterCard_Click(...) Handles btnMasterCard.Click
    TotalPurchase(1)
End Sub

Private Sub btnCash_Click(...) Handles btnCash.Click
    TotalPurchase(2)
End Sub

Private Sub btnReport_Click(...) Handles btnReport.Click
    Dim deptQuant(5), deptQuantT As Integer    'Quantity per department
    Dim deptSales(5), deptSalesT As Double     'Sales per department
    Dim methQuant(2), methQuantT As Integer    'Quantity per method
    Dim methAmnt(2), methAmntT As Double       'Sales per method
    Dim liability As Double                    'Amount of tax liability
    Dim fmtStr1 As String = "{0,-15} {1,6} {2,9:C}"
    Dim fmtStr2 As String = "{0,-15} {1,6:P} {2,9:C}"
    'Sum quantity and total amounts per department, without tax
    For i As Integer = 0 To count - 1
      'Sum quantity and total amounts per payment method
      methQuant(purchases(i).method) += 1
      methAmnt(purchases(i).method) += purchases(i).total
      For j As Integer = 0 To purchases(i).articleCount - 1
        deptQuant(purchases(i).articles(j).department) += _
          purchases(i).articles(j).quantity
        deptSales(purchases(i).articles(j).department) += _
          purchases(i).articles(j).price * purchases(i).articles(j).quantity
      Next
    Next
    'Display the quantity and sales per department
    lstOutput.Items.Clear()
    lstOutput.Items.Add("        Sales Report")
    lstOutput.Items.Add("")
    lstOutput.Items.Add(String.Format(fmtStr1, "Department ", "Qty", _
                              "    Sales"))
    lstOutput.Items.Add(String.Format(fmtStr1, "-----------", "---", _
                              "-----------"))
```

```
    For i As Integer = 0 To 5
        lstOutput.Items.Add(String.Format(fmtStr1, department(i), _
                            deptQuant(i), deptSales(i)))
        deptQuantT += deptQuant(i)
        deptSalesT += deptSales(i)
    Next
    lstOutput.Items.Add(String.Format(fmtStr1, "-----------", "---", _
                            "-----------"))
    lstOutput.Items.Add(String.Format(fmtStr1, "Grand Total", _
                            deptQuantT, deptSalesT))
    'Display the quantity and sales per payment method
    lstOutput.Items.Add("")
    lstOutput.Items.Add(String.Format(fmtStr1, "Payment      ", "Qty", _
                            "    Amount"))
    lstOutput.Items.Add(String.Format(fmtStr1, "-----------", "---", _
                            "-----------"))
    For i As Integer = 0 To 2
        lstOutput.Items.Add(String.Format(fmtStr1, method(i), _
                            methQuant(i), methAmnt(i)))
        methQuantT += methQuant(i)
        methAmntT += methAmnt(i)
    Next
    'Calculate The total amount of sales tax
    liability = methAmntT - deptSalesT
    lstOutput.Items.Add(String.Format(fmtStr1, "-----------", "---", _
                            "-----------"))
    lstOutput.Items.Add(String.Format(fmtStr1, "Gross Receipts:", _
                            methQuantT, methAmntT))
    lstOutput.Items.Add(String.Format(fmtStr2, "Tax Liability:", _
                            TAX_RATE, liability))
    lstOutput.Items.Add(String.Format(fmtStr1, "Net Receipts:", "", _
                            deptSalesT))
    txtQuantity.Focus()      'Focus on quantity for next article
End Sub
```

CHAPTER 7   SUMMARY

1. For programming purposes, tabular data are most efficiently processed if stored in an *array*. An array is declared with a *Dim* statement, which also can specify its *size* and initial values. The size of an already declared array can be specified or changed with a *ReDim* or *ReDim Preserve* statement. The highest subscript of the array is called its *upper bound* and is returned with the *GetUpperBound*(0) method. The *Erase* statement releases all memory allocated to an array.

2. An array of labels, text boxes, or buttons is referred to as a *control array*.

3. A *structure* is a composite programmer-designed data type with a fixed number of fields, each of which can be of any data type.

4. Two of the best-known methods for ordering (or *sorting*) arrays are the *bubble sort* and the *Shell sort*.

5. Any array can be searched *sequentially* to find the subscript associated with a sought-after value. Ordered arrays can be searched most efficiently by a *binary search*.

6. A table can be effectively stored in a *two-dimensional array*.

CHAPTER 7 PROGRAMMING PROJECTS

1. Table 7.21 contains some lengths in terms of feet. Write a program that displays the nine different units of measure; requests the unit to convert from, the unit to convert to, and the quantity to be converted, and then displays the converted quantity. A typical outcome is shown in Figure 7.15.

TABLE 7.21 **Equivalent lengths.**

1 inch = .0833 foot	1 rod = 16.5 feet
1 yard = 3 feet	1 furlong = 660 feet
1 meter = 3.28155 feet	1 kilometer = 3281.5 feet
1 fathom = 6 feet	1 mile = 5280 feet

FIGURE 7.15 **Possible outcome of Programming Project 1.**

2. Statisticians use the concepts of **mean** and **standard deviation** to describe a collection of data. The mean is the average value of the items, and the standard deviation measures the spread or dispersal of the numbers about the mean. Formally, if $x_1, x_2, x_3, \ldots, x_n$, is a collection of data, then

$$\text{mean} = m = \frac{x_1 + x_2 + x_3 + \cdots + x_n}{n}$$

standard deviation =

$$s = \sqrt{\frac{(x_1 - m)^2 + (x_2 - m)^2 + (x_3 - m)^2 + \cdots + (x_n - m)^2}{n}}$$

Write a computer program to

(a) place the exam scores 59, 60, 65, 75, 56, 90, 66, 62, 98, 72, 95, 71, 63, 77, 65, 77, 65, 50, 85, and 62 into an array;

(b) calculate the mean and standard deviation of the exam scores;

(c) assign letter grades to each exam score, ES, as follows:

$$ES \geq m + 1.5s \qquad\qquad A$$
$$m + .5s \leq ES < m + 1.5s \quad B$$
$$m - .5s \leq ES < m + .5s \quad C$$
$$m - 1.5s\ ES \leq m - .5s \quad D$$
$$ES < m - 1.5s \qquad\qquad F$$

For instance, if *m* were 70 and *s* were 12, then grades of 88 or above would receive A's, grades between 76 and 87 would receive B's, and so on. A process of this type is referred to as *curving grades*.

(d) Display a list of the exam scores along with their corresponding grades as shown in Figure 7.16.

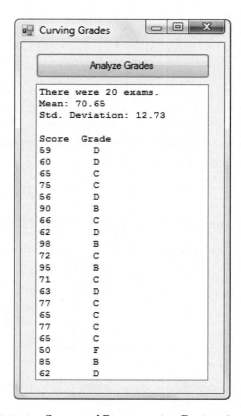

FIGURE 7.16   Output of Programming Project 2.

3. *Rudimentary Translator.* Table 7.22 gives English words and their French and German equivalents. Store these words in a text file and read them into a structure having a member for each language. Write a program that sorts the array according to the English words. The program should then request an English sentence as input and translate it into French and German. For example, if the English sentence given is MY PENCIL IS ON THE TABLE, then the French translation will be MON CRAYON EST SUR LA TABLE, and the German translation will be MEIN BLEISTIFT IST AUF DEM TISCH.

Note: Assume that the only punctuation in the sentence is a period at the end of the sentence. Use a binary search to locate each English word.

TABLE 7.22 **English words and their French and German equivalents.**

English	French	German	English	French	German
YES	OUI	JA	LARGE	GROS	GROSS
TABLE	TABLE	TISCH	NO	NON	NEIN
THE	LA	DEM	HAT	CHAPEAU	HUT
IS	EST	IST	PENCIL	CRAYON	BLEISTIFT
YELLOW	JAUNE	GELB	RED	ROUGE	ROT
FRIEND	AMI	FREUND	ON	SUR	AUF
SICK	MALADE	KRANK	AUTO	AUTO	AUTO
MY	MON	MEIN	OFTEN	SOUVENT	OFT

4. Write a program that allows a list of no more than 50 soft drinks and their percent changes in sales volume for a particular year to be input and displays the information in two lists titled *gainers* and *losers*. Each list should be sorted by the *amount* of the percent change. Try your program on the data for the ten soft drinks in Table 7.23.

Note: You will need to store the data initially in an array to determine the number of gainers and losers.

TABLE 7.23 **Changes in sales volume from 2005 to 2006 of leading soft-drink brands.**

Brand	% Change in Volume	Brand	% Change in Volume
Coke Classic	−2.0	Dr. Pepper	1.7
Pepsi-Cola	−2.5	Sprite	−1.0
Diet Coke	−0.1	Fanta	7.0
Mt. Dew	1.0	Diet Mt. Dew	8.5
Diet Pepsi	−1.0	Diet Dr. Pepper	6.4

Source: Beverage Digest, 2007

5. Each team in a six-team soccer league played each other team once. Table 7.24 shows the winners. Write a program to

(a) Place the team names in an array of structures that also holds the number of wins.

(b) Place the data from Table 7.24 in a two-dimensional array.

TABLE 7.24 Soccer league winners.

	Jazz	Jets	Owls	Rams	Cubs	Zips
Jazz	—	Jazz	Jazz	Rams	Cubs	Jazz
Jets	Jazz	—	Jets	Jets	Cubs	Zips
Owls	Jazz	Jets	—	Rams	Owls	Owls
Rams	Rams	Jets	Rams	—	Rams	Rams
Cubs	Cubs	Cubs	Owls	Rams	—	Cubs
Zips	Jazz	Zips	Owls	Rams	Cubs	—

(c) Place the number of games won by each team in the array of structures.

(d) Display a listing of the teams giving each team's name and number of games won. The list should be in decreasing order by the number of wins.

6. A poker hand can be stored in a two-dimensional array. The statement

```
Dim hand(3, 12) As Integer
```

declares an array with 52 elements, where the first subscript ranges over the four suits and the second subscript ranges over the thirteen denominations. A poker hand is specified by placing ones in the elements corresponding to the cards in the hand. See Figure 7.17.

	A	2	3	4	5	6	7	8	9	10	J	Q	K
Club ♣	0	0	0	0	0	0	0	0	1	0	0	0	0
Diamond ♦	1	0	0	0	0	0	0	0	0	0	0	0	0
Heart ♥	1	0	0	0	0	0	0	0	0	0	0	1	0
Spade ♠	0	0	0	0	1	0	0	0	0	0	0	0	0

FIGURE 7.17   Array for the poker hand A ♥ A ♦ 5 ♠ 9 ♣ Q ♥.

Write a program that requests the five cards as input from the user, creates the related array, and passes the array to procedures to determine the type of the hand: flush (all cards have the same suit), straight (cards have consecutive denominations—ace can come either before 2 or after King), straight flush, four-of-a-kind, full house (3 cards of one denomination, 2 cards of another denomination), three-of-a-kind, two pairs, one pair, or none of the above.

7. *Airline Reservations.* Write a reservation system for an airline flight. Assume the airplane has 10 rows with 4 seats in each row. Use a two-dimensional array of strings to maintain a seating chart. In addition, create an array to be used as a waiting list in case the plane is full. The waiting list should be "first come, first served," that is, people who are added early to the list get priority over those added later. Allow the user the following three options:

(a) Add a passenger to the flight or waiting list.

    1. Request the passenger's name.

    2. Display a chart of the seats in the airplane in tabular form.

    3. If seats are available, let the passenger choose a seat. Add the passenger to the seating chart.

    4. If no seats are available, place the passenger on the waiting list.

(b) Remove a passenger from the flight.

    1. Request the passenger's name.

    2. Search the seating chart for the passenger's name and delete it.

    3. If the waiting list is empty, update the array so the seat is available.

    4. If the waiting list is not empty, remove the first person from the list, and give him or her the newly vacated seat.

(c) Quit.

8. The Game of Life was invented by John H. Conway to model some genetic laws for birth, death, and survival. Consider a checkerboard consisting of an n-by-n array of squares. Each square can contain one individual (denoted by 1) or be empty (denoted by –). Figure 7.18(a) shows a 6-by-6 board with four of the squares occupied. The future of each individual depends on the number of his neighbors. After each period of time, called a *generation*, certain individuals will survive, others will die due to either loneliness or overcrowding, and new individuals will be born. Each nonborder square has eight neighboring squares. After each generation, the status of the squares changes as follows:

(a) An individual *survives* if there are two or three individuals in neighboring squares.

(b) An individual *dies* if he has more than three individuals or less than two in neighboring squares.

(c) A new individual *is born* into each empty square with exactly three individuals as neighbors.

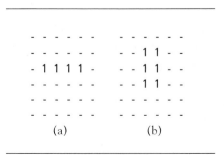

(a)   (b)

FIGURE 7.18 **Two generations.**

Figure 7.18(b) shows the status after one generation. Write a program to do the following:

1. Declare a two-dimensional array of size n, where n is input by the user, to hold the status of each square in the current generation. To specify the initial configuration, have the user input each row as a string of length n, and break the row into 1's or dashes with the Substring method.

2. Declare a two-dimensional array of size n by n to hold the status of each square in the next generation. Compute the status for each square and produce the display in Figure 7.18(b). **Note:** The generation changes all at once. Only current cells are used to determine which cells will contain individuals in the next generation.

3. Assign the next-generation values to the current generation and repeat as often as desired.

4. Display the individuals in each generation. **Hint:** The hardest part of the program is determining the number of neighbors a cell has. In general, you must check a 3-by-3 square around the cell in question. Exceptions must be made when the cell is on the edge of the array. Don't forget that a cell is not a neighbor of itself.

(Test the program with the initial configuration shown in Figure 7.19. It is known as the figure-eight configuration and repeats after eight generations.)

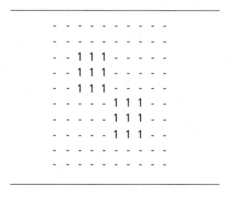

FIGURE 7.19   The figure eight.

9. Every book is identified by a ten-character International Standard Book Number (ISBN) that is usually printed on the back cover of the book. The first nine characters are digits and the last character is either a digit or the letter X (which stands for ten). Three examples of ISBNs are 0-13-030657-6, 0-32-108599-X, and 0-471-58719-2. The hyphens separate the characters into four blocks. The first block usually consists of a single digit and identifies the language (0 for English, 2 for French, 3 for German, etc.). The second block identifies the publisher (for example, 13 for Prentice Hall, 32 for Addison-Wesley-Longman, and 471 for Wiley); The third block is the number the publisher has chosen for the book. The fourth block, which always consists of a single character called the *check digit*, is used to test for errors. Let's

refer to the ten characters of the ISBN as d_1, d_2, d_3, d_4, d_5, d_6, d_7, d_8, d_9, and d_{10}. The check digit is chosen so that the sum

$$10 \cdot d_1 + 9 \cdot d_2 + 8 \cdot d_3 + 7 \cdot d_4 + 6 \cdot d_5 + 5 \cdot d_6 + 4 \cdot d_7 + 3 \cdot d_8 + 2 \cdot d_9 + 1 \cdot d_{10} \qquad (*)$$

is a multiple of 11. **Note:** A number is a multiple of 11 if it is exactly divisible by 11.). If the last character of the ISBN is an X, then in the sum $(*)$, d_{10} is replaced with 10. For example, with the ISBN 0-32-108599-X, the sum would be

$$10 \cdot 0 + 9 \cdot 3 + 8 \cdot 2 + 7 \cdot 1 + 6 \cdot 0 + 5 \cdot 8 + 4 \cdot 5 + 3 \cdot 9 + 2 \cdot 9 + 1 \cdot 10 = 165$$

Since 165/11 is 15, the sum is a multiple of 11. This checking scheme will detect every single-digit and transposition-of-adjacent-digits error. That is, if while copying an IBSN number you miscopy a single character or transpose two adjacent characters, then the sum $(*)$ will no longer be a multiple of 11.

(a) Write a program to accept an ISBN type number (including the hyphens) as input, calculate the sum $(*)$, and tell if it is a valid ISBN. (**Hint:** The number n is divisible by 11 if n Mod 11 is 0.) Before calculating the sum, the program should check that each of the first nine characters is a digit and that the last character is either a digit or an X.

(b) Write a program that begins with a valid ISBN (such as 0-13-030657-6) and then confirms that the checking scheme described above detects every single-digit and transposition-of-adjacent-digits error by testing every possible error. [**Hint:** If d is a digit to be replaced, then the nine possibilities for the replacements are $(d + 1)$ Mod 10, $(d + 2)$ Mod 10, $(d + 3)$ Mod 10, ..., $(d + 9)$ Mod 10.]

10. *User-Operated Directory Assistance.* Have you ever tried to call a person at their business and been told to type in some of the letters of their name on your telephone's keypad in order to obtain their extension? Write a program to simulate this type of directory assistance. Suppose the names and telephone extensions of all the employees of a company are contained in the text file EMPLOYEES.TXT. Each set of three lines of the file has the three pieces of information: last name, first and middle name(s), and telephone extension. (We have filled the file with the names of the U.S. presidents so that the names will be familiar.) The user should be asked to press buttons for the first three letters of the person's last name followed by the first letter of the first name. For instance, if the person's name is Gary Land, the user would type in 5264. The number 5264 is referred to as the "push-button encoding" of the name. (**Note:** People with different names can have the same push-button encoding— for instance, Herb James and Gary Land.)

The program should declare an array of structures to hold full names, extensions, and push-button encodings. The array should be filled while making a single pass through the file and then sorted by push-button encoding. After the user presses four keys on the keypad, the program should display the names and extensions of all the employees having the specified push-button encoding. See Figure 7.20.

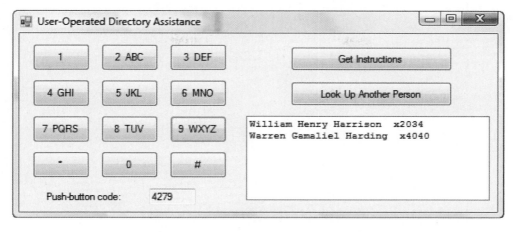

FIGURE 7.20   Sample run of Programming Project 10.

8

Sequential Files

8.1 Sequential Files

Throughout this text, we have processed data from text files created with the Visual Basic IDE and saved on a disk. Such files are stored on a disk as a sequence of characters. (Two special characters, called "carriage return" and "line feed", are inserted at the end of each line to indicate where new lines should be started.) These text files also are called **sequential files**. In this section, we create sequential files with Visual Basic programs and develop techniques for using sequential files.

■ Creating a Sequential File

There are many ways to organize data in a sequential file. As done throughout the book so far, we will continue to have each line contain just one piece of data. The following steps create a new sequential file and write data to it:

1. Choose a filename. The first part of a filename can contain up to 156 characters consisting of letters, digits, and other assorted characters (including spaces and periods). The second part of the filename is usually a three-character extension identifying the file type.

2. Choose the path for the folder to contain the file. The *filespec* is the full name of the file; that is, the string consisting of the path to the folder containing the file, followed by a backslash (\ ) and the filename (including the extension). An example of a filespec is "C:\Text files\INCOME FOR APRIL.TXT".

3. Execute a statement of the form

```
Dim sw As IO.StreamWriter = IO.File.CreateText(filespec)
```

where *sw* is a variable name. This process is referred to as **opening a file for output**. It establishes a communications link between the program and the disk drive for storing data onto the disk. It allows data to be output from the program and recorded in the specified file. (Visual Basic takes as the default path the *Debug* subfolder of the *bin* subfolder of the current project. Therefore, if the filename alone is used, the file will be placed in the *Debug* subfolder.) **Note:** The statement

```
Dim sr As IO.StreamReader = IO.File.OpenText(filespec)
```

used earlier in the book is said to **open a file for input**.

4. Place data into the file with the WriteLine method. If *datum* is either a string or a number, then the statement

```
sw.WriteLine(datum)
```

writes the information into a new line of the file.

5. After all the data have been recorded in the file, execute

```
sw.Close()
```

This statement is very important since the WriteLine method actually places data into a temporary buffer, and the Close method transfers the data to the disk. Therefore, if you omit the statement `sw.Close()` some data might be lost. The statement also breaks the communications link with the file. Therefore its omission might prevent other procedures from accessing the file.

Once a sequential file has been created, you can look at it in design mode with the Visual Basic Text Editor. Alternatively, the entire file can be displayed in a list box.

 Example 1 The following program creates a sequential file consisting of several names and then displays the entire contents of the file in a list box. If the list box is too short to display all the items from the file, Visual Basic automatically places a vertical scroll bar on the right side of the list box. The user can then scroll to see the remaining items.

```vb
Private Sub btnCreateFile_Click(...) Handles btnCreateFile.Click
  'Create the file PIONEERS.TXT
  Dim sw As IO.StreamWriter = IO.File.CreateText("PIONEERS.TXT")
  sw.WriteLine("Atanasoff")
  sw.WriteLine("Babbage")
  sw.WriteLine("Codd")
  sw.WriteLine("Dijkstra")
  sw.WriteLine("Eckert")
  sw.WriteLine("Faggin")
  sw.WriteLine("Gates")
  sw.WriteLine("Hollerith")
  sw.Close()
  MessageBox.Show("Names Recorded in File", "File Status")
End Sub

Private Sub btnDisplayFile_Click(...) Handles btnDisplayFile.Click
  'Display the contents of the file PIONEERS.TXT in a list box
  Dim sr As IO.StreamReader = IO.File.OpenText("PIONEERS.TXT")
  lstNames.Items.Clear()
  Do While sr.Peek <> -1
    lstNames.Items.Add(sr.ReadLine)
  Loop
  sr.Close()
End Sub
```

[Run, click the first button, and then click the second button.]

Note: In Example 1, if the file PIONEERS.TXT does not appear in the Solution Explorer window, you can press the Refresh button in the Solution Explorer toolbar to cause the file to appear.

Caution: If an existing file is opened for output, Visual Basic will erase the existing file and create a new empty file.

The WriteLine method allows us to create text files just like the ones that appear throughout this book. We already know how to read such files with the ReadLine method. The remaining major task is adding data to the end of a sequential file.

■ Adding Items to a Sequential File

Data can be added to the end of an existing sequential file with the following steps:

1. Execute the statement

```
Dim sw As IO.StreamWriter = IO.File.AppendText(filespec)
```

where *sw* is a variable name and *filespec* identifies the file. This process is called **opening a file for append**. It allows data to be output and recorded at the end of the specified file.

2. Place data into the file with the WriteLine method.

3. After all the data have been recorded into the file, close the file with the statement

```
sw.Close()
```

The IO.File.AppendText option is used to add data to an existing file. However, it also can be used to create a new file. If the file does not exist, then the IO.File.AppendText option creates the file.

The three options, CreateText, OpenText, and AppendText, are referred to as **modes**. A file should not be open in two modes at the same time. For instance, after a file has been opened for output and data have been written to the file, the file should be closed before being opened for input. For instance, had the statement `sw.Close()` in Example 1 been omitted, then the program would have crashed when the second button was clicked.

An attempt to open a nonexistent file for input terminates the program with a FileNotFoundException message box stating that the file could not be found. There is a method that tells us whether a certain file already exists. If the value of

```
IO.File.Exists(filespec)
```

is True, then the specified file exists. Therefore, prudence dictates that files be opened for input with code such as

```
Dim sr As IO.StreamReader
If IO.File.Exists(filespec) Then
  sr = IO.File.OpenText(filespec)
Else
  message = "Either no file has yet been created or the file "
  message &= filespec & " is not where expected."
  MessageBox.Show(message, "File Not Found")
End If
```

There is one file-management operation that we have yet to discuss: changing or deleting an item of information from a sequential file. An individual item of a file cannot be changed or deleted directly. A new file must be created by reading each item from the original file and recording it, with the single item changed or deleted, into the new file. The old file is then erased, and the new file renamed with the name of the original file. Regarding these last two tasks, the Visual Basic statement

```
IO.File.Delete(filespec)
```

removes the specified file from the disk, and the statement

```
IO.File.Move(oldfilespec, newfilespec)
```

changes the filespec of a file. (**Note:** The IO.File.Delete and IO.File.Move methods cannot be used with open files; doing so generates an error message.)

Creating a program that has extensive file handling can be simplified by placing the statement

```
Imports System.IO
```

at the top of the Code Editor, before the Class frmName statement. Then, there is no need to insert the prefix "IO." before the words StreamReader, StreamWriter, and File.

 Example 2   The following program manages a file of names and years of birth:

OBJECT	PROPERTY	SETTING
frmYOB	Text	Access YOB.TXT
lblName	Text	Name:
txtName		
lblYOB	Text	Year of Birth:
mtxtYOB	Mask	0000
btnAdd	Text	Add Above Person to File
btnLookUp	Text	Look up Year of Birth
btnDelete	Text	Delete Above Person from File

```
Imports System.IO     'Appears at top of Code Editor

Private Sub btnAdd_Click(...) Handles btnAdd.Click
  'Add a person's name and year of birth to file
  Dim message As String
  If (txtName.Text <> "") And (mtxtYOB.Text <> "") Then
    Dim sw As StreamWriter = File.AppendText("YOB.TXT")
    sw.WriteLine(txtName.Text)
    sw.WriteLine(mtxtYOB.Text)
    sw.Close()
```

```
      txtName.Clear()
      mtxtYOB.Clear()
      txtName.Focus()
      MessageBox.Show("Person added to file.")
   Else
      message = "You must enter a name and year of birth."
      MessageBox.Show(message, "Information Incomplete")
   End If
End Sub

Private Sub btnLookUp_Click(...) Handles btnLookUp.Click
   'Determine a person's year of birth
   Dim message As String
   If txtName.Text <> "" Then
      If File.Exists("YOB.TXT") Then
         DisplayYearOfBirth()
      Else
         message = "Either no file has yet been created or "
         message = message & "the file is not where expected."
         MessageBox.Show(message, "File Not Found")
      End If
   Else
      MessageBox.Show("You must enter a name.", "Information Incomplete")
   End If
   txtName.Focus()
End Sub

Private Sub btnDelete_Click(...) Handles btnDelete.Click
   'Remove a person from the file
   Dim message As String
   If txtName.Text <> "" Then
      If File.Exists("YOB.TXT") Then
         DeletePerson()
      Else
         message = "Either no file has yet been created or "
         message = message & "the file is not where expected."
         MessageBox.Show(message, "File Not Found.")
      End If
   Else
      MessageBox.Show("You must enter a name.", "Information Incomplete")
   End If
   txtName.Focus()
End Sub
```

```
Sub DisplayYearOfBirth()
  'Find the year of birth for the person in txtName
  Dim name As String, yob As Integer
  mtxtYOB.Clear()
  Dim sr As StreamReader = File.OpenText("YOB.TXT")
  Do While (name <> txtName.Text) And (sr.Peek <> -1)
    name = sr.ReadLine
    yob = CInt(sr.ReadLine)
  Loop
  If name = txtName.Text Then
    MessageBox.Show(name & " was born in " & yob, "Name Found")
    txtName.Clear()
  Else
    MessageBox.Show("Person is not in file.")
    txtName.Clear()
  End If
  sr.Close()
End Sub

Sub DeletePerson()
  'Remove the person in txtName from the file
  Dim name As String, yob As Integer
  Dim foundFlag As Boolean = False
  Dim sr As StreamReader = File.OpenText("YOB.TXT")
  Dim sw As StreamWriter = File.CreateText("TEMP.TXT")
  Do While (sr.Peek <> -1)
    name = sr.ReadLine
    yob = CInt(sr.ReadLine)
    If (name <> txtName.Text) Then
      sw.WriteLine(name)
      sw.WriteLine(yob)
    Else
      foundFlag = True
    End If
  Loop
  sr.Close()
  sw.Close()
  File.Delete("YOB.TXT")
  File.Move("TEMP.TXT", "YOB.TXT")   'Rename "TEMP.TXT" As "YOB.TXT"
  MessageBox.Show("Person deleted from file.")
  If Not foundFlag Then
    MessageBox.Show("The name was not found.")
  Else
    txtName.Clear()
    mtxtYOB.Clear()
  End If
End Sub
```

[Run. After several names have been added, the file might look as shown in Figure 8.1.]

```
Barbra
1942
Ringo
1940
Sylvester
1946
```

FIGURE 8.1   Sample contents of YOB.TXT.

■ Structured Exception Handling

There are two main types of problems that a software program might encounter when it executes. The first is a *bug*, which is caused by incorrect or faulty code. Common examples of bugs are typos, using the wrong formula, and accessing the wrong property value. The second type is an *exception*, which, as the term suggests, is a situation that happens occasionally, but not all the time. Two situations where exceptions occur are when invalid data are input and when a file cannot be accessed.

The fundamental difference between bugs and exceptions is that bugs are totally caused by the programmer while exceptions are caused by events beyond the programmer's control. For example, if a user enters a word when the program prompts for a number, an exception is generated and the program terminates abruptly. In this situation, the programmer did not employ faulty logic or mistype. If the user had followed the directions, no problem would have occurred. Even though the user is at fault, however, it is still the programmer's responsibility to anticipate exceptions and to include code to work around their occurrence.

The Visual Studio environment contains powerful tools that programmers can use to find and correct bugs. These debugging tools are discussed extensively in Appendix D. This section describes techniques used to anticipate and deal with exceptions (in programming terms, called "handling exceptions").

An unexpected problem causes Visual Basic first to throw an exception and then to handle it. If the programmer does not explicitly include exception-handling code in the program, then Visual Basic handles an exception with a default handler. This handler terminates execution, displays the exception's message in a window and highlights the line of code where the exception occurred. Consider a program that contains the following code:

```
Dim taxCredit As Double

Private Sub btnCompute_Click(...) Handles btnCompute.Click
  Dim numDependents As Integer
  numDependents = CInt(InputBox("How many dependents?"))
  taxCredit = 1000 * numDependents
End Sub
```

A user with no dependents might just leave the input dialog box blank and press the OK button. If so, Visual Basic terminates the program and displays the box shown

FIGURE 8.2   **Exception handled by Visual Basic.**

in Figure 8.2. (The problem was caused by the fact that the default value in an input dialog box, the empty string, cannot be converted to an integer. Text boxes also have the empty string as their default value.) It also highlights the fourth line of code since the exception was thrown while executing the CInt function. The program also would have crashed had the user typed in an answer like "TWO".

A robust program explicitly handles the previous exception by *protecting* the code in a Try-Catch-Finally block. This allows the program to continue regardless of whether an exception was thrown. The computer tries to execute the code in the Try block. As soon as an exception occurs, execution jumps to the code in the Catch block. Regardless of whether an exception occurred, the code in the Finally block is then executed. The following code is illustrative:

```
Dim taxCredit As Double

Private Sub btnCompute_Click(...) Handles btnCompute.Click
  Dim numDependents As Integer, message As String
  Try
    numDependents = CInt(InputBox("How many dependents?"))
  Catch
    message = "You did not answer the question with an " & _
              "integer value. We will assume your answer is zero."
    MessageBox.Show(message, "Improper Response")
    numDependents = 0
  Finally
    taxCredit = 1000 * numDependents
  End Try
End Sub
```

This type of exception handling is known as **data validation**. It catches situations where invalid data cannot be converted to a particular type. An exception is thrown if

| TABLE 8.1 | Some common exceptions. |

Exception Name	Description and Example
ArgumentOutOfRangeException	An argument to a method is out of range.
	```str = "Goodbye".Substring(12,3)```
IndexOutOfRangeException	An array's subscript is out of range.
	```Dim arr(3) As Integer```
	```arr(5) = 2```
InvalidCastException	A value cannot be converted to another type.
	```Dim num As Integer = CInt("one")```
NullReferenceException	A method is called on a variable that is set to Nothing.
	```Dim str As String, len As Integer```
	```len = str.Length```
OverflowException	A number too big for the data type is assigned.
	```Dim num As Integer = 2000000000```
	```num = 2 * num```
IO.DirectoryNotFoundException	A file within a missing folder is accessed.
	```Dim sr As IO.StreamReader = _```
	``` IO.File.OpenText("C:\BadDir\FILE.TXT")```
IO.FileNotFoundException	A missing file is accessed.
	```Dim sr As IO.StreamReader = _```
	``` IO.File.OpenText("MISSING.TXT")```
IO.IOException	Any file handling exception, including those mentioned above. For instance, an attempt is made to delete or rename an open file, to change the name of a closed file to an already used name, or when a disk drive specified contains no disk. **Note:** If a series of IO exceptions is being tested with Catch clauses, this exception should be the last one tested.
	```IO.File.Move(filespec, AlreadyExistingName)```

the user enters data that cannot be converted to an integer using the CInt function. Table 8.1 lists several exceptions and descriptions of why they are thrown.

The Catch block on the previous page will be executed whenever *any* exception occurs. Visual Basic also allows Try-Catch-Finally blocks to have one or more specialized Catch clauses that only handle a specific type of exception. The general form of a specialized Catch clause is

```
Catch exc As ExceptionName
```

where the variable *exc* will be assigned the name of the exception. The code in this block will be executed only when the specified exception occurs.

The general form of a Try-Catch-Finally block is

```
Try
  normal code
Catch exc1 As FirstException
  exception-handling code for FirstException
Catch exc2 As SecondException
  exception-handling code for SecondException
  .
  .
```

```
Catch
  exception-handling code for any remaining exceptions
Finally
  clean-up code
End Try
```

The *normal code* is the code that you want to monitor for exceptions. If an exception occurs during execution of any of the statements in this section, Visual Basic transfers control to the code in one of the Catch blocks. As with a Select Case block, the Catch clauses are considered one at a time until the proper exception is located. The last Catch clause in the preceding code functions like the Case Else clause. The *clean-up code* in the Finally block always executes last regardless of whether any *exception-handling code* has executed. In most situations, this code *cleans up* any resources such as files that were opened during the *normal code*. If clean-up is not necessary, then the Finally statement and its corresponding code can be omitted. However, to complete a Try block, a Catch block or a Finally block must appear.

In addition to data validation, a popular use of exception handling is to account for errors when accessing files. Visual Basic has the capability to access files stored on distant servers via the Internet. An exception is thrown if a desired file is missing (IO.FileNotFoundException) or if the file cannot be read because the Internet connection between the computer and the server is broken (IO.IOException).

Example 3   The following program reads the first line from a file on a CD. The program expects the file to reside in the folder DataFiles of the CD. Note that the clean-up code, `sr.Close()`, in the Finally block is enclosed in a Try-Catch block of its own. This protects the Close method from any exceptions that might occur.

```
Private Sub btnDisplay_Click(...) Handles btnDisplay.Click
  Dim sr As IO.StreamReader
  Dim message As String
  Try
    sr = IO.File.OpenText("E:\DataFiles\USPRES.TXT")
    message = "The first President was " & sr.ReadLine & "."
    MessageBox.Show(message, "President")
  Catch exp As IO.DirectoryNotFoundException
    message = "The requested folder is not on the CD."
    MessageBox.Show(message, "Error")
  Catch exp As IO.FileNotFoundException
    message = "The file is not in the specified folder of the CD."
    MessageBox.Show(message, "Error")
  Catch exp As IO.IOException
    message = "Check to see if there is a CD in drive E:."
    MessageBox.Show(message, "Error")
  Finally
    Try
      sr.Close()
    Catch
```

```
            'Disregard any exceptions during the Close() method
      End Try
   End Try
End Sub
```

[Remove the CD from the E: drive, run the program, and then click on the button.]

[Insert the CD containing the file USPRES.TXT (in the folder DataFiles) into the E: drive]

■ Comments

1. Sequential files make efficient use of disk space and are easy to create and use. Their disadvantages are as follows:

   (a) Often a large portion of the file must be read in order to find one specific item.
   (b) An individual item of the file cannot be changed or deleted easily.

   Another type of file, known as a **database**, has neither of the disadvantages of sequential files; however, databases use more disk space, and require greater effort to program. Databases are discussed in Chapter 10.

2. Consider the sequential file shown at the end of Example 2. This file is said to consist of three records of two fields each. A **record** holds all the data about a single individual. Each item of data is called a **field**. The three records are

Barbra	Ringo	Sylvester
1942	1940	1946

   and the two fields are the name field and the year-of-birth field.

3. Any variable declared within a Try-Catch-Finally block has block-level scope. That is, it will not be available after the block terminates.

4. Although we usually declare and assign values to StreamReader and StreamWriter variables in one statement, they can be declared with one statement and later assigned to a file with a second statement. This approach is especially useful when the variable is class-level and is assigned to a file in a procedure.

Practice Problems 8.1

1. Compose a Sub procedure RemoveDups that could be used in Example 2 to delete from YOB.TXT all repeated records except the first instance of a name matching the name in txtName. (Assume that the existence of YOB.TXT is checked prior to the execution of this Sub procedure.)

2. Compose a Sub procedure AddNoDuplicate to add a name and year of birth to the end of the file YOB.TXT only if the name to be added is not already present in the file. (Assume that the existence of YOB.TXT is checked prior to the execution of this Sub procedure.)

EXERCISES 8.1

In Exercises 1 through 10, determine the output displayed in the text box when the button is clicked.

1.
```
Private Sub btnDisplay_Click(...) Handles btnDisplay.Click
    Dim color As String
    Dim sw As IO.StreamWriter = IO.File.CreateText("COLORS.TXT")
    sw.WriteLine("Green")
    sw.WriteLine("Red")
    sw.Close()
    Dim sr As IO.StreamReader = IO.File.OpenText("COLORS.TXT")
    color = sr.ReadLine
    color = sr.ReadLine
    txtOutput.Text = color
    sr.Close()
End Sub
```

2.
```
Private Sub btnDisplay_Click(...) Handles btnDisplay.Click
    Dim color1, color2 As String
    Dim sw As IO.StreamWriter = IO.File.CreateText("COLORS.TXT")
    sw.WriteLine("Blue")
    sw.WriteLine("Red")
    sw.Close()
    Dim sr As IO.StreamReader = IO.File.OpenText("COLORS.TXT")
    color1 = sr.ReadLine
    color2 = sr.ReadLine
    txtOutput.Text = color1
    sr.Close()
End Sub
```

3.
```
Private Sub btnDisplay_Click(...) Handles btnDisplay.Click
    Dim color As String
    Dim sw As IO.StreamWriter = IO.File.CreateText("COLORS.TXT")
    sw.WriteLine("Blue")
    sw.WriteLine("Red")
    sw.WriteLine("Green")
    sw.Close()
    Dim sr As IO.StreamReader = IO.File.OpenText("COLORS.TXT")
    Do While (sr.Peek <> -1)
      color = sr.ReadLine
      txtOutput.Text = color
    Loop
    sr.Close()
End Sub
```

4. Assume that the contents of the file COLORS.TXT are:

Red
Green
Blue

FIGURE 8.3 Contents of the file GREETING.TXT.

```
Private Sub btnDisplay_Click(...) Handles btnDisplay.Click
    Dim file, color As String
    file = "COLORS.TXT"
    Dim sw As IO.StreamWriter = IO.File.AppendText(file)
    sw.WriteLine("Yellow")
    sw.Close()
    Dim sr As IO.StreamReader = IO.File.OpenText(file)
    For count As Integer = 1 To 4
      color = sr.ReadLine
      txtOutput.Text = color
    Next
    sr.Close()
End Sub
```

5.
```
Private Sub btnDisplay_Click(...) Handles btnDisplay.Click
    Dim num As Integer
    'Assume that txtBox has string "Yellow" in it.
    Try
      num = CInt(txtBox.Text)
      txtOutput.Text = "Your number is " & num
    Catch
      txtOutput.Text = "I don't recognize that number."
    End Try
End Sub
```

6.
```
Private Sub btnDisplay_Click(...) Handles btnDisplay.Click
   Dim colors() As String = {"Red", "Green", "Blue"}
   Try
      txtOutput.Text = "The third color is " & colors(3)
   Catch exc As IndexOutOfRangeException
      txtOutput.Text = "Index out of range."
   End Try
End Sub
```

7.
```
Private Sub btnDisplay_Click(...) Handles btnDisplay.Click
   Try
      Dim usPop As Integer = 304000000      'Approx population of U.S.
      Dim worldPop As Integer
      worldPop = 21 * usPop
      txtOutput.Text = CStr(worldPop)
   Catch exc As ArgumentOutOfRange
      txtOutput.Text = "Oops"
   Catch exc As OverflowException
      txtOutput.Text = "Error occurred."
   End Try
End Sub
```

8.
```
Private Sub btnDisplay_Click(...) Handles btnDisplay.Click
   Dim car As String = "Delorean", lastLetter As String
   Try
      lastLetter = car.Substring(8, 1)
      txtOutput.Text = lastLetter
   Catch exc As InvalidCastException
      txtOutput.Text = "It's a puzzlement"
   Catch exc As ArgumentOutOfRangeException
      txtOutput.Text = "That's going too far!"
   End Try
End Sub
```

9. Assume that the file PRICES.TXT is located in the Debug subfolder of the project-folder bin and the first line of the file is "Twelve Dollars".

```
Private Sub btnDisplay_Click(...) Handles btnDisplay.Click
   Dim sr As IO.StreamReader
   Dim age As Integer
   Try
      sr = IO.File.OpenText("PRICES.TXT")    'FileNotFound if fails
      price = CInt(sr.ReadLine) 'InvalidCast if fails
      txtOutput.Text = "Price is " & price
   Catch exc As IO.FileNotFoundException
      txtOutput.Text = "File PRICES.TXT not found"
   Catch exc As InvalidCastException
      txtOutput.Text = "File PRICES.TXT contains an invalid price."
   Finally
      Try
         sr.Close() 'This code executes no matter what happens above
```

```
    Catch
     'Disregard any exceptions thrown during the Close() method
    End Try
  End Try
End Sub
```

10. Redo Exercise 9 with the assumption that the file PRICES.TXT is not located in the *Debug* subfolder of the folder *bin*.

11. Assume that the contents of the file GREETING.TXT are as shown in Figure 8.3 (on page 416). What is the effect of the following program?

```
Private Sub btnDisplay_Click(...) Handles btnDisplay.Click
  Dim g As String
  Dim sr As IO.StreamReader = IO.File.OpenText("GREETING.TXT")
  Dim sw As IO.StreamWriter = IO.File.CreateText("WELCOME.TXT")
  Do While (sr.Peek <> -1)
    g = sr.ReadLine
    If (g <> "Aloha") Then
      sw.WriteLine(g)
    End If
  Loop
  sr.Close()
  sw.Close()
End Sub
```

12. Assume that the contents of the file YOB.TXT are as shown in Figure 8.1 (on page 410). What is the effect of the following program?

```
Private Sub btnDisplay_Click(...) Handles btnDisplay.Click
  Dim flag As Boolean, name As String, year As Integer
  Dim sr As IO.StreamReader = IO.File.OpenText("YOB.TXT")
  Dim sw As IO.StreamWriter = IO.File.CreateText("YOB2.TXT")
  flag = False
  name = ""
  Do While (name < "Clint") And (sr.Peek <> -1)
    name = sr.ReadLine
    year = CInt(sr.ReadLine)
    If name >= "Clint" Then
      sw.WriteLine("Clint")
      sw.WriteLine(1930)
      flag = True
    End If
    sw.WriteLine(name)
    sw.WriteLine(year)
  Loop
  Do While (sr.Peek <> -1)
    name = sr.ReadLine
    year = CInt(sr.ReadLine)
    sw.WriteLine(name)
    sw.WriteLine(year)
  Loop
```

```
    If Not flag Then
      sw.WriteLine("Clint")
      sw.WriteLine(1930)
    End If
    sr.Close()
    sw.Close()
  End Sub
```

In Exercises 13 through 18, identify any errors. Assume that the contents of the files YOB.TXT and GREETING.TXT are as shown in Figures 8.1 and 8.3.

13.
```
Private Sub btnDisplay_Click(...) Handles btnDisplay.Click
    Dim sw As IO.StreamWriter = IO.File.AppendText(YOB.TXT)
    sw.WriteLine("Michael")
    sw.WriteLine(1965)
    sw.Close()
End Sub
```

14.
```
Private Sub btnDisplay_Click(...) Handles btnDisplay.Click
    Dim name As String, yr As Integer
    Dim sw As IO.StreamWriter = IO.File.CreateText("YOB.TXT")
    name = sw.Readline
    yr = CInt(sw.ReadLine)
    txtOutput.Text = name
    sw.Close()
End Sub
```

15.
```
Private Sub btnDisplay_Click(...) Handles btnDisplay.Click
    'Copy the contents of the file GREETING.TXT into the file NEWGREET.TXT
    Dim name, greeting As String
    Dim sr As IO.StreamReader = IO.File.OpenText("GREETING.TXT")
    name = "NEWGREET.TXT"
    Dim sw As IO.StreamWriter = IO.File.CreateText("name")
    Do While (sr.Peek <> -1)
      greeting = sr.ReadLine
      sw.WriteLine(greeting)
    Loop
    sr.Close()
    sw.Close()
End Sub
```

16.
```
Private Sub btnDisplay_Click(...) Handles btnDisplay.Click
    Dim sw As IO.StreamReader = IO.File.CreateText("GREETING.TXT")
    "GREETING.TXT".Close()
End Sub
```

17.
```
Private Sub btnDisplay_Click(...) Handles btnDisplay.Click
    Try
      Dim age As Integer
      age = CInt(InputBox("Enter your age."))
```

```
      Catch
        MessageBox.Show("Invalid age.")
      End Try
      MessageBox.Show("You are " & age & " years old")
    End Sub
18. Private Sub btnDisplay_Click(...) Handles btnDisplay.Click
      Dim sw As IO.StreamWriter
      Try
        sw = IO.File.CreateFile("E:\LAKES.TXT")
      Catch IO.IOException
        MessageBox.Show("Is there a CD in the E: drive?")
      End Try
      sw.Close()
    End Sub
```

Exercises 19 through 24 are related and use the data in Table 8.2. The file created in Exercise 19 should be used in Exercises 20 through 24.

19. Write a program to create the sequential file COWBOY.TXT containing the information in Table 8.2.

TABLE 8.2	Prices paid by cowboys for certain items in mid-1800s.	
	Colt Peacemaker	12.20
	Holster	2.00
	Levi Strauss Jeans	1.35
	Saddle	40.00
	Stetson	10.00

20. Suppose the price of saddles is reduced by 20%. Use the file COWBOY.TXT to create a sequential file, COWBOY3.TXT, containing the new price list.

21. Write a program to add the data Winchester Rifle, 20.50 to the end of the file COWBOY.TXT.

22. Suppose an order is placed for 3 Colt Peacemakers, 2 Holsters, 10 pairs of Levi Strauss Jeans, 1 Saddle, and 4 Stetsons. Write a program to perform the following tasks:

    (a) Create the sequential file ORDER.TXT to hold the numbers 3, 2, 10, 1, and 4.

    (b) Use the files COWBOY.TXT and ORDER.TXT to display a sales receipt with three columns giving the name of each item, the quantity ordered, and the cost for that quantity.

    (c) Compute the total cost of the items and display it at the end of the sales receipt.

23. Write a program to request an additional item and price from the user. Then create a sequential file called COWBOY2.TXT containing all the information in the file COWBOY.TXT with the additional item (and price) inserted in its proper alphabetical sequence. Run the program for both of the following data items: Boots, 20.00 and Horse, 35.00.

24. Write a program to allow additional items and prices to be input by the user and added to the end of the file COWBOY.TXT. Include a method to terminate the process.

25. Suppose that the file YOBS.TXT contains many names and years and that the names are in alphabetical order. Write a program that requests a name as input and either gives the person's age in 2009 or reports that the person is not in the file. **Note:** Because the names are in alphabetical order, usually there is no need to search to the end of the file.

26. Suppose the file YOBS.TXT contains many names and years. Write a program that creates two files, called SENIORS.TXT and JUNIORS.TXT, and copies all the data on people born before 1955 into the file SENIORS.TXT and the data on the others into the file JUNIORS.TXT.

27. A publisher maintains two sequential files, HARDBACK.TXT and PAPER-BACK.TXT. Each record consists of the name of a book and the quantity in stock. Write a program to access these files. (The program should allow for the case when the book is not in the file.) A run of the program might look like Figure 8.4.

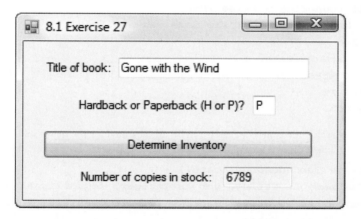

FIGURE 8.4 **A possible outcome of Exercise 27.**

28. Visual Basic cannot delete a file that is open. Attempting to do so generates an exception. Write a short program that uses structured exception handling to handle such an exception.

Solutions to Practice Problems 8.1

1. A record in YOB.TXT is kept if the name in the record does not match the search name, or if the name in the record matches the search name and a flag indicates that the search name has not been found previously.

```
Private Sub RemoveDups()
    Dim name As String, yob As Integer, foundFlag As Boolean
    foundFlag = False
    Dim sr As IO.StreamReader = IO.File.OpenText("YOB.TXT")
    Dim sw As IO.StreamWriter = IO.File.CreateText("TEMP.TXT")
```

```
      Do While sr.Peek <> -1
        name = sr.ReadLine
        yob = CInt(sr.ReadLine)
        If name <> txtName.Text Then
          sw.WriteLine(name)
          sw.WriteLine(yob)
        Else
          If Not foundFlag Then
            sw.WriteLine(name)
            sw.WriteLine(yob)
            foundFlag = True
          End If
        End If
      Loop
      sr.Close()
      sw.Close()
      IO.File.Delete("YOB.TXT")
      IO.File.Move("TEMP.TXT", "YOB.TXT")
      If foundFlag = False Then
        MessageBox.Show("The name was not found.")
      Else
        txtName.Clear()
        mtxtYOB.Clear()
      End If
    End Sub
```

2. The file YOB.TXT is first opened for input and scanned for the new name. If the name is not found, YOB.TXT is reopened for Append and the name and year of birth are added to the end of the file.

```
    Private Sub AddNoDuplicate()
      Dim name As String, yob As Integer, foundFlag As Boolean
      Dim sr As IO.StreamReader = IO.File.OpenText("YOB.TXT")
      foundFlag = False
      Do While (sr.Peek <> -1) And (Not foundFlag)
        name = sr.ReadLine
        yob = CInt(sr.ReadLine)
        If name = txtName.Text Then
          foundFlag = True
        End If
      Loop
      sr.Close()
      If Not foundFlag Then
        Dim sw As IO.StreamWriter = IO.File.AppendText("YOB.TXT")
        sw.WriteLine(txtName.Text)
        sw.WriteLine(mtxtYOB.Text)
        sw.Close()
      End If
    End Sub
```

8.2   Using Sequential Files

In addition to being accessed for information, sequential files are regularly updated by modifying certain pieces of data, removing some records, and adding new records. These tasks can be performed most efficiently if the files are first sorted.

■ Sorting Sequential Files

The records of a sequential file can be sorted on any field by first reading the data into an array of structures and then sorting on an individual element.

Example 1   The following program sorts the sequential file YOB.TXT of the previous section by year of birth:

```
Structure Individual
  Dim name As String
  Dim yearBorn As Integer
End Structure

Private Sub btnSort_Click(...) Handles btnSort.Click
  'Sort data from YOB.TXT file by year of birth
  Dim numPeople As Integer
  numPeople = NumberOfRecords("YOB.TXT")
  Dim person(numPeople - 1) As Individual
  ReadData(person, numPeople)
  SortData(person, numPeople)
  ShowData(person, numPeople)
  WriteData(person, numPeople)
End Sub

Function NumberOfRecords(ByVal filespec As String) As Integer
  Dim name As String, yearBorn As Integer
  Dim n As Integer     'Used to count records
  n = 0
  Dim sr As IO.StreamReader = IO.File.OpenText(filespec)
  Do While (sr.Peek <> -1)
    name = sr.ReadLine
    yearBorn = CInt(sr.ReadLine)
    n += 1     'Increase n by 1
  Loop
  sr.Close()
  Return n
End Function

Sub ReadData(ByRef person() As Individual, ByVal numPeople As Integer)
  'Read data from file into arrays
  Dim sr As IO.StreamReader = IO.File.OpenText("YOB.TXT")
```

```
    For index As Integer = 0 To numPeople - 1
      person(index).name = sr.ReadLine
      person(index).yearBorn = CInt(sr.ReadLine)
    Next
    sr.Close()
  End Sub

  Sub SortData(ByRef person() As Individual, ByVal numPeople As Integer)
    'Bubble sort arrays by year of birth
    For passNum As Integer = 1 To numPeople - 1
      For index As Integer = 1 To numPeople - passNum
        If person(index - 1).yearBorn > person(index).yearBorn Then
          SwapData(person, index - 1)
        End If
      Next
    Next
  End Sub

  Sub ShowData(ByVal person() As Individual, ByVal numPeople As Integer)
    'Display the sorted list
    lstShowData.Items.Clear()
    For index As Integer = 0 To numPeople - 1
      lstShowData.Items.Add(person(index).name & "      " & _
                            person(index).yearBorn)
    Next
  End Sub

  Sub SwapData(ByRef person() As Individual, ByVal index As Integer)
    Dim temp As Individual
    temp = person(index)
    person(index) = person(index + 1)
    person(index + 1) = temp
  End Sub

  Sub WriteData(ByVal person() As Individual, ByVal numPeople As Integer)
    'Write data back into file
    Dim sw As IO.StreamWriter = IO.File.CreateText("YOB2.TXT")
    For index As Integer = 0 To numPeople - 1
      sw.WriteLine(person(index).name)
      sw.WriteLine(person(index).yearBorn)
    Next
    sw.Close()
  End Sub
```

[Run, and then click the button.]

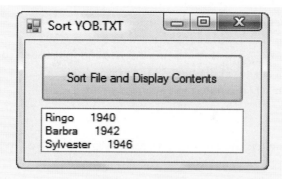

■ CSV Format

One common way to store data in a text file is to place each record on a single line with the fields separated by commas. This design is known as **CSV format**. (*Note:* CSV is an abbreviation for *Comma Separated Values*.) For example, the YOB.TXT file of the previous section would appear as follows in CSV format:

```
Barbra,1942
Ringo,1940
Sylvester,1946
```

Let's refer to the text file design we have been using as **LSV format**, where LSV stands for Line Separated Values. Also, let's make the convention of placing the prefix *csv* in front of the name of every file using CSV format. For instance, the preceding file would be named "csvYOB.TXT".

Visual Basic has a function called Split that facilitates working with CSV formatted files. Split can convert a line containing commas into a String array where the 0th element contains the text preceding the first comma, the 1st element contains the text between the first and second commas, . . . , and the last element contains the text following the last comma. For instance, suppose the String array *employees*( ) has been declared without an upper bound, and the String variable *line* has the value "Bob, 23.50, 45". Then the statement

```
employees = line.Split(","c)
```

sets the size of *employees*( ) to 3 and sets *employees*(0) = "Bob", *employees*(1) = "23.50", and *employees*(2) = "45". In the previous line of code, the character comma is called the **delimiter** for the Split function, and the letter *c* specifies that the comma have data type Character instead of String. (If Option Strict is Off, the letter *c* can be omitted.) Any character can be used as a delimiter. If no character is specified, the Split function will use the space character as delimiter.

Example 2   The following program illustrates the use of the Split function:

```
Private Sub btnRead_Click(...) Handles btnRead.Click
  Dim stateData(), line As String
```

```
    line = "California, 1850, Sacramento, Eureka"
    stateData = line.Split(",")c
    For i As Integer = 0 To stateData.GetUpperBound(0)
      stateData(i) = stateData(i).Trim    'Get rid of extraneous spaces
      lstOutput.Items.Add(stateData(i))
    Next
  End Sub
```

[Run, and then click the button. The following is displayed in the list box.]

```
California
1850
Sacramento
Eureka
```

Sequential files created with Visual Basic 6.0 (or earlier versions) are usually in CSV format. However, they can be converted easily to LSV format if desired.

Example 3   The following program converts any CSV file to an LSV file and then displays the contents of the new file. We will assume that the file to be converted is located in the *bin\Debug* subfolder for the program.

```
Private Sub btnConvert_Click(...) Handles btnConvert.Click
  Dim line, fields(), fromFile, toFile As String
  Dim sr As IO.StreamReader
  Dim sw As IO.StreamWriter
  fromFile = InputBox("Name of original file:", "Convert CSV to LSV")
  toFile = InputBox("Name of converted file:", "Convert CSV to LSV")
  sr = IO.File.OpenText(fromFile)
  sw = IO.File.CreateText(toFile)
  Do While (sr.Peek <> -1)
    line = sr.ReadLine
    fields = line.Split(",")c
    For i As Integer = 0 To fields.GetUpperBound(0)
      sw.WriteLine(fields(i).Trim)
    Next
  Loop
  sr.Close()
  sw.Close()
  sr = IO.File.OpenText(toFile)
  Do While (sr.Peek <> -1)
    lstFile.Items.Add(sr.ReadLine)
  Loop
  sr.Close()
End Sub
```

[Run, press the button, and respond to the two requests with csvSTATES.TXT and STATES.TXT. Assume that the file csvSTATES.TXT contains the two lines "California,

1850, Sacramento, Eureka" and "New York, 1788, Albany, Excelsior". The following will be displayed in the list box.]

```
California
1850
Sacramento
Eureka
New York
1788
Albany
Excelsior
```

The reverse of the Split function is the Join function, which concatenates the elements of a string array into a string containing the elements separated by a specified delimiter. For instance, the code

```
Dim greatLakes() As String = _
     {"Huron", "Ontario", "Michigan", "Erie", "Superior"}
Dim lakes As String
lakes = Join(greatLakes, ",")
txtOutput.Text = lakes
```

produces the output

```
Huron,Ontario,Michigan,Erie,Superior
```

■ Merging Sequential Files

In Section 7.2, we considered an algorithm for merging two ascending ordered arrays. This same algorithm can be applied to merging two ascending ordered files.

Suppose you have two ascending ordered LSV files (possibly with certain items appearing in both files), and you want to merge them into a third ordered file (without duplications). The technique for creating the third file is as follows:

1. Open the two files for input, and open a third file for output.
2. Try to get an item of data from each file.
3. Repeat the following steps until an item of data is not available in one of the files:
   (a) If one item precedes the other, write it into the third file and try to get another item of data from its file.
   (b) If the two items are identical, write one into the third file and try to get another item of data from each of the two ordered files.
4. At this point, an item of data has most likely been retrieved from one of the files and not yet written to the third file. In this case, write that item and all remaining items in that file to the third file.
5. Close the three files.

Example 4   The following program merges two ascending ordered files of numbers into a third ordered file:

OBJECT	PROPERTY	SETTING
frmMerge	Text	Merge Two Files
lblNameFirst	Text	Name of first file:
txtNameFirst		
lblNameSecond	Text	Name of second file:
txtNameSecond		
lblNameMerged	Text	Name for merged file:
txtNameMerged		
btnProceed	Text	Proceed to Merge
txtProgress	ReadOnly	True

```vb
Private Sub btnProceed_Click(...) Handles btnProceed.Click
  'Merge two ascending ordered files
  Dim file1, file2, file3 As String
  Dim have1data, have2data As Boolean
  Dim num1, num2 As Double
  Dim recCount As Integer      'Number of records in merged file
  file1 = txtNameFirst.Text
  file2 = txtNameSecond.Text
  file3 = txtNameMerged.Text
  Dim sr1 As IO.StreamReader = IO.File.OpenText(file1)
  Dim sr2 As IO.StreamReader = IO.File.OpenText(file2)
  Dim sw As IO.StreamWriter = IO.File.CreateText(file3)
  have1data = GetData(num1, sr1)
  have2data = GetData(num2, sr2)
  recCount = 0
  Do While (have1data And have2data)
    Select Case num1
      Case Is < num2
        sw.WriteLine(num1)
        have1data = GetData(num1, sr1)
      Case Is > num2
        sw.WriteLine(num2)
        have2data = GetData(num2, sr2)
      Case num2
        sw.WriteLine(num1)
        have1data = GetData(num1, sr1)
        have2data = GetData(num2, sr2)
    End Select
    recCount += 1
  Loop
  Do While have1data
    sw.WriteLine(num1)
    recCount += 1
    have1data = GetData(num1, sr1)
  Loop
```

```
    Do While have2data
      sw.WriteLine(num2)
      recCount += 1
      have2data = GetData(num2, sr2)
    Loop
    sr1.Close()
    sr2.Close()
    sw.Close()
    txtProgress.Text = recCount & " numbers written to " & file3
End Sub

Function GetData(ByRef num1 As Double, ByVal sr As IO.StreamReader) _
        As Boolean
  'If possible, read next value from file
  'Return value of True when new data are read; False if data
  'not available
  If (sr.Peek <> -1) Then
    num1 = CDbl(sr.ReadLine)
    Return True
  Else
    Return False
  End If
End Function
```

■ Control Break Processing

Suppose a small real estate company stores its sales data for a year in a sequential file in which each record contains four fields: month of sale, day of sale (1 through 31), address, and price. Typical data for the sales of the first quarter of a year are shown in Figure 8.5. The records are ordered by date of sale.

Month	Day	Address	Price
January	9	102 Elm Street	$203,000
January	20	1 Main Street	$315,200
January	25	5 Maple Street	$123,450
February	15	1 Center Street	$100,000
February	23	2 Vista Drive	$145,320
March	15	205 Rodeo Circle	$389,100

FIGURE 8.5   Real estate sales for first quarter of year.

Figure 8.6 shows the output of a program that displays the total sales for the quarter year, with a subtotal for each month.

A program to produce the output of Figure 8.6 must calculate a subtotal at the end of each month. The variable holding the month triggers a subtotal whenever its value changes. Such a variable is called a **control variable**, and each change of its value is called a **break**.

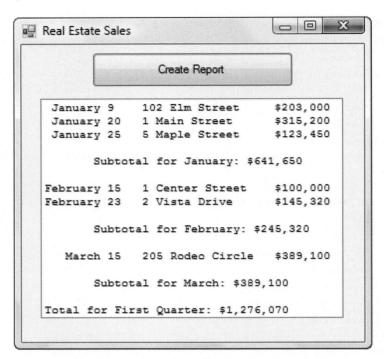

FIGURE 8.6   Output of Example 5.

Example 5   The following program produces the output of Figure 8.6. The data of Figure 8.5 are stored in the sequential file HOMESALE.TXT. The program allows for months with no sales. Because monthly subtotals will be displayed, the variable holding the current month is an appropriate control variable.

```
Private Sub btnCreateReport_Click(...) Handles btnCreateReport.Click
  'Display home sales by month
  Dim currentMonth As String = "", newMonth As String = ""
  Dim address As String = "", subtotalText As String = ""
  Dim dayNum As Integer, doneFlag As Boolean
  Dim price, monthTotal, yearTotal As Double
  Dim fmtStr As String = "{0,8} {1,-5}{2,-17}{3,10:C0}"
  Dim sr As IO.StreamReader = IO.File.OpenText("HOMESALE.TXT")
  doneFlag = False          'Flag to indicate end of list
  Do While (Not doneFlag)
    If (sr.Peek <> -1) Then
      newMonth = sr.ReadLine
      dayNum = CInt(sr.ReadLine)
      address = sr.ReadLine
      price = CDbl(sr.ReadLine)
    Else
      doneFlag = True                    'End of list
    End If
```

```
    If (newMonth <> currentMonth) Or doneFlag Then   'Ctrl break processing
      If currentMonth <> "" Then  'Don't print subtotal before 1st month
        lstReport.Items.Add("")
        subtotalText = "Subtotal for " & currentMonth & ": "
        lstReport.Items.Add("          " & subtotalText & _
                          FormatCurrency(monthTotal, 0))
        lstReport.Items.Add("")
      End If
      currentMonth = newMonth
      monthTotal = 0
    End If
    If (Not doneFlag) Then
      lstReport.Items.Add(String.Format(fmtStr, newMonth, dayNum, _
                        address, price))
      yearTotal += price
    End If
    monthTotal += price
  Loop
  sr.Close()
  lstReport.Items.Add("Total for First Quarter: " & _
                  FormatCurrency(yearTotal, 0))
End Sub
```

■ Comment

In the examples of this and the previous section, the files to be processed have been opened and closed within a single procedure. However, the solution to some programming problems requires that a file be opened just once the instant the program is run and stay open until the program is terminated. This is easily accomplished by opening the file in the form's Load event procedure and coding the Close method and End statement in the click event procedure for a button labeled "Quit."

Practice Problems 8.2

1. The program in Example 4 contains three Do loops. Explain why at most one of the last two loops will be executed. Under what circumstances will neither of the last two loops be executed?

2. Modify the program in Example 4 so that duplicate items will be repeated in the merged file.

EXERCISES 8.2

In Exercises 1 through 4, determine the output produced by the lines of code.

```
1. Dim someWords(), line As String
   line = "one,potato,two,potatoes,three,potatoes,four"
   someWords = line.Split(","c)
   txtOutput.Text = someWords(2)
```

2. ```
Dim someWords() As String
Dim line As String = "one,two,three"
someWords = line.Split(","c)
txtOutput.Text = someWords (someWords.GetUpperBound(0)).Trim
```

3. ```
Dim apart() As String = {"T","O","G","E","T","H","E","R"}
txtOutput.Text = Join(apart, ",")
```

4. ```
Dim line = "Easy come, easy go"
Dim apart() As String
apart = line.Split(","c)
txtOutput.Text = Join(apart, ",")
```

**Exercises 5 through 8 are related. They create and maintain the sequential file AVERAGE.TXT to hold batting averages of baseball players.**

5. Suppose the season is about to begin. Compose a program to create the sequential file that will contain the name of each player, his times at bat, and his number of hits. The program should allow the user to type a name into a text box and then click a button to add a record to the file. The times at bat and number of hits initially should be set to 0. (**Hint:** Declare and assign a value to the StreamReader variable at class level. Close the file when a "Quit" button is clicked.)

6. Each day, the statistics from the previous day's games should be used to update the file. Write a program to read the records one at a time and allow the user to enter the number of times at bat and the number of hits in yesterday's game for each player in appropriate text boxes on a form. When a button is clicked, a temporary file containing the updated data should replace the original file. (**Hint:** Declare and assign a value to the StreamReader and StreamWriter variables at class level. Close the files and end the program when all the data have been processed.)

7. Several players are added to the league. Compose a program to update the file.

8. Compose a program to sort the file AVERAGE.TXT with respect to batting averages and display the players with the top 5 batting averages. **Hint:** The file should be read once to determine the number of players and again to load the players into an array.

9. Write a program to convert any LSV file into a CSV file. **Note:** In addition to supplying the filenames, the user also must provide the number of fields in each record of the LSV file.

10. The file csvAgeAtInaugural.TXT contains the name and age at inaugural for each of the first 43 U.S. Presidents. (The first record is "George Washington, 57".) Write a program that requests an age as input and then displays in a list box the names of all U.S. Presidents of that age at their inaugurals.

11. Each record of the file csvUSSTATES.TXT has five fields: state name, abbreviation, when it entered the union, area (in square miles), population in 2006. The file is ordered by when the states entered the union. (The first record is "Delaware, DE, Dec. 1787, 2489, 853000".) Write a program to create a new file containing the same records, but ordered alphabetically by the state's abbreviation. The program
```

also should display the contents of the new file, neatly formatted into columns, in a list box.

12. A sentence is called a *chain-link* sentence if the last two letters of each word are the same as the first two letters of the next word, for instance, "The head administrator organized education on online networks." Write a program that accepts a sentence as input and determines whether it is a chain-link sentence. **Hint:** Use the space character as a delimiter for the Split method. To be robust, you can first remove commas by executing the statement `sentence = sentence.Replace(",", "")`, which replaces all commas in *sentence* with the empty string. Test the program with the sentence "Broadcast station, once certified, educates estimable legions."

Exercises 13 and 14 refer to the ordered file BLOCK.TXT containing the names of people on your block and the ordered file TIMES.TXT containing the names of all people who subscribe to the *New York Times*.

13. Write a program that creates a file consisting of the names of all people on your block who subscribe to the *New York Times*.

14. Write a program that creates a file consisting of the names of all *New York Times* subscribers who do not live on your block.

15. Suppose that a file of positive integers is in ascending order. Write a program to determine the maximum number of times any integer is repeated in the file. (For instance, if the entries in the file are 5, 5, 6, 6, 6, and 10, then the output is 3.)

16. Suppose that each record of the file SALES.TXT contains a salesperson's name and the dollar amount of a sale, and the records are ordered by the names. Write a program to display the name, number of sales, and average sale amount for each salesperson. For instance, if the first eight lines of the file contain the data: Adams, 123.45, Adams, 432.15, Brown, 89.95, Cook, 500.00, then the first two entries of the output would be

Salesperson	Number of Sales	Average Sale Amount
Adams	2	$277.80
Brown	1	$89.95

17. An elementary school holds a raffle to raise funds. Suppose that each record of the file RAFFLE.TXT contains a student's grade (1 through 6), name, and the number of raffle tickets sold and that the records are ordered by grade. Write a program using a control break to display the number of tickets sold by each grade and the total number of tickets sold.

18. *Multiple Control Breaks.* Suppose the sorted sequential file CENSUS.TXT contains names of all residents of a state, where each record consists of two lines of the form "last Name", "first Name". Write a program to determine, in one pass through the file, the most common last name and most common full name. (**Note:** In the unlikely event of a tie, the program should display the first occurring name.) For instance, the output in the list box might be as follows:

```
The most common last name is Brown.
The most common full name is John Smith.
```

In Exercises 19 and 20, suppose that the file MASTER.TXT contains the names and phone numbers of all members of an organization, where the records are ordered by name.

19. Suppose that the ordered file MOVED.TXT contains the names and new phone numbers of all members who have changed their phone numbers. Write a program to update the file MASTER.TXT.

20. Suppose that the ordered file QUIT.TXT contains the names of all members who have left the organization. Write a program to update the file MASTER.TXT.

Solutions to Practice Problems 8.2

1. Execution proceeds beyond the first Do loop only when the Peek method returns −1 for one of the input files. Because each of the last two Do loops executes only if the Peek method does not return −1, at most one loop can execute. Neither of the last two loops will be executed if each input file is empty or if the last entries of the files are the same.

2. Change the Select Case block to the following:

```
Select Case num1
  Case Is <= num2
    sw.WriteLine(num1)
    have1data = Get1data(num1, sr1)
  Case Is > num2
    sw.WriteLine(num2)
    have2data = Get2data(num2, sr2)
End Select
```

8.3   A Case Study: Recording Checks and Deposits

The purpose of this section is to take you through the design and implementation of a quality program for personal checkbook management. Nothing in this chapter shows off the power of Visual Basic better than the program in this section. That a user-friendly checkbook management program can be written in less than seven pages of code clearly shows Visual Basic's ability to improve the productivity of programmers. It is easy to imagine an entire finance program, similar to programs that have generated millions of dollars of sales, being written in only a few weeks by using Visual Basic!

■ Design of the Program

Though there are many commercial programs available for personal financial management, they include so many bells and whistles that their original purposes—keeping track of transactions and reporting balances—have become obscured. The program in this section was designed specifically as a checkbook program. It keeps track of expenditures and deposits and produces a report. Adding a reconciliation feature would be easy enough, although we did not include one.

The program is supposed to be user friendly. Therefore, it showcases many of the techniques and tools available in Visual Basic.

The general design goals for the program included the following abilities:

- Automatically enter the user's name on each check and deposit slip.
- Automatically provide the next consecutive check or deposit slip number. (The user can override this feature if necessary.)
- Automatically provide the date. (Again, this feature can be overridden.)
- For each check, record the payee, the amount, and optionally a memo.
- For each deposit slip, record the source, the amount, and optionally a memo.
- Display the current balance at all times.
- Produce a report detailing all transactions.

■ User Interface

With Visual Basic, we can place a replica of a check or deposit slip on the screen and let the user supply the information as if actually filling out a check or deposit slip. Figure 8.7 shows the form in its check mode. At the bottom of the check are a label and a text box for the current balance and four buttons.

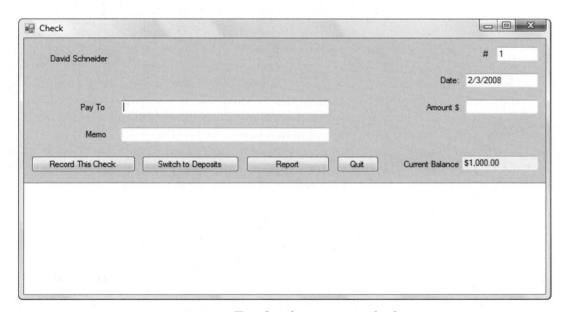

FIGURE 8.7   Template for entering a check.

The first time the program is run, the user is asked for his or her name, the starting balance, and the numbers of the first check and deposit slip. Suppose the user's name is David Schneider, the starting balance is $1000, and both the first check number and deposit slip number are 1. Figure 8.7 shows the form after the four pieces of input. The upper part of the form looks like a check. The form has a color of light gray when in check mode. The Date box is automatically set to today's date, but can be altered by the user. The user fills in the payee, amount, and optionally a memo. When the user pushes the Record This Check button, the information is written to a file, the balance is updated, and check number 2 appears.

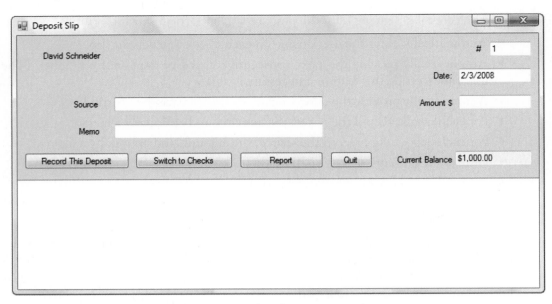

FIGURE 8.8 **Template for entering a deposit.**

To record a deposit, the user pushes the Switch to Deposits button. The form then appears as in Figure 8.8. The form's title bar now reads Deposit Slip, the words Pay To change to Source, and the color of the form changes to yellow. Also, in the buttons at the bottom of the slip, the words Check and Deposit are interchanged. A deposit is recorded in much the same way as a check. When the Report button is pushed, a report similar to the one in Figure 8.9 is displayed below the buttons.

The common design for the check and deposit slip allows one set of controls to be used for both items. The text of the label lblName is set to the user's name, while the text of the label lblToFrom will change back and forth between Pay To and Source.

Name: David Schneider	Starting balance: $1,000.00		5/6/2008
Date	Transaction	Amount	Balance
4/21/2008	Check #: 1 Paid to: Land's End Memo: shirts	$75.95	$924.05
4/29/2008	Check #: 2 Paid to: Bethesda Coop Memo: groceries	$125.00	$799.05
5/5/2008	Deposit #: 1 Source: Prentice Hall Memo: typing expenses	$245.00	$1,044.05
	Ending Balance: $1,044.05		

FIGURE 8.9 **Sample transaction report.**

TABLE 8.3   **Objects and initial property settings for the checkbook management program.**

Object	Property	Setting
frmAccount		
lblName	Font Size	10pt
lblNum	Text	#
txtNum		
lblDate	Text	Date:
txtDate		
lblToFrom		
txtToFrom		
lblAmount	Text	Amount $
txtAmount		
lblMemo	Text	Memo
txtMemo		
btnRecord	Text	&Record This Check
btnMode	Text	&Switch to Deposits
btnReport	Text	&Report
btnQuit	Text	&Quit
lblCurBal	Text	Current Balance
txtBalance	ReadOnly	True
lstTransactions	Font	Courier New

Table 8.3 lists the objects and their initial property settings. Because the program will always begin by displaying the next check, all the text for the labels and the BackColor property of the form could have been set at design time. We chose instead to leave these assignments to the SetupCheck method, which is normally used to switch from deposit entry to check entry, but also can be called by the form's Load event procedure to prepare the initial mode (check or deposit) for the form.

The transactions are stored in CSV format in a text file named CHECKBOOK.TXT. The first line of the file contains four entries: the name to appear on the check and deposit slip, the starting balance, the number of the first check, and the number of the first deposit slip. After that, each transaction is recorded on one line as a sequence of eight items: the type of transaction, the contents of txtToFrom, the current balance, the number of the last check, the number of the last deposit slip, the amount of money, the memo, and the date.

Coding the Program

The second row of Figure 8.10 identifies the different events to which the program must respond. Table 8.4 lists the corresponding event procedures and the general procedures they call.

Let's examine each event procedure:

1. *frmAccount_Load* first calls the InitializeData Sub procedure to process the text file. This procedure first looks to see if the file CHECKBOOK.TXT exists. The

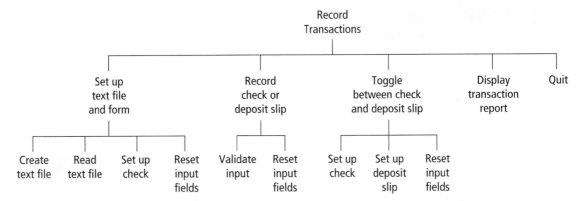

FIGURE 8.10   Hierarchy chart for checkbook management program.

TABLE 8.4   **Tasks and their procedures.**

	Task	Procedure
1.	Set up text file and form	frmAccount_Load
	1.1 Create text file	InitializeData
	1.2 Read text file	InitializeData
	1.3 Set up check	SetupCheck
	1.4 Reset input fields	ResetInput
2.	Record check or deposit slip	btnRecord_Click
	2.1 Validate input	DataValid
	2.2 Reset input fields	ResetInput
3.	Toggle between check & deposit slip	btnMode_Click
	3.1 Set up check	SetupCheck
	3.2 Set up deposit slip	SetupDeposit
	3.3 Reset input fields	ResetInput
4.	Display transaction report	btnReport_Click
5.	Quit	btnQuit_Click

function IO.File.Exists returns True if the file exists and False otherwise. If CHECKBOOK.TXT does exist, the procedure reads through the entire file to determine all information needed to proceed. If CHECKBOOK.TXT does not exist, the Sub procedure prompts the user for the name to appear on the checks and deposit slips, the starting balance, and the numbers of the first check and deposit slip and then writes these items to the text file. The event procedure calls the SetupCheck Sub procedure next to set the transaction type to Check and sets the appropriate text and background color for a check. The event procedure then calls ResetInput, which initializes all the text boxes.

The InitializeData Sub procedure employs structured exception handling to protect the code from four possible failures: The text file cannot be read, the text file has an invalid format, the user's input cannot be stored in a new file, and the user's input is invalid. In the first two situations, the program works around the exception by creating a new text file. In the third and fourth situation, the program displays an error message and terminates.

2. **btnRecord_Click** first confirms that the required fields contain valid entries. This is accomplished by calling the function DataValid. If the value returned is True, then btnRecord_Click updates the current balance, opens the text file in append mode, writes eight pieces of data to the file, and then closes the file. When DataValid returns False, the function itself pops up a message box to tell the user where information is needed or invalid. The user must type in the information and then press the Record button again. Both procedures employ structured exception handling to protect their code from failures. The btnRecord_Click procedure ensures that the new data can be stored in the file. If it can't, then an error message is displayed and the program terminates. The DataValid function ensures that the user's input is valid. If either the amount or number field is not a number, the InvalidCastException is thrown. The Catch block handles this exception by displaying an appropriate message asking the user to reenter the information.

3. **btnMode_Click** toggles back and forth from a check to a deposit slip. It calls SetupCheck, or its analog SetupDeposit, and then calls ResetInput.

4. **btnReport_Click** displays a complete history of all transactions as shown in Figure 8.9. This procedure reads the text file and displays each entry along with the beginning and ending balances. This procedure employs structured exception handling to protect its code from IO failures when the text file cannot be read correctly or has an invalid format.

5. **btnQuit_Click** ends the program.

```
'Class-level named constants and variables
'Text file that stores information
Const FILE As String = "CHECKBOOK.TXT"
'Variables used for each entry
Dim mode As Boolean           'Mode: check = True, deposit slip = False
Dim nameOnChk As String       'Name to appear on checks
Dim lastCkNum As Integer      'Number of last check written
Dim lastDpNum As Integer      'Number of last deposit slip processed
Dim curBal As Double          'Current balance in account

Private Sub frmAccount_Load(...) Handles MyBase.Load
  'Sets the class variables from a new or existing text file
  InitializeData()
  'Set name and balance labels
  lblName.Text = nameOnChk
  txtBalance.Text = FormatCurrency(curBal)
  'Set the date field to the current date. The value of CStr(Today)
  'is a string consisting of the current date (m/d/yr).
  txtDate.Text = CStr(Today)
  SetupCheck()
  ResetInput()
End Sub

Private Sub InitializeData()
  'Reads or creates the file and sets the class-level variables
  Dim sr As IO.StreamReader
```

```
    Dim exists As Boolean = False    'Set to True if text file exists
    Try
       'If text file exists, then read it.
       If IO.File.Exists(FILE) Then
          Dim data() As String    'Holds the data read from the file
          sr = IO.File.OpenText(FILE)
          'Split the first line of the text file using the separator
          data = sr.ReadLine.Split(","c)
          'Recover name to appear on checks, current balance, number of
          'last check written and number of last deposit slip processed
          nameOnChk = data(0)
          curBal = CDbl(data(1))
          lastCkNum = CInt(data(2))
          lastDpNum = CInt(data(3))
          Do While (sr.Peek <> -1)
             data = sr.ReadLine.Split(","c)
             curBal = CDbl(data(2))
             lastCkNum = CInt(data(3))
             lastDpNum = CInt(data(4))
          Loop
          exists = True
       End If
    Catch exc As IO.IOException
       'Display error message and set flag to False
       MessageBox.Show("Could not read " & FILE & _
                      ", will create a new file.", "Error")
       exists = False
    Catch
       'Display error message and set flag to False
       MessageBox.Show("File " & FILE & _
                      " is invalid, will create a new one.", "Error")
       exists = False
    Finally
       'Close the reader no matter what happens above
       Try
          sr.Close()
       Catch
       End Try
    End Try
    'If the file doesn't exist, then create one.
    If Not exists Then
       Dim sw As IO.StreamWriter
       Try
          'Text file does not exist, so get initial data from user
          nameOnChk = InputBox("Name to appear on checks:")
          curBal = CDbl(InputBox("Starting Balance:"))
```

```
      'Get numbers of last check and deposit slip
      lastCkNum = CInt(InputBox("Number of first check:")) - 1
      lastDpNum = CInt(InputBox("Number of first deposit slip:")) - 1
      'First record in text file records name to appear on checks
      'plus initial data for account
      Dim outputLine() As String = {nameOnChk, CStr(curBal), _
                                 CStr(lastCkNum), CStr(lastDpNum)}
      sw = IO.File.CreateText(FILE)
      sw.WriteLine(Join(outputLine, ","))
    Catch exc As IO.IOException
      'If an exception occurs then display message and quit
      MessageBox.Show("Cannot store data into file " & FILE & _
                  ". Program terminating.", "Error")
      End
    Catch
      'If a number cannot be converted then display message and quit
      MessageBox.Show("Invalid number. Program terminating.", "Error")
      End
    Finally
      'Close the writer no matter what happens above
      Try
        sw.Close()
      Catch
      End Try
    End Try
  End If
End Sub

Private Sub btnRecord_Click(...) Handles btnRecord.Click
  'Store the input into the text file
  Dim amt As Double
  Dim transType As String
  'Only store if all required fields are filled and valid
  If DataValid() Then
    amt = CDbl(txtAmount.Text)
    'Adjust balance by amount depending on check or deposit slip mode
    If mode Then
      curBal = curBal - amt
      lastCkNum = CInt(txtNum.Text)
      transType = "Check"
    Else
      curBal += amt
      lastDpNum = CInt(txtNum.Text)
      transType = "Deposit"
    End If
    txtBalance.Text = FormatCurrency(curBal)
```

```vb
        'String array contains info to be stored
        Dim transOutput() As String = {transType, txtToFrom.Text, _
          CStr(curBal), CStr(lastCkNum), CStr(lastDpNum), CStr(amt), _
          txtMemo.Text, txtDate.Text}
        Dim sw As IO.StreamWriter
        Try
          'Append the info to the text file, separated by the separator
          sw = IO.File.AppendText(FILE)
          sw.WriteLine(Join(transOutput, ","))
        Catch
          'Display error message and quit
          MessageBox.Show("Could not store data into file " & FILE & _
                          ". Program terminating.", "Error")
          End
        Finally
          'Close writer no matter what happens above
          Try
            sw.Close()
          Catch
          End Try
        End Try
        'Reset input controls to blank for next entry
        ResetInput()
    End If
End Sub

Function DataValid() As Boolean
    'Returns True if all data are valid, or displays a message if not
    Dim errorMessage As String
    'If one of the four required pieces of information
    'is missing, assign its name to errorMessage
    errorMessage = ""
    If txtToFrom.Text.Trim = "" Then
      If mode Then
        errorMessage = "Pay To"
      Else
        errorMessage = "Source"
      End If
      txtToFrom.Focus()
    ElseIf txtAmount.Text.Trim = "" Then
      errorMessage = "Amount"
      txtAmount.Focus()
    End If
    'If no errors yet then check syntax of the two numerical fields
    If errorMessage = "" Then
      'Check syntax of the amount field (Double)
      Try
        If CDbl(txtAmount.Text) <= 0 Then
          errorMessage = "The amount must be greater than zero."
```

```vb
          txtAmount.Focus()
        End If
      Catch exc As InvalidCastException
        errorMessage = "The amount " & txtAmount.Text & " is invalid."
        txtAmount.Focus()
      End Try
    Else
      errorMessage = "The '" & errorMessage & "' field must be filled."
    End If
    'Display error message if available
    If errorMessage = "" Then
      'All required data fields have been filled; recording can proceed
      Return True
    Else
      'Advise user of invalid data
      MessageBox.Show(errorMessage & " Please try again.")
      Return False
    End If
End Function

Private Sub btnMode_Click(...) Handles btnMode.Click
  'Toggle mode between Check and Deposit Slip
  If mode Then
    SetupDeposit()
  Else
    SetupCheck()
  End If
  'Set fields for next entry
  ResetInput()
End Sub

Sub SetupCheck()
  'Prepare form for the entry of a check
  mode = True
  Me.Text = "Check"    'Sets the title bar of the form
  lblToFrom.Text = "Pay To"
  btnRecord.Text = "&Record This Check"
  btnMode.Text = "&Switch to Deposits"
  Me.BackColor = Color.LightGray
End Sub

Sub SetupDeposit()
  'Prepare form for the entry of a deposit
  mode = False
  Me.Text = "Deposit Slip"    'Sets the title bar of the form
  lblToFrom.Text = "Source"
  btnRecord.Text = "&Record This Deposit"
  btnMode.Text = "&Switch to Checks"
  Me.BackColor = Color.Yellow
End Sub
```

```
Sub ResetInput()
  'Reset report listing
  lstTransactions.Items.Clear()
  'Reset all text entry fields except date
  txtToFrom.Clear()
  txtAmount.Clear()
  txtMemo.Clear()
  If mode Then
    'Make txtNum reflect next check number
    txtNum.Text = CStr(lastCkNum + 1)
  Else
    'Make txtNum reflect next deposit slip number
    txtNum.Text = CStr(lastDpNum + 1)
  End If
  'Set focus on to/from control for the next entry
  txtToFrom.Focus()
End Sub

Private Sub btnReport_Click(...) Handles btnReport.Click
  'Display report of all transactions in the text file
  Dim fmtStr As String = "{0, -18} {1, -35} {2, -12} {3, -12}"
  Dim data() As String      'Holds the data for each entry
  Dim balance As String
  Dim sr As IO.StreamReader
  lstTransactions.Items.Clear()
  Try
    'Display headings for the transaction data
    sr = IO.File.OpenText(FILE)
    data = sr.ReadLine.Split(","c)
    balance = data(1)
    'Display the name, starting balance, and today's date
    lstTransactions.Items.Add(String.Format(fmtStr, data(0), _
         "Starting Balance: " & FormatCurrency(balance), "", CStr(Today)))
    lstTransactions.Items.Add("")
    lstTransactions.Items.Add(String.Format(fmtStr, "Date", _
                      "Transaction", "Amount", "Balance"))
    fmtStr = "{0,-18} {1,-35} {2,-12:C} {3,-12:C}"
    'Loop until the end of file is reached
    Do While (sr.Peek <> -1)
      'Add a blank line in between entries
      lstTransactions.Items.Add("")
      'Fields are separated by a separator on one line for each entry
      data = sr.ReadLine.Split(","c)
      If data(0) = "Check" Then    'The entry is a check
        lstTransactions.Items.Add(String.Format(fmtStr, data(7), _
             "Check #: " & data(3), CDbl(data(5)), CDbl(data(2))))
        lstTransactions.Items.Add(String.Format(fmtStr, "", _
```

```
                      "Paid to: " & data(1), "", ""))
              lstTransactions.Items.Add(String.Format(fmtStr, "", _
                "Memo: " & data(6), "", ""))
          Else     'The entry is a deposit
              lstTransactions.Items.Add(String.Format(fmtStr, data(7), _
                "Deposit #: " & data(4), CDbl(data(5)), CDbl(data(2))))
              lstTransactions.Items.Add(String.Format(fmtStr, "", _
                "Source: " & data(1), "", ""))
              lstTransactions.Items.Add(String.Format(fmtStr, "", _
                "Memo: " & data(6), "", ""))
          End If
          balance = data(2)
        Loop
        'Display the ending balance
        lstTransactions.Items.Add("")
        lstTransactions.Items.Add(String.Format(fmtStr, "", _
                  "Ending Balance: " & FormatCurrency(balance), "", ""))
      Catch exc As IO.IOException
        'Any IO error reading the text file
        'Display an error message
        MessageBox.Show("Could not read file " & FILE & ".", "Error")
      Catch
        'Any non-IO error encountered. The two possibilities are:
        '1) The entry did not have 8 fields separated by the separator, or
        '2) The numeric data could not be displayed by FormatCurrency
        'Display an error message
        MessageBox.Show("File " & FILE & " has invalid format.", "Error")
      Finally
        'Close the reader no matter what happens above
        Try
          sr.Close()
        Catch
        End Try
      End Try
    End Sub

    Private Sub btnQuit_Click(...) Handles btnQuit.Click
      'Exit the program
      End
    End Sub
```

CHAPTER 8   SUMMARY

1. When sequential files are opened, we must specify whether they will be read from with a StreamReader or written to with a StreamWriter. Output files can be created anew (File.CreateText) or just added to (File.AppendText). A line of data is written to a file with the WriteLine method and read from a file with the ReadLine method.

2. *Structured exception handling* can reduce the likelihood that a program will crash. If an exception occurs while the code in the Try block is running, execution branches to the code in a Catch block that alerts the user of a mishap. The Finally block does its best to clean up before the program moves on to other tasks.

3. When data are stored with *CSV format*, an entire record is placed in a single line with fields separated by commas.

4. A sequential file can be ordered by placing its data in an array of structures, sorting the array, and then writing the ordered data into a file.

CHAPTER 8   PROGRAMMING PROJECTS

1. Table 8.5 gives the leading seven soft drinks in 2006 and their percentage share of the market. Write a program whose form contains two buttons and a list box. When the first button is clicked, these data should be placed into a sequential file. When the second button is clicked, the sequential file should be used to

   (a) display the seven brands and their sales in millions of gallons. (The entire soft drink industry sold about 15.2 billion gallons in 2006.)

   (b) calculate the total percentage market share of the leading seven soft drinks.

TABLE 8.5   **Leading soft-drink brands and 2006 market share.**

Coke Classic	17.3 %
Pepsi-Cola	11.0 %
Diet Coke	9.8 %
Mt. Dew	6.6 %
Diet Pepsi	6.0 %
Dr. Pepper	5.8 %
Sprite	5.7 %

Source: Beverage Digest, 2007

2. Suppose that the sequential file ALE.TXT contains the information shown in Table 8.6. Write a program to use the file to produce Table 8.7 in which the baseball teams are in descending order by the percentage of games won.

TABLE 8.6   **American League East games won and lost in 2007.**

Team	Won	Lost
Baltimore	69	93
Boston	96	66
New York	94	68
Tampa Bay	66	96
Toronto	83	79

TABLE 8.7	Final 2007 American League East standings.		
	W	L	Pct
Boston	96	66	0.593
New York	94	68	0.580
Toronto	83	79	0.512
Baltimore	69	93	0.426
Tampa Bay	66	96	0.407

3. Write a rudimentary word-processing program. The program should do the following:

   (a) Use InputBox to request the name of the sequential file to hold the document being created.

   (b) Set the label for a text box to "Enter Line 1," and allow the user to enter the first line of the document into the text box.

   (c) When the "Record Line" button is clicked, determine if the line is acceptable. Blank lines are acceptable input, but lines exceeding 60 characters in length should not be accepted. Advise the user of the problem with a message box, and then set the focus back to the text box so that the user can edit the line to an acceptable length. When an acceptable line is entered, write this line to the file and display it in a list box.

   (d) Change the label to "Enter Line 2," clear the text box, allow the user to enter the second line of the document into the text box, and carry out (c) for this line using the same list box.

   (e) Continue as in (d) with appropriate labels for subsequent lines until the user clicks on a Finished button.

   (f) Clear the list box, and display the number of lines written and the name of the text file created.

4. Write a program that counts the number of times a word occurs in the sequential file created in Programming Project 3. The filename and word should be read from text boxes. The search should not be sensitive to the case of the letters. For instance, opening a file that contained the first three sentences of the directions to this problem and searching for "the" would produce the output: "the" occurs six times.

5. *Create and Maintain Telephone Directories.* Write a program to create and maintain telephone directories. Each directory will be a separate sequential file. The following buttons should be available:

   (a) Select a directory to access. A list of directories that have been created should be stored in a separate sequential file. When a request is made to open a directory, the list of available directories should be displayed as part of an InputBox prompt requesting the name of the directory to be accessed. If the user responds with a directory name not listed, the desire to create a new directory should be confirmed and then the new directory created and added to the list of existing directories.

   (b) Add name and phone number (as given in the text boxes) to the end of the current directory.

    (c) Delete name (as given in the text box) from the current directory.

    (d) Sort the current directory into name order.

    (e) Display the names and phone numbers contained in the current directory.

    (f) Terminate the program.

6. Table 8.8 contains the statistics for a stock portfolio. (The current prices are given for January 17, 2008.)

TABLE 8.8   **Stock portfolio.**

Stock	Number of Shares	Date Purchased	Purchase Price/Share	Current Price/Share
Amgen	200	8/19/97	12.625	47.42
Delta Airlines	100	12/3/97	55.875	15.19
Novell	500	8/27/97	10.375	6.13
PPG	100	12/18/97	28.375	62.64
Timken	300	3/13/98	34.625	26.88

    (a) Compose a program to create the sequential file csvSTOCKS.TXT containing the information in Table 8.8.

    (b) Compose a program to perform the following tasks. A possible form design is shown in Figure 8.11.

FIGURE 8.11   **Possible form design for Programming Project 6.**

    (1) Display the information in the file csvSTOCKS.TXT as in Table 8.8 when the user clicks on a Display Stocks button.

    (2) Add an additional stock onto the end of the file csvSTOCKS.TXT when the user clicks on an Add Stock button. The data for the new stock should be read from appropriately labeled text boxes.

(3) Update the Current Price/Share of a stock in the file csvSTOCKS.TXT when the user clicks on an Update Stock button. The name of the stock to be updated and the new price should be read from the appropriate text boxes. The file csvSTOCKS.TXT should then be copied to a temporary file until the specified stock is found. The updated record for this stock should then be written to the temporary file, followed by all remaining records in csvSTOCKS.TXT. Finally, the original csvSTOCKS.TXT file should be erased and the temporary file renamed to csvSTOCKS.TXT.

(4) Process the data in the file csvSTOCKS.TXT, and produce the display shown in Figure 8.12 when a "Show Profit/Loss" button is clicked.

(5) Quit.

Stock	Cost	Current Value	Profit (or Loss)
Amgen	$2,525.00	$9,484.00	$6,959.00
Delta Airlines	$5,587.50	$1,519.00	($4,068.50)
Novell	$5,187.50	$3,065.00	($2,122.50)
PPG	$2,837.50	$6,264.00	$3,426.50
Timken	$10,387.50	$8,064.00	($2,323.50)

FIGURE 8.12   Output of Programming Project 6.

7. A department store has a CSV file (csvSTORE.TXT) containing all sales transacted for a year. Each record contains a customer's name, zip code, and amount of the sale. The file is ordered first by zip code and then by name. Write a program to display the total sales for each customer, the total sales for each zip code, and the total sales for the store. For instance, if the first six records of the file are

```
Adams, John, 10023, 34.50
Adams, John, 10023, 60.00
Jones, Bob, 10023, 62.45
Green, Mary, 12345, 54.00
Howard, Sue, 12345, 79.25
Smith, George, 20001, 25.10
```

then the output in the list box will begin as shown in Figure 8.13.

FIGURE 8.13   Sample output for Programming Project 7.

8. *Savings Account.* The sequential file csvACCOUNTS.TXT contains the name, account number, and beginning-of-month balance for each depositor. The sequential file csvTRANS.TXT contains all the transactions (deposits and withdrawals) for the month. Use csvTRANS.TXT to update the file csvACCOUNTS.TXT. Both files are sorted by account number. For each customer, display a statement similar to the one received from banks that shows all transactions and the end-of-month balance. Also, record all overdrawn accounts in a file. (As an optional embellishment, deduct a penalty if the balance fell below a certain level any time during the month. The penalty could include a fixed fee of $10, plus a charge of $1 for each check and deposit.)

9. A fuel economy study was carried out for five models of cars. Each car was driven for 100 miles, and then the model of the car and the number of gallons used were placed in a line of the sequential file csvMILEAGE.TXT. Table 8.9 shows the first entries of the file. Write a program to display the models and their average miles per gallon in decreasing order with respect to mileage. The program should utilize an array of structures with upper bound 4, where each structure has three members. The first member should record the name of each model of car. This member is initially empty; each car model name is added when first encountered in reading the file. The second member should record the number of test vehicles for each model. The third member should record the total number of gallons used by that model. **Note:** The first members of the elements of the array should be searched each time a record is read to determine the appropriate index to use with the other two members.

TABLE 8.9 Gallons of gasoline used in 100 miles of driving.

Model	Gal	Model	Gal	Model	Gal
Prius	2.1	Accord	4.1	Accord	4.3
Camry	4.1	Camry	3.8	Prius	2.3
Sebring	4.2	Camry	3.9	Camry	4.2
Mustang	5.3	Mustang	5.2	Accord	4.4

10. Each item in a supermarket is identified by its Universal Product Code (UPC), which consists of a sequence of 12 digits appearing below a rectangle of bars. See Figure 8.14. The bars have these digits encoded in them so that the UPC can be read by an optical scanner. Let's refer to the UPC as d_1-d_2 d_3 d_4 d_5 d_6-d_7 d_8 d_9 d_{10} d_{11}-d_{12}. The single digit on the left, d_1, identifies the type of product (for instance, 0 for general groceries, 2 for meat and produce, 3 for drug and health products, and 5 for coupons). The first set of five digits, d_2 d_3 d_4 d_5 d_6, identifies the manufacturer, and the second set of five digits, $0d_7$ d_8 d_9 d_{10} d_{11}, identifies the product. The twelfth digit on the right, d_{12}, is a check digit. It is chosen so that

$$3 \cdot d_1 + d_2 + 3 \cdot d_3 + d_4 + 3 \cdot d_5 + d_6 + 3 \cdot d_7 + d_8$$
$$+ 3 \cdot d_9 + d_{10} + 3 \cdot d_{11} + d_{12}. \qquad (*)$$

is a multiple of 10. For instance, for the UPC in Figure 8.11,

$$3 \cdot 0 + 7 + 3 \cdot 0 + 7 + 3 \cdot 3 + 4 + 3 \cdot 0 + 0 + 3 \cdot 9 + 0 \cdot 0 + 3 \cdot 3 + 4 = 40.$$

FIGURE 8.14   A Universal Product Code.

Since $40 = 4 \cdot 10$, 40 is a multiple of 10. In the event that the cashier has to enter the UPC manually and mistypes a digit, the above sum will usually not add up to a multiple of 10.

Write a program to simulate an automated check-out counter at a supermarket. A master sequential file, called UPC.TXT, should have a record for each item consisting of fields for the UPC, name of the item, and the price of the item. For instance, the file might contain the following record:

```
070734000034
Celestial Seasons Sleepytime Tea
2.59
```

The file should be ordered with respect to the UPCs. The program should allow the cashier to enter UPCs one at a time, should keep a running total of the number of items processed, and should place the UPCs in an array. Each UPC should be checked with the sum (*) as soon as it is entered and should be reentered if the sum is not a multiple of 10. After all items have been processed, the program should sort the array of UPCs and then produce a receipt similar to the one in Figure 8.15 after making just one pass through the master sequential file.

```
22-oz Jif Peanut Butter             2.29
Celestial Seasons Sleepytime Tea    2.59
365 Soda Root Beer                   .55
Total = = = = = = = = = = = = = >  $5.43
```

FIGURE 8.15   Sample output of Programming Project 10.

9

Additional Controls
and Objects

9.1   List Boxes, Combo Boxes, and the File-Opening Control

Throughout this book, we have used list boxes to display the output of a program. However, list boxes also provide a potent means for obtaining input by selecting an item from a list. Two other controls that allow us to choose an item from a list are the ComboBox and the OpenFileDialog controls.

■ The List Box Control

The list boxes discussed in this text display a single column of strings, referred to as **items**. The items to appear initially can either be specified at design time with the Items property or set with code in a procedure. Code is then used to access, add, or delete items from the list. We will first carry out all tasks with code and then show how the initial items can be specified at design time.

At any time, the value of

```
lstBox.Items.Count
```

is the number of items in the list box.

Each item in lstBox is identified by an **index number** ranging from 0 through lstBox.Items.Count − 1.

The Sorted property is perhaps the most interesting list box property. When it is set to True, the items will automatically be displayed in alphabetical (i.e., ANSI or ASCII) order. The default value of the Sorted property is False. When the Sorted property is set to True, the statement

```
num = lstBox.Items.Add(str)
```

inserts *str* into the list at the proper sorted position and assigns to the Integer variable *num* the index number of that position.

During run time, you can highlight an item from a list by clicking on it with the mouse or by moving to it with the up- and down-arrow keys when the list box has the focus. (The second method triggers the SelectedIndexChanged event each time an arrow key causes the highlight to move.) The value of

```
lstBox.SelectedIndex
```

is the index number of the item currently highlighted in lstBox. If no item is highlighted, the value of SelectedIndex is −1. The statement

```
lstBox.ListIndex = -1
```

will unhighlight any highlighted item in the list.

The list of items stored in the list box are held in lstBox.Items(). In particular, the value of

```
lstBox.Items(n)
```

is the item of lstBox having index *n*. The elements of the list are of a data type called Object. A variable of any type may be assigned to an element of the list. However, type casting must take place whenever an element of the list is assigned to a numeric or string variable or concatenated with another variable or literal. For instance, the statement

```
txtBox.Text = CStr(lstBox.Items(0))
```

displays the first item of lstBox. (**Note:** No casting need take place when the items of a list box are written to a text file.)

The value of

```
lstBox.Items(lstBox.SelectedIndex)
```

is the item currently highlighted in lstBox. Alternatively, the value of

```
lstBox.Text
```

is the currently highlighted item converted to a string. Setting this property to a String value (with a statement of the form `lstBox.Text = str`) selects the first item in the list box having value *str*.

The statement

```
lstBox.Items.RemoveAt(n)
```

deletes the item of index *n* from lstBox. The statement

```
lstBox.Items.Remove(str)
```

deletes the first occurrence of the value of *str* in lstBox.

When the user selects an item in a list box, an event is triggered. A program can respond to three main types of events. If the user clicks on an item, the Click event is processed. If the user clicks on a different item or uses the arrow keys to select it, the SelectedIndexChanged event is processed. If the user double-clicks on an item, then the Click, DoubleClick, and SelectedIndexChanged events are triggered.

 Example 1 An oxymoron is a pairing of contradictory or incongruous words. The following program displays a list of oxymorons. When you select an item, it is displayed in a text box. A button allows you to add an additional item with an input dialog box. You can delete an item by double-clicking on it with the mouse. After running the program, click on different items, add an item or two (such as "same difference" or "liquid gas"), and delete an item.

OBJECT	PROPERTY	SETTING
frmOxymoron	Text	OXYMORONS
lstOxys	Sorted	True
btnAdd	Text	Add an Item
lblDelete	AutoSize	False
	Text	[To delete an item, double-click on it.]
lblSelected	Text	Selected item:
txtSelected	ReadOnly	True

```
Private Sub lstOxys_SelectedIndexChanged(...) Handles _
          lstOxys.SelectedIndexChanged
  txtSelected.Text = CStr(lstOxys.Text)
End Sub

Private Sub btnAdd_Click(...) Handles btnAdd.Click
  Dim item As String
  item = InputBox("Item to Add:")
  lstOxys.Items.Add(item)
End Sub

Private Sub lstOxys_DoubleClick(...) Handles lstOxys.DoubleClick
  lstOxys.Items.RemoveAt(lstOxys.SelectedIndex)
  txtSelected.Clear()
End Sub
```

[Run, add some items and then click on an item of the list box.]

Filling a List Box at Design Time

The following steps show how to fill a list box at design time. (This method is used in Example 2.)

1. Select the Items property of the list box.
2. Click on the ellipsis button on the right side of the Settings box. (A window titled String Collection Editor will be displayed.)
3. Type in the first item, and press Enter.
4. Repeat Step 3 for each of the other items.
5. When you are finished entering items, click on the OK button.

Using an Array to Fill a List Box

After the elements of an array have been assigned values, these values can be placed in a list box with a single statement of the form

```
lstBox.DataSource = arrayName
```

Example 3 uses this type of statement to accomplish the same task as Example 2.

■ The Combo Box Control

A combo box is best thought of as a text box with a helping list box attached. With an ordinary text box, the user must type information into the box. With two types of combo boxes, the user has the option of either typing in information or just selecting the appropriate piece of information from a list. The information is then displayed at the top of the combo box. The three types of combo box, called Simple, DropDown, and DropDownList, are specified by the DropDownStyle property. See Figure 9.1. DropDown combo boxes are used in Windows applications as text boxes with a "history list" (list of past entries) from which you can either type a new entry or select an old entry. The standard prefix for the name of a combo box is *cbo*.

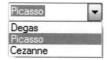

Simple combo box   DropDown (and DropDownList) combo box

FIGURE 9.1   Styles of combo boxes.

With a Simple combo box, the list is always visible. With a DropDown combo box, the list drops down when the user clicks on the arrow and then disappears after a selection is made. In either case, when an item from the list is highlighted, the item automatically appears in the text box at the top and its value is assigned to the Text property of the combo box. The DropDownList combo box looks like the DropDown combo box; the difference is that the user can only select an item from the list and cannot type into the text box.

Combo boxes have essentially the same properties, events, and methods as list boxes. In particular, all the statements discussed for list boxes also hold for combo boxes. The Text property determines what appears at the top of the combo box before the user accesses the combo box. The DropDownStyle property of a combo box must be specified at design time.

   Example 2   The following program uses a Simple combo box to obtain a person's title for the first line of the address of a letter. **Note:** At design time, first set the combo box's DropDownStyle property to Simple, and then lengthen the height of the combo box.

OBJECT	PROPERTY	SETTING
frmAddress	Text	Letter Address
lblTitle	Text	Title
cboTitle	Items	Mr.
		Ms.
		Dr.
		The Honorable
		Her Excellency
	DropDownStyle	Simple
	Text	(blank)
lblName	Text	Name:
txtName		
btnDisplay	Text	Display Full Name
txtDisplay	ReadOnly	True

```
Private Sub btnDisplay_Click(...) Handles btnDisplay.Click
  txtDisplay.Text = cboTitle.Text & " " & txtName.Text
End Sub
```

[Run, select an item from the combo box, type a name into the Name text box, and click the button.]

The same program with a style DropDown or DropDownList combo box produces the output shown below.

 Example 3 The following variation of Example 2 uses the same form design and settings as Example 2 except that there is no Items setting for cboTitle.

```
Private Sub frmAddress_Load(...) Handles MyBase.Load
  Dim titles() As String = {"Mr.", "Ms.", "Dr.", _
                            "The Honorable", "Her Excellency"}
  'Fill combo box with elements from array
  cboTitle.DataSource = titles
End Sub

Private Sub btnDisplay_Click(...) Handles btnDisplay.Click
  txtDisplay.Text = cboTitle.Text & " " & txtName.Text
End Sub
```

■ The OpenFileDialog Control

Windows applications, such as Word, Excel, and Notepad, all provide the same standard Open dialog box to help you specify the file you want to open. Figure 9.2 shows an Open dialog box that could be used with Notepad to open a text file. The same Open

FIGURE 9.2   An Open dialog box.

dialog box, with all its functionality, is available to Visual Basic programs courtesy of the OpenFileDialog control.

The OpenFileDialog control is in the Dialogs section of the Toolbox. When you place the control on a form it will not be visible. The icon and the default name, OpenFileDialog1, appear in the pane below the Main area. (We will not change the name since the default name completely describes the control's function.) The only property we will set for the control is the Filter property, which determines what text appears in the "Files of type:" combo box and what types of files will be displayed in the Main region of the dialog box. The simplest setting has the form

*text for combo box| * .ext*

where *ext* is a two- or three-letter extension describing the types of files to display. For our purposes, the most used setting for the Filter property will be

Text Documents (*.TXT)|*.TXT

The statement

OpenFileDialog1.ShowDialog()

brings the Open dialog box into play. After a file has been selected and the Open button pressed, the value of

OpenFileDialog1.*FileName*

will be the file's filespec; including drive, path, file name, and extension.

Example 4 The following program displays the contents of a text file selected by the user with an Open dialog box:

OBJECT	PROPERTY	SETTING
frmDisplayFile	Text	Display Contents of a File
btnSelect	Text	Select a Text File
lstOutput		
OpenFileDialog1	Filter	Text Documents (*.TXT) I *.TXT

```
Private Sub btnSelect_Click(...) Handles btnSelect.Click
  Dim textFile As String
  OpenFileDialog1.ShowDialog() 'Open dialog box appears and program
                               'pauses until a selection is made
  textFile = OpenFileDialog1.FileName
  Dim sr As IO.StreamReader = IO.File.OpenText(textFile)
  lstOutput.Items.Clear()
  Do While sr.Peek <> -1
    lstOutput.Items.Add(sr.ReadLine)
  Loop
  sr.Close()
End Sub
```

[Run, and press the button. (Assume that the user makes choices leading to the situation in Figure 9.2.) Select the file USPRES.TXT, and click on the Open button in the dialog box.]

Practice Problems 9.1

1. Write code to copy the contents of a list box into a file.
2. Give a statement that will display the last item in the combo box cboBox.

EXERCISES 9.1

For Exercises 1 through 16, suppose that the list box lstBox is as shown and determine the effect of the code. (Assume that the Sorted property is set to True.)

```
Bach
Beethoven
Chopin
Mozart
Tchaikovsky
```

1. ```
txtOutput.Text = lstBox.Text
```
2. ```
lstBox.Text = CStr(lstBox.Items(1))
```
3. ```
txtOutput.Text = CStr(lstBox.Items(lstBox.Items.Count - 1))
```
4. ```
txtOutput.Text = CStr(lstBox.Item(lstBox.SelectedIndex))
```
5. ```
txtOutput.Text = CStr(lstBox.SelectedIndex)
```
6. ```
txtOutput.Text = lstBox.Text & ", Hawaii!"
```
7. ```
lstBox.Items.Add("Molokai")
```
8. ```
lstBox.Items.Remove("Kauai")
```
9. ```
lstBox.Items.RemoveAt(0)
```
10. ```
lstBox.Items.RemoveAt(lstBox.SelectedIndex)
```
11. ```
lstBox.Items.RemoveAt(lstBox.Items.Count - 1)
```
12. ```
lstBox.Items.Clear()
```
13. ```
Dim total As Integer = 0
For n As Integer = 0 To lstBox.Items.Count - 1
  If InStr(lstBox.Items(n), "i") <> 0 Then
    total += 1
  End If
Next
txtOutput.Text = CStr(total)
```
14. ```
Dim sw As IO.StreamWriter = IO.File.CreateText("HAWAIIAN_ISLANDS.TXT")
For n As Integer = 0 To lstBox.Items.Count - 1
  sw.WriteLine(lstBox.Items(n))
Next
sw.Close()
```
15. ```
Dim island(10) As String
For n As Integer = 0 To lstBox.Items.Count - 1
  island(n) = CStr(lstBox.Items(n))
Next
lstBox.Items.Clear()
lstBox.Sorted = False
For n As Integer = lstBox.Items.Count - 1 To 0 Step -1
  lstBox.Items.Add(island(n))
Next
```
```

16.
```
Dim island(100) As String
Dim highestIndex As Integer = lstBox.Items.Count - 1
For n As Integer = 0 To highestIndex
  island(n) = CStr(lstBox.Items(n))
Next
lstBox.Items.Clear()
lstBox.Sorted = False
For n As Integer = highestIndex To 0 Step -1
  lstBox.Items.Add(island(n))
Next
```

In Exercises 17 through 26, assume that the Simple combo box cboBox appears as shown and that the Sorted property is set to True. Give a statement or statements that will carry out the stated task. (The statements should do the job even if additional items were added to the list.)

17. Highlight the name Moliere.

18. Highlight the first item of the list.

19. Delete the name Dante.

20. Delete the name Goethe.

21. Delete the last name in the list.

22. Insert the name Cervantes.

23. Display the odd indexed items in a list box, lstOutput.

24. Delete every item beginning with the letter S.

25. Determine if Cervantes is in the list.

26. Store the items in the file AUTHORS.TXT.

In Exercises 27 through 32, suppose that the form has a list box containing positive single-digit numbers, a button, and a text box. Write a Click event procedure for the button that displays the requested information in the text box.

27. The average of the numbers in the list box.

28. The largest number in the list box.

29. The smallest number in the list box.

30. The number of digits in the list box that are greater than the average.

31. The range of the numbers in the list box. The range is the difference betweeen the largest and smallest numbers.

32. The median of the numbers in the list. (The *median* of a set of *n* numbers is a number such that half the *n* numbers fall below the median, and half fall above. If the number of numbers *n* is odd, the median is the middle number when the numbers are arranged

in ascending order. If the number of numbers *n* is even, the median is the average of the two middle numbers when the numbers are arranged in ascending order.)

33. The file EURO_MEMBER_STATES.TXT contains the names of 15 member states that use the euro as their official currency. Use a list box to sort the names into alphabetical order, and then place the alphabetized list into a new ordered file named EURO_MEMBER_STATES_SORTED.TXT.

34. Write a program that contains a list box (with Sorted = False), a label, and two buttons captioned "Add an Item" and "Delete an Item". When the Add an Item button is clicked, the program should request an item with an input dialog box and then insert the item above the currently highlighted item. When the Delete an Item button is clicked, the program should remove the highlighted item from the list. At all times, the label should display the number of items in the list.

35. Consider the Length Converter in Figure 9.3. Write a program to place the items in the lists and carry out the conversion. (See the first programming project in Chapter 7 for a table of equivalent lengths.)

FIGURE 9.3   Form for Exercise 35.

36. Write a program that computes sales commissions using two combo boxes. One combo box is for the user to select a pre-set sales amount which ranges from $1,000 to $10,000 in $1,000 increments. Populate this combo box during the Form_Load event by using an appropriate loop. The other combo box lists the company's sales positions by full title. The positions are Senior Partner (SP), Partner (P), Senior Associate (SA), Junior Associate (JA) and Trainee (T). Each position earns a different sales commission. The commission rates are SP=25%, P=20%, SA=15%, JA=10%, and T=5%. Display the sales commission once the user has selected an amount and a position.

37. Write a program that allows a user to first select an mp3/video player *brand* from a combo box. Once the user selects a brand, display a list box of model choices (see table below) based upon the brand selected. This list box should not be visible until a brand is selected. When the user selects a model choice from the lsit box, display a descriptive phrase in a text box of what the user selected.

Brand	Model Options
SanDisk Sansa	1 GB Clip MP3 Player
	8 GB MP3 Video Player
Microsoft Zune	80 GB MP3 Video Player
	30 GB MP3 Video Player
	16 GB MP3 Video Player
Apple Ipod	Touch
	Classic
	Nano
	Shuffle

Solutions to Practice Problems 9.1

```
1. Sub SaveListBox()
     Dim sw As IO.StreamWriter = IO.File.CreateText("LISTDATA.TXT")
     For i As Integer = 0 To lstBox.Items.Count - 1
       sw.WriteLine(lstBox.Items(i))
     Next
     sw.Close()
   End Sub

2. txtBox.Text = CStr(cboBox.Items(cboBox.Items.Count - 1))
```

9.2   Seven Elementary Controls

■ The Group Box Control

Group boxes are passive objects used to group related sets of controls for visual effect. You rarely write event procedures for group boxes. The group box above has a group of three text boxes attached to it. When you move the group box, the attached controls follow as a unit. If you hide the group box, the attached controls will be hidden as well. To attach a control to a group box, just create the control any way you like, and drag it inside the group box. As shown later in this section, the group box control is particularly important when working with groups of radio button controls. The standard prefix for the name of a group box is *grp*. The title sunk into the border can be set with the Text property. Although group boxes cannot receive the focus, they can have an access key that sends the focus to the first control inside the group box that can receive the focus.

■ The Check Box Control

A check box, which consists of a small square and a caption (set with the Text property), presents the user with a yes/no choice. The form in Example 1 uses four check box controls. The Checked property of a check box has the value False when the square is empty and True when the square is checked. At run time, the user clicks on the square (or its accompanying caption) to toggle between the unchecked and checked states. So doing also triggers the CheckedChanged event.

 Example 1   The following program allows an employee to compute the monthly cost of various benefit packages:

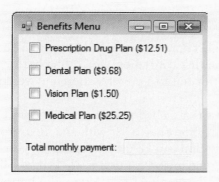

OBJECT	PROPERTY	SETTING
frmBenefits	Text	Benefits Menu
chkDrugs	Text	Prescription Drug Plan ($12.51)
chkDental	Text	Dental Plan ($9.68)
chkVision	Text	Vision Plan ($1.50)
chkMedical	Text	Medical Plan ($25.25)
lblTotal	Text	Total monthly payment:
txtTotal	ReadOnly	True

```
Private Sub Tally(...) Handles chkDrugs.CheckedChanged,_
                      chkDental.CheckedChanged,_
                      chkVision.CheckedChanged, chkMedical.CheckChanged
  Dim sum As Double = 0
  If chkDrugs.Checked Then
    sum += 12.51
  End If
  If chkDental.Checked Then
    sum += 9.68
  End If
  If chkVision.Checked Then
    sum += 1.5
  End If
  If chkMedical.Checked Then
    sum += 25.25
  End If
  txtTotal.Text = FormatCurrency(sum)
End Sub
```

[Run, and then click on the desired options.]

When a check box has the focus, the spacebar can be used to check (or uncheck) the box and invoke the CheckedChanged event. In addition, the state of a check box can be toggled from the keyboard without first setting the focus to the check box, if you create an access key for the check box by including an ampersand in the Text property. (At run time, access keys appear underlined after the Alt key is pressed.) For instance, if the Text property for the Dental Plan in Example 1 is set as "&Dental Plan", then the user can check (or uncheck) the box by pressing Alt + D.

■ The Radio Button Control

Radio buttons are used to give the user a single choice from several options. The name "radio button" comes from a reference to the first car radios, which had buttons that pressed in. Pressing one button would move the dial to a preset station and would raise any other button that was depressed.

Normally, a group of several radio buttons is attached to a group box. Each button consists of a small circle accompanied by a caption that is set with the Text property. (As with a button and a check box, an ampersand can be used to create an access key for a radio button.) When a circle or its accompanying caption is clicked, a solid dot appears in the circle and the button is said to be "on." At most one radio button in a group can be on at the same time. Therefore, if one button is on and another button in the group is clicked, the first button will turn off. By convention, the names of radio buttons have the prefix *rad*. A single form can have several groups of radio buttons. However, each group must be attached to its own group box or to the form itself (with only one group on the form).

The Checked property of a radio button tells if the button is on or off. The property

```
radButton.Checked
```

is True when radButton is on and False when radButton is off. The statement

```
radButton.Checked = True
```

turns on radButton and turns off all other buttons in its group. The statement

```
radButton.Checked = False
```

turns off radButton and has no effect on the other buttons in its group.

The CheckedChanged event for a radio button is triggered when an off button is turned on or an on button is turned off. Therefore, CheckedChanged events are usually triggered in pairs. In many programming situations, the best way to determine which radio button is selected is to employ a button control as in Example 2.

  Example 2   The following voting program allows undervotes (voting for neither), but prevents overvotes (voting for both):

OBJECT	PROPERTY	SETTING
frmBallot	Text	Vote for One
grpCandidates	Text	President
radCandidate1	Text	&Kennedy
	Checked	False
radCandidate2	Text	&Nixon
	Checked	False
btnVote	Text	Cast Vote
txtVote	ReadOnly	True

```
Private Sub btnVote_Click(...) Handles btnVote.Click
  If radCandidate1.Checked Then
    txtVote.Text = "You voted for Kennedy."
  ElseIf radCandidate2.Checked Then
    txtVote.Text = "You voted for Nixon."
  Else
    txtVote.Text = "You voted for neither."
  End If
End Sub
```

[Run, click on one of the radio buttons, and then click the Cast Vote button.]

■ The Timer Control

The **timer** control, which is invisible during run time, triggers an event after a specified amount of time has passed. (The timer control is found only in the *All Windows Forms* group of the Toolbox. When you double-click on the timer control in the Toolbox, it appears in a separate pane called the **tray**, at the bottom part of the Form Designer.) The length of time, measured in milliseconds, is set with the Interval property to be any integer from 1 to 2,147,483,647 (about 596 hours). The event triggered each time Timer1.Interval milliseconds elapses is called Timer1.Tick. In order to begin timing, a timer must first be turned on by setting its Enabled property to True. A timer is turned off by setting its Enabled property to False. The standard prefix for the name of a timer control is *tmr*.

Example 3 The following program creates a stopwatch that updates the time every tenth of a second.

OBJECT	PROPERTY	SETTING
frmStopwatch	Text	Stopwatch
btnStart	Text	Start
lblSeconds	Text	Seconds:
txtSeconds	ReadOnly	True
btnStop	Text	Stop
tmrWatch	Interval	100
	Enabled	False

```
Private Sub btnStart_Click(...) Handles btnStart.Click
  txtSeconds.Text = "0"      'Reset watch
  tmrWatch.Enabled = True
End Sub

Private Sub btnStop_Click(...) Handles btnStop.Click
  tmrWatch.Enabled = False
End Sub

Private Sub tmrWatch_Tick(...) Handles tmrWatch.Tick
  'Next line displays the time rounded to one decimal place
  txtSeconds.Text = CStr((CDbl(txtSeconds.Text) + 0.1))
End Sub
```

[Run, click the Start button, wait 10.5 seconds, and click the Stop button.]

■ The Picture Box Control

The **picture box** control is designed to hold drawings created with graphics commands or pictures stored in graphics files such as .BMP files created with Windows Paint, ICO files of icons that come with Windows, or GIF and JPEG images used on the World Wide Web.

A statement of the form

```
picBox.CreateGraphics.DrawRectangle(Pens.Blue, x, y, w, h)
```

where x, y, w, h are of type Integer, draws a blue rectangle of width w pixels and height h pixels in the picture box. The upper-left corner of the rectangle will be x pixels from the left side and *y* pixels from the top side of the picture box. (See Figure 9.4.) To get a feel for how big a pixel is, the initial size of the form when you create a new project is 300 pixels by 300 pixels.

FIGURE 9.4   Rectangle arguments.

The color Blue can be replaced by other colors. If DrawRectangle is replaced with DrawEllipse, the statement just displayed will draw the ellipse that would be inscribed in the rectangle just described. Also, if *w* and *h* have the same value, the ellipse will be a circle with a diameter of that value. In Figure 9.5, the picture box has a size of 140 by 140 pixels, a white background, and a FixedSingle border style. The circle is drawn with the statement

```
picBox.CreateGraphics.DrawEllipse(Pens.Red, 35, 35, 70, 70)
```

FIGURE 9.5   Picture box containing red circle.

A picture can be placed in a picture box control with the Image property. If you double-click on the Image property during design time, an Open dialog box appears and assists you in selecting an appropriate file. However, prior to setting the Image property, you should set the SizeMode property. If the SizeMode property is set to AutoSize, the picture box control will be resized to fit the picture. If the SizeMode property is set to StretchImage, the picture will be resized to fit the picture box control. Therefore, with the StretchImage setting, pictures can be reduced (by placing them into a small picture box control) or enlarged (by placing them into a picture box control bigger than the picture). Figure 9.6 shows a picture created with Paint and reduced by StretchImage to fit the picture box. By convention, names of picture box controls have the prefix *pic*.

FIGURE 9.6   Picture box with desert scene.

A picture also can be assigned to a picture box control at run time. However, a statement such as

```
picBox.Image = filespec
```

will not do the job. Instead, we must use the Image object with a statement such as

```
picBox.Image = Image.FromFile(filespec)
```

The SizeMode property can be altered at run time with a statement such as

```
picBox.SizeMode = PictureBoxSizeMode.AutoSize
```

■ The Horizontal and Vertical Scroll Bar Controls

Figure 9.7 shows the two types of **scroll bars**. When the user clicks on one of the arrow buttons, the scroll box moves a small amount toward that arrow. When the user clicks between the scroll box and one of the arrow buttons, the scroll box moves a large amount toward that arrow. The user can also move the scroll box by dragging it. The main properties of a scroll bar control are Minimum, Maximum, Value, SmallChange, and LargeChange, which are set to integers. At any time, hsbBar.Value is a number between hsbBar.Minimum and hsbBar.Maximum determined by the position of the left side of the scroll box. If the left side of the scroll box is halfway between the two arrows, then hsbBar.Value is a number halfway between hsbBar.Minimum and hsbBar.Maximum. If the scroll box is near the left arrow button, then hsbBar.Value is an appropriately proportioned value near hsbBar.Minimum. When an arrow button is clicked, hsbBar.Value changes by hsbBar.SmallChange and the scroll box moves accordingly. When the bar between the scroll box and one of the arrows is clicked, hsbBar.Value changes by hsbBar.LargeChange and the scroll box moves accordingly. When the scroll box is dragged, hsbBar.Value changes accordingly. The default values of Minimum, Maximum, Value, SmallChange, and LargeChange are 0, 100, 0, 1, and 10, respectively. However, these values are usually set at design time. The width of the scroll box is equal to the value of LargeChange. Since hsbBar.Value is determined by the left side of the scroll box, the greatest value it can assume is (hsbBar.Maximum − hsbBar.LargeChange + 1). Vertical scroll bars behave similarly.

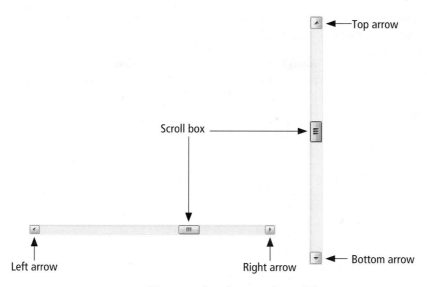

FIGURE 9.7 Horizontal and vertical scroll bars.

Note: The setting for the Minimum property must be less than the setting for the Maximum property. The Minimum property determines the values for the left and top arrows. The Maximum property determines the values for the right and bottom arrows.

The Scroll event is triggered whenever any part of the scroll bar is clicked.

✔ **Example 4** The following program uses scroll bars to move a smiling face around the form. The face is a large Wingdings character J inside a label. The values lblFace.Left and lblFace.Top are the distances in pixels of the label from the left side and top of the form. (One inch is about 88 pixels.)

OBJECT	PROPERTY	SETTING
frmFace	Text	Smiling Face
hsbXPos	Minimum	0
	Maximum	300
	SmallChange	10
	LargeChange	50
	Value	0
vsbYPos	Minimum	30
	Maximum	300
	SmallChange	10
	LargeChange	50
	Value	30
lblFace	Text	J
	Font	Wingdings, 24pt

```
Private Sub hsbXpos_Scroll(...) Handles hsbXpos.Scroll
  lblFace.Left = hsbXpos.Value
End Sub

Private Sub vsbYpos_Scroll(...) Handles vsbYpos.Scroll
  lblFace.Top = vsbYpos.Value
End Sub
```

[Run, and move the scroll boxes on the scroll bars.]

Practice Problem 9.2

What is the difference between a set of check boxes attached to a group box and a set of radio buttons attached to a group box?

EXERCISES 9.2

In Exercises 1 through 16, determine the effect of setting the property to the value shown.

1. `GroupBox1.Text = "Average Salary"`
2. `CheckBox1.Checked = True`
3. `CheckBox1.Checked = False`
4. `CheckBox1.Text = "&Spice"`
5. `RadioButton1.Checked = False`
6. `RadioButton1.Text = "Punt"`
7. `HScrollBar2.Value = HScrollBar2.Maximum - HScrollBar2.LargeChange + 1`
8. `HScrollBar2.Value = CInt((HScrollBar2.Maximum + HScrollBar2.Min) / 2)`
9. `VScrollBar2.SmallChange = VScrollBar2.LargeChange`

10. `Timer1.Interval = 3000`
11. `Timer1.Interval = CInt(intVar * 1000)`
12. `Timer1.Enabled = False`
13. `PictureBox1.SizeMode = PictureBoxSizeMode.StretchImage`
14. `PictureBox1.CreateGraphics.DrawEllipse(Pens.Blue, 20, 30, 100, 100)`
15. `PictureBox1.CreateGraphics.DrawRectangle(Pens.Green, 25, 50, 200, 100)`
16. `PictureBox1.Image = Image.FromFile("AIRPLANE.BMP")`

In Exercises 17 through 24, write one or more lines of code to carry out the task.

17. Set the caption for RadioButton1 to "Female".
18. Clear the small rectangular box of CheckBox1.
19. Turn off RadioButton1.
20. Move the scroll box of VScrollBar2 as low as possible.
21. Move the scroll box of HScrollBar2 one-third of the way from the left arrow to the right arrow.
22. Specify that Timer1 trigger an event every tenth of a second.
23. Draw a yellow circle of diameter 100 pixels in PictureBox1.
24. Specify that Timer1 cease to trigger the Tick event.

In Exercises 25 and 26, determine the state of the two radio buttons after the button is clicked.

25.
```
Private Sub Button1_Click(...) Handles Button1.Click
    RadioButton1.Checked = True
    RadioButton2.Checked = True
End Sub
```

26.
```
Private Sub Button1_Click(...) Handles Button1.Click
    RadioButton1.Checked = False
    RadioButton2.Checked = False
End Sub
```

27. Which of the controls presented in this section can receive the focus? Design a form containing all of the controls, and repeatedly press the Tab key to confirm your answer.

28. Create a form with two group boxes, each having two radio buttons attached to it. Run the program, and confirm that the two pairs of radio buttons operate independently of each other.

29. Suppose that a group box has two radio buttons attached to it. If the statement

    `GroupBox1.Visible = False`

    is executed, will the radio buttons also vanish? Test your answer.

30. Why are radio buttons also called "option buttons"?

A form contains a button and a group box with three check boxes named CheckBox1, CheckBox2, and CheckBox3 attached to it. In Exercises 31 and 32, write a Click event procedure for the button that displays the stated information in a text or list box when the button is clicked.

31. The number of boxes checked.

32. The captions of the checked boxes.

33. A hot dog street vender offers three types of hot dogs 'The Snack' ($1), 'The Sausage' ($2), or 'The Monster' ($4). The customer can order any of the following additional options: chili ($1), cheese ($.75), and sauerkraut ($.50). Write a program that computes the cost of the hot dog sale with options.

34. Write a program that lists 10 outdoor hobbies/activities as checkboxes inside of a group box. When a user clicks any checkbox, display the total number of checkboxes that are currently checked in a read-only text box control.

35. The Programs Ch09\Pictures folder contains files named MOON1.BMP, MOON2.BMP, ..., MOON8.BMP, which show eight phases of the moon. Create a form consisting of a picture box control and a timer control. Every two seconds assign another file to the Image property of the picture box control to see the moon cycle through its phases every 16 seconds. One phase is shown in Figure 9.8.

FIGURE 9.8   Form for Exercise 35.

36. Subscribers to the Matinee Series for a recent season at the Kennedy Center for the Performing Arts had to select four performances out of the six shown in the Matinee Series form in Figure 9.9 and had to indicate the method of payment. Write the Click event procedure for the button. The procedure should first determine whether exactly four performances have been checked. If not, the user should be so informed with a message dialog box. Then the method of payment should be examined. If no method has been indicated, the user must be reminded to select one. Depending on the method of payment, the user should be told with a message box to either mail in the check with the order form or give the credit card number with an input dialog box request. At the end of the process, the caption on the button should change to "Thank You".

37. Write a program to synchronize two speedometers (two horizontal scroll bars). The minimum speed (value) should be 0 and the max in mph should be 80. When the horizontal scroll box of either speedometer is moved, the other speedometer moves to the corresponding speed and each speed is displayed next to the speedometer. *Note*: 1 mph = 1.609344 kph.

38. Write a program to create a stopwatch with start, lap, stop, and reset functions. The stopwatch only needs to keep time in seconds accurate to a hundredth of second (000.0). Allow the program to store up to 10 lap times in a list box. In addition, display the current date in the lower right corner of the form. (*Hint*: Use `FormatDateTime(Now, DateFormat.LongDate)`).

39. *Simulation of Times Square Ball.* Create a form with a vertical scroll bar and a timer control. When the program is run, the scroll box should be at the top of the scroll bar. Each second the scroll box should descend one-tenth of the way down. When the scroll box reaches the bottom after 10 seconds, a message box displaying HAPPY NEW YEAR should appear.

FIGURE 9.9   Form for Exercise 36.

FIGURE 9.10   Form for Exercise 37.

FIGURE 9.11   Form for Exercise 38.

40. Write a program for a cannon ball game where the objective is to hit a stationary target (picTarget) with a cannon ball (picBall). The cannon ball should start at

the lower right corner on top of the ground image (picGround). A scroll bar should be used to change the launch velocity. The cannon ball should be launched at a 45 degree angle. A label should be used to indicate the current velocity setting. Include a button that fires the cannon ball and another that resets the cannon ball back to its original location. The fire button should be disabled after being clicked. The reset button should enable it again. Use message boxes to indicate a 'hit' or a 'miss' (a miss is when the cannon ball hits the ground or goes off the form to the right). Use a timer control to control the flight time of the cannon ball. Enable it when fired and disable the timer when the cannon ball strikes another object. Use Figure 9.X as a guide. The figure shows the cannon ball during its curved flight. *Notes:* Use class-level variables for the time, horizontal velocity, vertical velocity, initial starting point for the cannon ball and for the gravitational constant = 9.81. When the form loads, the initial location of the cannon ball object should be noted using the picture box's Left and Top properties. The horizontal and vertical velocities can be determined by the following equations:

```
vX = v * Math.Cos(45)
vY = v * Math.Sin(45)
```

Where vX is the horizontal velocity and vY is the vertical velocity and v is the velcoty obtained from the horizontal scroll bar value when the cannon ball is fired.

The timer event should contain the code to move the cannon ball by setting its Left and Top properties. The movement is controlled by the following equations:

```
ballX = vX * ftime + Xo
ballY = 0.5 * GRAV * ftime ^ 2 - (vY * ftime) + Yo
```

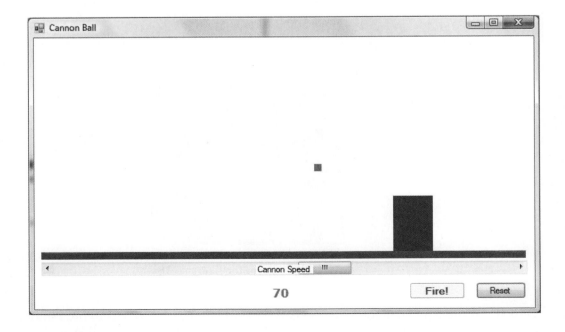

Where vX is the horizontal velocity and vY is the vertical velocity and v is the velocity obtained from the horizontal scroll bar value when the cannon ball is fired. The timer tick event should contain the code to move the cannon ball by setting its Left and Top properties. You may need to play with the timer interval setting and time increment amount in order to get an even flight. The movement is controlled by the following equations:

```
picBall.Left = ballX
picBall.Top  = ballY
```

Solution to Practice Problems 9.2

With radio buttons, at most one button can be on at any given time, whereas several check boxes can be checked simultaneously.

9.3 Four Additional Objects

■ The Clipboard Object

The **Clipboard** object is used to copy or move information from one location to another. It is maintained by Windows and therefore even can be used to transfer information from one Windows application to another. It is actually a portion of memory that holds information and has no properties or events.

If *str* is a string, then the statement

```
Clipboard.SetText(str)
```

replaces any text currently in the Clipboard with the value of *str*. The statement

```
str = Clipboard.GetText
```

assigns the text in the Clipboard to the string variable *str*. The statement

```
Clipboard.SetText("")
```

deletes the contents of the Clipboard.

A portion of the text in a text box or combo box can be **selected** by dragging the mouse across it or by moving the cursor across it while holding down the Shift key. After you select text, you can place it into the Clipboard by pressing Ctrl + C. Also, if the cursor is in a text box and you press Ctrl + V, the contents of the Clipboard will be pasted at the cursor position. These tasks also can be carried out in code. The SelectedText property of a text box holds the selected string from the text box, and a statement such as

```
Clipboard.SetText(txtBox.SelectedText)
```

copies this selected string into the Clipboard. The statement

```
txtBox.SelectedText = Clipboard.GetText
```

replaces the selected portion of txtBox with the contents of the Clipboard. If nothing has been selected, the statement inserts the contents of the Clipboard into txtBox at the cursor position. The Clipboard can actually hold any type of data, including graphics. Any time you use the Copy menu item, you are putting information into the Clipboard. The Paste menu item sends that data to your program.

■ The Random Class

Visual Basic has a useful object called a random number generator that is declared with a statement of the form

```
Dim randomNum As New Random
```

If m and n are whole numbers, with $m < n$, then the value of

```
randomNum.Next(m, n)
```

is a randomly selected whole number from m through n, including m but excluding n. The Next method of this built-in object allows us to produce some interesting applications.

 Example 1   The DC Lottery number is obtained by selecting a Ping-Pong ball from each of three separate bowls. Each ball is numbered with an integer from 0 through 9. The following program produces a lottery number. Such a program is said to **simulate** the selection of Ping-Pong balls.

```
Private Sub btnSelect_Click(...) Handles btnSelect.Click
  'Display the winning lottery number
  Dim randomNum As New Random
  Dim num1, num2, num3 As Integer
  num1 = randomNum.Next(0, 10)
  num2 = randomNum.Next(0, 10)
  num3 = randomNum.Next(0, 10)
  txtNumbers.Text = num1 & "   " & num2 & "   " & num3
End Sub
```

[Run, and then press the button.]

■ The MenuStrip Control

Visual Basic forms can have menu bars similar to those in most Windows applications. Figure 9.12 shows a typical menu, with the Order menu revealed. Here, the menu bar contains two menu items (Order and Color), referred to as **top-level** menu items. When the Order menu item is clicked, a drop-down list containing two second-level menu items (Ascending and Descending) appears. Although not visible here, the dropdown list under Color contains the two second-level menu items Foreground and Background. Each menu item is treated as a distinct control that responds to a click event. The click event is triggered not only by the click of the mouse button, but also for top-level items by pressing Alt + accessKey and for second-level items by just pressing the access key. The event procedure for the Ascending or Descending menu item also can be triggered by pressing the shortcut key combination Ctrl + A or Ctrl + D.

FIGURE 9.12   A simple menu.

Menus are created with the MenuStrip control, which is usually the third control in the Menus & Toolbars section of the Toolbox. Each menu item has a Text property (what the user sees) and a Name property (used to refer to the item in the code.) The following steps are used to create the Order-Color menu:

1. Start a new program.

2. Double-click on the MenuStrip control in the Toolbox. The control appears in a pane below the Main area, and a menu designer appears just below the title bar in the Form Designer. See Figure 9.13.

3. Click on the rectangle that says "Type Here", type in the text &Order, and press the Enter key. (The ampersand specifies O as an access key for the menu item.)

"Type Here" rectangles appear below and to the right of the Order menu item. The rectangle below is used to create a second-level item for the Order menu. The rectangle on the right is used to create a new first-level menu item.

4. Type the text "&Ascending" into the rectangle below the Order rectangle, and press the Enter key.

5. Click on the Ascending menu item to display its Property window. In the Property window, change the Name property of the menu item from AscendingToolStrip-MenuItem to mnuOrderAsc. Also, click on the down-arrow at the right of the ShortcutKeys setting box, click on the "Ctrl" Modifier check box, select "A" from the Key drop-down combo box, and then press the Enter key. (When the program is run, "Ctrl + A" will appear to the right of the word "Ascending".)

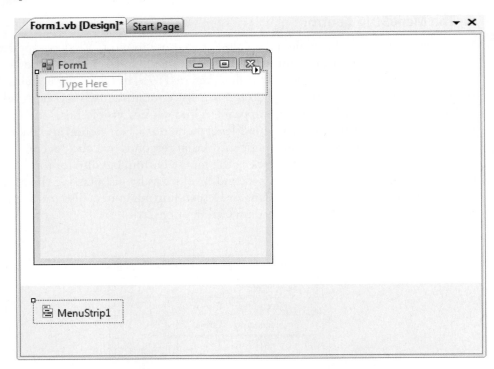

FIGURE 9.13 **The MenuStrip control added to a form.**

6. Type "&Descending" into the rectangle below the Ascending rectangle, set the Name property of the Descending menu item to mnuOrderDesc, and set the ShortcutKeys Property to Ctrl + D.

7. Click on the rectangle to the right of the Order rectangle and enter the text "&Color".

8. Type "&Foreground" into the rectangle below the Color rectangle, and set its Name property to mnuColorFore.

9. Type "&Background" into the rectangle below the Foreground rectangle, and set its Name property to mnuColorBack.

10. Click on the Foreground rectangle, and type "&Red" into the rectangle on its right. (We have just created a third-level menu item.) Set its Name property to mnuColorForeRed.

11. Type "&Blue" into the rectangle below the Red rectangle, and set its Name property to mnuColorForeBlue.

12. Click on the Background rectangle, type "&Yellow" into the rectangle on its right, and set its Name property to mnuColorBackYellow.

13. Type "&White" into the rectangle below the Yellow rectangle, and set its Name property to mnuColorBackWhite. Then set its Checked property to True. A check mark will appear to the left of the word "White."

14. Run the program; click on Order to see its menu items; click on Color and hover over the word Foreground to see its menu items. Each menu item has a Click event procedure. The menu items are only useful after we write code for the relevant event procedures.

Example 2   The following program uses the menu just created to alter the colors of a list box and the order of its items. The form has the text "Demonstrate Menus" in its title bar.

```
Private Sub frmDemo_Load(...) Handles MyBase.Load
  lstOutput.Items.Add("makes")
  lstOutput.Items.Add("haste")
  lstOutput.Items.Add("waste")
End Sub

Private Sub mnuOrderAsc_Click(...) Handles mnuOrderAsc.Click
  lstOutput.Sorted = True
End Sub

Private Sub mnuOrderDesc_Click(...) Handles mnuOrderDesc.Click
  'This code uses the fact that if a list is in ascending order,
  'then reading it backwards gives a descending list
  Dim temp(2) As String      'Hold ascending array of items
  lstOutput.Sorted = True    'Sort the items alphabetically
  For i As Integer = 0 To 2 'Place sorted items into the array
    temp(i) = CStr(lstOutput.Items(i))
  Next
  lstOutput.Sorted = False  'Turn off the Sorted property
  lstOutput.Items.Clear()
  For i As Integer = 2 To 0 Step -1
    lstOutput.Items.Add(temp(i))
  Next
End Sub

Private Sub mnuColorForeRed_Click(...) Handles mnuColorForeRed.Click
  lstOutput.ForeColor = Color.Red
End Sub

Private Sub mnuColorForeBlue_Click(...) Handles mnuColorForeBlue.Click
  lstOutput.ForeColor = Color.Blue
End Sub

Private Sub mnuColorBackYellow_Click(...) Handles _
          mnuColorBackYellow.Click
  'Make Yellow the background color of the list box, guarantee that a
  'check mark appears in front of the menu item Yellow and not in front
  'of the White menu item
  lstOutput.BackColor = Color.Yellow
  mnuColorBackYellow.Checked = True
  mnuColorBackWhite.Checked = False
End Sub
```

```
Private Sub mnuColorBackWhite_Click(...) Handles mnuColorBackWhite.Click
  lstOutput.BackColor = Color.White
  mnuColorBackYellow.Checked = False
  mnuColorBackWhite.Checked = True
End Sub
```

[Run, click on the Ascending item in the Order menu, click on the Color menu item, hover over the Foreground item, and click on Red.]

■ Multiple Forms

A Visual Basic program can contain more than one form. Additional forms are created from the Project menu with Add Windows Form (Alt/P/F), which brings up an Add New Item dialog box. See Figure 9.14. To add the new form, select Windows Form from the Templates pane, optionally type in a name, and press the Add button. The second form has default name Form2.

FIGURE 9.14 The Add New Item dialog box.

The name of each form appears in the Solution Explorer window (see Figure 9.15), and either form can be made the active form by double-clicking on its name. (When a form is active, its Form Designer and Code Editor are displayed in the Main area.) Also, the names of both forms appear on tabs in the Main area.

FIGURE 9.15   Solution Explorer after second form is added.

The most common use of a second form is as a customized dialog box that is displayed to present a special message or request specific information. When a Message or Input dialog box appears, the user cannot shift the focus to another form without first closing the dialog box by clicking on OK or Cancel. If a form is displayed with the ShowDialog method, then the form will exhibit this same behavior. The user will not be allowed to shift the focus back to the first form until the second form disappears. Such a form is said to be **modal**. It is customary to set the FormBorderStyle property of modal forms to Fixed Dialog. When a program is run, the first form created is the only one visible. After that, the second form will appear when its ShowDialog method is executed and disappear when its Close method is invoked.

Form2 is actually a template for a form in the same manner that the TextBox class denoted by the TextBox icon on the ToolBar is a template for the actual text boxes appearing on a form. A text box on a form is said to be an **instance** of the TextBox class. An instance of Form2 is created with a statement such as

```
Dim secondForm As New Form2()
```

which also provides a variable, *secondForm*, that will be used to refer to the instance of the form.

Variables declared with Dim statements are either local (visible only to the procedure where they are declared) or class-level (visible to the entire form where they were declared). If a variable is declared in the Declarations section of Form2 with the word "Dim" replaced with "Public," then the value of the variable will be available to all forms in the program. However, when such a Public variable is used in Form1, it is referred to by an expression such as secondForm.*variableName*. (As a personal analogy, at home you might be called John, but to strangers you might be introduced as "Fred's son John" to distinguish you from anyone else named John.)

Example 3   The following program uses a second form as a dialog box to total the different sources of income. Initially, only frmIncome is visible. The user types in his or her name and then either can type in the income or click on the button for assistance in totaling the different sources of income. Clicking on the button from frmIncome causes frmSources to appear and be active. The user fills in the three text boxes and then clicks on the button to have the amounts totaled and displayed in the Total Income text box of frmIncome.

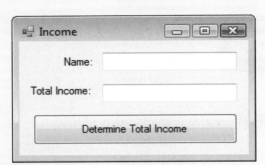

OBJECT	PROPERTY	SETTING
frmIncome	Text	Income
lblName	Text	Name:
txtName		
lblTotIncome	Text	Total Income:
txtTotIncome		
btnDetermine	Text	Determine Total Income

OBJECT	PROPERTY	SETTING
frmSources	Text	Sources of Income
	FormBorderStyle	FixedDialog
lblWages	Text	Wages:
txtWages		
lblIntIncome	Text	Interest Income:
txtIntIncome		
lblDivIncome	Text	Dividend Income:
txtDivIncome		
btnCompute	Text	Compute Total Income

```
'frmIncome's code
Private Sub btnDetermine_Click(...) Handles btnDetermine.Click
  Dim secondForm As New frmSources()      'Instantiate the second form
  secondForm.ShowDialog()  'Show second form and wait until it closes.
  '                  Then execute rest of the code in this procedure.
  txtTotIncome.Text = FormatCurrency(secondForm.sum)
End Sub


'frmSources's code
Public sum As Double   'Holds the sum of the text boxes' values
'The keyword Public makes the variable sum available to frmIncome.

Private Sub btnCompute_Click(...) Handles btnCompute.Click
  'Store the total into the Public variable sum
  sum = CDbl(txtWages.Text) + CDbl(txtIntIncome.Text) _
      + CDbl(txtDivIncome.Text)
  Me.Close() 'Close the form as it is not needed anymore
End Sub
```

[Run, enter name, click the button, and fill in the sources of income.] **Note:** After the Compute Total Income button is pressed, frmSources will disappear and the sum of the three numbers will be displayed in the Total Income text box of frmIncome.

Note: If a Structure is defined in frmIncome, it can be used as a data type in frmSources. However, in frmSources it must be referred to as frmIncome.*structureName*.

Practice Problem 9.3

What is the effect of the following event procedure?

```
Private Sub btnDisplay_Click(...) Handles btnDisplay.Click
  Dim randomNum As New Random
  Dim contestant() As String = {"Mary", "Pat", "Linda", _
                                "Barbara", "Maria"}
  Dim number As Integer, temp As String
  For i As Integer = 0 To 4
    number = randomNum.Next(i, 5)
    temp = contestant(i)
    contestant(i) = contestant(number)
    contestant(number) = temp
  Next
  lstOutput.Items.Clear()
  For i As Integer = 0 To 4
    lstOutput.Items.Add(contestant(i))
  Next
End Sub
```

EXERCISES 9.3

In Exercises 1 through 18, describe the effect of executing the statement(s).

1. ```
Clipboard.SetText("")
```

2. ```
Clipboard.SetText("Good Morning")
```

3. ```
Clipboard.SetText(txtBox.SelectedText)
```

4. ```
txtBox.SelectedText = Clipboard.GetText()
```

5. ```
txtBox.Text = Clipboard.GetText
```

6. ```
Dim strVar As String = "Option 10"
Clipboard.SetText(strVar)
```

7. ```
Dim strVar As String
strVar = Clipboard.GetText
```

8. ```
Dim randomNum As New Random
txtBox.Text = CStr(randomNum.Next(1, 100))
```

9. ```
Dim randomNum As New Random
Dim number As Integer
'Assume the array Euro() contains the names of 15 Member States using
the EURO as currency
number = randomNum.Next(0, 15)
txtBox.Text = Euro(number)
```

10. ```
Dim randomNum As New Random
'95 characters can be produced by the computer keyboard
txtBox.Text = Chr(randomNum.Next(32, 127))
```

11. ```
Dim randomNum As New Random
Dim number As Integer, temp As String
'Suppose the array golfer() contains the names of the 150 PGA golfers
number = randomNum.Next(0, 150)
lstBox.Items.Add(golfer(number))
temp = golfer(number)
golfer(number) = golfer(149)
golfer(149) = temp
lstBox.Items.Add(golfer(randomNum.Next(0, 149)))
```

12. ```
Dim randomNum As New Random
Dim suit() As String = {"Hearts", "Clubs", "Diamonds", "Spades"}
Dim denomination() As String = {"2", "3", "4", "5", "6", _
        "7", "8", "9", "10", "Jack", "Queen", "King", "Ace"}
txtBox.Text = denomination(randomNum.Next(0, 13)) & " of " & _
            suit(randomNum.Next(0, 4))
```

13. ```
mnuOrderAsc.Checked = True
```

14. ```
mnuOrderAsc.Checked = False
```

15. ```
mnuOrderAsc.Text = "Increasing Order"
```

16. ```
Me.Close()
```

17. ```
Public address As String   'In Declarations section of Form2
```
```

18. ```
Dim secondForm As New Form2()
secondForm.ShowDialog()
```

**In Exercises 19 through 34, write one or more lines of code to carry out the task.**

19. Replace the selected portion of txtBox with the contents of the Clipboard.
20. Clear out the contents of the Clipboard.
21. Place the word "Elephant" into the Clipboard.
22. Copy the selected text in txtBox into the Clipboard.
23. Delete the selected portion of txtBox.
24. Assign the contents of the Clipboard to the Integer variable *amount*.
25. Display in txtBox a randomly selected number from 1 to 10.
26. Twenty U.S. Stocks symbols are contained in the array *stocks*(). Display a randomly selected stock symbol in txtStock.
27. Display in txtBox a letter randomly selected from the alphabet.
28. The file PLAYERS.TXT contains the names of 75 professional football players. Display a randomly selected player in txtBox.
29. Display in txtBox the sum of the faces after tossing a pair of dice twice.
30. Twenty names are contained in the array *Rivers*(). Randomly select two different names from the array and display them in lstBox.
31. Remove the check mark in front of the menu item named mnuOrderDesc.
32. Change the text for mnuOrderDesc to "Decreasing Order".
33. Close the form containing the line of code.
34. Declare the Double variable *number* so that its value will be available to other forms.

**Exercises 35 and 36 refer to Example 2.**

35. Conjecture on the effect of the statement

    ```
    mnuOrderAsc.Enabled = False
    ```

    and test your conjecture.

36. Conjecture on the effect of the statement

    ```
    mnuOrderAsc.Visible = False
    ```

    and test your conjecture.

37. Write a program with a single text box and a menu with the three top-level items of File, Edit and Help. Under File are two second-level items, Hide and Exit. Hide should have a checkmark and toggle the visibility of the single text box. Exit should terminate the program. Cut, Copy and Paste are the three second-level items under Edit. Copy should place a copy of the selected portion of txtBox into the Clipboard. Paste should duplicate the contents of the Clipboard at the cursor position. Cut should delete a selected portion of the text box and place it in the Clipboard. Under Help the user can click About. When a user selects the About menu item show an About Box. The About Box can be added to your project by selecting Project–Add New Item–About Box. Figure 9.16 shows the generic About Box. You can edit the labels on the About Box by right mouse clicking on My Project in the Solution Explorer Window and clicking Open. The items are under the Assembly Information … button.
    ```

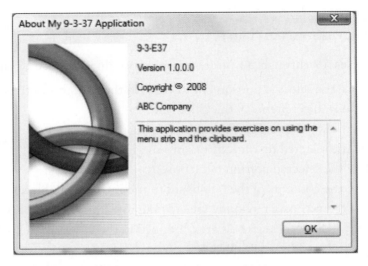

FIGURE 9.16 The About Box

38. Write a program that randomly selects three popular tourist destinations from a list box on the form. Populate the list box with the contents of the file DESTINA-TIONS.TXT on the form load event. The three randomly selected destinations should then replace the text of three radio buttons grouped together. The user then selects one of the three destination options and that destination is displayed on a label. Provide an Exit button to terminate the program.

39. The names of all the NBA teams are located in the file NBA_TEAMS.TXT. Write a program that randomly assigns a draft order for all 30 teams and displays them in order within a list box.

40. Write a program that repeatedly rolls a die and tallies the number of rolls and the number of time the number *one* was rolled. The program should stop when 1000 ones have been rolled. The program should then report the sample proportion of ones rolled by dividing 1000 by the total number of rolls. Store this proportion to the Clipboard and verify that you can paste it into a separate application such as Notepad.

41. Write a program using the form in Figure 9.17. Each time the button is pressed, a Random object is used to simulate a coin toss and the values are updated. The figure shows the status after the button has been pressed 400 times.

FIGURE 9.17 Sample run of Exercise 41.

Note: You can produce tosses quickly by just holding down the Enter key. Although the percentage of heads initially will fluctuate considerably, it should stay close to 50% after many (say, 1000) tosses.

42. Write a program containing the two forms shown in Figure 9.18. Initially, the Number to Dial form appears. When the Show Push Buttons button is clicked, the Push Button form appears. The user enters a number by clicking on successive push buttons and then clicks on Enter to have the number transferred to the read-only text box at the bottom of the first form.

FIGURE 9.18   Sample run of Exercise 42.

43. Add to the Cannon Ball program from 9-2-E40 by providing a pull-down menu options for the fire and reset buttons. Add an Exit button and a Menu item that terminates the program. The program should randomly place the target along the horizontal ground picture box every time the reset button is clicked and when the form loads. *Hint: Randomly set the picTarget.Left property using appropriate X values.*

44. *The Birthday Problem.* Given a random group of 23 people, how likely is it that two people have the same birthday? To answer this question, write a program that creates an array of 23 elements, randomly assigns to each subscripted variable one of the integers from 1 through 365, and checks to see if any of the subscripted variables have the same value. (Make the simplifying assumption that no birthdays occur on February 29.) Now expand the program to repeat the process 1000 times and determine the percentage of the time that there is a match.

45. Consider a dice game using a pair of dice in which dice are thrown and if 'snake eyes' (two 1's) are thrown you win ten dollars. If any other pair of numbers (two 2's, two 3's, etc.) is thrown you lose one dollar. Simulate playing the game 100 times and determine how much money you win or lose and display the results. Also display the number of snake eyes rolled.

Solution to Practice Problem 9.3

The event procedure places the names of the contestants in a randomly ordered list.

9.4 Graphics

In this section, we draw bar charts and pie charts in a picture box, and illustrate one method for creating animation on a form.

Caution: Since the programs in this section mix text and graphics, what you see on the monitor will vary with the monitor's DPI setting. To guarantee the intended outcomes, you should check that your monitor is set to display 96 DPI (Dots Per Inch). For details, see the first item under "Utilize the Windows Environment" in Appendix B.

■ Graphics Objects

A statement of the form

```
Dim gr As Graphics = picBox.CreateGraphics
```

declares *gr* to be a Graphics object for the picture box picBox.

The unit of measurement used in graphics methods is the **pixel**. To get a feel for how big a pixel is, the title bar of a form is 30 pixels high, and the border of a form is four pixels thick. The setting for the Size property of a picture box is two numbers separated by a comma. The two numbers give the width and height of the picture box in pixels. You can alter these numbers to specify a precise size. Each point of a picture box is identified by a pair of coordinates

```
(x, y)
```

where *x* (between 0 and picBox.Width) is its distance in pixels from the left side of the picture box, and *y* (between 0 and picBox.Height) is its distance in pixels from the top of the picture box.

Text is placed in a picture box with a statement of the form

```
gr.DrawString(string, Me.Font, Brushes.Color, x, y)
```

where *string* is either a string variable or literal, Me.Font specifies that the Form's font be used to display the text, and the upper-left corner of the first character of the text has coordinates (x, y). The color of the text is determined by *Color*. IntelliSense will provide a list of about 140 possible colors after **"Brushes."** is typed. As an example, the statements

```
Dim gr As Graphics = picBox.CreateGraphics
Dim strVar As String = "Hello"
gr.DrawString(strVar, Me.Font, Brushes.Blue, 4, 30)
gr.DrawString("World", Me.Font, Brushes.Red, 35, 50)
```

produce the output shown in Figure 9.19.

FIGURE 9.19   DrawString method.

■ Lines, Rectangles, Circles, and Sectors

Let *gr* be a Graphics object for picBox. Then the statement

```
gr.DrawLine(Pens.Color, x1, y1, x2, y2)
```

draws a straight line segment from the point with coordinates $(x1, y1)$ to the point with coordinates $(x2, y2)$. The color of the line is determined by *Color*. IntelliSense will provide an extensive list of possible colors after **"Pens."** is typed. For instance, the statement

FIGURE 9.20 **DrawLine method.**

```
gr.DrawLine(Pens.Blue, 50, 20, 120, 75)
```

draws a blue line from the point with coordinates (50, 20) to the point with coordinates (120, 75). See Figure 9.20.

The statement

```
gr.FillRectangle(Brushes.Color, x, y, w, h)
```

draws a solid rectangle of width w and height h in the color specified and having the point with coordinates (x, y) as its upper-left vertex. The left side of the rectangle will be x pixels from the left side of the picture box and the top side of the rectangle will be y pixels from the top of the picture box. For instance, the statement

```
gr.FillRectangle(Brushes.Blue, 50, 20, 70, 55)
```

draws the rectangle shown in Figure 9.21.

FIGURE 9.21 **FillRectangle method.**

The FillEllipse method draws a solid ellipse of a specified color, given the specifications of a circumscribed rectangle. The rectangle is specified by the coordinates of its upper-left point, its width, and its height. This method produces a circle when the width and height of the rectangle are the same. In particular, the statement

```
gr.FillEllipse(Brushes.Color, a - r, b - r, 2 * r, 2 * r)
```

draws a solid circle of the specified color with center (a, b) and radius r. For instance, the statement

```
gr.FillEllipse(Brushes.Blue, 80 - 40, 50 - 40, 2 * 40, 2 * 40)
```

draws a solid blue circle with center (80, 50) and radius 40. **Note:** If a rectangle were circumscribed about the circle, the rectangle would be a square with its upper-left vertex at (40, 10) and each side of length 80.

The FillPie method draws a solid sector of an ellipse in a color. The ellipse is specified by giving the coordinates, width, and height for the circumscribing rectangle, as in the FillEllipse method. The sector is determined by a radius line and the angle swept out by the radius line. We are interested solely in the case where the ellipse is a circle. The shaded region in Figure 9.22 is a typical sector (or pie shaped region) of a circle. The sector is determined by the two angles θ_1 and θ_2. The start angle, θ_1, is the angle through which the horizontal radius line must be rotated clockwise to reach the start-

FIGURE 9.22   A typical sector of a circle.

ing radius line of the sector. Angle θ_2 is the number of degrees through which the starting radius line must sweep (clockwise) to reach the ending radius line of the sector. The angles θ_1 and θ_2 are referred to as the **start angle** and the **sweep angle**, respectively. Figure 9.23 shows the start and sweep angles for three sectors of a circle.

FIGURE 9.23   FillPie method.

In general, a statement of the form

```
gr.FillPie(Brushes.Color, a - r, b - r, 2 * r, 2 * r, _
          startAngle, sweepAngle)
```

draws a sector of a circle of the specified color with center (a, b), radius r, and the given start and sweep angles. For instance, the middle image of Figure 9.22 can be drawn with a statement such as

```
gr.FillPie(Brushes.Blue, 80 - 40, 80 - 40, 2 * 40, 2 * 40, 45, 180)
```

The Brushes, Pens, and Fonts appearing in the drawing statements so far are literals of objects. Variables also can be used to provide these values. For instance, the statement **gr.FillRectangle(Brushes.Blue, 50, 20, 70, 55)** can be replaced by the pair of statements

```
Dim br As Brush = Brushes.Blue
gr.FillRectangle(br, 50, 20, 70, 55)
```

The first statement declares *br* to be a variable of type Brush and assigns it the value Brushes.Blue.

Numeric variables used in the Draw and Fill statements discussed in this section must be of type Integer or Single. The **Single data type** is similar to the Double data type, but has a smaller range. A variable of type Single can hold whole numbers, fractional, or mixed numbers between about $-3.4 \cdot 10^{38}$ and $3.4 \cdot 10^{38}$. The **CSng** function converts other data types to the Single data type.

■ Pie Charts

Consider the three pieces of data in Table 9.1. A pie chart can be used to graphically display the relative sizes of these numbers. The first step in creating a pie chart is to convert the numbers to percents. Since the total expenditures are $419 billion, the federal outlay is 33/419 ≈ .08 or 8%. Similarly, the state and local expenditures are 49% and 43%. See Table 9.2. Our goal is to write a program to display the information in the pie chart of Figure 9.24.

The blue sector in Figure 9.24 has start angle 0 and sweep angle .08 * 360. The red sector has start angle .08 * 360 and sweep angle .49 * 360. The tan sector has start angle .08 * 360 + .49 * 360 [or (.08 + .49) * 360] and sweep angle .43 * 360. Notice that

TABLE 9.1	Financing public schools (in billions).	
	Federal	$33
	State	$206
	Local	$180

TABLE 9.2	Financing public schools.	
	Federal	.08 or 8%
	State	.49 or 49%
	Local	.43 or 43%

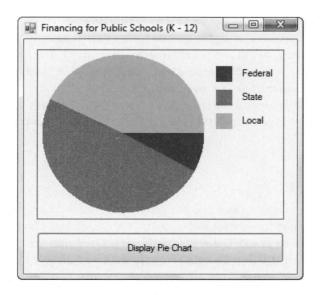

FIGURE 9.24 Pie chart for Example 1.

each start angle is (sum of previous percentages) * 360. The sweep angle for each sector is the corresponding percentage times 360.

 Example 1 The following program creates the pie chart (see Figure 9.22) for the financing of public schools. The program is written so that it can be easily converted to handle a pie chart with up to six sectors. All that is required is to change the first two Dim statements and the Me.Text statement. The "Dim br() As Brush" line, which creates an array of brushes, has six brushes in order to accommodate additional sectors.

```
Private Sub btnDisplay_Click(...) Handles btnDisplay.Click
  Dim legend() As String = {"Federal", "State", "Local"}
  Dim quantity() As Single = {33, 206, 180}
  Dim percent(quantity.GetUpperBound(0)) As Single
  Dim sumOfQuantities As Single = 0
  Dim sumOfSweepAngles As Single = 0
  Dim br() As Brush = {Brushes.Blue, Brushes.Red, Brushes.Tan, _
            Brushes.Green, Brushes.Orange, Brushes.Gray}
  Dim gr As Graphics = picOutput.CreateGraphics
  'The picture box has width 312 and height 215
  Dim r As Integer = 100     'Radius of circle
  Dim c As Integer = 105     'Center of circle has coordinates (c, c)
  Me.Text = "Financing for Public Schools (K - 12)"
  'Sum the numbers for the quantities
  For i As Integer = 0 To quantity.GetUpperBound(0)
    sumOfQuantities += quantity(i)
  Next
  'Convert the quantities to percents
  For i As Integer = 0 To quantity.GetUpperBound(0)
    percent(i) = quantity(i) / sumOfQuantities
  Next
  'Display the pie chart and the legends
  For i As Integer = 0 To quantity.GetUpperBound(0)
    gr.FillPie(br(i), c - r, c - r, 2 * r, 2 * r, _
            sumOfSweepAngles, percent(i) * 360)
    sumOfSweepAngles += percent(i) * 360
    gr.FillRectangle(br(i), 220, 20 + 30 * i, 20, 20)
    gr.DrawString(legend(i), Me.Font, Brushes.Black, 250, 22 + 30 * i)
  Next
End Sub
```

■ Bar Charts

Our goal here is to produce the bar chart of Figure 9.25 on the next page. The picture box for the chart has a width of 210 and height of 150 pixels. (Here, the BorderStyle property is set to FixedSingle for instructional reasons. In general, the bar chart will look better with the BorderStyle property left at its default setting: None.)

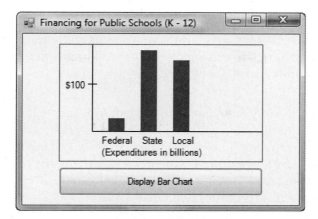

FIGURE 9.25   Bar chart for Example 2.

The three magnitudes for the graph are 33, 206, and 180. If we let a pixel correspond to one unit, then the largest rectangle will be 206 pixels high—a bit too large. With a pixel corresponding to 2 units, the largest rectangle will be 206 / 2 or 103 pixels high—a reasonable size. By setting the x-axis 110 pixels from the top of the picture box, the largest rectangle is accomodated comfortably. The top of the largest rectangle is $110 - 103$ [that is, $110 - (206/2)$] pixels from the top of the picture box. In general, a rectangle corresponding to the quantity q will be $110 - (q/2)$ pixels from the top of the picture box, and the height will be $q / 2$ pixels.

✔ **Example 2**   The following program produces the bar chart of Figure 9.24. Each rectangle is 20 pixels wide, and there are 20 pixels between rectangles.

```
Private Sub btnDisplay_Click(...) Handles btnDisplay.Click
  Dim quantity() As Single = {33, 206, 180}
  Dim gr As Graphics = picOutput.CreateGraphics
  'The picture box has width 210 and height 150
  gr.DrawLine(Pens.Black, 40, 110, picOutput.Width, 110) 'Draw x-axis
  gr.DrawLine(Pens.Black, 40, 110, 40, 0)                'Draw y-axis
  gr.DrawLine(Pens.Black, 35, 100 / 2, 45, 100 / 2)   'Draw tick mark
  gr.DrawString("$100", Me.Font, Brushes.Black, 5, 45)
  Me.Text = "Financing for Public Schools (K - 12)"
  For i As Integer = 0 To quantity.GetUpperBound(0)
    gr.FillRectangle(Brushes.Blue, 60 + i * 40, _
                  (110 - quantity(i) / 2), 20, quantity(i) / 2)
  Next
  gr.DrawString("Federal  State     Local", Me.Font, _
            Brushes.Black, 50, 115)
  gr.DrawString("(Expenditures in billions)", Me.Font, _
            Brushes.Black, 50, 130)
End Sub
```

■ Animation

One way to produce animation on a form is to place an image into a picture box and then move the picture by steadily changing the location of the picture box. Figure 9.25 shows a ball placed inside a small picture box.

 Example 3   In the following program, the ball in Figure 9.26 will initially move diagonally in a southeast direction and then bounce off any side of the form it hits. The **client area** of a form is the gray area within the title bar and borders of the form. The values of Me.ClientSize.Height and Me.ClientSize.Width are the height and width of the gray area. The values of picBox.Top and picBox.Left are the distances of the picture box from the top and left sides of the client area.

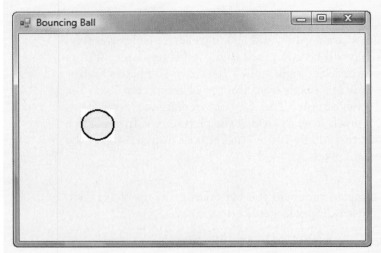

OBJECT	PROPERTY	SETTING
frmBall	Text	Bouncing Ball
picBall	Image	MOON5.BMP
Timer1	Interval	10

FIGURE 9.26   The form for Example 3.

The speed at which the ball moves is determined by the setting for the Interval property of Timer1. At each tick, the ball will move x pixels horizontally, where $x = 1$ or -1. When $x = 1$ the ball moves to the right, and when $x = -1$ the ball moves to the left. The value of x reverses when the ball strikes the right or left side of the form. The value of y determines the vertical motion of the ball in a similar manner,

```
Dim x As Integer = 1
Dim y As Integer = 1

Private Sub frmBall_Load(...) Handles MyBase.Load
  Timer1.Enabled = True
End Sub

Private Sub Timer1_Tick(...) Handles Timer1.Tick
  If picBall.Left <= 0 Or _
       picBall.Left >= (Me.ClientSize.Width - picBall.Width) Then
    x = -x
  End If
```

```
   picBall.Left += x
   If picBall.Top <= 0 Or _
        picBall.Top >= (Me.ClientSize.Height - picBall.Height) Then
      y = -y
   End If
   picBall.Top += y
End Sub
```

■ Comments

1. A statement of the form

```
Dim pn As Pen = Pens.Color
```

declares *pn* to be a variable of type Pen and assigns it the value Pens.*Color*.

2. A statement of the form

```
Dim fnt As Font = New Font(fontName, size)
```

declares *fnt* to be a variable of type Font and assigns it the specified font and size. For instance, the statements

```
Dim gr As Graphics = picBox.CreateGraphics
Dim fnt As Font = New Font("Courier New", 10)
gr.DrawString("Hello", fnt, Brushes.Blue, 4, 30)
```

display the word Hello in 10-point Courier New font.

3. The statement

```
picBox.Refresh()
```

clears all graphics and text from the picture box.

Practice Problems 9.4

1. (True or False) The Draw and Fill methods discussed in this section use colored Brushes.

2. Write lines of code that place a smiling face in the upper left corner of the form. (**Note:** The letter *J* corresponds to a smiling face in the Wingdings font.)

EXERCISES 9.4

In Exercises 1 through 4, write an event procedure to draw the given figures in a picture box.

1. Draw a circle whose center is located at the center of a picture box.

2. Draw a circle whose leftmost point is at the center of a picture box.

3. Use the FillEllipse method to create an unfilled red circle of radius 20.

4. Draw a triangle with three sides of the same length.

In Exercises 5 through 8, write a program to create the flag of the designated country. Refer to Figure 9.27. *Note:* The Swiss flag is square. For the other three flags, the width is 1.5 times the height.

Japan   Peru   Thailand   Greenland

FIGURE 9.27 Flags of four countries.

5. Japan   **6.** Peru   **7.** Thailand   **8.** Greenland

9. Write a program to draw displays such at the one in Figure 9.28. Let the user specify the maximum number (in this display, 8).

FIGURE 9.28 Drawing for Exercise 9.

10. Write a program to draw displays such as the one in Figure 9.29. Let the user specify the number of lines (in this display, 3).

──────────── Line 1
──────────── Line 2
──────────── Line 3

FIGURE 9.29 Drawing for Exercise 10.

11. Use the data in Table 9.3 to create a pie chart.

TABLE 9.3	Web Site Client Browsers.
Browser Name	**% of Total**
Internet Explorer 7 (IE7)	36%
Internet Explorer 6 (IE6)	24%
FireFox (Fx)	29%
Other	11%

12. Use the data in Table 9.4 to create a bar chart.

TABLE 9.4	User Resolution Data
Date	**Using 1024 × 768 or higher**
2008	79.5%
2007	65.3%
2006	60.1%
2005	54.8%
2004	46.1%
2003	30.9%

13. Write a program to create the line chart in Figure 9.30. Use the data in Table 9.5.

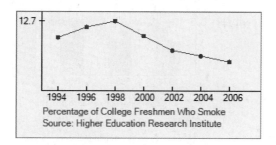

FIGURE 9.30   Line chart for Exercise 13.

TABLE 9.5	Percentage of college freshmen who smoke.						
	1994	**1996**	**1998**	**2000**	**2002**	**2004**	**2006**
Percent	9.7	11.6	12.7	10.0	7.4	6.4	5.3

Source: Higher Education Research Institute

14. Write a program to create the line chart in Figure 9.31. Use the data in Table 9.6

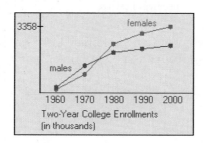

FIGURE 9.31   Line chart for Exercise 14.

TABLE 9.6	Two-year college enrollments (in thousands).				
	1960	**1970**	**1980**	**1990**	**2000**
Male	283	1375	2047	2233	2398
Female	170	945	2479	3007	3358

15. Write a program to create the bar chart in Figure 9.32.

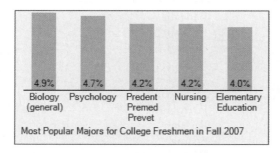

FIGURE 9.32   Bar chart for Exercise 15.

16. Write a program to create the bar chart in Figure 9.33. Use the data in Table 9.7

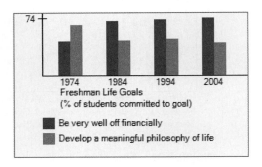

FIGURE 9.33 **Bar chart for Exercise 16.**

TABLE 9.7	Freshman life goals (% of students committed to goal).			
	1974	1984	1994	2004
Be very well off financially	44	70	72	74
Develop a meaningful philosophy of life	65	45	47	42

Source: Higher Education Research Institute

17. Write a program to create the bar chart in Figure 9.34. Use the data in Table 9.8. *Note:* Mandarin and Wu are spoken primarily in China.

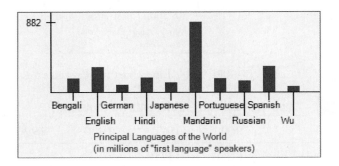

FIGURE 9.34 **Bar chart for Exercise 17.**

TABLE 9.8	Principal languages of the world.
Bengali	173
English	311
German	96
Hindi	182
Japanese	128
Mandarin	882
Portuguese	179
Russian	146
Spanish	326
Wu	78

18. Write a program that allows the user to display a budget as a pie chart. See Figure 9.35. After the user enters numbers into the four text boxes and presses the button, the pie chart should be displayed.

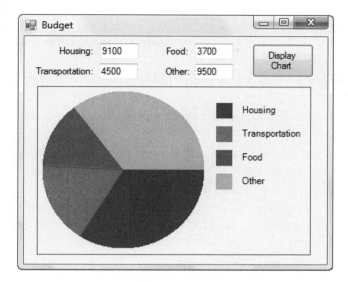

FIGURE 9.35 Form for Exercise 18.

19. Write a program in which an airplane flies horizontally and up across a form (with a white background color) to the upper right hand corner of the form. After it flies off the form, the airplane should reappear on the left and fly horizontally across the screen again in the same manner. **Note:** Use the image AIRPLANE.BMP found in the folder Ch09\Pictures.

Solutions to Practice Problems 9.4

---

1. False. Only the Fill methods and the DrawString method use colored Brushes. The DrawLine method uses colored Pens.

2.
```
Dim gr As Graphics = Me.CreateGraphics
Dim fnt As Font = New Font("Wingdings", 20)
gr.DrawString("J", fnt, Brushes.Red, 0, 0)
```

CHAPTER 9 SUMMARY

1. *List boxes* provide easy access to lists of strings. Items() holds the items stored in the list. Each item is identified by an index number $(0, 1, 2, \ldots)$. The lists can be automatically sorted (Sorted property = True) and altered (Items.AddItem, Items.RemoveAt, and Items.Remove methods), the currently highlighted item identified (Text property), and the number of items determined (Items.Count property).

2. *Combo boxes* are enhanced text boxes. They not only allow the user to enter information by typing it into a text box (read with the Text property), but also allow the user to select the information from a list of items.

3. The *OpenFileDialog control* provides a simple way to locate a file to be opened. The programmer can specify the types of files to display via the Filter property.

4. Selections are made with *check boxes* (allow several) and *radio buttons* (allow at most one). The state of the control (checked vs. unchecked or on vs. off) is stored in the Checked property. Clicking on a check box toggles its state. Clicking on a radio button gives it the on state and turns off the other radio buttons in its group.

5. *Group box controls* are used to band together other controls, especially radio buttons, as a unit.

6. The *timer control* triggers an event repeatedly after the duration of a specified time interval.

7. The *picture box control*, which displays pictures or geometric shapes, can expand to accommodate the size of the picture or have the picture alter its size to fit the control.

8. *Horizontal* and *vertical scroll bar controls* permit the user to select from among a range of integers by clicking or dragging with the mouse. The range is determined by the Minimum and Maximum properties, and changes trigger the Scroll event.

9. The *Clipboard* is filled with the SetText method or by pressing Ctrl + C, and is copied with the GetText method or by pressing Ctrl + V.

10. An object of type *Random* can generate a randomly selected integer from a specified range.

11. Menus, similar to the menus of Visual Basic itself, can be created with the *MenuStrip control*.

12. Additional forms can serve as customized dialog boxes. They are revealed with the ShowDialog method and removed with the Close method.

13. After a graphics object is produced with a *CreateGraphics* method, the *DrawString*, *DrawLine*, *FillRectangle*, *FillEllipse*, and *FillPie* methods can be used to display strings, lines, solid rectangles, solid ellipses, and solid sectors with colors supplied by Pen and Brush objects.

14. Animation can be produced by steadily moving a picture box containing an image.

CHAPTER 9   PROGRAMMING PROJECTS

1. *Membership List.* Write a menu-driven program to manage a membership list. See Figure 9.36 on the next page. Assume that the names and phone numbers of all members are stored in alphabetical order in the text file MEMBERPHONES.TXT. The names and phone numbers should be read into an array of structures, and the names should be displayed in a list box when the form is loaded. When a name is highlighted, both the name and phone number of the person should appear in the text boxes at the bottom of the screen. To delete a person, highlight his or her name and click on the Delete menu item. To change either the phone number or the spelling of the person's name, make the corrections in the text boxes, and click on the menu item Modify. To add a new member, type his or her name and phone number into the text boxes, and click on the menu item Add. When Exit is clicked, the new membership list should be written to the file, and the program should terminate.

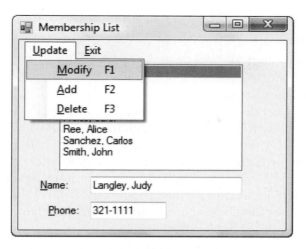

FIGURE 9.36 **Form for Programming Project 1.**

2. *Grade Book.* Write a comprehensive program that a professor could use to record student grades for several classes and save the records in sequential files. Each class has three one-hour exams and a final exam. The file for a single class should consist of the number of students in the class, call it *n*, and a record of five fields (name, grade1, grade2, grade3, and final) for each student, with the records ordered alphabetically by the student's name. (A typical name might appear as "Doe, John".) Initially, the four grade fields should contain zeros. The program should contain a top-level menu item, File, with second-level subitems for Open, Save, Add Student, and Remove Student. When a file is opened (via an OpenFileDialog control), the data for the students should be loaded into a list box. (The last two columns should remain blank.) The professor should be able to enter (or alter) exam data by double-clicking on a line of the list box to invoke a second form as a customized dialog box for inputting grades. See Figure 9.37. When a student is added, the student is in-serted in proper alphabetical position. When the Calculate Semester Grades button is clicked, the last two columns should be filled in by the program. (Assume that the final exam counts as two one-hour exams.) If a grade is changed after the

FIGURE 9.37 **Forms for Programming Project 2.**

last two columns have been filled in, the corresponding average and grade should be recomputed.

3. *Inventory Control.* Write an inventory program for a book store, and save the information in a sequential file. Each record should consist of five fields—title, author, category, wholesale price, and number in stock. (The two categories are fiction and nonfiction.) At any time, the program should display the titles of the books in stock in a list box, for which the user should have the option of displaying either all titles or just those in one of the two categories. When a book is selected from the list, its title, author, category, wholesale price, and number in stock should be displayed in a list box. The user should be able to add a new book, delete a book, or change the inventory level of a book in stock. At any time, the user should be able to calculate the total value of all books, or the total value of the books in either category.

4. *Voting Machine.* The members of the local "Gilligan's Island" fan club bring a computer to their annual meeting to use in the election of a new president. Write a program to handle the election. The program should add each candidate to a list box as he or she is nominated. After the nomination process is complete, club members should be able to approach the computer one at a time and double-click on the candidate of their choice. When a "Tally Votes" button is clicked, a second list box, showing the number of votes received by each candidate, should appear alongside the first list box. Also, the name(s) of the candidate(s) with the highest number of votes should be displayed in a list box.

5. *Airplane Seating Chart.* An airplane has 15 rows (numbered 1 through 15), with six seats (labeled A, B, C, D, E, and F) in each row. Write a program to display the seating chart in a list box with a line for each row. When the ticket agent clicks on the desired row in the list box, the row number and the status of the seats in the row are displayed in seven read-only text boxes. When the agent clicks on one of the text boxes, a second form containing four option buttons labeled Unoccupied, Regular, Low Calorie, and Vegetarian appears. See Figure 9.38 on the next page. Clicking on any radio button closes the second form and updates both the text box and the row for that seat in the list box. Unoccupied seats should be denoted with a period, while occupied seats are denoted with the first letter of their meal type. At any time, the agent can request the number of seats filled, the number of window seats vacant, and the numbers of each type of meal ordered.

6. *The Underdog and the World Series.* What is the probability that the underdog will win the World Series of Baseball? What is the average number of games for a World Series? Write an animated program to answer these questions. For instance, suppose that the underdog is expected to win 40% of the time. We say that the probability of the underdog winning a game is 40%. (**Note:** In order for a team to be the underdog, the probability that the team wins a game must be less than 50%.) Figure 9.39 on the next page shows that the probability that a 40% underdog wins the World Series is about 28.71% and that such a series should be expected to last an average of about 5.69 games. The program should simulate the playing of 10,000 World Series where the underdog has the probability of winning input in the text box. The values of the horizontal scroll bars should extend from 0 to 10,000 and should be calculated after each series so that the scroll boxes steadily move across the bars.

FIGURE 9.38 Forms for Programming Project 5.

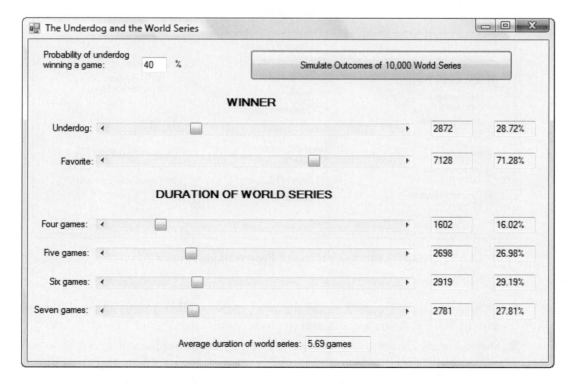

FIGURE 9.39 A sample run of Programming Project 6.

Note: In order for the text boxes to the right of the scroll bars to display data as the program progresses (and not just at the end of the program), execute a statement such as **txtUnderdog.Refresh** in about one-tenth of the 10,000 passes through the loop.

7. *College Admissions.* The admissions offices of large colleges often rely on a point system. A point system similar to the one in Figure 9.40 is used by a large state university. Write a program that displays the information in Figure 9.40 and allows an admissions officer to determine whether an applicant should be admitted. The numbers in brackets give the point count for each response. The GPA score displayed in the text box to the right of the horizontal scroll bar should change (from 2.0 to 4.0 in steps of .1) as the user clicks on the bar's right arrow. The point value in the brackets to the right of the text box is 20 times the GPA. A total of at most 40 points can be earned for the responses below the line. The program should calculate the total score and then admit every applicant whose score is at least 100.

FIGURE 9.40 **Sample run of Programming Project 7.**

8. *Monthly Rainfall.* Figure 9.41 on the next page is called a *range* chart. Using the data in Table 9.9, write a program to produce this chart.

9. *Speread of an Epidemic.* A community of 10,000 individuals is exposed to a flu epidemic in which infected individuals are sick for two days and then are immune from the illness. When we first start to observe the epidemic (that is, on

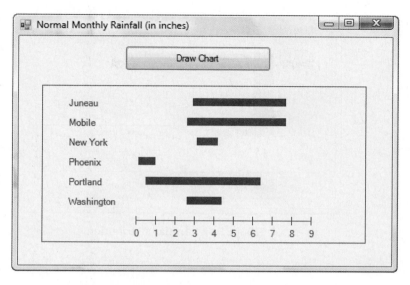

FIGURE 9.41   Range chart for Programming Project 8.

TABLE 9.9	**Range of normal monthly rainfall for selected cities (in inches).**	
	Lowest NMR	Highest NMR
Mobile	2.6	7.7
Portland	.5	6.4
Phoenix	.1	1.0
Washington	2.6	4.4
Juneau	2.9	7.7
New York	3.1	4.2

day 0), 200 people have had the illness for one day, and 100 people have had the illness for two days. At any time, the rate at which the epidemic is spreading is proportional to the product of the number currently ill and the number susceptible. Specifically, each day

[# of individuals in the first day of the illness] =

CInt(0.0001735 * [# sick the previous day] * [# susceptible the previous day])

Write a program that displays successive bar graphs illustrating the progress of the epidemic. When the "Show Day 0" button is pressed, the bar graph should show the distribution for day 0 (Figure 9.42). Each time the "Advance One Day" button is pressed, a bar graph showing the distribution for the next day should appear. Figure 9.43 shows the bar graph after this button has been pressed three times.

FIGURE 9.42 **Initial distribution.**

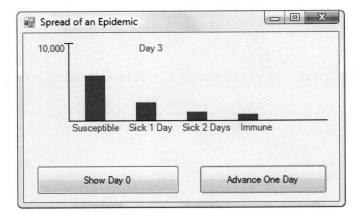

FIGURE 9.43 **Distribution on day 3 of epidemic.**

10. Simulate the playing of a baseball game. Each player on the Red team (the home team) is a .245 hitter. When a player gets a hit, 5% of the time it is a home run, 8% of the time it is a triple, 12% of the time it is a double, and 75% of the time it is a single. Each player on the Blue team is a .260 hitter. When a player gets a hit, 4% of the time it is a home run, 6% of the time it is a triple, 8% of the time it is a double, and 82% of the time it is a single. Assume that a single will advance each runner one base, whereas a double advances each runner two bases. Assume there are no walks or double plays. Show the scores for each inning of a nine-inning game and display the final outcome, which may be a tie.

10

Database Management

10.1 An Introduction to Databases

The management of databases is the number one use of computers today. Airlines use databases to handle nearly 1.5 billion passenger reservations per year. The 6,500 hospitals in the United States utilize databases to document the care of over 30 million patients per year. Banks in the United States utilize databases to monitor the use of 350 million credit cards. Although databases vary considerably in size and complexity, most of them adhere to the fundamental principles of design discussed in this chapter. That is, they are composed of a collection of interrelated tables.

A **table** is a rectangular array of data. Table 10.1 provides information about large cities. Each column of the table is called a **field**. (The third column gives the 2005 population in millions and the fourth column gives the projected 2015 population in millions.) The names of the fields are *city*, *country*, *pop2005*, and *pop2015*. Each row, called a **record**, contains the same type of information as every other row. Also, the pieces of information in each row are related; they all apply to a specific city. Table 10.2, Countries, has three fields and ten records.

TABLE 10.1   Cities.

city	country	pop2005	pop2015
Bombay	India	18.2	22.6
Calcutta	India	14.3	16.8
Delhi	India	15.1	20.9
Dhaka	Bangladesh	12.4	17.9
Jakarta	Indonesia	13.0	17.5
Lagos	Nigeria	11.0	17.0
Mexico City	Mexico	19.0	20.6
New York	USA	18.5	19.7
Sao Paulo	Brazil	18.2	20.0
Tokyo	Japan	35.2	36.2

Note: The population figures are for "urban agglomerations"—that is, contiguous densely populated urban areas.

TABLE 10.2   Countries.

country	pop2005	monetaryUnit
Bangladesh	141.8	taka
Brazil	186.4	real
China	1316.8	yuan
India	1103.4	rupee
Indonesia	222.8	rupiah
Japan	128.1	yen
Mexico	107.0	peso
Nigeria	131.5	naira
Russia	143.2	ruble
USA	298.2	dollar

Source: United Nations, Dept. for Economic and Social Information and Policy Analysis.

A **database** (or **relational database**) is a collection of one or more (usually related) tables that has been created with **database-management software**. Microsoft Access is one of the best known database-management products. Some other prominent ones are Oracle, SQL Server, and DB2. VB 2008 can manage, revise, and analyze a database that has been created with any of these products.

The database used in each example is found in the *Debug* subfolder of the *bin* folder for the program. The databases needed for the exercises are contained in the folder MajorDatabases located in the folder Ch10. The database files were created with Microsoft Access and have the extension .MDB. For instance, the file MEGACITIES.MDB is a database file containing the two tables presented on the preceding page. MDB files should be copied onto a hard drive and accessed from the hard drive. If the files originally resided on a CD, they might have the attribute "Read-only" set. If so, you should change this attribute for each file. To change the attribute setting, first use Windows Explorer to locate the file on the hard drive. Then right-click on the file, click Properties, and uncheck the "Read-only" box under Attributes.

■ Database Explorer

Visual Basic Express has a tool called Database Explorer that allows you to browse through the contents of a database. The other editions of Visual Basic have a tool called Server Explorer that can not only browse a database, but also view information on another computer. The following steps refer to Database Explorer, but are applicable to Server Explorer with slight modifications.

1. Invoke Database Explorer from the View menu. It will appear on the left side of the screen. (Server Explorer can be invoked from the Standard and Professional editions of Visual Basic 2008 with Alt/V/V.)

2. Right-click on "Data Connections", and click on "Add Connection". The Add Connection dialog box in Figure 10.1 appears. (**Note:** If a Change Data Source dialog box appears instead, select "Microsoft Access Database File" and click on OK.)

3. In the Add Connection dialog box that appears, the Data Source should be "Microsoft Access Database File (OLE DB)." If not, click on the Change button, select "Microsoft Access Database File" as the data source, and click on OK to return to the Add Connection dialog box.

4. Click on the "Browse. . ." button to the right of the "Database file name" text box. This will open up a file browser that allows you to locate any file. Select the file MEGACITIES.MDB from the folder Ch10\MajorDatabases, and press Open.

5. Clear the contents of the "User name" text box.

6. Press the Test Connection button at the bottom of the window. The message box stating "Test Connection Succeeded" will appear. Press the OK button on that message box, and then press the OK button on the Add Connection box.

7. An icon titled "MEGACITIES.MDB" should appear in the Database Explorer window. Click on the ⊞ sign to the left of the icon to expand this entry. Four subentries will appear: Tables, Views, Stored Procedures, and Functions.

8. Expand the Tables entry to reveal the two subentries, the tables Cities and Countries.

9. Expand the Cities entry to reveal the fields of the Cities table. See Figure 10.2.

FIGURE 10.1   Add Connection dialog box.

FIGURE 10.2   Database Explorer.

10. Right-click on Cities, and then click on "Retrieve Data." A grid similar to Figure 10.3 will appear. The grid not only displays all of the data in the Cities table, but also gives the names of the fields. **Note:** To remove the entry for the database MEGACITIES.MDB in Database Explorer, right-click on the entry, and select Delete.

	city	country	pop2005	pop2015
▶	Bombay	India	18.2	22.6
	Calcutta	India	14.3	16.8
	Delhi	India	15.1	20.9
	Dhaka	Bangladesh	12.4	17.9
	Jakarta	Indonesia	13	17.5
	Lagos	Nigeria	11	17
	Mexico City	Mexico	19	20.6
	New York	USA	18.5	19.7
	Sao Paulo	Brazil	18.2	20
	Tokyo	Japan	35.2	36.2
*	*NULL*	*NULL*	*NULL*	*NULL*

FIGURE 10.3   The Cities table of MEGACITIES.MDB.

The remainder of this section is devoted to creating programs that display information obtained from a database. A **DataTable** object is the representation of a table (with rows and columns) in ADO.NET. The ADO.NET technology allows programs to access data seamlessly from multiple, varied, and distant servers.

■ Accessing a Database with a Data Table

A DataTable object holds the contents of a table as a rectangular array. (A data table is similar to a two-dimensional array; it has rows and columns.) The following six lines of code create a DataTable variable named "dt" and fill it with the contents of the Cities table from the database MEGACITIES.MDB:

```
Dim dt As New DataTable()
Dim connStr As String = "Provider=Microsoft.Jet.OLEDB.4.0;" & _
                        "Data Source=MEGACITIES.MDB"
Dim sqlStr As String = "SELECT * FROM Cities"
Dim dataAdapter As New OleDb.OleDbDataAdapter(sqlStr, connStr)
dataAdapter.Fill(dt)
dataAdapter.Dispose()
```

Treat these six lines of code as a boiler plate to be inserted into a program.

Note: You can save yourself time by storing this code fragment in the Toolbox and dragging it into the Code Editor when needed.

A database resides on a disk, and a data table resides in memory. A **data adapter** is an intermediary object that serves as a conduit to allow bidirectional data transfers between the two. The first statement in the boiler plate, which declares *dt* to be a variable of type DataTable, is often placed in the Declarations section of the Code Editor. The fifth statement of the boiler plate uses the data adapter to fill the data table with data from the database. The sixth statement of the boiler plate releases all resources of the data adapter.

The variable *connStr* is called a **connection string**. A connection string has two parameters. The Provider parameter specifies the driver that is used to communicate with the database. The Data Source parameter gives the filespec of the database. When the database is in the *bin\Debug* folder of the current program, the filename can be used instead of the filespec.

The variable sqlStr is called an **SQL string**. SQL strings tell the data adapter which table to retrieve. SQL strings are discussed extensively in Section 10.2.

The second and third statements of the boiler plate have the following general form:

```
Dim connStr As String = "Provider=Microsoft.Jet.OLEDB.4.0;" & _
                        "Data Source=" & DataBaseName
Dim sqlStr As String = "SELECT * FROM " & TableName
```

where the database is assumed to be in the *Debug* subfolder of the *bin* subfolder of the program folder.

After the six lines of code are executed, the value of

```
dt.Rows.Count
```

is the number of records in the table, and the value of

```
dt.Columns.Count
```

is the number of fields in the table. The records are numbered 0 through `dt.Rows.Count - 1`, and the fields are numbered 0 through `dt.Columns.Count - 1`. The value of

```
dt.Columns(j).ToString
```

is the name of the *j*th field. The value of

```
dt.Rows(i)(j)
```

is the entry in the *j*th field of the *i*th record. The value of

```
dt.Rows(i)(fieldName)
```

is the entry in the specified field of the *i*th record. In Table 10.3, *dt* holds the Cities table of MEGACITIES.MDB.

TABLE 10.3   Some values from Cities table of MEGACITIES.MDB.

Expression	Value
`dt.Rows.Count`	10
`dt.Columns.Count`	4
`dt.Rows(7)(1)`	USA
`dt.Rows(1)("city")`	Calcutta

Note: The values of dt.Row(i)(j) and dt.Row(i)(fieldName) must be converted to strings with CStr before being placed in a text box or assigned to a String variable. However, they need not be converted when placed in a list box.

 Example 1   The following program displays one record at a time from Table 10.1 of the MEGACITIES.MDB database. The user can move forward or backward through the records, or specify the city to be displayed.

OBJECT	PROPERTY	SETTING
frmCities	Text	Cities Data
btnFind	Text	Find
btnNext	Text	Next
btnPrevious	Text	Previous
lblCity	Text	City:
txtCity	ReadOnly	True
lblCountry	Text	Country:
txtCountry	ReadOnly	True
lblPop2005	Text	Population 2005:
txtPop2005	ReadOnly	True
lblPop2015	Text	Population 2015:
txtPop2015	ReadOnly	True

```
Dim dt As New DataTable()
Dim rowIndex As Integer = 0

Private Sub frmCities_Load(...) Handles MyBase.Load
  'Get data from the database, put it into the DataTable object dt,
  'and display the initial record's data in text boxes.
  Dim connStr As String = "Provider=Microsoft.Jet.OLEDB.4.0;" & _
                     "Data Source=MEGACITIES.MDB"
  Dim sqlStr As String = "SELECT * FROM Cities"
  Dim dataAdapter As New OleDb.OleDbDataAdapter(sqlStr, connStr)
  dataAdapter.Fill(dt)
  dataAdapter.Dispose()
  UpdateTextBoxes()
End Sub


Private Sub btnFind_Click(...) Handles btnFind.Click
  'Search through each row looking for the requested city.
  'Update the fields if that city is found.
  'Otherwise display a message box.
  Dim cityName As String
  Dim cityFound As Boolean = False
  cityName = InputBox("Enter the name of the city to search for.")
  For i As Integer = 0 To (dt.Rows.Count - 1)
    If CStr(dt.Rows(i)("city")) = cityName Then
      cityFound = True
      rowIndex = i
```

```
      UpdateTextBoxes()
    End If
  Next
  If (Not cityFound) Then
    MessageBox.Show("Cannot find the requested city", "Not in Table")
  End If
End Sub

Private Sub btnNext_Click(...) Handles btnNext.Click
  'Show the next record if the current one is not the last.
  If (rowIndex < dt.Rows.Count - 1) Then
    rowIndex += 1   'Increase rowIndex by 1.
    UpdateTextBoxes()
  End If
End Sub

Private Sub btnPrevious_Click(...) Handles btnPrevious.Click
  'Show the previous record if the current one is not the first.
  If (rowIndex > 0) Then
    rowIndex = rowIndex - 1
    UpdateTextBoxes()
  End If
End Sub

Sub UpdateTextBoxes()
  'Display the contents of the row specified by the rowIndex variable.
  txtCity.Text = CStr(dt.Rows(rowIndex)("city"))
  txtCountry.Text = CStr(dt.Rows(rowIndex)("country"))
  txtPop2005.Text = CStr(dt.Rows(rowIndex)("pop2005"))
  txtPop2015.Text = CStr(dt.Rows(rowIndex)("pop2015"))
End Sub
```

[Run, and then click the Next button seven times.]

Example 2   The following program displays the contents of Table 10.1 of MEGACITIES.MDB in a list box, along with the percentage increases for the populations.

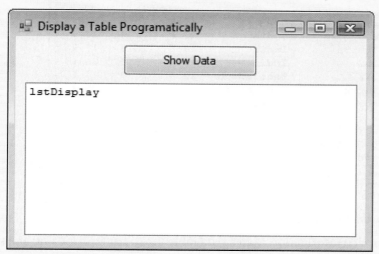

OBJECT	PROPERTY	SETTING
frmCities	Text	Display a Table Programatically
btnShow	Text	Show Data
lstDisplay	Font	Courier New

```vb
Private Sub btnShow_Click(...) Handles btnShow.Click
  Dim fmtStr As String = "{0,-15}{1,-10}{2,7:N1}{3,7:N1}{4,7:P0}"
  Dim percentIncrease As Double
  'Place contents of Cities table into a DataTable.
  Dim dt As New DataTable()
  Dim connStr As String = "Provider=Microsoft.Jet.OLEDB.4.0;" & _
                      "Data Source=MEGACITIES.MDB"
  Dim sqlStr As String = "SELECT * FROM Cities"
  Dim dataAdapter As New OleDb.OleDbDataAdapter(sqlStr, connStr)
  dataAdapter.Fill(dt)
  dataAdapter.Dispose()
  'Fill the list box.
  lstDisplay.Items.Add(String.Format(fmtStr, "CITY", "COUNTRY", _
                                "2005", "2015", "INCR."))
  For i As Integer = 0 To dt.Rows.Count - 1
    percentIncrease = (CDbl(dt.Rows(i)("pop2015")) - _
        CDbl(dt.Rows(i)("pop2005"))) / CDbl(dt.Rows(i)("pop2005"))
    lstDisplay.Items.Add(String.Format(fmtStr, dt.Rows(i)(0), _
        dt.Rows(i)(1), dt.Rows(i)(2), dt.Rows(i)(3), percentIncrease))
  Next
End Sub
```

[Run, and click the button.]

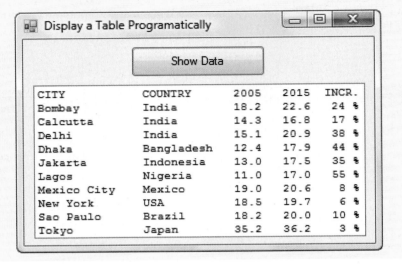

▨ Binding a List Box to a Data Table

In Example 2, we placed information from a data table into a list box one line at a time. However, a data table can be connected directly to a list box and have information transferred automatically into the list box. In such a situation, the list box is said to be **bound** to the data table. The statement

```
lstBox.DataSource = dt
```

binds the list box to the data table, and the statement

```
lstBox.DisplayMember = "country"
```

displays the contents of the specified field in the list box.

 Example 3 The following program uses a list box to display a column of data named "country" from a data table. When a particular country is selected, the event procedure retrieves the country's monetary unit from the corresponding record and displays it in a text box.

OBJECT	PROPERTY	SETTING
frmCountries	Text	Currency
lstCountries		
lblMonetaryUnit	Text	Monetary unit:
txtMonetaryUnit	ReadOnly	True

```
Dim dt As New DataTable()

Private Sub frmCountries_Load(...) Handles MyBase.Load
  Dim connStr As String = "Provider=Microsoft.Jet.OLEDB.4.0;" & _
                          "Data Source=MEGACITIES.MDB"
  Dim sqlStr As String = "SELECT * FROM Countries"
  Dim dataAdapter As New OleDb.OleDbDataAdapter(sqlStr, connStr)
  dataAdapter.Fill(dt)
  dataAdapter.Dispose()
  lstCountries.DataSource = dt    'Bind the list box to the data table.
  lstCountries.DisplayMember = "country"   'Display the specified field.
End Sub

Private Sub lstCountries_SelectedIndexChanged(...) _
          Handles lstCountries.SelectedIndexChanged
  txtMonetaryUnit.Text = _
     CStr(dt.Rows(lstCountries.SelectedIndex)("monetaryUnit"))
End Sub
```

[Run, and click on one of the countries.]

Importing an Existing Database into a Program

All databases required for the exercises are located in the subfolder *MajorDatabases* of the folder *Ch10* downloaded from the companion website. You can use the Visual Basic IDE to copy a database from the *MajorDatabases* folder and paste it into a program's *bin\Debug* folder. The steps are as follows:

1. Highlight the name of the program at the top of the Solution Explorer window. (**Note:** If the Solution Explorer window is not visible, click on Solution Explorer in the View menu.)

2. Click on "Add Existing Item" in the Project menu. (An "Add Existing Item" dialog box will appear.)

3. There is a drop-down combo box for displaying file types near the bottom of the dialog box. Click on its down-arrow and click on either "All Files (*.*)" or "Data Files (*.xsd, …)."

4. Locate the database file and double-click on it. (The database file will be copied, and the filename will appear in the Solution Explorer window. Also, a "Data Source Configuration Wizard" dialog box will appear.)

5. Click on the Cancel button in the "Data Source Configuration Wizard."

6. Locate the database file in the Solution Explorer window and move it to the *Debug* subfolder of *bin*. The move can be accomplished either by drag-and-drop or by Cut-and-Paste. (**Note:** If the *bin* folder does not show in the Solution Explorer window, click on the "Show All Files" icon in the Solution Explorer toolbar.)

Practice Problem 10.1

Determine the output displayed when the button is clicked.

```
Private Sub btnDisplay_Click(...) Handles btnDisplay.Click
  Dim dt As New DataTable()
  Dim connStr As String = "Provider=Microsoft.Jet.OLEDB.4.0;" & _
                          "Data Source=MEGACITIES.MDB"
  Dim sqlStr As String = "SELECT * FROM Countries"
  Dim dataAdapter As New OleDb.OleDbDataAdapter(sqlStr, connStr)
  dataAdapter.Fill(dt)
  dataAdapter.Dispose()
  lstOutput.Items.Add(dt.Columns(2).ToString)
  lstOutput.Items.Add(dt.Rows(5)(0))
  lstOutput.Items.Add(dt.Rows(8)(dt.Columns.Count - 2))
  lstOutput.Items.Add(dt.Rows(0)("monetaryUnit"))
  lstOutput.Items.Add(dt.Rows(dt.Rows.Count - 1)(2))
End Sub
```

EXERCISES 10.1

Exercises 1 through 16 refer to the database MEGACITIES.MDB. In Exercises 1 through 4, determine the output displayed when the button is clicked.

```
1. Private Sub btnDisplay_Click(...) Handles btnDisplay.Click
     Dim dt As New DataTable()
     Dim sum As Double
     Dim connStr As String = "Provider=Microsoft.Jet.OLEDB.4.0;" & _
                             "Data Source=MEGACITIES.MDB"
     Dim sqlStr As String = "SELECT * FROM Cities"
     Dim dataAdapter As New OleDb.OleDbDataAdapter(sqlStr, connStr)
     dataAdapter.Fill(dt)
     dataAdapter.Dispose()
     sum = 0
     For i As Integer = 0 To dt.Rows.Count - 1
       sum += CDbl(dt.Rows(i)("pop2015"))
     Next
     txtOutput.Text = sum & " million"
   End Sub
```

2.
```
Private Sub btnDisplay_Click(...) Handles btnDisplay.Click
    Dim dt As New DataTable()
    Dim connStr As String = "Provider=Microsoft.Jet.OLEDB.4.0;" & _
                            "Data Source=MEGACITIES.MDB"
    Dim sqlStr As String = "SELECT * FROM Cities"
    Dim dataAdapter As New OleDb.OleDbDataAdapter(sqlStr, connStr)
    dataAdapter.Fill(dt)
    dataAdapter.Dispose()
    For i As Integer = 0 To dt.Rows.Count - 1
      If CDbl(dt.Rows(i)("pop2015")) > 22 Then
        lstOutput.Items.Add(dt.Rows(i)(0))
      End If
    Next
  End Sub
```

3.
```
Private Sub btnDisplay_Click(...) Handles btnDisplay.Click
    Dim dt As New DataTable()
    Dim connStr As String = "Provider=Microsoft.Jet.OLEDB.4.0;" & _
                            "Data Source=MEGACITIES.MDB"
    Dim sqlStr As String = "SELECT * FROM Countries"
    Dim dataAdapter As New OleDb.OleDbDataAdapter(sqlStr, connStr)
    dataAdapter.Fill(dt)
    dataAdapter.Dispose()
    For i As Integer = 0 To dt.Rows.Count - 1
      If CStr(dt.Rows(i)("country")).Length = 5 Then
        lstOutput.Items.Add(dt.Rows(i)(0))
      End If
    Next
  End Sub
```

4.
```
Private Sub btnDisplay_Click(...) Handles btnDisplay.Click
    Dim dt As New DataTable()
    Dim connStr As String = "Provider=Microsoft.Jet.OLEDB.4.0;" & _
                            "Data Source=MEGACITIES.MDB"
    Dim sqlStr As String = "SELECT * FROM Countries"
    Dim dataAdapter As New OleDb.OleDbDataAdapter(sqlStr, connStr)
    dataAdapter.Fill(dt)
    dataAdapter.Dispose()
    For j As Integer = 0 To dt.Columns.Count - 1
      lstOutput.Items.Add(dt.Columns(j).ToString)
    Next
  End Sub
```

5. Write a program to place in a list box the names of the countries in the Countries table in the order that they appear in the table.

6. Write a program to place in a list box the names of the countries in the Countries table in the reverse order that they appear in the table.

7. Write a program to place in a list box the names of the cities in the Cities table whose populations are projected to exceed 20 million in the year 2015.

8. Write a program to place in a list box the names of the cities in the Cities table whose 2005 populations are between 12 and 16 million.

9. Write a program to place in a list box the names of the countries in the Countries table, where each name is followed by a hyphen and the name of its monetary unit.

10. Write a program to find and display the city in the Cities table that will experience the greatest percentage growth from 2005 to 2015. **Note:** The percentage growth is (pop2015 – pop2005) / pop2005.

11. Write a program to place the countries from the Countries table in a list box in descending order of their 2005 populations. **Hint:** Place the countries and their 2005 populations in an array of structures, and sort the array in descending order based on the populations.

12. Write a program to place the cities from the Cities table in a list box in descending order of their percentage population growth from 2005 to 2015.

13. Write a program to display the name and currency of each city in the table Cities.

14. Write a program to display in a list box the names of each country in Table 10.1 followed by the cities in that country that are listed in the Cities table.

15. Write a program to back up the contents of the Cities table in one sequential file and the Countries table in another sequential file. Run the program, and compare the sizes of these two sequential files with the size of the file MEGACITIES.MDB.

16. Write a program that allows the user to specify a city and then displays the percentage of its country's 2005 population that lives in that city. **Hint:** Use two Data-Tables.

Exercises 17 through 20 refer to the BIBLIO.MDB database from the folder Ch10\MajorDatabases.

17. How many tables are in the database? What are their names?

18. Give the names of the fields in the table Publishers.

19. How many records are in the table Publishers?

20. Write a program that requests the name of a publisher (such as Prentice Hall or Microsoft Press) and gives the publisher's address.

21. The folder Ch10\MajorDatabases contains the database COUNTRY_POP.MDB which consists of a single table, Countries, having four fields: an abbreviation for the country, the name of the country, the population of the country, and the size in square miles of the land that the country occupies. Write a program that allows the user to enter an abbreviation and obtain the name and population of the country. If the abbreviation entered does not correspond to any of the countries contained within the database, the user should be informed via a MessageBox.

The folder Ch10\MajorDatabases contains the database SALES.MDB, which contains two tables, Personnel and SalesPackages. The fields for the Personnel table are name, salesTeam, ytdSales (year to date), and mtdSales (month to date). The fields for the SalesPackages table are packageName, packageTitle, packageAvail (available to what sales team), and packageCost. The database has been filled with sample data, including the three sample records for each table as follows.

PERSONNEL

Brian Morgan, Purple, 6531, 300
Melissa Ellison, Green, 5329, 313
Alex Lewis, Blue, 5793, 279

SALESPACKAGES

Basic, Base Model One, Green, 95.00
Business, Business Class, Blue, 155.00
Premium, Premium with All Features, Red, 205.00

The database SALES.MDB should be used in Exercises 22 through 26.

22. Write a program to determine the salesperson with the largest number of sales for the current month. In the case of a tie, the program should list all salespeople with the largest number of sales.

23. Write a program to determine the salesperson who has made the most sales to date this year and also determines the salesperson who has made the fewest sales to date this year.

24. Write a program that displays all of the sales packages available by name in the salesPackages table within a list box. When the user clicks on one of the sales packages, the program should display the remaining attributes for that particular sales package within 3 textboxes on the form.

25. Write a program that displays all of the sales packages available by name from the salesPackages table within a list box. When the user clicks on one of the packages, the program will list all of the salespeople from the Personnel table that are eligible to sell that particular package. *Hint:* Use two DataTables.

26. Write a program to determine the number of sales made for each package by combining data from the Personnel and salesPackages tables.

Solution to Practice Problem 10.1

```
monetaryUnit
Japan
143.2
taka
dollar
```

10.2 Relational Databases and SQL

▨ Primary and Foreign Keys

A well-designed table should have a field (or set of fields) that can be used to uniquely identify each record. Such a field (or set of fields) is called a **primary key**. For instance, in the Countries table of Section 10.1 (Table 10.2), the country field is a primary key. In the Cities table (Table 10.1), because we are only considering very large cities (of over 1 million population), the city field is a primary key. Databases of student enrollments in a college usually use a field of Social Security numbers as the primary key. Names would not be a good choice because there could easily be two students having the same name.

When a table is created, a field can be specified as a primary key. If so, Visual Basic will insist that every record have an entry in the primary-key field and that the same entry does not appear in two different records. If the user tries to add a record with no data in the primary key, the error message "Index or primary key cannot contain a Null Value." will be generated. If the user tries to add a record with the same primary key data as another record, the error message "The changes you requested to the table were not successful because they would create duplicate values in the index, primary key, or relationship. Change the data in the field or fields that contain duplicate data, remove the index, or redefine the index to permit duplicate entries and try again." will be displayed.

When a database contains two or more tables, the tables are usually related. For instance, the two tables Cities and Countries are related by their country field. Let's refer to these two fields as Cities.country and Countries.country. Notice that every entry in Cities.country appears uniquely in Countries.country and that Countries.country is a primary key. We say that Cities.country is a **foreign key** of Countries.country. Foreign keys are usually specified when a database is first created. If so, Visual Basic will insist on the **Rule of Referential Integrity**, namely, that each value in the foreign key must also appear in the primary key of the other table.

In the database MEGACITIES.MDB, Cities.city and Countries.country have been specified as primary keys for their respective tables, and Cities.country has been specified as a foreign key of Countries.country. If the user tries to add a city to the Cities table whose country does not appear in the Countries table, then the error message "You cannot add or change a record because a related record is required in table 'Countries'." will be displayed. The message will also be generated if the user tries to delete a country from the Countries.country field that appears in the Cities.country field. Due to the interdependence of the two tables in MEGACITIES.MDB, this database is called a **relational database**.

A foreign key allows Visual Basic to link (or **join**) together two tables from a relational database in a meaningful way. For instance, when the two tables Cities and Countries from MEGACITIES.MDB are joined based on the foreign key Cities.country, the result is Table 10.4. The record for each city is expanded to show its country's population and its monetary unit. This joined table is very handy if, say, we want to navigate

TABLE 10.4   **A join of two tables.**

Cities. city	Cities. country	Cities. pop2005	Cities. pop2015	Countries. country	Countries. pop2005	Countries. monetaryUnit
Bombay	India	18.2	22.6	India	1103.4	rupee
Calcutta	India	14.3	16.8	India	1103.4	rupee
Delhi	India	15.1	20.9	India	1103.4	rupee
Dhaka	Bangladesh	12.4	17.9	Bangladesh	141.8	taka
Jakarta	Indonesia	13.0	17.5	Indonesia	222.8	rupiah
Lagos	Nigeria	11.0	17.0	Nigeria	131.5	naira
Mexico City	Mexico	19.0	20.6	Mexico	107	peso
New York	USA	18.5	19.7	USA	298.2	dollar
Sao Paulo	Brazil	18.2	20.0	Brazil	186.4	real
Tokyo	Japan	35.2	36.2	Japan	128.1	yen

through a table with buttons as in Example 1 of Section 10.1, but display a city's name and monetary unit. We only have to create the original two tables; Visual Basic creates the joined table as needed. The request for a joined table is made in a language called SQL.

■ SQL

Structured Query Language (SQL) was developed in the early 1970s at IBM for use with relational databases. The language was standardized in 1986 by ANSI (American National Standards Institute). Visual Basic uses a version of SQL that is compliant with ANSI-92 SQL. There are some minor variations that are of no concern in this book.

SQL is a very powerful language. One use of SQL is to request specialized information from an existing database or to have the information presented in a specified order.

■ Four SQL Requests (Queries)

We will focus on four basic types of requests that can be made with SQL.

Request I: Show the records of a table in a specified order.
Some variations of ordering with Cities are

- **(a)** alphabetical order based on the name of the city,
- **(b)** alphabetical order based on the name of the country, and within each country group, the name of the city,
- **(c)** descending order based on the projected 2015 population.

Request II: Show just the records that meet certain criteria.
Some examples of criteria with Cities are

- **(a)** cities that are in India,
- **(b)** cities whose 2015 population is projected to be at least 20 million,
- **(c)** cities whose name begins with the letter "D".

Request III: Join the tables together, connected by a foreign key, and present the records as in Requests I and II.
Some examples with MEGACITIES.MDB are

- **(a)** show the cities in descending order of the populations of their countries,
- **(b)** show the cities whose monetary unit has "u" as its second letter.

Request IV: Make available just some of the fields of either the basic tables or the joined table.
Some examples with MEGACITIES.MDB are

- **(a)** make available just the city and country fields of the Cities table,
- **(b)** make available just the city and monetary unit fields of the joined table.

Normally, we set the SQL statement of a data adapter to an entire table. Also, the records of the table are normally presented in the order they are physically stored in the table. We make the requests just discussed by specifying the SQL statement as one of the following types:

Request I: SELECT * FROM *Table1* ORDER BY *field1* ASC or SELECT * FROM *Table1* ORDER BY *field1* DESC

Request II: SELECT * FROM *Table1* WHERE *criteria*

Request III: SELECT * FROM *Table1* INNER JOIN *Table2* ON *foreign field* = *primary field* WHERE *criteria*

Request IV: SELECT *field1*, *field2*, ..., *fieldN* FROM *Table1* WHERE *criteria*

"ASC" and "DESC" specify ASCending and DESCending orders, respectively. A *criteria* clause is a string containing a condition of the type used with If blocks. In addition to the standard operators $<$, $>$, and $=$, *criteria* strings frequently contain the operator LIKE. Essentially, LIKE uses the wildcard characters "_" and "%" to compare a string to a pattern. An underscore character stands for a single character in the same position as the underscore character. For instance, the pattern "B_d" is matched by "Bid", "Bud", and "Bad". A percent sign stands for any number of characters in the same position as the percent sign. For instance, the pattern "C%r" is matched by "Computer", "Chair", and "Car". See Comments 3 through 5 for further information about LIKE.

In the sentence

```
SELECT fields FROM clause
```

fields is either * (to indicate all fields) or a sequence of the fields to be available (separated by commas), and *clause* is either a single table or a join of two tables. A join of two tables is indicated by a clause of the form

```
tblA INNER JOIN tblB ON foreign key of tblA = primary key of tblB
```

Appending

```
WHERE criteria
```

to the end of the sentence restricts the records to those satisfying *criteria*. Appending

```
ORDER BY field(s) ASC (or DESC)
```

presents the records ordered by the specified field or fields.

In general, the SQL statements we consider will look like

```
SELECT www FROM xxx WHERE yyy ORDER BY zzz
```

where SELECT *www* FROM *xxx* is always present and accompanied by one or both of WHERE *yyy* and ORDER BY *zzz*. In addition, the *xxx* portion might contain an INNER JOIN phrase.

The settings for the examples mentioned earlier are as follows:

I (a) Show the records from Cities in alphabetical order based on the name of the city with

```
SELECT * FROM Cities ORDER BY city ASC
```

I (b) Show the records from Cities in alphabetical order based first on the name of the country and, within each country group, the name of the city with

```
SELECT * FROM Cities ORDER BY country, city ASC
```

I (c) Show the records from Cities in descending order based on the projected 2015 population, using

```
SELECT * FROM Cities ORDER BY pop2015 DESC
```

II (a) Show the records for the Cities in India with

```
SELECT * FROM Cities WHERE country = 'India'
```

II (b) Show the records from Cities whose 2015 population is projected to be at least 20 million with

```
SELECT * FROM Cities WHERE pop2015 >= 20
```

II (c) Show the records from Cities whose name begins with the letter "D" with

```
SELECT * FROM Cities WHERE city LIKE 'D%'
```

III (a) Show the records from the joined table in descending order of the populations of their countries with

```
SELECT * FROM Cities INNER JOIN Countries ON Cities.country =
Countries.country ORDER BY Countries.pop2005 DESC
```

III (b) Show the records from the joined table whose monetary unit has "u" as its second letter with

```
SELECT * FROM Cities INNER JOIN Countries ON Cities.country =
Countries.country WHERE monetaryUnit LIKE '_u%'
```

IV (a) Make available just the city and country fields of the table Cities, using

```
SELECT city, country FROM Cities
```

IV (b) Make available just the city and monetaryUnit fields of the joined table with

```
SELECT city, monetaryUnit FROM Cities INNER JOIN Countries ON
Cities.country = Countries.country
```

Note: In several of the statements the single quote, rather than the normal double quote, was used to surround strings. This is standard practice with SQL statements.

We can think of an SQL statement as creating in essence a new "virtual" table from existing tables. For instance, we might regard the statement

```
SELECT city, pop2015 FROM Cities WHERE pop2015>=20
```

as creating the "virtual" table

city	pop2015
Bombay	22.6
Delhi	20.9
Mexico City	20.6
Sao Paulo	20.0
Tokyo	36.2

This table is a subtable of the original table Cities—that is, it consists of what is left after certain columns and rows are omitted.

As another example, the statement

```
SELECT Cities.city, Cities.Country, Countries.monetaryUnit FROM Cities
INNER JOIN Countries ON Cities.country = Countries.country
WHERE Countries.country>'K'
```

creates in essence the "virtual" table

Cities.city	Cities.country	Countries.monetaryUnit
Lagos	Nigeria	naira
Mexico City	Mexico	peso
New York	USA	dollar

which is a subtable of a join of the two tables Cities and Countries.

These "virtual" tables don't exist physically. However, for all practical purposes, Visual Basic acts as if they did. In standard relational database books, a "virtual" table is called a **view**.

The programs in Section 10.1 all contain a statement of the form

```
Dim sqlStr As String = "SELECT * FROM TableName"
```

that creates an entire existing table as a view. Replacing this string with a different SQL statement will result in a different "virtual" table for the data table when it is filled by the data adapter.

■ The DataGridView Control

In Section 10.1, information from databases is displayed in text boxes and list boxes. Another control, called the DataGridView, displays the values for an entire view in a table format identical to the table displayed by Database Explorer. The standard prefix for the name of a DataGridView control is *dgv*.

After a data table has been filled, the statement

```
dgvDisplay.DataSource = dt
```

displays the contents of the data table *dt* in the data grid view.

Example 1 The following program allows the user to alter the order and kinds of information displayed from a database. When the first button is pressed, the cities are presented in ascending order based on their 2005 populations. When the second button is pressed, the cities are presented in alphabetical order along with their monetary units.

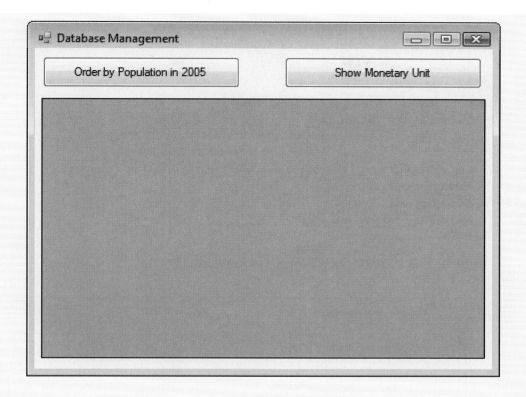

OBJECT	PROPERTY	SETTING
frmCities	Text	Database Management
btnOrderByPop	Text	Order by Population in 2005
btnShowMonUnit	Text	Show Monetary Unit
dgvDisplay		

```
Private Sub frmCities_Load(...) Handles MyBase.Load
  UpdateGrid("Select * From Cities")
End Sub

Private Sub btnOrderbyPop_Click(...) Handles btnOrderbyPop.Click
  'Display the data from the data table in the data grid.
  UpdateGrid("Select * From Cities Order By pop2005 ASC")
End Sub

Private Sub btnShowMonUnit_Click(...) Handles btnShowMonUnit.Click
  UpdateGrid("SELECT city, Cities.country, " & _
             "Cities.pop2005, monetaryUnit " & _
```

```
            "FROM Cities INNER JOIN Countries " & _
            "ON Cities.country = Countries.country " & _
            "ORDER BY city ASC")
End Sub

Sub UpdateGrid(ByVal sqlStr As String)
  Dim dt As New DataTable()
  Dim connStr As String = "Provider=Microsoft.Jet.OLEDB.4.0;" & _
                          "Data Source=MEGACITIES.MDB"
  Dim dataAdapter As New OleDb.OleDbDataAdapter(sqlStr, connStr)
  dataAdapter.Fill(dt)
  dataAdapter.Dispose()
  dgvDisplay.DataSource = dt
End Sub
```

[Run, and click on the Show Monetary Unit button.]

city	country	pop2005	monetaryUnit
Bombay	India	18.2	rupee
Calcutta	India	14.3	rupee
Delhi	India	15.1	rupee
Dhaka	Bangladesh	12.4	taka
Jakarta	Indonesia	13	rupiah
Lagos	Nigeria	11	naira
Mexico City	Mexico	19	peso
New York	USA	18.5	dollar
Sao Paulo	Brazil	18.2	real
Tokyo	Japan	35.2	yen

Database Management. Buttons: Order by Population in 2005, Show Monetary Unit.

The program in Example 3 of Section 10.1 searched a table for a specific record by looping through all the records. Whereas this technique is fine for small tables, it is not efficient for searches of large tables. A better way to find data that match a criteria is to include the criteria in the SQL string.

Example 2   The following program displays the large cities in a country specified by the user. Notice the single quotes surrounding the criteria in the SQL string.

OBJECT	PROPERTY	SETTING
frmCities	Text	Search with SQL
lblCountry	Text	Country:
txtCountry		
btnFindCities	Text	Find Cities
dgvDisplay		

```
Private Sub btnFindCities_Click(...) Handles btnFindCities.Click
  UpdateGrid("SELECT city FROM Cities WHERE country = '" & _
              txtCountry.Text & "' ORDER BY city ASC")
End Sub

Sub UpdateGrid(ByVal sqlStr As String)
  'Declare and populate the data table.
  Dim dt As New DataTable()
  Dim connStr As String = "Provider=Microsoft.Jet.OLEDB.4.0;" & _
                    "Data Source=MEGACITIES.MDB"
  Dim dataAdapter As New OleDb.OleDbDataAdapter(sqlStr, connStr)
  dataAdapter.Fill(dt)
  dataAdapter.Dispose()
  'Display the names of the cities in the specified country.
  If dt.Rows.Count = 0 Then
    MessageBox.Show("No cities from that country in the database")
  Else
    dgvDisplay.DataSource = dt
  End If
End Sub
```

[Run, type "India" into the text box, and press the button.]

Changing the Contents of a Database

The programs presented so far only read data from a database. Data grid views can be used to add, modify, and delete records from a database. After a DataAdapter has been created, the statement

```
Dim commandBuilder As New OleDb.OleDbCommandBuilder(dataAdapter)
```

will automatically enable any modifications to be stored. If *changes* is an Integer variable, then the statement

```
changes = dataAdapter.Update(dt)
```

will store all of the insertions, updates, and deletions made in the data table to the database and assign the number of records changed to the variable *changes*.

  Example 3   The following program demonstrates loading data from a database to a data grid view via a data adapter, allowing the user to make edits within the data grid view, and saving the changes back to the database. To update a record, highlight the field, and make the change. To insert a new record, click on the bottom row that begins with an asterisk and has blank fields. (The values in the fields are initially filled with "(null)" and should be changed.) To delete a row, click on the box to the left of the row so that the entire row is highlighted, and then click the Delete key. If you click the "Load Table From Database" button before clicking the "Save Changes To Database" button, any changes are lost. Run the program, and test it by clicking on the Load button, making some changes, and then clicking on the Save button.

OBJECT	PROPERTY	SETTING
frmCities	Text	Updating Databases
btnLoad	Text	Load Table From Database
btnSave	Text	Save Changes To Database
dgvDisplay		

```
'Class-level variables
Dim connStr As String = "Provider=Microsoft.Jet.OLEDB.4.0;" & _
                        "Data Source=MEGACITIES.MDB"
Dim sqlStr As String = "SELECT * FROM Cities"
Dim dt As New DataTable()

Private Sub btnLoad_Click(...) Handles btnLoad.Click
  'Displays the table's data in the data grid view
  'Clear the current contents of the table.
  dt.Clear()
  'Fill the data table with data from the database.
  Dim dataAdapter As New OleDb.OleDbDataAdapter(sqlStr, connStr)
  dataAdapter.Fill(dt)
  dataAdapter.Dispose()
  'Display the table in the data grid.
  dgvDisplay.DataSource = dt
End Sub

Private Sub btnSave_Click(...) Handles btnSave.Click
  'Save the tables's changes back to the database.
  Dim changes As Integer
  'Open a connection to the database for updating.
  Dim dataAdapter As New OleDb.OleDbDataAdapter(sqlStr, connStr)
  Dim commandBuilder As New OleDb.OleDbCommandBuilder(dataAdapter)
```

```
'Update the database with changes from the data table.
changes = dataAdapter.Update(dt)
dataAdapter.Dispose()
'Display the number of changes made.
If changes > 0 Then
  MessageBox.Show(changes & " changed rows were stored in the database.")
Else
  MessageBox.Show("No changes made.")
End If
End Sub
```

■ Calculated Columns with SQL

Suppose we want to display in a data grid the cities in the MEGACITIES.MDB database along with their expected population growth from 2005 to 2015. We could use Access to add a fifth field to the Cities table and fill it with the population growth. That is, for each record the entry in the new field would be the difference between its pop2015 and pop2005 fields. However, this would violate a fundamental principle of database design— *avoid fields whose values can be calculated from existing fields.* SQL provides a way to display a population growth column without creating a new field for the Cities table.

After the data table *dt* has been filled using the string

```
sqlStr = "SELECT city, (pop2015-pop2005) FROM Cities"
```

then the statement

```
dgvDisplay.DataSource = dt
```

causes the data grid view to display two columns, as shown in Figure 10.4, where the second column shows the population growth for each city. This column is called a **calculated column**.

city	Expr1001
Bombay	4.4000000000000021
Calcutta	2.5
Delhi	5.7999999999999989
Dhaka	5.4999999999999982
Jakarta	4.5
Lagos	6
Mexico City	1.6000000000000014
New York	1.1999999999999993
Sao Paulo	1.8000000000000007
Tokyo	1

FIGURE 10.4

The display in Figure 10.4 has two flaws—the second column does not have a meaningful name, and the numbers in the second column are not rounded to one decimal place. The first flaw can be corrected by adding the clause **AS popGrowth** after **(pop2015 - pop2005)**. This will give the column the heading *popGrowth*. The second flaw can be corrected by replacing **(pop2015-pop2005)** with **Round(pop2015-pop2005, 1)**. Therefore, using the string

```
sqlStr = "SELECT city, Round(pop2015-pop2005, 1) AS popGrowth " & _
         "FROM Cities"
```

to fill the table produces the output shown in Figure 10.5.

city	popGrowth
Bombay	4.4
Calcutta	2.5
Delhi	5.8
Dhaka	5.5
Jakarta	4.5
Lagos	6
Mexico City	1.6
New York	1.2
Sao Paulo	1.8
Tokyo	1

FIGURE 10.5

Note: The column title following the AS keyword can contain spaces. If so, the title should be surrounded by brackets. For instance, if the clause is AS [Population Growth], then the column title will be Population Growth.

Calculated values can be used in an ORDER clause to sort the displayed data. For instance, if the SQL string above is changed to

```
sqlStr = "SELECT city, Round(pop2015-pop2005, 1) AS popGrowth " & _
         "FROM Cities ORDER by (pop2015-pop2005) DESC"
```

then the cities will be sorted by their population growth.

■ Comments

1. Each record of the Countries table is related to one or more records of the Cities table, but each record of the Cities table is related to only one record of the Countries table. Therefore, we say that there is a **one-to-many relationship** from the Countries table to the Cities table.

2. SQL statements are insensitive to case. For instance, the following choices for criteria have the same effect: City = 'Tokyo', city = 'tokyo', CITY = 'tokyo', CiTy = 'TOKYO'.

3. When the LIKE operator is used, the "pattern" must appear on the right of the operator. For instance, the SQL statement

```
SELECT * FROM Cities WHERE city LIKE 'S%'
```

cannot be replaced by

```
SELECT * FROM Cities WHERE 'S%' LIKE city
```

4. The operator LIKE permits a refinement of the wildcard character "_". Whereas "_" is a placeholder for any letter, an expression such as "[letter1-letter2]" is a placeholder for any letter from letter1 to letter2. For instance, the pattern "[A-F]ad" is matched by Bad and Dad, but not Sad.

5. The LIKE operator can be used in If blocks in much the same way as the operators >, =, and <. In this situation, the operator is case sensitive. For instance, the condition ("bad" LIKE "[A-F]ad") is False. However, when LIKE is used in SQL statements, it is case insensitive. That is, ('bad' LIKE '[A-F]ad') is True. Furthermore, when LIKE is used in an If block, the asterisk is used instead of the percent sign to denote any number of characters, and the question mark stands for any one character.

6. The requirement that no record may have a null entry in a primary key and that entries for primary keys be unique is called the **Rule of Entity Integrity**.

Practice Problems 10.2

For each of the following grids, give an SQL statement that can be used to create the grid from the MEGACITIES.MDB database:

1.

country	pop2005	monetaryUnit
Indonesia	222.8	rupiah
India	1103.4	rupee

2.

country
Mexico
Brazil

EXERCISES 10.2

Exercises 1 through 4 refer to the database MEGACITIES.MDB, where the primary keys of Cities and Countries are city and country, respectively, and Cities.country is a foreign key to Countries.country. Determine whether the stated action could ever cause a problem. Explain.

1. Add a new record to the Cities table.

2. Delete a record from the Countries table.

3. Delete a record from the Cities table.

4. Add a new record to the Countries table.

The following tables are "virtual" tables derived from the MEGACITIES.MDB database. In Exercises 5 through 8, identify the "virtual" table associated with the SQL statement.

(A)		
country	pop2005	monetary-Unit
Russia	143.2	ruble
Indonesia	222.8	rupiah
India	1103.4	rupee
Brazil	186.4	real

(B)		
country	pop2005	monetary-Unit
China	1316.8	yuan

(C)		
country	pop2005	monetary-Unit
China	1316.8	yuan
India	1103.4	rupee

(D)		
country	pop2005	monetary-Unit
China	1316.8	yuan
Brazil	186.4	real
Bangladesh	141.8	taka

5. `SELECT * FROM Countries WHERE pop2005>1200 ORDER BY pop2005 ASC`

6. `SELECT * FROM Countries WHERE country<'E' ORDER BY pop2005 DESC`

7. `SELECT * FROM Countries WHERE monetaryUnit LIKE 'r%' ORDER BY country DESC`

8. `SELECT * FROM Countries WHERE pop2005>700 ORDER BY country ASC`

The following tables are "virtual" tables derived from the MEGACITIES.MDB database. In Exercises 9 through 12, identify the "virtual" table associated with the SQL statement.

(A)	
city	monetaryUnit
Sao Paulo	real

(B)	
city	monetaryUnit
Tokyo	yen
Bombay	rupee

(C)	
city	monetaryUnit
Bombay	rupee
Delhi	rupee
Calcutta	rupee

(D)	
city	monetaryUnit
Tokyo	yen

9. `SELECT city, monetaryUnit FROM Cities INNER JOIN Countries ON Cities.country = Countries.country WHERE city='Tokyo'`

10. `SELECT city, monetaryUnit FROM Cities INNER JOIN Countries ON Cities.country = Countries.country WHERE pop2015>22 ORDER BY pop2015 DESC`

11. `SELECT city, monetaryUnit FROM Cities INNER JOIN Countries`
    `ON Cities.country = Countries.country`
    `WHERE Cities.country = 'India' ORDER BY Cities.pop2005 DESC`

12. `SELECT city, monetaryUnit FROM Cities INNER JOIN Countries`
    `ON Cities.country = Countries.country`
    `WHERE city LIKE 'S%' ORDER BY Countries.pop2005 ASC`

For each grid in Exercises 13 through 20, give an SQL statement that can be used to create the grid from the MEGACITIES.MDB database. Then test your answer with a DataGridView filled from a table whose DataAdapter uses the SQL statement. *Note:* Several of the exercises here have more than one correct answer.

13.

country	monetaryUnit
Nigeria	naira
Bangladesh	taka
Russia	ruble
Brazil	real

14.

country	pop2005	monetaryUnit
India	1103.4	rupee
Indonesia	222.8	rupiah
Brazil	186.4	real
Russia	143.2	ruble

15.

city	country	pop2005	pop2015
Bombay	India	18.2	22.6
Delhi	India	15.1	20.9
Calcutta	India	14.3	16.8

16.

city	country	pop2005	pop2015
Sao Paulo	Brazil	18.2	20
Mexico City	Mexico	19	20.6
Delhi	India	15.1	20.9
Bombay	India	18.2	22.6
Tokyo	Japan	35.2	36.2

17.

city	country	pop2005	pop2015
Sao Paulo	Brazil	18.2	20
Bombay	India	18.2	22.6
New York	USA	18.5	19.7

18.

city	country	pop2005	pop2015
Sao Paulo	Brazil	18.2	20
Mexico City	Mexico	19	20.6

19.

city	pop2015	monetaryUnit
Bombay	22.6	rupee
Delhi	20.9	rupee
Calcutta	16.8	rupee

20.

city	Cities.pop2005	Countries.pop2005
Tokyo	35.2	128.1
Mexico City	19	107
New York	18.5	298.2

The folder Ch10\MajorDatabases contains the database COUNTRY_POP.MDB which consists of a single table, Countries, having four fields: an abbreviation for the country, the name of the country, the population of the country, and the size in square miles of the land that the country occupies.

The database COUNTRY_POP.MDB should be used in Exercises 21 through 25.

21. Write a program that displays a list of the countries within a data-bound list box. When the user clicks on one of the countries, the population and size of the country in square miles should be displayed.

22. Write a program that displays the names of the countries in a data-bound list box in ascending order determined by the population of that country. When the user clicks on one of the names, the population and size of the country in square miles should be displayed.

23. Write a program containing two data-bound list boxes, both containing a list of the countries available listed alphabetically. When the user selects a country from each list box and clicks on a button labeled Compare, the program should compare the population of the two countries and show the populations as a ratio of the first country chosen to the second one. *Hint*: Use two DataTables.

24. Create an SQL string that would be used to display a data grid view having two columns with the first column containing the names of the countries within the database and the second column containing their population. The countries should appear in decreasing order of their population densities.

25. Create an SQL string to find all countries whose code starts with an A and whose population is over 2,000,000.

26. The folder Ch10\MajorDatabases contains the database USPRESIDENTS.MDB which consists of two tables. The first is President and contains the fields, yearElected and President. The second table is named State and contains the fields President and homeState. Write an SQL string that can be used to display a data grid view having

two columns with the first column containing the year each President was elected and the second column containing the state the president was from. The list should appear in ascending order by year.

Exercises 27 through 34 use the database BASEBALL.MDB discussed in the exercises in Section 10.1. In Exercises 27 through 33, write a program to display the stated information in a DataGridView control.

27. The names of the players who play for a team based in New York.

28. The name(s) of the player(s) in the American League having the most hits.

29. The name(s) of the National League player(s) with the highest batting average for that league.

30. The names of all the players and their batting averages. The records should be sorted in descending order by batting average.

31. The names of all the teams, their home stadiums, and the team batting averages. Records should be sorted in ascending order by the team batting average.

32. The names of all the players, their leagues, and their team's batting averages.

33. The names of players and their batting averages. The records should be sorted in descending order by batting average and should only show the players whose batting average exceeded their team's batting average.

34. Write a program that requests a batting average and a league (American or National) and then displays the names of all the players in the league whose batting average is above the given batting average. The program should not permit the given batting average to be greater than 1 or less than 0.

Exercises 35 and 36 refer to the database PHONEBOOK.MDB, which holds all the information for the residence listings of a telephone book for a city. Assume the database consists of one table, Entries, with the six fields: lastName, firstName, middleInitial, houseNumber, street, and phoneNumber.

35. Write a program that will display the contents of the phone book in the standard form shown in Figure 10.8(a) on the next page.

36. Write a program that will display a "criss-cross" directory that gives phone numbers with the entries organized by street as in Figure 10.8(b) on the next page.

AAKER Larry 3 Main St	874-2345	APPLE ST 3 Carl Aaron	405-2345
AARON Alex 23 Park Ave	924-3456	5 John Smith	862-1934
Bob R 17 Elm St	347-3456	7 Ted T Jones	405-1843
Carl 3 Apple St	405-2345	ARROW RD 1 Ben Rob	865-2345
(a)		(b)	

FIGURE 10.8 (a) Standard phone directory and (b) criss-cross directory.

Solutions to Practice Problems 10.2

1. `SELECT * FROM Countries WHERE country LIKE 'I%'`
   `ORDER BY pop2005 ASC`

2. `SELECT country FROM Countries WHERE country='Mexico'`
   `OR country='Brazil' ORDER BY pop2005 ASC`

CHAPTER 10 SUMMARY

1. A *table* is a group of data items arranged in a rectangular array, each row containing the same categories of information. Each data item (row) is called a *record*. Each category (column) is called a *field*. Two tables with a common field are said to be *related*. A *database* is a collection of one or more tables that are usually related.

2. Visual Basic's Database Explorer can be used to identify and view the tables of a database.

3. The *DataTable* object is used to access the information in a table. This information is supplied via a *data adapter*. The data adapter must be provided three pieces of information—the software serving as the database provider, the location of the database, and a statement telling it what part of the database to access. The first two pieces of information are combined into a string called a *connection string*.

4. When a list box is *bound* to a data table, information from the database can be inserted automatically into the list box.

5. A *primary key* is a field or set of fields that uniquely identifies each row of a table. The *Rule of Entity Integrity* states that no record can have a null entry in a primary key and that entries for primary keys must be unique. A foreign key is a field or set of fields in one table that refers to a primary key in another table. The *Rule of Referential Integrity* states that each value in the foreign key must also appear in the primary key.

6. Structured Query Language (SQL) is used to create a "virtual" table, or *view*, consisting of a subtable of a table or of a join of two tables and imposes an order on the records. The subtable or join is specified with the reserved words SELECT, FROM, WHERE, ORDER BY, and INNER JOIN ... ON. The WHERE clause of an SQL statement commonly uses the LIKE operator in addition to the standard operators. Data adapters use SQL statements to specify the views they will use to fill data tables.

7. The *data grid view control* can show an entire "virtual" table in a spreadsheetlike display. It can also be used to make changes in a database.

8. A *computed column* of a data grid does not contain values from a field in a database table, but rather, it contains values that are computed from one or more fields.

CHAPTER 10 PROGRAMMING PROJECTS

1. The database MICROLAND.MDB is maintained by the Microland Computer Warehouse, a mail-order computer-supply company. Tables 10.5 through 10.7 show parts of three tables in the database. The table Customers identifies each customer by an ID number and gives, in addition to the name and address, the total amount of purchases during the current year prior to today. The table Inventory identifies each product in stock by an ID number and gives, in addition to its description and price (per unit), the quantity in stock at the beginning of the day. The table Orders gives the orders received today. Suppose that it is now the end of the day. Write a program that uses the three tables to do the following:

   (a) Display in a list box the items that are out of stock and therefore must be reordered.

   (b) Display in a list box bills for all customers who ordered during the day. The bill should indicate if an item is currently out of stock.

2. *Grade Book.* A teacher maintains a database containing two tables—Students and Grades. The Students table has six fields: *socSecNumber, lastName, firstName, streetAddress, cityAndState,* and *zipCode.* The Grades table has four fields: *socSecNumber, firstExam, secondExam,* and *finalExam.* At the beginning of the semester, the Students table is filled in completely with a record for each student in a class, and the Grades table has a record for each student that contains only the student's social security number. (**Note:** The database is contained in the file GRADEBOOK.MDB from the folder Ch10\MajorDatabases.) Write a program that allows the instructor to record and process the grades for the semester. The program should do the following.

   (a) Create a data grid view that can be used to fill in the grades for each student after each exam.

   (b) At the end of the semester, display a data grid view showing the name of each student and his or her semester average. The semester average should be calculated as (firstExam + secondExam + 2*finalExam)/4.

   (c) Display a list of semester grades that the instructor can post on his or her office door. The list should contain the last four digits of each student's social security number and the student's semester grade. The semester grade should be determined by the semester average with an A for 90–100, a B for 80–89, and so on. The list should be ordered by semester average.

   (d) Display a letter for a student (identified by his or her social security number) similar to the one shown below.

TABLE 10.5   First three records of the Customers table.

custID	name	street	city	amtPurchases
1	Michael Smith	2 Park St.	Dallas, TX 75201	234.50
2	Brittany Jones	5 Second Ave	Tampa, FL 33602	121.90
3	Warren Pease	7 Maple St.	Boston, MA 02101	387.20

TABLE 10.6   First three records of the Inventory table.

itemID	description	price	quantity
PL208	Visual Basic	89.50	12
SW109	MS Office Upgrade	195.95	2
HW913	Scanner	49.95	8

TABLE 10.7   First four records of the Orders table.

custID	itemID	quantity
3	SW109	1
1	PL208	3
1	HW913	2
2	PL208	1

George Jackson
123 Main Street
Washington, DC 20015

Dear George,

Your grades for CMSC 100 are as follows:
  Final Exam: 87
  Semester Grade: B

Best wishes for a good summer,
Professor Jones

11

Object-Oriented Programming

11.1 Classes and Objects

noun A word used to denote or name a person, place, thing, quality, or act.

verb That part of speech that expresses existence, action, or occurrence.

adjective Any of a class of words used to modify a noun or other substantive by limiting, qualifying, or specifying.

The American Heritage Dictionary of the English Language

"A good rule of thumb for object-oriented programming is that classes are the nouns in your analysis of the problem. The methods in your object correspond to verbs that the noun does. The properties are the adjectives that describe the noun."

Gary Cornell & David Jezak

Practical experience in the financial, scientific, engineering, and software design industries has revealed some difficulties with traditional program design methodologies. As programs grow in size and become more complex, and as the number of programmers working on the same project increases, the number of dependencies and interrelationships throughout the code increases exponentially. A small change made by one programmer in one place may have many effects, both intended and unintended, in many other places. The effects of this change may ripple throughout the entire program, requiring the rewriting of a great deal of code along the way.

A partial solution to this problem is "data hiding" where, within a unit, as much implementation detail as possible is hidden. Data hiding is an important principle underlying object-oriented programming. An object is an encapsulation of data and procedures that act on the data. The only things of concern to a programmer using an object are the tasks that the object can perform and the parameters used by these tasks. The details of the data structures and procedures are hidden within the object.

Two types of objects will be of concern to us: **control objects** and **code objects**. Examples of control objects are text boxes, list boxes, buttons, and all the other controls that can be created from the Toolbox. So far, most of our programs have contained a single class block beginning with a line, such as "Public Class frmName" and ending with the line "End Class." A code object is a specific instance of a user-defined type, called a **class**, which is defined similarly to a structure, but in a separate class block of the form

```
Class ClassName
   statements
End Class
```

Each class block is delineated in the Code Editor by an elongated left bracket appearing to the left of the block. Both control objects and class objects have properties, methods, and events. The main differences are that control objects are predefined and have physical manifestations, whereas the programmer must create the class blocks for code objects. In this section, when we use the word "object" without a qualifier, we mean "code object."

Whenever you double-click on the TextBox icon in the Toolbox, a new text box is created. Although each text box is a separate entity, they all have the same properties, methods, and events. Each text box is said to be an **instance** of the class TextBox. In some sense, the TextBox icon in the Toolbox is a template or blueprint for creating text boxes.

When you look at the Properties window for a text box, the drop-down list box at the top of the window reads something like "TextBox1 System.Windows.Forms.TextBox." TextBox1 is the name of the control object and it is said to be an instance of the class "TextBox." You can't set properties or invoke methods of the TextBox class; you can only set properties or invoke methods of the specific text boxes that are instances of the class. The analogy is often made between a class and a cookie cutter. The cookie cutter is used to create cookies that you can eat, but you can't eat the cookie cutter.

Object-oriented programs are populated with objects that hold data, have properties, respond to methods, and raise events. (The generation of events will be discussed in the next section.) Six examples are as follows:

1. In a professor's program to assign and display semester grades, a student object might hold a single student's name, social security number, midterm grade, and final exam grade. A CalcSemGrade method might calculate the student's semester grade. Events might be raised when improper data are passed to the object.

2. In a payroll program, an employee object might hold an employee's name, hourly wage, and hours worked. A CalculatePay method would tell the object to calculate the wages for the current pay period.

3. In a checking account program, a check register object might have methods that record and total the checks written during a certain month, a deposit slip object might record and total the deposits made during a certain month, and an account object might keep a running total of the balance in the account. The account object would raise an event to alert the bank when the balance gets too low.

4. In a bookstore inventory program, a textbook object might hold the name, author, quantity in stock, and wholesale price of an individual textbook. A CalculateRetailPrice method might instruct the textbook object to calculate the selling price of the textbook. An event could be triggered when the book goes out of stock.

5. In a game program, an airplane object might hold the location of an airplane. At any time, the program could tell the object to display the airplane at its current location or to drop a bomb. An event can be triggered each time a bomb is released so that the program can determine if anything was hit.

6. In a card game program, a card object might hold the denomination and suit of a specific card. An IdentifyCard method might return a string such as "Ace of Spades." A deck of cards object might consist of an array of card objects and a ShuffleDeck method that thoroughly shuffles the deck. A Shuffling event might indicate the progress of the shuffle.

The most important object-oriented term is **class**. A class is a template from which objects are created. The class specifies the properties and methods that will be common to all objects that are instances of that class. Classes are formulated in class blocks. An object, which is an instance of a class, can be created in a program with a pair of statements of the form

```
Dim objectName As ClassName
objectName = New ClassName(arg1, arg2, ...)
```

The first of these two lines of code declares what type of object the variable will refer to. The actual object does not exist until it is created with the New keyword, as done in the second line. This is known as creating an **instance** of an object and is where an object is actually created from its corresponding class. After this second line of code executes, the object is then ready for use. The first line can appear either in the Declarations section of a program (to declare a class-level variable) or inside a procedure (to declare a local variable). The instantiation line can only appear in a procedure; however, any object variable can be instantiated when declared (as either class-level or local) by using the single line

```
Dim objectName As New ClassName(arg1, arg2, ...)
```

In a program, properties, methods, and events of the object are accessed with statements of the form shown in the following table:

TASK	STATEMENT
Assign a value to a property	`objectName.propertyName = value`
Assign the value of a property to a variable	`varName = objectName.propertyName`
Carry out a method	`objectName.methodName(arg1, ...)`
Raise an event	`RaiseEvent eventName`

The program in Example 1 uses a class named Student to calculate and display a student's semester grade. The information stored by an object of the type Student consists of a student's name, Social Security number, and grades on two exams (midterm and final). This data is stored in variables declared with the statements

```
Private m_name As String        'Name
Private m_ssn As String         'Social security number
Private m_midterm As Double     'Numerical grade on midterm exam
Private m_final As Double        'Numerical grade on final exam
```

The word Private guarantees that the variables cannot be accessed directly from outside the object. In object-oriented programming terminology, these variables are called **member variables** (or **instance variables**). We will follow the common convention of beginning the name of each member variable with the prefix "m_". Each of these variables is used to hold the value of a property. However, instead of being accessed directly, each member variable is accessed indirectly by a **property block**. For instance, the following property block consists of a Get property procedure to retrieve (or *read*) the value of the Name property and a Set property procedure to assign (or *write*) the value of the Name property:

```
Public Property Name() As String
  Get
    Return m_name
  End Get
  Set(ByVal value As String)
    m_name = value
  End Set
End Property
```

In a property block, additional code can be added after the Get and Set statements to validate the data before they are returned or stored. The word Public allows the property to be accessed from outside the code for the Student class block. For instance, the Name property can be accessed by code in the form's class block. On the other hand, since the member variables were declared as Private, they cannot be accessed directly from code in the form's block. They can only be accessed through Property procedures that allow values to be checked and perhaps modified. Also, a Property procedure is able to take other steps necessitated by a change in the value of a member variable.

A property block needn't contain both Get and Set property procedures. For instance, the block

```
Public WriteOnly Property Midterm() As Double
   Set(ByVal value As double)
     m_midterm = value
   End Set
End Property
```

specifies the Midterm property as "write only." This property could be specified to be "read only" with the block

```
Public ReadOnly Property Midterm() As Double
   Get
      Return m_midterm
   End Get
End Property
```

Methods are constructed with Sub or Function procedures. A Function procedure is used when the method returns a value; otherwise a Sub procedure will suffice. For instance, the method CalcSemGrade, which is used to calculate a student's semester grade, is created as follows:

```
Function CalcSemGrade() As String
   Dim grade As Double
   grade = (m_midterm + m_final) / 2
   grade = Math.Round(grade)   'Round the grade.
   Select Case grade
     Case Is >= 90
       Return "A"
     Case Is >= 80
       Return "B"
     Case Is >= 70
       Return "C"
     Case Is >= 60
       Return "D"
     Case Else
       Return "F"
   End Select
End Function
```

An object of the type Student is declared in the code for the form with a pair of statements such as

```
Dim pupil As Student    'Declare pupil as object of type Student
pupil = New Student()    'Create an instance of Student
```

After these two statements are executed, properties and methods can be utilized with statements such as

```
pupil.Name = "Adams, Al"                  'Assign a value to m_name
txtBox.Text = pupil.Name                  'Display the student's name
lstBox.Items.Add(pupil.CalcSemGrade)      'Display semester grade.
```

The first statement calls the Set property procedure for the Name property, the second statement calls the Get property procedure for the Name property, and the third statement calls the method CalcSemGrade.

 Example 1 The following program uses the class Student to calculate and display a student's semester grade:

OBJECT	PROPERTY	SETTING
frmGrades	Text	Semester Grade
lblName	Text	Name:
txtName		
lblSSN	Text	SSN:
mtxtSSN	Mask	000-00-0000
lblMidterm	Text	Midterm:
txtMidterm		
lblFinal	Text	Final:
txtFinal		
btnEnter	Text	&Enter Information
btnDisplay	Text	&Display Grade
btnQuit	Text	&Quit
lstGrades	Font	Courier New

```
Public Class frmGrades
  Dim pupil As Student    'pupil is an object of class Student

  Private Sub btnEnter_Click(...) Handles btnEnter.Click
    pupil = New Student()    'Create an instance of Student.
    'Read the values stored in the text boxes.
    pupil.Name = txtName.Text
    pupil.SocSecNum = mtxtSSN.Text
    pupil.Midterm = CDbl(txtMidterm.Text)
    pupil.Final = CDbl(txtFinal.Text)
    'Clear text boxes and list box
    txtName.Clear()
    mtxtSSN.Clear()
    txtMidterm.Clear()
    txtFinal.Clear()
```

```
      lstGrades.Items.Clear()
      'Notify user that grades for the student have been recorded.
      lstGrades.Items.Add("Student Recorded.")
    End Sub

    Private Sub btnDisplay_Click(...) Handles btnDisplay.Click
      Dim fmtStr As String = "{0,-20}{1,-15}{2,-4}"
      lstGrades.Items.Clear()
      lstGrades.Items.Add(String.Format(fmtStr, pupil.Name, _
                      pupil.SocSecNum, pupil.CalcSemGrade))
    End Sub

    Private Sub btnQuit_Click(...) Handles btnQuit.Click
      End
    End Sub
End Class        'frm Grades

Class Student
    Private m_name As String        'Name
    Private m_ssn As String         'Social security number
    Private m_midterm As Double     'Numerical grade on midterm exam
    Private m_final As Double       'Numerical grade on final exam

    Public Property Name() As String
      Get
        Return m_name
      End Get
      Set(ByVal value As String)
        m_name = value
      End Set
    End Property

    Public Property SocSecNum() As String
      Get
        Return m_ssn
      End Get
      Set(ByVal value As String)
        m_ssn = value
      End Set
    End Property

    Public WriteOnly Property Midterm() As Double
      Set(ByVal value As Double)
        m_midterm = value
      End Set
    End Property

    Public WriteOnly Property Final() As Double
      Set(ByVal value As Double)
        m_final = value
      End Set
    End Property
```

```
Function CalcSemGrade() As String
   Dim grade As Double
   grade = (m_midterm + m_final) / 2
   grade = Math.Round(grade)   'Round the grade.
   Select Case grade
     Case Is >= 90
       Return "A"
     Case Is >= 80
       Return "B"
     Case Is >= 70
       Return "C"
     Case Is >= 60
       Return "D"
     Case Else
       Return "F"
   End Select
 End Function
End Class        'Student
```

[Run, enter the data for a student (such as "Adams, Al", "123-45-6789", "82", "87"), press the Enter Information button to send the data to the object, and press the Display Grade button to display the student's name, Social Security number, and semester grade.]

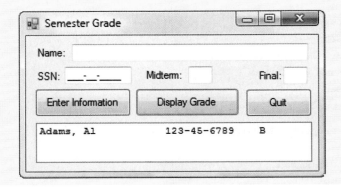

In summary, the following six steps are used to create a class:

1. Identify a *thing* in your program that is to become an object.
2. Determine the properties and methods that you would like the object to have. (As a rule of thumb, properties should access data, and methods should perform operations.)
3. A class will serve as a template for the object. The code for the class is placed in a class block of the form

```
Class ClassName
   statements
End Class
```

4. For each of the properties in Step 2, declare a private member variable with a statement of the form

```
Private variableName As DataType
```

Member variables can be preceded with the keyword Public, which allows direct access to the member variables from the code in the form. However, this is considered poor programming practice. By using Set property procedures to update the data, we can enforce constraints and carry out validation.

5. For each of the member variables in Step 4, create a Property block with Get and/or Set procedures to retrieve and assign values of the variable. The general forms of the procedures are

```
Public Property PropertyName() As DataType
  Get
    (Possibly additional code.)
    Return variableName
  End Get
  Set(ByVal value As DataType)
    (Possibly additional code.)
    variableName = value
  End Set
End Property
```

In the Get or Set code, additional code can be added to prevent the object from storing or returning invalid or corrupted data. For example, an If block could be added to only allow valid Social Security numbers, alerting the user in the event of an invalid number.

6. For each method in Step 2, create a Sub procedure or Function procedure to carry out the task.

Example 2   The following modification of the program in Example 1 calculates semester grades for students who have registered on a "Pass/Fail" basis. We create a new class, named PFStudent, with the same member variables and property procedures as the class Student. The only change needed in the class block occurs in the CalcSemGrade method. The new code for this method is

```
Function CalcSemGrade() As String
  Dim grade As Double
  grade = (m_midterm + m_final) / 2
  grade = Math.Round(grade)   'Round the grade.
  If grade >= 60 Then
    Return "Pass"
  Else
    Return "Fail"
  End If
End Function
```

The only change needed in the form's code is to replace the two occurrences of *Student* with *PFStudent*. When the program is run with the same input as in Example 1, the output will be

```
Adams, Al    123-45-6789   Pass
```

■ Object Constructors

Each class has a special method called a **constructor** that is always invoked when an object is instantiated. The constructor takes zero or more arguments, and the code inside the procedure block performs any tasks needed for initializing an object. It is often used to set default values for member variables and to create other objects associated with this object. The first line of the constructor for a class has the form

```
Public Sub New(ByVal par1 As DataType1, ByVal par2 As DataType2, ...)
```

The graphical program in Example 3 illustrates the use of a constructor to specify the size and placement of a circle. This task involves pixels. To get a feel for how big a pixel is, the initial size of the form when you create a new project is 300 pixels by 300 pixels. Section 9.4 explains how graphics are created inside a picture box with the Graphics object gr = picBox.CreateGraphics. In Example 3, the statement

```
gr.DrawEllipse(Pens.Black, Xcoord, Ycoord, Diameter, Diameter)
```

draws a circle inside a picture box, where Xcoord and Ycoord are the distances (in pixels) of the circle from the left side and top of the picture box.

 Example 3　The following program contains a circle object. The object keeps track of the location and diameter of the circle. (The location is specified by two numbers, called the coordinates, giving the distance from the left side and top of the picture box. Distances and the diameter are measured in pixels.) A Show method displays the circle and a Move method adds 20 pixels to each coordinate of the circle. Initially, the (unseen) circle is located at the upper-left corner of the picture box and has a diameter of 40. The form has a button captioned "Move and Show Circle" that invokes both methods. Notice that the Xcoord, Ycoord, and Diameter properties, rather than the member variables, appear in the methods.

OBJECT	PROPERTY	SETTING
frmCircle	Text	Moving Circle
btnMove	Text	Move and Show Circle
btnQuit	Text	Quit
picCircle		

```
Public Class frmCircle
  Dim round As New Circle()

  Private Sub btnMove_Click(...) Handles btnMove.Click
    round.Move(20)
    round.Show(picCircle.CreateGraphics)
  End Sub

  Private Sub btnQuit_Click(...) Handles btnQuit.Click
    End
  End Sub
End Class          'frmCircle

Class Circle
  Private m_x As Integer   'Dist from left side of picture box to circle
  Private m_y As Integer   'Distance from top of picture box to the circle
  Private m_d As Integer   'Diameter of circle
  Public Sub New()
    'Set the initial location of the circle to the upper left
    'corner of the picture box, and set its diameter to 40.
    Xcoord = 0
    Ycoord = 0
    Diameter = 40
  End Sub

  Public Property Xcoord() As Integer
    Get
      Return m_x
    End Get
    Set(ByVal value As Integer)
      m_x = value
    End Set
  End Property

  Public Property Ycoord() As Integer
    Get
      Return m_y
    End Get
    Set(ByVal value As Integer)
      m_y = value
    End Set
  End Property

  Public Property Diameter() As Integer
    Get
      Return m_d
    End Get
    Set(ByVal value As Integer)
```

```
      m_d = value
    End Set
  End Property

  Sub Show(ByRef gr As Graphics)
    'Draw a circle with the given graphics context.
    gr.DrawEllipse(Pens.Black, Xcoord, Ycoord, Diameter, Diameter)
  End Sub

  Sub Move(ByVal distance As Integer)
    Xcoord += distance
    Ycoord += distance
  End Sub
End Class        'Circle
```

[Run, and press the Move button ten times.]

When the line that instantiates an object contains arguments, the values of these arguments are passed to the object's New procedure. For instance, in Example 3, the first line typed in the form's code can be changed to

```
Dim round As New Circle(0, 0, 40)
```

and the New procedure for the Circle class can be changed to

```
Public Sub New(ByVal x As Integer, ByVal y As Integer, _
              ByVal d As Integer)
  'Set the initial location of the circle to x pixels from
  'the left side and y pixels from the top of the picture box.
  'Set the diameter to d pixels.
  Xcoord = x
  Ycoord = y
  Diameter = d
End Sub
```

Practice Problems 11.1

1. Which of the following analogies is out of place?
   (a) class : object
   (b) sewing pattern : garment
   (c) blueprint : house
   (d) programmer : program
   (e) cookie cutter : cookie

2. In Example 1, suppose that the first five lines of the event procedure btnEnter_Click are replaced with

```
Private Sub btnEnter_Click(...) Handles btnEnter.Click
  Dim ssn As String = "123-45-6789"    'Social Security Number
  'Create an instance of Student.
  pupil = New Student(ssn)
  pupil.Name = txtName.Text
```

Create a New procedure and revise the SocSecNum property block for the Student class to be consistent with the last line in the preceding code.

EXERCISES 11.1

Exercises 1 through 14 refer to the class Student. When applicable, assume that *pupil* is an instance of the class.

1. What will be the effect if the *Midterm* property block is changed to the following?

```
Public WriteOnly Property Midterm() As Double
  Set(ByVal value As Double)
    Select Case value
      Case Is < 0
        m_midterm = 0
      Case Is > 100
        m_midterm = 100
      Case Else
        m_midterm = value
    End Select
  End Set
End Property
```

2. What will be the effect if the *Midterm* property block is changed to the following?

```
Public WriteOnly Property Midterm() As Double
  Set(ByVal value As Double)
    m_midterm = value + 10
  End Set
End Property
```

3. Modify the class block for *Student* so that the following statement will display the student's midterm grade:

```
lstGrades.Items.Add(pupil.Midterm)
```

4. Modify the class block for *Student* so that the student's semester average can be displayed with a statement of the form

```
lstGrades.Items.Add(pupil.Average)
```

5. In the class block for Student, why can't the third line of the CalcSemGrade method be written

```
grade = (Midterm + Final) / 2
```

6. Write code for the class block that sets the two grades to 10 whenever an instance of the class is created.

7. What is the effect of adding the following code to the class block:

```
Public Sub New()
   SocSecNum = "999-99-9999"
End Sub
```

In Exercises 8 through 14, determine the errors in the given form code.

8.
```
Dim scholar As Student

Private Sub btnGo_Click(...) Handles btnGo.Click
   Dim firstName as String
   scholar.Name = "Warren"
   firstName = scholar.Name
End Sub
```

9.
```
Dim scholar As Student

Private Sub btnGo_Click(...) Handles btnGo.Click
   Dim nom as String
   scholar = Student()
   scholar.Name = "Peace, Warren"
   nom = scholar.Name
End Sub
```

10.
```
Dim scholar As Student

Private Sub btnGo_Click(...) Handles btnGo.Click
   Dim nom as String
   scholar = New Student()
   m_name = "Peace, Warren"
   nom = scholar.Name
End Sub
```

11.
```
Dim scholar As Student

Private Sub btnGo_Click(...) Handles btnGo.Click
   Dim nom As String
   scholar = New Student()
```

```
      scholar.Name = "Peace, Warren"
      nom = m_name
    End Sub
```

12. ```
    Dim scholar As Student

    Private Sub btnGo_Click(...) Handles btnGo.Click
      Dim grade As String
      scholar = New Student()
      scholar.CalcSemGrade = "A"
      grade = scholar.CalcSemGrade()
    End Sub
    ```

13. ```
    Dim pupil, scholar As Student

    Private Sub btnGo_Click(...) Handles btnGo.Click
      scholar = New Student()
      pupil = New Student()
      scholar.Midterm = 89
      pupil.Midterm = scholar.Midterm
      lstGrades.Items.Add(pupil.Midterm)
    End Sub
    ```

14. ```
    Dim scholar As Student
    scholar = New Student()

    Private Sub btnGo_Click(...) Handles btnGo.Click
      scholar.Name = "Transmission, Manuel"
    End Sub
    ```

15. In the following program, determine the output displayed in the list box when the button is pressed:

    ```
    Public Class frmCountry
      Dim nation As New Country("Canada", "Ottawa")

      Private Sub btnDisplay_Click(...) Handles btnDisplay.Click
        nation.Population = 31
        lstBox.Items.Add("Country: " & nation.Name)
        lstBox.Items.Add("Capital: " & nation.Capital)
        lstBox.Items.Add("Pop: " & nation.Population & " million")
      End Sub
    End Class        'frmCountry

    Class Country
      Private m_name As String
      Private m_capital As String
      Private m_population As Double

      Sub New(ByVal name As String, ByVal capital As String)
        m_name = name
        m_capital = capital
      End Sub
    ```
    ```

```
Public ReadOnly Property Name() As String
  Get
    Return m_name
  End Get
End Property

Public ReadOnly Property Capital() As String
  Get
    Return m_capital
  End Get
End Property

Public Property Population() As Double
  Get
    Return m_population
  End Get
  Set(ByVal value As Double)
    m_population = value
  End Set
End Property
End Class        'Country
```

Exercises 16 through 18 refer to the class *Circle*.

16. Create a class called Rectangle that will contain length and width variables, length and width properties, and a new Sub procedure.

17. Add a function to the rectangle class that can be used to calculate and return the area of the rectangle.

18. Add a function to the rectangle class that can be used to calculate and return the perimeter of the rectangle. Also create code that would create an object of the class, populate it, and calculate the value.

Exercises 19 through 21 refer to the class *Circle* contained within the chapter.

19. Enhance the program in Example 3 so that it stores the radius of the circle instead of the diameter of the circle. Change any variables, properties, or procedures/functions necessary to implement this change.

```
Dim poly As Square

Private Sub btnGo_Click(...) Handles btnGo.Click
  poly = New Square()
  poly.Area = 25
  txtLength.Text = CStr(poly.Length)
  txtPerimeter.Text = CStr(poly.Perimeter)
End Sub
```

20. Enhance the program in Example 3 and add a function to the Circle class that can be used to calculate and return the area of a circle.

21. Enhance the program in Example 3 and add a function to the Circle class that can be used to calculate and return the circumference of the circle.

```
Dim cubes As PairOfDice

Private Sub btnGo_Click(...) Handles btnGo.Click
  cubes = New PairOfDice()
  cubes.Roll()
  txtOne.Text = CStr(cubes.Die1)
  txtTwo.Text = CStr(cubes.Die2)
  txtSum.Text = CStr(cubes.SumOfFaces)
End Sub
```

22. Write a program to roll a pair of dice 1000 times, and display the number of times that the sum of the two faces is 7. The program should use an instance of the class PairOfDice discussed in the previous exercise.

23. Write the code for a class called College. The class should have properties Name, NumStudents, and NumFaculty. The method SFRatio should compute the student–faculty ratio. When the following form code is executed, the number 12.4 should be displayed in the text box:

```
Dim school As College

Private Sub btnGo_Click(...) Handles btnGo.Click
  school = New College()
  school.Name = "University of Maryland, College Park"
  school.NumStudents = 36041
  school.NumFaculty = 2896
  txtBox.Text = FormatNumber(school.SFRatio, 1)
End Sub
```

24. Write a program that calculates an employee's pay for a week based on the hourly wage and the number of hours worked. All computations should be performed by an instance of the class Wages.

25. Write a program to implement the cash register in Figure 11.1. The program should have a class called CashRegister that keeps track of the balance and allows deposits and withdrawals. The class should not permit a negative balance.

FIGURE 11.1   Form for Exercise 25.

26. Write a program that calculates the average of up to 50 numbers input by the user and stored in an array. See Figure 11.2. The program should use a class named Statistics and have an AddNumber method that stores numbers into an array one at a time. The class should have a Count property that keeps track of the number of numbers stored and a method called Average that returns the average of the numbers.

FIGURE 11.2   Form for Exercise 26.

27. Write a program that a college bookstore can use to keep track of and determine the retail prices of textbooks. All computations should be performed by an instance of the class Textbook. The class should have properties Title, Author, Cost (wholesale cost), Quantity (number of copies in stock), and the method Price, that is, the retail price. Assuming that the bookstore marks up books by 25%, the Price should be 1.25 times the Cost.

28. Write a program that calculates an employee's FICA tax, with all computations performed by an instance of a class FICA. The FICA tax has two components: the Social Security benefits tax, which in 2008 is 6.2 percent of the first $102,000 of earnings for the year, and the Medicare tax, which is 1.45 percent of earnings.

29. Write a program that adds two fractions and displays their sum in reduced form. The program should use a Fraction class that stores the numerator and denominator of a fraction and has a Reduce method that divides each of the numerator and denominator by their greatest common divisor. Exercise 39 of Section 6.1 contains an algorithm for calculating the greatest common divisor of two numbers.

Solutions to Practice Problems 11.1

1. (d) A programmer is not a template for creating a program.

2.
```
Public Sub New(ByVal ssn As String)
    'Assign the value of ssn to the member variable m_ssn.
  m_ssn = ssn
End Sub

Public ReadOnly Property SocSecNum() As String
  Get
    Return m_ssn
  End Get
End Property
```

Note: Since a student's Social Security number never changes, there is no need to have a Set property procedure for SocSecNum.

11.2 Arrays of Objects; Events; Containment

"An object without an event is like a telephone without a ringer."

Anonymous

■ Arrays of Objects

The elements of an array can have any data type—including a user-defined class. The program in Example 1 uses an array of type Student.

 Example 1   In the following program, which uses the same form design as Example 1 of the previous section, the user enters four pieces of data about a student into text boxes. When the Enter Information button is pressed, the data are used to create and initialize an appropriate object and the object is added to an array. When the Display Grades button is pressed, the name, Social Security number, and semester grade for each student in the array are displayed in the list box.

```
Public Class frmGrades
  Dim students(50) As Student
  Dim lastStudentAdded As Integer = -1      'Position in array of student
  '                                          most recently added
  Private Sub btnEnter_Click(...) Handles btnEnter.Click
    'Create an instance of student.
    'Read the values stored in the text boxes.
    Dim pupil As New Student()
    pupil.Name = txtName.Text
    pupil.SocSecNum = mtxtSSN.Text
    pupil.Midterm = CDbl(txtMidterm.Text)
    pupil.Final = CDbl(txtFinal.Text)
    'Add the student to the array
    lastStudentAdded += 1
    students(lastStudentAdded) = pupil
    'Clear text boxes
    txtName.Clear()
    mtxtSSN.Clear()
    txtMidterm.Clear()
    txtFinal.Clear()
    lstGrades.Items.Add("Student Recorded.")
  End Sub

  Private Sub btnDisplay_Click(...) Handles btnDisplay.Click
    Dim fmtStr As String = "{0,-20}{1,-15}{2,-1}"
    lstGrades.Items.Clear()
    lstGrades.Items.Add(String.Format(fmtStr, "Student Name", _
                                      "SSN", "Grade"))
```

```vb
      For i As Integer = 0 To lastStudentAdded
        lstGrades.Items.Add(String.Format(fmtStr, students(i).Name, _
                      students(i).SocSecNum, students(i).CalcSemGrade))
      Next
    End Sub

    Private Sub btnQuit_Click(...) Handles btnQuit.Click
      End
    End Sub
  End Class         'frmGrades

  Class Student
    Private m_name As String
    Private m_ssn As String
    Private m_midterm As Double
    Private m_final As Double

    Public Property Name() As String
      Get
        Return m_name
      End Get
      Set(ByVal value As String)
        m_name = value
      End Set
    End Property

    Public Property SocSecNum() As String
      Get
        Return m_ssn
      End Get
      Set(ByVal value As String)
        m_ssn = value
      End Set
    End Property

    Public WriteOnly Property Midterm() As Double
      Set(ByVal value As Double)
        m_midterm = value
      End Set
    End Property

    Public WriteOnly Property Final() As Double
      Set(ByVal value As Double)
        m_final = value
      End Set
    End Property

    Function CalcSemGrade() As String
      Dim grade As Double
      grade = (m_midterm + m_final) / 2
      grade = Math.Round(grade)   'Round the grade.
```

```
    Select Case grade
      Case Is >= 90
        Return "A"
      Case Is >= 80
        Return "B"
      Case Is >= 70
        Return "C"
      Case Is >= 60
        Return "D"
      Case Else
        Return "F"
    End Select
  End Function
End Class      'Student
```

[Run, type in data for Al Adams, press the Enter Information button, repeat the process for Brittany Brown and Carol Cole, press the Display Grades button, and then enter data for Daniel Doyle.]

■ Events

In the previous section, we drew a parallel between classes and controls and showed how to define properties and methods for classes. In addition to the predefined event New for classes, other events can be defined by the programmer to communicate changes of properties, errors, and the progress of lengthy operations. Such events are called **user-defined events**. The statement for triggering an event is located in the class block, and the event is dealt with in the form's code. Suppose that the event is named UserDefinedEvent and has the parameters *par1*, *par2*, and so on. In the class block, the statement

```
Public Event UserDefinedEvent(ByVal par1 As DataType1, _
                          ByVal par2 As DataType2, ...)
```

should be placed in the Declarations section, and the statement

```
RaiseEvent UserDefinedEvent(arg1, arg2, ...)
```

should be placed at the locations in the class block code at which the event should be triggered. In the form's code, an instance of the class, call it *object1*, must be declared with a statement of the type

```
Dim WithEvents object1 As ClassName
```

or the type

```
Dim WithEvents object1 As New ClassName
```

in order to be able to respond to the event. That is, the keyword WithEvents must be inserted into the declaration. The header of an event procedure for *object1* will be

```
Private Sub object1_UserDefinedEvent(ByVal par1 As DataType1, _
                            ByVal par2 As DataType2,...) _
                            Handles object1.UserDefinedEvent
```

 Example 2   Consider the Circle class defined in Example 3 of Section 11.1. In the following program, we add a user-defined event that is triggered whenever the location of a circle changes. The event has parameters to pass the location and diameter of the circle. The form's code uses the event to determine if part (or all) of the drawn circle will fall outside the picture box. If so, the event procedure displays the message "Circle Off Screen" in a text box. Let's call the event PositionChanged.

OBJECT	PROPERTY	SETTING
frmCircle	Text	Moving Circle
btnMove	Text	Move and Show Circle
btnQuit	Text	Quit
txtCaution	ReadOnly	True
picCircle		

```
Public Class frmCircle
  Dim WithEvents round As New Circle()

  Private Sub btnMove_Click(...) Handles btnMove.Click
    round.Move(20)
    round.Show(picCircle.CreateGraphics)
  End Sub
```

```
      Private Sub btnQuit_Click(...) Handles btnQuit.Click
        End
      End Sub

      Private Sub round_PositionChanged(ByVal x As Integer, _
        ByVal y As Integer, ByVal d As Integer) Handles round.PositionChanged
        'This event is triggered when the location of the circle changes.
        'The code determines if part of the circle is off the screen.
        If (x + d > picCircle.Width) Or _
           (y + d > picCircle.Height) Then
          txtCaution.Text = "Circle Off Screen"
        End If
      End Sub
    End Class        'frmCircle

    Class Circle
      Private m_x As Integer 'Dist from left side of picture box to circle
      Private m_y As Integer 'Distance from top of picture box to circle
      Private m_d As Integer 'Diameter of circle

      Public Event PositionChanged(ByVal x As Integer, _
                                   ByVal y As Integer, ByVal d As Integer)
      'Event is triggered when the circle moves.

      Public Sub New()
        'Set the initial location of the circle to the upper-left
        'corner of the picture box, and set its diameter to 40.
        Xcoord = 0
        Ycoord = 0
        Diameter = 40
      End Sub

      Public Property Xcoord() As Integer
        Get
          Return m_x
        End Get
        Set(ByVal value As Integer)
          m_x = value
        End Set
      End Property

      Public Property Ycoord() As Integer
        Get
          Return m_y
        End Get
        Set(ByVal value As Integer)
          m_y = value
        End Set
      End Property
```

```
Public Property Diameter() As Integer
  Get
    Return m_d
  End Get
  Set(ByVal value As Integer)
    m_d = value
  End Set
End Property

Sub Show(ByRef gr As Graphics)
  'Draw a circle with the given graphics context.
  gr.DrawEllipse(Pens.Black, Xcoord, Ycoord, Diameter, Diameter)
End Sub

Sub Move(ByVal distance As Integer)
  Xcoord += distance
  Ycoord += distance
  RaiseEvent PositionChanged(Xcoord, Ycoord, Diameter)
End Sub
End Class      'Circle
```

[Run, and press the "Move and Show Circle" button eleven times.]

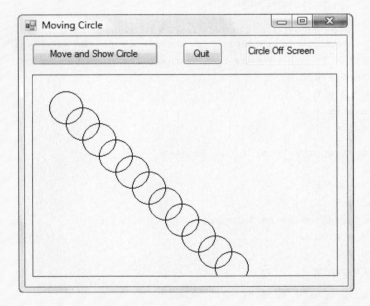

Note: As the last circle appears, the words "Circle Off Screen" are displayed in the text box.

■ Containment

We say that class A **contains** class B when a member variable of class A makes use of an object of type class B. In Example 3, the class DeckOfCards contains the class Card.

Example 3   The following program deals a five-card poker hand. The program has a deck-of-cards object containing an array of 52 card objects. The card object has two properties, Denomination and Suit, and one method, IdentifyCard. The IdentifyCard method returns a string such as "Ace of Spades." In the DeckOfCards object, the New event procedure assigns denominations and suits to the 52 cards. The method ReadCard(n) returns the string identifying the *n*th card of the deck. The method ShuffleDeck uses the Random class to mix up the cards while making 2000 passes through the deck. The event

```
Shuffling(n As Integer, nMax As Integer)
```

is triggered during each shuffling pass through the deck, and its parameters communicate the number of the pass and the total number of passes, so that the program that uses it can keep track of the progress.

OBJECT	PROPERTY	SETTING
frmPoker	Text	Poker Hand
lstHand		
btnShuffle	Text	&Shuffle
btnDeal	Text	&Deal
btnQuit	Text	&Quit

```
Public Class frmPoker
  Dim WithEvents cards As New DeckOfCards()

  Private Sub btnShuffle_Click(...) Handles btnShuffle.Click
    cards.ShuffleDeck
  End Sub

  Private Sub btnDeal_Click(...) Handles btnDeal.Click
    Dim str As String
    lstHand.Items.Clear()
    For i As Integer = 0 To 4
      str = cards.ReadCard(i)
      lstHand.Items.Add(str)
    Next
  End Sub

  Private Sub btnQuit_Click(...) Handles btnQuit.Click
    End
  End Sub

  Private Sub cards_Shuffling(ByVal n As Integer, _
                   ByVal nMax As Integer) Handles cards.Shuffling
    'n is the number of the specific pass through the deck (1, 2, 3...).
    'nMax is the total number of passes when the deck is shuffled.
    lstHand.Items.Clear()
    lstHand.Items.Add("Shuffling Pass: " & n & " out of " & nMax)
```

```
      For i As Integer = 1 To 1000000      'Slow down the shuffle.
      Next
      lstHand.Update()   'Refresh contents of list box
    End Sub
  End Class        'frmPoker

  Class Card
    Private m_denomination As Integer   'A number from 0 through 12
    Private m_suit As String              'Hearts, Clubs, Diamonds, Spades

    Public Property Denomination() As Integer
      Get
        Return m_denomination
      End Get
      Set(ByVal value As Integer)
        'Only store valid values.
        If (value >= 0) And (value <= 12) Then
          m_denomination = value
        End If
      End Set
    End Property

    Public Property Suit() As String
      Get
        Return m_suit
      End Get
      Set(ByVal value As String)
        'Only store valid values.
        If (value = "Hearts") Or (value = "Clubs") Or _
          (value = "Diamonds") Or (value = "Spades") Then
          m_suit = value
        End If
      End Set
    End Property

    Function IdentifyCard() As String
      Dim denom As String = ""
      Select Case m_denomination + 1
        Case 1
          denom = "Ace"
        Case Is <= 10
          denom = CStr(m_denomination + 1)
        Case 11
          denom = "Jack"
        Case 12
          denom = "Queen"
        Case 13
          denom = "King"
      End Select
      Return denom & " of " & m_suit
```

```vb
    End Function
End Class      'Card

Class DeckOfCards
   Private m_deck(51) As Card 'Class DeckOfCards contains class Card
   Public Event Shuffling(ByVal n As Integer, ByVal nMax As Integer)

   Public Sub New()
     'Make the first thirteen cards hearts, the
     'next thirteen cards diamonds, and so on.
     Dim suits() As String = {"Hearts", "Clubs", "Diamonds", "Spades"}
     For i As Integer = 0 To 3
       'Each pass corresponds to one of the four suits.
       For j As Integer = 0 To 12
         'Assign numbers from 0 through 12 to the
         'cards of each suit.
         m_deck(i * 13 + j) = New Card()
         m_deck(i * 13 + j).Suit = suits(i)
         m_deck(i * 13 + j).Denomination = j
       Next
     Next
   End Sub

   Function ReadCard(ByVal cardNum As Integer) As String
     Return m_deck(cardNum).IdentifyCard()
   End Function

   Sub Swap(ByVal i As Integer, ByVal j As Integer)
     'Swap the ith and jth card in the deck.
     Dim tempCard As Card
     tempCard = m_deck(i)
     m_deck(i) = m_deck(j)
     m_deck(j) = tempCard
   End Sub

   Sub ShuffleDeck()
     'Do 2000 passes through the deck.  On each pass,
     'swap each card with a randomly selected card.
     Dim index As Integer
     Dim randomNum As New Random()
     For i As Integer = 1 To 2000
       For k As Integer = 0 To 51
         index = randomNum.Next(0, 52)   'Randomly select a number
         'from 0 through 51 inclusive.
         Swap(k, index)
       Next
       RaiseEvent Shuffling(i, 2000)
     Next
   End Sub
End Class      'DeckOfCards
```

[Run, click on the Shuffle button, and click on the Deal button after the shuffling is complete.]

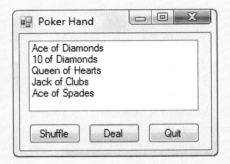

Practice Problems 11.2

Consider the program in Example 1 of Section 11.1, and suppose that mtxtSSN is an ordinary text box.

1. Alter the Set SocSecNum property procedure to raise the event ImproperSSN when the Social Security number does not have 11 characters. The event should pass the length of the Social Security number and the student's name to the form's code.

2. What statement must be placed in the Declarations section of the class block?

3. Write an event procedure for the event ImproperSSN.

4. What statement in the form's code must be altered?

EXERCISES 11.2

1. In Example 1, modify the event procedure btnDisplay_Click so that only the students who receive a grade higher than a C are displayed.

The folder Ch10\MajorDatabases contains the database COUNTRY_POP.MDB which consists of a single table, Countries, having four fields: an abbreviation for the country, the name of the country, the population of the country, and the size in square miles of the land that the country occupies. This database was used in chapter 10 and is also used in Exercise 2 through 5 below.

```
Delaware
DE
Dec. 1787
1954
759000
```

2. Create (a) a class Country with four properties to hold the information about a single country from the database and (b) a method that calculates the density (people per square mile) of the country.

3. Write a program that requests a country's name in an input dialog box and displays the Country's code, population, and population density. The program should use an array of Country objects.

4. Write a program that displays the names of the countries and their population densities in a list box ordered by population density. The program should use an array of Country objects.

5. Write a program that reads the data from the database into an array of Country objects and raises an event whenever the population of a country exceeds one hundred million. Countries with a large population should have their names and populations displayed in a list box by the corresponding event procedure. **Hint:** Create a class called WorldCountries that contains the array and defines a method Add that adds a new country to the array. The Add method should raise the event.

6. Create a class Student that contains a student's name and their final exam grade. Also add an event IllegelGradeEntry that is raised when a grade below 0 or above 100 is attempted to be entered as a grade. Show the entire class block and write an event procedure for the event that would generate an error message.

7. Consider the CashRegister class in Exercise 25 of Section 11.1. Add the event AttemptToOverdraw that is raised when the user tries to subtract more money than is in the cash register.

8. Consider the class PairOfDice discussed in Exercise 21 of Section 11.1. Add the event SnakeEyes that is raised whenever two ones appear during a roll of the dice. Write a program that uses the event.

9. Consider the Fraction class in Exercise 29 of Section 11.1. Add the event ZeroDenominator, that is triggered whenever a denominator is set to 0. Write a program that uses the event.

10. Write a program for the fraction calculator shown in Figure 11.3. After the numerators and denominators of the two fractions to the left of the equals sign are placed in the four text boxes, one of four operations buttons should be pressed. The result appears to the right of the equals sign. The program should use a Calculator class, which contains three members of the type Fraction discussed in Exercise 29 of Section 11.1. **Note:** In Figure 11.3, the fraction bars are very short list boxes.

FIGURE 11.3   Sample Output for Exercise 10.

11. Write a program that takes orders at a fast food restaurant. See Figure 11.4 on the next page. The restaurant has two menus, a regular menu and a kids menu. An item is ordered by highlighting it in one of the list boxes and then pushing the ≫ or ≪ button to place it in the order list box in the center of the form. As each item is ordered, a running total is displayed in the text box at the lower right part of the form. The program should use a Choices class, which contains a Food class. (The contents of each of the three list boxes should be treated as Choices objects.) Each Food object should hold the name and price of a single food item. The Choices class should have a ChoiceChanged event that can be used by the form code to update the cost of the order.

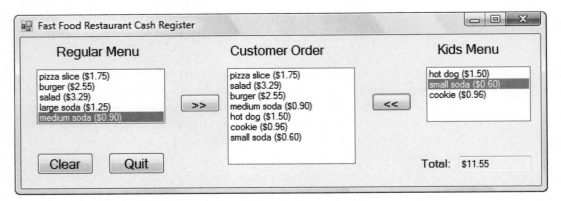

FIGURE 11.4 Sample Output for Exercise 11.

12. Write a program for a simple game in which each of two players rolls a pair of dice. The person with the highest tally wins. See Figure 11.5. The program should use a Game class (HighRoller) having two member variables of the type PairOfDice discussed in Exercise 21 of Section 11.1.

FIGURE 11.5 Sample output for Exercise 12.

13. Write a program to produce an employee's weekly paycheck receipt. The receipt should contain the employee's name, amount earned for the week, total amount earned for the year, FICA tax deduction, withholding tax deduction, and take-home amount. The program should use an Employee class and a Tax class. The Tax class must have properties for the amount earned for the week, the prior total amount earned for the year, the number of withholding allowances, and marital status. It should have methods for computing FICA and withholding taxes. The Employee class should store the employee's name, number of withholding allowances, marital status, hours worked this week, hourly salary, and previous amount earned for the year. The Employee class should use the Tax class to calculate the taxes to be deducted. The formula for calculating the FICA tax is given in Exercise 28 of Section 11.1. To compute the withholding tax, multiply the number of withholding allowances by $67.31, subtract the product from the amount earned, and use Table 11.1 or Table 11.2.

TABLE 11.1   2008 Federal income tax withheld for a single person paid weekly.

Adjusted Weekly Income	Income Tax Withheld
$0 to $51	$0
Over $51 to $198	10% of amount over $51
Over $198 to $653	$14.70 + 15% of amount over $198
Over $653 to $1,533	$82.95 + 25% of amount over $653
Over $1,533 to $3,202	$302.95 + 28% of amount over $1,533
Over $3,202 to $6,916	$770.27 + 33% of amount over $3,202
Over $6,916	$1,995.89 + 35% of amount over $6,916

TABLE 11.2   2008 Federal income tax withheld for a married person paid weekly.

Adjusted Weekly Income	Income Tax Withheld
$0 to $154	$0
Over $154 to $453	10% of amount over $154
Over $453 to $1,388	$29.90 + 15% of amount over $453
Over $1,388 to $2,651	$170.15 + 25% of amount over $1,388
Over $2,651 to $3,994	$485.90 + 28% of amount over $2,651
Over $3,994 to $7,021	$861.94 + 33% of amount over $3,994
Over $7,021	$1,860.85 + 35% of amount over $7,021

Solutions to Practice Problems 11.2

```
1. Public Property SocSecNum() As String
     Get
       Return m_ssn
     End Get
     Set(ByVal value As String)
       If value.Length = 11 Then
         m_ssn = value
       Else
         RaiseEvent ImproperSSN(value.Length, m_name)
       End If
     End Set
   End Property

2. Public Event ImproperSSN(ByVal length As Integer, _
                       ByVal studentName As String)

3. Private Sub pupil_ImproperSSN(ByVal length As Integer, _
           ByVal studentName As string) Handles pupil.ImproperSSN
     MessageBox.Show("The social security number entered for " & _
         studentName & " consisted of " & length & _
         " characters. Reenter the data for " & studentName & ".")
   End Sub
```

4. The statement

```
Dim pupil As Student
```

must be changed to

```
Dim WithEvents pupil As Student
```

11.3 Inheritance

The three relationships between classes are "use," "containment," and "inheritance." One class **uses** another class if it manipulates objects of that class. We say that class A **contains** class B when a member variable of class A makes use of an object of type class B. Sections 11.1 and 11.2 present examples of use and containment.

Inheritance is a process by which one class (the **child** or **derived** class) inherits the properties, methods, and events of another class (the **parent** or **base** class). The child has access to all of its parent's properties, methods and events as well as to all of its own. If the parent is itself a child, then it and its children have access to all of its parent's properties, methods and events. Consider the classes shown in Figure 11.6. All three children inherit Property A and Sub B from their parent. Child2 and Child3 have an additional event and a property, respectively. GrandChild1 has access to Property A, Sub B, and Event C from its parent and adds Function E and Sub F. The collection of a parent class along with its descendants is called a **hierarchy**.

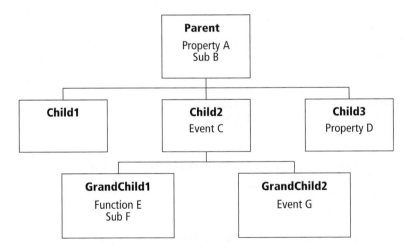

FIGURE 11.6 **Example of inheritance hierarchy.**

There are two main benefits gained by using inheritance: First, it allows two or more classes to share some common features yet differentiate themselves on others. Second, it supports code reusability by avoiding the extra effort required to maintain duplicate code in multiple classes. For these reasons, inheritance is one of the most powerful tools of object-oriented programming. Considerable work goes into planning and defining the member variables and methods of the parent class. The child classes are beneficiaries of this effort.

Just as structured programming requires the ability to break complex problems into simpler subproblems, object-oriented programming requires the skill to identify useful hierarchies of classes and derived classes. Software engineers are still working on the guidelines for when and how to establish hierarchies. One useful criterion is the **ISA test**: If one class *is a* more specific case of another class, the first class should be derived from the second class.

The Visual Basic keyword Inherits identifies the parent of a class. The code used to define the class Parent and its child class Child2 as illustrated in Figure 11.6 is

```
Class Parent
  Public Property A
    'Property Get and Set blocks
  End Property

  Sub B()
    'Code for Sub procedure B
  End Sub
End Class

Class Child2
  Inherits Parent
  Event C()
End Class
```

As Child2 is itself a parent, its child GrandChild1 can be declared using a similar statement:

```
Class GrandChild1
  Inherits Child2

  Function E()
    'Code for function E
  End Sub

  Sub F()
    'Code for Sub procedure F
  End Sub
End Class
```

 Example 1   In the following program, the user is presented with a basic adding machine. The Calculator class implements the Multiply and Divide methods and inherits the FirstNumber and SecondNumber properties and the Add and Subtract methods from its AddingMachine parent. When the Adding Machine radio button is selected, the user may add or subtract two numbers using an AddingMachine object. When the Calculator radio button is selected, the user may add, subtract, multiply, or divide two numbers using a Calculator object. Notice that the multiply and divide buttons are hidden when the Adding Machine is selected, and how the Click event procedures for the btnAdd and btnSubtract buttons examine the state of the radio button to determine which machine to use.

OBJECT	PROPERTY	SETTING
frmCalculate	Text	Calculations
lblNumber1	Text	First Number:
txtNumber1		
lblNumber2	Text	Second Number:
txtNumber2		
lblResult	Text	Result:
txtResult	ReadOnly	True
grpMachine	Text	Machine
radAddingMachine	Text	Adding Machine
	Checked	True
radCalculator	Text	Calculator
btnAdd	Text	+
btnSubtract	Text	−
btnMultiply	Text	×
btnDivide	Font	Symbol
	Text	¸ (Cedilla)

```vb
Public Class frmCalculate
  'Create both machines.
  Dim adder As New AddingMachine()
  Dim calc As New Calculator()

  Private Sub radAddingMachine_CheckedChanged(...) _
                     Handles radAddingMachine.CheckedChanged
    'Hide the multiply and divide functionality.
    btnMultiply.Visible = False
    btnDivide.Visible = False
  End Sub

  Private Sub radCalculator_CheckedChanged(...) _
                     Handles radCalculator.CheckedChanged
    'Show the multiply and divide functionality.
    btnMultiply.Visible = True
    btnDivide.Visible = True
  End Sub

  Private Sub btnAdd_Click(...) Handles btnAdd.Click
    'Add two numbers.
    If radAddingMachine.Checked Then
      'If adding machine selected, use it to get the result.
      adder.FirstNumber = CDbl(txtNumber1.Text)
      adder.SecondNumber = CDbl(txtNumber2.Text)
      txtResult.Text = CStr(adder.Add)
    Else
      'If calculator selected, use it to get the result.
      calc.FirstNumber = CDbl(txtNumber1.Text)
      calc.SecondNumber = CDbl(txtNumber2.Text)
      txtResult.Text = CStr(calc.Add)
    End If
  End Sub
```

```
    Private Sub btnSubtract_Click(...) Handles btnSubtract.Click
        'Subtract two numbers.
      If radAddingMachine.Checked Then
          'If adding machine selected, use it to get the result.
          adder.FirstNumber = CDbl(txtNumber1.Text)
          adder.SecondNumber = CDbl(txtNumber2.Text)
          txtResult.Text = CStr(adder.Subtract)
      Else
          'If calculator selected, use it to get the result.
          calc.FirstNumber = CDbl(txtNumber1.Text)
          calc.SecondNumber = CDbl(txtNumber2.Text)
          txtResult.Text = CStr(calc.Subtract)
      End If
    End Sub

    Private Sub btnMultiply_Click(...) Handles btnMultiply.Click
        'Multiply two numbers.
      calc.FirstNumber = CDbl(txtNumber1.Text)
      calc.SecondNumber = CDbl(txtNumber2.Text)
      txtResult.Text = CStr(calc.Multiply)
    End Sub

    Private Sub btnDivide_Click(...) Handles btnDivide.Click
        'Divide two numbers.
      calc.FirstNumber = CDbl(txtNumber1.Text)
      calc.SecondNumber = CDbl(txtNumber2.Text)
      txtResult.Text = CStr(calc.Divide)
    End Sub
End Class         'frmCalculate

Class AddingMachine
  Private m_num1, m_num2 As Double

  Public Property FirstNumber() As Double
    Get
      Return m_num1
    End Get
    Set(ByVal value As Double)
      m_num1 = value
    End Set
  End Property

  Public Property SecondNumber() As Double
    Get
      Return m_num2
    End Get
    Set(ByVal value As Double)
      m_num2 = value
    End Set
  End Property
```

```
Function Add() As Double
   Return FirstNumber + SecondNumber
End Function

Function Subtract() As Double
   Return FirstNumber - SecondNumber
End Function
End Class        'AddingMachine

Class Calculator
  Inherits AddingMachine
  'Calculator inherits properties FirstNumber and SecondNumber
  'and functions Add() and Subtract().

  Function Multiply() As Double
     Return FirstNumber * SecondNumber
  End Function

  Function Divide() As Double
     Return FirstNumber / SecondNumber
  End Function
End Class        'Calculator
```

[Run, type in 12 and 3, and press the + and − buttons. Click the Calculator radio button, and press the +, −, ×, and ÷ buttons.]

■ Polymorphism and Overriding

The set of properties, methods, and events for a class is called the class **interface**. In essence, the interface of a class defines how it should behave. The interfaces of the classes AddingMachine and Calculator used in Example 1 are shown in Table 11.3.

Consider the classes used in Examples 1 and 2 of Section 11.1. Both Student and PFStudent have the same interface even though they carry out the task of computing a semester grade differently. See Table 11.4.

TABLE 11.3   Interfaces used in Example 1.

		AddingMachine	Calculator
Properties		FirstNumber	FirstNumber
		SecondNumber	SecondNumber
Methods		Add	Add
		Subtract	Subtract
			Multiply
			Divide
Events		(none)	(none)

TABLE 11.4   Interfaces used in Examples 1 and 2 in Section 11.1.

		Student	PFStudent
Properties		Name	Name
		SocSecNum	SocSecNum
		Midterm	Midterm
		Final	Final
Methods		CalcSemGrade	CalcSemGrade
Events		(none)	(none)

If a programmer wants to write a program that manipulates objects from these two classes, he or she need only know how to use the interface. The programmer need not be concerned with what specific implementation of that interface is being used. The object will then behave according to its specific implementation.

The programmer need only be aware of the CalcSemGrade method and needn't be concerned about its implementation. The feature that two classes can have methods that are named the same and have essentially the same purpose, but different implementations, is called **polymorphism**.

A programmer may employ polymorphism in three easy steps. First, the properties, methods, and events that make up an interface are defined. Second, a parent class is created that performs the functionality dictated by the interface. Finally, a child class inherits the parent and overrides the methods that require different implementation than the parent. The keyword Overridable is used to designate the parent's methods that can be overridden, and the keyword Overrides is used to designate the child's methods that are doing the overriding.

There are situations where a child class needs to access the parent class's implementation of a method that the child is overriding. Visual Basic provides the keyword MyBase to support this functionality.

Consider the code from Example 1 of Section 11.1. To employ polymorphism, the keyword Overridable is inserted into the header of the CalcSemGrade method in the Student class:

```
Overridable Function CalcSemGrade() As String
```

The PFStudent class inherits all of the properties and methods from its parent, overriding the CalcSemGrade method as follows:

```
Class PFStudent
  Inherits Student

  Overrides Function CalcSemGrade() As String
    'The student's grade for the semester
    If MyBase.CalcSemGrade = "F" Then
      Return "Fail"
    Else
      Return "Pass"
    End If
  End Function
End Class        'PFStudent
```

 Example 2   In the following program, the user can enter student information and display the semester grades for the class. The PFStudent class inherits all of the properties from its parent Student, but overrides the CalcSemGrade method with its own implementation. The btnEnter_Click event procedure stores an element created by either class into the *students* array. However, the btnDisplay_Click event procedure does not need to know which elements are from which class, thus demonstrating polymorphism. (**Note:** In the 6th line of the btn_Enter event procedure, the statement **pupil=NewPFStudent()** is valid since, due to inheritance, every PFStudent *is a* Student.)

OBJECT	PROPERTY	SETTING
frmGrades	Text	Semester Grade
lblName	Text	Name:
txtName		
lblSSN	Text	SSN:
mtxtSSN	Mask	000-00-0000
lblMidterm	Text	Midterm:
txtMidterm		
lblFinal	Text	Final:
txtFinal		
grpGradingOption	Text	Grading Option
radLetterGrade	Text	Letter Grade
	Checked	True
radPassFail	Text	Pass/Fail
btnEnter	Text	&Enter Information
btnDisplay	Text	&Display Grades
btnQuit	Text	&Quit
lstGrades	Font	Courier New

```
Public Class frmGrades
  Dim students(50) As Student            'Stores the class
  Dim lastStudentAdded As Integer = -1   'Last student added to students()

  Private Sub btnEnter_Click(...) Handles btnEnter.Click
    'Stores a student into the array.
    Dim pupil As Student
    'Create the appropriate object depending upon the radio button.
    If radPassFail.Checked Then
```

```vbnet
      pupil = New PFStudent()
    Else
      pupil = New Student()
    End If
    'Store the values in the text boxes into the object.
    pupil.Name = txtName.Text
    pupil.SocSecNum = mtxtSSN.Text
    pupil.Midterm = CDbl(txtMidterm.Text)
    pupil.Final = CDbl(txtFinal.Text)
    'Add the student to the array.
    lastStudentAdded += 1
    students(lastStudentAdded) = pupil
    'Clear text boxes and list box.
    txtName.Clear()
    mtxtSSN.Clear()
    txtMidterm.Clear()
    txtFinal.Clear()
    lstGrades.Items.Add("Student #" & lastStudentAdded + 1 _
                    & " recorded.")
    txtName.Focus()
  End Sub

  Private Sub btnDisplay_Click(...) Handles btnDisplay.Click
    'Display the students' information and semester grade.
    Dim fmtStr As String = "{0,-20}{1,-15}{2,-4}"
    lstGrades.Items.Clear()
    'Loop over all available elements of the Student array.
    For i As Integer = 0 To lastStudentAdded
      lstGrades.Items.Add(String.Format(fmtStr, students(i).Name, _
                    students(i).SocSecNum, students(i).CalcSemGrade))
    Next
  End Sub

  Private Sub btnQuit_Click(...) Handles btnQuit.Click
    'Quit the program
    End
  End Sub
End Class      'frmGrades

Class Student
  'Member variables to hold the property values
  Private m_name As String
  Private m_ssn As String
  Private m_midterm As Double
  Private m_final As Double

  Public Property Name() As String
    'The student's name
    Get
      Return m_name
```

```
      End Get
      Set(ByVal value As String)
        m_name = value
      End Set
    End Property

    Public Property SocSecNum() As String
      'The student's Social Security Number
      Get
        Return m_ssn
      End Get
      Set(ByVal value As String)
        m_ssn = value
      End Set
    End Property

    Public WriteOnly Property Midterm() As Double
      'The student's score on the midterm exam
      Set(ByVal value As Double)
        m_midterm = value
      End Set
    End Property

    Public WriteOnly Property Final() As Double
      'The student's score on the final exam
      Set(ByVal value As Double)
        m_final = value
      End Set
    End Property

    Overridable Function CalcSemGrade() As String
      'The student's grade for the semester
      Dim grade As Double
      'The grade is based upon average of the midterm and final exams.
      grade = (m_midterm + m_final) / 2
      grade = Math.Round(grade)   'Round the grade.
      Select Case grade
        Case Is >= 90
          Return "A"
        Case Is >= 80
          Return "B"
        Case Is >= 70
          Return "C"
        Case Is >= 60
          Return "D"
        Case Else
          Return "F"
      End Select
    End Function
  End Class       'Student
```

```
Class PFStudent
  Inherits Student

  Overrides Function CalcSemGrade() As String
    'The student's grade for the semester
    If MyBase.CalcSemGrade = "F" Then
      Return "Fail"
    Else
      Return "Pass"
    End If
  End Function
End Class        'PFStudent
```

[Enter the data and press the Enter Information button for three students. Then press the Display Grades button, and finally enter the data for another student.]

Example 2 employs inheritance and overriding to provide functionality to one child class. If a program contains two or more children of a class, however, the technique of overriding can lead to confusing programs. Visual Basic provides a cleaner design through the use of abstract classes.

■ Abstract Properties, Methods, and Classes

Sometimes you want to insist that each child of a class have a certain property or method that it must implement for its own use. Such a property or method is said to be **abstract** and is declared with the keyword MustOverride. An **abstract** property or method consists of just a header with no code following it. It has no corresponding **End Property**, **End Sub**, or **End Function** statement. Its class is called an **abstract base class** and must be declared with the keyword MustInherit. Abstract classes cannot be instantiated, only their children can be instantiated.

Example 3   The following program calculates the area of several regular two-dimensional shapes given the length of one side. (A regular shape is a shape whose sides have identical length and whose interior angles are identical.) The abstract parent class Shape implements the Length property and declares the Name and Area functions as MustOverride. Notice that methods declared with MustOverride do not have any implementation code. Each child class inherits the property from the parent and implements the two functions. The btnDisplay_Click event procedure uses polymorphism to set the shapes' length and display the shapes' names and areas.

OBJECT	PROPERTY	SETTING
frmShapes	Text	Two-Dimensional Shapes
lblLength	Text	Length of a side:
txtLength		
btnDisplay	Text	Display
lstOutput		

```vb
Public Class frmShapes
    'Declare shape array.
    Dim shape(3) As Shape

    Private Sub frmShapes_Load(...) Handles MyBase.Load
        'Populate the array with shapes.
        shape(0) = New EquilateralTriangle()
        shape(1) = New Square()
        shape(2) = New Pentagon()
        shape(3) = New Hexagon()
    End Sub

    Private Sub btnDisplay_Click(...) Handles btnDisplay.Click
        Dim length As Double
        'Set lengths of all shapes.
        length = CDbl(txtLength.Text)
        For i As Integer = 0 To 3
            shape(i).Length = length
        Next
        'Display results.
        lstOutput.Items.Clear()
        For i As Integer = 0 To 3
            lstOutput.Items.Add("The " & shape(i).Name & " has area " _
                            & FormatNumber(shape(i).Area)) & "."
        Next
    End Sub
End Class        'frmShapes

MustInherit Class Shape
    Private m_length As Double        'Stores the value of Length property
```

```vbnet
  Public Property Length() As Double
    'Length of a side
    Get
      Return m_length
    End Get
    Set(ByVal value As Double)
      m_length = value
    End Set
  End Property

  MustOverride Function Name() As String
  'Returns the name of the shape.

  MustOverride Function Area() As Double
  'Returns the area of the shape.
End Class        'Shape

Class EquilateralTriangle
  Inherits Shape

  Overrides Function Name() As String
    'The name of this shape
    Return "Equilateral Triangle"
  End Function

  Overrides Function Area() As Double
    'Formula for the area of an equilateral triangle
    Return Length * Length * Math.Sqrt(3) / 4
  End Function
End Class          'EquilateralTriangle

Class Square
  Inherits Shape

  Overrides Function Name() As String
    'The name of this shape
    Return "Square"
  End Function

  Overrides Function Area() As Double
    'Formula for the area of a square
    Return Length * Length
  End Function
End Class        'Square

Class Pentagon
  Inherits Shape

  Overrides Function Name() As String
    'The name of this shape
    Return "Pentagon"
  End Function
```

```
Overrides Function Area() As Double
  'Formula for the area of a pentagon
  Return Length * Length * Math.Sqrt(25 + (10 * Math.Sqrt(5))) / 4
End Function
End Class        'Pentagon

Class Hexagon
  Inherits Shape

  Overrides Function Name() As String
    'The name of this shape
    Return "Hexagon"
  End Function

  Overrides Function Area() As Double
    'Formula for the area of a hexagon
    Return Length * Length * 3 * Math.Sqrt(3) / 2
  End Function
End Class        'Hexagon
```

[Run the program, enter 5, and press the Display button.]

Comments

1. Visual Basic uses inheritance in every Windows application that is written. Examination of any program's code reveals that the form's class inherits from the class System.Windows.Forms.Form.

2. In Example 2, the btnDisplay_Click event procedure does not need to know which elements of the Student array are instances of the Student class and which are instances of the PFStudent class. In some situations, however, the program may want to know this. Visual Basic provides the expression **TypeOf...Is** to test if an instance was created from a particular class (or from the class' parents, grandparents, etc.) For example, the following procedure counts the number of pass/fail students in the *students* array:

```
Sub CountPassFail()
  Dim count As Integer = 0
  For i As Integer = 0 To lastStudentAdded
    If TypeOf students(i) Is PFStudent Then
      count += 1
    End If
  Next
  MessageBox.Show("There are " & count & " pass/fail students out of " _
    & lastStudentAdded & " students in the class.")
End Sub
```

3. Child classes do not inherit or have access to the parent's Private member variables.

1. In the class AddingMachine of Example 1, the Add function could have been defined with

```
Function Add() As Double
  Return m_num1 + m_num2
End Function
```

Explain why the Multiply function of the class Calculator cannot be defined with

```
Function Multiply() As Double
  Return m_num1 * m_num2
End Function
```

2. Consider the hierarchy of classes shown below. What value is assigned to the variable *phrase* by the following two lines of code?

```
Dim mammal As New Mammals()
Dim phrase As String = mammal.Msg

Class Animals

  Overridable Function Msg() As String
    Return "Can move"
  End Function
End Class

Class Vertebrates
  Inherits Animals

  Overrides Function Msg() As String
    Return MyBase.Msg & " " & "Has a backbone"
  End Function
End Class

Class Mammals
  Inherits Vertebrates

  Overrides Function Msg() As String
    Return MyBase.Msg & " " & "Nurtures young with mother's milk"
  End Function
End Class

Class Anthropods
  Inherits Animals

  Overrides Function Msg() As String
    Return MyBase.Msg & " " & "Has jointed limbs and no backbone"
  End Function
End Class
```

In Exercises 1 through 4, identify the output of the code that uses the following two classes:

```
Class Person
  Public m_name as string
  Public m_age as integer

  Overridable Function PrintData() as String
    Return m_name & ", " & m_age
  End Function

  Overridable Sub SetData(byVal name as string, byVal age as integer)
  m_name = name
  m_age = age
  End Function
End Class

Class Employee
  Inherits Person
  Private m_salary as Double
  Private m_department as String
  Overrides Function PrintData() As String
    Return m_name & ", " & m_department & ", " & m_salary.toString("C")
  End Function

  Overridable Sub SetData(byVal name as string, byVal age as integer, _
  byVal salary as double, byVal department as string)
  m_name = name
  m_age = age
  m_salary = salary
  m_department = department
  End Function
End Class
```

1. ```
   Dim student as Person = New Person()
     student.SetData("Brian", 19)
     txtOutput.text = student.PrintData()
   ```

2. ```
   Dim assistant as Employee = New Employee()
     assistant.SetData("Jill", 27, 23323.00, "Accounting")
     txtOutput.text = assistant.PrintData()
   ```

3. ```
   Dim student as Person = New Person()
     Dim assistant as Employee = New Employee()
     assistant.SetData("Jill", 27, 23323.00, "Accounting")
     student.PrintData()
   ```

4. ```
   Dim student as Person = New Person()
     Dim assistant as Employee = New Employee()
     assistant.SetData("Jill", 27, 23323.00, "Accounting")
     student.SetData("Brian", 19)
     assistant.PrintData()
   ```

In Exercises 5 through 6, identify the output of the code that uses the following two classes:

```
Class Base
  Overridable Function Msg() As String
    Return "This is from the Base Class."
  End Function
End Class

Class Derived
  Inherits Base
  Overrides Function Msg() As String
    Return MyBase.msg & " And this is from the Derived Class."
  End Function
End Class
```

5. What value is assigned to the variable phrase by the following two lines of code?

```
Dim myClass as New Derived()
Dim phrase As String = myClass.Msg
```

6. What value is assigned to the variable phrase by the following two lines of code?

```
Dim myClass As New Base()
Dim phrase As String = myClass.Msg
```

In Exercises 7 through 16, identify the errors in the code.

7.
```
Class Hello
    Function Hi() As String
      Return "hi!"
    End Function
  End Class

  Class Greetings
    Overrides Hello
    Function GoodBye() As String
      Return "goodbye"
    End Function
  End Class
```

8.
```
Class Hello
    Function Hi() As String
      Return "hi!"
    End Function
  End Class

  Class Greetings
    Inherits Hi()
    Function GoodBye() As String
      Return "goodbye"
    End Function
  End Class
```

9.
```
Class Hello
  Function Hi() As String
    Return "hi!"
  End Function
End Class

Class Aussie
  Inherits Hello
  Function Hi() As String
    Return "G'day mate!"
  End Function
End Class
```

10.
```
Class Hello
  Function Hi() As String
    Return "hi!"
  End Function
End Class

Class WithIt
  Inherits Hello
  Overrides Function Hi() As String
    Return "Hey"
  End Function
End Class
```

11.
```
Class Hello
  Overridable Function Hi() As String
    Return "hi!"
  End Function
End Class

Class Cowboy
  Inherits Hello
  Function Hi() As String
    Return "howdy!"
  End Function
End Class
```

12.
```
Class Hello
  MustOverride Function Hi() As String
    Return "hi!"
  End Function
End Class

Class DragRacer
  Inherits Hello
  Overrides Function Hi() As String
    Return "Start your engines!"
  End Function
End Class
```

13.
```
Class Hello
    MustInherit Function Hi() As String
End Class

Class Gentleman
  Inherits Hello
  Overrides Function Hi() As String
    Return "Good day"
  End Function
End Class
```

14.
```
Class Hello
    MustOverride Function Hi() As String
End Class

Class Euro
  Inherits Hello
  Overrides Function Hi() As String
    Return "Caio"
  End Function
End Class
```

15.
```
MustOverride Class Hello
    MustOverride Function Hi() As String
End Class

Class Southerner
  Inherits Hello
  Overrides Function Hi() As String
    Return "Hi y'all"
  End Function
End Class
```

16.
```
MustInherit Class Hello
    MustOverride Function Hi() As String
End Class

Class NorthEasterner
  Inherits Hello
  Overrides Function Hi(ByVal name As String) As String
    Return "How ya doin', " & name
  End Function
End Class
```

17. Expand Example 1 to use a class ScientificCalculator that is derived from the class Calculator and has an exponentiation button in addition to the four arithmetic buttons.

18. Rewrite Example 2 so that the class Student has an abstract method CalcSemGrade and two derived classes called LGStudent (LG stands for "Letter Grade") and PFStudent.

19. Consider the class CashRegister from Exercise 25 of Section 11.1. Create a derived class called FastTrackRegister that could be used at a toll booth to collect money

from vehicles and keep track of the number of vehicles processed. Write a program using the class and having the form in Figure 11.7. One dollar should be collected from each car and two dollars from each truck.

FIGURE 11.7   Form for Exercise 19.

20. Write a program that keeps track of a bookstore's inventory. The store orders both trade books and textbooks from publishers. The program should define an abstract class Book that contains the MustOverride property Price, and the ordinary properties Quantity, Name, and Cost. The Textbook and Tradebook classes should be derived from the class Book and should override property Price by adding a markup. (Assume that the markup is 40% for a trade book and 20% for a textbook.) The program should accept input from the user on book orders and display the following statistics: total number of books, number of textbooks, total cost of the orders, and total value of the inventory. (The value of the inventory is the amount of money that the bookstore can make if it sells all of the books in stock.) A sample output is shown in Figure 11.8 on the next page.

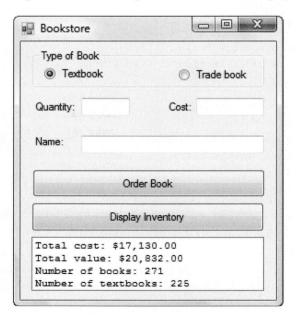

FIGURE 11.8   Sample output for Exercise 20.

21. Write a program that records the weekly payroll of a department that hires both salaried and hourly employees. The program should accept user input and display the number of employees, the number of salaried employees, the total payroll, and the average number of hours worked. The abstract class Employee should contain Name and Rate properties. (The Rate text box should be filled in with the weekly salary for salaried workers and the hourly wage for hourly workers.) The Salaried and Hourly classes should inherit the Employee class and override the method GrossPay that accepts the number of hours worked as a parameter. A sample output is shown in Figure 11.9. **Hint:** Use an array of a structure that holds the employee object and the number of hours worked during the week.

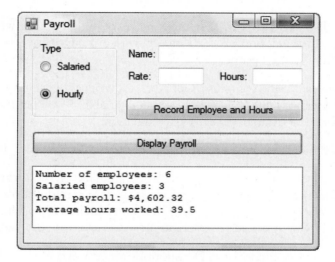

FIGURE 11.9 Sample output for Exercise 21.

22. Consider the class Statistics from Exercise 26 of Section 11.1. Create a derived class called CompleteStats that also provides a Spread function and an event called NewSpread. This event should be raised whenever the spread changes. (The *spread* is the difference between the highest and the lowest grades.) Write a program that uses the classes to analyze up to 50 exam grades input by the user. The program should display the number of grades and the current spread at all times. When the Calculate Average button is pressed, the program should display the average of the grades. A sample output is shown in Figure 11.10.

FIGURE 11.10 Sample output for Exercise 22.

Solutions to Practice Problems 11.3

1. While the derived class Calculator has access to the Properties and Methods of the base class AddingMachine, it does not have access to its Private member variables.
2. The string "Can move Has a backbone Nurtures young with mother's milk"

CHAPTER 11 SUMMARY

1. An *object* is an entity that stores data, has methods that manipulate the data, and can trigger events. A *class* is a template from which objects are created. A *method* specifies the way in which an object's data are manipulated. An *event* is a message sent by an object to signal the occurrence of a condition.

2. Each class is defined in a separate block of code starting with Class *ClassName* and ending with End Class. Data are stored in member variables and accessed by procedures called properties.

3. A property routine contains a Get block to retrieve the value of a member variable or a Set block to assign a value to a member variable. These procedures can also be used to enforce constraints and carry out validation.

4. Visual Basic automatically invokes a New procedure when an object is created.

5. An object variable is declared with a statement of the form `Dim objectName As ClassName`, and the object is created with a statement of the form `objectName = New ClassName(arg1, arg2, ...)`. These two statements are often combined into the single statement `Dim objectName As New ClassName(arg1, arg2, ...)`.

6. Events are declared in the Declarations section of a class with a statement of the form `Public Event UserDefinedEvent(arg1, arg2, ...)` and triggered with a `RaiseEvent` statement. The declaration statement for the object must include the keyword `WithEvents` in order for the events coming from the object to be processed. The header of an event-handling procedure has the form `Private Sub procedureName(par1, par2, ...) Handles objectName.UserDefinedEvent`.

7. The properties, methods, and events of a class are referred to as its *interface*.

8. Inheritance, which is implemented with the keyword Inherits, allows a new class (called the *derived* or *child* class) to be created from an existing class (called the *base* or *parent* class) and to gain its interface.

9. Polymorphism is the feature that two classes can have methods that are named the same and have essentially the same purpose, but different implementations.

10. The keywords, Overridable, Overrides, MustInherit, and MustOverride allow derived classes to customize inherited properties and methods.

CHAPTER 11 PROGRAMMING PROJECTS

1. *Son of Deep Blue.* Write a program that plays a game of tic-tac-toe in which a person competes with the computer. The game should be played in a control array of nine labels. See Figure 11.11. After the user moves by placing an X in a label the program should determine the location for the O. The program should use a tic-tac-toe object that raises events when a player moves and when the game is over. The outcome of the game should be announced in a message dialog box.

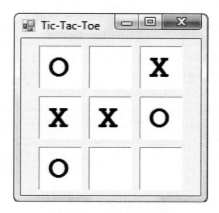

FIGURE 11.11   Tic-Tac-Toe.

2. *Bank Account.* Write a program to maintain a person's Savings and Checking accounts. The program should keep track of and display the balances in both accounts, and maintain a list of transactions (deposits, withdrawals, fund transfers, and check clearings) separately for each account. The two lists of transactions should be stored in sequential files so that they will persist between program sessions.

Consider the form in Figure 11.12. The two drop-down combo boxes should each contain the items Checking and Savings. Each of the four group

FIGURE 11.12   Bank accounts.

boxes corresponds to a type of transaction. (When Savings is selected in the Account combo box, the Check group box should disappear.) The user makes a transaction by typing data into the text boxes of a group box and pressing the button. The items appearing in the Transactions list box should correspond to the type of account that has been selected. The caption of the second label in the Transfer group box should toggle between "to Checking" and "to Savings" depending on the item selected in the "Transfer from" combo box. If a transaction cannot be carried out, a message (such as "Insufficient funds") should be displayed.

The program should use two classes, Transaction and Account. The class Transaction should have properties for transaction name, amount, date, and whether it is a credit (deposit) or debit (withdrawal/check).

The class Account, which will have both a checking account and a savings account as instances, should use an array of Transaction objects. In addition, it should have properties for name (Checking or Savings) and balance. It should have methods to carry out a transaction (if possible), to display the list of transactions, and to load and retrieve the set of transactions into or from a sequential file. The events InsufficientFunds and TransactionCommitted should be triggered at appropriate times. The value of CStr(Today) is a string giving the current date.

Hint: In order for an Account object to display a list of transactions, a list box should be passed to a method as an argument. The method might be declared with
`Sub EnumerateTransactions(ByVal lb As ListBox).`

3. Write a program for the game BlackJack. See Figure 11.13. The program should use a Blackjack class (Blackjack) that contains a member variable of the type DeckOfCards presented in Example 3 of Section 11.2.

FIGURE 11.13 Sample output for Programming Project 3.

APPENDIX A

ANSI VALUES

ANSI Value	Character	ANSI Value	Character	ANSI Value	Character
000	(null)	041	)	082	R
001	□	042	*	083	S
002	□	043	+	084	T
003	□	044	,	085	U
004	□	045	–	086	V
005	□	046	.	087	W
006	□	047	/	088	X
007	□	048	0	089	Y
008	□	049	1	090	Z
009	(tab)	050	2	091	[
010	(line feed)	051	3	092	\
011	□	052	4	093	]
012	□	053	5	094	^
013	(carriage return)	054	6	095	_
014	□	055	7	096	`
015	□	056	8	097	a
016	□	057	9	098	b
017	□	058	:	099	c
018	□	059	;	100	d
019	□	060	<	101	e
020	□	061	=	102	f
021	□	062	>	103	g
022	□	063	?	104	h
023	□	064	@	105	i
024	□	065	A	106	j
025	□	066	B	107	k
026	□	067	C	108	l
027	□	068	D	109	m
028	□	069	E	110	n
029	□	070	F	111	o
030	□	071	G	112	p
031	□	072	H	113	q
032	(space)	073	I	114	r
033	!	074	J	115	s
034	"	075	K	116	t
035	#	076	L	117	u
036	$	077	M	118	v
037	%	078	N	119	w
038	&	079	O	120	x
039	'	080	P	121	y
040	(	081	Q	122	z

ANSI Value	Character	ANSI Value	Character	ANSI Value	Character
123	{	170	ª	217	Ù
124	|	171	«	218	Ú
125	}	172	¬	219	Û
126	~	173	-	220	Ü
127	□	174	®	221	ý
128	□	175	‾	222	ip
129	□	176	°	223	ß
130	,	177	±	224	à
131	ƒ	178	²	225	á
132	"	179	³	226	â
133	…	180	´	227	ã
134	†	181	µ	228	ä
135	‡	182	¶	229	å
136	^	183	·	230	æ
137	‰	184	¸	231	ç
138	Š	185	¹	232	è
139	‹	186	º	233	é
140	Œ	187	»	234	ê
141	□	188	1/4	235	ë
142	Ž	189	1/2	236	ì
143	□	190	3/4	237	í
144	□	191	¿	238	î
145	'	192	À	239	ï
146	'	193	Á	240	ð
147	"	194	Â	241	ñ
148	"	195	Ã	242	ò
149	•	196	Ä	243	ó
150	–	197	Å	244	ô
151	—	198	Æ	245	õ
152	~	199	Ç	246	ö
153	™	200	È	247	÷
154	š	201	É	248	ø
155	›	202	Ê	249	ù
156	œ	203	Ë	250	ú
157	□	204	Ì	251	û
158	ž	205	Í	252	ü
159	Ÿ	206	Î	253	ý
160	(no-break space)	207	Ï	254	þ
161	¡	208	Ð	255	ÿ
162	¢	209	Ñ		
163	£	210	Ò		
164	¤	211	Ó		
165	¥	212	Ô		
166	¦	213	Õ		
167	§	214	Ö		
168	¨	215	×		
169	©	216	Ø		

APPENDIX B
HOW TO

Invoke and Exit Visual Basic

Note: Visual Basic is part of a suite of programs called Visual Studio, which also contains the C# (pronounced "C-sharp") and C++ ("C-plus-plus") programming languages.

A. Invoke Visual Basic Express Edition

    1. Click the Start button.
    2. Hover over All Programs.
    3. Click on Microsoft Visual Basic 2008 Express Edition.

B. Exit Visual Basic

    1. Press Alt/F/X or click on Exit in the File menu.

    or

    1. Click on the Close button; that is, the small square button containing an "X" located at the upper-right corner of the window.

Note: If an unsaved program is present, Visual Basic will prompt you about saving it.

Manage Programs

A. Run a program from Visual Basic

    1. Click on the Start Debugging icon (play button) in the Toolbar.

    or

    1. Press F5.

    or

    1. Press Alt/Debug/Start Debugging.

B. Save the current program.

    1. Click on Save All in the File menu, or click the Save All icon (shows three diskettes) on the Toolbar.

C. Begin a new program.

    1. Click on New Project in the File menu, or click on the New Project icon on the Toolbar, or Press Ctrl + N. (If the previous program has not been saved, Visual Basic will prompt you about saving it.)
    2. Check that Windows Forms Application is highlighted.

3. Optionally type a name for the program into the Name box.
4. Press the OK button.

D. Open a recent program.

1. Hover over Recent Projects in the File menu. (A new panel listing numbered recent programs will appear on the right.)
2. Click on a recent program, or press the corresponding number.

E. Open a program stored on a disk.

1. Click on Open Project in the File menu, or press Ctrl + O.
2. Navigate to the program's folder.
3. Double-click on the folder, or highlight the folder and click on OK or Open. (Three subfolders and two files will be displayed.)
4. Double-click on the file with extension *sln*.

Note 1: In Step 1, if an unsaved program is present, Visual Basic will prompt you about saving it.

Note 2: If neither the Form Designer nor the Code Editor for the program appears, double-click on *formName*.vb in the Solution Explorer window.

F. Change the name of a program.

1. Create a new program with the new name.
2. Give the form the same name as the form in the program to be renamed.
3. Without writing any code or placing any controls on the form, save the program with the new name.
4. Click on "Close Project" in the File menu to close the program.
5. Use Windows Explorer to open the folder for the program with the old name, and Copy the two files having the extension .vb; that is *formName*.Designer.vb and *formName*.vb.
6. Paste the two .vb files into the folder for the program having the new name.
7. Open the *Debug* subfolder of the *bin* folder for the program having the old name and Copy all text files and databases.
8. Paste the text files and databases into the corresponding subfolder of the program having the new name.
9. Delete the folder for the program having the old name.

G. Use the Solution Explorer to view the Code Editor or the Form Designer.

Note: If the Solution Explorer window is not visible, click on Solution Explorer in the View menu.

1. In the Solution Explorer window, right-click on *fileName*.vb.
2. Click on either View Code or View Designer.

H. Import an existing database into a program.

1. Highlight the name of the program at the top of the Solution Explorer window. (**Note:** If the Solution Explorer window is not visible, click on Solution Explorer in the View menu.)

2. Click on "Add Existing Item" in the Project menu. (An "Add Existing Item" dialog box will appear.)
3. There is a drop-down combo box for displaying file types near the bottom of the dialog box. Click on its down-arrow and click on either "All Files (*.*)" or "Data Files (*.xsd, …)."
4. Locate the database file and double-click on it. (The database file will be copied, and the filename will appear in the Solution Explorer window. Also, a Data Source Configuration Wizard dialog box will appear.)
5. Click on the Cancel button in the Data Source Configuration Wizard box.
6. Locate the database file in the Solution Explorer window and move it to the *Debug* subfolder of *bin*. The move can be accomplished either by drag-and-drop or by Cut-and-Paste. (**Note:** If the *bin* folder does not show in the Solution Explorer window, click on the "Show All Files" button in the Solution Explorer toolbar.)

Use the Code and Text Editor

A. Select (or highlight) text as a block.

1. Move the cursor to the beginning or end of the text.
2. Hold down a Shift key and use the direction keys to highlight a block of text.
3. Release the Shift key.

or

1. Move the mouse to the beginning or end of the text.
2. Hold down the left mouse button and move the mouse to the other end of the text.
3. Release the left mouse button.

Note 1: To de-select text, press the Esc key or click outside the text.

Note 2: To select a word, double-click on it. To select a line, move the mouse pointer just far enough into the left margin so that the pointer changes to an arrow, and then single-click there.

B. Delete text.

1. Select the text as a block. (See item A of this section.)
2. Press Alt/E/T, or press Ctrl + X.

Note: In the preceding maneuver, the text is placed in the Clipboard and can be retrieved by pressing Ctrl + V. To delete the text without placing it in the Clipboard, select it as a block, and press the Delete key.

C. Move text.

1. Select the text as a block, and drag it to the new location with the mouse.

D. Use the Clipboard to move or duplicate text.

1. Select the text as a block.
2. Press Ctrl + X to delete the block and place it into the Clipboard, or press Ctrl + C to place a copy of the block into the Clipboard.

    3. Move the cursor to the location where you desire to place the block.

    4. Press Ctrl + V to place a copy of the text from the Clipboard at the cursor position.

E. Search for specific text.

    1. Click on Quick Find in the Edit menu or press Ctrl + F.

    2. Type the desired text into the "Find what:" rectangle. (Alternatively, press the down-arrow button on the right side of the rectangle to select from a list of the text items most recently searched for.)

    3. If you would like to specify certain search options, such as "Match case," click on the plus button to the left of "Find Options," and check one or more boxes.

    4. Press the Find Next button.

    5. To repeat the search, press F3 or Enter.

F. Find and Replace.

    1. Click on Quick Replace in the Edit menu or press Ctrl + H.

    2. Type the text to be replaced into the "Find what:" rectangle. (Alternatively, press the down-arrow button on the right side of the rectangle to select from a list of the text items most recently searched for.)

    3. Type the replacement text into the "Replace with:" rectangle. (Alternatively, press the down-arrow button on the right side of the rectangle to select from a list of the text items most recently used as replacements.)

    4. If you would like to specify certain search options, such as "Match case," click on the plus button to the left of "Find Options," and check one or more boxes.

    5. Press either the "Replace All" button to replace all occurrences of the text to be replaced, or press "Find Next" to highlight the first occurrence of the text to be replaced. With the second option, either click "Replace" to replace the highlighted text, or press "Find Next" to highlight (and possibly replace) the next occurrence of the sought-after text.

G. Rename all instances of a variable, Sub procedure, or Function. (Code Editor only.)

    1. Select the name.

    2. Right-click on the name and click on "Rename". A "Rename" dialog box will appear.

    3. Type the new name into the "New Name" text box.

    4. Click the OK button to carry out the changes.

Note 1: This process is known as *symbolic rename*.

Note 2: If the name of a local variable is changed, the change will be limited to the procedure containing the variable.

H. Undo a change.

    1. Click on Undo in the Edit menu or press Ctrl + Z to undo the last change made.

Note: If desired, an undone change can be redone by pressing Shift + Alt + Backspace.

I. Turn off the IntelliSense feature. (Code Editor only)

    1. Click on Options in the Tools menu.
    2. If the check box to the left of "Show all settings" is unchecked, check it.
    3. In the left pane, expand "Text Editor."
    4. Expand the subheading "Basic."
    5. Click on the subtopic "General."
    6. Ensure that all the check boxes under the "Statement completion" heading are unchecked and then click on OK.

J. Wrap words to the next line in the Code Editor rather than having a horizontal scrollbar.

    1. Follow steps 1 through 5 of part I above.
    2. In the right pane, place a check mark in the check box labeled "Word wrap."

K. Hide a long procedure. (Code Editor only)

    1. Scroll to the top of the procedure.
    2. Click on the box with a minus sign in it that is to the left of the header of the procedure. (Notice that the box now contains a plus sign and that the entire procedure is hidden on the one line. Click on the box again to show the procedure.)

L. Add a collapsible region. (Code Editor only)

    1. Type #Region *"regionName"* on the line before the code to be included in the region.
    2. Type #End Region on the line after the last line of code in the region.
    3. The region of code can then be collapsed by clicking on the minus box and restored by clicking on the plus box.

    Note: A region cannot be defined within an event, Function, or Sub procedure.

M. Instruct the Code Editor to indent by two spaces.

    1. Follow steps 1 through 4 of part I.
    2. Click on the subtopic "Tabs."
    3. In the right pane, change the number in the "Indent size:" text box to 2.

Managing Text Files

Note 1: If the Solution Explorer window is not visible, click on Solution Explorer in the View menu.

Note 2: If the *bin* folder does not show in the Solution Explorer window, click on the "Show All Files" icon in the Solution Explorer toolbar.

A. Display a text file associated with an open program.

    1. In the Solution Explorer window, open the *bin* folder by double-clicking on it.
    2. Open the *Debug* subfolder of the *bin* folder by double-clicking on it. (The text file should appear in a list of several files. If the file is not listed in the *Debug* subfolder, click the Refresh button and reopen the folders.)

    3. Double-click on the text file to open it. (The contents of the file will be displayed in a Text Editor in the Main area, and a tab containing the filename will appear at the top of the Main area.)

B. Close an open text file.

    1. Click on Close in the File menu.

or

    1. Right-click on the tab containing the filename at the top of the Main area.
    2. Click on Close.

C. Import an existing text file into an open program.

    Note: This task is especially useful when importing a file from a "Text_Files_for_Exercises" folder.

    1. Highlight the name of the program at the top of the Solution Explorer window.
    2. Click on "Add Existing Item" in the Project menu. (An "Add Existing Item" dialog box will appear.)
    3. There is a drop-down combo box for displaying file types near the bottom of the dialog box. Click on its down-arrow and click on "All Files (*.*)."
    4. Locate the text file and double-click on it. (The text file will be copied, and the filename will appear in the Solution Explorer window.)
    5. Locate the text file in the Solution Explorer window and move it to the *Debug* subfolder of *bin*. The move can be accomplished either by drag-and-drop or by Cut-and-Paste.

D. Create a new text file in an open program.

    1. Highlight the name of the program at the top of the Solution Explorer window.
    2. Click on Add New Item in the Project menu. (An Add New Item input dialog box will appear.) Alternately, click on the Add New Item icon in the toolbar.
    3. Select the Text File icon in the input dialog box, and enter a name for the file in the Name text box. (Visual Basic will automatically add the extension ".txt" to the name.)
    4. Click on the Add button. (The Text Editor will appear in the Main area.)
    5. Type the contents of the file into the Text Editor. (Our convention is to enter each item of data on a new line.)
    6. Right-click on the tab containing the filename and click on Save *filename*.
    7. Right-click on the tab containing the filename and click on Close.
    8. Locate the text file at the bottom of the Solution Explorer window.
    9. Move the text file to the *Debug* subfolder of *bin*. (The move can be accomplished either by drag-and-drop or by Cut and Paste.)

E. Modify an existing text file in an open program.

    1. In the Solution Explorer window, locate the text file in the subfolder *Debug* of the *bin* folder.
    2. Double-click on the filename of the text file to open the file. (The contents of the file will be displayed in the Text Editor, and a tab containing the filename will appear at the top of the Main area.)
    3. Alter or add items in the file.

    4. Right-click on the tab containing the filename, and click on Save *filename*.

    5. Right-click on the tab containing the filename, and click on Close.

F. Delete an existing text file in an open program.

    1. In the Solution Explorer window, locate the text file in the subfolder *Debug* of the *bin* folder.

    2. Right-click on the filename and click on Delete.

    3. Click on the OK button in the message box that appears.

Get Help

A. Obtain information about a Visual Basic topic.

    1. Press Alt/H/I to invoke the index.

    2. Type the topic into the "Look for:" box.

    3. Click on the topic or a subheading under the topic.

B. View the syntax and purpose of a Visual Basic keyword.

    1. Type the word into a Code Editor.

    2. Place the cursor on, or just following, the keyword.

    3. Press F1.

C. Obtain a list of Visual Basic's reserved words.

    1. Press Alt/H/I to invoke the index.

    2. Type "reserved words" into the "Look for:" box.

    3. Click on the subheading "Visual Basic keywords."

D. Obtain a list of shortcut keys.

    1. Press Alt/H/I to invoke the index.

    2. Type "access keys" into the "Look for:" box.

    3. Click on the subheading "Visual Basic."

    4. Click on one of the underlined links.

E. Obtain information about a control.

    1. Click on the control in the Form Designer.

    2. Press F1.

Manipulate a Dialog Box

A. Use a dialog box.

Note: A dialog box contains three types of items: rectangles (text or list boxes), option lists, and buttons. An option list is a sequence of radio buttons or check boxes.

    1. Move from item to item with the Tab key. (The movement is from left to right and top to bottom. Use Shift + Tab to reverse the direction.)

    2. Inside a rectangle, either type in the requested information, or use the direction keys to make a selection.

3. In an option list, a radio button can be selected or by clicking on it. A dot inside the circle indicates that the button has been selected.

4. In an option list, a selected check box can be checked or unchecked by pressing the spacebar. An X or "✓" inside the square indicates that the option has been checked.

5. A highlighted button is invoked by pressing the Enter key.

B. Cancel a dialog box.

1. Press the Esc key.

or

1. Press the Tab key until the button captioned "Cancel" is highlighted, and then press the Enter key.

Use Menus

A. Open a drop-down menu.

1. Click on the menu name.

or

1. Press Alt.
2. Press the underlined letter in the name of the menu. Alternatively, use the right-arrow key to move the highlighted cursor bar to the menu name, and then press the down-arrow key.

B. Make a selection from a drop-down menu.

1. Click on the drop-down menu.
2. Click on the desired item.

or

1. Press the Alt key and then click on the drop-down menu. One letter in each item that is eligible to be used will be underlined.
2. Press the underlined letter. Alternatively, use the down-arrow key to move the cursor bar to the desired item, and then press the Enter key.

C. Look at all the menus in the Menu bar.

1. Press Alt/F.
2. Press the right-arrow key to cycle through available menus.

D. Close a drop-down menu.

1. Press the Esc key, or click anywhere outside the menu.

Utilize the Windows Environment

A. Determine and/or change the DPI setting for the monitor.

<u>Windows XP</u>

1. Right-click the Windows desktop to display a context menu.

2. Click Properties on the context menu to bring up the Display Properties dialog box.
3. Click the Settings tab on the Display Properties dialog box.
4. Click the Advanced button to display the monitor properties dialog box. The current DPI setting will be shown in the "DPI setting" box.
5. If you would like to change the setting, select a different DPI setting in the "DPI setting" drop-down box. [**Note:** The screen captures in this book were done with a DPI setting of "Normal Size (96 DPI)." With that setting, the forms you see on your computer will look exactly like those in the book.]
6. If you changed the DPI setting, click on "Restart the computer before applying the new display settings."
7. Click the OK button. (If you did not change the DPI setting, nothing will happen. You will be returned to the Display Properties dialog box, and can press the OK button to return to the desktop.)
8. If you changed the DPI setting, a message box will be displayed. Click OK twice, answer Yes to the question posed, click the Close button at the bottom of the Display Properties dialog box, and click on the Yes button to restart your computer and allow the changes to take effect.

Windows Vista

1. Right-click the Windows desktop to display a context menu.
2. Click Personalize on the context menu to display the "Personalize appearance and sounds" window.
3. In the left pane, click "Adjust font size (DPI)." (If you are prompted for an administrator password or confirmation, type the password or provide confirmation by pressing the Continue button.) The current DPI setting will be indicated.
4. If you would like to select the other DPI setting, click on it. [**Note:** The screen captures in this book were done with a DPI setting of "Default scale (96 DPI)." With that setting, the forms you see on your computer will look exactly like those in the book.]
5. Click the OK button. (If you did not change the DPI setting, nothing will happen. You will be returned to the Personalize window, and can close the window to return to the desktop.)
6. If you changed the DPI setting, restart your computer to allow the changes to take effect.

B. Place text in the Windows Clipboard.

1. Select the text as a block as described in the How to Use the Editor section.
2. Press Ctrl + C.

C. Display all characters in a font.

1. Click the Start button.
2. Point to All Programs.
3. Click on Accessories.
4. Click on System Tools.
5. Click on Character Map.
6. Click on the down-arrow at the right end of the Font box.
7. Highlight the desired font, and press the Enter key, or click on the desired font.

Manage Files and Folders with Windows Explorer

A. Invoke Windows Explorer

1. Right-click the Windows Start button. (A context menu will appear).
2. Click on Explore in the context menu.

or

Windows XP

1. Click on the Windows Start button.
2. Click on Run. (A Run dialog box will appear.)
3. Type the word "Explorer" into the Run dialog box.
4. Click on the OK button.

Windows Vista

1. Click the Windows Start button.
2. Click your user name.

or

1. Click the Windows Start button.
2. Type Explorer into the "Start Search" box.
3. Click on the Enter key.

B. Create a new folder.

1. Open the folder you want to contain the new folder as a subfolder.
2. Right-click on an empty section of the open folder.
3. In the context menu that appears, point to New.
4. In the new menu that appears, click Folder. (A new folder appears with the temporary name "New Folder.")
5. Type a name for the folder, and then press the Enter key.

C. Rename a file or folder.

1. Right-click on the file or folder.
2. In the context menu that appears, click Rename. (The current name will appear highlighted inside a rectangle.)
3. Type the new name, and then press the Enter key.

D. Delete a file or folder.

1. Right-click on the file or folder.
2. In the context menu that appears, click Delete. (A dialog box containing the name of the file or folder and asking you to confirm the deletion will appear.)
3. Click the Yes button.

or

1. Click on the file or folder.
2. Press the Delete key. (A dialog box containing the name of the file or folder and asking you to confirm the deletion will appear.)
3. Click the Yes button.

E. Copy a file or folder.

    1. Right-click on the file or folder to be copied.
    2. In the context menu that appears, click on Copy.
    3. Right-click on the folder in which the copy is to be placed.
    4. In the context menu that appears, click on Paste.

F. Move a file or folder.

    1. Right-click on the file or folder to be moved.
    2. In the context menu that appears, click on Cut.
    3. Right-click on the folder to which the file or folder is to be moved.
    4. In the context menu that appears, click on Paste.

or

    1. Click on the file or folder to be moved.
    2. Hold down the left mouse button and drag the file or folder to the new location.
    3. Release the left mouse button.

G. Configure Windows to display filename extensions.

    <u>Windows XP</u>

    1. Click on Folder Options in the Tools menu. (A dialog box will appear.)
    2. Click on the View tab in the dialog box.
    3. If there is a check mark in the box next to "Hide extensions for known file types," click on the box to remove the check mark.
    4. Click on the OK button to close the Folders Options dialog box.

    <u>Windows Vista</u>

    1. Click on the Start button.
    2. Type "Folder Options" into the Start Search box and press the Enter key.
    3. Click on the View tab in the Folder Options dialog box.
    4. If there is a check mark in the box next to "Hide extensions for known file types," click on the box to remove the check mark.
    5. Click on the OK button to close the Folders Options dialog box.

Design a Form

A. Display the Toolbox containing the available controls.

    1. Click on Toolbox in the Veiw menu.

B. Place a new control on the form.

    Option I: (new control with default size)

    1. Drag the control onto the form and release the mouse button.

    Option II: (new control with default size and position)

    1. Double-click on the control's icon in the Toolbox. The new control will be placed on top of the last-drawn control.

2. Size and position the control as described in items G and H, which follow.

Option III: (a single new control sized and positioned as it is created)

1. Click on the control's icon in the Toolbox.
2. Move the mouse to the approximate position on the form desired for the upper-left corner of the control.
3. Press and hold the left mouse button.
4. Move the mouse to the position on the form desired for the lower-right corner of the control. A rectangle will indicate the overall shape of the new control.
5. Release the left mouse button.
6. The control can be resized and repositioned as described in items G and H.

C. Create a related group of controls.

1. Place a group box on the form to hold the related group of controls.
2. Use the options in item B of this section to place controls in the group box.

D. Select a particular control.

1. Click on the control.

or

1. Press the Tab key until the control is selected.

E. Delete a control.

1. Select the control to be deleted.
2. Press the Delete key.

F. Delete a related group of controls.

1. Select the group box holding the related group of controls.
2. Press the Delete key.

G. Move a control or related group of controls to a new location.

1. Move the mouse onto the control or the group box containing the related group of controls.
2. Drag the object to the new location.

H. Change the size of a control.

1. Select the desired control.
2. Move the mouse to one of the sizing handles located around the edge of the control. The mouse pointer will change to a double-arrow, which points in the directions that resizing can occur.
3. Drag to the desired size.

I. Change the size of a form.

1. Move the mouse to the edge or corner of the selected form that is to be stretched or shrunk. The mouse pointer will change to a double-arrow, which points in the directions that resizing can occur.
2. Drag to the desired size.

Work with the Properties of a Form or Control

A. Activate the Properties window.

   1. Press Alt/V/W.

or

   1. Press F4.

or

   1. Click on an object on the form with the right mouse button.
   2. In the context menu that appears, click on Properties.

B. Highlight a property in the Properties window.

   1. Activate the Properties window.
   2. Use the up- or down-arrow keys to move the highlight bar to the desired property.

or

   1. Activate the Properties window.
   2. Click on the up or down arrow located at the ends of the vertical scrollbar at the right side of the Properties window until the desired property is visible.
   3. Click on the desired property.

C. Obtain a description of a property.

   1. If the Description pane is not visible, right-click on the Properties window and then click on "Description."
   2. Highlight the property in the Properties window. Its purpose will appear in the Description pane.

D. Select or specify a setting for a property.

   1. Highlight the property whose setting is to be changed.
   2. Click on the Settings box or press Tab to place the cursor in the Settings box.

      a. If a down-arrow button appears at the right end of the Settings box, click on the down arrow to display a list of all allowed settings, and then click on the desired setting.
      b. If an ellipsis (three periods: . . .) appears at the right end of the Settings box, press F4, or click on the ellipsis to display a dialog box. Answer the questions in the dialog box, and click on OK or Open, as appropriate.
      c. If the cursor moves to the Settings box, type in the new setting for the property.

E. Use the Color palette to set foreground and background colors.

   1. Select the desired control or the form.
   2. Press Alt/V/W or F4 to activate the Properties window.
   3. To set the foreground color, click on the down-arrow to the right of the ForeColor settings box, click on the Custom tab, and click on the desired color.
   4. To set the background color, click on the down-arrow to the right of the BackColor settings box, click on the Custom tab, and click on the desired color.

F. Let a label change size to accommodate its caption (that is, the setting of its Text property.)

   1. Keep the label's AutoSize property set to True. (The label will shrink to the smallest size needed to hold the current caption. If the caption is changed, the label automatically will grow or shrink horizontally to accommodate the new caption.)

G. Let a label caption use more than one line.

   1. Change the label's AutoSize property setting to False and increase its height. (If the label is not wide enough to accommodate the entire caption on one line, part of the caption will wrap to additional lines. If the label height is too small, then part or all of these additional lines will not be visible.)

H. Let a text box display more than one line.

   1. Set the text box's MultiLine property to True. (If the text box is not wide enough to accommodate the text entered by the user, the text will wrap down to new lines. If the text box is not tall enough, lines will scroll out of view, but can be displayed with the cursor up or down keys.)

I. Assign an access key to a button, check box, or radio button.

   1. When assigning a value to the Text property, precede the desired access-key character with an ampersand (&).

J. Allow a particular button to be activated by a press of the Enter key.

   1. Set the form's AcceptButton property to the particular button.

K. Allow the pressing of Esc to activate a particular button.

   1. Set the form's CancelButton property to the particular button.

L. Adjust the order in which the Tab key moves the focus.

   1. Select the first control in the tabbing sequence.
   2. Change the setting of the TabIndex property for this control to 0.
   3. Select the next control in the tabbing sequence.
   4. Change the setting of the TabIndex property for this control to 1.
   5. Repeat Steps 3 and 4 (adding 1 to the Tab Index property) until all controls on the form that belong in the tabbing sequence have been assigned a new TabIndex setting with the desired order.

   or

   1. Press Alt/V/B to show the current tab order. (Each control on the form has a small box in its upper-left corner with a number in it. This number is the TabIndex property setting.)

2. Hover over the first control in the new tabbing sequence. (Notice that the cursor becomes a cross.) Click on the control to change its TabIndex property to 0.

3. Hover over the second control in the new tabbing sequence. Click on the control to change its TabIndex property to 1.

4. Repeat Steps 2 and 3 until all controls on the form that belong in the tabbing sequence have been assigned a new TabIndex setting in the desired order.

5. Press Alt/V/B to hide the tab order numbers.

M. Change a common property in more than one control.

1. Click on the first control.
2. While holding the Ctrl key down, click on the second control.
3. Repeat Step 2 for each additional control.
4. Press F4. (The Properties window is shown.)
5. Click on a property and change its setting.

Note: Only properties that are available in all of the selected controls (such as background color) may be changed in this manner.

N. Have the form appear in the center of the screen when a program executes.

1. Click on the form.
2. Press F4. (The properties window is shown.)
3. Click on the StartPosition property.
4. Set the property to CenterScreen.

O. Change the Name property of Form1 to frmElse.

1. In the Solution Explorer window, right-click on the file Form1.vb.
2. Click on Rename in the context menu that appears.
3. Change the name of the file Form1.vb to frmElse.vb. (**Caution:** Don't forget to retain the extension ".vb.")

P. Specify a custom background or foreground color for a control.

1. In the Properties window, select the BackColor or ForeColor property.
2. Click on the down arrow in the right part of the Settings box.
3. Click on the Custom tab to display a grid of colors.
4. Right-click on one of the sixteen white boxes at the bottom of the grid to display the Define Color dialog box. (The dialog box theoretically allows you to create over 48 million custom colors. The large variegated square is called the *color field* and the narrow rectangle is called the *color slider*.)
5. To select a custom color, click on any point in the color field and then use the arrow head to move along the color slider (At any time, the rectangle labeled "Color | Solid" displays the current color.)
6. Click the Add Color button.

Manage Procedures

A. Access the Code Editor.

   1. Press Alt/V/C or F7.

or

   1. With the Form Designer active, right-click anywhere on the form.
   2. Click on View Code.

or

   1. Press Alt/V/P to activate the Solution Explorer window.
   2. Right-click on the file *formName*.vb.
   3. Click on View Code.

B. Create a general procedure.

   1. Access the Code Editor.
   2. Move to a blank line that is not inside a procedure.
   3. Type "Sub" (for a Sub procedure) or "Function" (for a Function procedure) followed by the name of the procedure and any parameters.
   4. Press the Enter key. (The Code Editor will now display the new procedure heading and an End Sub or End Function statement.)
   5. Type the body of the procedure into the Code Editor.

C. Create an event procedure.

   1. Access the Code Editor.
   2. Click on the down-arrow at the right of the Class Name box, and then select an object.
   3. Click on the down-arrow at the right of the Method Name box, and then select an event. (An empty event procedure that handles the event is created.)

D. Alter a procedure.

   1. View the procedure in the Code Editor.
   2. Make changes as needed.

E. Remove a procedure.

   1. Bring the procedure into the Code Editor.
   2. Select the entire procedure as a block.
   3. Press the Delete key.

F. Insert an existing procedure into a program.

   1. Open the program containing the procedure.
   2. View the procedure in the Code Editor.
   3. Select the entire procedure as a block.
   4. Press Ctrl + C to place the procedure into the Clipboard.
   5. Open the program in which the procedure is to be inserted, and access the Code Editor.
   6. Move the cursor to a blank line.
   7. Press Ctrl + V to place the contents of the Clipboard into the program.

Manage Windows

A. Enlarge the active window to fill the entire screen.

    1. Click on the Maximize button (page icon; second icon from the right) on the title bar of the window.

    2. To return the window to its original size, click on the Restore (double-page) button that has replaced the Maximize button.

B. Move a window.

    1. Move the mouse to the title bar of the window.

    2. Drag the window to the desired location.

C. Change the size of a window that has not been enlarged.

    1. Move the mouse to the edge of the window that is to be adjusted or to the corner joining the two edges to be adjusted.

    2. When the mouse becomes a double arrow, drag the edge or corner until the window has the desired size.

D. Close a window.

    1. Click on the Close button (X) on the far right corner of the title bar.

Use the Printer

A. Obtain a printout of a program.

    1. Invoke the Code Editor.

    2. Click on Print in the File menu. Or, press Ctrl + P.

    3. Press the OK button.

Use the Debugger

(See Appendix D for more details.)

A. Break a program at a specified line.

    1. Place the cursor on the desired line.

    2. Press F9. A red dot will appear to the left of the line on the gray bar to indicate that the line has been set as a *breakpoint*. Whenever the running program reaches the breakpoint, it will go into debug mode.

    Note: To remove this breakpoint, repeat Steps 1 and 2.

or

    1. Click on the thick gray bar at a point to the left of the line. Click again to remove the breakpoint.

or

    1. Place the cursor on the line, press the right mouse button, and click on "Run to Cursor." In this case, the line is not set as a breakpoint; however, execution will stop the first time the line is reached.

B. Remove all breakpoints.

  1. Press Alt/D/D or Ctrl + Shift + F9.

C. Run a program one statement at a time.

  1. Break the program at a specific line using one of the techniques described in Item A of this section.

  2. Press the F8 key to execute each statement.

D. Run the program one statement at a time, but execute each general procedure call without stepping through the statements in the procedure one at a time.

  1. Break the program at a specific line using a technique described in Item A of this section.

  2. Repeatedly press the Shift + F8 key combination to execute successive liines and each general procedure without stepping through each statement in the procedure.

E. Continue execution of a program that has been suspended.

  1. Press F5.

F. Set the next statement to be executed in the current procedure.

  1. Place the cursor anywhere in the desired statement.

  2. Right-click on the line, and click on "Set next statement."

G. Determine the value of an expression during debug mode.

  1. Click on QuickWatch in the Debug menu.

  2. Type the expression into the Expression box.

  3. Click on the Add Watch button. The expression and its value will appear in the Watch window.

  or

  1. In debug mode, hover the cursor over the variable to have its value displayed.

H. Clear the contents of the Watch window.

  1. Right-click anywhere on the Watch window.

  2. Click Clear All.

APPENDIX C

CONVERTING FROM VISUAL BASIC 6.0 TO VISUAL BASIC 2008

This appendix, which shows how the language has changed from VB6 to VB2008, is intended for people who have used Visual Basic 6.0. The language changes from VB6 to VB2008 are vast, much greater than in any previous upgrade of Visual Basic. The topics covered in this appendix are restricted to material discussed in this textbook.

Section 2.2

In VB2008, programs can be given a name as soon as they are started.

The Command Button of VB6 is called a Button in VB2008, and its naming convention calls for the use of the prefix *btn*. The default name has changed from Command1 to Button1.

In VB2008, the default name for a text box has been changed from VB6's Text1 to TextBox1.

The Caption property for a button, form, or label in VB6 is called the Text property in VB2008

The Alignment property for a label or text box in VB6 is called the TextAlign property in VB2008.

In VB2008, Shift + Ctrl + *letter* cannot be used to navigate the Properties window as was possible in VB6.

In VB2008, the Name property of a form cannot be altered by just changing the contents of the Settings box in the Properties window. (See Appendix B for details.)

Section 2.3

In a VB2008 event procedure header line, the event(s) is specified following the Handles keyword. The default procedure name for the event can be altered.

In VB2008, controls do not have default properties. For instance, the VB6 statement **txtBox="Hello,World"** must be replaced with **txtBox.Text="Hello,World"**.

In VB2008, the form object is referred to inside the form's code as Me, not Form1. For instance, the phrase in the form's title bar is specified with a statement such as **Me.Text = "New Caption"**.

The events LostFocus and GotFocus can still be used in VB2008. However, the preferred names for these events are Leave and Enter.

The DblClick event procedure of VB6 is called DoubleClick in VB2008.

In VB2008, font properties can be altered during run time; however, not with statements such as **txtBox.Font.Bold = True**.

In VB2008, all of the code required for creating a form is contained in the file *formName*.Designer.vb. Whenever the form is modified with the Form Designer, those changes are reflected by changes to the code in this file.

Section 3.1

In VB2008, you can declare multiple variables of the same data type on a single line without having to repeat the type keyword. For instance, a statement such as **Dim m, n As Double** specifies that both variables have data type Double. (In VB6, only *n* would have type Double.)

In VB2008, all variables must be declared as being of a specific type.

In VB2008 variables can be given an initial value when they are declared.

VB2008 does not allow the use of the Print method to display text in a picture box or on a form.

In VB2008, Option Explicit defaults to On.

The built-in functions Sqr and Round from VB6 are replaced in VB2008 by the functions Math.Sqrt and Math.Round.

In VB2008, the +=, −=, *=, /= and ^= operators are available as shortcuts for certain types of assignment statements.

Section 3.2

In VB2008, the positions of the characters in a string are now numbered beginning with 0.

Option Strict, which enforces the proper use of variable types, has been added in VB2008 and defaults to Off.

TABLE C.1 **Replacements for Functions.**

VB6	VB2008
UCase(str)	**str.ToUpper**
Len(str)	**str.Length**
Left(str, n)	**str.Substring(0, n)**
Mid(str, m, n)	**str.Substring(m - 1, n)**
Right(str, n)	**str.Substring(str.Length - n)**
Instr(str1, str2)	**str1.IndexOf(str2)**
Trim(str)	**str.Trim**

Section 3.3

In VB2008, strings can be formatted and tables organized with the String.Format method.

In VB2008, files are not accessed with Open statements. Instead they are read with an IO.StreamReader object.

In VB2008, text files are located by default in the folder *bin\Debug* rather than in *bin*.

Section 5.1

In VB2008, every parameter in the header of a Sub or Function procedure must explicitly be declared as ByVal or ByRef. If neither is stated, VB2008 will automatically insert ByVal before the parameter name.

In a VB2008 Call statement, the name of the Sub procedure must be followed with parentheses even if there are no arguments.

Section 5.2

In VB2008, the default way of passing a variable to a procedure is ByVal instead of ByRef.

Section 5.3

In VB2008, the Return statement is the preferred way to set the value returned by a Function.

Section 6.3

In VB2008, the control variable of a For...Next loop can be declared in the For statement, either explicitly or implicitly. Also, the **Continue For** statement allows an iteration of the loop to be skipped.

Section 7.1

In VB2008, there are no fixed-sized arrays; all arrays are dynamic. That is, no matter how an array is declared, it can always be resized.

In VB2008, arrays must have a lower bound 0. A range cannot be specified using the To keyword.

In VB2008, statements of the form **Dim *arrayName*(*intVar*) As *DataType*** are valid.

In VB2008, you cannot use ReDim in the initial declaration of an array. You can use it only to change the size of an array that already has been declared.

In VB2008, ReDim no longer accepts an As clause to change the type of an array.

In VB2008, when an array is an argument of a procedure call, the name of the array is not followed by parentheses.

In VB2008, statements of the form **array1 = array2** can be used to assign all of array2's values to array1.

Section 7.3

The control arrays discussed in this section are not the same as those available in VB6; they are really just arrays of controls. Lost is the ease of creating the controls in code and the ease of handling event procedures.

The Type blocks from VB6 are replaced by Structure blocks in VB2008.

VB2008 does not support fixed-length strings

Section 8.1

The **Name** method of VB6 is replaced in VB2008 by **File.Move.** For instance, **Name *oldfilespec* As *newfilespec*** becomes **File.Move(*oldfilespec, newfilespec)*.**

Although GoSub is not supported by VB2008, On Error GoTo is supported. However, structured exception handling with Try-Catch-Finally blocks is preferable to the unstructured error handling available with VB6.

Section 9.1

TABLE C.2	List box or combo box name changes.	
VB6	**VB2008**
List property	Items
AddItem method	Items.Add
RemoveItem method	Items.RemoveAt
Clear method	Items.Clear
Style property	DropDownStyle
ListIndex property	SelectedIndex

The favored event procedure for list boxes and combo boxes has changed from Click in VB6 to SelectedItemChanged in VB2008.

In VB2008, list boxes no longer have an ItemData property.

The common dialog control from VB6, which was an amalgam of five controls, has been replaced in VB2008 by five individual controls.

Section 9.2

For the check box and radio button controls, the Value property of VB6 has been replaced in VB2008 with the Checked property.

The Frame control of VB6 has been replaced in VB2008 by the GroupBox control.

VB2008 does not have a Line, Shape, or Image control. As alternatives, VB2008's Label control can be used to draw lines and rectangular shapes, and VB2008's PictureBox control has most of the capabilities of VB6's Image control.

For the picture box control, the Picture property of VB6 has been replaced in VB2008 by the Image property.

In VB2008, the picture box control has a StretchImage property that is analogous to the Stretch property for the image control in VB6.

With VB2008, a Timer is turned off with the statement `Timer1.Enabled = False` instead of with the statement `Timer1.Interval = 0`.

The Max and Min properties for scroll bars of VB6 have been changed to Maximum and Minimum. The default value for Maximum is 100. (The Max property had a default value of 32,767.) In VB6, Min could be set to a value greater than Max; in VB2008, this is not allowed.

In VB2008, the unit of measure for graphics is pixels. (Twips was the unit in VB6.)

The graphics Scale method of VB6 is not supported in VB2008.

For the timer control, the Timer event of VB6 has been replaced with the Tick event in VB2008.

In VB2008, the Timer control is not visible on the form in the Form Designer.

Section 9.3

In VB2008, a primary Form (usually called Form1) is displayed when the program is executed. Secondary forms may be defined and displayed using the form's ShowDialog method.

The SelText property of a text box in VB6 is called SelectedText in VB2008.

In VB2008, menus are created with the MenuStrip control found in the Toolbox instead of VB6's Menu Editor that was invoked from the Tools menu.

The Random object of VB2008 is much easier to use than the Rnd function of VB6.

Section 9.4

The PSet, Line, and Circle methods of picture boxes from VB6 are no supported in VB2008. Instead, points, lines, and circles are drawn with the SetPixel, DrawLine, and DrawEllipse methods of a Graphics object.

The FillColor property of VB6 is replaced by colors passed via a Brushes object to either the FillRectangle, FillEllipse, or FillPie methods of a Graphics object.

Section 10.1

VB2008's Database Explorer displays a database's tables and data.

In VB6, data are accessed through a data control. In VB2008, database data are loaded with a database adapter into a data table. The rows and columns of the data table may be accessed similarly to a two-dimensional array.

Section 10.2

VB6 uses Find methods and bookmarks to locate records within a data table. VB2008 uses the WHERE clause in the SQL statement to establish search criteria.

In VB2008, a data table can be bound to a DataGridView control that displays the entire table or a ListBox control that displays an entire column.

In VB2008, changes to data are saved in the database using the database adapter.

Section 11.1

VB6 has separate Property Let and Property Get procedures. VB2008 has a Property block that contains Set and Get procedures.

In VB2008, classes can be written in the Code Editor using Class blocks.

VB6's Initialize event is called New in VB2008 and takes optional parameters.

Section 11.3

VB2008's classes have full object-oriented capability, including inheritance, polymorphism, and abstraction.

APPENDIX D
VISUAL BASIC DEBUGGING TOOLS

Errors in programs are called **bugs**, and the process of finding and correcting them is called **debugging**. Since the Visual Basic editor does not discover errors due to faulty logic, these errors present the most difficulties in debugging. One method of discovering a logical error is by **desk-checking**, that is, tracing the values of variables on paper by writing down their expected value after "mentally executing" each line in the program. Desk checking is rudimentary and highly impractical except for small programs.

Another method of debugging involves placing MessageBox.Show statements at strategic points in the program and displaying the values of selected variables or expressions until the error is detected. After correcting the error, the MessageBox.Show statements are removed. For many programming environments, desk checking and MessageBox.Show statements are the only debugging methods available to the programmer.

The Visual Basic debugger offers an alternative to desk checking and MessageBox.Show statements. It allows you to pause during the execution of your program in order to view and alter values of variables. These values can be accessed through the Immediate, Watch, and Locals windows, known as debugging windows.

The Three Program Modes

At any time, a program is in one of three modes—**design mode**, **run mode**, or **debug mode**. (Debug mode is also known as **break mode**.) When the current

Title bar, Menu bar, and Toolbar during design mode.

Title bar, Menu bar, and Toolbar during run mode.

Title bar, Menu bar, and Toolbar during debug mode.

mode is "run" or "debug," the words "Running" or "Debugging" are displayed (in parentheses) in the Visual Basic title bar. The absence of these words indicates that the current mode is "design."

With the program in design mode, you place controls on a form, set their initial properties, and write code. Run mode is initiated by pressing F5 or the Start Debugging button. Debug mode is invoked automatically when a run-time error occurs. You can use Debug options to break the program at specified places. While the program is in debug mode, you can hover the cursor over any variable to obtain its current value. Also, you can use the debugging windows, such as the Immediate, Watch, and Locals windows, to examine values of expressions. When you enter debug mode, the Toolbar contains a Continue button. You can click on it to continue with the execution of the program.

Stepping through a Program

The program can be executed one statement at a time, with each press of an appropriate function key executing a statement. This process is called **stepping**. After each step, values of variables, expressions, and conditions can be displayed in the debugging windows, and the values of variables can be changed.

When a procedure is called, the lines of the procedure can be executed one at a time, referred to as **stepping into** the procedure, or the entire procedure can be executed at once, referred to as **stepping over** a procedure. A step over a procedure is called a **procedure step**. In addition, you can execute the remainder of the current procedure at once, referred to as **stepping out** of the procedure. The three toolbar buttons shown in Figure D.1 can be used for stepping.

FIGURE D.1   The Toolbar buttons used to Step Into, Step Over, and Step Out.

As another debugging tool, Visual Basic allows the programmer to specify certain lines as **breakpoints**. Then, when the program is run, execution will stop at the first breakpoint reached. The programmer can then either step through the program or continue execution to the next breakpoint. Also, the programmer can place the cursor on any line in the program and have execution stop at that line with a "Run to Cursor" command. Program execution normally proceeds in order through the statements in a procedure. However, at any time the programmer can specify the next statement to be executed.

The tasks discussed previously are summarized next, along with a means to carry out each task. The tasks invoked with function keys also can be produced from the menu bar, the context menu (produced by clicking the right mouse button), or the Toolbar.

Run to cursor	Press Ctrl + F8
Step Into	Press F8
Step Over	Press Shift + F8
Step Out	Press Ctrl + Shift + F8
Set a breakpoint	Move cursor to line, press F9

Remove a breakpoint	Move cursor to line containing breakpoint, press F9
Clear all breakpoints	Press Ctrl + Shift + F9
Continue execution of the program	Press F5
Stop debugging	Ctrl + Alt + Break

The Immediate Window

While in break mode, you can set the focus to the **Immediate window** by clicking on it (if visible), by pressing Ctrl + Alt + I, or by hovering the cursor over "Windows" in the Debug menu and clicking on Immediate. When you type a statement into the Immediate window and press the Enter key, the statement is executed at once. A statement of the form

? expression

displays the value of the expression on the next line of the Immediate window. (The question mark is shorthand for Debug.Print.) A statement of the form

var = value

assigns a value to a variable. In Figure D.2, the variable *numVar* had the value 10 when the program was interrupted.

```
Immediate Window                                          ☒

? 2 * numVar
20
numVar = 100
? 2 * numVar
200
```

FIGURE D.2   Three statements executed in the Immediate window.

The Watch Window

The **Watch window**, which only can be viewed in Break mode, permits you to view the values of variables and expressions. The Watch window in Figure D.3 shows the values of one variable and two expressions. If you don't see a Watch window when you enter Break mode, hover the cursor over Windows in the Debug menu, and then click on Watch.

Name	Value	Type
num	100	Integer
5 * num	500	Integer
num > 90	True	Boolean

FIGURE D.3   A typical Watch window.

Although you can type directly into the Watch window, the easiest way to add an expression to the window is to right-click on a variable in the Code Editor and then click on "Add Watch" in the context menu. You can then alter the expression in the Name column of the Watch window. To delete an expression from the Watch window, right-click on the expression and then click on "Delete Watch." Also, you can directly change the value of any variable in the Watch window and have the values of the other expressions change accordingly.

The Locals Window

While in break mode, you can invoke the Locals window from the Debug menu by positioning the cursor over Windows and then clicking on Locals. This window automatically displays the names, values, and types of all variables in the current procedure. See Figure D.4. You can alter the values of variables at any time.

Name	Value	Type
⊞ ◆ Me	{WindowsApplication1.Form1}	WindowsApplication1.Form1
⊞ ◆ e	{X = 43 Y = 9 Button = Left {1048576}}	System.EventArgs
◆ num1	3	Integer
◆ num2	4	Integer
◆ phrase	"Hello world."	String
⊞ ◆ sender	{Text = "Button1"}	Object

FIGURE D.4   A typical Locals window.

Six Walkthroughs

The following walkthroughs use the debugging tools with the programming structures covered in Chapters 3, 4, 5, and 6.

Stepping through an Elementary Program: Chapter 3

The following walkthrough demonstrates several capabilities of the debugger:

1. Create a form with a button (btnPush) and a text box (txtBox).

2. Double-click on the button and enter the following event procedure:

```
Private Sub btnPush_Click(...) Handles btnPush.Click
  Dim num As Integer
  num = CInt(InputBox("Enter a number:"))
  num += 1
  num += 2
  txtBox.Text = CStr(num)
End Sub
```

3. Place the cursor on the line beginning Private Sub, press the right mouse button, and click on "Run to Cursor." The program will execute, and the form will appear.

4. Click on the button. The Code Editor appears and a yellow arrow points to the Private Sub statement.

5. Press F8. The yellow arrow now points to the statement containing InputBox to indicate that it is the next statement to be executed. (Pressing F8 is referred to as *stepping into*. You can also step to the next statement of a program with the Step Into option from the Debug menu or with the Step Into icon.)

6. Press F8. The statement containing InputBox is executed, and an Input dialog box requesting a number appears. Respond to the request by typing 5 and clicking the OK button.

7. Press F8 again to execute the statement **num += 1.**

8. Let the mouse hover over any occurrence of the variable *num* for a second or so. The current value of the variable will be displayed in a small box. See Figure D.5.

FIGURE D.5   Obtaining the value of a variable.

9. Press Ctrl + Alt + Break to stop debugging. (You also can stop debugging by clicking on "Stop Debugging" in the Debug menu.)

10. Move the cursor to the line

    num +=   2

    and then press F9. A red dot appears on the gray border to the left of the line. This indicates that the line is a breakpoint. Pressing F9 is referred to as *toggling a breakpoint*.

11. Press F5 and click on the button. Respond to the request by entering 5 and pressing OK. The program executes the first three lines inside the procedure and stops at the breakpoint. The breakpoint line is not executed.

12. Open the Immediate window by pressing Ctrl + Alt + I. If necessary, clear the contents of the window by pressing the right mouse button and selecting "Clear All." Type the statement

    ```
    ? num
    ```

    into the Immediate window, and then press Enter to execute the statement. The appearance of "6" on the next line of the Immediate window confirms that the breakpoint line was not executed.

13. Click on the Code Editor.

14. Move the cursor to the line "num += 1," click the right mouse button, and then click on "Set next Statement."

15. Press F8 to execute the selected line.

16. Return to the Immediate window by clicking on it. Type the statement "? num," and press Enter to confirm that the value of *num* is now 7. Then return to the Code Editor.

17. Move the cursor to the breakpoint line, and press F9 to deselect the line as a breakpoint.

18. Press F5 to execute the remaining lines of the program. Observe that the value displayed in the text box is 9.

Stepping through Programs Containing Selection Structures: Chapter 4

If Blocks

The following walkthrough demonstrates how an If statement evaluates a condition to determine whether to take an action:

1. Create a form with a button (btnPush), a text box (txtBox), and the following code:

    ```
    Private Sub btnPush_Click(...) Handles btnPush.Click
      Dim wage As Double
      wage = CDbl(InputBox("Wage:"))
      If wage < 7.25 Then
        txtBox.Text = "Below minimum wage."
      Else
        txtBox.Text = "Wage Ok."
      End If
    End Sub
    ```

2. Place the cursor on the line beginning "Private Sub," press the right mouse button, and click on "Run to Cursor." The program will execute and the form will appear.

3. Click on the button, and then press F8. The yellow arrow points to the statement containing InputBox.

4. Press F8 once to execute the statement containing InputBox. Type a wage of 6.25, and press the Enter key. The If statement is highlighted, but has not been executed.

5. Press F8 once, and notice that the yellow arrow has jumped to the statement `txtBox.Text = "Below minimum wage."` Because the condition "wage < 7.25" is true, the action associated with Then was chosen.

6. Press F8 to execute the txtBox.Text statement. Notice that Else is skipped and the yellow arrow points to End If.

7. Press F8 again. We are through with the If block, and the statement following the If block, End Sub, is highlighted.

8. Press Ctrl + Alt + Break to terminate debugging.

9. If desired, try stepping through the program again with 7.75 entered as the wage. Since the condition "wage < 7.25" will be false, the Else action will be executed instead of the Then action.

Select Case Blocks

The following walkthrough illustrates how a Select Case block uses the selector to choose from among several actions.

1. Create a form with a button (btnPush) and a text box (txtBox). Double-click on the button and enter the following procedure:

```
Private Sub btnPush_Click(...) Handles btnPush.Click
   Dim age, price As Double
   age = CDbl(InputBox("Age:"))
   Select Case age
     Case Is < 12
       price = 0
     Case Is < 18
       price = 3.5
     Case Is >= 65
       price = 4
     Case Else
       price = 5.5
   End Select
   txtBox.Text = "Your ticket price is " & _
              FormatCurrency(price)
End Sub
```

2. Place the cursor on the line beginning "age =", press the right mouse button, and click on "Run to Cursor." The program will execute, and the form will appear.

3. Click on the button. The arrow will point to the statement beginning "age =".

4. Press F8 once to execute the statement beginning "age =". Type an age of 8, and press the Enter key. The arrow points to the Select Case statement, but the statement has not been executed.

5. Press F8 twice, and observe that the arrow points to the action associated with "Case Is < 12".

6. Press F8 once to execute the assignment statement. Notice that the arrow now points to End Select. This demonstrates that when more than one Case clause is true, only the first is acted upon.

7. Press Ctrl + Alt + Break to terminate debugging.

8. If desired, step through the program again, entering a different age and predicting which Case clause will be acted upon. (Some possible ages to try are 12, 14, 18, 33, and 67.)

Stepping through a Program Containing a General Procedure: Chapter 5

The following walkthrough uses the single-stepping feature of the debugger to trace the flow through a Sub procedure.

1. Create a form with a button (btnPush) and a text box (txtBox). Then enter the following two procedures:

```
Private Sub btnPush_Click(...) Handles btnPush.Click
  Dim p, b As Double
  p = 1000           'Principal
  GetBalance(p, b)
  txtBox.Text = "The balance is " & FormatCurrency(b)
End Sub

Sub GetBalance(ByVal prin As Double, ByRef bal As Double)
  'Calculate the balance at 5% interest rate
  Dim interest As Double
  interest = 0.05 * prin
  bal = prin + interest
End Sub
```

2. Place the cursor on the line beginning "Private Sub," press the right mouse button, and click on "Run to Cursor." The program will execute, and the form will appear.

3. Click on the button. In the Code Editor, a yellow arrow points to the Private Sub statement.

4. Press F8 once, and observe that the yellow arrow now points to the statement "p = 1000." This statement will be executed when F8 is next pressed.

5. Press F8 again. The statement "p = 1000" was executed, and the yellow arrow now points to the statement calling the Sub procedure GetBalance.

6. Press F8, and observe that the yellow arrow is now pointing to the header of the Sub procedure.

7. Press F8 three times to execute the assignment statements. The yellow arrow now points to the End Sub statement. (Notice that the Dim and comment statements were skipped.)

8. Press F8, and notice that the yellow arrow has moved back to the btnPush_Click event procedure and is pointing to the calling statement. By hovering the cursor over the variable *b*, you can verify that the Sub procedure was executed.

9. Press Ctrl + Alt + Break to terminate debugging.

10. Repeat Steps 2 through 5, and then press Shift + F8 to *step over* the Sub procedure GetBalance. The Sub procedure has been executed in its entirety.

11. Press Ctrl + Alt + Break to terminate debugging.

Communicating between Arguments and Parameters: Chapter 5

The following walkthrough uses the Locals window to monitor the values of arguments and parameters during the execution of a program.

1. If you have not already done so, type the preceding program into the Code Editor.

2. Place the cursor on the line beginning "Private Sub," press the right mouse button, and click on "Run to Cursor." The program will execute, and the form will appear.

3. Click on the button.

4. Select the Debug menu, hover the cursor over "Windows," and then click on "Locals." Notice that the variables *b* and *p* from the btnPush_Click event procedure appear in the Locals window. The other variables in the list (Me, sender, and e) needn't concern us.

5. Press F8 twice to point to the calling statement. Notice that the value of the variable *p* has changed.

6. Press F8 to call the Sub procedure. Notice that the variables displayed in the Locals window are now those of the procedure GetBalance.

7. Press F8 three times to execute the procedure.

8. Press F8 to return to the btnPush_Click event procedure. Notice that the value of the variable *b* has inherited the value of the variable *bal*.

9. Press Ctrl + Alt + Break to terminate debugging.

Stepping through a Program Containing a Do Loop: Chapter 6

Do Loops

The following walkthrough demonstrates the use of the Watch window to monitor the value of a condition in a Do loop that searches for a name:

1. Create a form with a button (btnPush) and a text box (txtBox). Then double-click on the button, and enter the following event procedure:

```
Private Sub btnPush_Click(...) Handles btnPush.Click
  'Look for a specific name.
  Dim searchName As String, name As String = ""
  Dim sr As IO.StreamReader = IO.File.OpenText("DATA.TXT")
```

```
        searchName = InputBox("Name:") 'Name to search for in list
        Do While (name <> searchName) And (sr.Peek <> -1)
          name = sr.ReadLine
        Loop
        sr.Close()
        If name = searchName Then
          txtBox.Text = name
        Else
          txtBox.Text = "Name not found"
        End If
    End Sub
```

2. Create a text file with the name DATA.TXT, save the file in the program's *Debug* subfolder inside the *bin* folder, and close the file.

   Bert
   Ernie
   Grover
   Oscar

3. Place the cursor on the line beginning "Private Sub," press the right mouse button, and click on "Run to Cursor." The program will execute, and the form will appear.

4. Click on the button. The yellow arrow points to the header of the event procedure.

5. Right-click on the variable *searchName*, and click on "Add Watch." The variable *searchName* has been added to a window titled Watch.

6. Repeat Step 5 for the variable *name*.

7. Drag the mouse across the words **name <> searchName** to highlight them. Then click the right mouse button, and click on "Add Watch." The Boolean expression has been added to the Watch window.

8. Press F8 four times to execute the File.OpenText statement and the statement containing InputBox. Enter the name "Ernie" in the input dialog box, and then click OK.

9. Press F8 repeatedly until the entire event procedure has been executed. Pause after each keypress, and notice how the values of the expressions in the Watch window change.

10. Press the Close button on the form to terminate debugging.

APPENDIX E

A BIOGRAPHICAL HISTORY
OF COMPUTING

The following people made important contributions to the evolution of the computer and the principles of programming. While we think of the computer as a modern technology, it is interesting to note that many of its technologies and concepts were developed decades before Silicon Valley became an address in American culture.

■ 1800s

George Boole: a self-taught British mathematician; devised an algebra of logic that later became a key tool in computer design. The logical operators presented in Section 5.1 are also known as Boolean operators.

Charles Babbage: a British mathematician and engineer; regarded as the father of the computer. Although the mechanical "analytical engine" that he conceived was never built, it influenced the design of modern computers. It had units for input, output, memory, arithmetic, logic, and control. Algorithms were intended to be communicated to the computer via punched cards, and numbers were to be stored on toothed wheels.

Augusta Ada Byron: a mathematician and colleague of Charles Babbage; regarded as the first computer programmer. She encouraged Babbage to modify the design based on programming considerations. Together they developed the concepts of decision structures, loops, and a library of procedures. Decision structures, procedures, and loops are presented in Chapters 4, 5, and 6 of this text, respectively.

Herman Hollerith: the founder of a company that was later to become IBM; at the age of 20 he devised a computer that made it possible to process the data for the U.S. Census of 1890 in one-third the time required for the 1880 census. His electromagnetic "tabulating machine" passed metal pins through holes in punched cards and into mercury-filled cups to complete an electric circuit. Each location of a hole corresponded to a characteristic of the population.

■ 1930s

Alan Turing: a gifted and far-sighted British mathematician; made fundamental contributions to the theory of computer science, assisted in the construction of some of the early large computers, and proposed a test for detecting intelligence within a machine. His theoretical "Turing machine" laid the foundation for the development of general-purpose programmable computers. He changed the course of the Second World War by breaking the German "Enigma" code, thereby making secret German messages comprehensible to the Allies.

John V. Atanasoff: a mathematician and physicist at Iowa State University; declared by a federal court in Minnesota to be the inventor of the first electronic digital special-purpose computer. Designed with the assistance of his graduate assistant, Clifford Berry, this computer used vacuum tubes (instead of the less efficient relays) for storage and arithmetic functions.

1940s

Howard Aiken: a professor at Harvard University; built the Mark I, a large-scale digital computer functionally similar to the "analytical engine" proposed by Babbage. This computer took five years to build and used relays for storage and computations. It was technologically obsolete before it was completed.

Grace M. Hopper: retired in 1986 at the age of 79 as a rear admiral in the United States Navy; wrote the first major subroutine (a procedure that was used to calculate sin x on the Mark I computer) and one of the first assembly languages. In 1945, she found that a moth fused onto a wire of the Mark I was causing the computer to malfunction, thus the origin of the term "debugging" for finding errors. As an administrator at Remington Rand in the 1950s, Dr. Hopper pioneered the development and use of COBOL, a programming language for the business community written in English-like notation.

John Mauchley and J. Presper Eckert: electrical engineers working at the University of Pennsylvania; built the first large-scale electronic digital general-purpose computer to be put into full operation. The ENIAC used 18,000 vacuum tubes for storage and arithmetic computations, weighed 30 tons, and occupied 1500 square feet. It could perform 300 multiplications of two 10-digit numbers per second, whereas the Mark I required 3 seconds to perform a single multiplication. Later they designed and developed the UNIVAC I, the first commercial electronic computer.

John von Neumann: a mathematical genius and member of the Institute for Advanced Study in Princeton, New Jersey; developed the stored program concept used in all modern computers. Prior to this development, instructions were programmed into computers by manually rewiring connections. Along with Hermann H. Goldstein, he wrote the first paper on the use of flowcharts.

Maurice V. Wilkes: an electrical engineer at Cambridge University in England and student of von Neumann; built the EDSAC, the first computer to use the stored program concept. Along with D. J. Wheeler and S. Gill, he wrote the first computer-programming text, *The Preparation of Programs for an Electronic Digital Computer* (Addison–Wesley, 1951), which dealt in depth with the use and construction of a versatile subroutine library.

John Bardeen, Walter Brattain, and William Shockley: physicists at Bell Labs; developed the transistor, a miniature device that replaced the vacuum tube and revolutionized computer design. It was smaller, lighter, more reliable, and cooler than the vacuum tube.

1950s

John Backus: a programmer for IBM; in 1953, headed a small group of programmers who wrote the most extensively used early interpretive computer system, the IBM 701 Speedcoding System. An interpreter translates a high-level language program into machine language one statement at a time as the program is executed. In 1957, Backus and his team produced the compiled language Fortran, which soon became the primary academic and scientific language. A compiler translates an entire program into efficient machine language before the program is executed. (Visual Basic combines the best of both worlds. It has the power and speed of a compiled language and the ease of use of an interpreted language.)

Reynold B. Johnson: IBM researcher; invented the computer disk drive. His disk drive, known as the Ramac, weighed a ton and stored five megabytes of data. Mr. Johnson's other inventions included an electromechanical device that can read pencil-marked multiple-choice exams and grade them mechanically, the technology behind children's "Talk to Me Books," and major advances in the quality of tapes used in VCRs. He was a 1986 recipient of the National Medal of Technology.

Donald L. Shell: in 1959, the year that he received his Ph.D. in mathematics from the University of Cincinnati, published an efficient algorithm for ordering (or sorting) lists of data. Sorting consumes a significant amount of running time on computers. The Shell sort is presented in Chapter 7 of this text.

1960s

John G. Kemeny and Thomas E. Kurtz: professors of mathematics at Dartmouth College and the inventors of BASIC; led Dartmouth to national leadership in the educational uses of computing. Kemeny's distinguished career included serving as an assistant to both John von Neumann and Albert Einstein, serving as president of Dartmouth College, and chairing the commission to investigate the Three Mile Island nuclear power plant accident. In later years, Kemeny and Kurtz devoted considerable energy to the promotion of structured BASIC.

Corrado Bohm and Guiseppe Jacopini: European mathematicians; proved that any program can be written with the three structures discussed in Section 1.4: sequence, decisions, and loops. This result led to the systematic methods of modern program design known as structured programming.

Edsger W. Dijkstra: professor of computer science at the Technological University at Eindhoven, The Netherlands; stimulated the move to structured programming with the publication of a widely read article, "Go To Statement Considered Harmful." In that article, he proposes that GoTo statements be abolished from all high-level languages such as BASIC. The modern programming structures available in Visual Basic do away with the need for GoTo statements.

Harlan B. Mills: IBM Fellow and professor of computer science at the University of Maryland; advocated the use of structured programming. In 1969, Mills was asked to write a program creating an information database for the *New York Times*, a project that was estimated to require 30 person-years with traditional programming techniques. Using structured programming techniques, Mills single-handedly completed the project in six months. The methods of structured programming are used throughout this text.

Donald E. Knuth: professor of computer science at Stanford University; generally regarded as the preeminent scholar of computer science in the world.

He is best known for his monumental series of books, *The Art of Computer Programming*, the definitive work on algorithms.

Ted Hoff, Stan Mazer, Robert Noyce, and Federico Faggin: engineers at the Intel Corporation; developed the first microprocessor chip. Such chips, which serve as the central processing units for microcomputers, are responsible for the extraordinary reduction in the size of computers. A computer with greater power than the ENIAC now can be held in the palm of the hand.

Douglas Engelbart: human interface designer at the Stanford Research Institute; inventor of the computer mouse. While most of us would believe that the mouse is a new technology, the prototype was actually developed in the 1960s. Funded by a government project, Engelbert and his team developed the idea of a mouse to navigate a computer screen with pop-up "windows" to present information to the user. In a contest to choose the best navigation tool, the mouse won over the light pen, a joystick, a "nose-pointing" device, and even a knee-pointing device!

1970s

Ted Codd: software architect; laid the groundwork for relational databases in his seminal paper, "A Relational Model of Data for Large Shared Data Banks," which appeared in the June 1970 issue of the *Communications of the* ACM. Relational databases are studied in Chapter 10 of this text.

Paul Allen and Bill Gates: cofounders of Microsoft Corporation; developed languages and the original operating system for the IBM PC. The operating system, known as MS-DOS, is a collection of programs that manage the operation of the computer. In 1974, Gates dropped out of Harvard after one year, and Allen left a programming job with Honeywell to write software together. Their initial project was a version of BASIC for the Altair, the first microcomputer. Microsoft is one of the most highly respected software companies in the World and a leader in the development of applications and programming languages.

Stephen Wozniak and Stephen Jobs: cofounders of Apple Computer Inc.; started the microcomputer revolution. The two had met as teenagers while working summers at Hewlett–Packard. Another summer, Jobs worked in an orchard, a job that inspired the names of their computers. Wozniak designed the Apple computer in Jobs's parents' garage, and Jobs promoted it so successfully that the company was worth hundreds of millions of dollars when it went public. Both men resigned from the company in 1985. Jobs founded a new company that developed the "Next" computer. He later returned to Apple and incorporated aspects of the Next computer into the Apple operating system.

Dan Bricklin and Dan Fylstra: cofounders of Software Arts; wrote VisiCalc, the first electronic spreadsheet program. An electronic spreadsheet is a worksheet divided into rows and columns, which analysts use to construct budgets and estimate costs. A change made in one number results in the updating of all numbers derived from it. For instance, changing a person's housing expenses will immediately produce a change in total expenses. Bricklin got the idea for an electronic spreadsheet after watching one of his professors at Harvard Business School struggle while updating a spreadsheet at the blackboard. VisiCalc became so popular that many people bought personal computers just so they could run the program.

Dennis Ritchie: member of the team at Bell Labs, creator of the C programming language. C is often referred to as a "portable assembly language." Programs developed in C benefit from speed of execution by being fairly low-level and close to assembly language, yet not being tied up in the specifics of a particular hardware architecture. This characteristic was particularly important to the development of the Unix operating system, which occurred around the same time as the development of C. Throughout the 1970s, 1980s, 1990s, and even today, C has been a widely used language, particularly in situations where very fast program execution time is important.

Ken Thompson: member of the team at Bell Labs that created the Unix operating system as an alternative to the operating system for IBM's 360 mainframe computers. Unlike many other earlier operating systems, Unix was written in C instead of assembly language. This allowed it to be adapted to a wide variety of computer architectures. Programmers could then develop programs in C that were intended to run on a Unix operating system, avoiding much of the rewriting involved in porting (adapting) these programs from one type of machine to another. Over the past 30 years, many variants upon Unix have emerged, often referred to as different "flavors" of Unix. Unix and its variants have played a tremendous role in the growth of the Internet, as well as being an operating system used by many commercial, scientific, and academic institutions.

Alan Kay: a brilliant programmer at the University of Utah; crystallized the concept of reuseable building blocks of code to develop software programs. He developed a new language, Smalltalk, a pure object-oriented language, while at Xerox Palo Alto Research Center (PARC) in the 1970s. Most of today's programming languages such as C++, C#, Java, and Visual Basic make use of object-oriented features first developed in Smalltalk. Still, because of its conceptual purity, Kay believes that Smalltalk "is the only real object-oriented language."

Don Chamberlain: a Stanford Ph.D. and National Science Foundation scholar working at IBM; created a database programming language, later known as SQL (Structured Query Language). This innovative language was built on a "relational" model for data, where related data groups could be put into tables, then linked in various ways for easy programming and access. Very few people know that one of the world's largest software companies, Oracle Corporation, was founded on this technology, developed by IBM and published for all to use. SQL is covered in Chapter 10 of this book.

1980s

Phillip "Don" Estridge: head of a product group at IBM; directly responsible for the success of the personal computer. The ubiquity of the PC today can be attributed to a marketing decision by Estridge to make off-the-shelf, easily producible computers for a mass market, and to back that with IBM's huge marketing resources. Estridge's "skunk-works" group in Boca Raton broke many established IBM rules for product introduction. The IBM PC, introduced in 1981, chose an operating system from Microsoft and a processor chip from Intel over other vendors. This licensing deal opened the way for Microsoft's and Intel's successes today.

Mitchell D. Kapor: cofounder of Lotus Corporation; wrote the business software program Lotus 1-2-3, one of the most successful pieces of software for personal computers in its time. Lotus 1-2-3 is an integrated program consisting of a spreadsheet, a database manager, and a graphics package.

Tom Button: group product manager for applications programmability at Microsoft; headed the team that developed QuickBasic, QBasic, and Visual Basic. These modern, yet easy-to-use, languages greatly increased the productivity of programmers.

Alan Cooper: director of applications software for Coactive Computing Corporation; considered the father of Visual Basic. In 1987, he wrote a program called Ruby that delivered visual programming to the average user. A few years later, Ruby was combined with QuickBasic to produce Visual Basic, the remarkably successful language that allows Windows programs to be written from within Windows easily and efficiently.

Tim Berners–Lee: British computer scientist; father of the World Wide Web. He proposed the Web project in 1989 while working in Switzerland. His brainchild has grown into a global phenomenon. Berners-Lee, currently a senior research scientist at MIT, was awarded the first Millenium Technology Prize in 2004.

Charles Simonyi: a Hungarian programmer; known to the industry as the "father of Word." He left his native Budapest as a 17-year-old prodigy to work at Xerox's prestigious Palo Alto Research Center (PARC), where he developed the capability of "What You See Is What You Get" (WYSIWYG) software. This technology, which allows users to define the fonts and presentations for computer output, opened the door to desktop publishing on the personal computer. In 1980, Simonyi joined a fledgling software company called Microsoft and developed Microsoft Word into one of the most widely used software programs ever.

Bjarne Stroustrup: a native of Denmark; creator of the C++ programming language. Stoustrup came to the United States to work for Bell Labs, during which time he created C++ to extend the C programming language with additional capabilities for object-oriented and generic programming. C++ has been one of the most widely used programming languages, combining the speed and efficiency of C with features that make the development of large-scale programs much simpler. Because of its ability to work at a low level in a manner similar to C, C++ remains the language of choice for many projects where other programming languages such as Java and Visual Basic are not suitable.

Richard M. Stallman: a star programmer at MIT's Artificial Intelligence Lab and a MacArthur Foundation Fellow; founded the Free Software Foundation (FSF). The FSF is an organization dedicated to promoting the free availability of software for public access, modification, and improvement. This philosophy contrasts with that of a large part of the commercial software development world, where software is developed for sale, but the full rights to the source code are maintained by the company writing the software. Among his many technical accomplishments, Stallman created free versions of EMACS (a highly popular text editor on Linux/Unix systems) and GCC (a free C language compiler).

1990s

Marc Andreessen: a former graduate student at the University of Illinois; inventor of the Web browser. He led a small band of fellow students to develop Mosaic, a program that allowed the user to move around the World Wide Web by clicking on words and symbols. Andreessen went on to cofound NCSA and Netscape Communications Corporation. Netscape's was the leading Web browser throughout the mid 1990s before being surpassed by Microsoft's Internet Explorer.

James Gosling: corporate vice president and Sun Fellow at Sun Microsystems; creator of the Java programming language. What started as an attempt to create a simple language for a networked world, Java, an object-oriented language, became a popular language for Internet programming. Java has become the primary teaching language at many universities. Visual Basic has many of the features and capabilities of Java.

Linus Torvalds: a graduate of the University of Helsinki in Finland; developed the popular Linux operating system. Linux began as a project by Linus to create a Unix operating system that could be used on personal computers. In the early 1990s, he began sharing the Linux source code with other OS programmers over the Internet, allowing them to contribute to and improve it. This philosophy resonated with the Internet culture, and the popularity of Linux grew quickly. Today, Linux is widely used, particularly as an operating system for Web servers. It is an open-source operating system, meaning that the source code (instructions) is made freely available for anyone to obtain, view, modify and use.

APPENDIX F
FILES AND FOLDERS

We use the word **disk** to refer to either the hard disk, a diskette, a CD, or DVD. Each drive is identified by a letter. Normally, the hard drive is identified by C, the diskette drive by A, and the CD (or DVD) drive by D or E. Disk management is handled by Windows.

Disks hold not only programs, but also collections of data stored in files. The term **file** refers to either a program file, a text file, or some other kind of data file. Each file has a name consisting of a base name followed by an optional extension consisting of a period and one or more characters. The term **filename** refers to the combination of the base name, the period, and the extension. A filename can contain up to 215 characters, typically consisting of letters, digits, spaces, periods, and other assorted characters. (The only characters that cannot be used in filenames are \, /, :, *, ?, <, >, ", and |.) Extensions are normally used to identify the type of file. For example, spreadsheets created with Excel have the extension *xlsx* or *xls* (eXceL Spreadsheet), documents created with Word have the extension *docx* or *doc* (DOCument), and files created with Notepad have the extension *txt* (TeXT document). Some examples of filenames are "Annual Sales.xlsx," "Letter to Mom.docx," and "Phone.txt".

Because a disk is capable of holding thousands of files, locating a specific file can be quite time consuming. Therefore, related files are grouped into collections called **folders**. For instance, one folder might hold all your Visual Basic programs, and another the documents created with your word processor.

Think of a disk as a large folder, called the **root folder**, that contains several smaller folders, each with its own name. (The naming of folders follows the same rules as the naming of files.) Each of these smaller folders can contain yet other named folders. Any folder contained inside another folder is said to be a **subfolder** of that folder. Each folder is identified by listing its name preceded by the names of the successively larger folders that contain it, with each folder name preceded by a backslash. Such a sequence is called a **path**. For instance, the path \Sales\NY08\July identifies the folder July, contained in the folder NY08, which in turn is contained in the folder Sales. Think of a file, along with its name, as written on a slip of paper that can be placed into either the root folder or one of the smaller folders. The combination of a drive letter followed by a colon, a path, and a filename is called a **filespec**, an abbreviation of "file specification." Some examples of filespecs are C:\VB01\VB.EXE and E:\Personal\INCOME08.TXT.

Neither Windows nor Visual Basic distinguishes between uppercase and lowercase letters in folder names and filenames. For instance, the names COSTS02.TXT, Costs02.Txt, and costs02.txt are equivalent. We use uppercase letters in this book for filenames.

In early operating systems such as MS-DOS, folders were called **directories**. Many Visual Basic objects and commands still refer to folders as directories. The terms "root folder" and "path" are a reference to the "tree" metaphor commonly used to describe a computer's disk. In this metaphor, the large folder at the lowest level of the disk is called the "root" folder. The smaller folders contained in the root folder can be thought of as "branches" that emanate from the root. Each branch may have smaller branches, which in turn may have their own smaller branches, and so on. Finally, a file in one of these folders can be thought of as a leaf on a branch. The leaf is reached by starting at the root and following a "path" through the branches.

ANSWERS

To Selected Odd-Numbered Exercises

EXERCISES 2.2

1. After a button is clicked, it has a blue border.

(In Exercises 3 through 24, begin by pressing Alt/F/N/P to begin a new project.)

3. Click on the form to make it the selected object.
Click on the Properties window or Press F4 to activate the Properties window.
Move around with the up- and down-arrow keys until the Text property is highlighted.
Type "CHECKING ACCOUNT".

5. Double-click the TextBox icon in the Toolbox.
Activate the Properties window, and highlight the BackColor property.
Click on the down-arrow button to the right of the Settings box.
Click on the Custom tab.
Click on the desired yellow in the palette.
Click on the form to see the empty, yellow text box.

7. Double-click on the Label icon in the Toolbox.
Activate the Properties window, and highlight the AutoSize property.
Set the AutoSize property to False.
Highlight the Text property.
Type the requested sentence.
Highlight the TextAlign property.
Click on the down-arrow button to the right of the Settings box, and click on one of the center rectangles.
Click on the form.
Use the mouse to resize the label so that the sentence occupies three lines.

9. Double-click on the TextBox icon in the Toolbox.
Activate the Properties window, and highlight the Text property.
Type "Visual Basic 2008".
Set the Name property to txtLanguage.
Highlight the Font property.
Click on the ellipsis to the right of the Settings box.
Scroll up the font list box, and click on Courier New in the Font box.
Click OK.
Resize the text box to accommodate its text.
Click on the form to see the resulting text box.

11. Double-click on the Button icon in the Toolbox.
    Activate the Properties window, and highlight the BackColor property.
    Click on the down-arrow button to the right of the Settings box.
    Click on the Custom tab, and then click on the white square in the palette.
    Highlight the Text property.
    Type "PUSH".
    Highlight the Font property, and click on the ellipsis.
    Click on Italic in the Font style box.
    Click on 24 in the Size box.
    Click OK.
    Click on the form to see the resulting button.

13. Double-click on the Button icon in the Toolbox.
    Activate the Properties window, and highlight the Text property.
    Type "PUS&H".
    Click on the form to see the resulting button.

15. Double-click on the Label icon in the Toolbox.
    Activate the Properties window, and highlight the Name property.
    Type "lblAKA". (The name will appear in the Settings box.)
    Highlight the Text property.
    Type "ALIAS".
    Highlight the AutoSize property.
    Set the AutoSize property to False.
    Highlight the Font property, and click on the ellipsis.
    Click on Italic in the Font style box.
    Click OK.
    Highlight the TextAlign property.
    Click on the down-arrow box to the right of the Settings box, and click on one of the center rectangles.

17. Double-click on the Label icon in the Toolbox.
    Highlight the AutoSize property.
    Set the AutoSize property to False.
    Activate the Properties window, and highlight the TextAlign property.
    Click on the down-arrow box to the right of the Settings box, and click on one of the rectangles on the right.
    Highlight the Text property.
    Type "VISUAL BASIC" and press Enter.
    If the words "VISUAL BASIC" are on one line, make the label narrower and longer, until the words appear on two lines.

19. Double-click on the Label icon in the Toolbox.
    Activate the Properties window, and highlight the Font property.
    Click on the ellipsis to the right of the Settings box.
    Click on Wingdings in the Font box.
    Click on the largest size available (72) in the Size box.
    Click OK.
    Highlight the Text property.
    Change the setting to a less than sign ($<$).
    Click on the label.

Note: If you didn't know that the less than symbol corresponded to a diskette in the Wingdings font, you could double-click on the diskette character in the Character Map, click the Copy button, highlight the Text property, and press Ctrl + V. The less than character would appear in the Text settings box.

21. Double-click on the ListBox icon in the Toolbox.
    Activate the Properties window, and highlight the BackColor property.
    Click on the down-arrow button to the right of the Settings box.
    Click on the Custom tab.
    Click on the desired yellow square in the palette.
    Click on the form to see the yellow list box.

23. In the Solution Explorer window, right click on "Form1.vb" and select Rename from the Context menu.
    Type "frmYellow.vb".
    Right-click on the form in the Form Designer, and select Properties from the Context menu.
    Click on the BackColor property in the Properties Window.
    Click on the down-arrow button in the right part of the Settings box, and then click on the Custom tab.
    Click on a square colored yellow.

25. Begin a new project.
    Change the text in the form's title bar to "Dynamic Duo".
    Place two buttons on the form.
    Enter "Batman" as the text of the first button, and enter "Robin" as the text of the second button.
    Increase the font size for both buttons to 14.

27. Begin a new project.
    Change the text in the form's title bar to "Fill in the Blank".
    Place a label, a text box, and another label on the form at appropriate locations.
    Change the Text setting of the first label to "Go ahead, make my" and of the second label to "A Quote by Clint Eastwood".
    Position the labels and text box as needed.

29. Begin a new project.
    Change the text in the form's title bar to "An Uncle's Advice".
    Place on the form five labels and three buttons.
    Set the AutoSize properties of the first and last labels to False.
    Set the BackColor property of the last label to Blue, and set its ForeColor property to Yellow.
    Change the Text property of each label as indicated.
    Change the settings of the buttons' Text properties to "1", "2", and "3". Resize and position the labels and buttons as is appropriate.

33. 1

35. Each arrow key moves the text box in the indicated direction.

37. Pressing the right- and left-arrow keys widens and narrows the text boxes, buttons, and list boxes in the group of selected controls. The up- and down-arrow keys shorten and lengthen the buttons and list boxes in the group. The arrow keys have no effect on the labels, and only the left- and right-arrow keys affect the text boxes.

39. Drag a label and a list box onto the form.
Click on the label.
Hold down the Ctrl key and click on the list box. (You have now selected a group of two controls.)
In the Properties window, click on the ⊞ sign to the left of the Font property.
Click on the Size property and change the setting to 12.
Press the Enter key.

(*Alternative:* Replace the last three steps with the following steps.)

In the Properties window, highlight the Font property.
Click on the ellipsis button to the right of the Settings box.
Click on 12 in the Size list.
Click OK.

41. The label is positioned just to the left of the text box, and the two middles are aligned.

43. "Center" refers to the midpoint horizontally, whereas "middle" refers to the midpoint vertically.

45. The setting toggles between True and False.

EXERCISES 2.3

1. The word "Hello"

3. The word "Hello" on an orange-colored background

5. The text box vanishes; nothing is visible.

7. The word "Hello" in green letters

9. The word "Hello" on a gold background

11. Form1.Text should be Me.Text.

13. Red should be replaced with Color.Red.

15. Font.Size is a read-only property. The statement `txtOutput.Text = txtBox.Font.Size` is valid since it is reading the value of txtBox.Font.Size. However, `txtBox.Font.Size = 20` is not valid since it is setting the value of txtBox.Font.Size.

17. `lblTwo.Text = "E.T. phone home."`

19. `txtBox.ForeColor = Color.Red`
`txtBox.Text = "The stuff that dreams are made of."`

21. `txtBox.Enabled = False`

23. `lblTwo.Visible = False`

25. `btnOutcome.Enabled = True`

27. `txtBoxTwo.Focus()`

29. The Enter event occurs when the object gets the focus.

```
33. Private Sub btnLeft_Click(...) Handles btnLeft.Click
      txtBox.Text = "Left Justify"
      txtBox.TextAlign = HorizontalAlignment.Left
    End Sub

    Private Sub btnCenter_Click(...) Handles btnCenter.Click
      txtBox.Text = "Center"
      txtBox.TextAlign = HorizontalAlignment.Center
    End Sub

    Private Sub btnRight_Click(...) Handles btnRight.Click
      txtBox.Text = "Right Justify"
      txtBox.TextAlign = HorizontalAlignment.Right
    End Sub

35. Private Sub btnRed_Click(...) Handles btnRed.Click
      txtBox.BackColor = Color.Red
    End Sub

    Private Sub btnBlue_Click(...) Handles btnBlue.Click
      txtBox.BackColor = Color.Blue
    End Sub

    Private Sub btnWhite_Click(...) Handles btnWhite.Click
      txtBox.ForeColor = Color.White
    End Sub

    Private Sub btnYellow_Click(...) Handles btnYellow.Click
      txtBox.ForeColor = Color.Yellow
    End Sub

37. Private Sub txtLife_Enter(...) Handles txtLife.Enter
      txtQuote.Text = "I like life, it's something to do."
    End Sub

    Private Sub txtFuture_Enter(...) Handles txtFuture.Enter
      txtQuote.Text = "The future isn't what it used to be."
    End Sub

    Private Sub txtTruth_Enter(...) Handles txtTruth.Enter
      txtQuote.Text = "Tell the truth and run."
    End Sub

39. Private Sub btnOne_Click(...) Handles btnOne.Click
      btnOne.Visible = False
      btnTwo.Visible = True
      btnThree.Visible = True
      btnFour.Visible = True
    End Sub

    Private Sub btnTwo_Click(...) Handles btnTwo.Click
      btnOne.Visible = True
      btnTwo.Visible = False
      btnThree.Visible = True
      btnFour.Visible = True
    End Sub

    Private Sub btnThree_Click(...) Handles btnThree.Click
      btnOne.Visible = True
      btnTwo.Visible = True
      btnThree.Visible = False
      btnFour.Visible = True
    End Sub
```

```
Private Sub btnFour_Click(...) Handles btnFour.Click
  btnOne.Visible = True
  btnTwo.Visible = True
  btnThree.Visible = True
  btnFour.Visible = False
End Sub
```

41.
```
Private Sub btnVanish_Click(...) Handles btnVanish.Click
  lblFace.Visible = False
End Sub

Private Sub btnReappear_Click(...) Handles btnReappear.Click
  lblFace.Visible = True
End Sub
```

43.
```
Private Sub btnAny_Click(...) Handles btnOne.Click, btnTwo.Click
  txtOutput.Text = "You just clicked on a button."
End Sub
```

CHAPTER 3

EXERCISES 3.1

1. 12

3. .125

5. 1

7. 2

9. 1

11. Not valid

13. Valid

15. Not valid

17. 2

19. 16

21. 9

23.
```
Private Sub btnCompute_Click(...) Handles btnCompute.Click
  lstOutput.Items.Add((7 * 8) + 5)
End Sub
```

25.
```
Private Sub btnCompute_Click(...) Handles btnCompute.Click
  lstOutput.Items.Add(0.025 * 25)
End Sub
```

27.
```
Private Sub btnCompute_Click(...) Handles btnCompute.Click
  lstOutput.Items.Add(17 * (3 + 162))
End Sub
```

29.

	x	y
`Private Sub btnEvaluate_Click(...) Handles` `        btnEvaluate.Click`		
`Dim x, y As Double`	0	0
`x = 1`	1	0
`y = 3 + x`	1	4
`x = y + 5`	9	4
`lstResults.Items.Clear()`	9	4
`lstResults.Items.Add(x + 4)`	9	4
`y = y + 1`	9	5
`End Sub`		

31. 6

33. 1
8
9

35. 1
64

37. 49
28

39. The third line should read `c = a + b`

41. In the second line number 1,000,5 should have no commas. The number should be written as 10005. In the third line $100 should have no $. The number should be written as 100.

43. 9W is not a valid variable name; `lstOutput.Add` should be `lstOutput.Items.Add`

45. `Dim quantity As Integer = 12`

47. 10

49. 6

51. 3.128

53. –3

55. 1

57. 6

59.
```
Private Sub btnCompute_Click(...) Handles btnCompute.Click
    Dim revenue, costs, profit As Double
    revenue = 98456
    costs = 45000
    profit = revenue - costs
    lstOutput.Items.Add(profit)
End Sub
```

61.
```
Private Sub btnCompute_Click(...) Handles btnCompute.Click
    Dim price, discountPercent, markdown As Double
    price = 19.95
    discountPercent = 30
    markdown = (discountPercent / 100) * price
```

```
      price = price - markdown
        lstOutput.Items.Add(price)
    End Sub
```

63.
```
   Private Sub btnCompute_Click(...) Handles btnCompute.Click
      Dim balance As Double
      balance = 500
      balance += 0.03 * balance
      balance += 0.03 * balance
      lstOutput.Items.Add(balance)
   End Sub
```

65.
```
   Private Sub btnCompute_Click(...) Handles btnCompute.Click
      Dim balance As Double
      balance = 100
      balance = balance * (1.05 ^ 10)
      lstOutput.Items.Add(balance)
   End Sub
```

67.
```
   Private Sub btnCompute_Click(...) Handles btnCompute.Click
      Dim acres, yieldPerAcre, corn As Double
      acres = 30
      yieldPerAcre = 18
      corn = yieldPerAcre * acres
      lstOutput.Items.Add(corn)
   End Sub
```

69.
```
   Private Sub btnCompute_Click(...) Handles btnCompute.Click
      Dim distance, elapsedTime, averageSpeed As Double
      distance = 233
      elapsedTime = 7 - 2
      averageSpeed = distance / elapsedTime
      lstOutput.Items.Add(averageSpeed)
   End Sub
```

71.
```
   Private Sub btnCompute_Click(...) Handles btnCompute.Click
      Dim waterPerPersonPerDay, people, days, waterUsed As Double
      waterPerPersonPerDay = 1600
      people = 304000000
      days = 365
      waterUsed = waterPerPersonPerDay * people * days
      lstOutput.Items.Add(waterUsed)
   End Sub
```

EXERCISES 3.2

1. `Computer Science`

3. `Mathematics`

5. `action`

7. `222`

9. `The cost is 25 dollars and 70 cents.`

11. `TO BE OR NOT TO BE`

13. `5.5`

15. `goodbye`

17. `LIBER LIBERTAS`

19. `ABC`
    `2`
    `4`
    `55 mph`
    `STU`

21. `12`
    `MUNICIPALITY`
    `city`
    `6`

23. 16 (0 through 15)

25. True

27. The variable *phoneNumber* should be declared as type String, not Double.

29. The word sub cannot be cannot be used as a variable name.

31. The IndexOf method cannot be applied to a number, only a String.

33.
```
Private Sub btnDisplay_Click(...) Handles btnDisplay.Click
    Dim firstName, middleName, lastName As String
    Dim yearOfBirth As Integer
    firstName = "Thomas"
    middleName = "Alva"
    lastName = "Edison"
    yearOfBirth = 1847
    txtOutput.Text = firstName & " " & middleName & " " & lastName & _
                    ", " & yearOfBirth
End Sub
```

35.
```
Private Sub btnDisplay_Click(...) Handles btnDisplay.Click
    Dim publisher As String
    publisher = "Prentice Hall, Inc."
    txtOutput.Text = "(c)" & publisher
End Sub
```

37. `Dim str As String` 'Place in the Declarations section of the program

39.
```
Private Sub btnCompute_Click(...) Handles btnCompute.Click
    Dim distance As Double
    distance = CDbl(txtNumSec.Text) / 5
    distance = Math.Round(distance, 2)
    txtOutput.Text = "The distance of the storm is " & distance & _
                    " miles."
End Sub
```

41.
```
Private Sub btnCompute_Click(...) Handles btnCompute.Click
    Dim cycling, running, swimming, pounds As Double
    cycling = CDbl(txtCycle.Text)
    running = CDbl(txtRun.Text)
    swimming = CDbl(txtSwim.Text)
    pounds = (200 * cycling + 475 * running + 275 * swimming) / 3500
    pounds = Math.Round(pounds, 1)
    txtWtLoss.Text = pounds & " pounds were lost."
End Sub
```

43.
```
Private Sub btnCompute_Click(...) Handles btnCompute.Click
    Dim income As Double
```

```
    income = CDbl(txtRevenue.Text) - CDbl(txtExpenses.Text)
    txtNetIncome.Text = CStr(income)
  End Sub
```

45. ```
Private Sub btnCompute_Click(...) Handles btnCompute.Click
    Dim tip As Double
    tip = CDbl(txtAmount.Text) * CDbl(txtPercentage.Text) / 100
    txtTip.Text = CStr(Math.Round(tip, 2))
  End Sub
```

47. ```
Private Sub btnIncrease_Click(...) Handles btnIncrease.Click
      txtOutput.Text = CStr(CInt(txtOutput.Text) + 1)
  End Sub
```

49. ```
Private Sub btnCompute_Click(…) Handles btnCompute.Click
    Dim sentence, word As String
    Dim position As Integer
    sentence = txtSentence.Text
    word = txtWord.Text
    position = sentence.IndexOf(word)
    txtOutput.Text = sentence.Substring(0, position) & _
                     sentence.Substring(position + word.Length)
  End Sub
```

51. ```
Private Sub btnDisplay_Click(...) Handles btnDisplay.Click
      'Estimate the speed of a car given the stopping distance.
    Dim speed, distance As Double
    distance = CDbl(txtDistanceSkidded.Text)
    speed = Math.Sqrt(24 * distance)
    txtEstimatedSpeed.Text = speed & " mph"
  End Sub
```

53. ```
  'Class-level variables
  Dim sum As Double   'Sum of the scores entered
  Dim num As Integer 'Number of scores entered

  Private Sub btnRecord_Click(...) Handles btnRecord.Click
    num += 1
    sum += CDbl(txtScore.Text)
    txtScore.Clear()
    txtScore.Focus()
  End Sub

  Private Sub btnCalculate_Click(...) Handles btnCalculate.Click
    txtAverage.Text = CStr(sum / num)
  End Sub

  Private Sub txtScore_TextChanged(...) Handles txtScore.TextChanged
    txtAverage.Clear()
  End Sub
```

55. ```
Private Sub txtEitherNum_TextChanged(...) Handles _
              txtFirstNum.TextChanged, txtSecondNum.TextChanged
    txtSum.Clear()
  End Sub
```

EXERCISES 3.3

1. `123.5`

3. `1,234.0`

5. `0.12`

7. `-0.67`

9. `19,877.000`

11. `56`

13. `$123`

15. `($0.23)`

17. `$0.80`

19. `5.50%`

21. `100.00%`

23. `66.67%`

25. `Pay amount $222,222.00`

27. `25.6% of the U.S. population 25+ years old are college graduates.`

29. `The likelihood of Heads is 50%`

31.
```
1234567890123456789012345
   5                     3
```

33.
```
1234567890123456789012345
           5   3
```

35.
```
12345678901234567890
    A       Alice
```

37.
```
12345678901234567890
      College    Mascot
  Univ. of MD    Terrapins
         Duke    Blue Devils
```

39.
```
123456789012345678901234567890
Element  Weight   Percent
Oxygen   97.5     65.0 %
Carbon   27.0     18.0 %
```

41. `20`

43. `softball`

45. `Age: 20`

47. `The White House has 132 rooms.`

49. `Sum = 333 and average = 166.5.`

51.
```
Metropolitan
Metropolitan
```

53. `You might win 360 dollars.`

55. `Hello John Jones`

57. `MessageBox.Show("Dies diem docet", "Latin Quote")`

59. In the text file, an expression was used where a numerical literal was expected.

61. Input box returns String which should be converted to Double by using function CDbl().

63. FormatNumber(123456) is a string and therefore cannot be assigned to a Double variable.

65. You must insert **String.Format(** after the left parenthesis.

67.
```
Private Sub btnDisplay_Click(...) Handles btnDisplay.Click
    'Displays information about Americans' eating habits
    Dim food, units As String, quantityPerDay As Double
    Dim sr As IO.StreamReader = IO.File.OpenText("SODA.TXT")
    food = sr.ReadLine
    units = sr.ReadLine
    quantityPerDay = CDbl(sr.ReadLine)
    lstOutput.Items.Add("Americans consume " & quantityPerDay & _
                        " " & units)
    lstOutput.Items.Add("of " & food & " per day.")
    sr.Close()
End Sub
```

69.
```
Private Sub btnDisplay_Click(...) Handles btnDisplay.Click
    'Report percent increase for a basket of goods.
    Dim begOfYearPrice, endOfYearPrice As Double
    Dim percentIncrease As Double
    begOfYearPrice = 200
    endOfYearPrice = CDbl(InputBox("Enter price at the end of year:"))
    percentIncrease = 100 * (endOfYearPrice - _
                        begOfYearPrice) / begOfYearPrice
    txtOutput.Text = "The percent increase for the year is " & _
                        percentIncrease & "."
End Sub
```

71. 000

73. LLL000

75. 0-00-000000-&

77.
```
Private Sub btnDisplay_Click(...) Handles btnDisplay.Click
    'Report checking account balances.
    Dim account As String
    Dim beginningBalance, deposits, withdrawals As Double
    Dim endOfMonthBalance, total As Double
    Dim sr As IO.StreamReader = IO.File.OpenText("3-3-E77.TXT")
    Dim fmtStr As String = "{0,-10}{1,10:C}"
    lstOutput.Items.Clear()
    lstOutput.Items.Add(String.Format(fmtStr, "Account", "Balance"))
    '1st account
    account = sr.ReadLine
    beginningBalance = CDbl(sr.ReadLine)
    deposits = CDbl(sr.ReadLine)
    withdrawals = CDbl(sr.ReadLine)
    endOfMonthBalance = beginningBalance + deposits - withdrawals
    lstOutput.Items.Add(String.Format(fmtStr, account, _
                        endOfMonthBalance))
    total = endOfMonthBalance
    '2nd account
    account = sr.ReadLine
    beginningBalance = CDbl(sr.ReadLine)
    deposits = CDbl(sr.ReadLine)
    withdrawals = CDbl(sr.ReadLine)
    endOfMonthBalance = beginningBalance + deposits - withdrawals
    lstOutput.Items.Add(String.Format(fmtStr, account, _
                        endOfMonthBalance))
```

```vb
        total += endOfMonthBalance    'Increase total by endOfMonthBalance.
        '3rd account
        account = sr.ReadLine
        beginningBalance = CDbl(sr.ReadLine)
        deposits = CDbl(sr.ReadLine)
        withdrawals = CDbl(sr.ReadLine)
        endOfMonthBalance = beginningBalance + deposits - withdrawals
        lstOutput.Items.Add(String.Format(fmtStr, account, _
                        endOfMonthBalance))
        total += endOfMonthBalance    'Increase total by endOfMonthBalance.
        lstOutput.Items.Add(String.Format(fmtStr, "Total", total))
        sr.Close()
    End Sub

79. Private Sub btnDisplay_Click(...) Handles btnDisplay.Click
        'Compute semester averages.
        Dim socNmb As String
        Dim exam1, exam2, exam3, final, average, total As Double
        Dim fmtStr As String = "{0,-15}{1,8:N0}"
        Dim sr As IO.StreamReader = IO.File.OpenText("3-3-E79.TXT")
        lstOutput.Items.Clear()
        lstOutput.Items.Add(String.Format(fmtStr, "Soc. Sec. No.", _
                        "Average"))
        '1st student
        socNmb = sr.ReadLine
        exam1 = CDbl(sr.ReadLine)
        exam2 = CDbl(sr.ReadLine)
        exam3 = CDbl(sr.ReadLine)
        final = CDbl(sr.ReadLine)
        average = (exam1 + exam2 + exam3 + final * 2) / 5
        lstOutput.Items.Add(String.Format(fmtStr, socNmb, average))
        total = average
        '2nd student
        socNmb = sr.ReadLine
        exam1 = CDbl(sr.ReadLine)
        exam2 = CDbl(sr.ReadLine)
        exam3 = CDbl(sr.ReadLine)
        final = CDbl(sr.ReadLine)
        average = (exam1 + exam2 + exam3 + final * 2) / 5
        lstOutput.Items.Add(String.Format(fmtStr, socNmb, average))
        total += average  'Increase value of total by value of average.
        '3rd student
        socNmb = sr.ReadLine
        exam1 = CDbl(sr.ReadLine)
        exam2 = CDbl(sr.ReadLine)
        exam3 = CDbl(sr.ReadLine)
        final = CDbl(sr.ReadLine)
        average = (exam1 + exam2 + exam3 + final * 2) / 5
        lstOutput.Items.Add(String.Format(fmtStr, socNmb, average))
        total += average  'Increase value of total by value of average.
        lstOutput.Items.Add(String.Format(fmtStr, "Class Average", _
                        total / 3))
        sr.Close()
    End Sub

81. Private Sub txtName_Enter(…) Handles txtName.MouseEnter
        MessageBox.Show("Enter first name, middle initial, and " & _
                        "last name separated by spaces.")
    End Sub
```

```
Private Sub txtAddress_Enter(…) Handles txtAddress.MouseEnter
   MessageBox.Show("Enter street address, city, state, and " & _
                   "zip code separated by commas.")
End Sub
```

83.
```
Private Sub btnCompute_Click(...) Handles btnCompute.Click
    'Show growth of money in a savings account.
    Dim principal, intRate, yrs, amt As Double
    lstOutput.Items.Clear()
    principal = CDbl(txtPrincipal.Text)
    intRate = CDbl(txtIntRate.Text)
    yrs = 10
    amt = principal * (1 + intRate) ^ yrs
    lstOutput.Items.Add("When " & FormatCurrency(principal))
    lstOutput.Items.Add("is invested at " & FormatPercent(intRate))
    lstOutput.Items.Add("interest for " & yrs & " years,")
    lstOutput.Items.Add("the balance is " & FormatCurrency(amt))
End Sub
```

85.
```
Private Sub btnCompute_Click(...) Handles btnCompute.Click
    Dim pricePerGallon, numberOfGallons, cost As Double
    pricePerGallon = CDbl(InputBox("Enter price per gallon", "Price"))
    numberOfGallons = CDbl(InputBox("Enter number of gallons", _
                                    "Quantity"))
    cost = pricePerGallon * numberOfGallons
    txtOutput.Text = "Total cost is " & cost & "."
End Sub
```

```
Programming Project 5
Private Sub btnCompute_Click(…) Handles btnCompute.Click
  Dim changeAmount As Double
  Dim amount, quarters, dimes, nickels, pennies As Integer
  changeAmount = CDbl(txtInput.Text)
  amount = CInt(100 * changeAmount)
   quarters = amount \ 25
   amount = amount - quarters * 25
   dimes = amount \ 10
   amount = amount - dimes * 10
   nickels = amount \ 5
   amount = amount - nickels * 5
   pennies = amount
   txtQ.Text = CStr(quarters)
   txtD.Text = CStr(dimes)
   txtN.Text = CStr(nickels)
   txtP.Text = CStr(pennies)
End Sub
```

CHAPTER 4

EXERCISES 4.1

1. HI

3. The letter after M is: N

5. "We're all in this alone." - Lily Tomlin

7. True

9. True

11. False

13. True

15. False

17. False

19. True

21. True

23. False

25. False

27. True

29. True

31. Equivalent

33. Not Equivalent

35. Equivalent

37. Equivalent

39. Equivalent

41. `a >= c`

43. `(a <= b) And (c <> d)`

45. `(b = 5) Or (c >= d) or (c.length >=7)`

47. True

49. False

EXERCISES 4.2

1. `a is greater than 5.`

3. `Visual Basic Programming is Fun.`

5. `10`

7. `Cost of call: $11.26`

9. `A is a vowel.`

11. `positive`

13. Incorrect condition. Should be `If ((1 < num) And (num < 3)) Then`

15. `The if statement requires a "Then"`

```
Private Sub btnDisplay_Click(ByVal sender As System.Object, ByVal e As
System.EventArgs) Handles btnDisplay.Click
  If ("a" <> "A") Then
    txtOutput.Text = "The values are not equal"
  End If
End Sub
```

17. Comparing numeric and string values in line 5

19. Incorrect condition. Should be `If ((j = 4) Or (k = 4)) Then`

21. `a = 5`

23.
```
If j = 7 Then
    b = 1
Else
    b = 2
End If
```

25.
```
message = "Is Alaska bigger than Texas and California combined?"
answer = InputBox(message)
If (answer.Substring(0, 1) = "Y") Then
  txtOutput.Text = "Correct"
Else
  txtOutput.Text = "Wrong"
End If
```

27.
```
Private Sub btnCompute_Click(...) Handles btnCompute.Click
    'Give server a tip.
    Dim cost, tip As Double
    cost = CDbl(InputBox("Enter cost of meal:"))
    tip = cost * 0.15
    If tip < 1 Then
      tip = 1
    End If
    txtOutput.Text = "Leave " & FormatCurrency(tip) & " for the tip."
End Sub
```

29.
```
Private Sub btnCompute_Click(...) Handles btnCompute.Click
    'Order widgets.
    Dim num, cost As Double
    num = CDbl(InputBox("Number of widgets:"))
    If num < 100 Then
      cost = 0.25 * num   '25 cents each
    Else
      cost = 0.2 * num    '20 cents each
    End If
    txtOutput.Text = "The cost is " & FormatCurrency(cost) & "."
End Sub
```

31.
```
Private Sub btnProcess_Click(ByVal sender As System.Object, ByVal e As
System.EventArgs) Handles btnProcess.Click
    Dim answer As String
    answer = InputBox("Who Created Mickey Mouse?")
    If answer = ("Walt Disney") Or answer = ("Ub Iwerks") Then
      txtOutput.Text = "Correct"
    Else
      txtOutput.Text = "Sorry,Incorrect"
    End If
End Sub
```

33.
```
Private Sub btnProcess_Click(ByVal sender As System.Object, ByVal e As
System.EventArgs) Handles btnProcess.Click
    Dim balance, purchase As Double
    balance = CDbl(InputBox("Enter the balance on the Gift Card: "))
    purchase = CDbl(InputBox("Enter the amount of the purcase: "))
```

```vb
   If (balance < purchase) Then
     txtOutput.Text = "Transaction denied,insufficient funds"
   Else
     txtOutput.Text = "Transaction approved"
     balance -= purchase
     txtOutput.Text += "Remaining Balance on card is: " & FormatCurrency(balance)
   End If
   If balance < 10.0 Then
     txtOutput.Text += " Notice:Balance is less than $10.00"
   End If
 End Sub
```

35.
```vb
Private Sub btnCompute_Click(...) Handles btnCompute.Click
   'Display change from a transaction.
   Dim weight, cost, amount, change As Double
   weight = CDbl(txtWeight.Text)
   amount = CDbl(txtAmount.Text)
   cost = weight * 1.7
   If (amount >= cost) Then
     change = amount - cost
     txtOutput.Text = "Your change is " & FormatCurrency(change) & "."
   Else
     txtOutput.Text = "I need " & FormatCurrency(cost - amount) & _
                      " more."
   End If
 End Sub
```

37.
```vb
Private Sub btnCompute_Click(...) Handles btnTranslate.Click
   'Convert to Pig Latin.
   Dim word, first As String
   word = InputBox("Enter a word (use all lowercase):")
   first = word.Substring(0, 1)
   If "aeiou".IndexOf(first) <> -1 Then
     word &= "way"
   Else
     word = word.Substring(1) & first & "ay"
   End If
   txtOutput.Text = "The word in pig latin is " & word & "."
 End Sub
```

39.
```vb
Dim numLines As Integer = 0  'In Declarations section
 'numLines tells the number of lines displayed.

 Private Sub btnBogart_Click(...) Handles btnBogart.Click
   If numLines = 0 Then
     lstOutput.Items.Add("I came to Casablanca for the waters.")
     numLines += 1
   ElseIf numLines = 2 Then
     lstOutput.Items.Add("I was misinformed.")
     numLines += 1
   End If
 End Sub

 Private Sub btnRaines_Click(...) Handles btnRaines.Click
   If numLines = 1 Then
     lstOutput.Items.Add("But we're in the middle of the desert.")
     numLines += 1
   End If
 End Sub
```

41.
```
Private Sub btnEvaluate_Click(...) Handles btnEvaluate.Click
  'Assume that the Text property of txtNumberOfGuesses
  'was set to 0 in the Form Designer
  Dim msg As String
  txtNumberOfGuesses.Text = CStr(CInt(txtNumberOfGuesses.Text) + 1)
  If txtAnswer.Text.ToUpper.IndexOf("COOLIDGE") <> -1 Then
    MessageBox.Show("Calvin Coolidge was born on July 4, 1872.", "Correct")
    End
  ElseIf CInt(txtNumberOfGuesses.Text) = 3 Then
    msg = "He once said, 'If you don't say anything," & _
          " you won't be called upon to repeat it.'"
    MessageBox.Show(msg, "Incorrect")
  ElseIf CInt(txtNumberOfGuesses.Text) = 7 Then
    MessageBox.Show("His nickname was 'Silent Cal.'", "Incorrect")
  ElseIf CInt(txtNumberOfGuesses.Text) = 10 Then
    msg = "Calvin Coolidge was born on July 4, 1872."
    MessageBox.Show(msg, "You've run out of Guesses")
    End
  Else
    MessageBox.Show("Sorry.", "Incorrect")
  End If
  txtAnswer.Clear()
  txtAnswer.Focus()
End Sub
```

43.
```
Private Sub btnCalculateTax_Click(...) Handles btnCalculateTax.Click
  'Calculate state income tax.
  Dim income, tax As Double
  income = CDbl(InputBox("Taxable income:"))
  If income <= 20000 Then
    tax = 0.02 * income
  Else
    If income <= 50000 Then
      tax = 400 + 0.025 * (income - 20000)
    Else
      tax = 1150 + 0.035 * (income - 50000)
    End If
  End If
  txtOutput.Text = "Tax is " & FormatCurrency(tax)
End Sub
```

45.
```
Private Sub btnDisplay_Click(ByVal sender As System.Object, ByVal e As
  System.EventArgs) Handles btnDisplay.Click
  Dim number, cost As Double
  number = Cint(InputBox("Enter number of T-Shirts to purchase: " ))
  If (number = 1) Then
    cost = (8.0 * 90%)
  ElseIf (number = 2) Then
    cost = (8.0 * 2 * 80%)
  Else
    cost = (8.0 * number * 70%)
  End If
  txtOutput.Text = "The cost of the T-Shirt purchase is: " &
FormatCurrency(cost)
End Sub
```

EXERCISES 4.3

1. ```
The price is $3.75
The price is $3.75
```

3. ```
1933 - Greatest Generation
1960 - Baby Boomer
2000 - Generation Y
```

5. ```
Nope.
He worked with the developer, von Neumann, on the ENIAC.
Correct.
```

7. ```
The more things change, the less they remain the same.
Less is more.
Time keeps everything from happening at once.
```

9. Case statement is required:

```
Private Sub btnDisplay_Click(ByVal sender As System.Object, ByVal e As
System.EventArgs) Handles btnDisplay.Click
  Dim a As String = "Hi"
  Select Case a
    Case a = "Hi"
    txtOutput.Text = "Hello"
  End Select
End Sub
```

11. Case comparision is incorrect:

```
Dim color As String
color = InputBox ("Enter a color")
Select Case color
  Case Is = "red"
    txtOutput.Text = "I like red"
  Case Else
End Select
```

13. Error in second Case clause

15. Logical error: `>= "Peach"` should be `>= "PEACH"`.
    Syntax error: `"ORANGE TO PEACH"` should be `"ORANGE" To "PEACH"`.

17. Valid

19. Invalid

21. Valid

23. ```
Select Case input
   Case Is = "R"
     txtOutput.Text = "Color is Red"
   Case Is = "B"
     txtOutput.Text = "Color is Blue"
   Case Else
     txtOutput.Text = "Color is Black"
End Select
```

25. ```
Select Case input
  Case input >= 90
    txtOutput.Text = "Letter Grade is A"
```

```
      Case input >= 80
        txtOutput.Text = "Letter Grade is B"
      Case input >= 70
        txtOutput.Text = "Letter Grade is C"
      Case input >= 60
        txtOutput.Text = "Letter Grade is D"
      Case Else
        txtOutput.Text = "Letter Grade is F"
    End Select
```

27.
```
Private Sub btnDescribe_Click(...) Handles btnDescribe.Click
    'Determine degree of cloudiness.
    Dim percent As Double
    percent = CDbl(InputBox("Percentage of cloud cover:"))
    Select Case percent
      Case 0 To 30
        txtOutput.Text = "Clear"
      Case 31 To 70
        txtOutput.Text = "Partly cloudy"
      Case 71 To 99
        txtOutput.Text = "Cloudy"
      Case 100
        txtOutput.Text = "Overcast"
      Case Else
        txtOutput.Text = "Percentage must be between 0 and 100."
    End Select
End Sub
```

29.
```
Private Sub btnFindNumDays_Click(...) Handles btnFindNumDays.Click
    Dim monthName, answer As String
    Dim numberOfDays As Integer
    monthName = InputBox("Enter a month (do not abbreviate):")
    'Compute number of days in the month
    Select Case monthName.ToUpper
      Case "FEBRUARY"
        answer = InputBox("Is it a leap year?")
        If answer.ToUpper.Substring(0, 1) = "Y" Then
          numberOfDays = 29
        Else
          numberOfDays = 28
        End If
      Case "APRIL", "JUNE", "SEPTEMBER", "NOVEMBER"
        numberOfDays = 30
      Case "JANUARY", "MARCH", "MAY", "JULY", "AUGUST", _
           "OCTOBER", "DECEMBER"
        numberOfDays = 31
    End Select
    txtoutput.Text = monthName & " has " & numberOfDays & " days."
End Sub
```

31.
```
Private Sub btnAssign_Click(...) Handles btnAssign.Click
    Dim score As Integer, letterGrade As String
    'Give letter grade for number score.
    score = CInt(InputBox("What is the score?"))
    Select Case score
      Case 90 To 100
        letterGrade = "A"
```

```
      Case 80 To 89
        letterGrade = "B"
      Case 70 To 79
        letterGrade = "C"
      Case 60 To 69
        letterGrade = "D"
      Case 0 To 59
        letterGrade = "F"
      Case Else
        letterGrade = "Invalid"
    End Select
    txtOutput.Text = "The letter grade is " & letterGrade & "."
  End Sub
```

33.
```
Private Sub btnDescribe_Click(...) Handles btnDetermine.Click
    'Determine cash reward.
    Dim amountRecovered, payment As Double
    amountRecovered = CDbl(InputBox("How much was recovered?"))
    Select Case amountRecovered
      Case Is <= 75000
        payment = 0.1 * amountRecovered
      Case Is <= 100000
        payment = 7500 + 0.05 * (amountRecovered - 75000)
      Case Is > 100000
        payment = 8750 + 0.01 * (amountRecovered - 100000)
        If payment > 50000 Then
          payment = 50000
        End If
    End Select
    txtOutput.Text = "The amount given as reward is " & _
                    FormatCurrency(payment) & "."
  End Sub
```

35.
```
Private Sub btnDisplay_Click(...) Handles btnDisplay.Click
    Dim pres, state, trivia, whichBush As String
    pres = txtLastName.Text
    Select Case pres.ToUpper
      Case "CARTER"
        state = "Georgia"
        trivia = "The only soft drink served in the Carter " & _
                 "White House was Coca-Cola."
      Case "REAGAN"
        state = "California"
        trivia = "His secret service code name was Rawhide."
      Case "BUSH"
        state = "Texas"
        whichBush = InputBox("Are his middle initials HW or W?")
        Select Case whichBush.ToUpper
          Case "HW"
            trivia = "He was the third left-handed president."
          Case "W"
            trivia = "He once owned the Texas Rangers baseball team."
        End Select
        state = "Texas"
      Case "CLINTON"
        state = "Arkansas"
        trivia = "In college he did a good imitation of Elvis Presley."
```

```
        Case Else
          state = ""
          trivia = ""
      End Select
      If state <> "" Then
        lstOutput.Items.Clear()
        lstOutput.Items.Add("President " & pres & "'s" & _
                            " home state was " & state & ".")
        lstOutput.Items.Add(trivia)
      End If
      txtLastName.Clear()
      txtLastName.Focus()
  End Sub
```

CHAPTER 5

EXERCISES 5.1

1. There's no great loss
   without some small gain.

3. Nothing is certain but
   Death and Taxes

5. All's well
   that ends well.

7. HOOLAHOOP

9. 88 keys on a piano

11. It was the best of times.
    It was the worst of times.

13. Your name has 7 letters.
    The first letter is G

15. abcde

17. 144 items in a gross

19. 30% of M&M's Plain Chocolate Candies are brown.

21. 1440 minutes in a day

23. t is the 6th letter of the word.

25. According to the Bureau of Labor Statistics,
    the average salaries for computer occupations
    in 2006 were as follows:

    Computer support specialists earned $44,350.
    Database administrators earned $67,460.
    Computer programmers earned $69,500.
    Computer systems analysts earned $72,230.

27. President B. Clinton is a graduate of Georgetown University.
    President G. Bush is a graduate of Yale University.

29. The first 6 letters are Visual.

31. The negative of worldly is unworldly

33.
```
24 blackbirds
baked in
a pie.
```

35. There is a parameter in the Sub procedure, but no argument in the statement calling the Sub procedure.

37. Since Handles is a keyword, it cannot be used as the name of a Sub procedure.

39.
```
Private Sub btnDisplay_Click(...) Handles btnDisplay.Click
    'Display a lucky number.
    Dim num As Integer = 7
    Lucky(num)
End Sub

Sub Lucky(ByVal num As Integer)
    'Display message.
    txtOutput.Text = num & " is a lucky number."
End Sub
```

41.
```
Private Sub btnDisplay_Click(...) Handles btnDisplay.Click
    'Information about trees
    Dim tree As String, ht As Double
    Dim sr As IO.StreamReader = IO.File.OpenText("TREES.TXT")
    lstBox.Items.Clear()
    tree = sr.ReadLine
    ht = CDbl(sr.ReadLine)
    Tallest(tree, ht)
    tree = sr.ReadLine
    ht = CDbl(sr.ReadLine)
    Tallest(tree, ht)
    sr.Close()
End Sub

Sub Tallest(ByVal tree As String, ByVal ht As Double)
    'Display information about tree.
    lstBox.Items.Add("The tallest " & tree & " in the U.S. is " & _
                     ht & " feet.")
End Sub
```

43.
```
Private Sub btnTriple_Click(...) Handles btnTriple.Click
    'Given a number, display its triple.
    Dim num As Double
    num = CDbl(InputBox("Enter a number:"))
    Triple(num)
End Sub

Sub Triple(ByVal num As Double)
 'Multiply the value of the number by 3.
    txtResult.Text = "The triple of " & num & " is " & 3 * num & "."
End Sub
```

45.
```
Private Sub btnDisplay_Click(...) Handles btnDisplay.Click
    Dim word As String, widthOfZone As Integer
    'Enter a word and column number to display.
    word = InputBox("Enter a word of at most ten letters.")
    widthOfZone = CInt(InputBox("Enter a number between 10 and 20."))
    PlaceNShow(word, widthOfZone)
End Sub

Sub PlaceNShow(ByVal word As String, _
               ByVal widthOfZone As Integer)
```

```
        'Display the word at the given column number.
        Dim fmtStr As String = "{0," & widthOfZone & "}"
        lstOutput.Items.Add("12345678901234567890")
        lstOutput.Items.Add(String.Format(fmtStr, word))
    End Sub
47. Private Sub btnDisplay_Click(...) Handles btnDisplay.Click
        'Intended college majors
        lstOutput.Items.Clear()
        DisplaySource()
        Majors(17.7, "business")
        Majors(1.1, "computer science")
    End Sub

    Sub DisplaySource()
     'Display the source of the information.
     Dim phrase As String
     phrase = "According to a 2007 survey of college freshmen"
     lstOutput.Items.Add(phrase)
     phrase = "taken by the Higher Educational Research Institute:"
     lstOutput.Items.Add(phrase)
     lstOutput.Items.Add("")
    End Sub

    Sub Majors(ByVal students As Double, ByVal field As String)
        'Display the information about the major
        lstOutput.Items.Add(students & _
                   " percent said they intend to major in " & field & ".")
    End Sub
49. Private Sub btnDisplay_Click(...) Handles btnDisplay.Click
        'Favorite number
        Dim num As Double
        lstOutput.Items.Clear()
        num = CDbl(txtBox.Text)
        Sum(num)
        Product(num)
    End Sub

    Sub Sum(ByVal num As Double)
      Dim phrase As String
      phrase = "The sum of your favorite number with itself is "
      lstOutput.Items.Add(phrase & (num + num) & ".")
    End Sub

    Sub Product(ByVal num As Double)
      Dim phrase As String
      phrase = "The product of your favorite number with itself is "
      lstOutput.Items.Add(phrase & (num * num) & ".")
    End Sub
51. Private Sub btnDisplay_Click(...) Handles btnDisplay.Click
        'Old McDonald Had a Farm.
        Dim animal, sound As String
        Dim sr As IO.StreamReader = IO.File.OpenText("FARM.TXT")
        animal = sr.ReadLine
        sound = sr.ReadLine
        ShowVerse(animal, sound)
        animal = sr.ReadLine
        sound = sr.ReadLine
        ShowVerse(animal, sound)
```

```
    animal = sr.ReadLine
    sound = sr.ReadLine
    ShowVerse(animal, sound)
    sr.Close()
  End Sub

  Sub ShowVerse(ByVal animal As String, ByVal sound As String)
    'Display a verse from Old McDonald Had a Farm
    lstOutput.Items.Add("Old McDonald had a farm. Eyi eyi oh.")
    lstOutput.Items.Add("And on his farm he had a " & animal & _
                        ". Eyi eyi oh.")
    lstOutput.Items.Add("With a " & sound & " " & sound & _
                        " here, and a " & sound & " " & sound & " there.")
    lstOutput.Items.Add("Here a " & sound & ", there a " & sound & _
                        ", everywhere a " & sound & " " & sound & ".")
    lstOutput.Items.Add("Old McDonald had a farm. Eyi eyi oh.")
    lstOutput.Items.Add("")
  End Sub
```

53.
```
  Private Sub btnDisplay_Click(...) Handles btnDisplay.Click
    Dim occupation As String, num06, num16 As Double
    Dim sr As IO.StreamReader = IO.File.OpenText("GROWTH.TXT")
    Dim fmtStr As String = "{0,-30}{1,4}      {2,4}       {3,8}"
    lstOutput.Items.Clear()
    lstOutput.Items.Add(String.Format(fmtStr, "Occupation", 2006, _
                        2016, "Increase"))
    occupation = sr.ReadLine
    num06 = CDbl(sr.ReadLine)
    num16 = CDbl(sr.ReadLine)
    CalculateAndDisplay(occupation, num06, num16)
    occupation = sr.ReadLine
    num06 = CDbl(sr.ReadLine)
    num16 = CDbl(sr.ReadLine)
    CalculateAndDisplay(occupation, num06, num16)
    occupation = sr.ReadLine
    num06 = CDbl(sr.ReadLine)
    num16 = CDbl(sr.ReadLine)
    CalculateAndDisplay(occupation, num06, num16)
    occupation = sr.ReadLine
    num06 = CDbl(sr.ReadLine)
    num16 = CDbl(sr.ReadLine)
    CalculateAndDisplay(occupation, num06, num16)
    sr.Close()
  End Sub

  Sub CalculateAndDisplay(ByVal occupation As String, _
                          ByVal num06 As Double, ByVal num16 As Double)
    Dim perIncrease As Double
    Dim fmtStr As String = "{0,-30}{1,4}        {2,4}       {3,8:P0}"
    perIncrease = (num16 - num06) / num06
    lstOutput.Items.Add(String.Format(fmtStr, occupation, num06, _
                        num16, FormatPercent(perIncrease, 1)))
  End Sub
```

55.
```
  Dim answer As String

  Private Sub btnQuestion_Click(...) Handles btnQuestion.Click
    'Quiz
    Dim category As Integer
```

```
      category  = CInt(InputBox("Enter question number (1, 2, or 3):"))
      Select Case category
        Case 1
          AskQuestion1()
          CheckAnswer()
        Case 2
          AskQuestion2()
          CheckAnswer()
        Case 3
          AskQuestion3()
          CheckAnswer()
        Case Else
          txtOutput.Text  = "That is not a valid question number."
      End Select
    End Sub

    Sub AskQuestion1()
      'Ask question number 1.
      'Answer is stored in a class-level variable.
      Dim question As String = "Who was the only living artist to have " & _
           "his work displayed in the Grand Gallery of the Louvre?"
      answer = InputBox(question, "Question #1")
    End Sub

    Sub AskQuestion2()
      'Ask question number 2.
      'Answer is stored in a class-level variable.
      Dim question As String = "Who said 'Computers are useless. " & _
                    "They can only give you answers.'"
      answer = InputBox(question, "Question #2")
    End Sub

    Sub AskQuestion3()
      'Ask question number 3.
      'Answer is stored in a class-level variable.
      Dim question As String = "By what name is Pablo Blasio better known?"
      answer = InputBox(question, "Question #3")
    End Sub

    Sub CheckAnswer()
      'Check the answer for its correctness
      'Correct answer to all questions is the same.
      'Answer is stored in a class-level variable.
      If (answer.ToUpper = "PABLO PICASSO") Or _
         (answer.ToUpper = "PICASSO") Then
        txtOutput.Text = "Correct! Pablo Picasso."
      Else
        txtOutput.Text = "I'm sorry, that is incorrect."
      End If
    End Sub
```

EXERCISES 5.2

1. 9

3. Can Can

5. 25

7. Less is more.

9. `Gabriel was born in the year 1980`

11. `Buckeyes`

13. `0`

15. `1`
    `1`

17. `4 overwhelming`
    `8 whelming`
    `4 whelming`
    `4 ming`
    `4 whelming`

19. The variable *c* should be a parameter in the Sub procedure. That is, the header for the Sub procedure should be

```
Sub Sum(ByVal x As Double, ByVal y As Double, ByRef c As Double)
```

Also, the Dim statement in the Sub procedure should be deleted.

21.
```
Private Sub btnCompute_Click(...) Handles btnCompute.Click
    'Calculate sales tax
    Dim price, tax, cost As Double
    lstOutput.Items.Clear()
    InputPrice(price)
    Compute(price, tax, cost)
    ShowData(price, tax, cost)
End Sub

Sub InputPrice(ByRef price As Double)
  'Get the price of the item
  price = CDbl(InputBox("Enter the price of the item:"))
End Sub

Sub Compute(ByVal price As Double, ByRef tax As Double, _
            ByRef cost As Double)
  'Calculate the cost
  tax = 0.05 * price
  cost = price + tax
End Sub

Sub ShowData(ByVal price As Double, ByVal tax As Double, _
             ByVal cost As Double)
  'Display bill
  lstOutput.Items.Add("Price: " & price)
  lstOutput.Items.Add("Tax:    " & tax)
  lstOutput.Items.Add("-------")
  lstOutput.Items.Add("Cost:   " & cost)
End Sub
```

23.
```
Private Sub btnDisplay_Click(...) Handles btnDisplay.Click
    'Determine the area of a rectangle.
    Dim length, width, area As Double
    InputSize(length, width)
    ComputeArea(length, width, area)
    ShowArea(area)
End Sub

Sub ComputeArea(ByVal length As Double, ByVal width As Double, _
                ByRef area As Double)
```

```vb
     'Calculate the area.
     area = length * width
   End Sub

   Sub InputSize(ByRef length As Double, ByRef width As Double)
     'Get the dimensions of the rectangle.
     length = CDbl(txtLength.Text)
     width = CDbl(txtWidth.Text)
   End Sub

   Sub ShowArea(ByVal area As Double)
     'Display the area of the rectangle.
     txtOutput.Text = "The area of the rectangle is " & area
   End Sub
```

25.
```vb
   Function checkTriangle(ByVal side1 As Double, ByVal side2 _
     As Double, ByVal side3 As Double) As String
     If (side1 <= 0) Or (side2 <= 0) Or (side3 <= 0) Then
       Return "data error"
     End If
     If (side1 = side2) And (side2 = side3) Then
       Return "Equilateral"
     ElseIf (side1 = side2) Or (side2 = side3) Or _
       (side3 = side1) Then
       Return "Isosceles"
     Else
       Return "Scalene"
     End If
   End Function
```

27.
```vb
   Dim high, low, guess, guesscount As Integer 'Class level
     Private Sub btnPlayHiLo_Click(…) Handles btnPlayHiLo.Click
       MessageBox.Show("Think of a number between 1 and 100")
       high = 101
       low = 1
       guesscount = 0
       GetGuess(high, low)
     End Sub

     Private Sub btnTooHigh_Click(…) Handles btnTooHigh.Click
       high = guess
       GetGuess(high, low)
     End Sub

     Private Sub btnTooLow_Click(…) Handles btnTooLow.Click
       low = guess
       GetGuess(high, low)
     End Sub

     Private Sub btnCorrect_Click(…) Handles btnCorrect.Click
       lstBox.Items.Add("Gameover")
       btnTooHigh.Enabled = False
       btnTooLow.Enabled = False
       btnCorrect.Enabled = False
     End Sub

     Private Sub GetGuess(ByVal high As Integer, ByVal low As Integer)
       guess = (high + low) \ 2
       guesscount += 1
       lstBox.Items.Add("Guess# " & guesscount & "guess is " & guess)
     End Sub
```

29.
```
Private Sub Convert()
    Dim original as String
    Dim answer,b As Integer
    original = _
    InputBox("enter a 4 digit value in some base 2..10")
    b = CInt(InputBox("what base is that number in?(2-10)"))
    Dim d1, d2, d3, d4 As Integer
    d1 = CInt(original.Substring(3, 1))
    d2 = CInt(original.Substring(2, 1))
    d3 = CInt(original.Substring(1, 1))
    d4 = CInt(original.Substring(0, 1))
    answer = (((d4 * b + d3) * b) + d2) * b + d1
    MessageBox.Show(CStr(answer))
End Sub
```

31.
```
Function TaxiCab(ByVal x1 As Double, ByVal y1 As Double, _
    ByVal x2 As Double, ByVal y2 As Double) As Double
    Dim x As Double = abs(x2 - x1)
    Dim y As Double = abs(y2 - y1)
    Return 10 * (x + y)
End Function

Function abs(byval z as Double) as Double
  abs = z
  If z < 0 Then
    Return -z
    End If
    Return z
End Function
```

33.
```
Private Sub btnsum_Click(…) Handles btnsum.Click
    Dim n As Integer
    n = CInt(txtinput.Text)
    lblAnswer.Text = sumints(n)
End Sub

Function sumints(ByVal n As Integer) As Integer
  Return n * (n + 1) / 2
End Function
```

EXERCISES 5.3

1. `203`

3. `The population will double in 24 years.`

5. `Volume of cylinder having base area 3.14159 and height 2 is 6.28318`
   `Volume of cylinder having base area 28.27431 and height 4 is 113.09724`

7. `train`

9. `moral has the negative amoral`
   `political has the negative apolitical`

11. The function header should end with "As String", not "As Integer".

13.
```
Dim total As Double    'In Declarations section of Code Editor

Private Sub btnDetermine_Click(...) Handles btnDetermine.Click
    'Tin Needed for a Tin Can
    Dim radius, height As Double
```

```
        lstOutput.Items.Clear()
        InputDims(radius, height)
        ShowAmount(radius, height)
    End Sub

    Sub InputDims(ByRef radius As Double, ByRef height As Double)
        radius = CDbl(InputBox("Enter radius of can:"))
        height = CDbl(InputBox("Enter height of can:"))
    End Sub

    Sub ShowAmount(ByVal radius As Double, ByVal height As Double)
        lstOutput.Items.Add("A can of radius " & radius & " and height " & _
                          height)
        lstOutput.Items.Add("requires " & CanArea(radius, height) & _
                          " square centimeters to make.")
    End Sub

    Function CanArea(ByVal radius As Double, ByVal height As Double) _
                  As Double
        'Calculate surface area of a cylindrical can.
        Return 6.283 * (radius ^ 2 + radius * height)
    End Function
```

15.
```
    Private Sub btnCalculate_Click(...) Handles btnCalculate.Click
        txtBMI.Text = CStr(BMI(CDbl(txtWeight.Text), CDbl(txtHeight.Text)))
    End Sub

    Function BMI(ByVal w As Double, ByVal h As Double) As Double
        'Calculate body mass index.
        Return Math.Round((703 * w) / (h ^ 2))
    End Function
```

17.
```
    Private Sub btnDetermine_Click(...) Handles btnDetermine.Click
        'Popcorn profits
        Dim popcorn, butter, bucket, price As Double
        InputAmounts(popcorn, butter, bucket, price)
        ShowProfit(popcorn, butter, bucket, price)
    End Sub

    Sub InputAmounts(ByRef popcorn As Double, ByRef butter As Double, _
                     ByRef bucket As Double, ByRef price As Double)
        Dim phrase As String = "What is the cost (in dollars) of the "
        popcorn = CDbl(InputBox(phrase & "popcorn kernels?"))
        butter = CDbl(InputBox(phrase & "butter?"))
        bucket = CDbl(InputBox(phrase & "bucket?"))
        price = CDbl(InputBox("What is the sale price?"))
    End Sub

    Function Profit(ByVal popcorn As Double, ByVal butter As Double, _
                    ByVal bucket As Double, ByVal price As Double) As Double
        'Calculate the profit on a bucket of popcorn.
        Return price - (popcorn + butter + bucket)
    End Function

    Sub ShowProfit(ByVal popcorn As Double, ByVal butter As Double, _
                   ByVal bucket As Double, ByVal price As Double)
        txtProfit.Text = FormatCurrency(Profit(popcorn, butter, bucket, _
                                        price))
    End Sub
```

19.
```
    Private Sub btnCompute_Click(...) Handles btnCompute.Click
        'Original Cost of Airmail
        Dim weight As Double
```

```
      InputWeight(weight)
      ShowCost(weight)
   End Sub

   Function Ceil(ByVal x As Double) As Double
      Ceil = -Int(-x)
   End Function

   Function Cost(ByVal weight As Double) As Double
      'Calculate the cost of an airmail letter.
      Return 0.05 + 0.1 * Ceil(weight - 1)
   End Function

   Sub InputWeight(ByRef weight As Double)
      weight = CDbl(txtWeight.Text)
   End Sub

   Sub ShowCost(ByVal weight As Double)
      txtOutput.Text = "The cost of mailing the letter was " & _
                  FormatCurrency(Cost(weight)) & "."
   End Sub
```

21.
```
   Private Sub btnAddressNGreet_Click(...) Handles btnAddressNGreet.Click
      'Display a greeting for a senator.
      Dim name As String
      name = InputBox("Enter the senator's name:")
      lstOutput.Items.Clear()
      lstOutput.Items.Add("The Honorable " & name)
      lstOutput.Items.Add("United States Senate")
      lstOutput.Items.Add("Washington, DC 20001")
      lstOutput.Items.Add("")
      lstOutput.Items.Add("Dear Senator " & LastName(name) & ",")
   End Sub

   Function LastName(ByVal name As String) As String
      'Determine the last name of a two part name.
      Dim spaceNmb As Integer
      spaceNmb = name.IndexOf(" ")
      Return name.Substring(spaceNmb + 1)
   End Function
```

CHAPTER 6

EXERCISES 6.1

1. `17`

3. `You are a super programmer!`

5. `2`

7. The value of *q* keeps growing until the program crashes when the value reaches the upper limit for a variable of type Double.

9. Do and Loop interchanged

11. `While num >= 7`

13. `Until response <> "Y"`

15. `Until name = ""`

17. `Until (a <= 1) Or (a >= 3)`

19. `While n = 0`

21.
```
Private Sub btnDisplay_Click(...) Handles btnDisplay.Click
    'Request and display three names.
    Dim name As String, num As Integer = 0
    Do While num < 3
      name = InputBox("Enter a name:")
      lstOutput.Items.Add(name)
      num += 1      'Add 1 to value of num.
    Loop
End Sub
```

23.
```
Private Sub btnDisplay_Click(...) Handles btnDisplay.Click
    'Convert Celsius to Fahrenheit.
    Dim fmtStr As String = "{0,7}  {1,10}"
    Dim celsius As Double = -40
    lstOutput.Items.Add(String.Format(fmtStr, "Celsius", "Fahrenheit"))
    Do While celsius <= 40
      lstOutput.Items.Add(String.Format(fmtStr, celsius, _
                          Fahrenheit(celsius)))
      celsius += 5
    Loop
End Sub

Function Fahrenheit(ByVal celsius As Double) As Double
    'Convert Celsius to Fahrenheit.
    Return (9 / 5) * celsius + 32
End Function
```

25.
```
Private Sub btnDetermine_Click(...) Handles btnDetermine.Click
    'Determine the year that the world population will exceed
    '10 billion, assuming a 1.17% rate of increase.
    Dim yr As Integer, pop As Double
    yr = 2008          'Start at 2008.
    pop = 6.64         'Population of 6.64 billion
    Do While pop <= 10
      pop = (1 + 0.0117) * pop
      yr += 1
    Loop
    txtOutput.Text = "The world population will reach 10 billion in " _
                     & yr & "."
End Sub
```

27.
```
Private Sub btnDetermine_Click (. . .) Handles btnDetermine.Click
    'Display first terms in the Fibonacci sequence
    Dim x As Integer = 1
    Dim y As Integer = 1
    Dim z As Integer = x + y
    lstOutput.Items.Clear()
    lstOutput.Items.Add(x)
    lstOutput.Items.Add(y)
    Do While z <= 100
      lstOutput.Items.Add(z)
      x = y
      y = z
      z = x + y
```

```
      Loop
   End Sub
```

29.
```
Private Sub btnDetermine_Click(...) Handles btnDetermine.Click
   'When after 6:30, do clock hands exactly overlap?
   Dim minuteHandPos, hourHandPos, difference As Double
   minuteHandPos = 0
   hourHandPos = 30
   Do While hourHandPos - minuteHandPos >= 0.0001
     difference = hourHandPos - minuteHandPos
     minuteHandPos = minuteHandPos + difference
     hourHandPos += difference / 12
   Loop
   txtOutput.Text = "The hands overlap at " & _
                 FormatNumber(minuteHandPos, 2) & " minutes after six."
End Sub
```

31.
```
Private Sub btnBounceBall_Click(...) Handles btnBounceBall.Click
   'Drop a ball, and find number of bounces and total distance traveled.
   Dim height, bounceFactor, distance As Double
   Dim bounces As Integer
   InputData(height, bounceFactor)
   BounceBall(height, bounceFactor, bounces, distance)
   ShowData(bounces, distance)
End Sub

Sub InputData(ByRef height As Double, _
            ByRef bounceFactor As Double)
   'Input height and coefficient of restitution.
   Dim prompt As String
   prompt = "What is the coefficient of restitution of the " & _
            "ball (0 to 1)? Examples are .7 for a tennis ball, " & _
            ".75 for a basketball, .9 for a super ball, and " & _
            ".3 for a softball."
   bounceFactor = CDbl(InputBox(prompt))
   prompt = "From how many meters will the ball be dropped?"
   height = CDbl(InputBox(prompt))
   height = 100 * height    'Convert to centimeters.
End Sub

Sub BounceBall(ByVal hght As Double, ByVal bFactor As Double, _
            ByRef bounces As Integer, ByRef dist As Double)
   bounces = 1             'First bounce
   dist = hght
   Do While hght * bFactor >= 10
     bounces += 1
     hght = bFactor * hght
     dist += 2 * hght       'Up then down again
   Loop
End Sub

Sub ShowData(ByVal bounces As Integer, _
            ByVal distance As Double)
   txtOutput.Text = "The ball bounced " & bounces & _
                 " times and traveled about " & _
                 FormatNumber(distance / 100) & " meters."
End Sub
```

33.
```
Private Sub btnCompute_Click(...) Handles btnCompute.Click
   'Calculate number of years to deplete savings account.
   Dim amt As Double, yrs As Integer
```

```
   amt = CDbl(InputBox("Enter initial amount in account:"))
   yrs = 0
   If amt * 1.05 - 1000 >= amt Then
     txtOutput.Text = "Account will never be depleted."
   Else
     Do
       amt = amt * 1.05 - 1000
       yrs += 1
     Loop Until amt <= 0
     txtOutput.Text = "It takes " & yrs & _
                      " years to deplete the account."
   End If
 End Sub
```

35.
```
Private Sub btnCompute_Click(...) Handles btnCompute.Click
   'Compute age when year is the square of age.
   Dim age As Integer = 1
   Do While (1980 + age) <> (age * age)
     age += 1
   Loop
   txtOutput.Text = age & " years old"
 End Sub
```

37.
```
Private Sub btnCapitalizeAll_Click(...) Handles btnCapitalizeAll.Click
   txtOutput.Text = txtSentence.Text.ToUpper
 End Sub

Private Sub btnCapitalizeFirstLetters_Click(...) Handles _
            btnCapitalizeFirstLetters.Click
   'Capitalize first letter of each word.
   Dim info As String = txtSentence.Text.Trim
   Dim word As String
   Dim newSentence As String = ""
   Dim positionOfSpace As Integer = info.indexOf(" ")
   info = txtSentence.Text.Trim
   Do While info <> ""
     positionOfSpace = info.IndexOf(" ")
     If positionOfSpace <> -1 Then
       word = info.Substring(0, positionOfSpace + 1)
       info = info.Substring(positionOfSpace + 1)
       newSentence &= word.Substring(0, 1).ToUpper & word.Substring(1)
     Else
       newSentence &= info.Substring(0, 1).ToUpper & info.Substring(1)
       info = ""
     End If
   Loop
   txtOutput.Text = newSentence
 End Sub
```

39.
```
Private Sub btnFind_Click(...) Handles btnFind.Click
   'Compute the greatest common divisor of two numbers.
   Dim m, n, t As Integer
   InputIntegers(m, n)
   Do While n <> 0
     t = n
     n = m Mod n     'Remainder after m is divided by n.
     m = t
```

```
    Loop
    txtOutput.Text = "The greatest common divisor is " & m & "."
  End Sub

  Sub InputIntegers(ByRef m As Integer, ByRef n As Integer)
    'Input two integers.
    m = CInt(InputBox("Enter first integer:", "GCD"))
    n = CInt(InputBox("Enter second integer:", "GCD"))
  End Sub
```

EXERCISES 6.2

1. `At least one word contains the letter A.`

3. `pie`
   `cake`
   `melon`

5.
```
      A
   Apple
   Apricot
   Avocado

      B
   Banana
   Blueberry

      G
   Grape

      L
   Lemon
   Lime
```

7. `A brace of ducks.`

9. `counters`

11. Loop statement missing. Also, loop cannot be entered because the (default) value of *num* is 0.

13. Last president in file will not be displayed.

15.
```
Private Sub btnFind_Click(...) Handles btnFind.Click
    'Find largest of a collection of numbers.
    Dim largest, num As Double
    largest = 0
    Dim sr As IO.StreamReader = IO.File.OpenText("POSNUMS.TXT")
    Do While sr.Peek <> -1
      num = CDbl(sr.ReadLine)
      If num > largest Then
        largest = num
      End If
    Loop
    txtOutput.Text = "The largest number is " & largest & "."
    sr.Close()
End Sub
```

17.
```
Private Sub btnDisplay_Click(...) Handles btnDisplay.Click
    'Display percentage of grades that are above average.
    Dim total, grade, average As Double
```

```
    Dim numGrades, aaCount As Integer
    Dim sr As IO.StreamReader = IO.File.OpenText("FINAL.TXT")
    total = 0
    numGrades = 0
    Do While sr.Peek <> -1
      grade = CDbl(sr.ReadLine)
      total += grade
      numGrades += 1
    Loop
    sr.Close()
    If numGrades > 0 Then
      average = total / numGrades
      aaCount = 0
      sr = IO.File.OpenText("FINAL.TXT")
      Do While sr.Peek <> -1
        grade = CDbl(sr.ReadLine)
        If grade > average Then
          aaCount += 1
        End If
      Loop
      sr.Close()
      txtOutput.Text = FormatPercent(aaCount / numGrades) & _
                       " of grades are above the average of " & _
                       FormatNumber(average) & "."
    End If
  End Sub
```

19.
```
Private Sub btnDisplay_Click(...) Handles btnDisplay.Click
    'Display the name of the requested president.
    Dim n, num As Integer
    Dim name As String
    Dim sr As IO.StreamReader = IO.File.OpenText("USPRES.TXT")
    n = CInt(txtPresNum.Text)
    If (1 <= n) And (n <= 43) Then
      num = 0
      Do
        name = sr.ReadLine
        num += 1
      Loop Until num = n
      lstOutput.Items.Add(name & " was president number " & n & ".")
      sr.Close()
    End If
    txtPresNum.Clear()
    txtPresNum.Focus()
  End Sub
```

21.
```
Private Sub btnCompute_Click(...) Handles btnCompute.Click
    'Generate sequence with algorithm
    Dim n, numSteps As Double
    lstOutput.Items.Clear()
    n = CDbl(txtInitialNumber.Text)
    numSteps = 0
    Do While n <> 1
      numSteps += 1
      If (n Mod 2 = 0) Then
        n = n / 2
        lstOutput.Items.Add(n)
```

```vbnet
      Else
        n = (3 * n) + 1
        lstOutput.Items.Add(n)
      End If
    Loop
    txtOutput.Text = "It took " & numSteps & " steps to reach 1."
  End Sub
```

23.
```vbnet
Private Sub btnFind_Click(...) Handles btnFind.Click
    'Analyze a Shakespearean sonnet.
    Dim totalWords, lineCount As Double
    Dim wordCount, positionOfSpace As Integer
    Dim sonnetLine, word As String
    Dim sr As IO.StreamReader = IO.File.OpenText("SONNET.TXT")
    totalWords = 0
    lineCount = 0
    Do While sr.Peek <> -1
      sonnetLine = sr.ReadLine
      lineCount += 1
      wordCount = 0
      Do While sonnetLine <> ""
        positionOfSpace = sonnetLine.IndexOf(" ")
        If positionOfSpace <> -1 Then
          word = sonnetLine.Substring(0, positionOfSpace + 1)
          sonnetLine = sonnetLine.Substring(positionOfSpace + 1)
        Else
          sonnetLine = ""
        End If
        wordCount += 1
      Loop
      totalWords += wordCount
    Loop
    sr.Close()
    txtOutput.Text = "The sonnet contains an average of " & _
                    FormatNumber(totalWords / lineCount) & _
                    " words per line and a total of " & _
                    totalWords & " words."
  End Sub
```

25.
```vbnet
Private Sub btnRemoveParens_Click(...) Handles btnRemoveParens.Click
    'Remove parentheses and their contents from a sentence.
    Dim sentence, letter, newSentence As String
    Dim parensFlag As Boolean, position As Integer
    sentence = txtSentence.Text
    newSentence = ""
    parensFlag = False
    position = 0
    Do Until position > sentence.Length - 1
      letter = sentence.Substring(position, 1)
      Select Case letter
        Case "("
          parensFlag = True
        Case ")"
          parensFlag = False
          position = position + 1
        Case Else
          If parensFlag = False Then
```

```
              newSentence &= letter
            End If
        End Select
        position += 1
    Loop
    txtOutput.Text = newSentence
End Sub
```

27.
```
Private Sub btnDisplay_Click(...) Handles btnDisplay.Click
    'Display liquids available, given an amount of money.
    Dim money, price As Double
    Dim liquid, top As String
    lstOutput.Items.Clear()
    money = CDbl(txtAmount.Text)
    top = "You can purchase one gallon of any of the following liquids:"
    lstOutput.Items.Add(top)
    Dim sr As IO.StreamReader = IO.File.OpenText("LIQUIDS.TXT")
    Do While sr.Peek <> -1
        liquid = sr.ReadLine
        price = CDbl(sr.ReadLine)
        If price <= money Then
            lstOutput.Items.Add(liquid)
        End If
    Loop
    sr.Close()
End Sub
```

EXERCISES 6.3

1.
```
Pass #1
Pass #2
Pass #3
Pass #4
```

3.
```
2
4
6
8
Who do we appreciate?
```

5.
```
5
6
7
```

7.
```
Hicham El Guerrouj   3:43.13
Alan Webb   3:46.91
Svetlana Masterkova   4:12.56
```

9.
```
1    4    7    10
2    5    8    11
3    6    9    12
```

11. `*******Hooray*******`

13. Loop is never executed since 1 is less than 25, and the step is negative.

15. The For...Next loop will not execute since 20 is greater than 0. You must add **step -1** to end of the For statement.

17.
```
Private Sub btnDisplay_Click(...) Handles btnDisplay.Click
    For num As Integer = 1 To 9 Step 2
        lstBox.Items.Add(num)
```

```vb
   Next
End Sub
```

19.
```vb
Private Sub btnDisplay_Click(...) Handles btnDisplay.Click
   Dim row As String = ""
   For i As Integer = 1 To 9
     row &= "*"
   Next
   txtOutput.Text = row
End Sub
```

21.
```vb
Private Sub btnDisplay_Click(...) Handles btnDisplay.Click
   'Display 10 x 10 array of stars.
   Dim row As String
   For i As Integer = 1 To 10
     row = ""
     For j As Integer = 1 To 10
       row &= "*"
     Next
     lstOutput.Items.Add(row)
   Next
End Sub
```

23.
```vb
Private Sub btnCompute_Click(...) Handles btnCompute.Click
   'Compute the sum 1 + 1/2 + 1/3 + 1/4 + ... + 1/100.
   Dim sum As Double = 0
   For denominator As Integer = 1 To 100
     sum += 1 / denominator
   Next
   txtOutput.Text = "The sum is " & FormatNumber(sum, 5) & "."
End Sub
```

25.
```vb
Private Sub btnAnalyzeOptions_Click(...) Handles _
              btnAnalyzeOptions.Click
   'Compare salaries.
   Dim opt1, opt2 As Double
   opt1 = Option1()
   opt2 = Option2()
   lstOutput.Items.Add("Option 1 = " & FormatCurrency(opt1))
   lstOutput.Items.Add("Option 2 = " & FormatCurrency(opt2))
   If opt1 > opt2 Then
     lstOutput.Items.Add("Option 1 pays better.")
   Else
     lstOutput.Items.Add("Option 2 pays better.")
   End If
End Sub

Function Option1() As Double
   'Compute total salary for 10 days,
   'with a flat salary of $100/day.
   Dim sum As Integer
   sum = 0
   For i As Integer = 1 To 10
     sum += 100
   Next
   Return sum
End Function

Function Option2() As Double
   'Compute the total salary for 10 days,
```

```
      'starting at $1 and doubling each day.
      Dim sum, daySalary As Integer
      sum = 0
      daySalary = 1
      For i As Integer = 1 To 10
        sum += daySalary
        daySalary = 2 * daySalary
      Next
      Return sum
    End Function
```

27.
```
    Private Sub btnComputeIdealWeights_Click(...) Handles _
                  btnComputeIdealWeights.Click
      'Ideal weights for men and women
      Dim lower, upper As Integer
      lstWeightTable.Items.Clear()
      InputBounds(lower, upper)
      ShowWeights(lower, upper)
    End Sub

    Function IdealMan(ByVal height As Integer) As Double
      'Compute the ideal weight of a man given the height.
      Return 4 * height - 128
    End Function

    Function IdealWoman(ByVal height As Integer) As Double
      'Compute the ideal weight of a woman given the height.
      Return 3.5 * height - 108
    End Function

    Sub InputBounds(ByRef lower As Integer, ByRef upper As Integer)
      'Input the lower and upper bounds on height.
      lower = CInt(InputBox("Enter lower bound on height in inches:"))
      upper = CInt(InputBox("Enter upper bound on height in inches:"))
    End Sub

    Sub ShowWeights(ByVal lower As Integer, ByVal upper As Integer)
      'Display table of weights.
      Dim fmtStr As String = "{0,-11}{1,-13}{2,-11}"
      lstWeightTable.Items.Add(String.Format(fmtStr, "Height", _
                              "Wt-Women", "Wt-Men"))
      lstWeightTable.Items.Add("")
      For height As Integer = lower To upper
        lstWeightTable.Items.Add(String.Format(fmtStr, height, _
                              IdealWoman(height), IdealMan(height)))
      Next
    End Sub
```

29.
```
    Private Sub btnAnalyze_Click(...) Handles btnAnalyze.Click
      'Determine number of sibilants in sentence.
      txtOutput.Text = "There are " & Sibilants(txtSentence.Text) & _
                    " sibilants in the sentence."
    End Sub

    Function Sibilants(ByVal sentence As String) As Integer
      'Count the number of sibilants (i.e., the letters S and Z).
      Dim numSibs As Integer
      Dim letter As String
      numSibs = 0
      For i As Integer = 0 To sentence.Length - 1
        letter = sentence.Substring(i, 1).ToUpper
```

```
      If (letter = "S") Or (letter = "Z") Then
        numSibs += 1
      End If
    Next
    Return numSibs
  End Function
```

31.
```
Private Sub btnCalculate_Click(...) Handles btnCalculate.Click
    'Savings account balance after 10 years
    Dim amt As Double = 800
    For yearNum As Integer = 1 To 10
      amt = (1.04 * amt) + 100 '(Growth due to interest) + deposit
    Next
    txtOutput.Text = "The final amount is " & FormatCurrency(amt) & "."
End Sub
```

33.
```
Private Sub btnAnalyze_Click(...) Handles btnAnalyze.Click
    'Radioactive decay; cobalt-60 decays at a rate of about 12% per year
    Dim grams As Double = 10
    For yearNum As Integer = 1 To 5
      grams = 0.88 * grams
    Next
    lstOutput.Items.Add("Of 10 grams of cobalt-6,")
    lstOutput.Items.Add(FormatNumber(grams) & _
                        " grams remain after 5 years.")
End Sub
```

35.
```
Private Sub btnDisplay_Click(...) Handles btnDisplay.Click
    'Draw a hollow box.
    Dim stars As Integer
    lstOutput.Items.Clear()
    stars = CInt(InputBox("Number of stars?"))
    DrawSide(stars)
    For i As Integer = 1 To stars - 2
      DrawRow(stars)
    Next
    DrawSide(stars)
End Sub

Sub DrawSide(ByVal stars As Integer)
    'Draw a solid side of stars for top and bottom.
    Dim row As String = ""
    For i As Integer = 1 To stars
      row &= "*"
    Next
    lstOutput.Items.Add(row)
End Sub

Sub DrawRow(ByVal stars As Integer)
    'Draw a row (put spaces between the two stars).
    Dim row As String = "*"
    For i As Integer = 1 To stars - 2
      row &= " "
    Next
    row &= "*"
    lstOutput.Items.Add(row)
End Sub
```

37.
```
Private Sub btnDetermine_Click(...) Handles btnDetermine.Click
    'Gambling casino problem
```

```
     Dim testValue, amount As Double
     testValue = 4
     Do
       testValue += 1     'Start test with $5.
       amount = testValue
       For i As Integer = 1 To 3        'One iteration for each casino
         amount = amount - 1     'Entrance fee
         amount = amount / 2     'Funds lost
         amount = amount - 1     'Exit fee
       Next
     Loop Until amount = 0
     txtOutput.Text = "Beginning amount = " & FormatCurrency(testValue)
   End Sub
```

39.
```
   Private Sub btnCompute_Click(...) Handles btnCompute.Click
     'Compute total earnings at retirement
     'get 5% raise per year, retire at age 65
     Dim name As String, age As Integer, salary As Double
     Dim earnings As Double = 0
     name = InputBox("Enter the person's name: ")
     age = CInt(InputBox("Enter the person's age: "))
     salary = CDbl(InputBox("Enter the person's starting salary: "))
     For i As Integer = age To 64
       earnings += salary
       salary = (1.05) * salary
     Next
     txtOutput.Text = name & " will earn about " & _
                    FormatCurrency(earnings, 0)
   End Sub
```

CHAPTER 7

EXERCISES 7.1

1. 501

3. `Have a soup spoon.`

5. `9`
   `4`

7. `18`

9. `A rook is worth more than a bishop`

11. `Your total is 280.`

13. The `ReDim` statement should not end with an `As String` clause.

15. When $k > 5$, the array subscript will be a negative number.

17. The number 2 in the second statement should be deleted.

19.
river(0)	river(1)	river(2)	river(3)	river(4)
Thames	Ohio	Amazon	Volga	Nile

river(0)	river(1)	river(2)	river(3)	river(4)
Ohio	Amazon	Volga	Nile	Thames

21. (a) 11   (b) −3   (c) 15   (d) 18

23. Replace the `btnDisplay_Click` event with the following:

```
Private Sub btnDisplay_Click(...) Handles btnDisplay.Click
  'Display the numbers of the games won by the team in the text box.
  Dim i As Integer
  Dim foundFlag As Boolean = False
  lstGamesWon.Items.Clear()
  For i = 0 To upperBound
    If teamName(i) = txtName.Text Then
      lstGamesWon.Items.Add(i + 1)
      foundFlag = True
    End If
  Next
  If Not foundFlag Then
    lstGamesWon.Items.Add("Never won a Super Bowl.")
  End If
End Sub
```

25. `ReDim inventory (1000)`

27.
```
Dim marx(3) As String   'In Declarations section of Code window

Private Sub frmMarx_Load(...) Handles MyBase.Load
  marx(0) = "Chico"
  marx(1) = "Harpo"
  marx(2) = "Groucho"
  marx(3) = "Zeppo"
End Sub
```

29.
```
'Store in b() the reverse of the values in a().
For i As Integer = 0 To 4
  b(i) = a(4 - i)
Next
```

31.
```
'Display the elements of the array a() in columns.
Dim fmtStr As String = "{0,15}{1,15}{2,15}{3,15}{4,15}"
For i As Integer = 0 To 25 Step 5
  lstOutput.Items.Add(String.Format(fmtStr, a(i), a(i + 1), _
                                    a(i + 2), a(i + 3), a(i + 4)))
Next
```

33.
```
'Compare arrays a() and b() for same values.
Dim differFlag As Boolean = False
For i As Integer = 0 To 9
  If a(i) <> b(i) Then
    differFlag = True
  End If
Next
If differFlag Then
  txtOutput.Text = "The arrays are not identical."
Else
  txtOutput.Text = "The arrays have identical values."
End If
```

35.
```
'Curve grades by adding 5.
For i As Integer = 0 To 9
  exams(i) += 5
Next
```

37.
```
Private Sub btnScores_Click(...) Handles btnScores.Click
    'Read data from a file, and display their frequencies.
    Dim frequency(4) As Integer    'Stores the results
    Dim num As Integer
    Dim fmtStr As String = "{0,-12} {1,-9:N0}"
    'Open the data file for input.
    Dim sr As IO.StreamReader = IO.File.OpenText("SCORES.TXT")
    'Loop over the 30 lines in the file.
    For i As Integer = 1 To 30
      num = CInt(sr.ReadLine)
      'Increment the frequency element that belongs to the number.
      'Divide by 10, and get the integer part.
      frequency(CInt(Int(num / 10))) += 1
    Next
    sr.Close()       'Always close the reader when finished with it.
    'Display the results.
    lstOutput.Items.Add(String.Format(fmtStr, "Interval", "Frequency"))
    For i As Integer = 0 To 4
      lstOutput.Items.Add(String.Format(fmtStr, (i * 10) & " to " & _
                          ((i + 1) * 10 - 1), frequency(i)))
    Next
End Sub
```

39.
```
Dim pres(42) As String     'Holds the presidents' names
Private Sub frmPres_Load(...) Handles MyBase.Load
    'Loads the data from the file into the array
    Dim sr As IO.StreamReader = IO.File.OpenText("USPRES.TXT")
    For i As Integer = 0 To 42
      pres(i) = sr.ReadLine
    Next
    sr.Close()
End Sub

Private Sub btnDisplayFullNames_Click(...) _
            Handles btnDisplayFullNames.Click
    'Display the presidents who have the requested first name.
    Dim space As Integer
    Dim firstName As String
    Dim foundFlag As Boolean = False
    lstFullNames.Items.Clear()
    'Loop over all presidents.
    For i As Integer = 0 To 42
      'The first name is the string before the first space.
      space = pres(i).IndexOf(" ")
      firstName = pres(i).Substring(0, space)
      'If the first name matches, then display the president.
      If firstName = txtFirstName.Text Then
        lstFullNames.Items.Add(pres(i))
        foundFlag = True
      End If
    Next
    'If not found, display message.
    If Not foundFlag Then
    lstFullNames.Items.Add("Name not found.")
    End If
End Sub

Private Sub lstDisplayPres_Click(...) Handles lstDisplayPres.Click
    'Display the presidents between two numbers, inclusive.
```

```
      lstPres.Items.Clear()
      'Loop from the lower number to the upper number.
      For i As Integer = CInt(txtLowerNum.Text) To CInt(txtUpperNum.Text)
        lstPres.Items.Add(i & ". " & pres(i - 1))
      Next
    End Sub
```

41.
```
    Private Sub btnShow_Click(...) Handles btnShow.Click
      'Test two phrases to see if they are anagrams.
      Dim first(25), second(25) As Integer   'Holds frequencies
      Dim letter As String
      Dim result As Boolean = True
      'Convert both phrases to uppercase.
      txtFirst.Text = txtFirst.Text.ToUpper
      txtSecond.Text = txtSecond.Text.ToUpper
      'Count the frequencies of the first phrase.
      For i As Integer = 0 To txtFirst.Text.Length - 1
        letter = txtFirst.Text.Substring(i, 1)
        'Increment the frequency element belonging to the letter.
        If (letter >= "A") And (letter <= "Z") Then
          first(Asc(letter) - Asc("A")) += 1
        End If
      Next
      'Count the frequencies of the second phrase.
      For i As Integer = 0 To txtSecond.Text.Length - 1
        letter = txtSecond.Text.Substring(i, 1)
        'Increment the frequency element belonging to the letter.
        If (letter >= "A") And (letter <= "Z") Then
          second(Asc(letter) - Asc("A")) += 1
        End If
      Next
      'Compare the two frequencies.
      For i As Integer = 0 To 25
        'If the frequencies differ, set the result flag to False.
        If first(i) <> second(i) Then
          result = False
        End If
      Next
      'Display the result.
      If result Then
        txtOutput.Text = "The two phrases are anagrams."
      Else
        txtOutput.Text = "The two phrases are not anagrams."
      End If
    End Sub
```

EXERCISES 7.2

1. No

3. Superior

5. greater than
   less than
   greater than
   less than
   equals

7. total rainfall for second quarter: 7 inches.

9. Change `txtOutput.Text = city` to `txtOutput.Text = city(1)`. You can't display an entire array with one statement.

11. *n* is incremented by 1 even if the user enters a negative number to stop and see the product. Move the incrementing inside the If block just before the statement *num(n) = number*.

13. In the Sub procedure *CopyArray*, the parentheses should be removed in the line `b() = a()`

15.
```
Sub Ascending()
    'Determine if array is ascending.
    Dim i As Integer = 0
    Dim orderFlag As Boolean = True
    Do While (i < scores.GetUpperBound(0)) And (orderFlag)
      If scores(i) > scores(i + 1) Then
        orderFlag = False
      End If
      i += 1
    Loop
    If orderFlag Then
      txtOutput.Text = "Array is ascending."
    Else
      txtOutput.Text = "Array is not ascending."
    End If
End Sub
```

17.
```
Sub WhatOrder()
    'Determine if order is ascending, descending, both, or neither.
    Dim ascFlag As Boolean = True
    Dim descFlag As Boolean = True
    Dim i as Integer = 0
    Do While (i < scores.GetUpperBound(0)) And (ascFlag Or descFlag)
      If scores(i) > scores(i + 1) Then
        ascFlag = False
      End If
      If scores(i) < scores(i + 1) Then
        descFlag = False
      End If
      i += 1
    Loop
    If ascFlag And descFlag Then
      txtOutput.Text = "Array is both ascending and descending."
    ElseIf (Not ascFlag) And (Not descFlag) Then
      txtOutput.Text = "Array is neither ascending nor descending."
    ElseIf ascFlag Then
      txtOutput.Text = "Array is ascending."
    Else
      txtOutput.Text = "Array is descending."
    End If
End Sub
```

19.
```
Sub MergeOrderedWithDups()
    Dim indexA, indexB As Integer
    Dim doneA, doneB As Boolean
    'Merge ascending arrays, with duplications.
    ReDim c(39)
    indexA = 0
    indexB = 0
```

```
        doneA = False
        doneB = False
        'Loop over each element of the resulting array.
        For indexC As Integer = 0 To 39
          'If a's element is less than b's, add a's to c.
          If ((a(indexA) <= b(indexB)) And Not doneA) Or (doneB) Then
            c(indexC) = a(indexA)
            'Get next element from a.
            If indexA < 19 Then
              indexA = indexA + 1
            Else
              doneA = True
            End If
          Else
            'Otherwise, add b's element to c.
            c(indexC) = b(indexB)
            'Get next element from b
            If indexB < 19 Then
              indexB = indexB + 1
            Else
              doneB = True
            End If
          End If
        Next
      End Sub
```

21.
```
    Dim states(49) As String      'Holds state data
    Dim count As Integer          'Number of states stored

    Private Sub btnInsert_Click(...) Handles btnInsert.Click
      'Insert a state into the array.
      Dim position As Integer
      'If there is no more room in the array, display a message.
      If count >= 50 Then
        MessageBox.Show("Fifty states have already been entered.", _
              "No more room.")
      Else
        'Store the new state as the next element.
        states(count) = txtState.Text
        'Find the place to insert the state.
        position = 0
        Do While states(position) < txtState.Text
          position += 1
        Loop
        'If the position already holds the state, then display message.
        If (states(position) = txtState.Text) And (position < count) Then
          MessageBox.Show("State already exists in the list.", "Exists")
        Else
          'Shift the states above the position.
          For i As Integer = count - 1 To position Step -1
            states(i + 1) = states(i)
          Next
          'Insert the new state in the position, and increment counter.
          states(position) = txtState.Text
          count += 1
        End If
```

```vb
    'Clear input and output, and reset focus for next input.
    lstOutput.Items.Clear()
    txtState.Clear()
    txtState.Focus()
  End If
End Sub

Private Sub btnDelete_Click(...) Handles btnDelete.Click
  'Remove a state from the list.
  Dim position As Integer = 0
  'Find the state within the array.
  Do While (position < count - 1) And (txtState.Text > states(position))
    position += 1
  Loop
  'If the state is not found or no states stored, then display message.
  If (count = 0) Or (txtState.Text <> states(position)) Then
    MessageBox.Show("The state is not in the list.", "Not found")
  Else
    count = count — 1      'Decrement counter.
    'Shift array above position down by one.
    For i As Integer = position To count - 1
      states(i) = states(i + 1)
    Next
    lstOutput.Items.Clear()
    txtState.Clear()
    txtState.Focus()
  End If
End Sub

Private Sub btnDisplay_Click(...) Handles btnDisplay.Click
  'Display the array in the list box.
  lstOutput.Items.Clear()
  For i As Integer = 0 To count - 1
    lstOutput.Items.Add(states(i))
  Next
  txtState.Clear()
  txtState.Focus()
End Sub
```

23.
```vb
Dim grades(99) As Integer     'Stores grade data
Dim count As Integer          'Number of grades stored

Private Sub btnRecord_Click(...) Handles btnRecord.Click
  'Add a score to the array.
  'If no more room, then display error message.
  If count >= 100 Then
    MessageBox.Show("100 scores have been entered.", "No more room.")
  Else
    'Store the input into the array.
    grades(count) = CInt(txtScore.Text)
    count += 1
    'Reset input.
    lstOutput.Items.Clear()
    txtScore.Clear()
    txtScore.Focus()
  End If
End Sub
```

```vb
Private Sub btnDisplay_Click(...) Handles btnDisplay.Click
  'Display average of grades and the number above average.
  Dim avg As Double, aboveAvg As Integer
  avg = Average(grades, count)
  aboveAvg = AboveAverage(grades, count, avg)
  lstOutput.Items.Clear()
  lstOutput.Items.Add("The average is " & FormatNumber(avg, 2) & ".")
  lstOutput.Items.Add(FormatNumber(aboveAvg, 0) & _
                        " students scored above the average.")
End Sub

Function Average(ByVal scores() As Integer, ByVal cnt As Integer) _
          As Double
  'Calculate the average score.
  Dim sum As Double = 0
  For i As Integer = 0 To cnt - 1
    sum += scores(i)
  Next
  'The average is the sum divided by the count; account for 0 count.
  If cnt = 0 Then
    Return 0
  Else
    Return sum / cnt
  End If
End Function

Function AboveAverage(ByVal scores() As Integer, _
                      ByVal cnt As Integer, _
                      ByVal average As Double) As Integer
  'Count the number of scores above the average score.
  Dim num As Integer = 0
  For i As Integer = 0 To cnt - 1
    If scores(i) > average Then
      num += 1
    End If
  Next
  Return num
End Function
```

25.
```vb
Private Sub btnUpdate_Click(...) Handles btnUpdate.Click
  'Merge two sets of data into a master set.
  Dim colors(71), retired(7), added(55) As String
  Dim i, j As Integer
  LoadArray(colors, "PRE1990COLORS.TXT")
  LoadArray(retired, "RETIREDCOLORS.TXT")
  LoadArray(added, "ADDEDCOLORS.TXT")
  'Remove the retired colors from the array.
  ReDim Preserve colors(120)
  i = 0
  j = 0        'Shift the array by the amount in j.
  Do While i <= 71 - 7
    If colors(i) = retired(j) Then
      j += 1
    End If
    colors(i) = colors(i + j)
    i += 1
  Loop
```

```
   'Insert the added colors into the master set.
   i = 0
   j = 0
   Do While j <= 55
     If added(j) < colors(i) Then      'Insert new color.
       For k As Integer = 63 + j To i Step -1
         colors(k + 1) = colors(k)     'Shift array.
       Next
       colors(i) = added(j)
       j += 1
     End If
     lstOutput.Items.Add(colors(i))
     i += 1
   Loop
   'Display the rest of the colors.
   For k As Integer = i To 119
     lstOutput.Items.Add(colors(k))
   Next
 End Sub

 Sub LoadArray(ByRef data() As String, ByVal fileName As String)
   'Load string data from a file.
   Dim sr As IO.StreamReader = IO.File.OpenText(fileName)
   'Fill the array, and close the reader.
   For i As Integer = 0 To data.GetUpperBound(0)
     data(i) = sr.ReadLine()
   Next
   sr.Close()
 End Sub
```

EXERCISES 7.3

1. `Utility expenses for spring: $484.62`

3. `Summer bills top spring bills by $235.68`

5. `heights are not the same`
   `150`

7. `Bill Gates lives in Medina, Washington`

9. *peace* should be *prize.peace*, and *year* should be *prize.year*.

11. The condition `(game1 > game2)` is not valid. Structures can only be compared one field at a time.

13.
```
Private Sub btnDisplay_Click(...) Handles btnDisplay.Click
  lstOutput.Items.Clear()
  For i As Integer = 0 To club.GetUpperBound(0)
    lstOutput.Items.Add(club(i).name)
  Next
End Sub
```

15.
```
Private Sub btnDisplay_Click(...) Handles btnDisplay.Click
  'Displays the students who are enrolled in CMSC 100
  Dim subject As String = "CMSC 100"
  'Loop over all students in the club.
  For i As Integer = 0 To club.GetUpperBound(0)
    'Loop over all courses for that student.
```

```
        For j As Integer = 0 To club(i).courses.GetUpperBound(0)
          'If a course matches, display the student's name.
          If club(i).courses(j) = subject Then
            lstOutput.Items.Add(club(i).name)
          End If
        Next
      Next
    End Sub
```

17.
```
    Dim grades(5) As TextBox        'Refers to grade textboxes
    Dim hours(5) As TextBox         'Refers to hours textboxes

    Structure Course
      Dim grade As String           'Grade in the course
      Dim hours As Double           'Number of credit-hours
    End Structure

    Private Sub frmGrades_Load(...) Handles MyBase.Load
      'Associate the textbox arrays with the textboxes
      grades(0) = txtGrade1
      grades(1) = txtGrade2
      grades(2) = txtGrade3
      grades(3) = txtGrade4
      grades(4) = txtGrade5
      grades(5) = txtGrade6
      hours(0) = txtHours1
      hours(1) = txtHours2
      hours(2) = txtHours3
      hours(3) = txtHours4
      hours(4) = txtHours5
      hours(5) = txtHours6
    End Sub

    Private Sub btnDisplay_Click(...) Handles btnDisplay.Click
      'Calculate and display the grade point average.
      Dim courses(5) As Course      'Holds the courses
      Dim numGrades As Integer
      'Read the data into the courses array until there is no more data.
      numGrades = 0
      For count As Integer = 0 To 5
        If (grades(count).Text <> "") Then
          numGrades += 1
          courses(count).grade = grades(count).Text
          courses(count).hours = CDbl(hours(count).Text)
        End If
      Next
      If numGrades > 0 Then
        'Redimension the array for the final count.
        ReDim Preserve courses(numGrades — 1)
        'Compute the GPA, and display the result.
        DisplayGPA(GPA(courses))
      Else
        'Display the error message.
        txtOutput.Text = "No grade(s) entered."
      End If
    End Sub

    Function GPA(ByVal c() As Course) As Double
      'Compute the GPA of a set of courses.
```

```
Dim credits, hours As Double
'Add up the credits and hours based upon the grade.
For i As Integer = 0 To c.GetUpperBound(0)
   'Ignore invalid grades.
   Select Case c(i).grade.ToUpper
     Case "A"
        credits += 4 * c(i).hours
        hours += c(i).hours
     Case "B"
        credits += 3 * c(i).hours
        hours += c(i).hours
     Case "C"
        credits += 2 * c(i).hours
        hours += c(i).hours
     Case "D"
        credits += 1 * c(i).hours
        hours += c(i).hours
     Case "F"
        hours += c(i).hours
   End Select
Next
'The GPA is the points divided by the total credit hours.
If hours = 0 Then
   Return 0
Else
   Return credits / hours
End If
End Function

Sub DisplayGPA(ByVal gpa As Double)
   'Display the GPA and a congratulatory message.
   txtGPA.Text = FormatNumber(gpa, 2)
   If gpa >= 3 Then
      txtOutput.Text = "Congratulations, you made the Honor Roll."
   Else
      txtOutput.Text = "Congratulations on completing the semester."
   End If
End Sub
```

19.
```
Structure Building
   Dim name As String        'Name
   Dim city As String        'City
   Dim height As Double      'Height in feet
   Dim stories As Integer    'Number of stories
End Structure

Dim buildings(4) As Building      'Holds data

Private Sub frmBuildings_Load(...) Handles MyBase.Load
   'Load data from file into structure array.
   Dim count As Integer = 0
   Dim sr As IO.StreamReader = IO.File.OpenText("BUILDINGS.TXT")
   'Loop until the end of file is reached.
   Do While sr.Peek <> -1
      'Make sure there is enough room to store data.
      If count > buildings.GetUpperBound(0) Then
         ReDim Preserve buildings(count + 5)
      End If
```

```
     'Store data from file into structure members.
     buildings(count).name = sr.ReadLine()
     buildings(count).city = sr.ReadLine()
     buildings(count).height = CDbl(sr.ReadLine())
     buildings(count).stories = CInt(sr.ReadLine())
     count += 1
   Loop
   sr.Close()
   'Resize array to exact number stored.
   ReDim Preserve buildings(count - 1)
 End Sub

 Private Sub btnDisplay_Click(...) Handles btnDisplay.Click
   'Look up building name, and display information.
   'Clear output.
   txtCity.Clear()
   txtHeight.Clear()
   txtStories.Clear()
   'Loop over all buildings in the array.
   For i As Integer = 0 To buildings.GetUpperBound(0)
     'If the name matches, display the information.
     If txtName.Text.ToUpper = buildings(i).name.ToUpper Then
       txtCity.Text = buildings(i).city
       txtHeight.Text = CStr(buildings(i).height)
       txtStories.Text = CStr(buildings(i).stories)
     End If
   Next
   'If no building matched, then display a message.
   If txtCity.Text = "" Then
     MessageBox.Show("Building not found.", "Not found.")
   End If
 End Sub
```

21.
```
 Structure Franchise
     Dim name As String     'Franchise Name
     Dim stores As Integer 'Number of stores
 End Structure

 Private Sub btnDisplay_Click(...) Handles btnDisplay.Click
   'Loads data and displays a report on percentage of stores
   Dim pizza(9) As Franchise
   Dim count As Integer = 0
   Dim fmtStr As String = "{0,-20} {1,7:P}"
   'Load data into array. Determine total number of stores
   Dim sr As IO.streamReader = IO.File.OpenText("7-3-E21.TXT")
   For i As Integer = 0 To 9
     pizza(i).name = sr.ReadLine
     pizza(i).stores = CInt(sr.ReadLine)
     count += pizza(i).stores
   Next
   'Display report
   lstOutput.Items.Add(String.Format(fmtStr, "NAME", "PERCENT"))
   For i As Integer = 0 To 9
     lstOutput.Items.Add(String.Format(fmtStr, pizza(i).name, _
                                   pizza(i).stores / count))
   Next
 End Sub
```

EXERCISES 7.4

1. 500
   300

3. 8
   8

5. Items are not properly swapped.

7. Sequential, since the array in not ordered

9. 4 swaps

11. $(n-1) + (n-2) + \cdots + 1$. A shorter version of this formula is $n(n-1)/2$.

13. 4 swaps

15. 8 comparisons

17. 32; 16 1/2; 6

19.
```
Sub SwapThree(ByRef x As String, ByRef y As String, _
              ByRef z As String)
  Dim temp As String
  temp = x
  x = y
  y = z
  z = x
End Sub
```

21.
```
Structure CapitalEvent
  Dim name As String
  Dim crowd As Integer              'Estimate in thousands.
End Structure

Private Sub btnDisplay_Click(...) Handles btnDisplay.Click
  'Read and sort the event data.
  Dim sr As IO.StreamReader = IO.File.OpenText("7-4-E21.TXT")
  Dim temp, evt(8) As CapitalEvent     'Nine events total
  Dim fmtStr As String = "{0,-50} {1,5}"
  For i As Integer = 0 To 8
    evt(i).name = sr.ReadLine()
    evt(i).crowd = CInt(sr.ReadLine())
  Next
  sr.Close()
  'Use bubble sort to order.
  For i As Integer = 1 To 8
    For j As Integer = 1 To 9 - i
      If evt(j - 1).name > evt(j).name Then
        'Swap.
        temp = evt(j - 1)
        evt(j - 1) = evt(j)
        evt(j) = temp
      End If
    Next
  Next
  'Display the events.
  lstOutput.Items.Clear()
  lstOutput.Items.Add(String.Format(fmtStr, "EVENT", "CROWD"))
```

```
    For i As Integer = 0 To 8
      lstOutput.Items.Add(String.Format(fmtStr, evt(i).name, _
                                        evt(i).crowd))
    Next
  End Sub
```

23.
```
  Private Sub btnStore_Click(...) Handles btnStore.Click
    'Read 10 sorted words, then add one more.
    Dim i As Integer
    Dim temp, words(10) As String    'Eleven words to store
    'Get all eleven words from the user.
    For j As Integer = 0 To 10
      words(j) = InputBox("Enter word #" & "Enter word #" & j + 1, "")
    Next
    'Find correct position of eleventh word.
    i = 0
    Do While words(i) < words(10)
      i += 1
    Loop
    'Shift the array, and insert the new word.
    temp = words(10)
    For j As Integer = 9 To i Step -1
      words(j + 1) = words(j)
    Next
    words(i) = temp
  End Sub
```

25.
```
  Private Sub btnSort_Click(...) Handles btnSort.Click
    'Read and sort a list of numbers
    Dim n As Integer = CInt(txtN.Text)
    Dim temp, nums(n - 1) As Double
    For i As Integer = 0 To n - 1 'Get numbers from the user
      nums(i) = CDbl(InputBox("Enter number #" & i + 1))
    Next
    'Use bubble sort to swap
    For i As Integer = 1 To n - 1
      For j As Integer = 1 To n - i
        If nums(j - 1) > nums(j) Then
          'Swap
          temp = nums(j - 1)
          nums(j - 1) = nums(j)
          nums(j) = temp
        End If
      Next
    Next
    'Display the ordered list of numbers
    For i As Integer = 0 To n - 1
      lstOutput.Items.Add(nums(i))
    Next
  End Sub
```

27.
```
Dim codes(25) As String

  Private Sub frmCode_Load(...) Handles MyBase.Load
    'Read in the code for the 26 letters of the alphabet.
    Dim sr As IO.StreamReader = IO.File.OpenText("7-4-E27.TXT")
    For i As Integer = 0 To 25
      codes(i) = sr.ReadLine()
```

```
    Next
    sr.Close()
  End Sub

  Private Sub btnDisplay_Click(...) Handles btnDisplay.Click
    'Display a word in Morse code.
    Dim word, result As String
    'Convert input to uppercase.
    word = txtWord.Text.ToUpper
    result = ""
    'Loop over each character of the string. Note that the index starts at 0.
    For i As Integer = 0 To word.Length - 1
      If (word.Substring(i, 1) >= "A") And _
         (word.Substring(i, 1) <= "Z") Then
        result = result & codes(Asc(word.Substring(i, 1)) - Asc("A")) & " "
      End If
    Next
    txtOutput.Text = result
  End Sub
```

29.
```
  Private Sub btnDisplay_Click(...) Handles btnDisplay.Click
    'Get seven scores from the user, and display the average.
    Dim scores(6), temp As Integer
    Dim sum As Integer
    'Read the seven scores into the array.
    For i As Integer = 0 To 6
      scores(i) = CInt(InputBox("Enter score #" & i + 1, ""))
    Next
    'Bubble sort the scores.
    For i As Integer = 1 To 6
      For j As Integer = 1 To 7 - i
        If scores(j - 1) > scores(j) Then
          'Swap scores.
          temp = scores(j - 1)
          scores(j - 1) = scores(j)
          scores(j) = temp
        End If
      Next
    Next
    'Calculate and display the average.
    sum = 0
    For i As Integer = 2 To 6      'Throw out the two lowest scores.
      sum += scores(i)
    Next
    txtOutput.Text = FormatNumber(sum / 5)
  End Sub
```

31.
```
  Private Sub btnDisplay_Click(...) Handles btnDisplay.Click
    'Get data from the user, and display the median.
    Dim data(), temp, median As Double
    Dim n, p, q As Integer
    'Read the number of elements.
    n = CInt(InputBox("Enter number of data elements:"))
    ReDim data(n - 1)
    'Read the data into the array.
    For i As Integer = 0 To data.GetUpperBound(0)
      data(i) = CDbl(InputBox("Enter element #" & (i + 1)))
    Next
```

```
'Bubble sort the data.
For i As Integer = 1 To data.GetUpperBound(0)
  For j As Integer = 1 To data.GetUpperBound(0) + 1 - i
    If data(j - 1) > data(j) Then
       'Swap scores.
       temp = data(j - 1)
       data(j - 1) = data(j)
       data(j) = temp
    End If
  Next
Next
'Determine median based upon even or odd number of numbers
q = data.GetUpperBound(0) + 1          'number of numbers
p = CInt(Int((q - 1) / 2))
If Math.Round(q / 2) = q / 2 Then
  'If q even, median is average of two middle elements
  median = (data(p) + data(p + 1)) / 2
Else
  'If q odd, median is the middle element
  median = data(p)
End If
txtOutput.Text = CStr(median)
End Sub
```

EXERCISES 7.5

1. 12

3. Dorothy

5. 5
   11
   10

7. 1
   2
   3
   4

9. The declaration statement should read **Dim a(3, 2) As Integer.** (Once *j* gets to 3, there will be an "Index Out of Range" error.)

11.
```
Sub FillArray(ByRef a() As Integer)
    'Fill an array.
    For row As Integer = 0 To 5
      For col As Integer = 0 To 5
        a(row, col) = col
      Next
    Next
End Sub
```

13.
```
Sub Exchange(ByRef a() As Double)
    'Interchange values in rows 3 and 4.
    Dim temp As Double
    For col As Integer = 0 To 5
      temp = a(3, col)
      a(3, col) = a(4, col)
      a(4, col) = temp
    Next
End Sub
```

15.
```
Private Sub btnDisplay_Click(...) Handles btnDisplay.Click
    'Display a company's inventory from its two stores
    'Declare the inventory and sales arrays
    Dim inventory(,) As Integer = {{25, 64, 23}, {12, 82, 19}}
    Dim sales(,) As Integer = {{7, 45, 11}, {4, 24, 8}}
    Dim total(2) As Integer
    Dim fmtStr As String = "{0,1} {1,2} {2,2} {3,2} {4,3}"
    'Adjust the inventory values to reflect todays sales
    For store As Integer = 1 To 2
      For item As Integer = 1 To 3
        inventory(store - 1, item - 1) = _
              inventory(store - 1, item - 1) - sales(store - 1, item - 1)
        'Accumulate the total inventory per store
        total(store) += inventory(store - 1, item - 1)
      Next
    Next
    'Display the store's inventory and totals
    lstOutput.Items.Add(String.Format(fmtStr, "", "1", "2", "3", "TOT"))
    For store As Integer = 1 To 2
      lstOutput.Items.Add(String.Format(fmtStr, store, _
                          inventory(store - 1, 0), _
                          inventory(store - 1, 1), _
                          inventory(store - 1, 2), total(store)))
    Next
End Sub
```

17.
```
Private Sub btnDisplay_Click(...) Handles btnDisplay.Click
    'Display the course and campus enrollments
    'Define and fill the enrollment array
    Dim er(,) As Integer = {{5, 15, 22, 21, 12, 25, 16, 11, 17, 23}, _
                            {11, 23, 51, 25, 32, 35, 32, 52, 25, 21}, _
                            {2, 12, 32, 32, 25, 26, 29, 12, 15, 11}}
    'Define the arrays to accumulate the information
    Dim campusTotal(2), courseTotal(9) As Integer
    For campus As Integer = 0 To 2
      For course As Integer = 0 To 9
        campusTotal(campus) += er(campus, course)
        courseTotal(course) += er(campus, course)
      Next
    Next
    'Display the campus enrollment
    lstOutput.Items.Add("CAMPUS ENROLLMENT")
    For campus As Integer = 0 To 2
      lstOutput.Items.Add((campus + 1) & ": " & campusTotal(campus))
    Next
    'Display the course enrollment
    lstOutput.Items.Add("COURSE ENROLLMENT")
    For course As Integer = 0 To 9
      lstOutput.Items.Add((course + 1) & ": " & courseTotal(course))
    Next
End Sub
```

19.
```
Private Sub btnDisplay_Click(...) Handles btnDisplay.Click
    'Load golf data, cumulate totals and display results
    Dim scores(3,3) As Integer
    Dim golfers(3) As String
    Dim sr As IO.StreamReader = IO.File.OpenText("GOLF.TXT")
```

```
    Dim golferTotal(3) As Integer, roundTotal(3) As Integer
    For golfer As Integer = 0 To 3
      golfers(golfer) = sr.ReadLine
      For round As Integer = 0 To 3
        scores(golfer, round) = CInt(sr.ReadLine)
      Next
    Next
    sr.Close()
    'Aggregate the figures
    For golfer As Integer = 0 To 3
      For round As Integer = 0 To 3
        golferTotal(golfer) += scores(golfer, round)
        roundTotal(round) += scores(golfer, round)
      Next
    Next
    'Display golfer's totals
    lstOutput.Items.Add("GOLFER TOTALS")
    For golfer As Integer = 0 To 3
      lstOutput.Items.Add(golfers(golfer) & ": " & golferTotal(golfer))
    Next
    lstOutput.Items.Add("")
    'Display average per round
    lstOutput.Items.Add("ROUND AVERAGE")
    For round As Integer = 0 To 3
      lstOutput.Items.Add(round + 1 & ": " & _
                          FormatNumber(roundTotal(round) / 4))
    Next
  End Sub
```

21.
```
    Private Sub btnDisplay_Click(...) Handles btnDisplay.Click
      'Display the high ranking disciplines for a university
      Dim sr As IO.StreamReader = IO.File.OpenText("RANKINGS.TXT")
      Dim ranking(2,4) As String
      Dim disciplines(2) As String
      For field As Integer = 0 To 2
        disciplines(field) = sr.ReadLine
        For rank As Integer = 0 To 4
          ranking(field, rank) = sr.ReadLine
        Next
      Next
      Sr.Close()
      'Look up the specified university in the rankings
      Dim result = ""
      For category As Integer = 0 To 2
        For rank As Integer = 0 To 4
          If txtName.Text.ToUpper = ranking(category, rank).ToUpper Then
            'Append category name to result
            result &= disciplines(category) & "    "
          End If
        Next
      Next
      'Display result
      If result = "" Then
        txtOutput.Text = "None."
      Else
        txtOutput.Text = result
      End If
    End Sub
```

23.
```
Dim scores(14, 4) As Integer    'Stores students' exam scores
Dim count As Integer            'Current number of students stored
Dim names(14) As String         'Stores students' names
Private Sub btnAdd_Click(...) Handles btnAdd.Click
  'Add student to array.
  If (count = 15) Then
    MessageBox.Show("Fifteen students already stored", "Warning")
  Else
    count += 1
    names(count - 1) = txtName.Text
    scores(count - 1, 0) = CInt(txtExam1.Text)
    scores(count - 1, 1) = CInt(txtExam2.Text)
    scores(count - 1, 2) = CInt(txtExam3.Text)
    scores(count - 1, 3) = CInt(txtExam4.Text)
    scores(count - 1, 4) = CInt(txtExam5.Text)
    'Reset input
    txtName.Clear()
    txtExam1.Clear()
    txtExam2.Clear()
    txtExam3.Clear()
    txtExam4.Clear()
    txtExam5.Clear()
    txtName.Focus()
  End If
End Sub

Private Sub btnDisplay_Click(...) Handles btnDisplay.Click
  'Aggregate totals and display report.
  Dim n, temp As Integer
  Dim sum, median As Double
  Dim even As Boolean
  'Display student's semester grades.
  lstOutput.Items.Clear()
  lstOutput.Items.Add("Students' Semester Average")
  For i As Integer = 0 To count - 1
    'Accumulate sum of scores for each student.
    sum = 0
    For exam As Integer = 0 To 4
      sum += scores(i, exam)
    Next
    'Display the student's name and semester average.
    lstOutput.Items.Add(names(i) & ": " & FormatNumber(sum / 5))
  Next
  'Display median on the exams.
  lstOutput.Items.Add("Exam Medians")
  'Determine whether the count is even or odd.
  even = (Int(count / 2) = count / 2)
  For exam As Integer = 0 To 4
    'Bubble sort the scores array based upon the exam score.
    For i As Integer = 1 To count - 1
      For j As Integer = 1 To count - i
        If scores(j - 1, exam) > scores(j, exam) Then
          'Swap scores.
          temp = scores(j - 1, exam)
          scores(j - 1, exam) = scores(j, exam)
          scores(j, exam) = temp
        End If
```

```
      Next
    Next
    'Calculate median depending upon even or odd.
    n = CInt(Int(count / 2))
    If even Then
      'Median is average of two middle scores.
      median = (scores(n - 1, exam) + scores(n, exam)) / 2
    Else
      'Median is middle score.
      median = scores(n, exam)
    End If
    'Display median score for exam.
    lstOutput.Items.Add((exam + 1) & ": " & FormatNumber(median))
    Next
  End Sub
```

25.
```
Private Sub btnDisplay_Click(...) Handles btnDisplay.Click
  'Load data into an array, cumulate totals, and display a report
  Dim totalSales As Double
  Dim sales(,) As Integer = {{25, 64, 23, 45, 14}, _
                             {12, 82, 19, 34, 63}, _
                             {54, 22, 17, 43, 35}}
  Dim price() As Double = {12, 17.95, 95, 86.5, 78}
  'Cumulate totals
  Dim totals(2) As Double
  For store As Integer = 0 To 2
    For item As Integer = 0 To 4
      totals(store) += sales(store, item) * price(item)
    Next
  Next
  'Display report, storing grand total in totalSales
  lstOutput.Items.Add("Sales per store")
  For store As Integer = 0 To 2
    lstOutput.Items.Add((store + 1) & ": " & _
                        FormatCurrency(totals(store)))
    totalSales += totals(store)
  Next
  lstOutput.Items.Add("Total sales: " & FormatCurrency(totalSales))
    End Sub
```

CHAPTER 8

EXERCISES 8.1

1. `Red`

3. `Green`

5. `I don't recognize that number.`

7. `Error occurred.`

9. `File PRICES.TXT contains an invalid price.`

11. The file WELCOME.TXT is created and has the following lines:
```
Hello
Bon Jour
```

13. The filespec YOB.TXT needs to be delimited with quotation marks.

15. There should be no quotations around the variable name as the parameter to the CreateText method.

17. The variable *age* is declared within the Try-Catch-Finally block and therefore is not available below the line *End Try*.

19.
```
Private Sub btnCreate_Click(...) Handles btnCreate.Click
    'Create a sequential file, and populate it.
    Dim sw As IO.StreamWriter = IO.File.CreateText("COWBOY.TXT")
    sw.WriteLine("Colt Peacemaker")
    sw.WriteLine("12.20")
    sw.WriteLine("Holster")
    sw.WriteLine("2.00")
    sw.WriteLine("Levi Strauss Jeans")
    sw.WriteLine("1.35")
    sw.WriteLine("Saddle")
    sw.WriteLine("40.00")
    sw.WriteLine("Stetson")
    sw.WriteLine("10.00")
    sw.Close()          'Always close the writer when finished.
    MessageBox.Show("The file has been created.", "DONE")
End Sub
```

21.
```
Private Sub btnAdd_Click(...) Handles btnAdd.Click
    'Append to a sequential file.
    Dim sw As IO.StreamWriter = IO.File.AppendText("COWBOY.TXT")
    sw.WriteLine("Winchester Rifle")
    sw.WriteLine("20.50")
    sw.Close()
    MessageBox.Show("The item has been added to the file.", "DONE")
End Sub
```

23.
```
Private Sub btnAdd_Click(...) Handles btnAdd.Click
    'Add new item to list from COWBOY.TXT,
    'and save in alphabetical order into COWBOY2.TXT.
    Dim flag As Boolean
    Dim item, price As String
    'Open COWBOY for input and COWBOY2 for output.
    Dim sr As IO.StreamReader = IO.File.OpenText("COWBOY.TXT")
    Dim sw As IO.StreamWriter = IO.File.CreateText("COWBOY2.TXT")
    flag = False
    item = ""
    'Loop until we reach the new item to add or run out of room.
    Do While (item < txtItem.Text) And (sr.Peek <> -1)
      'Read the current item from the file.
      item = sr.ReadLine
      price = sr.ReadLine
      'If we have reached the new item, add the new item.
      If item > txtItem.Text Then
        'Add the new item and the new item's price.
        sw.WriteLine(txtItem.Text)
        sw.WriteLine(txtPrice.Text)
        'Set flag true so we don't add it again at the end.
        flag = True
      End If
      'Add the current item and price.
      sw.WriteLine(item)
      sw.WriteLine(price)
```

```
      Loop
      'If there are any more items to read, write them to the output.
      Do While (sr.Peek <> -1)
        item = sr.ReadLine
        price = sr.ReadLine
        sw.WriteLine(item)
        sw.WriteLine(price)
      Loop
      'If the new item hasn't been written yet, write it.
      If Not flag Then
        sw.WriteLine(txtItem.Text)
        sw.WriteLine(txtPrice.Text)
      End If
      sr.Close()    'Always close the reader when finished.
      sw.Close()    'Always close the writer when finished.
      'Display a message, and clear the input text boxes.
      MessageBox.Show("Item added to COWBOY2.TXT")
    End Sub
```

25.
```
    Private Sub btnLookup_Click(...) Handles btnLookup.Click
      'Lookup person in data file to get age.
      Dim found As Boolean = False
      Dim name As String, yob As Integer
      Dim sr As IO.StreamReader = IO.File.OpenText("YOBS.TXT")
      'Loop through file until end or name found.
      Do While (sr.Peek <> -1) And (Not found)
        name = sr.ReadLine
        yob = CInt(sr.ReadLine)
        If name.ToUpper >= txtName.Text.ToUpper Then
          If name.ToUpper > txtName.Text.ToUpper Then
            Exit Do
          Else
            'If name matches, display the age
            txtOutput.Text = CStr(2008 - yob)
            found = True
          End If
        End If
      Loop
      sr.Close()
      'If name not found, then display message.
      If Not found Then
        txtOutput.Text = "Not found."
      End If
    End Sub
```

27.
```
    Private Sub btnLookup_Click(...) Handles btnLookup.Click
      'Lookup book title in sequential file.
      Dim fileName As String
      Dim title As String, quantity As Integer
      'Determine file to open, and then open it for input.
      If mtxtType.Text.ToUpper = "P" Then
        fileName = "PAPERBACK.TXT"
      Else
        fileName = "HARDBACK.TXT"
      End If
      Dim sr As IO.StreamReader = IO.File.OpenText(fileName)
      'Loop until title is found or end of file.
      title = ""
```

```
      Do While (title.ToUpper <> txtTitle.Text.ToUpper) And _
            (sr.Peek <> -1)
        title = sr.ReadLine
        quantity = CInt(sr.ReadLine)
      Loop
      sr.Close()
      'Display result.
      If title.ToUpper = txtTitle.Text.ToUpper Then
        txtQuantity.Text = CStr(quantity)
      Else
        txtQuantity.Text = "n/a"
        MessageBox.Show("Book not found in file.")
      End If
    End Sub
```

EXERCISES 8.2.

1. Two

3. T,O,G,E,T,H,E,R

5. ```
Dim sw As IO.StreamWriter = IO.File.CreateText("AVERAGE.TXT")

Private Sub btnAdd_Click(...) Handles btnAdd.Click
  'Add a name with 0 times and 0 hits to the file.
  sw.WriteLine(txtName.Text)
  sw.WriteLine(0)
  sw.WriteLine(0)
  'Reset input text boxes.
  txtName.Clear()
  txtName.Focus()
End Sub

Private Sub btnQuit_Click(...) Handles btnQuit.Click
  sw.Close()
  End   'Terminate the program.
End Sub
```

7. ```
Dim sw As IO.StreamWriter

Private Sub frmBaseball_Load(...) Handles MyBase.Load
  sw = IO.File.AppendText("AVERAGE.TXT")
End Sub

Private Sub btnAdd_Click(...) Handles btnAdd.Click
  'Add a name with 0 times and 0 hits to the file.
  sw.WriteLine(txtName.Text)
  sw.WriteLine(0)
  sw.WriteLine(0)
  'Reset input text box.
  txtName.Clear()
  txtName.Focus()
End Sub

Private Sub btnQuit_Click(...) Handles btnQuit.Click
  sw.Close()
  End           'Terminate the program.
End Sub
```

9. ```
Private Sub btnConvert_Click(...) Handles btnConvert.Click
  'Convert a sequential file in LSV format to a sequential file
  'in "Comma Separated Values" (CSV) format.
```
```

```vb
    Dim numFields As Integer       'Number of fields per record
    numFields = CInt(txtFields.Text)
    Dim field(numFields - 1) As String  'String array to hold fields
    Dim sr As IO.StreamReader = IO.File.OpenText(txtLSV.Text)
    Dim sw As IO.StreamWriter = IO.File.CreateText(txtCSV.Text)
    'Loop over all lines in the LSV file.
    Do While (sr.Peek <> -1)
      'Set each field to a line from the LSV file.
      For i As Integer = 0 To numFields - 1
        field(i) = sr.ReadLine
      Next
      'Join the fields with a comma, and write to the CSV file.
      sw.WriteLine(Join(field, ","))
    Loop
    sw.Close()
    sr.Close()
    MessageBox.Show("Conversion completed.", "DONE")
  End Sub
```

11.
```vb
Structure State
    Dim name As String       'State name
    Dim abbr As String       'Abbreviation
    Dim entered As String    'Date entered union
    Dim area As Double       'Area in square miles
    Dim pop As Double        'Population in 2006
End Structure

Private Sub btnDisplay_Click(...) Handles btnDisplay.Click
    'Load data from CSV file, sort on abbreviation, write to new file,
    'and display records in list box.
    Dim temp As State
    Dim state(4) As String     'Current state data, five fields total
    Dim states(49) As State    'Holds all states
    Dim fmtStr As String = "{0,-4} {1,-17} {2,-10} {3,10:N0} {4,13:N0}"
    'Read the data into the states array.
    Dim sr As IO.StreamReader = IO.File.OpenText("csvUSSTATES.TXT")
    For i As Integer = 0 To 49
      state = sr.ReadLine.Split(","c)
      'The field order is name, abbr, entered, area, pop.
      states(i).name = state(0)
      states(i).abbr = state(1)
      states(i).entered = state(2)
      states(i).area = CDbl(state(3))
      states(i).pop = CDbl(state(4))
    Next
    sr.Close()
    'Bubble sort the array based upon abbreviation name.
    For i As Integer = 1 To 49
      For j As Integer = 1 To 50 - i
        If states(j - 1).abbr > states(j).abbr Then
          'Swap elements.
          temp = states(j - 1)
          states(j - 1) = states(j)
          states(j) = temp
        End If
      Next
    Next
    'Write the data to the output file and to the list box.
```

```vb
        Dim sw As IO.StreamWriter = IO.File.CreateText("csvSORTED.TXT")
        lstOutput.Items.Add(String.Format(fmtStr, "ABBR", "STATE", _
                                          "ENTERED", "AREA", "POPULATION"))
    For i As Integer = 0 To 49
        'Copy data into string array.
        state(0) = states(i).name
        state(1) = states(i).abbr
        state(2) = states(i).entered
        state(3) = CStr(states(i).area)
        state(4) = CStr(states(i).pop)
        'Join string array using commas, and write to file.
        sw.WriteLine(Join(state, ","))
        'Write data to list box.
        lstOutput.Items.Add(String.Format(fmtStr, states(i).abbr, _
                                   states(i).name, states(i).entered, _
                                   states(i).area, states(i).pop))
    Next
    sw.Close()
  End Sub
```

13.
```vb
    Private Sub btnCreate_Click(...) Handles btnCreate.Click
        'Write matching records from two input files into a third file.
        Dim name, subscriber As String
        'Open files for reading.
        Dim srBlock As IO.StreamReader = IO.File.OpenText("BLOCK.TXT")
        Dim srTimes As IO.StreamReader = IO.File.OpenText("TIMES.TXT")
        Dim sw As IO.StreamWriter = IO.File.CreateText("NAMES.TXT")
        'Loop over all records in the BLOCK reader.
        subscriber = ""
        Do While srBlock.Peek <> -1
          'Read in the name from BLOCK.
          name = srBlock.ReadLine
          'Loop until the subscriber has been reached.
          Do While (subscriber < name) And (srTimes.Peek <> -1)
            'Read the next subscriber.
            subscriber = srTimes.ReadLine
          Loop
          'If we have a match, then write it to output file.
          If subscriber = name Then
            sw.WriteLine(name)
          End If
        Loop
        srBlock.Close()
        srTimes.Close()
        sw.Close()
        MessageBox.Show("The file has been created.", "DONE")
    End Sub
```

15.
```vb
    Private Sub btnCount_Click(...) Handles btnCount.Click
        'Count the maximum number of repeated integers.
        Dim max, lastNum, numRepeats, number As Integer
        'Open data file.
        Dim sr As IO.StreamReader = IO.File.OpenText("NUMBERS.TXT")
        max = 0
        lastNum = 0
        numRepeats = 0
        'Loop over all input.
        Do While sr.Peek <> -1
```

```
    number = CInt(sr.ReadLine)
    'If number has changed, then compare its count.
    If number <> lastNum Then
      'If its count is more than the max, update the max.
      If numRepeats > max Then
        max = numRepeats
      End If
      'Store this number as the last number.
      lastNum = number
      numRepeats = 1
    Else
      numRepeats += 1    'Increment the count
    End If
  Loop
  sr.Close()
  txtOutput.Text = CStr(max)      'Display the result
End Sub
```

17.
```
Private Sub btnDisplay_Click(...) Handles btnDisplay.Click
  'Display a report on count of raffle tickets by grade.
  Dim grade, gradeTotal, total As Integer
  Dim currentGrade, tickets As Integer
  Dim name As String
  Dim fmtStr As String = "{0,5} {1,7:N0}"
  'Open data file for input.
  Dim sr As IO.StreamReader = IO.File.OpenText("RAFFLE.TXT")
  'Reset cumulative totals.
  grade = 0
  gradeTotal = 0
  total = 0
  'Loop over all records in the file.
  lstOutput.Items.Add(String.Format(fmtStr, "GRADE", "TICKETS"))
  Do While sr.Peek <> -1
    'Read in student's data.
    currentGrade = CInt(sr.ReadLine)
    name = sr.ReadLine
    tickets = CInt(sr.ReadLine)
    'If grade changes, then display current grade's totals.
    If grade <> currentGrade Then
      'If not first pass, display totals.
      If grade <> 0 Then
        lstOutput.Items.Add(String.Format(fmtStr, grade, gradeTotal))
        'Update cumulative total.
        total += gradeTotal
      End If
      'Reset grade.
      grade = currentGrade
      gradeTotal = 0
    End If
    'Add student's tickets to grade's total.
    gradeTotal += tickets
  Loop
  sr.Close()
  'Display last grade's totals.
  lstOutput.Items.Add(String.Format(fmtStr, grade, gradeTotal))
  total += gradeTotal
  'Display grand total.
```

```
       lstOutput.Items.Add(String.Format(fmtStr, "TOTAL", total))
    End Sub
19. Private Sub btnUpdate_Click(...) Handles btnUpdate.Click
       'Update phone number master file with file of those who have moved.
       Dim masterName, masterNumber As String   'Master info
       Dim movedName, movedNumber As String      'Moved info
       'Open input files for reading.
       Dim srMaster As IO.StreamReader = IO.File.OpenText("MASTER.TXT")
       Dim srMoved As IO.StreamReader = IO.File.OpenText("MOVED.TXT")
       'Open temporary file to hold output.
       Dim sw As IO.StreamWriter = IO.File.CreateText("TEMP.TXT")
       'Loop over all records in the move input file.
       Do While srMoved.Peek <> -1
         'Read in name that has moved.
         movedName = srMoved.ReadLine
         movedNumber = srMoved.ReadLine
         'Loop until find a matching record in master file.
         Do
           'Read a name from the master file.
           masterName = srMaster.ReadLine
           masterNumber = srMaster.ReadLine
           If movedName = masterName Then
             'If found a match, then write the new number.
             sw.WriteLine(masterName)
             sw.WriteLine(movedNumber)
           Else
             'Otherwise, write the master number.
             sw.WriteLine(masterName)
             sw.WriteLine(masterNumber)
           End If
         Loop Until masterName = movedName
       Loop
       'Write the rest of the master file.
       Do While srMaster.Peek <> -1
         masterName = srMaster.ReadLine
         masterNumber = srMaster.ReadLine
         sw.WriteLine(masterName)
         sw.WriteLine(masterNumber)
       Loop
       srMaster.Close()
       srMoved.Close()
       sw.Close()
       'Delete the old master, and rename the temporary file.
       IO.File.Delete("MASTER.TXT")
       IO.File.Move("TEMP.TXT", "MASTER.TXT")
       MessageBox.Show("The file has been updated.", "DONE")
    End Sub
```

CHAPTER 9

EXERCISES 9.1

1. The currently selected item in **lstBox**, Mozart, is displayed in **txtOutput**.

3. The last item, O`ahu, from **lstBox** is displayed in **txtOutput**.

5. 3

7. The item Moloka`i is inserted into `lstBox` between Maui and O`ahu.

9. The first item, Hawai`i, is removed from `lstBox`.

11. The last item, O`ahu, is removed from `lstBox`.

13. The number 4 is displayed in the text box, `txtOutput`.

15. `The list box will be empty.`

17. `cboBox.Text = CStr(cboBox.Items(2))`

19. `cboBox.Items.Remove("Dante")`

21. `cboBox.Items.RemoveAt(cboBox.Items.Count - 1)`

23.
```
For i As Integer = 0 To For i = 1 To cboBox.Items.Count - 1 Step 2
    lstOutput.Items.Add(cboBox.Items(i))
Next
```

25.
```
Dim found As Boolean = False
Dim i As Integer
For i = 0 To cboBox.Items.Count - 1
  If CStr(cboBox.Items(i)) = "Cervantes" Then
    found = True
  End If
Next
If found Then
  txtOutput.Text = "Cervantes is in the list."
Else
  txtOutput.Text = "Cervantes not found."
End If
```

27.
```
Private Sub btnDisplay_Click(...) Handles btnDisplay.Click
    Dim i As Integer
    Dim total As Double = 0
    For i = 0 To lstNumbers.Items.Count - 1
    Next
    txtOutput.Text = "The average of the numbers is " & _
                     total / lstNumbers.Items.Count
End Sub
```

29.
```
Private Sub btnDisplay_Click(...) Handles btnDisplay.Click
    lstNumbers.Sorted = True
    txtOutput.Text = "The largest value in the list is " & _
                 CStr(lstNumbers.Items(lstNumbers.Items.Count - 1))
End Sub
```

31.
```
Private Sub btnDisplay_Click(...) Handles btnDisplay.Click
    Dim range As Double
    lstData.Sorted = True
    range = lstData.Items(lstData.Items.Count - 1) - lstData.Items(0)
    txtOutput.Text = "Range: " & CStr(range)
End Sub
```

33.
```
Private Sub btnSort_Click(...) Handles btnSort.Click
    'Load names from a file into a sorted List Box
    'and write them to another file.
    Dim sr As IO.StreamReader = IO.File.OpenText("POPULAR_NAMES.TXT")
    Do While sr.Peek <> -1
      lstOutput.Items.Add(sr.ReadLine)
```

```
       Loop
       sr.Close()
       'Open the output file.
       Dim sw As IO.StreamWriter = IO.File.CreateText("SORTED_NAMES.TXT")
       For i As Integer = 0 To lstOutput.Items.Count - 1
         sw.WriteLine(lstOutput.Items(i))
       Next
       sw.Close()
       MessageBox.Show("The ordered file has been created.", "DONE")
     End Sub

35. Private Sub btnDisplay_Click(...) Handles btnDisplay.Click
       'Convert a length from one unit to the other.
       'The inches array stores the number of inches in each unit.
       Dim inches() As Double = {1, 12, 3 * 12, 100 / 2.54, 12 * 5280}
       Dim result As Double
       'If input is not specified, display message.
       If (lstFrom.SelectedIndex < 0) Or _
          (lstTo.SelectedIndex < 0) Or _
          (txtAmount.Text = "") Then
         MessageBox.Show("Please select both units and enter a length.", _
                     "Incomplete")
       Else
         'Convert the first units to inches, then convert to second units.
         result = CDbl(txtAmount.Text) * inches(lstFrom.SelectedIndex) _
                  / inches(lstTo.SelectedIndex)
         'Display the decimal places in the result depending upon the size.
         If result < 1 Then
           txtOutput.Text = FormatNumber(result, 6)
         Else
           txtOutput.Text = FormatNumber(result, 2)
         End If
       End If
     End Sub

37. 'Note: This event procedure handles events from all three combo boxes.

     Private Sub SelectedIndexChanged(...) Handles _
                       cboBrand.SelectedIndexChanged, _
                       cboMemory.SelectedIndexChanged, _
                       cboMonitor.SelectedIndexChanged
       'Update output if all choices have been made.
       If (cboBrand.SelectedIndex >= 0) And _
          (cboMemory.SelectedIndex >= 0) And _
          (cboMonitor.SelectedIndex >= 0) Then
         txtOutput.Text = "You have a " & cboBrand.Text & _
                       " computer with " & cboMemory.Text & _
                       " of memory and a " & cboMonitor.Text & _
                       " monitor."
       End If
     End Sub
```

EXERCISES 9.2

1. The word "Average Salary" becomes the caption embedded in the top of GroupBox1.

3. The CheckBox1 check box becomes (or remains) unchecked.

5. The radio button becomes (or remains) unselected.

7. The scroll box moves to its rightmost position.

9. Clicking on the arrow on either end of the scroll bar will move the button the same ("large") distance as clicking on the bar between the scroll box and an arrow.

11. The Tick event will be triggered every *intVar* seconds.

13. Any picture placed into the picture box will be automatically enlarged or contracted to fit the picture box.

15. A green rectangle of width 200 pixels and height 100 pixels will be drawn in the picture box. Its upper-left corner will be 25 pixels from the left side of the picture box and 50 units from the top side.

17. RadioButton1.Text = "Female"

19. RadioButton1.Checked = False

21.
```
HScrollBar2.Value = CInt(HScrollBar2.Minimum + _
                   (HScrollBar2.Maximum - HScrollBar2.Minimum) / 3)
```

23.
```
PictureBox1.CreateGraphics.DrawEllipse(Pens.Yellow, _
                   10, 10, 100, 100)
```

25. RadioButton2 is selected and RadioButton1 is unselected.

27. Check boxes, combo boxes, horizontal scroll bars, list boxes, radio buttons, and vertical scroll bars can receive the focus.

29. Yes

31.
```
Dim box(2) As CheckBox

Private Sub frmCount_Load(...) Handles MyBase.Load
  box(0) = CheckBox1
  box(1) = CheckBox2
  box(2) = CheckBox3
End Sub

Private Sub btnDisplay_Click(...) Handles btnDisplay.Click
  Dim numChecked As Integer = 0
  For i As Integer = 0 To 2
    If box(i).Checked Then
      numChecked += 1
    End If
  Next
  txtOutput.Text = CStr(numChecked)
End Sub
```

33.
```
'This event procedure is called when any of the checkboxes
'or radio buttons change.

Private Sub CheckedChanged(...) Handles _
      radDeluxe.CheckedChanged, _
      radSuper.CheckedChanged, _
      chkUpgradedVideo.CheckedChanged, _
      chkModem.CheckedChanged, _
      chkMemory.CheckedChanged
  'Update the cost of the system.
  Dim cost As Double
  cost = 0
  'Add amounts to the cost based upon selections.
  If radDeluxe.Checked Then
    cost += 1000
```

```
      Else
        'Super model
        cost += 1500
      End If
      If chkUpgradedVideo.Checked Then
        cost += 200
      End If
      If chkModem.Checked Then
        cost += 30
      End If
      If chkMemory.Checked Then
        cost += 120
      End If
      txtOutput.Text = FormatCurrency(cost)
    End Sub
```

35.
```
  Dim phase As Integer          'Current phase of the moon

  Private Sub tmrMoon_Tick(...) Handles tmrMoon.Tick
    'Update the phase, and display the image.
    'Timer Interval setting is 2000.
    'Timer Enabled setting is True.
    phase += 1
    If phase = 9 Then
      phase = 1
    End If
    picBox.Image = Image.FromFile("Moon" & phase & ".BMP")
  End Sub
```

37.
```
  Public Sub vsbFahren_Scroll(...) Handles vsbFahren.Scroll
    'When Fahrenheit value changes, update the Celsius value.
    'vsbFahren.Minimum = 32, vsbFahren.Maximum = 225
    'vsbFahren.SmallChange = 1, vsbFahren.LargeChange = 14
    Dim celsius As Integer
    txtFahren.Text = CStr(vsbFahren.Value)
    celsius = CInt((5 / 9) * (vsbFahren.Value - 32))
    vsbCelsius.Value = celsius
    txtCelsius.Text = CStr(vsbCelsius.Value)
  End Sub

  Public Sub vsbCelsius_Scroll(...) Handles vsbCelsius.Scroll
    'When Celsius value changes, update the Fahrenheit value
    'vsbCelsius.Minimum = 0, vsbCelsius.Maximum = 125
    'vsbCelsius.SmallChange = 1, vsbCelsius.LargeChange = 10
    Dim fahrenheit As Integer
    txtCelsius.Text = CStr(vsbCelsius.Value)
    fahrenheit = CInt((9 / 5) * vsbCelsius.Value + 32)
    vsbFahren.Value = fahrenheit
    txtFahren.Text = CStr(vsbFahren.Value)
  End Sub
```

39.
```
  Dim count As Integer = 10

  Private Sub tmrBall_Tick(...) Handles tmrBall.Tick
    'Update the value of the scroll bar and label.
    'Timer Interval setting is 1000.
    'vsbBall.Minimum = 0, vsbBall.Maximum = 10
    count = count - 1
    vsbBall.Value = 10 - count
    lblBall.Text = CStr(count)
```

```
      'If at zero, display the message and end program.
      If count = 0 Then
        tmrBall.Enabled = False
        MessageBox.Show("HAPPY NEW YEAR!!!!", "NYE")
        End
      End If
    End Sub
```

EXERCISES 9.3

1. The contents of the Clipboard are deleted.

3. The text currently selected in txtBox, if any, is copied into the clipboard.

5. The contents of the Clipboard are displayed in txtBox.

7. The contents of the Clipboard are assigned to the variable *strVar*.

9. The name of one of the 15 listed member states using the EURO is selected at random and displayed in txtBox.

11. Two different PGA golfers are selected at random and displayed in the list box.

13. A check mark appears in front of the mnuOrderAsc menu item.

15. The text appearing on the mnuOrderAsc item will be changed to Increasing Order.

17. The string variable *address* will be available to all forms in the program.

19. txtBox.SelectedText = Clipboard.GetText

21. Clipboard.SetText("Elephant")

23. txtBox.SelectedText = ""

25.
```
Dim randomNum As New Random()
txtBox.Text = CStr(randomNum.Next(1, 11))
```

27.
```
Dim randomNum As New Random()
'A and Z have ANSI values 65 and 90.
txtBox.Text = Chr(randomNum.Next(65, 91))
```

29.
```
Dim randomNum As New Random()
txtBox.Text = CStr(randomNum(1, 7) + randomNum(1, 7)+ randomNum(1, 7)
+ randomNum(1, 7))
```

31. mnuOrderDesc.Checked = False

33. Me.Close()

35. The menu item mnuOrderAsc is greyed out and cannot be selected.

37.
```
Private Sub mnuCopy_Click(...) Handles mnuCopy.Click
    'Copy selected text into Clipboard.
    Clipboard.SetText(txtBox.SelectedText)
End Sub

Private Sub mnuPaste_Click(...) Handles mnuPaste.Click
    'Paste Clipboard into text box.
    txtBox.SelectedText = Clipboard.GetText
End Sub

Private Sub mnuCut_Click(...) Handles mnuCut.Click
    'Copy selected text into Clipboard, and delete selected text.
```

```
    Clipboard.SetText(txtBox.SelectedText)
    txtBox.SelectedText = ""
End Sub


Private Sub mnuExit_Click(...) Handles mnuExit.Click
    End         'Terminate the program.
End Sub
```

39.
```
Private Sub btnDeal_Click(...) Handles btnDeal.Click
    'Deal five cards at random.
    Dim deckOfCards(51) As String
    Dim suits() As String = {"Hearts", "Diamonds", "Clubs", _
                             "Spades"}
    Dim n As Integer
    Dim randomNum As New Random()
    Dim temp As String
    'Populate each suit of the deck.
    For i As Integer = 0 To 3
      'Populate numbers 2 through 10.
      For j As Integer = 2 To 10
        deckOfCards(i * 13 + j) = j & " of " & suits(i)
      Next
      'Populate the honors cards.
      deckOfCards(i * 13 + 0) = "King of " & suits(i)
      deckOfCards(i * 13 + 1) = "Ace of " & suits(i)
      deckOfCards(i * 13 + 11) = "Jack of " & suits(i)
      deckOfCards(i * 13 + 12) = "Queen of " & suits(i)
    Next
    lstOutput.Items.Clear()
    'Choose five cards at random.
    For i As Integer = 1 To 5
      'Choose a card at random.
      n = randomNum.Next(0, 53 - i)
      lstOutput.Items.Add(deckOfCards(n))
      'Swap the chosen card with the one at the end.
      temp = deckOfCards(n)
      deckOfCards(n) = deckOfCards(52 - i)
      deckOfCards(52 - i) = temp
    Next
End Sub
```

41.
```
Dim randomNum As New Random()     'Random number generator

Private Sub btnToss_Click(...) Handles btnToss.Click
    'Toss a coin, and keep track of results.
    If randomNum.Next(0, 2) = 0 Then
      txtOutcome.Text = "Heads"
      txtHeads.Text = CStr(CInt(txtHeads.Text) + 1)
    Else
      txtOutcome.Text = "Tails"
      txtTails.Text = CStr(CInt(txtTails.Text) + 1)
    End If
    'Display total tosses and percentage.
    txtTosses.Text = CStr(CInt(txtTosses.Text) + 1)
    txtPercentHeads.Text = FormatPercent(CDbl(txtHeads.Text) / _
                                    CDbl(txtTosses.Text))
End Sub
```

EXERCISES 9.4

1.
```
Private Sub btnDraw_Click(...) Handles btnDraw.Click
    Dim gr As Graphics = picBox.CreateGraphics
    Dim x, y, r As Double
    x = picBox.Width / 2
    y = picBox.Height / 2
    r = x / 2
    If r > y / 2 Then
      r = y / 2
    End If
    gr.FillEllipse(Brushes.Black, CSng(x - r), CSng(y - r), _
                                  CSng(2 * r), CSng(2 * r))
End Sub
```

3.
```
Private Sub btnDraw_Click(...) Handles btnDraw.Click
    Dim gr As Graphics = picBox.CreateGraphics
    Dim x, y, r As Double
    x = picBox.Width / 2
    y = picBox.Height / 2
    r = 20
    gr.FillEllipse(Brushes.Red, CSng(x - r), CSng(y - r), _
                                CSng(2 * r), CSng(2 * r))
    r = 19
    gr.FillEllipse(Brushes.White, CSng(x - r), CSng(y - r), _
                                  CSng(2 * r), CSng(2 * r))
End Sub
```

5.
```
Private Sub btnCreate_Click(...) Handles btnCreate.Click
    Dim gr As Graphics = picFlag.CreateGraphics
    Dim br() As Brush = {Brushes.Green, Brushes.White, Brushes.Red}
    'picFlag.Width = 99
    'picFlag.Height = 149
    For i As Integer = 0 To 2
      gr.FillRectangle(br(i), 0 + i * 50, 0, 50, 99)
    Next
    gr.DrawLine(Pens.Black, 0, 0, 148, 0)    'top border
    gr.DrawLine(Pens.Black, 0, 0, 0, 98)      'left border
    gr.DrawLine(Pens.Black, 0, 98, 148, 98)  'bottom border
    gr.DrawLine(Pens.Black, 148, 0, 148, 98) 'right border
End Sub
```

7.
```
Private Sub btnCreate_Click(...) Handles btnCreate.Click
    Dim gr As Graphics = picFlag.CreateGraphics
    Dim br() As Brush = {Brushes.Orange, Brushes.White, Brushes.Green}
    Dim r As Integer = 12    'radius of circle
    'picFlag.Width = 99
    'picFlag.Height = 149
    For i As Integer = 0 To 2
      gr.FillRectangle(br(i), 0, 0 + i * 33, 149, 33)
    Next
    gr.FillPie(Brushes.Orange, 75 - r, 49 - r, 2 * r, 2 * r, 0, 360)
    gr.DrawLine(Pens.Black, 0, 0, 148, 0)    'top border
    gr.DrawLine(Pens.Black, 0, 0, 0, 98)      'left border
    gr.DrawLine(Pens.Black, 0, 98, 148, 98)  'bottom border
    gr.DrawLine(Pens.Black, 148, 0, 148, 98) 'right border
End Sub
```

```
9. Private Sub btnDraw_Click(...) Handles btnDraw.Click
     Dim n As Integer
     Dim numbers As String = ""
     Dim gr As Graphics = picBox.CreateGraphics
     picBox.Refresh()
     n = CInt(txtNumber.Text)
     'Font is Microsoft Sans Serif
     For i As Integer = 0 To n
       If i < 9 Then
         numbers &= i & "        "
       Else
         numbers &= i & "       "
       End If
       gr.DrawLine(Pens.Blue, 12 + (24 * i), 5, 12 + (24 * i), 15)
     Next
     gr.DrawLine(Pens.Blue, 0, 10, 24 * (n + 1), 10)
     gr.DrawString(numbers, Me.Font, Brushes.Blue, 8, 20)
   End Sub
```

CHAPTER 10

EXERCISES 10.1

1. Combined population of the 10 most populous cities in 2015: **209.2 million**

3. **China**
   India
   Japan

```
5. Private Sub btnDisplay_Click(...) Handles btnDisplay.Click
     'Display the country names in the order they are stored.
     'Open a connection to the database.
     Dim connStr As String = "Provider=Microsoft.Jet.OLEDB.4.0;" & _
                       "Data Source=MEGACITIES.MDB"
     Dim sqlStr As String = "SELECT * FROM Countries"
     Dim dataAdapter As New OleDb.OleDbDataAdapter(sqlStr, connStr)
     'Fill the data table with data from the database.
     Dim dt As New DataTable()
     dataAdapter.Fill(dt)
     dataAdapter.Dispose()
     'Display the country names (field/column 0) in the list box.
     For i As Integer = 0 To dt.Rows.Count - 1
       lstOutput.Items.Add(dt.Rows(i)(0))
     Next
   End Sub
```

```
7. Private Sub btnDisplay_Click(...) Handles btnDisplay.Click
     'Displays the cities whose populations in 2015 will exceed 20 mil
     'Open a connection to the database.
     Dim connStr As String = "Provider=Microsoft.Jet.OLEDB.4.0;" & _
                       "Data Source=MEGACITIES.MDB"
     Dim sqlStr As String = "SELECT * FROM Cities"
     Dim dataAdapter As New OleDb.OleDbDataAdapter(sqlStr, connStr)
     'Fill the data table with data from the database.
     Dim dt As New DataTable()
```

```
   dataAdapter.Fill(dt)
   dataAdapter.Dispose()
   'Display the city name (column 0) where the 2015 pop exceeds 20.
   For i As Integer = 0 To dt.Rows.Count - 1
     If CDbl(dt.Rows(i)("pop2015")) > 20 Then
       lstOutput.Items.Add(dt.Rows(i)(0))
     End If
   Next
 End Sub
```

9.
```
 Private Sub btnDisplay_Click(...) Handles btnDisplay.Click
   'Displays countries and monetary units
   'Open a connection to the database.
   Dim connStr As String = "Provider=Microsoft.Jet.OLEDB.4.0;" & _
                           "Data Source=MEGACITIES.MDB"
   Dim sqlStr As String = "SELECT * FROM Countries"
   Dim dataAdapter As New OleDb.OleDbDataAdapter(sqlStr, connStr)
   'Fill the data table with data from the database.
   Dim dt As New DataTable()
   dataAdapter.Fill(dt)
   dataAdapter.Dispose()
   'Display the country (column 0) and its monetary unit (column 2).
   For i As Integer = 0 To dt.Rows.Count - 1
     lstOutput.Items.Add(CStr(dt.Rows(i)(0)) & " - " & _
                         CStr(dt.Rows(i)(2)))
   Next
 End Sub
```

11.
```
 Structure Country
   Dim name As String
   Dim pop2005 As Double
   Dim monetaryUnit As String
 End Structure

 Private Sub btnDisplay_Click(...) Handles btnDisplay.Click
   'Displays countries in descending order of their population
   'Open a connection to the database.
   Dim connStr As String = "Provider=Microsoft.Jet.OLEDB.4.0;" & _
                           "Data Source=MEGACITIES.MDB"
   Dim sqlStr As String = "SELECT * FROM Countries"
   Dim dataAdapter As New OleDb.OleDbDataAdapter(sqlStr, connStr)
   'Fill the data table with data from the database.
   Dim dt As New DataTable()
   dataAdapter.Fill(dt)
   dataAdapter.Dispose()
   'Declare an array of structures to hold the data.
   Dim temp, countries(dt.Rows.Count - 1) As Country
   'Load the data into the array.
   For i As Integer = 0 To dt.Rows.Count - 1
     countries(i).name = CStr(dt.Rows(i)(0))
     countries(i).pop2005 = CDbl(dt.Rows(i)(1))
     countries(i).monetaryUnit = CStr(dt.Rows(i)(2))
   Next
   'Bubble sort on population.
   For i As Integer = 1 To dt.Rows.Count - 1
     For j As Integer = 1 To dt.Rows.Count - i
       If countries(j - 1).pop2005 < countries(j).pop2005 Then
         temp = countries(j - 1)
         countries(j - 1) = countries(j)
```

```
                countries(j) = temp
              End If
          Next
      Next
      'Display the country names.
      For i As Integer = 0 To dt.Rows.Count - 1
        lstOutput.Items.Add(countries(i).name)
      Next
    End Sub
```

13.
```
Private Sub btnDisplay_Click(...) Handles btnDisplay.Click
    'Displays cities and monetary units
    Dim j As Integer
    'Open a connection to the database.
    Dim connStr As String = "Provider=Microsoft.Jet.OLEDB.4.0;" & _
                            "Data Source=MEGACITIES.MDB"
    Dim sqlStr As String = "SELECT * FROM Cities"
    Dim dataAdapter As New OleDb.OleDbDataAdapter(sqlStr, connStr)
    'Fill the data table with data from the database.
    Dim dt As New DataTable()
    dataAdapter.Fill(dt)
    dataAdapter.Dispose()
    'Load data from Countries table into second data table.
    sqlStr = "SELECT * FROM Countries"
    dataAdapter = New OleDb.OleDbDataAdapter(sqlStr, connStr)
    Dim dt2 As New DataTable()
    dataAdapter.Fill(dt2)
    dataAdapter.Dispose()
    'Loop for each city.
    For i As Integer = 0 To dt.Rows.Count - 1
      j = 0
      'When the city's country is found, then quit the loop.
      Do While CStr(dt2.Rows(j)(0)) <> CStr(dt.Rows(i)(1))
        j += 1
      Loop
      'Display the city and monetary unit.
      lstOutput.Items.Add(CStr(dt.Rows(i)(0)) & " - " & _
                          CStr(dt2.Rows(j)(2)))
    Next
  End Sub
```

15. The two sequential files have a combined size of 498 bytes, while the database file has size 196 KB.

17. Two tables: Publishers and Titles

19. 10

21.
```
Dim dt As New DataTable()    'Data table holds the data.

Private Sub frmStates_Load(...) Handles MyBase.Load
    'Loads the information into the data table
    'Open a connection to the database.
    Dim connStr As String = "Provider=Microsoft.Jet.OLEDB.4.0;" & _
                            "Data Source = STATE_ABBR.MDB"
    Dim sqlStr As String = "SELECT * FROM States"
    Dim dataAdapter As New OleDb.OleDbDataAdapter(sqlStr, connStr)
    'Fill the data table with data from the database.
```

```
      dataAdapter.Fill(dt)
      dataAdapter.Dispose()
  End Sub

  Private Sub btnDisplay_Click(...) Handles btnDisplay.Click
      'Display the state that matches the abbreviation.
      'Convert the abbreviation to uppercase.
      mtxtAbbr.Text = mtxtAbbr.Text.ToUpper
      If mtxtAbbr.Text = "" Then
        'Display error message.
        txtOutput.Text = "Enter a state."
      Else
        txtOutput.Clear()
        'Loop over all states.
        For i As Integer = 0 To 49
          'If the abbreviation matches, then display the name.
          If mtxtAbbr.Text = CStr(dt.Rows(i)(0)) Then
            txtOutput.Text = CStr(dt.Rows(i)(1))
          End If
        Next
        If txtOutput.Text = "" Then
          'Display error message.
          txtOutput.Text = "Not found."
        End If
      End If
      'Set focus back on abbreviation.
      mtxtAbbr.Focus()
  End Sub
```

EXERCISES 10.2

1. Could cause a problem if the country added is not one of the countries in the Countries table

3. No problem

5. (B)

7. (A)

9. (D)

11. (C)

13.
```
SELECT country, monetaryUnit FROM Countries WHERE pop2005>130 AND pop2005<200
ORDER BY pop2005 ASC
```

15.
```
SELECT * FROM Cities WHERE country='India' ORDER BY pop2015 DESC
```

17.
```
SELECT * FROM Cities WHERE pop2005>18 AND pop2005<19 ORDER BY pop2005 ASC,
pop2015 ASC
```

19.
```
SELECT city, pop2015, monetaryUnit FROM Cities INNER JOIN Countries
ON Countries.country=Cities.country
WHERE Countries.country='India' ORDER BY pop2015 DESC
```

21.
```
Dim dt As New DataTable()    'Holds the data

Private Sub frmCurrency_Load(...) Handles MyBase.Load
    'Get all fields from the Rates table sorted by country.
    Dim connStr As String = "Provider = Microsoft.Jet.OLEDB.4.0;" & _
                            "Data Source = EXCHRATE.MDB"
```

```vb
   Dim sqlStr As String = "SELECT * FROM Rates ORDER BY Country"
   Dim dataAdapter As New _
            OleDb.OleDbDataAdapter(sqlStr, connStr)
   'Fill the data table, and close the data adapter.
   dataAdapter.Fill(dt)
   dataAdapter.Dispose()
   'Set the list box's data source to the countries field.
   lstCountries.DataSource = dt
   lstCountries.DisplayMember = "Country"
End Sub

Private Sub lstCountries_SelectedIndexChanged(...) _
            Handles lstCountries.SelectedIndexChanged
   'Display the country's monetary unit and exchange rate.
   txtCurrency.Text = CStr(dt.Rows(lstCountries.SelectedIndex)(1))
   txtRate.Text = FormatNumber((dt.Rows(lstCountries.SelectedIndex)(2)), 5)
End Sub
```

23.
```vb
Structure Rate
   Dim country As String
   Dim monetaryUnit As String
   Dim dollarRate As Double
End Structure

Dim rateTable As New DataTable()
Dim rateTable2 As New DataTable()

Private Sub frmCurrency_Load(...) Handles MyBase.Load
   'Get all fields from the Rates table sorted by country.
   Dim connStr As String = "Provider = Microsoft.Jet.OLEDB.4.0;" & _
                        "Data Source = EXCHRATE.MDB"
   Dim sqlStr As String = "SELECT * FROM Rates ORDER BY Country"
   Dim dataAdapter As New OleDb.OleDbDataAdapter(sqlStr, connStr)
   'Fill the from and to table and close the data adapter
   dataAdapter.Fill(rateTable)
   dataAdapter.Fill(rateTable2)
   dataAdapter.Dispose()
   'Set the list boxes' data sources to the respective data tables.
   lstFrom.DataSource = rateTable
   lstFrom.DisplayMember = "Country"
   lstTo.DataSource = rateTable2
   lstTo.DisplayMember = "Country"
End Sub

Private Sub btnConvert_Click(...) Handles btnConvert.Click
   'Convert the monetary unit, and display the result.
   Dim result, amount As Double
   Dim fromRate, toRate As Rate
   Dim fromIndex As Integer = lstFrom.SelectedIndex
   Dim toIndex As Integer = lstTo.SelectedIndex
   'Display an error message if input is insufficient.
   If (fromIndex < 0) Or (toIndex < 0) Or _
      (txtAmount.Text.Trim = "") Then
     MessageBox.Show("Both countries and an amount must be provided.", _
            "Insufficient Input")
   Else
      'Get each row from the data table, and store into a structure.
      fromRate = GetRate(fromIndex)
      toRate = GetRate(toIndex)
      'Convert the amount
```

```
        amount = CDbl(txtAmount.Text)
        result = Convert(fromRate.dollarRate, toRate.dollarRate, amount)
        'Display the result formatted with the rates.
        txtResult.Text = FormatNumber(amount) & " " & _
                fromRate.monetaryUnit & "s from " & fromRate.country & _
                " equals " & FormatNumber(result) & " " & _
                toRate.monetaryUnit & "s from " & toRate.country
    End If
    txtAmount.Focus()
End Sub

Function GetRate(ByVal rowNum As Integer) As Rate
    'Store the fields from a row into a structure.
    Dim rateInfo As Rate
    rateInfo.Country = CStr(rateTable.rows(rowNum)("Country"))
    rateInfo.monetaryUnit = CStr(rateTable.Rows(rowNum)("monetaryUnit"))
    rateInfo.dollarRate = CDbl(rateTable.Rows(rowNum)("dollarRate"))
    Return rateInfo
End Function

Function Convert(ByVal fromRate As Double, _
                ByVal toRate As Double, _
                ByVal amount As Double) As Double
    'Convert the amount from the from Currency to the to Currency.
    Return amount * toRate / fromRate
End Function
```

27.
```
Private Sub btnDisplay_Click(...) Handles btnDisplay.Click
    'Display the data from the data table in the data grid
    Dim sqlStr As String
    sqlStr = "Select player From Players INNER JOIN Teams ON " & _
            "Players.team=Teams.team WHERE location='New York'"
    UpdateGrid(sqlStr)
End Sub

Sub UpdateGrid(ByVal sqlStr As String)
    Dim dt As New DataTable()
    Dim connStr As String = "Provider=Microsoft.Jet.OLEDB.4.0;" & _
                        "Data Source=BASEBALL.MDB"
    Dim dataAdapter As New OleDb.OleDbDataAdapter(sqlStr, connStr)
    dataAdapter.Fill(dt)
    dataAdapter.Dispose()
    dgvDisplay.DataSource = dt
End Sub
```

35.
```
Private Sub btnDisplay_Click(...) Handles btnDisplay.Click
    'Display a telephone directory.
    Dim lastName, str As String
    Dim fmtStr As String = "{0,-30} {1,7}"
    Dim connStr As String = "Provider = Microsoft.Jet.OLEDB.4.0;" & _
                        "Data Source = PHONEBOOK.MDB"
    Dim sqlStr As String = "SELECT * FROM Entries ORDER BY " & _
                        "lastName, firstName, middleInitial ASC"
    Dim dataAdapter As New OleDb.OleDbDataAdapter(sqlStr, connStr)
    Dim dt As New DataTable()
    dataAdapter.Fill(dt)
    dataAdapter.Dispose()
    'Loop over all rows, remembering the current lastname.
    lastName = ""
```

```
lstOutput.Items.Add(String.Format(fmtStr, "NAME, ADDRESS", _
                                  "PHONE #"))
For i As Integer = 0 To dt.Rows.Count - 1
  If lastName <> CStr(dt.Rows(i)(0)) Then
    'If the last name has changed, then remember it.
    lastName = CStr(dt.Rows(i)(0))
    'LASTNAME firstName middleInitial streetNumber street
    str = lastName.ToUpper & " " & CStr(dt.Rows(i)(1)) & " " & _
        CStr(dt.Rows(i)(2)) & "   " & _
        CStr(dt.Rows(i)(3)) & " " & CStr(dt.Rows(i)(4))
  Else
    'firstName middleInitial streetNumber street
    str = "    " & CStr(dt.Rows(i)(1)) & " " & _
        CStr(dt.Rows(i)(2)) & "   " & _
        CStr(dt.Rows(i)(3)) & " " & CStr(dt.Rows(i)(4))
  End If
  lstOutput.Items.Add(String.Format(fmtStr, str, _
                                    dt.Rows(i)(5)))
Next
End Sub
```

CHAPTER **11**

EXERCISES **11.1**

1. Any negative grade will be recorded as 0, and any grade greater than 100 will be recorded as 100.

3. Remove the keyword WriteOnly from the Midterm property block, and add the following *Get* property procedure to it:

```
Get
   Return m_midterm
End Get
```

5. The properties Midterm and Final are write only.

7. The property SocSecNum is initialized to the value **999-99-9999.**

9. The keyword New is missing from the third line of the event procedure.

11. The statement **nom = m_name** is not valid.

13. The statements

```
pupil.Midterm  = scholar.Midterm
```

and

```
lstGrades.Items.Add(pupil.Midterm)
```

are not valid. The property Midterm is write only; it can be set, but cannot return a value.

15. ```
Country: Canada
Capital: Ottawa
Pop: 31 million
```
```

17. Create a **formLoad** event procedure with the following lines, and change 20 to −20 in the **btnMove_Click** event procedure:

```
round.Xcoord = picCircle.Width - 40
round.Ycoord = picCircle.Height - 40
```

21.
```
Class PairOfDice

    Private m_die1, m_die2 As Integer
    Dim randomNum As New Random()

    Public ReadOnly Property Die1() As Integer
      Get
        Return m_die1
      End Get
    End Property

    Public ReadOnly Property Die2() As Integer
      Get
        Return m_die2
      End Get
    End Property

    Public ReadOnly Property SumOfFaces() As Integer
      Get
        Return m_die1 + m_die2
      End Get
    End Property

    Sub Roll()
      m_die1 = randomNum.Next(1, 7)
      m_die2 = randomNum.Next(1, 7)
    End Sub
End Class
```

25.
```
Public Class frmCashRegister
    Dim register As New CashRegister()

    Private Sub btnAdd_Click(...) Handles btnAdd.Click
      'Add an amount to the balance.
      register.Add(CDbl(txtAmount.Text))
      'Display the new result.
      txtBalance.Text = FormatCurrency(register.Balance)
      txtAmount.Clear()
      txtAmount.Focus()
    End Sub

    Private Sub btnSubtract_Click(...) Handles btnSubtract.Click
      'Subtract an amount from the balance.
      register.Subtract(CDbl(txtAmount.Text))
      'Display the new result.
      txtBalance.Text = FormatCurrency(register.Balance)
      txtAmount.Clear()
      txtAmount.Focus()
    End Sub
End Class           'frmCashRegister

Class CashRegister
    Private m_balance As Double
```

```vb
Public ReadOnly Property Balance() As Double
  Get
    Return m_balance
  End Get
End Property

Sub Add(ByVal amount As Double)
  'Make sure balance does not go negative for negative amounts.
  If (m_balance + amount) >= 0 Then
    m_balance += amount
  End If
End Sub

Sub Subtract(ByVal amount As Double)
  'Make sure balance does not go negative.
  If (m_balance - amount) >= 0 Then
    m_balance = m_balance - amount
  End If
End Sub
End Class      'CashRegister
```

EXERCISES 11.2

1.
```vb
Sub btnDisplay_Click(...) Handles btnDisplay.Click
  Dim fmtStr As String = "{0,-20}{1,-15}{2,-1}"
  lstGrades.Items.Clear()
  lstGrades.Items.Add(String.Format(fmtStr, "Student Name", _
                                   "SSN", "Grade"))
  For i As Integer = 0 To lastStudentAdded
    If students(i).CalcSemGrade = "A" Then
      lstGrades.Items.Add(String.Format(fmtStr, students(i).Name, _
                          students(i).SocSecNum, _
                          students(i).CalcSemGrade))
    End If
  Next
End Sub
```

7.
```vb
Public Class frmCashRegister
  Dim WithEvents register As New CashRegister()

  Private Sub btnAdd_Click(...) Handles btnAdd.Click
    'Add an amount to the balance.
    register.Add(CDbl(txtAmount.Text))
    'Display the new result.
    txtBalance.Text = FormatCurrency(register.Balance)
    txtAmount.Clear()
    txtAmount.Focus()
  End Sub

  Private Sub btnSubtract_Click(...) Handles btnSubtract.Click
    'Subtract an amount from the balance.
    register.Subtract(CDbl(txtAmount.Text))
    'Display the new result.
    txtBalance.Text = FormatCurrency(register.Balance)
    txtAmount.Clear()
    txtAmount.Focus()
  End Sub
```

```
      Private Sub AttemptToOverdraw(ByVal amt As Double) _
                          Handles register.AttemptToOverdraw
        MessageBox.Show("You would have been overdrawn by " & _
              FormatCurrency(-1 * amt) & ".", "Withdrawal Denied")
      End Sub
    End Class    'frmCashRegister

  Class CashRegister
    Private m_balance As Double
    Public Event AttemptToOverdraw(ByVal amt As Double)

    Public ReadOnly Property Balance() As Double
      Get
        Return m_balance
      End Get
    End Property

    Sub Add(ByVal amount As Double)
      'Make sure balance does not go negative for negative amounts.
      If m_balance + amount >= 0 Then
        m_balance += amount
      Else
        RaiseEvent AttemptToOverdraw(m_balance - amount)
      End If
    End Sub

    Sub Subtract(ByVal amount As Double)
      'Make sure balance does not go negative.
      If m_balance - amount >= 0 Then
        m_balance = m_balance - amount
      Else
        RaiseEvent AttemptToOverdraw(m_balance - amount)
      End If
    End Sub
  End Class       'CashRegister
```

EXERCISES 11.3

1. 4

3. 64

5. `Can move Has jointed limbs and no backbone`

7. The keyword Overrides should be Inherits.

9. The Hi function should be declared with the Overridable keyword in class Hello and with the keyword Overrides keyword in class Aussie.

11. The Hi function should be declared with the Overrides keyword in class Cowboy.

13. The Hello class should be declared with the MustInherit keyword, and the function Hi should be declared with the MustOverride keyword.

15. The Hello class should be declared with the MustInherit keyword, not MustOverride.

19. `Public Class frmRegister`
`    Dim tollBooth As New FastTrackRegister()`

```vb
Private Sub btnProcess_Click(...) Handles btnProcess.Click
  'Process the vehicle
  If radCar.Checked Then
    tollBooth.ProcessCar()
  Else
    tollBooth.ProcessTruck()
  End If
  'Display the revenue and number of vehicles
  txtRevenue.Text = FormatCurrency(tollBooth.Balance)
  txtNumVehicles.Text = CStr(tollBooth.Count)
End Sub
End Class        'frmRegister

Class CashRegister
  Private m_balance As Double

  Sub Deposit(ByVal amount As Double)
    m_balance += amount              'Add the amount to the balance.
  End Sub

  Sub WithDrawal(ByVal amount As Double)
    m_balance = m_balance - amount   'Subtract the amount from balance.
  End Sub

  Public ReadOnly Property Balance() As Double
    Get
      Return m_balance
    End Get
  End Property
End Class          'CashRegister

Class FastTrackRegister
  Inherits CashRegister
  Private m_count As Integer

  Public ReadOnly Property Count() As Integer
    Get
      Return m_count
    End Get
  End Property

  Sub ProcessCar()
    m_count += 1     'Process a car: $1.00.
    Deposit(1)
  End Sub

  Sub ProcessTruck()
    m_count += 1     'Process a truck: $2.00.
    Deposit(2)
  End Sub
End Class        'FastTrackRegister
```

INDEX

G